Latin American Development Priorities

Many countries in Latin America and the Caribbean (LAC) have achieved considerable economic growth, yet the region still faces many seemingly intractable problems. The conventional wisdom in development agencies – that prioritization is impossible and that everything must be done – is simply not effective.

Latin American Development Priorities shows how limited resources could be used for the greatest benefit of the LAC region. A panel of economists met over three days in San José to review proposals to tackle the ten most important challenges, which emerged from a survey by the Inter-American Development Bank (IDB). The Expert panel was asked a question which appears simple but is actually very difficult to answer: What should LAC governments do with an additional nominal $10 billion?

Hard choices are needed if the region's problems are to be tackled effectively. This book provides the means to make those choices as objectively as possible.

BJØRN LOMBORG is Director of the Copenhagen Consensus Center and Adjunct Professor in the Department of Management, Politics and Philosophy at Copenhagen Business School. He is the author of the controversial bestseller, *The Skeptical Environmentalist* (Cambridge, 2001), and was named as one of the top 100 public intellectuals by *Foreign Policy* and *Prospect* magazines in 2008.

Latin American Development Priorities

Edited by
BJØRN LOMBORG

CAMBRIDGE
UNIVERSITY PRESS

CAMBRIDGE UNIVERSITY PRESS
Cambridge, New York, Melbourne, Madrid, Cape Town, Singapore, São Paulo, Delhi

Cambridge University Press
The Edinburgh Building, Cambridge CB2 8RU, UK

Published in the United States of America by Cambridge University Press, New York

www.cambridge.org
Information on this title: www.cambridge.org/9780521747523

© Copenhagen Consensus Center 2009

First published 2009

Printed in the United Kingdom at the University Press, Cambridge

A catalogue record for this publication is available from the British Library

ISBN 978-0-521-76690-6 hardback
ISBN 978-0-521-74752-3 paperback

Contents

Figures

Tables

Contributors

Susan Rose-Ackerman
Yale University

Max A. Alier
IMF

Miguel Braun
IDB and CIPPEC

Benedict Clements
IMF

Mark A. Cohen
Resources for the Future

Amy Damon
Macalester College

Alejandra Cox Edwards
California State University, Long Beach

Ronald Fischer
Universidad de Chile

Sebastian Galiani
Washington University in St. Louis

Paul Glewwe
University of Minnesota

Julio A. Gonzalez
World Bank

José Luis Guasch
World Bank

Mark P. Jones
Rice University

Randall A. Kramer
Duke University

Adriana Kugler
University of Houston

Bjørn Lomborg
Copenhagen Consensus Center

Andrew Morrison
World Bank

Philip Musgrove
Health Affairs

Ugo Panizza
UNCTAD

Mauricio Rubio
Universidad Externado de Colombia (UEC)

William D. Savedoff
Social Insight

Roger A. Sedjo
Resources for the Future

Tomas Serebrisky
World Bank

Juha Siikamäki
Fellow, Resources for the Future

Miguel Urquiola
Columbia University

Stephen D. Younger
Cornell University

Acknowledgments

I would like to extend my gratitude to all those who helped make this important volume possible. Special thanks must go to the Costa Rican government and President Oscar Arias for his support and enthusiasm for the Consulta de San José. We must also thank the Inter-American Development Bank for their partnership with the Copenhagen Consensus Center, and dedication and interest in this project. We are indebted, also, to all of the chapter and alternative view contributors for taking part in the project and for the interesting analyses and results they have brought about. The power of new research is at the core of the success of the Copenhagen Consensus project, and the quality of work on a wide range of topics presented in this volume is remarkable. The Copenhagen Consensus team and especially Maria Jakobsen, Tommy Petersen, and Henrik Meyer, deserve personal acknowledgment for their dedication, energy, and commitment. We also thank David Young and David Livermore for their valuable assistance.

This volume is dedicated to all of those people who took part in the Consulta de San José, with gratitude for their insight and effort.

Bjørn Lomborg
Copenhagen, June 2008

Abbreviations and acronyms

AAA	Accountability and Anticorruption Project
ADR	alternative dispute resolution
AIOS	International Association of Pension Fund Supervisor Organizations
APA	Administrative Procedure Act (US)
ASEAN	Association of Southeast Asian Nations
AUGE	Programa de Acceso Universal de Garantías Explícitas
B/C	benefit-cost
BCR	benefit-cost ratio
BDH	Bono de Desarrollo Humano (Ecuador)
CBA	cost-benefit analysis
CBO	Congressional Budget Office
CCT	conditional cash transfer
CEDLAS	Center for Distributive, Labor, and Social Research
CER	cost-effectiveness ratio
CGD	Center for Global Development
CIPPEC	Centro de Implementacíon de Politicas Públicas
CONAFE	Consejo Nacional de Fomento Educativo
CPI	consumer prices index
CPI	Corruption Perceptions Index (TI)
CPMF	bank debit tax
CPTED	crime prevention through environmental design
CV	contingent valuation
CVM	contingent valuation method
DALY	disability adjusted life year
DARE	Drug Abuse Resistance Education
DB	defined benefits
DC	defined contributions
DCPP	Disease Control Priorities Project
DIP	Devolución de Impuestos a los Pobres

DPT	diphtheria, pertussis, and tetanus
DWL	deadweight loss
ECA	East Europe and Central Asia
ECD	early child development
ECH	Encuesta Continua de Hogares (Uruguay)
ECLAC	Economic Commission for Latin America and the Caribbean
EITC	earned income tax credit
EPA	Environmental Protection Agency (US)
ESU	evolutionarily significant unit
FAO	Food and Agricultural Organization (UN)
FOIA	Freedom of Information Act
FONASA	National Health Fund (Chile)
FRL	fiscal responsibility law
FTA	free-trade agreement
GAO	Government Accountability Office (US)
GDP	gross domestic product
GIS	geographic information systems
GNI	gross national income
HC	Hogares Comunitarios (Colombia)
HDI	Human Development Index
HDIs	human development indicators
HRM	human resource management
IBP	International Budget Partnership
IFC	International Finance Corporation (World Bank)
IFIs	International Financial Institutions
IMF	International Monetary Fund
IMSS	Instituto Mexicano de Seguridad Social
INE	Instituto Nacional de Estadísticas
IPCC	Intergovernmental Panel on Climate Change
IPV	intimate partner violence
IRR	internal rate of return
IRS	Internal Revenue Service (US)
ISAPRE	private insurer (Chile)
ISSTE	Instituto de Seguridad Social de los Trabajadores del Estado
IUCN	International Union for the Conservation of Nature and Natural Resources (World Conservation Union)
IUGR	intrauterine growth retardation

JIT	just-in-time
LAC	Latin America and the Caribbean
LAPO	Latin American Public Opinion Project
LBW	low birthweight
LMIC	low- and middle-income countries
MDG	Millennium Development Goal
MIRR	modified internal rate of return
MMR	measles, mumps, and rubella
MOH	Ministry of Health
NAFTA	North American Free Trade Agreement
NGO	non-governmental organization
NPM	new public management
NPV	net present value
OECD	Organization for Economic Cooperation and Development
OOP	out-of-pocket (spending)
OPS	Organización Panamericana de la Salud
OR	operations research
ORT	oral rehydration therapy
PACES	Programa de Ampliacíon de Cobertura de la Educatión Secundaria
PAHO	Pan American Health Organization
PAYG	pay-as-you-go (social security)
PB	Participatory Budgeting
PDV	present discounted value
PELA	Proyecto de Elites Latinoamericanas
PIDI	Proyecto Integral de Desarrollo Infantil
PIRLS	Program in International Reading and Literacy Studies
PISA	Program for International Student Assessment
PL	plurality (electoral formula)
PMP	fiscal policymaking process
PPP	public–private partnership
PPP	purchasing power parity
PR	proportional representation
PRAF	Programa de Asignación Familiar (Honduras)
PSF	Programa da Saúde da Família
PV	present value
QALY	quality adjusted life year
R&D	research and development

REP	Reentry Partnership Initiative
RES	Research Department (Inter-American Development Bank)
RPS	Red de Protección Social (Nicaragua)
SEDLAC	Socio-Economic Database for Latin America and Caribbean
SGF	Solidarity and Guarantees Fund
SGSSS	Sistema General de Seguridad Social en Salud
SMD	single-member district
SME	small and medium-sized enterprise
SP	stated preference
SPSA	severance payment saving accounts
SSA	sub-Saharan Africa
SSRs	structural surplus rules
STATUS	Student Training Through Urban Strategies
SUS	Sistema Única da Saúde
TFP	total factor productivity
TI	Transparency International
TIMSS	Trends in International Mathematics and Science Studies
UEC	Universidad Externado de Colombia
UI	unemployment insurance
UIA	unemployment insurance account
UNEP	UN Environmental Program
UNODC	UN Office on Drugs and Crime
USDA	US Department of Agriculture
USDOI	US Department of the Interior
VAT	value added tax
WEF	World Economic Forum
WHO	World Health Organization
WSIPP	Washington State Institute for Public Policy
WTP	willingness-to-pay
ZMVS	Zona Metropolitana del Valle del Sulla

Expert panel findings

An expert panel of nine distinguished economists who gathered for the Consulta de San José met to consider the research presented in this volume. The panel comprised:

- Orazio Attanasio, Professor of University College London
- Jere Behrman, Professor of the University of Pennsylvania
- Nancy Birdsall, President of the Center for Global Development
- John H. Coatsworth, Professor of Columbia University
- Ricardo Hausmann, Professor of Harvard University
- Finn E. Kydland, Nobel Laureate and Professor of the University of California
- Nora Lustig, Visiting Professor of George Washington University and Former Director of the UNDP Poverty Group
- José Antonio Ocampo, Professor of Columbia University and Former United Nations Under Secretary General
- Andrés Velasco, Professor of Harvard University and Minister of Finance for Chile.

Over three days, this panel was presented with more than forty solutions to regional challenges. For each challenge, the members heard the arguments from expert authors and an alternate view. The panel then deliberated and ranked the proposals, in descending order of desirability, as follows:

1. Early Childhood Development (Poverty)
2. Fiscal Rules (Fiscal Problems)
3. Increase Investment in Infrastructure, Including Maintenance (Infrastructure)
4. Policy and Program Evaluation Agency (Fiscal Problems)
5. Conditional Cash Transfers (Poverty and Education)
6. Universal Health Insurance: Basic Package (Health)

7. Nutrition Programs for Pre-School Age Children (Poverty and Education)
8. Crime Prevention through Environment Design (Violence and Crime)
9. Replace Taxes on Formal Employment with Other Taxes (Employment)
10. Adopt Policies and Services to Reduce Transaction Costs for Trade (Infrastructure)
11. Cash Awards to Journalists for Publication in Major International Media of Governance Failures (Public Administration)
12. Implement Protocols and Publish Outcomes (Health)
13. Training for Disadvantaged Workers (Employment)
14. Automated Computer-Based System for Revenue Collection (Public Administration)
15. Tobacco Tax and Other Measures to Reduce Smoking (Health)
16. Program Targeting At-Risk Mothers and Young Children (Violence and Crime)
17. Comprehensive Program to Deal with Youth and Gang Violence (Violence and Crime)
18. Merit Recruitment and Promotion in the Civil Service (Public Administration)
19. Civil Society Monitoring and Information Provisions (Public Administration)
20. Contingent Debt Instruments (Fiscal Problems)
21. Reduction of the Minimum Wage and Transfers to the Working Poor (Employment)
22. Government Monitoring: Audit Agencies and Ombudsmen (Public Administration)
23. Improve Judicial and Prosecutorial Independence and Performance (Public Administration)
24. Universal Health Insurance: Full Package (Health)
25. Women's Representation: Quotas (Democracy)
26. Make Tax System More Progressive (Fiscal Problems)
27. Voucher Programs (Education)
28. Alcohol Tax, Restriction of Alcohol Sales, Elimination of Alcohol Advertising (Health)
29. Comprehensive Prison Treatment and Reintegration Program (Violence and Crime)

More information on the Expert panel's methodology and approach can be found in the Introduction to this volume.

The top five solutions

Top priority was given to **Early Childhood Development** programs. These are interventions that improve the physical, intellectual, and social development of children early in their life. The interventions range from growth monitoring, daycare services, pre-school activities, improved hygiene and health services to parenting skills. Besides improving children's welfare directly, the panel concluded that these programs create further benefits for family members, releasing women and older siblings to work outside the home or to further their own education. Evidence shows that the benefits are substantially higher than the costs. Promoting early childhood development is a regional solution that provides both immediate and long-term benefits.

Improving **Fiscal Rules** was generally seen as a great opportunity to improve the budget process within many countries in the LAC region. Consolidating the budget process through procedural rules that would set structural deficit targets and limit deficits, spending and debt levels, and increase budget transparency, would help avoid insolvency and excess spending in good times. At a low cost, this could potentially increase nations' growth rate substantially.

Next on the panel's list was **Increased Investment in Infrastructure, Including Maintenance**. The panel found that the LAC region under-invests in infrastructure. Improving roads, seaport, water, sanitation, electricity, and telecommunication would considerably stimulate growth. Boosting infrastructure and improving maintenance was found to yield a very high return on investment, while also providing and increasing access to markets and thus generating more prosperity.

The panel found that idea of establishing independent **Policy and Program Evaluation Agencies** very promising. An independent (public or private) and possibly international agency should provide evaluation and cost-benefit analysis to monitor social conditions and government programs over time. Between nations, the agencies should share information on effective policies. This would ensure that more effective programs are prioritized by both policymakers and the public.

The panel also recommended **Conditional Cash Transfer** (CCT) programs to provide monthly cash payments to poor households conditioned on parents sending their children to school, health clinics, etc. The panel found that this is a well-proven way to permanently reduce poverty. Furthermore, the panel found that CCTs could address several different problem areas such as poverty, inequality, and inadequate health and education, especially if adapted to local conditions.

Promising solutions that require further research

During the panel's deliberation, a number of very promising proposals were identified as needing further research as there is still a lack of knowledge of impact and effectiveness. The panel found that they addressed very important problems. The proposals were:

- Prevention of Domestic Violence (Violence and Crime)
- Improving the Quality of Education (Education)
- Rural Infrastructure (Poverty)
- Financial Services for the Poor (Poverty)
- Improve Efficiency of Delivery (Health)

Introduction

BJØRN LOMBORG

In May 2004, the first Copenhagen Consensus was held in Denmark's capital. This was a groundbreaking event, which for the first time brought together a group of the world's most eminent economists to jointly prioritize additional spending on some of the world's most pressing problems. A second global event took place in 2008 and, in the meantime, other focused projects have been run in conjunction with the United Nations. While these processes are all global in focus, this volume brings together the material from the first regional process: the Consulta de San José, held in Costa Rica in October 2007.

The need for prioritization is as real as ever. Good progress has been made in a number of areas in recent years, particularly on the overall economic front, but a number of problems in the Latin American and Caribbean (LAC) region are seemingly intractable. Potential solutions based on best practice, either in the region or more widely, form the basis of this volume, but to make real progress over the coming years, limited resources need to be committed where they are likely to do most good.

The LAC region is part of the developing world, but many countries within it have achieved considerable economic growth in recent years and can certainly not be considered among the world's poorest. This in itself is a compelling reason to focus an event purely on the region. If issues are assessed globally, the vast problems of extreme poverty in sub-Saharan Africa (SSA) and parts of Asia dominate considerations. When basic needs are unfulfilled for hundreds of millions of people, and some states are dysfunctional, assuring food and water security and providing basic healthcare often becomes a prerequisite for further successful interventions.

This is not to suggest that the LAC region does not have problems of poverty and less-than-ideal government. Unfortunately, it does. Haiti is among the world's poorest states by any reckoning, and Bolivia has particularly high levels of rural poverty, for example. Inefficient and corrupt bureaucracies hold back growth. But there has been considerable progress in the region, both economically and in terms of governance. Encouraging though this is, it also means that it is not immediately obvious which of the remaining problems can be addressed most cost-effectively.

The essence of the Copenhagen Consensus process is to assess, as objectively as possible, both the extent of the problems and the cost and benefits of interventions aimed at tackling them. Expert authors have been commissioned to produce a series of Challenge papers (chapters 1–10), and these in turn have been critically reviewed by other experts in alternative view papers (2.1–10.1). An eminent Expert panel has been set up to make the prioritization.

For the Consulta de San José, the challenges presented to the Expert panel were selected via a survey conducted by the IDB: 1,800 professionals in LAC – policymakers, academics, business representatives, journalists, and researchers – were asked to list the most important challenges facing the region. The top ten issues that emerged from this exercise, and which form the framework of the volume, were:

- Democracy
- Education
- Employment and social security
- Environment
- Fiscal policy reforms
- Health
- Infrastructure
- Poverty
- Public administration
- Violence and crime

The Expert panel was asked a question which appears simple, but is actually very difficult to answer: What should LAC governments do with an additional nominal $10 billion which becomes available? The straightforward answer, of course, is to spend it on the projects which give the greatest results. In the language of economics, we should choose the projects with the largest benefit-cost ratios (BCRs).

The difficulty comes in estimating the true costs and placing a value on the benefits which flow from the intervention. Economics provides us with a powerful intellectual framework to compare choices, but relies on placing a value on things which a layperson may consider have no monetary value (or, alternatively, may be considered priceless). One of the biggest criticisms of economic evaluation is the need to place a price on human life itself. Yet this has to be done if priorities are to be evaluated.

But the fact that there is inevitable room for debate about the exact value we place on certain benefits means that BCRs of this type can never be definitive and accurate; rather, they are indicative. In other words, prioritization is not necessarily simply a case of choosing projects which have the highest BCRs. Many contributors look at the sensitivity of the figure to the assumptions which are made. If an intervention appears cost-effective across a range of assumptions, we can assume that any conclusions we draw are robust. But that also means comparing projects on the basis of a range of BCR values rather than simply ranking by a single value.

Time preference is also an important matter to consider. In an economist's view, benefits received (and costs outlaid) in years to come are worth less than similar amounts in the present. Most laypeople would agree with this principle. Faced with taking $100 now or in a year's time, there is no reason for delay. However, if the choice was between $100 and $110 in a year, or even $200 in five years, then it would possibly be rational to choose the larger amount in future, assuming that our current needs were met. Economists assign an annual discount rate to indicate the degree of time preference and in the case of Copenhagen Consensus process evaluations, interventions are generally assessed at both 3% and 6% rates. If BCRs are favorable at both rates, we can again be quite confident in the robustness of the conclusion.

However, many of the solutions proposed to the LAC region's problems have benefits which will accrue over long periods of time; in the case of interventions aimed at young children or pregnant mothers, for example, this can be for a whole lifetime, or even extend to later generations. Taking typical discount rates, even the ones used here which are, by economic standards, relatively low, means that benefits which may be very significant to individuals or societies in several decades' time will have a very low discounted value today. While this may seem unreasonable, it is important always to keep in mind that resources spent on solutions that will achieve their benefits only many decades from now are resources that can not be used to achieve more immediate benefits (which in turn may lead to greater, long-term benefits).

The Consulta de San José, in common with other Copenhagen Consensus process events, held a Youth Forum in parallel with the deliberations of the Expert panel. The young people in the Forum assessed the same material as the experts and, like them, were asked to prioritize the solutions put forward. However, they were not obliged to base their conclusions on purely economic analysis. It is interesting to see how the priorities of expert economists are validated by the rather similar rankings of the Youth Forum.

The Expert panel had a difficult task in choosing between a range of options on which to spend the nominal $10 billion. Some critics of the process would argue that they should be doing no such thing, that all the problems of developing countries deserve attention and that to choose between them is iniquitous. But we believe, on the contrary, that the best way to help poor people in the LAC region is to do things which improve lives a lot rather than a little. This may involve some hard choices, but generalized, unfocused attempts at help will simply mean doing less good at higher cost.

Another criticism of the Copenhagen Consensus process is that the answer to poverty lies not in specific interventions launched by governments or international organizations on behalf of the poor, but in creating the right conditions in developing countries so that they can undertake their own development. This is not lightly to be dismissed since, in an ideal world, such self-help should arguably be the norm. Indeed, the transformation of a number of Southeast Asian countries since the 1960s has been to a great degree due solely to their own efforts.

Nevertheless, there remain in the LAC region not only great disparities between countries, but also enormous inequality within countries. Across the region, it is the rural population which often suffers to an undue degree. Countries have not made the rapid progress of many dynamic Asian economies. Focused interventions could provide a kickstart for progress across a range of issues.

Prioritization produces losers and winners. In this case, the winners – the top priority interventions chosen by the Expert panel – were educational (childhood development programs), financial (better fiscal rules), and infrastructural (greater investment). At the bottom of the priority list came projects including the introduction of quota systems for female politicians, voucher systems for education, restrictions on alcohol sales, and prison rehabilitation programs. However, some proposals could not be ranked with the current level of information, and thus the Expert panel emphasized the need for more research for several areas, including options for reducing domestic violence, improving the quality of education and healthcare delivery, and improving rural infrastructure and financial services for the poor.

But, whether they are deemed "winners" or "losers," all the proposed interventions are thoughtful and deserve our consideration. The rest of this introduction gives a brief summary of the issues and solutions put forward in the chapters and alternative views which form the core of this book. You, the reader, may form your own conclusions. Although the Expert panel has made a well-argued set of choices, this is not the final word. By re-analyzing the evidence and proposing different approaches, it is perhaps possible to make a different argument for prioritization. What is important with this collection of essays, which represents our best knowledge on policy choices in the LAC region assessed by the Copenhagen Consensus framework, is that such a debate can now be based on the best available facts, focusing on the pressing need for setting smart priorities.

The challenges

Democracy is the topic covered by Mark P. Jones of Rice University (chapter 1). Although the political systems of Chile, Costa Rica, and Uruguay bear comparison with those of North America and Western Europe, Haiti and Venezuela stretch the concept of democracy to its limits, while a group of countries including Bolivia, Colombia, and Paraguay are considered only partly free. The specific issues discussed by Jones are the weakness of political parties (thus encouraging short-term, populist policies) and the vast under-representation of women in national politics.

Reforming the party system to encourage consistent policies and reduce the plethora of short-lived, personality based parties could in principle be achieved via several specific systematic changes. However, the conclusion is that, while such reform would have benefits in some countries, in many others it would be likely to fail – and, indeed, merely consolidate corrupt systems. It seems that other conditions need to be in place for a fully functioning democracy to thrive.

The under-representation of women in national government can be considered not only a flaw in democracy, but also to prevent their fundamentally different policy approach from influencing politics. It is proposed that this be corrected via a system of quotas, closed-candidate lists, and multi-representative electoral districts. While this would undoubtedly increase representativeness and government legitimacy, the benefits are difficult to quantify.

Amy Damon and Paul Glewwe of Macalester College and the University of Minnesota discuss the issue of **Education** in their contribution (chapter 2). In their view, although many claims are made for the benefits of education *per se*, it is the outcomes which are important, and Damon and Glewwe propose three policies which they suggest will benefit the region. With a few notable exceptions, such as Haiti, large strides have been made in the LAC region in recent decades, and yet the educational outcomes in even the best-performing countries, such as Argentina and Chile, do not compare with those in the rich countries of the industrialized world.

Better-educated people not only have the potential for higher earnings, but the quality of life both for them and for their children is better. Although not directly educational, the authors' proposal to implement nutritional programs for pre-school children would have the benefit of improving both the number of years of schooling and the achievement of the children during that time. The benefits of this are significant, and the Expert panel made this intervention their top-priority recommendation.

Secondly, conditional cash transfers to families (CCTs), made while children attend school, can certainly increase years of schooling, although the quality of teaching remains an important but ill-defined issue. Thirdly, providing vouchers to enable parents to choose to send their children to private schools appears to improve outcomes via increased competition.

Miguel Urquiola of Columbia University provides an alternative view (hereafter, AV) of the educational issue (AV 2.1). He points out that although education has improved, the LAC region is still losing ground in comparison to East Asia, and that reducing the repetition of years would be more cost-effective than merely increasing the number of years spent at school. He also argues that the improved outcomes found in some private schools can be accounted for by socio-economic factors, and questions the perception that private education is necessarily better.

Labor market reforms are perhaps not the most instantly crowd-pleasing subject, but that does not make them any less important. Alejandra Cox Edwards of California State University, Long Beach, argues in chapter 3 that current labor laws restrict job creation and productivity, and prevent the LAC region from seizing the benefits of globalization. Nevertheless, these laws were enacted to protect workers, and their reform is politically difficult, despite the fact that a shortage of jobs in the formal, regulated sector means that countries in the region have large informal (and hence unprotected) sectors.

Edwards suggests that social security payments are currently seen purely as a tax, since the link with benefits is indirect. By reforming the system to reduce the tax element, workers will value their contributions more, and those who do not benefit will no longer be taxed. The overall objective of her proposals is to increase the flexibility of the labor market, and other interventions suggested include defined severance pay for all who leave jobs and replacement of the minimum wage by earned income tax credits (EITC) to give more job opportunities to unskilled workers.

Edwards argues that these interventions would increase formal sector employment, reduce the size of the informal sector but improve the lot of those still working in it, reduce overall unemployment, and raise productivity. Adriana Kugler of the University of Houston and Stanford's Center for the Study of Poverty and Inequality suggests, in her alternative view (AV 3.1), that the benefits of the proposed interventions may actually be lower than estimated.

Roger A. Sedjo and Juha Siikamäki of Resources for the Future focus on proposals concerning **Forests and biodiversity** (chapter 4). Actions within this area currently tend to be decided on a political basis because of the difficulty of doing a conventional economic analysis. The chapter attempts to put in place a more evidence-based foundation for future decisions. The region is rich in forests, particularly tropical ones, which are especially high in biodiversity. This species richness is threatened by deforestation.

Species can have a direct value – for example, to hunters – but also a public good value which can be estimated in terms of willingness-to-pay (WTP) surveys. Valuing forest ecosystems is also difficult, but this has increasingly now been done by way of their carbon sequestration potential; in the LAC region, this has been estimated to be over

$3 trillion. There are various conceptual ways of protecting forests, including compensation of owners and even paying up-front for the whole area to be protected. Costs are high, but far lower than the benefits.

Randall A. Kramer of Duke University argues in his alternative view (AV 4.1) that Sedjo and Siikamäki under-estimate the difficulties of moving away from timber extraction, and thereby over-state the net benefits. Kramer proposes as an alternative the protection of forests on the basis of non-use values, using WTP studies to justify the cost-effectiveness of this. Ultimately, of course, this intrinsic value is likely to be estimated significantly higher by prosperous non-residents of the region.

In his discussion of **Fiscal policy reform**, Miguel Braun of IDP and CIPPEC describes the region in chapter 5 as a historical "basket case." Fortunately, much progress has been made, but Braun's concern is that an underlying structural deficit may have been disguised by the healthy international economic climate (at least, until recently). The problem is compounded by a procyclical fiscal policy in many countries: expansionary when the economy is growing, and contractionary during recessions.

Finding long-term solutions means addressing root causes: an inherent volatility when countries have high levels of foreign currency debt, coupled with decentralized political systems which do not encourage responsible policymaking. The solutions proposed are improved debt management, consolidating and reforming the budget process to promote greater responsibility and accountability, and tax reform coupled with a more rigorous process of prioritizing cost-effective expenditure. Implemented together, these reforms could give a 3% annual boost to growth.

Max A. Alier and Benedict Clements of the IMF provide an alternative view (AV 5.1). While largely agreeing with Braun's analysis and proposals, they think that he has been too pessimistic about recent progress. The key issue, in their view, is to promote economic growth, and this is best achieved by introducing a more progressive tax system and spending government revenues more effectively. Nevertheless, they caution against introducing excessive rigidities into the budget process, which introduce distortions and limit the possibilities for the introduction of counter-cyclical policies.

Health is clearly an important topic which still provides many challenges in the region. Philip Musgrove, Deputy Editor, *Health Affairs*, proposes in chapter 6 a very different approach to earlier Copenhagen Consensus studies. Rather than focus on specific disease states, he proposes a systemic approach to increase access to quality healthcare. In practice, this is complementary to the disease-driven approach, looking at ways in which specific interventions can be delivered better to more people.

Musgrove quotes evidence of poorer people in particular being unaware that they are in the early stages of chronic diseases such as diabetes. For those who know they need medical help, services may not be accessible or may be delivered inefficiently, or to a low standard. Musgrove's first proposal is to provide better access by introducing some form of universal health insurance, which will particularly benefit the poorer members of society. This should be accompanied by policies designed to raise treatment standards and deliver care more efficiently. However, it is very difficult to estimate quantitative benefits and costs for such approaches.

William D. Savedoff of Social Insight, in his alternate view (AV 6.1), supports Musgrove's proposals for systemic change, which he suggests is particularly relevant for a region which is relatively prosperous and where non-communicable diseases (NCDs) are an important problem. He adds to this by estimating BCRs, which for a range of assumptions look very favorable. He also suggests an additional, low-cost intervention of increasing taxes and restrictions on the sale of alcohol and tobacco.

Infrastructure is less obviously a priority than something as basic as healthcare. However, Julio A. Gonzalez, José Luis Guasch, and Tomas Serebrisky of the World Bank make a convincing case in chapter 7 for increased investment. With international trade becoming freer, logistics costs are now a larger proportion of the total costs of trade than are tariff barriers. While by no means the worst region, LAC growth is constrained by infrastructure limitations, and investment needs to be increased from the present approximately 2% of GDP to between 3 and 6% to keep pace with China, for example.

Increasing the number of phone lines has a marked effect on overall growth, with power-generation and transport networks also being significant. But this investment is not in itself sufficient: policies must also be adopted which foster improved logistics efficiency and facilitate trade. Although physical infrastructure costs are large, policy reforms have low monetary costs but are often politically difficult to institute. The rewards, however, would be significant in terms of increased economic growth.

Ronald Fischer of the Universidad de Chile supports this analysis and set of proposals in his alternative view (AV 7.1). However, he suggests that the effect on growth may be over-stated, and that major infrastructure projects may not be warranted in sparsely populated countries. Reform proposals such as these have been held back for many years by political and bureaucratic difficulties. Nevertheless, Fischer points towards the creation of an open and efficient economy in Chile as an example of what can be achieved.

The LAC region, although by no means the world's poorest, still has deep-rooted problems of **Poverty** in many countries, as discussed in chapter 8 by Sebastian Galiani of Washington University in St. Louis. The poverty issue is compounded by high rates of inequality, with indigenous and rural populations being most severely affected. This means that economic growth alone is not sufficient to solve the problem: there must also be an element of redistribution. It is remarkable that, even in economically progressive Chile, the tax system itself is still slightly regressive, and the situation is even worse in other countries.

Interventions such as nutritional supplementation, CCTs (generally linked to school enrollment), and investment in early childhood development (ECD) can help to build human capital, lift people out of poverty, and reduce inequality in a cost-effective way. For rural areas, where poverty is most widespread, land reform, creation and enforcement of secure property titles, and infrastructure investment can provide additional benefits.

Stephen D. Younger of Cornell University makes two criticisms of Galiani's proposals in his alternative view (AV 8.1). First, he thinks that too little attention is paid to inequality. Second, he believes that investment in ECD, while good in itself, will have benefits only in the longer term. For more immediate poverty alleviation, transfer payment schemes are more appropriate. These can be made even more effective by weighting them with respect to income distribution.

Susan Rose-Ackerman of Yale University addresses the thorny issue of problems with **Public administration and institutions** in chapter 9.

Poorly functioning and corrupt public administration and legal systems have negative social effects and reduce economic growth. Overall, corruption can be seen as a symptom of underlying frailties in the state. But regulatory reform can be difficult if both the bureaucracy and legislature are weak, so an alternative solution is to change the way that goods and services are provided.

Reforms of the tax system – in particular, simplification and better management – can significantly increase the proportion of tax actually collected. Peru has even reduced corruption levels by recruiting large numbers of new and better-qualified staff. Similar reforms to the civil service to increase its level of professionalism, appropriate use of the private sector to deliver services, greater public accountability, and more transparency and freedom for public discussion in the media can all provide benefits at modest cost.

Ugo Panizza of UNCTAD regards Rose-Ackerman's contribution as a comprehensive *tour de force*, but highlights a few specific issues in his alternative view (AV 9.1). In particular, he argues that money cannot buy good public administration. He points not to civil servants being poorly paid, for example (as is often argued), but to compressed salary scales, which effectively reward low skills but are a disincentive to the better qualified, and also argues for the need to incentivize political reformers.

Violence and crime remains a major concern in the region. In the final chapter 10, Mark A. Cohen of Resources for the Future, and Mauricio Rubio of Universidad Externado de Colombia (UEC), discuss the background and ways to improve the situation. Despite public perceptions, the overall situation has not deteriorated in recent years, although the firearms death rate remains about three times the world average. But the overall figures mask a continuous drop in fatalities in Central America (particularly Colombia and El Salvador) offset by a larger rise in South America. Homicide rates vary enormously between different districts, and the majority of offenders are young men, most often gang members. Violence against women also runs at a high level.

Unfortunately, there is little hard evidence from other countries to identify the most effective solutions. Nevertheless, evidence is building that targeting at-risk mothers and their young children can help them to develop proper social skills and reduce the chance of later offending. For the current generation, there are a number of interventions which can help to reduce gang membership, although reducing school drop-out rates may be one of the most effective, and is beyond the scope of the chapter. Similarly, prison treatment and rehabilitation programs can reduce the extremely high rate of re-offending.

Andrew Morrison of the World Bank criticizes some aspects of Cohen and Rubio's contribution in his alternative view (AV 10.1), in particular questioning the cost-effectiveness of prisoner rehabilitation given the poor state of LAC prison infrastructure. Morrison proposes as an additional solution crime prevention through environmental design (CPTED). A further alternative – "hot spot" policing – is attractive, but would require massive changes to the culture and organization of policing.

Conclusions

These were the ten challenges and sets of solutions considered in detail by the Expert panel. Top of their rankings were a number of solutions which address both real and present human problems (childhood development and CCTs for schooling) and some of the broader structural issues which have held back development in the region (improved fiscal policies and greater infrastructure investment).

These are all interventions which should have long-term benefits in the LAC region, and may be what it needs to help it fulfill its global potential. We now invite you, the reader, to read the contributions critically and make your own prioritization.

1 | Democracy in the LAC region, challenges and solutions: political party and party system institutionalization and women's legislative representation

MARK P. JONES

1 Introduction

The countries of the LAC region confront numerous challenges to the quality of their democracies. A 2006 survey conducted by the Research Department (RES) at the Inter-American Development Bank evaluated the challenges faced by the region in sixteen thematic areas, one of which was democracy (Berkman and Cavallo 2006). Among the sixteen thematic areas, democracy was considered by the respondents to represent one of the top ten problems faced by the region, and the survey evaluated six principal challenges to democracy, in order of importance for the survey respondents: "Little real enforcement of rules and accountability for politicians," "Weak democratic culture," "Crisis of representation," "Political intimidation and violence," "Traditional parties losing traditional constituencies," and "No real separation of powers."

The challenges that LAC democracies face today are very real, and quite daunting. However, when discussing them, and any potential solutions, we must be cognizant of the considerable diversity in the objective conditions of the region's democracies. The extent and nature of any specific challenge varies considerably, depending on the country in question. Therefore any solution offered to a challenge will vary in many important respects, depending on country-specific factors (Spiller and Tommasi 2007; Stein and Tommasi 2008). This is not to say that it is not possible to make general recommendations for solutions for the region, but rather that some of the specifics of these recommendations

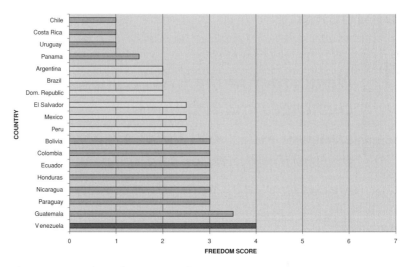

Figure 1.1 Freedom (democracy): the Americas, 2007

will be different, depending on which specific country (or subsets of countries that share common institutional, developmental, or other relevant features) one is referring to.

The broad diversity in the current state of democracy in the LAC region is illustrated in figure 1.1, which provides the average 2007 Freedom Score for the Latin American countries (Freedom House 2008). While these scores can be problematic when used for cross-temporal analysis, they are the most valid and reliable measures we have of the quality of democracy in a country at a particular juncture in time.

The Freedom Score (the average of a Political Rights score and a Civil Liberties score) ranges from 1 (most free/democratic) to 7 (least free/undemocratic). Virtually all Western European countries have a Freedom Score of 1 (as do Canada and the United States, among others), while scores of 7 are possessed by the world's most brutal and oppressive dictatorships (e.g. Cuba, North Korea, Sudan). Figure 1.1 underscores the wide variance in the level of democracy in the LAC region, and suggests that the extent and nature of the challenges to democracy in these countries also vary considerably in nature, breadth, and intensity.

The LAC region has several countries whose democracies are directly comparable in terms of their political rights and civil liberties to those found in Western Europe. Chile, Costa Rica, and Uruguay all possess

Freedom Scores of 1, and Panama (1.5) is not far behind. A second group of countries have Freedom Scores of 2 and 2.5 (still classified as "Free" by Freedom House) which, while indicative of a reasonably well-functioning democracy, reveal that compared to the Western European countries, as well as their more democratic counterparts listed above, the functioning of these countries' democracies is deficient in many important respects. The countries that fall in this category are Argentina, Brazil, the Dominican Republic, El Salvador, Mexico, and Peru. A third group of countries is located in the Freedom House category of "Partly Free," with Freedom Scores of 3 and 3.5 (Bolivia, Colombia, Ecuador, Nicaragua, Paraguay, and Guatemala). In these countries, the level and quality of democracy is markedly inferior to that found in Chile, Costa Rica, Uruguay, and Panama. Their respective democratic systems also possess more flaws and problems than those of the second group of twelve countries listed above (i.e. those with Freedom Scores between 2 and 3.5). Finally, Venezuela's democracy suffers from a litany of maladies, such that the continued use of the term "democracy" to describe the country stretches the concept of democracy to its very limits (if not beyond them).

The above review of the level and quality of democracy in the countries of the region highlights the tremendous diversity of the region's democratic systems. Several countries have democracies that rival the world's best. Other countries, however, have democracies that suffer from serious deficiencies, with a few sufficiently deficient that the question of whether or not the country can even be considered a democracy is raised.

The challenges faced by LAC democracies are numerous. In this chapter I draw on the results of the RES survey to examine two serious challenges faced by the region's democracies. The first relates to the weak (and declining) level of institutionalization of the political parties and party systems in the region. Several of the challenges identified in the RES survey are directly linked to the crisis of the region's parties and party systems (i.e. "Little real enforcement of rules and accountability for politicians," "Crisis of representation," "Traditional parties losing traditional constituencies"). The second challenge is linked to the dramatic under-representation of women (in particular) and other social groups in the region's national legislatures (i.e. the challenge of "Crisis of representation"). While women are but one of the many social groups under-represented in LAC's legislatures, they are the most important, and therefore for reasons of space here I focus exclusively on issues related to women's under-representation. Nonetheless, many lessons drawn from the analysis of this challenge and the solutions to it will be applicable in many important respects to other under-represented social groups (e.g. ethnic and racial minorities, youth, the poor).

2 Political Party Institutionalization

The problem and solution, background

A crucial characteristic of political party systems is their level of insti-tutionalization. While it is true that there is such as thing as too much institutionalization, which can have a deleterious effect on the func-tioning of a democracy, with the pre-1993 Venezuelan party system a classic example (Coppedge 1997; Crisp 2000), in general party institu-tionalization is seen as a positive trait for the functioning of a democ-racy (Mainwaring 1998, 1999; Mainwaring and Scully 1995).

The more institutionalized a party system is, the greater the likeli-hood that it will have programmatic political parties.[1] In a party sys-tem dominated by programmatic political parties, the parties compete with each other based primarily on policy proposals. Furthermore, the policy orientations of the parties tends to be relatively stable, thereby allowing for higher levels of democratic (i.e. voter) accountability and identifiability than occurs in countries with weakly institutionalized party systems (Mainwaring 1999; Shugart and Mainwaring 1997). Institutionalized party systems also provide for greater levels of policy consistency due to the strong role played by parties in political recruit-ment and the concerted efforts made by political elites to promote the party label (as a unique policy brand) and protect its value (which implies maintaining relatively consistent policy positions over time, with dramatic changes in policy stances occurring only infrequently).

It is difficult, if not impossible, for a programmatic party to exist within a weakly institutionalized party system. In weakly institution-alized systems, political parties compete based far more on personal appeals or short-term populist policy proposals designed to win over

---

[1] It is, however, possible to have high levels of party institutionalization along with political parties with a clientelist, non-programmatic, base (Kitschelt 2000).

voters and then be forgotten after the election (Mainwaring 1998, 1999). The parties also play a much less prominent role in the political recruitment process. In weakly institutionalized party systems, political parties often are ephemeral in life-span, with their policy positions on specific issues highly flexible.

For voters in weakly institutionalized party systems it is much more difficult to hold political parties accountable than in institutionalized party systems. It is also more difficult to identify how one's vote will translate into a governance option, and what that governance option will do once in power (Shugart and Mainwaring 1997). Furthermore, since political parties play a weak role in the recruiting process, are often short-lived, and place less importance on the policy brand name and value of their party label, there is much less policy consistency in weakly institutionalized party systems than in their institutionalized counterparts. Lastly, given the lack of commitment of political elites to their parties in particular and to the party system in general, weakly institutionalized party systems are much more conducive breeding grounds for anti-system politics than institutionalized party systems.

Scott Mainwaring is widely regarded as the leading authority on party system institutionalization in the LAC region (Mainwaring 1998, 1999; Mainwaring and Scully 1995; Mainwaring and Zoco 2007). Mainwaring identifies four key components that together influence the level of party system institutionalization in a country: Stability in patterns of inter-party competition; Party roots in society; The legitimacy of parties and elections; and Party organization. Below I briefly examine each of these components, first discussing the conceptual base for the component, then operationalizing this concept as a set of empirical indicators, and finally providing values for these indicators for the LAC democracies. The section concludes with the presentation of an index of party institutionalization for the eighteen LAC democracies (table 1.1).

Stability in inter-party patterns of competition

In institutionalized party systems the relevant parties tend to be the same, year in and out, and to garner relatively similar shares of votes and seats over time. In weakly institutionalized party systems, parties that are relevant in one year are often irrelevant a few years later. Furthermore, the percentage of the vote and seats parties win in these

Table 1.1 *Party institutionalization index*

Country	Institutionalization Index	Electoral volatility	Party roots	PE legitimacy	Party organization
Uruguay	80	77	80	66	97
El Salvador	75	89	71	43	98
Honduras	73	94	76	40	82
Dominican Republic	73	73	89	48	80
Panama	71	86	76	43	79
Chile	71	97	55	54	78
Argentina	69	81	56	47	91
Paraguay	68	72	89	36	73
Nicaragua	67	69	76	36	86
Mexico	65	76	66	37	82
Costa Rica	64	74	71	51	61
Brazil	61	85	45	37	76
Venezuela	57	53	57	55	65
Ecuador	52	57	59	28	64
Colombia	51	64	56	38	46
Peru	50	43	58	34	67
Guatemala	44	41	51	36	49
Bolivia	43	26	68	29	51

weakly institutionalized systems tend to vary considerably from one election to the next.

The stability of inter-party competition is measured using the following indicator: the level of seat (percentage of the seats) volatility (Seat volatility) in the most recent lower/single house election.[2] Latin America presents a wide range of volatility, with countries such as Chile, Honduras, and El Salvador possessing volatility levels comparable to those found in Western Europe (Bartolini and Mair 1990). In these democracies the same parties tend to win comparable vote and seat shares over time. In contrast, the region is home to other countries with extremely high levels of volatility, such as Peru, Guatemala, and Bolivia. Here, parties that were among the most relevant in the country

---

[2] In table 1.1, this value is subtracted from 100, so that lower values signify higher volatility. For greater measurement and operationalization details on many of the variables presented in this section, see Jones (2005).

either ceased to exist or saw their popular support plummet over a very short time period. At the same time, parties that either did not exist, or were inconsequential players only a few years earlier were, a few years later, among the most prominent.

Party roots in society

In institutionalized party systems, parties have strong roots in society (Mainwaring 1998, 1999). Voters tend to cast their ballots for the same party election after election, and the parties possess a high level of linkage with society. In weakly institutionalized party systems, parties are only loosely rooted in society. Voters commonly lack loyalty to parties, and instead cast their votes based more on the traits and characteristics of the individual candidates or their electoral campaign messages. In addition, parties possess relatively weak and ephemeral ties with society.

The extent of party roots in society (Party roots) is measured employing three indicators. The first is the percentage of the population that possessed some form of identification with a party.[3] The second is the percentage of legislators who believe that there exists a strong-to-moderate level of party identification in their country (PELA 2007). The third is calculated by subtracting from 100 the percentage of legislators who believe that parties are distant from society in their country (PELA 2007).

In terms of overall party roots in society, one extreme is represented by Paraguay, the Dominican Republic, and Uruguay, all of which have parties with deeply entrenched roots in society. In contrast, party roots in society are quite shallow at the other extreme of this measure, such as in Chile, Guatemala, and Brazil.

The legitimacy of political parties and elections

A basic prerequisite for an institutionalized party system is that both parties and the elections in which they compete are viewed as legitimate by the population (Mainwaring 1998, 1999). Furthermore, for an institutionalized party system to exist, parties must be viewed as institutions that are vital to the functioning of the democratic system. In contrast, in weakly institutionalized party systems neither parties nor elections enjoy a high level of legitimacy. Furthermore, a significant

---

[3] All public opinion data come from the Latinobarómetro survey (2000–5).

proportion of citizens are skeptical of the usefulness of parties as institutions.

Two aspects of political party legitimacy are examined. The first is the percentage of citizens who stated that parties were indispensable for the functioning of the country. The second is the percentage of the population that had a great deal or some confidence in parties. The average of these two is the Party legitimacy measure.

Election legitimacy is assessed using two measures. The first asked respondents to rate elections in their country on a 1 to 5 scale of clean to not clean. The second asked respondents the extent to which they agreed with the statement that "elections offer voters a real choice between parties and candidates" on a scale of 1 (strongly agree) to 4 (strongly disagree). In each case the average score (1 to 5, and 1 to 4, respectively) for all valid responses is calculated. This result is then divided by the high score for the scale (5 and 4, respectively). Finally, this resulting percentage is subtracted from 100 to produce the two measures.

P&E legitimacy is an aggregate measure of Political party and election legitimacy. One extreme on this aggregate measure is represented by Uruguay, Venezuela, and Chile, where both political parties and elections enjoy considerable legitimacy among the population. At the other extreme, represented by Peru, Bolivia, and Ecuador, both elections and political parties suffer from a serious crisis of legitimacy.

Political party organization
In institutionalized party systems, the parties possess a noteworthy level of material and human resources, intra-party processes are predictable and routinized, and the party as an institution is prescient over individual party leaders (Mainwaring 1998). In weakly institutionalized party systems, parties have limited resources, internal processes are unpredictable, and individual leaders dominate the parties, with the party as an institution weak to non-existent.

Party organization is measured using two variables: Political party age (Mainwaring 1998, 1999) and Elite opinion that their party is a continuously functioning organization, and not primarily an electoral vehicle. The Political party age variable is itself the average of two variables. The first is the percentage of parties (those that held at least 10% of the seats in the lower/single house) that as of 2004 had been in existence for at least ten years. The second is the percentage of the same parties that as of 2004 had been in existence for at least twenty-five years. The second measure of party organization is based on a PELA (2007) question that asked legislators if they considered their party organization to be continuous, or if they thought the party organization was merely an electoral vehicle.

Party organization is the strongest in El Salvador, Uruguay, and Argentina. It is the weakest in Bolivia, Guatemala, and Colombia.

Party institutionalization index

In table 1.1 the four aggregate measures discussed above are presented, and then aggregated, to create a Party institutionalization index. Based on this index, countries such as Uruguay, El Salvador, Honduras, the Dominican Republic, Panama, and Chile possess well-institutionalized party systems, while countries such as Venezuela, Ecuador, Colombia, Peru, Guatemala, and Bolivia possess weakly institutionalized party systems. Intermediate cases are Argentina, Paraguay, Nicaragua, Mexico, Costa Rica, and Brazil.

There is a very strong relationship between the level of party institutionalization and crucial factors such as the quality of a country's democratic system and the level of corruption. For instance, the institutionalized party systems possess an average Freedom House Freedom Score of 1.8, notably better than that possessed by either the intermediate (2.3) or the weakly institutionalized (3.2) party systems. By the same token the institutionalized party systems are noticeably less corrupt than their weakly institutionalized counterparts. According to the World Bank's Control of corruption indicator (with lower scores indicating higher levels of corruption), the institutionalized, intermediate, and weakly institutionalized party systems have average scores of 54.1, 39.8, and 32.0 respectively (Kaufmann *et al.* 2007).

The solution

The previous concise overview of political party and party system institutionalization reveals the great diversity that exists within the LAC democracies. The first set of more institutionalized party systems tends to have the basic building blocks necessary for a well-institutionalized party system comparable to those found in the exemplary democracies of Western Europe. While these party systems have some modest problems, it is clear that there exists a solid foundation upon which to construct a solid institutionalized party system. At the other extreme, the current state of the political party system is sufficiently dilapidated that it is unclear if current conditions are auspicious for any serious efforts to construct a more institutionalized party system. In these countries it is possible that the political party system is sufficiently degraded such that any efforts to improve the level of political party and party system institutionalization may meet with only limited success. The intermediate party systems occupy a mid-point between these two extremes, with the setting conducive to the establishment of a more institutionalized party system, but with the amount of effort (and level of uncertainty surrounding the possibility of success) greater than in the more institutionalized party systems.

The general solution proposed for the crisis of LAC's political parties and party systems is to increase the level of political party and party system institutionalization. A set of reforms are proposed whose purpose would be to increase such institutionalization in the region. The goal of these reforms focuses principally on increasing the value of the party label, bolstering the incentives for politicians to engage in activities designed to enhance the stability, reputation, and functioning of political parties, and improving the legitimacy of political parties and elections.

The political party marketplace

The institutionalization of political parties in many LAC countries is undermined by the widespread defection of existing legislators and politicians, the constant formation and extinction of different political parties, the failure of legislators to follow party directives within legislative bodies, and a general lack of concern exhibited by politicians for their party's reputation in the eyes of the public. These deficiencies are in many countries the consequence of the low barriers to entry for new political parties and low thresholds for political party survival. Below is a set of proposals designed to enhance the level of political party and party system institutionalization in the region (the focus here is on political parties competing in national-level elections).

A first reform is to establish a relatively high barrier to entry for new political parties. The goal of this reform is to make the formation of a new political party a non-trivial matter, thereby providing incentives for politicians to remain within their existing party as well as to follow party mandates and directives. At the same time, it is desirable that these barriers to entry not be prohibitively high. Mexico provides a good example that both protects against the proliferation of parties but at the same time allows for reasonable entry for new political parties that demonstrate an important level of popular support. The basic components of Mexico's law require the party to have a small number of registered members (3,000) in two-thirds (20 of 32) of Mexico's states, a smaller number of members in two-thirds (200 of 300) of Mexico's single-member districts, and a total number of members that equals 0.26% of the number of registered voters in the country. In addition to these requisites, a requirement (such as in Honduras) that the party possess a functioning organization in at least half of all departments and in at least half of all municipalities provides an important additional barrier to entry.

The proposed reforms that should be adopted by all countries (except in the event that the existing barriers to entry in that area are greater) are the following. To achieve formal registration as a political party, a party must have a number of members equal to 1% of the registered voters in two-thirds of the country's largest subnational territorial units (i.e. states, provinces, departments, regions) as well as have a number of members equal to 1% of the registered voters in the country as a whole. The party must also possess a functioning organization in at least two-thirds of the largest subnational territorial units and in at least half of the country's municipalities (those with populations above a certain threshold that will vary by country).

The second proposed reform relates to the extinction of political parties. In order to promote an institutionalized political party system, weak political parties must be culled from the herd of existing parties, and not allowed to remain around to serve as "parties of convenience" and/or crowd the ballot. This is accomplished through a reform that establishes a minimum percentage of the vote that parties must win in each legislative election (lower- or single-house). El Salvador and Nicaragua's rules are instructive in this case. They require that parties receive at least 3% (El Salvador) and 4% (Nicaragua) of the valid vote at the national level to maintain their official registration as a party (in El Salvador, for coalitions, this number is multiplied by the number of parties in the coalition). Nicaragua (similar to other countries, such as Mexico) also requires parties to run candidates for a minimum percentage of public offices. The proposed reform here would follow these models and require that a party be disbanded if it fails to win at least 4% of the valid vote at the national level (multiplied by the number of coalition partners for coalitions, up to a maximum of 12%) in the election for members of the lower/single house. It would also require the parties to run candidates for at least half of the positions being contested in all national legislative elections.

The third reform relates to the formation of alliances in national elections. Following the general model of Brazil for presidential elections, all electoral alliances among parties must be national in scope, in that alliance partners in one legislative district must be the same as in all other legislative districts and at the national level (i.e. for presidential elections). All decisions regarding the formation of alliances would be made by the political party's national leadership.

Party and campaign finance

The next set of reforms is designed to influence the system of campaign and party finance in the country. Following the lead of many European countries (e.g. Germany) the state should provide the political parties with very generous resources designed to promote education, mobilization, and recruitment efforts by the parties between elections, in order to deepen the ties political parties have with the country's electorate. The amount of this financing will vary by country, but it should be of sufficient size (e.g. 0.1%–0.4% of the country's annual national budget, depending on the overall size of the budget) that it will allow the parties to engage in considerable outreach activities and at the same time enhance the incentives for politicians to remain within their party and work to enhance its national reputation. In order to bolster a reduced set of the most relevant and viable parties, these funds should be limited to parties with a minimum percentage of seats in the lower/single house (e.g. 5%).

The next reform is comparable in intent, in that it would provide ample campaign financing to parties that receive a minimum percentage of the vote in national elections. Parties that surpassed a minimum percentage of the vote (such as 5% as in France) would be reimbursed for campaign expenses up to a set amount (an amount sufficiently high that it represents a significant proportion of a party's overall expenditures).

A final reform in this vein would have the national government allocate copious amounts of time on national television and radio to political parties in proportion to the number of legislative seats occupied by the party members (e.g. following the general concept of the Brazilian model). A related reform would restrict television and radio advertisements to those allocated by the national government.

Candidate selection

A problem faced by many political parties is insuring that elected representatives support general party positions in their elected office. The responsiveness of these elected officials can be enhanced by two reforms. The first provides the party leadership with control over the candidate nomination process, and access to the ballot using the party label. In order to promote intra-party democracy while still maintaining a prominent role for the party leadership, a mixed-selectorate multi-stage selection process such as that advocated by Rahat (2007) would be utilized. A second, more drastic reform (and perhaps one that it would be best not to implement in some countries), would follow the example of Mexico and prohibit immediate re-election to national offices (thereby placing the fate of elected public officials in the hands of the party leadership to a considerable extent).

Voting reforms

A final set of reforms relates to increasing the linkages among candidates for public office, and thereby increasing the extent of "party" oriented voting. First, in those countries where the presidential and legislative elections are not held concurrently, the constitution should be reformed so that the presidential and legislative elections are held on the same day. This is especially the case for those countries that do not have a mixed timing cycle (e.g. half of the presidential and legislative contests held concurrently and half held non-concurrently), such as Colombia, El Salvador, the Dominican Republic, and Venezuela. In these countries all or virtually all legislative elections are held separately from the presidential contest. The situation in the mixed systems that hold half of the lower-house elections (Mexico) and lower- and upper-house elections (Argentina) would also be improved by reforming the constitution to allow for concurrent elections.[4] These

---

[4] Given the six-year presidential terms in Mexico, in the event of this type of reform it would be wise to consider a reduction in the length of the presidential term to four or five years (similar to the term lengths in force at present throughout the rest of the region).

concurrent elections would enhance the national nature of the electoral process and enhance the extent of a "party oriented" vote.

The second reform in this area relates to the ballot structure. The logic behind this reform is to link the different votes for different offices together such that the voter casts a vote based more on party than on individual candidate characteristics. The most extreme form of vote linkage (and one that is not advocated here) is the use of a fused vote where voters are provided with only one vote for multiple offices. For instance, Bolivian voters have but one vote with which to select candidates for three offices (President, Senator, Chamber of Deputies–Party List), as do Uruguayans (President, Senator, Chamber of Deputies). A middle option is to embrace the model of many US states and allow voters the option of casting a straight party ticket vote. This middle option is similar to the option Argentine voters have of placing an unaltered party-supplied ballot (as opposed to an Australian ballot) for all offices in their ballot envelope that they then deposit in the ballot box.

Summary of benefits and costs

Overall, and *ceteris paribus*, democracies with more institutionalized party systems should have more programmatic politics and less personalist- and clientelist-based politics. These reforms should thus increase the extent of programmatic politics in these countries, providing incentives for political parties and politicians to compete based more on their party's programmatic platform than on personalist or populist appeals.

This increased focus by the political parties and politicians on programmatic politics should also provide for greater public policy consistency, as parties and politicians will be evaluated by the electorate based on the extent to which they successfully implement their proposed/promised public policy agenda.

Irrespective of the increase in programmatic politics, inducing a greater level of political party and party system institutionalization will result in a significantly greater level of accountability and of identifiability. In contrast to the present situation in a majority of LAC countries, citizens will be better able to hold an executive (through their party) accountable for the performance in office. The presence of institutionalized parties should also increase the linkage between citizens and politicians, thereby providing for greater support for and confidence in the functioning of the democratic system.

The potential costs of these reforms are three-fold. From a monetary perspective the increased financial support will represent a modest drain on the national budget (in an amount that will vary considerably depending on the current level of state support for political parties in the different countries and the economies of scale present in the different countries). There is also a danger that, by supporting existing political parties and creating somewhat high barriers to entry, the political party system may ossify and become unrepresentative and detached from the electorate. The historic case of Venezuela is instructive in this respect (Coppedge 1997; Crisp 2000).

Finally, it is possible that the increased resources provided to the political parties will not foster the development and consolidation of programmatic parties, but rather will result in the consolidation of strong clientelist political parties with marginal programmatic orientations (Kitschelt 2000). The likelihood of this adverse scenario is highest in the more corrupt countries of the region, where it is quite possible that the increasing power of parties will result more in the consolidation of clientelist machines than in the generation of policy oriented parties. For example, the World Bank provides the global percentile ranking of these eighteen countries in terms of the extent to which corruption is controlled in the country (Kaufmann *et al.* 2007). A higher ranking means that the country is less corrupt and a lower ranking means that it is more corrupt. The high levels of corruption present in the region make it quite possible that any attempts to increase the power of parties will have the undesired effect of increasing the power of clientelist machines – the greater the level of corruption in a country, the greater the potential "cost" associated with the empowering of clientelist politics (Kitschelt 2000). Thus we would expect these reforms designed to enhance party institutionalization to have the least risk of resulting in an entrenchment of clientelist machines in those countries with the lowest levels of corruption (i.e. Chile, Costa Rica, Uruguay, El Salvador, Colombia, and Panama) and the most risk of resulting in an entrenchment of clientelist politics in those countries with the highest levels of corruption (i.e. Venezuela, Paraguay, Honduras, Nicaragua, Ecuador, and Guatemala).

The benefits of these four categories of reforms were determined based on the extent to which an adoption of them would improve the

Table 1.2 *Benefit and cost information: proposed party institutionalization solution*

Country	Solution benefit	Solution cost	BCR
Argentina	5	2	2.50
Bolivia	2	3	0.67
Brazil	3	1	3.00
Chile	1	1	1.00
Colombia	5	1	5.00
Costa Rica	3	1	3.00
Dominican Republic	6	4	1.50
Ecuador	4	4	1.00
El Salvador	2	2	1.00
Guatemala	3	3	1.00
Honduras	3	4	0.75
Mexico	2	2	1.00
Nicaragua	1	3	0.33
Panama	2	1	2.00
Paraguay	4	3	1.33
Peru	4	2	2.00
Uruguay	5	1	5.00
Venezuela	6	5	1.20

Note: The theoretical range for the benefits and costs is 0 (no benefit/ no cost) to 8/6 (high benefit/high cost).

level of party institutionalization compared to that existing under the present rules (Payne *et al.* 2007). The costs were based on the monetary cost associated with the reform compared to existing expenditures in the area, the potential that the reforms may block out legitimate political competitors and promote party system ossification, and the probability that the reforms will work to strengthen clientelist machines in a country (Payne *et al.* 2007). The costs and benefits for each category were evaluated on a three-point scale, ranging from 0 (low benefit/low cost) to 2 (high benefit/high cost), with the values then summed for a cost and benefit score that, respectively, can range from 0 (no benefit, no cost) to 8/6 (very high benefit, very high cost). These benefit and cost values as well as the BCR are provided in table 1.2.

The values in table 1.2 have no absolute meaning. They do, however, assist in evaluating across countries the relative benefits of the

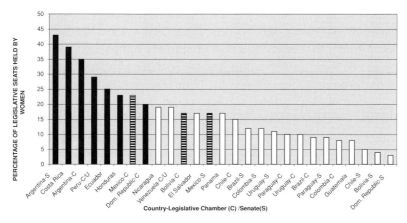

Figure 1.2 The representation of women: LAC region, 2007

proposed reforms compared to the relative costs of these reforms. In some instances, reforms are likely to have a high BCR (e.g. Colombia, Uruguay), while in others the costs appear to be noticeably greater than the benefits (e.g. Bolivia, Nicaragua).

3 Women's representation

The problem and solution, background

The 1995 UN Fourth World Conference on Women, held in Beijing, highlighted the dramatic under-representation of women in decision-making bodies and advocated a series of policies that governments should adopt to rectify this under-representation (UN 1995). The under-representation of women in legislatures is criticized as problematic for two principal reasons. First, inadequate descriptive representation of women represents a serious flaw in the functioning of a democracy (Inter-Parliamentary Union 1994; Phillips 1995). Second, numerous studies show there are several significant differences between male and female legislators in legislative behavior and policy preferences (Thomas 1994; Bratton and Ray 2002).

One of the most prominent recommendations to emerge from the Beijing Conference was that governments should adopt positive action policies to increase the number of women holding public office. Figure 1.2 details the level of women's representation in LAC's national legislatures. The dramatic and embarrassing under-representation of women in these legislative bodies is still clearly evident a dozen years after the Conference, and has been recognized as a serious democratic deficit facing the region by a host of scholars and policymakers, with the gap between current reality and the goal of parity a principal focus of the Economic Commission for Latin America and the Caribbean X Session of the Regional Conference on Women in Latin America and the Caribbean (Montaño 2007). Of the twenty-seven legislative bodies in figure 1.2, only one has a composition that is at least 40% female (Argentine Senate) while only three have a composition that is at least 30% female (Argentine Senate, Costa Rican Legislative Assembly, Argentine Chamber of Deputies). In contrast, in nine of the legislatures women represent 10% or fewer of the members, and a further eleven have a membership that is between 11% and 20% female.

Nowhere in the world has the Beijing Conference's recommendation been followed more than in the LAC region, where between 1996 and 2000 eleven countries adopted legislation requiring a minimum percentage of women on the party lists used for the election of national legislators. In spite of the adoption of this legislation, the percentage of women legislators in many countries remains very low, with only a handful of cases that can be considered an unqualified success. In order to address the current dismal representation of women in LAC's legislatures a series of reforms must be adopted, reforms that depend in part on a country's existing electoral legislation.

In figure 1.2, the percentage bars for the legislative bodies are in one of three shadings. Black indicates that the country employs well-designed gender quota legislation to elect members of that legislative body. Striped indicates that the country employs well-designed gender quota legislation to select a portion of that legislative body. White indicates that the country employs no quota rules or has flawed quota rules governing the election of members of the legislature.

Htun and Jones (2002) underscore the combined importance of the use of closed lists, placement mandates, moderate-to-large-sized electoral districts (which on average generate moderate-to-large-sized party magnitudes), and strict compliance rules in insuring the effectiveness of quota legislation. They underscore that quota legislation will, *ceteris paribus*, result in a larger percentage of women elected when it is used in concert with closed lists and placement mandates than when the same quota legislation is used in conjunction with open lists (where placement mandates are not effective).

The type of party list (closed or open) is highly consequential for the effectiveness of a quota law. A prominent advantage of closed-list systems when used in concert with gender quotas and placement mandates is that when combined with adequate enforcement of compliance, they guarantee a minimum floor of women's representation across all parties/districts. For example, in Argentina, Costa Rica, and Mexico (where a closed list, placement mandates, and strict compliance are in force), we can be assured, at the minimum, that if a party wins three seats in a district, at least one of the seats will be occupied by a woman. In some districts, more than one woman will occupy the party's garnered seats, but at the minimum one always will. In contrast to closed-list systems, open-list systems provide no such guarantee. Thus while in some districts women will do quite well electorally (as is also the case in closed-list systems), in others they do quite poorly, even when their party wins a substantial number of seats. In sum, the potential distribution of women elected under closed-list systems (once party magnitude reaches two in an overwhelming number of cases in Argentina and Costa Rica, and when it reaches three in all other cases in these two countries as well as in Bolivia (with a few exceptions due to compliance failure) and Mexico) is truncated at a low of between 20% and 50% depending on party magnitude and country-specific rules. In contrast, the distribution of women elected under open-list systems is never truncated (i.e. its low value is always 0%). Based on this logic, most scholars (e.g. Norris 2001; Htun and Jones 2002; Krook, 2005) posit that, *ceteris paribus*, the combined use of quotas with placement mandates and closed party lists should result in a greater number of women elected to Congress than is the case when quotas without placement mandates are utilized in concert with open-party lists. Nonetheless, some scholars (Schmidt 2005; Matland 2006) have questioned the above logic, concluding that the two arrangements are equally effective in terms of the election of women legislators.

In the absence of gender quota legislation, the effect of the use of a closed vs. open list will depend in large part on whether the party elites who largely decide the composition of the party lists are more or less favorable to the election of women than the electorate (Matland 2005). If the elites are more progressive than the electorate, then women are more likely to be elected under the closed-list arrangement, while the obverse would be the case if the electorate is more progressive than the elites.

In all of the above cases, the greater the number of seats a party wins (i.e. the larger the party magnitude), the greater the percentage of women legislators who are likely to be elected (Matland 2005). Whether this relationship is linear, logarithmic, or follows some other distribution is a question for which the literature provides little guidance.

Recent research (Jones 2009) concludes that when non-flawed quota legislation is in force, a higher percentage of women is likely to be elected when, *ceteris paribus*, closed lists are used instead of open lists. However, the gap between these closed- and open-list systems that possess effective quota legislation is substantially smaller than one would expect based on the existing literature, and is principally the consequence of the superiority of the closed-list systems when a party elects two legislators in a district.

Jones (2009) also finds the relationship between party magnitude and the percentage of women elected varies considerably depending on the type of party list utilized (closed or open) and on the presence or absence of well-designed quota legislation. In the open-list systems (both with and, especially, with flawed/without quotas) party magnitude is not significantly related to the percentage of women elected. The most salient relationship between party magnitude and the election of women is present in the systems with well-designed quota legislation and closed lists. In these systems, what is of particular importance is whether or not party magnitude is one. When party magnitude is one, the probability a woman will be elected is comparatively very low.

The solution

The review above highlights three principal areas in which reforms should be adopted in the LAC region to improve the representation of women in the region's national legislatures: Quota legislation, List format, and Party magnitude.

The most fundamental reform is the adoption of the most effective gender quota legislation for the election of the members of their national legislature. If a country wants to significantly increase its percentage of women legislators in the short (or even medium) term, the best option is the adoption of quota legislation.

All countries should be required to adopt quota legislation that provides for the following. No more than half of the legislative candidates for the party in each district can be of the same sex (where the number of candidates is odd, the odd candidate can be of either sex). In the closed-list systems, the candidate lists must be zippered. The first candidate can be of either sex, but all subsequent candidates must alternate by sex. In the open-list systems, a similar 50% quota should be adopted (pending future analysis that demonstrates that an increase in the number of women candidates above a certain threshold, such as 30%, does not diminish the percentage of women elected). This legislation must also have rigid compliance standards that are reviewed and enforced by the governmental electoral authorities/courts. Parties that do not comply with the legislation in a district will not be able to run candidates in that district.

For the closed-list systems with effective quotas, the above reform would have a modest, but important, impact on women's representation via the increase in the quota percentage (from the present 30%, 33%, or 40% to 50%), through a more effective placement mandate (i.e. zippering), and through the assurance of 100% compliance. For instance, in the Argentine Chamber (30% quota, placement mandate), had this reform been in force in the previous election cycle, the percentage of women elected (*ceteris paribus*) would have been 44% (significantly higher than the actual value of 35%).

At present it is not possible to predict with any accuracy the impact of an increase in the quota percentages in the open-list systems. However, if these countries were to replace their open lists with closed lists, we would expect, *ceteris paribus*, an increase in the percentage of women elected of around 10%.

For the countries that currently have either flawed quota legislation or no quota legislation at all, the adoption of quota legislation (with quota percentages comparable to those existing in the quota systems) would result, *ceteris paribus*, in an increase in the percentage of women elected of approximately 19% (if the closed-list and quota option was utilized) and an increase in the percentage of women elected of around 12% (if the open-list and quota option was utilized).

In those countries that possess or adopt effective quota legislation, closed lists should be adopted where open lists are currently employed. This is particularly the case for those countries that have recently (in the past ten years) switched from the use of closed lists to open lists (Dominican Republic, Ecuador, Honduras), for whose political systems the switch back to a closed list should not be overly traumatic.

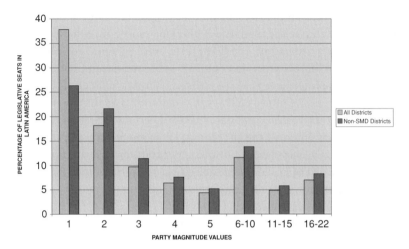

Figure 1.3 Where legislators come from: LAC region, with and without single-member districts

Finally, figure 1.3 highlights a current deficiency of the LAC electoral systems: 38% (all districts) and 26% (non-single-member district) of LAC legislators are the only legislator from their party elected in a district. As noted earlier, women have the most difficulty reaching office when their party wins only one seat in the electoral district in the preferred electoral system for the election of women (closed lists and quotas). Therefore reforms need to be adopted to increase the average size of party magnitude in the event that closed lists and quotas are employed (in the other systems, party magnitude is of little relevance for the election of women, and thus any electoral reforms in this realm are unlikely to have a positive effect on the election of women).

The principal determinant of party magnitude is district magnitude. Therefore a first, and fundamental, reform should be to eliminate all small-magnitude districts (especially any single-member districts). As district magnitude advances beyond five, the percentage of seats won in the district by a party winning only one seat also drops. This reform should therefore promote the creation of district magnitude values that are above five and ideally below twenty (assuming the use of proportional representation, or PR), although the former point is much more crucial than the latter.

Secondary electoral law reforms that will work with district magnitude changes to increase average party magnitude values include electoral formula modifications and the adoption of thresholds. Given its tendency to favor larger parties, where proportional representation is used for seat allocation, the d'Hondt formula should be utilized in place of the LR–Hare formula (although the reality in the region is that all but a handful of countries already employ the d'Hondt formula) (Payne *et al.* 2007). Other alternatives that will work to improve the size of party magnitude are the adoption of a requirement that a party surpass a district-level vote threshold, as in Argentina (especially in electoral districts with large district magnitudes) or national-level vote thresholds, as in Peru. For instance, parties could be required to win at least 5% of the votes in a district to be eligible to receive seats in the district or to win 5% of the national-level vote to be eligible to receive any seats (regardless of district-level results).

In sum, in order to promote the equal representation of women, all countries should adopt an electoral system with the following features: (1) Quota legislation mandating that no more than 50% of the candidates (with the odd number of candidates' exception) be of the same sex and that the sex of the candidates on the party lists alternate (i.e. zippered); (2) Lists that do not comply with the quota legislation requisites will be rejected; (3) Closed lists should be utilized for the election of legislators; (4) Legislators should be elected from medium-sized multi-member districts (e.g. with six–twenty members, with reaching the minimum value of six of paramount importance); (5) The d'Hondt formula should be utilized for seat allocation where proportional representation is the indicated seat allocation methodology; (6) In large-magnitude districts a 5% threshold should be utilized, and/or at the national level a 5% vote threshold should be used.

The adoption of these reforms would result in a substantial increase in the percentage of women elected throughout the region. The magnitude of this increase would vary by country and, within countries with a bicameral parliament by legislature, depending in large part on the current methods utilized. However, the overall percentage of women in most of the legislative bodies would most likely reach approximately 40%.

The case of Costa Rica is instructive on this point, as among the existing electoral system arrangements in the region it most closely approximates the electoral system proposed here. It differs from the ideal system in that its quota percentage (40%) and placement mandate rules do not require men and women to alternate on the party lists

Table 1.3 *The 2006 Legislative Assembly elections: Costa Rica*

Province	District magnitude	Political parties (women elected/seats won)					
		Total women (%)	PLN[a]	PAC[b]	ML[c]	PUSC[d]	Others (4 total)
San José	20	8 (40)	3/7	3/5	1/2	1/2	0/1, 0/1, 0/1
Alajuela	11	5 (46)	2/5	2/4	0/1	1/1	
Cartago	7	4 (57)	2/3	2/3	0/1		
Heredia	5	2 (40)	1/3	1/2			
Limón	5	1 (20)	1/2	0/1	0/1	0/1	
Puntarenas	5	1 (20)	1/2	0/1	0/1	0/1	
Guanacaste	4	1 (25)	1/3	0/1			
TOTAL	57	22 (39)	11/25	8/17	1/6	2/5	0/4

Note: [a] PLN = Partido Liberación Nacional (National Liberation Party).

[b] PAC = Partido Acción Ciudadana (Citizen Action Party).

[c] ML = Movimiento Libertario (Libertarian Movement).

[d] PUSC = Partido Unidad Social Cristiana (Social Christian Unity Party).

(although the actual distribution does not deviate far from this ideal), it employs the LR–Hare formula (with a 1/2 quota district-level vote threshold) which exercises a modest reductive impact on party magnitude (for instance, had the d'Hondt formula been used in 2006, the average party magnitude would have been 2.48, and not 2.11 as was actually the case), and in several electoral districts the district magnitude is less than ideal (in three provinces district magnitude is five, and in one province it is four). In the 2006 elections, twenty-two (39%) of the fifty-seven deputies elected were women. Table 1.3 provides a distribution of the seats won by electoral district and party. In the three larger electoral districts, women won seventeen of the thirty-eight seats in play (45%). However in the four districts that elected five or fewer deputies, women won only five of the nineteen seats being contested (26%). Had the district magnitude in these districts been larger, the overall percentage of women elected would have been notably higher.

Summary of benefits and costs

The benefits of the above reform proposal are three-fold. First, and most importantly, the reform will immediately improve the descriptive representation of women in the region's legislative bodies. This enhanced presence of women in the legislature will in turn enhance the legitimacy of the country's democratic system of government. Second, by increasing the presence of women in positions of power, the reform will aid in the creation of an autonomous and powerful cadre of women political leaders in the country. Third, the presence of an increased contingent of women in the legislature will allow for a greater degree of substantive representation of issues and policies of importance to women in the region, whose interests are often not adequately represented by overwhelmingly male legislative bodies.

The direct costs of these reforms can be divided into two groups. The first are the political costs associated with the reforms, in particular the extent to which the reforms recommended above require changes in the existing electoral legislation and the degree to which the current rules are embedded in the political system (for instance, have the current rules been in place for decades or only a few years?). The other direct costs of this reform are those engendered by the positive action nature of the reform, which by definition "discriminates" against male candidates by limiting their ability to compete for public office. Given the extremely limited and constrained nature of these latter costs, they will not be considered in the cost-benefits analysis (CBA), however some information on them is provided in the following paragraph.

It should be noted that this reform provides for equal representation, and charges of "discrimination" are based on a vision that views the current dramatic under-representation of women (itself the product of the considerable level of discrimination suffered by women in the region's political systems) as the status quo. There is also the concern that women who arrive in office under the quota system will hold a diminished status as legislators. However, there is no empirical evidence that this is in fact the case in any of the region's democracies. In fact, an advantage of these types of formal quota systems (in contrast to reserved seat systems) is that they dovetail nicely with the informal quotas that already exist in the candidate selection process throughout the region (e.g. factional quotas, regional quotas, union quotas).

This reform has three main components. The first is the employment of effective gender quota legislation, the second is the utilization of closed lists, and the third is the manner in which the system promotes moderate levels of party magnitude (in particular, the use of moderate-sized electoral districts, the use of the d'Hondt formula, and the use of district- or national-level thresholds).

The benefits of these changes are measured in terms of the expected impact on the goal of achieving gender parity in the national legislature (in particular, how the reform would move the country from its present status towards the goal of gender parity). The costs of these changes are measured in terms of the impact the reforms would have on aspects of representativeness, effectiveness, and participation (Payne *et al.* 2007).

Three general solutions are presented and then applied to the legislatures of the region. The first solution (A) entails the employment of the ideal gender quota legislation as described above (e.g. 50% quota, zippered lists, full compliance), closed party lists, and electoral rules conducive to moderate-sized party magnitude values (in particular, limiting the number of single seats won by parties at the district level). The second solution (B) entails the employment of the ideal gender quota legislation (50% quota, zippered lists), but no other changes to the existing legislation. The third solution (C) entails employment of the ideal gender quota legislation (50% quota, zippered lists) and closed party lists, but no changes regarding magnitude.

Solution A would provide the greatest benefits in terms of the election of women legislators, virtually insuring a legislature that would be between 40% and 50% female.

Solution B's benefits would vary, depending on the existing party magnitude values and list format in the region's legislatures. Its impact would the greatest (resulting in an approximately 20% jump in the percentage of women elected) among the systems that presently do not have effective quota legislation but at the same time employ medium-sized-to-large-sized electoral districts (and, to a lesser extent, the d'Hondt formula and/or district-level or national-level thresholds) as well as utilizing closed party lists. It would also have a positive effect (albeit weaker than that in the systems mentioned immediately above) in systems that do not have effective quota legislation and at the same time employ open lists (approximately 15%). This solution's impact would be the weakest among the systems that presently have effective quota legislation (in the closed-list systems a 10% increase would be expected, while it is unclear what the expectations would be for the open-list systems).

Solution C's benefits would be greatest (15%–20%) in those systems that presently do not have effective quota legislation and employ medium-sized-to-large-sized electoral districts (and, to a lesser extent, the d'Hondt formula and/or district-level or national-level thresholds). It would also have a noteworthy impact (approximately 10%) in open-list systems that currently have effective quota legislation, as long as party magnitude values are not predominantly one. For instance, were the open-list converts of the Dominican Republic (Chamber), Ecuador, and Honduras to shift back to closed lists, we would expect the percentage of women elected to office to increase by approximately 7%, 6%, and 12%, respectively (with the differences due to the higher party magnitude values existing in Honduras).

The most direct cost of the reforms above would be in the replacing of male legislators with female legislators. As there is no existing literature that demonstrates that male legislators are superior in their legislative capacities to female legislators, this cost is considered to be negligible.

A series of indirect costs (and perhaps benefits) would be associated with the extent to which the reforms related to increasing party magnitude (Solution A) and changing the type of party list used (Solutions A and C) would affect the degree of representativeness, effectiveness, and

Table 1.4 *Cost-benefit analysis (CBA) of the three quota solutions, by system type*

Current system	Solution A				Solution B				Solution C			
	Increase in % of women	Impact on Rep	Impact on Effect	Impact on Part	Increase in % of women	Impact on Rep	Impact on Effect	Impact on Part	Increase in % of women	Impact on Rep	Impact on Effect	Impact on Part
Quotas + Closed lists + Ideal PM	Low	=	=	=	Low	=	=	=	Low	=	=	=
Quotas + Closed lists + Low PM	Moderate	+/=	−/=	=/−	Moderate	=/=	=/=	=/=	Low	=/=	=/=	=/=
Quotas + Open lists + Ideal PM	Moderate	=	+	−	Low	=	=	=	Moderate	+	+	−
Quotas + Open lists + Low PM	Moderate	+	=	−	Low	=	=	=	Low	+	+	−
No/flawed quotas + Closed lists + Ideal PM	High	=	=	=	High	=	=	=	High	=	=	=
No/flawed quotas + Closed lists + Low PM	High	+/=	−/=	=/−	High	=/=	=/=	=/=	Moderate	=/=	=/=	=/=
No/flawed quotas + Open lists + Ideal PM	High	=	+	−	Low	=	=	=	High	+	+	−
No/flawed quotas + Open lists + Low PM	High	+	=	−	Low	=	=	=	Moderate	+	+	−

Note: PM = Party magnitude.
Increase in the % of women
Very High (35% +)
High (25%–34%)
Moderate (15%–24%)
Low (5%–14%)
Very Low (less than 5%)
+ (positive), − (negative), = (neutral).
In the Low PM/Closed List category the first entry is for the PR systems and the second is for the mixed systems.

participation of the electoral system (Payne *et al.* 2007). Here I follow Payne *et al.* (2007) in assessing the impact of these reforms on these three crucial consequences of an electoral system for the functioning of politics.

The most substantial reform would be adopting medium-sized-to-large-sized districts for the election of national legislators. For systems that currently possess a large number of small-sized PR districts, this reform would increase the level of representativeness, reduce the level of effectiveness, and perhaps result in a modest increase in participation. For systems that currently employ mixed-member PR, this reform would have no effect on representativeness, a minor negative effect on effectiveness, and a negative effect on participation. For the few single-member-district systems, this reform would strongly increase representativeness, strongly reduce effectiveness, and strongly reduce participation. The more modest party magnitude-related reforms (national or district thresholds, d'Hondt formula) would exercise a very modest negative effective on representativeness and a very modest positive effect on effectiveness (and no impact on participation).

The adoption of closed lists to replace open lists would have no impact on representativeness. In contrast, it would have a positive impact on effectiveness and a negative impact on participation.

Table 1.4 provides a summary of the benefits and costs (perhaps better thought of as the consequences of the solutions for representativeness, effectiveness, and participation in the political system) of the three solutions. In general, the reforms that would most increase the percentage of women elected to national legislative office would improve representativeness (due to the reforms designed to increase party magnitude), have a mixed to negative effect on effectiveness (due to the reforms designed to increase party magnitude, but tempered in some instances by the move from open to closed lists), and a neutral and at times negative impact on participation (with the negative impact occurring where mixed-member systems are eliminated and where open lists are replaced by closed lists). The benefits would be greatest in those systems that presently do not employ effective quota legislation and implement Solution A. It should be noted that as Solution B requires no other changes to the existing electoral laws (other than the adoption of the specified quota legislation), its implementation would have no effect on representation, effectiveness, or participation.

4 Conclusion

The democracies of the LAC region are currently facing a myriad of difficult problems. In this chapter I have identified two critical challenges facing the region's democracies, and proposed two solutions that will aid them in addressing these challenges. It is crucial to keep in mind that LAC's democracies are incredibly diverse and that, given the dramatically different democratic contexts in these countries, any reforms proposed must take into account the specific situation in each country. Reiterating a point made earlier, in the area of democracy, several LAC democracies are models for the region and the world (e.g. Chile, Costa Rica, Uruguay), while others are severely deficient across a wide range of democratic indicators (e.g. Guatemala, Venezuela).

Bibliography

Bartolini, Stefano and Peter Mair, 1990. *Identity, Competition and Electoral Availability: The Stabilization of European Electorates, 1885–1985.* Cambridge: Cambridge University Press

Berkman, Heather and Eduardo Cavallo, 2006. "The Challenges in Latin America: Identifying what Latin Americans Believe to be the Main Problems Facing their Countries." Washington, DC: Inter-American Development Bank, unpublished manuscript

Bratton, Kathleen A. and Leonard P. Ray, 2002. "Descriptive Representation, Policy Outcomes, and Municipal Day-Care Coverage in Norway." *American Journal of Political Science* **46**: 428–37

Coppedge, Michael, 1997. *Strong Parties and Lame Ducks: Presidential Partyarchy and Factionalism in Venezuela.* Stanford, CA: Stanford University Press

Crisp, Brian F., 2000. *Democratic Institutional Design: The Powers and Incentives of Venezuelan Politicians and Pressure Groups.* Stanford, CA: Stanford University Press

Freedom House, 2008. "Freedom in the World 2007." New York: Freedom House, www.freedomhouse.org

Htun, Mala N. and Mark P. Jones, 2002. "Engendering the Right to Participate in Decision-Making: Electoral Quotas and Women's Leadership in Latin America." In Nikki Craske and Maxine Molyneux, eds., *Gender and the Politics of Rights and Democracy in Latin America.* New York: Palgrave

Inter-Parliamentary Union, 1994. *Plan of Action: To Correct Present Imbalances in the Participation of Men and Women in Political Life.* Series Reports and Documents, **22**. Geneva: Inter-Parliamentary Union

Jones, Mark P., 2005. "The Role of Parties and Party Systems in the Policymaking Process." Workshop on "State Reform, Public Policies, and Policymaking Processes." Inter-American Development Bank, Washington, DC, February 28–March 2

  2009. "Gender Quotas, Electoral Laws, and the Election of Women: Evidence from the Latin American Vanguard." *Comparative Political Studies* **42**: 56–81

Kaufmann, Daniel, Aart Kraay, and Massimo Mastruzzi, 2007. *Governance Matters VI: Governance Indicators for 1996–2006.* Washington, DC: World Bank Development Economics Research Group

Kitschelt, Herbert, 2000. "Linkages Between Citizens and Politicians in Democratic Polities." *Comparative Political Studies* **33**: 845–79

Krook, Mona Lena, 2005. *Politicizing Representation: Campaigns for Candidate Gender Quotas Worldwide.* PhD dissertation, Columbia University

Mainwaring, Scott, 1998. "Rethinking Party Systems Theory in the Third Wave of Democratization: The Importance of Party System Institutionalization." Kellogg Institute Working Paper **260**, University of Notre Dame

  1999. *Rethinking Party Systems in the Third Wave of Democratization: The Case of Brazil.* Stanford, CA: Stanford University Press

Mainwaring, Scott and Timothy R. Scully, 1995. "Introduction: Party Systems in Latin America." In Scott Mainwaring and Timothy R. Scully, eds., *Building Democratic Institutions: Party Systems in Latin America.* Stanford, CA: Stanford University Press

Mainwaring, Scott and Edurne Zoco, 2007. "Political Sequences and the Stabilization of Interparty Competition: Electoral Volatility in Old and New Democracies." *Party Politics* **13**: 155–78

Matland, Richard E., 2005. "Enhancing Women's Political Participation: Legislative Recruitment and Electoral Systems." In Julie Ballington and Azza Karam, eds., *Women in Parliament: Beyond Numbers, A Revised Edition.* Stockholm: International IDEA

  2006. "Electoral Quotas: Frequency and Effectiveness," In Drude Dahlerup, ed., *Women, Quotas, and Politics.* New York: Routledge

Moñtano, Sonia, 2007. *Women's Contribution to Equality in Latin America and the Caribbean.* Santiago de Chile: ECLAC

Norris, Pippa, 2001. "Breaking the Barriers: Positive Discrimination Policies for Women." In Jyette Klausen and Charles S. Maier, eds., *Has*

Liberalism Failed Women? Parity, Quotas, and Political Representation. New York: St. Martin's Press

Payne, J. Mark, Daniel Zovatto G., and Mercedes Mateo Díaz, 2007. *Democracies in Development: Politics and Reform in Latin America (Expanded and Updated Edition).* Washington, DC: Inter-American Development Bank

Phillips, Anne, 1995. *The Politics of Presence.* New York: Oxford University Press

Proyecto de Elites Latinoamericanas (PELA), 2007. Manuel Alcántara Sáez, Director, Universidad de Salamanca, 1994–2007

Rahat, Gideon, 2007. "Candidate Selection: The Choice Before the Choice." *Journal of Democracy* **18**(1): 157–70

Schmidt, Gregory D., 2005. "Is Closed List PR Really Optimal for the Election of Women?: A Cross-National Analysis." Paper prepared for the Annual Meeting of the American Political Science Association, Washington, DC

Shugart, Matthew Soberg and Scott Mainwaring, 1997. "Presidentialism and Democracy in Latin America: Rethinking the Terms of the Debate." In Scott Mainwaring and Matthew Soberg Shugart, eds., *Presidentialism and Democracy in Latin America.* New York: Cambridge University Press

Spiller, Pablo T. and Mariano Tommasi, 2007. *The Institutional Foundations of Public Policy in Argentina: A Transactions Cost Approach.* New York: Cambridge University Press

Stein, Ernesto and Mariani Tommasi (with Pablo T. Spiller and Carlos Scartascini), 2008. *Policymaking in Latin America: How Politics Shape Policies.* Washington, DC: Inter-American Development Bank

Thomas, Sue, 1994. *How Women Legislate.* New York: Oxford University Press

UN, 1995. *Report on the Fourth World Conference on Women: Beijing, September 4–15.* New York: United Nations

2 | *Three proposals to improve education in the LAC region: estimates of the costs and benefits of each strategy*

AMY DAMON AND PAUL GLEWWE[*]

1 Introduction

Many macroeconomists have claimed that increased levels of education lead to increased economic growth (Lucas 1988; Barro 1991; Mankiw, Romer, and Weil 1992), although others have questioned these findings (Bils and Klenow 2000; Pritchett 2001). Among microeconomists, many studies have provided evidence of the impact of education on individuals' incomes (see Glewwe 2002, for a review). Education is also seen as a means to improve health and reduce fertility (Strauss and Thomas 1995; Schultz 1997, 2002) and is seen as an intrinsic good in itself (Sen 1999: 292–7).

This support for education among economists is matched by even greater enthusiasm in, and financial support from, international development institutions (World Bank 2001; UNDP 2003). As discussed below, developing countries have massively expanded their education systems since the 1960s, perhaps in response to the enthusiasm of donors. One example of the focus policymakers have placed on education is that two of the eight Millennium Development Goals (MDGs) adopted at the UN Millennium Summit in September 2000 focus on education: first, all children should complete primary school by 2015, and second, gender equality should be attained at all levels of education by 2015.

[*] We would like to thank Miguel Urquiola and staff members at the Copenhagen Consensus Center and at the IDB for helpful comments on previous versions of this chapter. Of course, we alone are responsible for any errors in our contribution.

These claims about the value of education are not necessarily correct. And even if they were correct, they do not provide any advice on which policies are most effective at raising educational outcomes, such as years of completed schooling and skills learned while in school. Finally, most of the discussion has focused on developing countries in general, without specific attention to the LAC countries. This chapter presents three proposals for improving education outcomes in the LAC region, assesses their impact on education outcomes, and, most importantly, presents estimates of their value as measured by the economic returns they generate by raising individuals' incomes when they are adults. The three policy proposals are: (1) Nutrition programs for infants and pre-school age children; (2) Conditional cash transfer programs, which provide cash payments to parents if their children are regularly attending school; and (3) Vouchers that can be used to pay for most of the cost of attending private schools. For each proposal, the estimated value of these benefits is then compared to the costs. For three different countries, Bolivia, Guatemala, and the Philippines, early childhood nutrition programs generated benefits that far exceeded the costs. In contrast, the benefits produced by conditional cash transfer programs in three different countries (Honduras, Mexico, and Nicaragua) almost always exceeded the costs if a 3% discount rate is used; in constrast, using a 6% discount rate sometimes yielded benefits that were less than the costs. Finally, a study of a voucher program in Colombia appears to have produced benefits that greatly exceed the costs, although one should be cautious about drawing general conclusions based on results from a single country. A final point is that some benefits, such as health benefits, could not be easily evaluated, so the benefits from all of these studies may well under-estimate the true picture.

This rest of this chapter is organized as follows. Section 2 provides an overview of education in the LAC region. Section 3 provides a brief review of the determinants of education outcomes, and the impact of education on income and other socio-economic phenomena. The three policy proposals are presented and evaluated in section 4. Section 5 discusses the benefits of undertaking more randomized evaluations to strengthen the knowledge base for education policies. The final section 6 summarizes the findings and draws several conclusions.

Table 2.1 *Trends in educational outcomes: LAC region, 1960–2004*

	1960	1980	2000	2004
Pre-primary gross enrollment rate (%)	–	28	59	64
Primary gross enrollment rate (%)	77	97	127	110
Primary net enrollment rate (%)	–	70	96	94
Primary repetition rate (%)	–	15	12	5
Primary school completion rate (%)	–	–	98	99
Primary pupil–teacher ratio	34	31	26	26
Secondary gross enrollment rate (%)	31	49	86	77
Secondary net enrollment rate (%)	–	16	64	61
Secondary repetition rate (%)	–	–	11	11
Secondary pupil–teacher ratio	–	–	19	18
Tertiary gross enrollment rate (%)	3	14	21	30

Source: World Bank World Development Indicators, 2007.

2 Progress and problems with education in the LAC region

The LAC countries have made great progress since 1960, and especially since 1980, in ensuring that all children complete primary school and most children enroll in secondary school. This can be seen in table 2.1. In 1960, most – but not all – children enrolled in primary school but less than one-third were enrolled in secondary school. By 1980, almost all children in the LAC countries were enrolled in primary school, and about half were enrolled in secondary school. In more recent years (2000 and 2004), virtually all children enroll in primary school and complete the primary cycle. Pre-primary enrollment has also increased dramatically, from about one-quarter in 1980 to about two-thirds in 2004. In addition, a large majority of children were enrolled in secondary school (although the exact percentage of children who complete secondary school has not been documented for most LAC countries). Grade repetition rates were not high, on average, and have come down in recent years to about 5% at the primary level and 11% at the secondary level. Finally, participation in post-secondary education has increased rapidly, to almost one-third of the population.

These generally favorable trends mask fairly large differences across the thirty-one countries in the LAC region. Table 2.2 presents detailed

Table 2.2 *Basic education statistics: LAC region, 2004*

	Pre-primary gross enrollment rate (%)	Primary gross enrollment rate (%)	Primary net enrollment rate (%)	Primary repetition rate (% of total enrollment)	Primary completion rate (% of relevant age group)	Secondary gross enrollment rate (%)	Secondary net enrollment rate (%)	Tertiary gross enrollment rate (%)
	2004	2004	2004	2004	2004	2004	2004	2004
Argentina	62	118	..	6	100	97	79	53
Barbados	89	107	97		108	110	95	38
Belize	28	124	95	11	103	85	71	3
Bolivia	50	113	95	2	101	80	73	41
Brazil	68	151	92	25	108	104	69	16
Chile	52	104	..	2	95	89	..	43
Colombia	38	111	83	4	94	75	55	27
Costa Rica	64	112	..	7	92	77	..	25
Cuba	116	100	96	1	93	93	87	54
Dominica	65	95	88	4	107	107	90	33
Dominican Republic	32	112	86	7	91	68	49	
Ecuador	77	117	98	2	101	61	52	..
El Salvador	51	114	92	7	86	63	44	19
Grenada	81	92	84	3	106	101	78	
Guatemala	28	113	93	13	70	49	34	..
Guyana	106	132	..	2	89	102	..	9

Haiti	..	..	..	..	*40*	..	..	16
Honduras	33	113	91	8	79	65	..	*15*
Jamaica	92	95	91	3	84	88	79	23
Mexico	84	109	98	5	99	80	64	..
Nicaragua	35	112	88	11	73	64	41	45
Panama	55	112	98	5	97	70	64	*16*
Paraguay	31	..	..	8	*78*	*60*	..	33
Peru	60	114	97	8	100	92	69	
St. Kitts and Nevis	101	101	94	..	114	94	87	
St. Lucia	71	106	98	2	102	81	71	14
St. Vincent and the Grenadines	86	106	94	6	93	78	62	
Suriname	*91*	..	..	..	..	..	..	
Trinidad and Tobago	86	102	92	5	94	84	72	12
Uruguay	*61*	*109*	..	9	98	*98*	..	37
Venezuela	55	105	92	7	89	72	61	41
LAC	65	118	95	6	88	86	67	28

Notes: **Bold italic** = 2003 estimate.

.. = Missing data.

Source: World Development Indicators, 2007.

information, by country, for 2004 (the most recent data available). Pre-primary enrollment rates vary from 28% in Belize and Guatemala to over 100% in Cuba, Guyana and St. Kitts and Nevis. Primary enroll-ment rates (both net and gross rates) are close to 100%, although there are a few exceptions (discussed in the next paragraph).[1] Repeti-tion rates are generally low, with one important exception: the primary repetition rate in Brazil is 25%, double or more than double the rate in all the other countries. Secondary enrollment rates, both gross and net, show a large amount of variation. The gross rates (which cover more countries) range from a low of 49% (Guatemala; Haiti is pre-sumably lower, but no data are available) to close to 100% (Barbados, Brazil, Dominica, Grenada, Guyana, and Uruguay).[2] Tertiary enroll-ment rates also vary widely, from a low of 3% in Belize to slightly over 50% in Argentina and Cuba.

A few countries in table 2.2 stand out as low performers. The low-est performer is Haiti, for which very little data are available. The sole statistic available, the primary completion rate, is only 40%, much lower than that of any other country (the next-lowest rate is Guatemala's 70%). Other countries with weak performance are Paraguay and three Central American countries, Guatemala, Hon-duras, and Nicaragua; the primary school completion rates for these four countries vary from 70 to 79%. Guatemala also had the low-est secondary enrollment rates: a net rate of 34% and a gross rate of 49%. (Haiti probably has even lower rates, but no data are available.)

The progress in education in recent years, as seen in table 2.1, sug-gests that the education levels in the LAC countries are moving closer to those of high-income countries, with almost universal primary school enrollment, a large majority of students enrolled in (and presumably

---

[1] The gross enrollment rate is the ratio of the number of children enrolled in a given level of schooling divided by all children in the age range associated with that level. Net rates include as enrolled only those children in the associated age range, excluding children outside that range. Thus gross enrollment rates are almost always larger than net enrollment rates, and they can exceed 100% if many "over-age" children are enrolled in a given level of schooling due to grade repetition and late enrollment into the first grade of primary school.

[2] Note that Brazil's *net* secondary enrollment rate (69) is much lower than its *gross* rate (104), and that the net rate is not particularly high compared to the net rates in other LAC countries. This large difference between Brazil's net and gross rate reflects the unusually high rate of grade repetition in Brazil.

Table 2.3 *Mean mathematics and reading achievement, TIMSS and PIRLS studies*

Country	Mathematics (TIMSS) 1999 Grade 8	Reading (PIRLS)	
		2003 Grade 8	2001 Grade 4
France	–	–	525
Japan	579	570	–
UK	–	–	553
USA	502	504	542
Argentina	–	–	420
Belize	–	–	327
Chile	392	387	–
Colombia	–	–	422
Indonesia	403	411	–
Korea (South)	587	589	–
Malaysia	519	508	–
Thailand	467	–	–
Turkey	429	–	449

Source: IAEEA (2000, 2003).

a large majority finishing) secondary school, and a tertiary (gross) enrollment rate of 30%. However, there are serious problems regarding how much children actually learn in school that cannot be seen in these statistics. International comparisons of learning from three international studies are shown in tables 2.3 (TIMSS and PIRLS studies) and 2.4 (PISA study), focusing on the results for the LAC countries and several developed countries and developing countries outside of the LAC region.

The four developed countries in table 2.3 (France, Japan, the United Kingdom and the United States) have grade 8 mathematics and grade 4 reading scores that range from 502 to 579. This range can be seen as a goal for developing countries to achieve. Yet the four LAC countries in table 2.3 (Argentina, Chile, Belize, and Colombia) have scores that fall far short of this goal, ranging from 327 (grade 4 reading score in Belize) to 422 (grade 4 reading score in Colombia). This performance is particularly worrisome because two of these four countries (Argentina and Chile) are relatively well-off LAC countries, with above-average

Table 2.4 *Mathematics and reading achievement of*
15-year-olds, PISA study

		Reading	
Country	Mathematics Mean score	Mean score	% with very low skills
France[a]	517	505	4.2
Japan[a]	557	522	2.7
UK[a]	529	523	3.6
USA[a]	493	504	6.4
Argentina[b]	388	418	22.6
Brazil[a]	334	396	23.3
Chile[b]	384	410	19.9
Mexico[a]	387	422	16.1
Peru[b]	292	327	54.1
Indonesia[b]	367	371	31.1
South Korea[a]	547	525	0.9
Thailand[b]	432	431	10.4

Notes: [a] Data are for 2000.
[b] Data are for 2002.
Source: OECD and UNESCO (2003).

education performance (as seen in table 2.2). It is also important to note
that students in one Middle Eastern and several East Asian developing
countries (Indonesia, South Korea, Malaysia, Thailand, and Turkey)
seem to perform better than all four of these LAC countries. (*Note:*
These four LAC countries are the only countries from that region that
participated in the TIMSS and PIRLS studies.)

The international comparisons in the PISA study shown in table 2.4
present a similarly sobering assessment of learning in the LAC region.
The scores for the developed countries range from 493 to 557, and
the percentage with very low reading skills in those countries varies
from 2.7% to 6.4%. In contrast, the scores in the five LAC countries
(Argentina, Brazil, Chile, Mexico, and Peru) range from 292 (math
score in Peru) to 422 (reading score in Mexico), and the percentage
of children with very low reading skills ranges from 16.1% (Mexico)
to 54.1% (Peru). Finally, the three East Asian countries in table 2.4

Table 2.5 *Trends in education finance: LAC region, 1980–2004*

	1980	2000	2004
Expenditure per student, as % of GDP *per capita*:			
Primary	6	13	16
Secondary	10	13	17
Tertiary	44	48	26
Total public spending on education, as % of GDP	5	4	4

Source: World Bank (various years).

(Indonesia, South Korea, and Thailand) scored as well as, and often much better than, the top-performing LAC countries.

It is also useful to look at trends in education finance. Table 2.5 shows that spending per student (as a proportion of GDP *per capita*) has steadily increased at the primary and secondary levels since 1980, while spending per student at the tertiary level increased slightly from 1980 to 2000 and dropped sharply from 2000 to 2004. Total spending on education (as a percentage of total GDP) has changed little since 1980, except for a small decline from 1980 to 2000.

There is also substantial variation among the LAC countries in spending on education. This is shown in table 2.6. Relative to GDP *per capita*, government spending per student on primary and secondary education is highest in Barbados, Cuba, and St. Vincent and the Grenadines. It is lowest in Dominica, Peru, and Uruguay. As a percentage of total GDP, government spending on education at all levels is highest in Cuba and St. Vincent and the Grenadines and lowest in the Dominican Republic and Venezuela. Table 2.6 also shows primary and secondary student–teacher ratios, which are an (admittedly crude) indicator of school quality. The lowest ratios in primary school are in Barbados and Cuba, while the highest ratios are in Guatemala, Honduras, and Nicaragua. At the secondary level, the lowest levels are Cuba, St. Kitts and Nevis, Paraguay, and Ecuador, while the highest are in the Dominican Republic, Honduras, and Nicaragua.

The LAC countries have made notable progress in achieving gender equity at all education levels. Duryea *et al.* (2007) report that the gender gap closed starting with the forty-five-year-old age cohort and has since reversed, with girls receiving higher average years of education than boys. More specifically, women born between 1940 and

Table 2.6 *Statistics on spending and teacher–pupil ratios, by country, 2004*

	Expenditure per student, primary (% of GDP *per capita*)	Expenditure per student, secondary (% of GDP *per capita*)	Expenditure per student, tertiary (% of GDP *per capita*)	Public spending on education, total (% of GDP)	Pupil–teacher ratio, primary	Pupil–teacher ratio, secondary
	2004	2004	2004	2004	2004	2004
Argentina	11	14	10	4	..	17
Barbados	24	29	..	7	15	17
Belize	13	18	218	5	23	19
Bolivia	16	13	36	6	24	24
Brazil	..	..	..	..	..	17
Chile	13	14	15	4	27	25
Colombia	20	20	27	5	29	25
Costa Rica	17	17	36	5	21	19
Cuba	38	41	87	10	10	11
Dominica	9	6	..	..	18	17
Dominican Republic	..	..	..	1	24	30
Ecuador	..	..	..	..	23	13
El Salvador	10	10	12	3	30	..
Grenada	12	13	..	5	18	20
Guatemala	..	..	..	..	31	15
Guyana	11	15	37	6	28	16

Haiti	..	20	..	..	..	-
Honduras	***14***	..	..	..	**33**	33
Jamaica	12	..	41	4	28	19
Mexico	***15***	***17***	44	6	28	18
Nicaragua	9	10	..	3	34	32
Panama	10	12	***26***	4	24	16
Paraguay	***13***	***14***	30	***4***	..	***12***
Peru	7	9	12	3	22	17
St. Kitts and Nevis	8	..	0	4	18	9
St. Lucia	16	18	***0***	5	24	17
St. Vincent and the Grenadines	29	20	..	11	18	20
Suriname	..	..	..	..	19	***15***
Trinidad and Tobago	..	..	..	..	18	19
Uruguay	***6***	7	19	2	..	***16***
Venezuela	..	..	..	..	19	..
LAC	..	..	..	5	23	***19***

Notes: **Bold italic** = 2000 estimate.

.. = Missing data.

Source: World Development Indicators, 2007.

1942 on average received 5 years of education while males in this cohort received 5.8. However, women born between 1979 and 1981 received 9.6 years of schooling, while their male counterparts received 9.3. On average the gender gap declined by 0.27 years of schooling per decade. This reversal is primarily explained by increased educational attainment by females at higher education levels, as opposed to changes in primary education. Within the LAC region there is considerable diversity in educational attainment. Four countries (Bolivia, Guatemala, Mexico, and Peru) within the region still have a significant gender difference favoring boys. However, this disparity is found only in the lowest-income quintile and primarily among the indigenous populations.

Indigenous populations in the LAC region have lagged behind the non-indigenous populations in terms of educational attainment, gender parity, and test scores. In Peru, Duryea *et al.* (2007) found that indigenous males and females attend school at lower rates than non-indigenous people in the same age cohort, and that the years of schooling of indigenous females, on average, were 2 years less than those of their male counterparts. Similar trends were found for indigenous populations in Bolivia, Guatemala, and Mexico. For example, Hernandez-Zavala *et al.* (2006) found that indigenous adults in Guatemala had attained only half the years of schooling that non-indigenous adults attained. In Mexico, this disparity is even wider, indigenous adults attaining only 3 years of education, vs. 8 years for non-indigenous adults. There are many reasons for this disparity; some have suggested high rates of poverty in indigenous communities, low quality of the educational environment at home, and failure to accommodate linguistic differences in the classroom.

Turning to disparities in test scores, Hernandez-Zavala *et al.* (2006) compared math and reading scores between indigenous and non-indigenous populations among 3rd and 4th year primary school students in Guatemala and Peru, and 5th grade students in Mexico. For (Spanish) language testing, they found standardized gaps between indigenous and non-indigenous students of 0.77, 0.73, and 1.06 standard deviations for Peru, Mexico, and Guatemala, respectively. They also found similar gaps (0.69 in Peru and Mexico and 0.89 in Guatemala) for math scores. An analysis of the contributing factors to this gap reveals that family and school characteristics explain between 41% (Guatemala, language test) and 75% (Mexico, language test).

In summary, the LAC countries have been very successful in ensuring that almost all children complete primary school and that most children obtain at least several years of secondary education. Yet some serious problems remain. First, a few countries – particularly Haiti and three Central American countries – are lagging behind. Second, the skills attained per year of schooling are much lower than the skills obtained per year by children in high-income countries, and even in some other developing countries. Third, in many countries the indigenous population has much lower educational outcomes than the non-indigenous population, and in a few countries substantial gender gaps remain. What can these countries do to improve the educational outcomes for their children? The remainder of this chapter attempts to answer this question.

3 Economic analysis of the causes and consequences of education outcomes

Policy recommendations for education should be based on sound research. This research involves analyzing education data from the country (or countries) in question. Such data are used to estimate relationships that can then be used to assess the impact of education policies on education outcomes, and of education outcomes on income, health status, and other objectives of economic development. Unfortunately, there are many potential estimation problems that can confound attempts to assess the impacts of education policies. This section reviews these issues, using standard microeconomic theory. For further discussion of estimation issues and reviews of the literature, see Glewwe (2002) and Glewwe and Kremer (2006). This section begins by presenting a simple economic model of schooling attainment and learning. It then expands the model to incorporate more general types of government education policies, after which it discusses the impacts of schooling on individuals' incomes and their health. The final subsection explains how estimates of the impacts of education policies on education outcomes and estimates of the impacts of education outcomes on individuals' incomes can be used to calculate rates of return and BCRs for specific education policies or programs.

A simple economic model of schooling and learning

To assess the effectiveness of education policies, one needs to understand the causal impacts of those policies on education outcomes. Estimation of these impacts is quite difficult. Before examining problems
of estimation regarding some causal relationship that one may want to
estimate, it is important to be very clear about what that relationship
is. This subsection presents a simple model of household behavior that
leads to well-defined causal relationships that one can attempt to estimate. These estimates can serve as the basis for assessing the impact
of various education policies on outcomes of interest.

For simplicity, assume that parents have a utility function that they
attempt to maximize, and one of the decisions they must make concerns
the education for their children. Again for simplicity, assume that the
household has only one child, and that there are only two time periods,
the first when the child is of school age and the second when the child
is an adult of working age. The utility function is assumed to have
only three variables, consumption in time period 1 (C_1), consumption
in time period 2 (C_2), and the academic skills that the child acquires
from his or her schooling (A):

$$U = U(C_1, C_2, A) \tag{1}$$

Parents attempt to maximize this utility function subject to a time
constraint and the production function for cognitive skills.

The production function for cognitive skills is a structural (technological) relationship between various "inputs," all factors that determine learning, and the "output," academic skills attained. It can be
specified as follows:

$$A = A_p(\textbf{EI}, PS, \alpha, \textbf{SC}, YS) \tag{2}$$

where the "p" subscript indicates that this is a production function.
Every variable in (2) refers to the first time period. There are five
types of causal factors that determine academic skills: **EI** is a vector
of educational inputs provided by parents (e.g. school supplies, books,
education toys, and – perhaps most importantly – time spent by parents
with the child that has pedagogical value) in the first time period,
PS is parental schooling, which can make parents' time (one of the
components of **EI**) more valuable, α is the child's innate intelligence
("ability"), **SC** is a vector of school (and teacher) characteristics, which

can be thought of as specific aspects of school quality, and YS is years of schooling attained in time period 1A is defined in (1). All variables in (2) have positive impacts on A.

The other constraint faced by parents is the intertemporal budget constraint. Let W_0 be the initial wealth of the household, and assume that the household can borrow and lend between the two time periods at an interest rate r.[3] Normalizing the price of the consumption good to equal 1 in time period 1, the budget constraint is:

$$W_0 = C_1 + p_{C,2}C_2/(1+r) + p_{EI}EI + p_S YS \qquad (3)$$

where $p_{C,2}$ is the price of the consumption good in time period 2, p_{EI} is the price of educational inputs, and p_S is the price of a year of schooling. Note that, for simplicity, this budget constraint assumes that parents do not receive any transfers from their children after they finish school and start working; to the extent that such transfers do occur they will, in effect, increase parental demand for schooling via the A term in the utility function (assuming that the transfers received increase with the level of schooling of the child).

Optimizing the utility in (1) with respect to the constraints in (2) and (3) gives the following standard demand functions for the four endogenous variables that can be purchased in the market:[4]

$$C_1 = C_{1,D}(W_0; r, p_{C,2}, p_{EI}, p_S; SC, PS; \alpha, \sigma) \qquad (4)$$

$$C_2 = C_{2,D}(W_0; r, p_{C,2}, p_{EI}, p_S; SC, PS; \alpha, \sigma) \qquad (5)$$

$$EI = EI_D(W_0; r, p_{C,2}, p_{EI}, p_S; SC, PS; \alpha, \sigma) \qquad (6)$$

$$YS = YS_D(W_0; r, p_{C,2}, p_{EI}, p_S; SC, PS; \alpha, \sigma) \qquad (7)$$

where the "D" subscript indicates that these are standard demand functions, and σ is parental tastes for child education (which determine the shape of the utility function). Note that all of the variables on

---

[3] For simplicity, this budget constraint does not explicitly show parental income in the two time periods. Yet income in both time periods can be included as part of lifetime wealth (W_0), where income in the second time period is discounted by dividing it by $1 + r$. Note that this assumes that income is exogenous in both time periods, which is also done to maintain simplicity.

[4] The term "endogenous" is used here in terms of its meaning in an economic model: endogenous variables are variables that can be influenced by household behavior. Whether these variables are endogenous in an *econometric* sense – that is, correlated with the error term in an equation to be estimated – is a separate question, which will be discussed below.

the right-hand side of these demand functions are exogenous; that is, none of them is under the control of the parents.[5] A final point regarding these demand functions is that they do not explicitly account for parents' time preference for consumption; in general, "impatient" parents will have higher demand for C_1, lower demand for C_2, and no clear effect on the demand for EI and YS (as long as parents do not face credit constraints).

A final important relationship is the demand for the child's academic skills. This can be obtained by inserting (6) and (7) directly into (2):

$$A = A_D(W_0; r, p_{C,2}, p_{EI}, p_S; SC, PS; \alpha, \sigma) \tag{8}$$

where the "D" subscript indicates that this is a demand equation, and as in the other demand equations all the variables on the right-hand side are exogenous in the sense discussed above.

It is very important to understand the difference between (2), the production function for academic skills, and (8), the demand function for academic skills. Consider what happens when some aspect of school quality, call it SC_j, increases. Equation (2) shows how that increase in school quality affects academic skills, *holding constant all other variables in* (2). This can be depicted as $\partial A_p / \partial SC_j$. In contrast, (8) shows how this increase in school quality affects academic skills *after the household adjusts educational inputs and years of schooling.* The derivative for this relationship is:

$$\partial A_D / \partial SC_j = \partial A_p / \partial SC_j + (\partial A_p / \partial YS)(\partial YS_D / \partial SC_j)$$
$$+ (\partial A_p / \partial EI)(\partial EI_D / \partial SC_j) \tag{9}$$

The first term in (9) is the structural impact of school quality on academic achievement, which is what is measured in (2), but there are also the "indirect" effects via changes in the demand for years of schooling and educational inputs, which are the second and third terms in (9). One possibility is that parents reduce their demand for YS and EI in response to an improvement in school quality; if all three arguments in the utility function are normal goods, the household will have an

---

[5] Whether these variables are exogenous in the econometric sense of being uncorrelated with the error term in an equation to be estimated is a separate question; this is discussed below.

incentive to reduce *YS* and **EI** in order to "balance" the increase in *A* that comes from an increase in school quality with increases in C_1 and C_2 (which can be increased if *YS* and **EI** are reduced). Yet even if all arguments in the utility function are normal goods the direction of this adjustment is uncertain because the increase in SC_j in effect reduces the implicit price of academic skills (*A*); this price effect will increase demand for those skills, and raises the possibility that $\partial A_D/\partial SC_j$ will be greater than $\partial A_p/\partial SC_j$. For further discussion of these points, see Glewwe and Miguel (2008).

Many economists and education researchers have attempted to estimate the determinants of years of schooling as given in (7). These attempts have been only partially successful due to a variety of estimation problems, including omitted variable bias, measurement error in the explanatory variables, and potential problems of endogenous program placement. Omitted variable bias occurs if some of the variables in that equation are not in the data, and so in effect they end up in the error term in the regression equation. If these "omitted" variables are correlated with one or more of the observed variables, the observed variables are endogenous in the econometric sense that they are correlated with the error term, and the estimated impacts of *all* of the observed variables are likely to be biased estimates of the true impacts. For example, suppose that one is interested in the impact on years of schooling of various school and teacher characteristics (the variables in **SC**), many of which can be changed by introducing a new education policy. Schools and teachers that are "above average" are likely to be above average in many ways. If some of those ways are not measured by any of the variables in the data set, and they are positively correlated with the school and teacher characteristics that are in the data set, the impacts of the variables that are in the data set are likely to be over-estimated because they are positively correlated with the error term in the regression model (which includes the unobserved school characteristics) and thus they are endogenous in the econometric sense. Similarly, if parents with higher "tastes" for their children's education (higher σ) are more likely to send their children to better-quality schools, then the variables in **SC** will be positively correlated with the error term (if σ is not observed, which is usually the case); those parents encourage their children to stay in school and thus the positive correlation will lead to over-estimation of the impact of school quality on years of completed schooling.

Random measurement error in the explanatory variables in any regression equation will tend to lead to under-estimation of the impacts of those variables that are measured with error. For example, if data on the tuition and fees charged by schools (p_S) are measured with error (which often appears to be the case when such data are collected from household surveys and/or schools surveys), then the estimated impact of tuition and fees on years of schooling is likely to be under-estimated.

Bias from endogenous program placement occurs if government ministries introduce new educational programs or policies in areas where conditions are particularly poorly suited for raising educational outcomes. This will tend to lead to under-estimation of the impact of those programs or policies on educational outcomes. For example, suppose that parents' attitudes toward (tastes for) education are rather negative in a particular area. In order to raise educational outcomes in that area, and in others like it, the government may provide additional support to or programs for education in those areas. But if these attitudes toward education are not observed, regression estimates of the impact of this type of policy will tend to under-estimate the true impact because the policy variable would be negatively correlated with the error term (which includes tastes for education) in the regression equation. A final point is that another form of endogenous program placement bias could lead to over-estimation of the impacts of government programs; this is possible if "elite" groups, who may have higher tastes for education and higher unobserved educational inputs, are able to pressure the government to implement new policies in the schools their children attend.

These estimation problems have led researchers to use more rigorous methods in recent years to avoid these types of biases. Methods include the use of instrumental variables (although finding credible instruments can be very difficult), panel data methods, "natural" experiments, and randomized trials. For a detailed discussion, see Glewwe and Kremer (2006). The three proposals presented in section 4 are based on studies that have used these methods to estimate the impact of school characteristics or other variables on years of schooling. The estimation methods used are explained in more detail there.

Policymakers are interested not only in factors that determine years of schooling, but also in factors that determine how much children learn while in school. As explained above, there are two relationships to consider, the production function in (2) and the demand relationship in (8). Focusing on variables that are most relevant for policy decisions, (2) shows how learning changes when school and teacher characteristics change *if there are no changes in years of schooling or in educational inputs provided by parents.* On the other hand, (8) shows how changes in school and teacher characteristics, as well as changes in school fees (p_S) and the price of educational inputs (p_{EI}), will change learning *after parents' behavioral responses have taken place.* Both of these relationships are of interest. Equation (8) shows exactly what will happen in the real world when a policy is implemented, because in the real world households will adjust their behavior after the policy is implemented. Yet (2) is also of interest because it better captures the full benefit to society as a whole, since (8) does not measure the benefits households receive when they readjust their demand for educational inputs (**EI**) and years of schooling (*YS*) in response to the program. That is, if a household decides to reduce spending on educational inputs in response to the program or policy change, it raises its utility by spending more on other items (C_1 and C_2), but this benefit is ignored in (8). See Glewwe *et al.* (2004) for a more complete explanation of this point.

Expanding the model to include government policies

The discussion thus far has been rather narrow in that it assumes that education policies can be measured in terms of changes in teacher and school characteristics, and changes in school fees and the prices of educational inputs. Fortunately, this framework can be extended to examine policies that do not directly change **SC**, p_S, and p_{EI} but instead change them indirectly by changing the way schools are organized. This allows for the analysis of education policies such as decentralization, promoting competition by removing restrictions on private schools, or developing incentive schemes that link teacher pay to student performance. In principle, these types of policies affect schooling outcomes by changing what happens in the classroom. For example, increased competition may change the behavior of teachers, and these behaviors can be included as components of the vector **SC**. Formally, education policies, denoted by **EP**, may interact with local community characteristics, denoted by **CC**, to determine the quality of a school and even the prices of educational inputs in some cases (e.g. policies that allow communities to set school fees):

$$SC = sc(\mathbf{CC}, \mathbf{EP}) \tag{10}$$

$$p_S = p_S(\mathbf{CC}, \mathbf{EP}) \tag{11}$$

$$p_{EI} = p_{EI}(\mathbf{CC}, \mathbf{EP}) \tag{12}$$

Estimating (10), (11), and (12) would require very detailed data on what happens in schools such as the many dimensions of teacher behavior. An alternative is to substitute (10), (11), and (12) into (7) and (8) to obtain the reduced-form relationships:

$$YS = YS_I(W_0; r, p_{C,2}, PS; \mathbf{CC}, \mathbf{EP}; \alpha, \sigma) \tag{13}$$

$$A = A_I(W_0; r, p_{C,2}, PS; \mathbf{CC}, \mathbf{EP}; \alpha, \sigma) \tag{14}$$

where the "*I*" subscript indicates that this reduced-form relationship focuses on institutional aspects of how schools are organized. Knowledge of the relationships in (13) and (14) would directly link education policies to the main outcomes of interest to policymakers.

Estimating the impact of education policies on years of schooling and on learning – that is, estimating (13) and (14) – faces many of the estimation problems discussed above. For example, policies such as offering teacher incentives or decentralizing control of schools are not randomly introduced in some schools and not others, but instead are implemented in schools that are chosen for a particular reason, or that volunteer to participate. Thus, just as in the problem of bias from non-random program placement, schools that implement a policy of interest may differ from schools that do not in systematic and unobserved ways. This will cause the education policy variable to be correlated with the error term in the regression equation and thus to be endogenous in the econometric sense, leading to biased estimates. One way to get around many of these estimation problems, which is discussed more in section 5, is to implement new education policies in a random sample of schools.

The impact of schooling on income

The discussion thus far has been limited to the relationships that determine years of schooling and the learning that takes place within schools. But to assess the merits of any education policy one must also consider the value of the schooling, in terms of both its income and non-income benefits. This information can then be used to calculate BCRs for specific education policies.

Economists and other social scientists have conducted a large amount of research on the impact of schooling on the incomes of individuals, in both developed and developing countries. Unfortunately, as with the literature on the determinates of learning and years of schooling, there are many estimation problems that can lead to biased estimates. On a more positive note, a large amount of research has been done on how to overcome these estimation problems, including some research done in developing countries. This subsection presents a brief review of the most relevant issues, beginning with wage earners and then turning to farmers and other self-employed individuals.

In a well-functioning competitive labor market, employers will pay wage earners the marginal product of their labor. This marginal product will depend on their skills, broadly defined, which are primarily determined by their schooling and their experience. This can be depicted as follows:

$$
\begin{aligned}
w = w(A) &= w(A_p(\text{EI}, PS, \alpha, \text{SC}, YS; EXP)) \\
&= w(\text{EI}, PS, \alpha, \text{SC}, YS; EXP)
\end{aligned} \tag{15}
$$

where A is a vector of the many kinds of skills learned, EXP is years of experience, and a modified version of (2) has been used to show how skills acquired from schooling evolve over time as individuals accumulate more years of work experience.

Among the determinants of wages in (15), it is relatively easy to collect information on years of schooling and on experience. It is harder, though not impossible, to collect data on educational inputs (EI), parental schooling (PS), innate ability (α), and school "quality" (SC). Many labor economists have, following the pioneering work of Gary Becker and Jacob Mincer, estimated the following log linear functional form for (15):

$$
\begin{aligned}
\log(w) &= \beta_0 + \beta_1 YS + \beta_2 EXP + \beta_3 EXP_2 + u \\
&= \beta_0 + \beta_1 YS + \beta_2 EXP + \beta_3 EXP_2 + u(\text{EI}, PS, \alpha, \text{SC})
\end{aligned} \tag{15'}
$$

where the error term u is some function of educational inputs provided by parents, parental schooling, learning ability, and school quality, which are usually unavailable and thus are relegated to the error term.

Most attempts to estimate $(15')$ use data sets that contain variables for wages (w) and years of schooling (YS). Years of work experience (EXP) is either directly measured or (more often) calculated as current age minus years of education minus 6. The latter approach for measuring work experience assumes that individuals start schooling at age 6, do not repeat any years of schooling, start working full time immediately after finishing their schooling, and continue working full time up until the time of the interview; all of these assumptions could be erroneous in many developing countries, which will introduce measurement error (not necessarily random) in the work experience variable, which in turn is likely to lead to biased estimates.

Perhaps the most serious problem with estimates of (15) is that the error term – that is, $u(\text{EI, PS}, \alpha, \text{and SC})$ – is likely to be correlated with years of schooling (YS) and years of work experience (EXP), which introduces biases in the estimate of the impact of schooling on wages (β_1). For example, the model presented above (and common sense) suggests that parents will tend to increase their child's years in school if either the child is more talented (higher α) or the quality of the school is higher (higher SC). Both of these phenomena will cause u to be positively correlated with YS and thus will lead to overestimation of β_1. It is also possible that educational inputs (EI) are positively correlated with years of schooling. Parents with high "tastes" for schooling are likely to purchase more educational inputs and are likely to keep their children in school for more years, leading to positive correlation in YS and EI and thus positive correlation between YS and the error term in $(15')$. On the other hand, YS could be measured with random error, which will tend to lead to under-estimation of β_1. Overall, it is unclear whether simple estimates of β_1 obtained from estimates of equations similar to $(15')$ over-estimate or under-estimate the true impact of schooling on wages.

When calculating the benefits of education, in particular the impact of schooling on wages, one should exercise caution. Many estimates of $(15')$ have been published that are likely to be biased. See Glewwe (1996) for an example from Ghana. Thus even published estimates need to be scrutinized, as opposed to blindly accepting their accuracy.

If doubt arises about estimates of β_1 for a particular country, the wisest approach may be to use an estimate of about 0.08 or 0.09. These values are similar to very careful estimates of β_1 by Duflo (2001) for Indonesia, which use a "natural experiment" of rapid school construction as an instrumental variable for educational attainment of adult males.

A final issue is that many people in developing countries are not wage earners; instead they are self-employed, operating farms or small family-run businesses. This is particularly true in rural areas. This raises two problems. First, estimates of the impact of schooling on the earnings of wage earners could suffer from sample selection bias. Second, and more importantly, there is no reason to expect the impact of education on wages to be the same as the impact of education on self-employment income. Indeed, Duflo (2001) found that the impact of years of schooling on the incomes of the self-employed was smaller than the impact on the incomes of wage earners. This suggests that, for countries with many self-employed individuals, it would be prudent to use estimates of β_1 ranging from 0.05 to 0.07.[6] Based on these results, the BCRs presented below use two different assumptions about the impact of an additional year of schooling on labor income, an "upper bound" rate of 10%, and a "lower bound" rate of 5%.

The impact of schooling on health and other outcomes

Education provides not only higher incomes but also improves the quality of life in other ways. Perhaps most importantly, better-educated people are healthier and have healthier children (Glewwe 1999; Grossman 2006). This benefit of education is not captured in estimates of the impact of education on income. Unfortunately, for most developing countries there are no reliable estimates of the impact of education on health outcomes, so this benefit is not included in this chapter. Thus the BCRs presented in section 4 are under-estimates of the true benefits. Future research should attempt to measure these non-income benefits.

[6] In rural areas of developing countries, where many of the programs evaluated in this chapter were implemented, a large fraction of the labor force consists of self-employed farmers. Thus the rate of return to education in rural areas will, in general, be lower than the rate of return prevailing in urban areas.

Using estimates of causal relationships to calculate rates of return and BCRs for education policies

Standard CBA uses estimates of the cost and of the expected benefits (which often accrue over many years) of a program or policy, to calculate either an economic rate of return or a BCR for that program or policy. Turn first to estimates of economic rates of return. Once one has the costs and benefits of the program or policy, both in monetary terms, for all years, the economic rate of return is the discount rate that sets the present discounted value of the cost of the project equal to the present discounted value of its benefits. For example, suppose that the cost of the project at time zero is C_0, and that there are no other costs, and that the benefits accrue steadily from year 1 to year 30. Denoting the benefits for each of these years as $B_1, B_2, \ldots B_{30}$, the economic rate of return is the value of r that makes the following equality hold:

$$C_0 = \sum_{t=1}^{30} B_t/(1+r)^t \tag{16}$$

Sometimes costs are incurred for more than one year, so the most general definition of the economic rate of return is the value of r that ensures that the following equality holds:

$$\sum_{t=0}^{T_c} C_t/(1+r)^t = \sum_{t=0}^{T_b} B_t/(1+r)^t \tag{17}$$

where T_c is the last year for which costs are incurred and T_b is the last year for which benefits are generated. If there is no cost or no benefit for a given time period, then the corresponding C_t or B_t can be set equal to zero. Note also that in practice it is not necessary to go out beyond $t = 50$ because the value of $1/(1+r)^t$ becomes close to zero. For example, $1/(1+0.05)^{50} = 0.0872$.

Now turn to BCRs. These are very easy to calculate. Instead of finding the value of r that sets both sides of (17) equal to each other, choose a "reasonable" r (i.e. a reasonable discount rate), and then calculate the BCR as:

$$\text{BCR} = \left[\sum_{t=0}^{T_c} B_t/(1+r)^t \right] \Big/ \left[\sum_{t=0}^{T_b} C_t/(1+r)^t \right] \tag{18}$$

This is simply the present discounted value of the benefits divided by the present discounted value of the costs, for a given discount rate.

In practice, it is useful to use two or three different discount rates; section 4 uses discount rates of 3% and 6% for each intervention.

For most types of education policies, the direct costs are relatively easy to calculate. In addition, there is an important indirect cost to consider. If children go to school for a longer period of time because of a certain policy, the opportunity cost of that additional time spent in school must also be included as part of the cost. This is usually done by valuing that time in terms of the wages or income that would have been earned had the child worked during that additional period of time.

Assessing the monetary value of the benefits of an education policy is more complicated. In the simplest case, the policy has increased children's skills, which are measured by the vector A in (15), and this in turn increases wages. If most or all of the increases in skills occur through increases in years of schooling, then it is not necessary to measure A directly, but instead one can use estimates of β_1 in (15') to calculate the impact of the education policy, via its impact on years of schooling, on wages. On the other hand, if much of the benefit is in terms of increasing skills learned for a given number of years of schooling, the contribution of this increase in skills to labor productivity, and thus to labor income, should be calculated directly. One way to do so is to convert an increase in skills into the number of additional years of schooling required to obtain that increase in skills, and then use estimates of the impact of years of schooling on wages (or other types of labor income) to measure the value of the increase in skills.

While benefit-cost analyses can be important guides for policy, governments and development organizations must keep in mind several limitations that they have. First, they are only as reliable as the estimates on which they are based. As explained above, there are many problems with estimating the causal relationships (in particular, estimates of the impact of education policies on education outcomes, and of education outcomes on incomes) so those estimates need to be scrutinized with a critical eye. Second, strictly speaking, estimates of both costs and benefits of a particular program or policy apply only to that program or policy in that country, and seemingly minor changes in those programs or policies, or even precisely the same program or policy in a different country, could have very different costs and benefits. Third, in principle, raising funds via taxes in order to fund a program or policy can lead to distortions in economic activity that, in effect, raise the social cost of implementing the project or program. Keeping these limitations in mind, section 4 presents estimates of BCRs for several different types of education policies.

4 Estimates of BCRs for three types of education intervention

This section presents CBAs of the three education interventions that seem most promising (in terms of high BCRs) for LAC countries, based on many recent studies. All three of these interventions operate by increasing the demand for education: nutrition programs for pre-school children; conditional cash transfers; and vouchers that can be used to attend private schools. For each specific program studied, BCRs are presented using two different annual discount rates, 3% and 6% (these are the rates requested by the Copenhagen Consensus Center).

Before turning to the specific interventions, it is important to point out an issue which limited the analysis, which is that CBAs could be done only for interventions that had been rigorously evaluated. There are many other interventions that appear to be promising, but since no careful studies have been done of those interventions it is not possible to calculate reliable estimates of the benefits (calculation of the costs is usually less of a problem). Indeed, the benefit estimates of some of the programs included in this chapter may also suffer from serious biases, as explained in detail below.

Nutrition programs for pre-school-age children

There are several studies that have presented credible evidence showing that children who are better nourished in the first years of life stay in school longer and learn more per year of schooling (for a detailed review, see Glewwe and Miguel 2008). This subsection presents estimates of BCRs based on three recent, and rigorous, studies, two from the LAC region (Bolivia and Guatemala) and one from Asia (the Philippines).

Perhaps the most well-known, and arguably the first, study of the impact of a child nutrition program on health and education outcomes in a developing country is the INCAP study that was initiated in four Guatemalan villages in 1969. In two villages, a nutritious porridge (*atole*) was provided to pre-school-age children for a period of up to three years. In the other two villages, a much less nutritious cool drink (*fresco*) was provided for the same period of time. Assignment of the four villages to receive *atole* or *fresco* was random. The annual cost of the *atole* intervention, in US dollars, was $18.25 per child. Primary medical care was also provided in all four villages, for an additional $5 per child per year, so the total annual cost of the program was $23.25 per child per year.[7] Studies of the benefits (see below) have focused on children who were in the program for three years.[8] For children who participated in the program for three full years, the present discounted value of the cost of the program was $67.74 using a 3% discount rate and $65.88 using a 6% discount rate. (All BCRs presented in this chapter use the first year of program operation as the base year for discounting.)

Turning to the benefits of the INCAP child nutrition intervention, Maluccio *et al.* (2006) estimate that the *atole* supplementation increased grade attainment by 1.2 years for girls, but there was no impact for boys. Technically speaking, this estimate is the benefit of the *atole* program relative to the *fresco* program, but the nutritional content of the *fresco* drink was small compared to the nutritional content of the *atole* porridge, so this estimate is fairly close to (though a slight under-estimate of) the impact of the *atole* intervention relative to no intervention at all. The difference in the impact by sex is puzzling and may reflect random variation; perhaps the most reasonable conclusion is that this intervention increases the years of schooling of the average student by 0.6 years. Since the villages were assigned to *atole* or *fresco* randomly, there is a good reason to believe that the coefficient estimate of the impact of being exposed to the *atole* program is unlikely to be biased. Patrinos and Velez (1994) estimate that an additional year of schooling in Guatemala increases wages by about 10.7%, based on data from wage earners.[9] This may over-estimate the actual benefit because no attempt is made to account for unobserved child ability and these estimates are based on a national sample, whereas

[7] We would like to thank John Maluccio for providing us with this information on the costs of the INCAP program in Guatemala.
[8] Any child, and indeed any adult, was allowed to come to the feeding centers, which were open from about 10 a.m. to 2 p.m., for the entire eight years that they operated, but most analyses of the benefits focus on children who participated for three years.
[9] We use the estimate in table A-6 that includes the largest number of control variables.

the INCAP intervention was implemented in rural areas (many rural residents are self-employed farmers, who generally have lower rates of return to education, as discussed above). As explained already, because of this potential for over-estimation of the impact of an additional year of schooling on wages, two scenarios are presented, one using an upper bound of 10% and the other using a lower bound of 5%, for calculating the benefits. Taking a 10% increase in wages as an upper bound, the present discounted value of the increase in wages from an increase of 0.6 years of schooling is $622 for a 3% discount rate and $261 for a 6% discount rate. Table 2.7 shows the associated BCRs, which are 9.19 and 3.96, respectively. Using a 5% increase in wages per year of schooling as a lower bound leads to an increase in wages of $312 for a 3% discount rate and $131 for a 6% discount rate, with associated BCRs of 4.61 and 1.99, respectively.

A second program from Latin America that has recently been evaluated is the Proyecto Integral de Desarrollo Infantil (PIDI) program that was implemented in Bolivia in the 1990s. This program included not only a nutritional component (the cost of which was about 40% of the cost of the program) but also educational activities; both nutrition supplementation and educational activities are common components of early child development (ECD) programs.[10] It was implemented in low-income neighborhoods of urban areas, and children between 6 months and 72 months were eligible to enroll in it. It is much more expensive than the Guatemalan intervention, with an average cost of $516 per child per year. In their analysis of the program, Behrman, Cheng, and Todd (2004) assume that the average child is enrolled in the program for three years, which implies that the present discounted value of the cost is $1,394 for a 3% discount rate and $1,256 for a 6% discount rate.

Behrman, Cheng, and Todd use matching methods to estimate the impact of a typical child's participation in the program on several outcomes: (1) Child height; (2) Grades completed; (3) Cognitive skills,

---

[10] The evaluation of the PIDI program, as in the evaluations of almost all ECD programs, could not separate the impact of the nutritional component from that of the educational activity component. Grantham-McGregor *et al.* (1997) present evidence from Jamaica that both components contribute to children's cognitive development. See Schady (2006) for a more recent review of the limited evidence from the LAC countries on the impact of ECD programs on child development.

conditional on grade completed; and (4) Age at the time of school completion, conditional on grades completed. The study provides estimates of the impact of the program on all these outcomes. To assess the value of these outcomes in terms of increased wages, the authors use previously published studies from different countries (Brazil for impact of height on wages and Pakistan for impact of cognitive skills on earnings). The authors estimate that the present discounted value of the benefits is $4,647 using a 3% discount rate, and $2,781 using a 6% discount rate. As seen in table 2.7, the associated BCRs are 3.33 for the 3% discount rate and 2.21 for the 6% discount rate.[11]

A third set of BCR figures combines estimates from the Philippines of the impact of child nutritional status on educational outcomes and the impacts of those outcomes on wages with the estimated cost of a nutritional intervention program in India. The feeding program is the Narangwal Project, which operated in the Indian State of Punjab in the late 1960s and early 1970s. Kielmann and associates (1983) estimate that this program increased child height by about 2 cm. The cost of the Narangwal Project program was about $100 per child.

The benefits of an increase in height of 2 cm were estimated, using data from the Philippines, by Glewwe, Jacoby, and King (2001). The increase in test scores from better nutrition (as measured by a 2 cm increase in child height) is equivalent to an increase of about six months of schooling for the average child. The authors estimate that a six-month increase in schooling leads to an increase in wages of $57 per year (this is based on a wage regression similar to that shown in (15′), which finds that an additional year of schooling increases wages by 7%). Assuming that a child works for 45 years when an adult, the discounted value of this additional income is $929 using a 3% discount rate and $390 using a 6% discount rate, respectively. The associated BCRs, again shown in table 2.7, are 9.29 for the 3% discount rate and 3.90 for the 6% discount rate. An alternative approach is to assume that students achieve the same level of cognitive skills but can do so

[11] The calculations presented in Behrman, Cheng, and Todd (2004) were very complicated, and we were unable to replicate their results given the information in the paper. Thus we could not measure how the BCR changed when the increase in wages from an additional year of schooling was set to either 5% or 10%. Presumably the results are not very sensitive to altering this effect because years of completed schooling is only one of four pathways by which the program affected wages.

Table 2.7 *Estimates of BCRs, by type of education intervention*

Program	Country	3% discount rate			6% discount rate		
		Cost	Benefit	BCR	Cost	Benefit	BCR
Early childhood nutrition programs							
INCAP (10% return)	Guatemala	68	622	9.2	66	261	4.0
INCAP (5% return)	Guatemala	68	312	4.6	66	131	2.0
PIDI	Bolivia	1394	4647	3.3	1256	2781	2.2
Narangwal: 1st scenario	India/Philip.	100	929	9.3	100	390	3.9
Narangwal: 2nd scenario	India/Philip.	100	417	4.2	100	271	2.7
CCT							
Progresa/Oportunidades	Mexico						
3-year program (10% ret.)		391	1081	2.8	380	453	1.2
3-year program (5% ret.)		391	541	1.4	380	227	0.6
Perm. program (10% ret.)		839	1081	1.3	754	453	0.6

Perm. program (5% ret.)		839	541	0.6	754	227	0.3
RED	Nicaragua						
10% ret., excl. attend.		268	557	2.1	264	233	0.9
5% ret., excl. attend.		268	278	1.0	264	117	0.4
10% ret., incl. attend.		268	1409	5.3	264	591	2.2
5% ret., incl. attend.		268	721	2.7	264	302	1.1
PRAF	Honduras						
10% ret., excl. attend.		131	875	6.7	128	367	2.9
5% ret., excl. attend.		131	438	3.3	128	183	1.4
10% ret., incl. attend.		131	1113	8.5	128	467	3.7
5% ret., incl. attend.		131	557	4.2	128	233	1.8
Vouchers for private secondary schools							
PACES (0.12 increase)	Colombia	193	1215	6.3	188	872	4.6
PACES (1 year increase)	Colombia	193	4914	25.5	188	2060	10.9

Note: All costs and benefits are in USD.
Source: Authors' calculations, as explained in text.

by leaving school six months earlier (and thus start their working life six months earlier). This leads to a one-time benefit of $650 when the child is about 15 years old; the present discounted value of this figure is $417 using a 3% discount rate and $271 using a 6% discount rate. The associated BCRs are 4.17 for the 3% discount rate and 2.71 for the 6% discount rate, respectively.

CCT programs

Several LAC countries, and a few countries in other regions of the world, have implemented programs that provide monthly cash payments to poor households if the school-age children in those households attend school regularly. Most of these programs have been carefully evaluated because they were implemented in a randomized way: from a sample of a large number of communities half or more than half were randomly selected to implement the program while the other communities served as controls. This greatly eases (but does not eliminate) many estimation problems regarding the impact of these programs on children's educational outcomes. While these programs increase enrollment and attendance in the program areas, CCTs generally do not address the often low quality of education. It is possible that combining CCTs with increases in school quality is more cost-effective than either intervention by itself; regrettably, there is little reliable evidence on whether this conjecture is correct. Keeping this in mind, this subsection presents BCRs for CCT programs that have been implemented in Honduras, Mexico, and Nicaragua.

The earliest, largest, and most well-known CCT program is the Progresa program that was implemented in 314 communities in rural Mexico in 1998 (another 181 rural communities served as a control group for the first two years of the program). (The program was later renamed Oportunidades and was expanded to urban areas.) For children of primary school age and lower secondary school age in poor households (about two-thirds of the households in these communities were officially designated as poor), monthly payments were provided to families if their children attended school for 85% or more of the days that the schools were open. The families were initially told that the program would last only for three years, although in fact the program has continued to operate. If the program had operated for only three years, the (discounted) average cost per child would be about

$391 for a 3% discount rate and about $380 for a 6% discount rate, respectively. However, if parents had assumed that the program would operate indefinitely when making their enrollment decisions then the estimated benefit of the program pertains to a child going through the program for seven years (grades 3–9), so the (discounted) average cost per child would be about $839 for a 3% discount rate and about $754 for a 6% discount rate, respectively. Note that these costs are averaged over all eligible children, including those who did not fully participate because they dropped out of school, because the estimated benefits were for all children, not just those who fully participated. Thus the BCRs presented below are for all children who had the opportunity to participate in the program – that is, they are based on estimates of the impact of "offering" the program on the average years of schooling of all poor children in the "treatment" communities.

Schultz (2004) estimates that the cumulative impact of the Progresa program is to increase the years of schooling of the children in the "treatment" communities by 0.66 years. Note that this estimated impact is the impact of being offered the program, not the impact of participating in it; the latter would be higher since some children in the communities where Progresa was implemented dropped out of school and thus did not fully participate. Citing a study of estimates of the determinants of wages in urban areas of Mexico, Schultz assumes that each additional year of schooling increases wages by 12%. This could over-estimate the rate of return to years of schooling among beneficiaries of the program, for two reasons. First, children with higher levels of schooling may have higher innate ability. Second, and more importantly, these estimates are for urban areas and, as discussed above, the returns to schooling in rural areas (where a substantial portion of the labor force consists of self-employed farmers) are likely to be much lower. The results presented in table 2.7 use two different assumptions, one that an additional year of schooling raises wages by 10% (perhaps because many educated people in rural areas will eventually migrate to urban areas) and the other that it raises wages by 5% (assuming that most rural residents remain in rural areas). Based on wages of youth in the Progresa data set, Schultz (2004) estimates an average wage of US$1,002 per year, so an increase in 0.66 years of schooling implies a wage increase of $66 per year (1,002*0.10*0.66) if an additional year of schooling raises wages by 10%, or $33 per year if an additional year of schooling raises wages by 5%. Assuming that the typical rural youth in Mexico will work from age 15 to age 60, the present discounted value of the wage gain from the Progresa program, assuming that a year of schooling raises wages by 10%, is estimated to be $1,081 using a 3% discount rate and $453 using a 6% discount rate, respectively. The more conservative assumption that one more year of schooling raises wages by only 5% leads to lower values: $541 using a 3% discount rate and $227 using a 6% discount rate, respectively.

Combining the estimates of the discounted costs and benefits yields four sets of results. If one assumes that the impact estimated by Schultz (2004) corresponds to operating the program for only three years and that a year of schooling raises wages by 10%, then the BCRs are 2.8 for a 3% discount rate and 1.2 for a 6% discount rate, respectively. In contrast, if one assumes that Schultz's estimates correspond to a permanent program, in which case an individual child is eligible to receive benefits for seven years, then the BCRs are lower, 1.3 for a 3% discount rate and 0.6 for a 6% discount rate, respectively (continuing to assume that each year of schooling increases wages by 10%). If a more conservative assumption about the impact of schooling on wages is used – namely, that each year increases wages by 5% – then the BCRs (assuming that the estimated effects are for a three-year program) are 1.4 for a 3% discount rate and 0.6 for a 6% discount rate, respectively. The lowest BCRs result from assuming that a year of schooling increases wages by only 5% and that the estimated effects reflect a program that has operated for seven years: they are 0.6 for a 3% discount rate and 0.3 for a 6% discount rate, respectively.

Two Central American countries, Honduras and Nicaragua, have followed Mexico's lead and also implemented CCT programs, and have also done so in a randomized way that facilitates assessment of the impact of those programs on schooling outcomes. Nicaragua's program is called RED (Red de Protection Social, Social Safety Net). The implementation of the first phase of this program began in 2000 and ended in 2003. The education component of the program focused on providing cash payments to families with children age 7–13 who were in grades 1–4 (the health and nutrition component provided benefits for families with pre-school-age children). As in Mexico, the child had to attend at least 85% of the days that school was open to receive the transfer. These transfers were provided every other month.

The average annual payment for participating students was about $136. The first phase of the program, which is all that has been analyzed thus far, lasted for two years. The present discounted value (PDV) of the cost of the first two years of the program was $268 for a 3% discount rate and $264 for a 6% discount rate, respectively.

Turning to the benefits, Maluccio and Flores (2005) estimate that the program increased school enrollment rates by 13 percentage points and increased attendance, conditional on enrollment, by 20%. Since these estimates are based on the randomized design of the program, they are fairly credible. For simplicity, one can assume that the 13-percentage point increase in enrollment leads to a 13-percentage point increase in eventual years of schooling attained. Average years of schooling for adults in Nicaragua is 4.58 years, which is similar to the education levels of 15–20-year-olds in the control communities in the second year of the study. Thus a 13% increase in years of schooling corresponds to a 0.59 increase in years of schooling. An increase of 0.59 years of schooling implies an income increase from the RED program, assuming that one additional year of schooling increases wages by 10%, of $34 (0.59 × 57) per year.[12] Discounting this increase in income by 3% implies a present discounted value of $557, while using a 6% discount rate leads to a lower figure, $233. The more conservative estimate that a year of schooling raises wages by only 5% implies an increase in wages of $17. Discounting this increase in income by 3% implies a present discounted value of $278, while using a 6% discount rate leads to a lower figure, $117.

A more optimistic scenario can be constructed by noting that the RED program also increased daily attendance by 20 percentage points. Assuming that this augments human capital by 20% for a given number of years of schooling, this is equivalent to an additional 20% increase in years of schooling without any change in daily attendance, which adds 0.92 years to the 0.59 "direct" increase in years of schooling and so leads to an increase of 1.51 years (for a total increase of

---

[12] We could not find data on average wages in Nicaragua, but (as seen below) survey data from neighboring Honduras yield an average annual wage of $763. World Bank data on gross national income *per capita* for 2003 show figures of $730 for Nicaragua and $970 for Honduras, which suggests an average annual wage of $574 for Nicaragua. Therefore an increase of 10% per year of schooling means an increase of $57 per year, or $29 per year for a 5% return to education.

33% in years of schooling). Assuming that each additional year of schooling raises wages by 10%, this implies an increase in wages of $86 (1.51 × 57) per year. Discounting this increase in income by 3% yields a PDV of $1,409, while using a 6% discount rate leads to a lower figure, $591. The assumption that another year of schooling raises wages by only 5% per year implies an annual wage increase of $44, and discounting this increase in income by 3% implies a present discounted value of $721, while using a 6% discount rate gives a lower figure, $302.

Finally, consider the BCRs. Assuming a program impact equivalent to an increase in 0.59 years of schooling, comparing the costs and benefits gives a BCR of 2.1 when using the 3% discount rate and 0.9 when using the 6% discount rate, if one also assumes that an additional year of schooling increases wages by 10%. The more pessimistic assumption that each year of schooling raises wages by only 5% implies a BCR of 1.0 for the 3% discount rate and 0.4 for the 6% discount rate. Higher BCRs are obtained when the program is assumed to increase years of schooling by 1.51 years. If an additional year of schooling increases wages by 10%, then one obtains a BCR of 5.3 given the 3% discount rate and 2.2 using the 6% discount rate. On the other hand, if an additional year of schooling increases wages by only 5%, the corresponding BCRs are 2.7 for a 3% discount rate and 1.1 for a 6% discount rate, respectively.

The last CCT program considered in this chapter is Honduras' Programa de Asignacion Familiar (PRAF). In its current form, known as PRAF II, the education component provided cash transfers to families of children age 6–12 who were enrolled in the first four years of primary school. (PRAF II also had a health and nutrition program for pre-school children, which is not analyzed here; there was also a plan to provide assistance to schools, but that plan was never implemented.) Families were supposed to receive the transfer only if their child's daily attendance rate was 85% or higher, but in fact this attendance requirement was not enforced. As in Mexico and Nicaragua, the program was implemented as a randomized trial. It is not clear how long parents expected the PRAF program to last, but a reasonable compromise is to assume that they expected it to last three years, which was the length of the pilot program (even if the program lasted longer, any given child can stay in the program only four years, since it covers only children in grades 1–4).

The PRAF cash transfers for school attendance were smaller than those in Mexico and Nicaragua. They amounted to $5 per month, or $45 per year (school is in session for nine months of the year). Assuming that the beneficiaries made decisions on the assumption that the program would operate for three years, the present discounted value of the costs per child are $131 using a 3% discount rate and $128 using a 6% discount rate, respectively.

Taking advantage of the experimental design of the study, Glewwe, Olinto, and de Souza (2004) estimate that the PRAF II program increased children's completed years of schooling from 4.2 to 4.9 years, or by 0.7 years. Psacharopoulos and Patrinos (2004) cite a 1991 study for Honduras that estimates that an increase of one year of education increases wages by 9.3%. Since Honduras and Nicaragua are neighboring countries, it is useful to use the same set of assumptions about the impact of an additional year of education on wages – i.e. that it increases wages by 10% (if most children in rural areas migrate to urban areas) or by 5% (if most children remain in rural areas). The 10% figure implies that a 0.7 increase in years of education increases wages by 7%, while the 5% figure implies that such an increase will increase wages by 3.5%. Bedi and Gaston (1997) report that a typical monthly wage in Honduras is $63, which implies an annual wage of $763. Thus a 7% increase in annual wages implies an annual increase in wages of $53.44 and a 3.5% increase would raise annual wages by $26.72. A more optimistic scenario is to note that the PRAF II program also increased daily attendance by 4.6%. Assuming that this augments human capital by 4.6% for a given number of years of schooling, this is equivalent to an additional 4.6% increase in years of schooling without any change in daily attendance, which adds 0.19 years to the 0.7 "direct" increase in years and so leads to an increase of 0.89 years. This implies increases in wages per year of $67.95 (assuming that a year of schooling raises wages by 10%) or, more conservatively, $33.97 (assuming that a year of schooling raises wages by 5%).

Finally, consider BCRs, which are shown in table 2.7. Turning to the more pessimistic scenario that PRAF II increased years of schooling by only 0.7 years, but the more optimistic assumption that an additional year of schooling raises wages by 10%, the present discounted value of the benefits is $875 using the 3% discount rate and $367 using the 6% discount rate, respectively. Given the cost estimates discussed above, the implied BCRs are 6.7 for the 3% discount rate and

2.9 for the 6% discount rate, respectively. The more optimistic scenario converts higher attendance rates into an equivalent amount of years of schooling, so that the program increases "effective" years of schooling by 0.89 years. The present discounted value of the benefits is $1,113 using the 3% discount rate and $467, etc. using the 6% discount rate, and the implied BCRs are 8.5 for the 3% discount rate and 3.7 for the 6% discount rate, respectively. All of these figures drop when the more pessimistic assumption that an additional year of schooling raises wages by only 5% is imposed. In particular, using this assumption with the more pessimistic scenario of the impact of the program (that it increases years of schooling by only 0.7 years) yields a present discounted value of the benefits of only $438 using the 3% discount rate and only $183 using the 6% discount rate, and the implied BCRs are 3.3 and 1.4, respectively. On the other hand, combining this lower assumption about the contribution of schooling to wages with the scenario that the program raises effective years of schooling by 0.89 yields a present discounted value of the benefits of $557 using the 3% discount rate and $233 using the 6% discount rate, and the implied BCRs are 4.2 and 1.8, respectively.

To summarize the results for the CCT programs, under most sets of assumptions the benefits exceed the costs. However, in the case of Progresa, benefits only barely exceed costs using a 3% discount rate, but when the 6% discount rate is used benefits exceed the costs only under the most optimistic assumptions. The Honduran CCT program seems to have the highest BCR, but it is not clear why this is the case.

Voucher programs

Two LAC countries, Chile and Colombia, have implemented voucher programs that allow students to use government funds to pay for the cost of private schooling. The underlying motivation for these programs is that competition among schools will increase school quality, and providing vouchers is one way to promote competition among schools.

The Colombian voucher program PACES (Programa de Ampliacíon de Cobertura de la Educatión Secundaria) was implemented in a quasi-randomized way, which reduces many estimation problems. It awarded three-year scholarships to over 125,000 students from poor urban neighborhoods from 1992 to 1997, which could be used to attend private schools. In most communities where the demand for vouchers exceeded the supply, voucher eligibility was determined by a lottery, hence the natural experiment.

Following Angrist *et al.* (2002), the cost to society as a whole of the PACES program is as follows. First, providing a student with a voucher cost the government $24 per year more than the cost of enrolling the student in a public school. Second, although households of lottery winners were able to reduce spending on their child's education by $22, they also reduced the amount of time that their children worked, which had an opportunity cost of $41. Thus the net cost to parents was $19 per year. Therefore the net cost to society as a whole was $43 per lottery winner per year. In fact, this cost needs to be increased because it is based on data from the survey year, in which only 49% of winners were using vouchers, while 88% of voucher winners eventually used the vouchers, so these costs need to be multiplied by 0.88/0.49. Doing this, and applying a discount rate of 3% for the three years, gives a present discounted value of $193 for the cost using a 3% discount rate, and $188 using a 6% discount rate, respectively.

Angrist *et al.* (2002) estimate that poor urban students who received scholarships completed 0.12 more years of schooling than did poor urban students who were randomly denied scholarships. In urban areas of Colombia, it is reasonable to assume that an additional year of schooling raises wages by 10%, so an increase of 0.12 years would raise wages by 1.2%. The parents of the children in the sample had annual earnings of about $2,400 and an average of 5.9 years of schooling. The children have an average of about 7.5 years of schooling, which suggests an average income of $3,000. Thus an increase in wages of 1.2% amounts to a benefit per year of $36. The present discounted value of this benefit over the lifetime of the child is $1,215 using a 3% discount rate and $872 using a 6% discount rate, which imply BCRs of 6.3 and 4.6, respectively.

In fact, the benefits of these vouchers may be higher because students who received them performed 0.2 standard deviations higher on standardized tests, which is equivalent to attaining about one additional year of schooling. The implied increase of one year of schooling suggests that vouchers raised incomes by $300 per year, the present discounted value of which is $4,914 at a 3% discount rate and $2,060 at a 6% discount rate, respectively. The corresponding BCRs are quite high, at 25.5 and 10.9, respectively. These results are summarized in table 2.7.

In contrast, an analysis of a voucher program in Chile by Hsieh and Urquiola (2006) found no effect of vouchers on students' test scores, repetition rates, and years of schooling. Indeed, the main effect of the program seems to have been to encourage the "best" students in public schools to switch to private schools. Overall, then, the evidence on the impact of vouchers on education in the LAC countries is mixed.

Programs that could not be evaluated

Many readers of this chapter will ask why other education programs and policies were not evaluated. This subsection explains why specific programs, some of which are well known, were excluded.

1. *Decentralized management.* The World Bank and other aid organizations have encouraged many developing countries to decentralize the administration and decisionmaking in primary and secondary schools, in order to allow those schools to respond in a more flexible way to local needs and to give local communities more power over decisionmaking. Two examples of this are the EDUCO program in El Salvador, which was analyzed by Jimenez and Sawada (1999), and the autonomous schools program in Nicaragua, which was studied by King and Ozler (2000). However, as explained in Glewwe (2002), both of these studies have serious shortcomings which raise the possibility that their estimates of the impact of these programs on education outcomes suffer from serious biases. Thus there are no reliable studies that have assessed these types of programs.

2. *Deworming.* Miguel and Kremer (2004) found that providing medicine to control infections of intestinal worms increased school enrollment and attendance at very little cost, which implies very high BCRs. However, the intervention examined an area in Kenya with very high levels of helminth infections and, more generally, the LAC countries have much lower levels of such infections than do countries in SSA. Thus it is not clear that BCRs derived from this study are applicable to the LAC countries.

3. *Bilingual education.* A paper by Shapiro and Trevino (2004) examined the impact of the CONAFE program in Mexico. This program

is difficult to evaluate because it combines bilingual with decentralized education. Moreover, there is also a potential problem of under-estimation of the impacts due to endogenous program placement given that the program was targeted to disadvantaged areas. Finally, Shapiro and Trevino's estimated impacts of the program are quite small; for example, it decreased the drop-out rate by only 0.13 percentage points.

4. *Teacher incentives and professional training*. Some LAC countries have implemented programs that provide teachers with monetary incentives and professional training to improve their teaching, but there are no reliable studies showing that they have sizeable impacts on student outcomes. An example is the Carrera Magisterial program, which is one component of a larger educational decentralization reform that was implemented in Mexico in 1992. The goal of this program was to raise the quality of basic education through professional training and improved working conditions. It tied salary increases to teacher performance as assessed by voluntary evaluation in the classroom. Despite these efforts, Lopez-Acevedo (2004) found no significant impact of this program on student outcomes.

5 Recommendations to strengthen the knowledge base for education policy

Section 4 provides several pieces of evidence that early childhood nutrition programs, and to a lesser extent CCT programs, are worthwhile investments in the sense that the benefits are much larger than the costs, although the BCRs show a fair amount of variation depending on the assumptions made and the program evaluated. There is also one study that shows that vouchers to attend private secondary schools are a worthwhile investment, but we should be cautious about basing policies on a single study. Perhaps the most frustrating conclusion is that there are many other education policies, some of which may be even more effective investments than these, for which there is little or no reliable evidence on impact on education outcomes. Until more rigorous evidence is available on these other policies, many effective interventions may go unfunded and many less effective policies may be implemented, wasting government resources.

From the authors' viewpoint, the biggest blind spot in our current knowledge is the impact of various education policies on education outcomes. Many studies are done every year, but most do not address in a convincing manner the serious econometric problems raised in section 3. In our view, the best way to reduce this gap in current knowledge is to conduct more randomized experiments similar to those that were done for CCT programs in Honduras, Mexico, and Nicaragua. Economists and other social scientists have increasingly conducted such studies in Africa, Asia, and Latin America, but it is difficult to know whether the results for African or Asian countries would apply to the LAC countries.

Although some LAC countries have conducted randomized trials of education interventions, others have not, and many governments may be reluctant to do so because it would be embarrassing if an evaluation shows that a program is ineffective. In contrast, non-governmental organizations (NGOs) in developing countries may be very well placed to conduct randomized evaluations. Unlike governments, NGOs are not expected to serve entire populations. Also unlike governments, financial and administrative constraints often lead NGOs to phase in programs over time, and randomization will often be the fairest way to determine the phase-in order. However, while NGOs are well placed to conduct randomized evaluations, expecting them to finance the research is less reasonable, as the results are regional, if not global, public goods.

This suggests that large international aid organizations, such as the World Bank and the IDB, should finance more randomized evaluations and, more generally, more program evaluations. After all, such evaluations are a global "public good" that will be under-supplied if no efforts are made to finance them. The results of these evaluations should be broadly disseminated, which will not be easy for these organizations because many studies will find that existing programs do not work as intended. Finally, if possible, randomized studies should always compare their findings with standard cross-sectional and/or panel data estimates based on the control group data.

A final point regarding randomized evaluations is that they may also have problems of sample selection bias, attrition bias, and spillover effects, just as retrospective evaluations do. Yet correcting for these limitations is often easier for randomized evaluations than for evaluations based on retrospective studies. For example, sample selection problems could arise if factors other than random assignment influence program allocation. For example, parents may attempt to move their children from a class (or a school) without the program to a class (or school) with the program. Conversely, individuals allocated to a treatment group may not receive the treatment (for example, because they decide not to take up the program). Even if randomized methods have been employed and the intended allocation of the program was random, the actual allocation may not be. This problem can be addressed through intention to treat methods or by using random assignment as an instrumental variable for actual assignment. It is much harder to address in retrospective studies, since it is often difficult to find factors that plausibly affect exposure to the program that would not affect education outcomes through other channels.

6 Summary and conclusions

This chapter has examined three proposals for improving education outcomes in the LAC region and assessed their impacts on education outcomes. More importantly, it has presented estimates of the value of each of these three types of projects in terms of the economic returns they generate by raising individuals' incomes when they are adults. Three policy proposals were examined: (1) Nutrition programs for infants and pre-school-age children; (2) CCT programs, which provide cash payments to parents if their children are regularly attending school; and (3) Vouchers that can be used to pay for most of the cost of attending private schools. For each proposal, the estimated value of these benefits was compared to the costs. For three different countries, early childhood nutrition programs generated benefits that far exceeded the costs. In contrast, the benefits produced by CCT programs in three different countries (Honduras, Mexico, and Nicaragua) consistently exceeded the costs only if a 3% discount rate was used; using a 6% discount rate often produced benefits that were less than the costs. Finally, a study of a voucher program in Colombia appears to have produced benefits that greatly exceed the costs, although one should be cautious about results from a single country since a voucher program in Chile had no discernable impacts on students' education outcomes. A final point that applies to all three types of program is that some benefits, such as health benefits, could not be easily evaluated, so the benefits from all of these studies may well under-estimate the true impact.

While this information should be very useful to policymakers, there is still much that is unknown. As noted above, there are many more interventions that one would like to be assessed, such as decentralized management, bilingual education and teacher training, and incentive programs, but there are almost no rigorous studies of these. Governments, non-profit aid agencies, and large international organizations need to develop effective systems for evaluating education projects and publicizing their results. This will not be a simple task, but the alternative of doing little or nothing to analyze new policies or programs will do nothing to help children in the LAC countries catch up to the education levels of children in developed countries.

Bibliography

Angrist, Joshua, Eric Bettinger, Erik Bloom, Elizabeth King, and Michael Kremer, 2002. "Vouchers for Private Schooling in Colombia: Evidence from a Randomized Natural Experiment." *American Economic Review* **92**(5): 1535–58

Barro, Robert, 1991. "Economic Growth in a Cross-Section of Countries." *Quarterly Journal of Economics* **106**(2): 407–43

Bedi, Arjun S. and Noel Gaston, 1997. "Returns to Endogenous Education: The Case of Honduras." *Applied Economics* **29**(4): 519–28

Behrman, Jere, Yingmei Cheng, and Petra Todd, 2004. "Evaluating Preschool Programs when Length of Exposure to the Program Varies: A Nonparametric Approach." *Review of Economics and Statistics* **86**(1): 108–32

Bils, Mark and Peter Klenow, 2000. "Does Schooling Cause Growth?" *American Economic Review* **90**(5): 1160–83

Duflo, Esther, 2001. "Schooling and Labor Market Consequences of School Construction in Indonesia: Evidence from an Unusual Policy Experiment." *American Economic Review* **91**(4): 795–813

Duryea, Suzanne, Sebastian Galiani, Hugo Nopo, and Claudia Piras, 2007. "The Educational Gender Gap in Latin America and the Caribbean." IADB Research Department Working Paper **300**

Glewwe, Paul, 1996. "The Relevance of Standard Estimates of Rates of Return to Schooling for Education Policy: A Critical Assessment." *Journal of Development Economics* **51**(2): 267–90

1999. "Why Does Mother's Schooling Raise Child Health in Developing Countries? Evidence from Morocco." *Journal of Human Resources* **34**(1): 124–59

2002. "Schools and Skills in Developing Countries: Education Policies and Socioeconomic Outcomes." *Journal of Economic Literature* **40**(2): 436–82

Glewwe, Paul, Hanan Jacoby, and Elizabeth King, 2001. "Early Childhood Nutrition and Academic Achievement: A Longitudinal Analysis." *Journal of Public Economics* 81(3): 345–68

Glewwe, Paul and Michael Kremer, 2006. "Schools, Teachers, and Education Outcomes in Developing Countries." In E. Hanushek and F. Welch, eds., *Handbook of the Economics of Education.* Amsterdam: North-Holland

Glewwe, Paul, Michael Kremer, Sylvie Moulin, and Eric Zitzewitz, 2004. "Retrospective vs. Prospective Analyses of School Inputs: The Case of Flip Charts in Kenya." *Journal of Development Economics* 74(1): 251–68

Glewwe, Paul and Edward Miguel, 2008. "The Impact of Child Health and Nutrition on Education in Less Developed Countries." In T. P. Schultz and J. Strauss, eds., *Handbook of Development Economics, Volume 4.* Amsterdam: Elsevier

Glewwe, Paul, Pedro Olinto, and Priscila de Souza, 2004. "Evaluating the Impacts of Conditional Cash Transfers on Schooling in Honduras: An Experimental Approach." Draft. Department of Applied Economics, University of Minnesota

Grantham-McGregor, Sally, Susan Walker, Susan Chang, and Christine Powell, 1997. "Effects of Early Childhood Supplementation with and without Stimulation on Later Development in Stunted Jamaican Children." *American Journal of Clinical Nutrition* 66: 247–53

Grossman, Michael, 2006. "Education and Nonmarket Outcomes." In E. Hanushek and F. Welch, eds., *Handbook of the Economics of Education.* Amsterdam: North-Holland

Hernandez-Zavala, Martha, Harry Patrinos, Chris Sakellariou, and Joseph Shapiro, 2006. "Quality of Schooling and Quality of Schools for Indigenous Students in Guatemala, Mexico, and Peru." World Bank Policy Research Working Paper 3982, available at http://ssrn.com/abstract=923289

Hsieh, Chang-Tai and Miguel Urquiola, 2006. "The Effects of Generalized School Choice on Achievement and Stratification: Evidence from Chile's Voucher Program." *Journal of Public Economics* 90(8–9): 1477–1503

IAEEA, 2000. "TIMSS 1999: International Mathematics Report." International Study Center, Boston College, International Association for the Evaluation of Educational Achievement

2003. "PIRLS 2001 International Mathematics Report." International Study Center, Boston College, International Association for the Evaluation of Educational Achievement

Jimenez, Emmanuel and Yasuyuki Sawada, 1999. "Do Community-Managed Schools Work? An Evaluation of El Salvador's EDUCO Program." *World Bank Economic Review* **13**(3): 415–41

Kielmann, Arnfried A. and Associates, 1983. *Child and Maternal Health Services in Rural India: The Narangwal Experiment.* Baltimore, MD: Johns Hopkins University Press

King, Elizabeth and Berk Ozler, 2000. "What's Decentralization Got to Do with Learning: Endogenous School Quality and Student Performance in Nicaragua." World Bank Development Research Group

Lopez-Acevedo, Gladys, 2004. "Professional Development and Incentives for Teacher Performance in Schools in Mexico." World Bank Policy Research Working Paper **3236**, March

Lucas, Robert, 1988. "On the Mechanics of Economic Development." *Journal of Monetary Economics* **22**: 3–42

Maluccio, John and Rafael Flores, 2005. "Impact Evaluation of a Conditional Cash Transfer Program: The Nicaraguan *Red de Protección Social.*" Research Report **141**. International Food Policy Research Institute, Washington, DC

Maluccio, John, John Hoddinott, Jere Behrman, Reynald Martorell, Agnes Quisumbing, and Aryeh Stein, 2006. "The Impact of Nutrition During Early Childhood on Education Among Guatemalan Adults." PIER Working Paper **06–026**, Department of Economics, University of Pennsylvania

Mankiw, N. Gregory, David Romer, and David Weil, 1992. "A Contribution to the Empirics of Economic Growth." *Quarterly Journal of Economics* **107**(2): 407–37

Miguel, Ted and Michael Kremer, 2004. "Worms: Identifying Impacts on Education and Health in the Presence of Treatment Externalities." *Econometrica* **72**(1): 159–217

OECD and UNESCO, 2003. "Literacy Skills for the World of Tomorrow: Further Results from PISA 2000." Programme for International Student Assessment Paris: OECD

Patrinos, Harry and Eduardo Velez, 1994. "Education and the Labor Market in Guatemala." Education and Social Policy Department. Washington, DC: World Bank

Pritchett, Lant, 2001. "Where Has All the Education Gone?" *World Bank Economic Review* **15**(3): 367–91

Psacharopoulos, George and Harry Patrinos, 2004. "Returns to Investment in Education: A Further Update." *Education Economics* **12**(2): 111–34

Schady, Norbert, 2006. "Early Child Development in Latin America and the Caribbean." World Bank Policy Research Working Paper **3869**

Schultz, T. Paul, 1997. "Demand for Children in Low Income Countries." In M. Rosenzweig and O. Stark, eds., *Handbook of Population and Family Economics*. Amsterdam: North-Holland

2002. "Why Governments Should Invest More to Educate Girls." *World Development* **30**: 207–25

2004. "School Subsidies for the Poor: Evaluating the Mexico Progresa Poverty Program." *Journal of Development Economics* **74**(1): 199–50

Sen, Amartya, 1999. *Development as Freedom*. New York: Knopf

Shapiro, Joseph and Jorge Moreno Trevino, 2004. "Compensatory Education for Disadvantaged Mexican Students: An Impact Evaluation Using Propensity Score Matching." Policy Research Working Paper **3334**

Strauss, John and Duncan Thomas, 1995. "Human Resources." In J. Behrman and T. N. Srinivasan, eds., *Handbook of Development Economics: Volume 3*. Amsterdam: North-Holland

UNDP, 2003. *Human Development Report 2003*. New York: United Nations Development Programme

World Bank, various years. *World Development Indicators*. Washington, DC: World Bank

World Bank, 2001. *World Development Report 2000/2001: Attacking Poverty*. Washington, DC: World Bank

2.1 | *Education: an alternative view*

MIGUEL URQUIOLA

In their Solution chapter, Damon and Glewwe present a useful summary of options to improve education in the LAC region. This alternative view presents three comments. The first simply seeks to complement the authors' sound diagnosis, making the case that while they are correct to emphasize educational quality, some issues concerning quantity remain. Specifically, achieving acceptable enrollment and particularly grade completion rates is still a challenge in many countries, which reflects issues related to delayed entry, drop-out, and repetition rates.

The second comment arises because the Consulta de San José takes the interesting approach of comparing interventions across sectors, which necessitates the calculation of BCRs. Damon and Glewwe note that this in turn requires knowledge of interventions' *causal* impact. They therefore reasonably choose to focus on "interventions that have been rigorously evaluated," and use an appropriately high standard to select them. This gives the chapter a sharp focus but entails a cost, because the menu of options considered must originate from a limited list – excluding, for instance, some options to reduce repetition or raise school quality.

The final comment concerns the chapter's third proposal: school choice. One point here is that this is not a clearly defined option – the term can stand for different interventions with potentially different results. Second, a broader look at the evidence on choice, both within and outside the LAC region, suggests that the specifics of these programs matter, and I would thus be wary of a blanket "most-promising" classification.

1 Educational quantity

The literature makes an arbitrary but often useful distinction between educational *quantity* and *quality*, where the former captures the extent of contact individuals have with the school system (through measures such as enrollment rates), and the latter the skills they gain from this contact (using measures such as test scores). Regarding quantity, the chapter gives the sense that while all may not be well in the LAC region, it is well on its way:

The progress . . . suggests that education levels in [LAC] are moving closer to those of higher income countries . . . virtually all children enroll in primary school and complete the primary cycle and follow . . . Repetition rates are generally low . . .

A first issue is that such assessments depend a bit on the reference point. For instance, Vegas and Petrow (2007) point out that regional primary completion rates did not approach 90% until about 2000, and that at least relative to some sets of countries, the LAC region has been losing ground: while in 1960 the proportion of adults who had completed upper secondary education was 7% in the LAC region and 11% in East Asia, by the turn of the century these numbers were 18 and 44%, respectively.

Perhaps more importantly, the aggregate evidence conceals relevant inter-country heterogeneity. To provide a sense of this, figure 2.1.1 draws on household survey data to plot age-specific enrollment rates in Chile and Honduras. These two countries illustrate the range of enrollment outcomes in the LAC region, and point to some relevant facts. First, delayed entry continues to be an issue. Even in Chile, where primary schooling is close to universal, the net enrollment rate for age 6 (the normative starting age) is below 90% overall, and below 80% in rural areas. In Honduran rural areas, roughly 50 and 40% of 6- and 7-year-olds, respectively, do not enroll. Second, in the 8–13 range, enrollment rates are relatively high – in urban areas they exceed 90% all over the region – although in a few countries they never quite approach 100. Third, as is well known, enrollment begins to drop in the 13–15 age range. All this leads to an "inverted-U" age–enrollment profile, which is evident for rural populations in almost all countries, and marked even for the aggregate population in countries such as Bolivia, Brazil, Colombia, and Nicaragua.

The data in figure 2.1.1 can be summarized by a measure which we term *average years in school*, obtained by cumulatively adding the observed age-specific enrollment rates. This yields the expected number of years that individuals will spend in school by a given age, given the enrollment patterns *currently* observed in their country. This

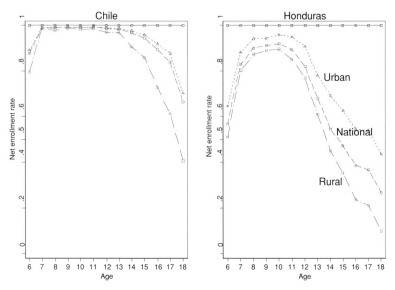

Figure 2.1.1 Age–enrollment profiles: Chile and Honduras
Source: This and all subsequent figures are based on Urquiola and Calderón
(2006)

measure provides a useful benchmark against which to compare countries' performance in producing *years of schooling* – i.e. actual grades
completed.[1]

To illustrate the usefulness of this measure, figure 2.1.2 first graphs
the maximum feasible attainment (measured in years of schooling)

---

[1] The calculation of average years in school is illustrated below. For age 6, the
measure equals the enrollment rate expressed as a proportion – e.g. by the time
they are 6, children have spent an average 0.88 years in school in Chile, and
0.57 in Honduras (columns (2) and (4)). These entries are then cumulated.

	Chile		Honduras	
	Net enrollment rate	Average years in school	Net enrollment rate	Average years in school
Age	(1)	(2)	(3)	(4)
6	87.7	0.88	56.8	0.57
7	98.9	1.87	82.8	1.40
8	98.9	2.86	90.1	2.3
9	99.2	3.85	91.3	3.2
...				

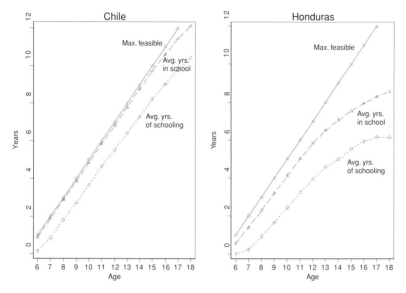

Figure 2.1.2 Maximum schooling, average years *in school*, and average years *of schooling*

that an individual of a given age could reach if she entered school at age 6 and made "normal" progress. For instance, this person could complete a maximum of one year of schooling by age 6, two by age 7, and so on. The middle line plots our average *years in school* measure.

Focusing first on Honduras, even at age 6 there is a clear gap between the top two segments, partly because of delayed entry. These then run roughly parallel up to age 10, reflecting the high enrollment rates in this age range. After that, they diverge markedly, as drop-out rates increase. For Chile, the average-years-in-school segment begins slightly below the maximum, reflecting the non-zero-delayed entry observed even in this case, but the low drop-out rates limit the divergence between the two top segments.

The third segment plots average years *of schooling* – the grades individuals report they have actually passed. Comparing the second and third segments thus indicates how effectively an educational system turns average years *in school* (contact with the system) into average years *of schooling*. In other words, figure 2.1.2 answers the

Table 2.1.1 *Average years in school and years of schooling, age 18*

Country	Avg. years in school (1)	Avg. years of schooling (2)	Difference ((1)–(2))
Brazil	11.4	7.3	4.1
Nicaragua	9.7	5.9	3.8
Dominican Republic	11.8	8.3	3.5
Jamaica	11.7	8.8	2.9
Uruguay	11.4	8.7	2.7
...			
El Salvador	10.0	8.0	2.0
Panama	11.5	9.5	2.0
Mexico	10.6	8.7	1.9
Ecuador	10.4	8.7	1.7
Chile	12.1	10.4	1.7

Note: Based on data in Urquiola and Calderón (2006).

question "Why doesn't every 18-year-old in Honduras achieve 12 years of schooling?" It makes clear this is due to two factors: the lack of universal attendance (the gap between the first and the second segment), and the failure to turn years in school into years of schooling (the gap between the second and the third segment), largely but not exclusively due to repetition.

Of particular relevance is the growth in the gap between the two lower segments – by age 18 this has grown to about one year in Chile, and more than two in Honduras. To further illustrate the variation in this gap, table 2.1.1 lists ten "extreme" countries, showing that it ranges from 1.7 years in Chile and Ecuador to 4.1 in Brazil. These data thus suggest that many countries produce significantly less attainment than they could.

Figure 2.1.3 summarizes the consequences of some of the above information by describing the years of schooling observed at the 25th and 75th percentiles of the distribution in Chile and Honduras. It shows that a non-trivial proportion of Honduran children leave the system with only three or four years of schooling. Even in the context of rapid progress, therefore, there are still countries/areas in the LAC region where attainment, even in terms of quantity, is quite low.

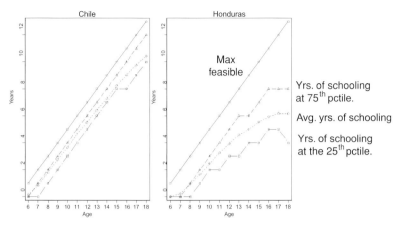

Figure 2.1.3 Maximum schooling, average years *in school*, and average years *of schooling*

To summarize, while Damon and Glewwe are right to emphasize educational quality, some issues concerning quantity remain. Specifically, achieving acceptable enrollment and particularly completion rates is still a substantial challenge in many countries. Indeed, the gist of the comparison by Vegas and Petrow (2007), cited at the beginning of this alternative view, is that the region has made less progress in attainment than in enrollment.

2 Restrictive focus

The Consulta de San José calls for cost-benefit comparisons of interventions across sectors. Damon and Glewwe note that this requires knowledge of interventions' *causal* impact, and therefore reasonably restrict their attention to "interventions that have been rigorously evaluated." This gives the chapter a sharp focus, but at the cost of omitting interventions that might have high returns.

For example, CCTs are one of the solutions proposed, which might reflect that perhaps no other social policy in the LAC region has been as rigorously evaluated. Section 1 suggests, however, that in some countries tackling repetition might deliver greater results: while many children do show up for school, they and/or the system fail to turn this into years of schooling. In terms of figure 2.1.2, CCTs address the gap between the top and the middle segment, but in many countries that between the middle and the bottom segment (which largely reflects repetition) is larger.

More specifically, Schultz (2004) estimates that Progresa raised years of schooling in Mexico by 0.5–0.7 years. Table 2.1.1 (loosely) suggests that eliminating repetition – admittedly, a tall order – could have three to four times that impact in Mexico, and seven to eight times that effect in Brazil. This is not to argue we should abandon CCTs, but to point out that initiatives to understand and reform what actually goes on in schools in terms of repetition might have a higher return. Of course, Damon and Glewwe do not cover such interventions – in most cases, they are not clearly defined or (to my knowledge and apparently to theirs) clearly evaluated.

Similarly, the chapter stresses that improving quality should be a priority. Yet one issue with CCTs, as raised by Reimers *et al.* (2006), is that they do not target quality, and Behrman, Parker, and Todd (2006) suggest that Progresa indeed did not raise test scores.

To summarize, my sense is that Damon and Glewwe make a reasonable decision to focus on interventions that have been credibly evaluated, but this comes at a cost. Noting this also serves to underline my agreement regarding their call to expand the knowledge base of educational interventions in the LAC region (and around the world) – expanding the list of solidly evaluated options will require aggressive long-term research.[2]

3 School choice

The evidence on the impact of school choice, when one looks around the world, is mixed. There has been a lot of work beyond the (high-quality and highly influential) study by Angrist *et al.* (2002) that the authors highlight. To elaborate, the gains from choice are expected to originate in two sources: (i) if private schools are more effective, there will be gains from transferring students to the private sector,

---

[2] One intervention the authors might want to consider involves tutoring for lower-achieving students. For evidence on India and Chile, see Banerjee, Cole, and Duflo (2007) and Chay *et al.* (2005), respectively. Additionally, the discussion on decentralization could note Galiani, Gertler, and Schargrodsky (2005), although this would probably not affect the results of their review.

and (ii) competition may force all schools, particularly public ones, to improve.

The international evidence suggests that private schools do have higher tests scores than public ones, but this difference largely disappears if one controls for socio-economic status, leaving open the possibility that private productivity is at best modestly higher. Indeed, controversies in this area often concern whether the difference is zero or modest – see the evidence on Chile, Milwaukee, and New York, among other cases.[3] In part, these discussions reflect difficulties in identifying causal effects, but in some cases they persist despite experimental data.

Further, even if one could get clear answers from public/private comparisons (such as the study the authors focus on arguably produces), Hsieh and Urquiola (2003, 2006) illustrate that these would mainly answer the question "Would a randomly selected student perform better in a private than in a public school?" If part of that better performance is due to peer effects, for example, such evidence would not answer the question "What would happen to achievement if we shifted a substantial proportion of children to the private sector?" To answer the latter question, one needs to examine the effects of school choice on aggregate outcomes and/or public sector performance, which turns out to be empirically even more challenging and has likewise often resulted in controversy – see, for instance, studies on Chile, Sweden, the United Kingdom, and the United States.[4]

While much of this evidence is from outside the LAC region, a few words should be added about Chile, which has undertaken the largest expansion of school choice in the region and arguably the world. (Suffice it to note that more than half of all urban schools in Chile are private, that these are often run for-profit, and that parents can use any subsidized school – religious or not – willing to take their children).

Surprisingly, national and international testing data leave open the possibility that this initiative has not improved average performance substantially. Indeed, within Chile there is a generalized perception

---

[3] On Milwaukee see, for example, Greene *et al.* (1997), Rouse (1998), and Witte (1998); on New York, Peterson, Myers, and Howell (1998) and Krueger and Zhu (2004); on Chile, Mizala and Romaguera (2000) and Contreras (2005).
[4] On Chile see, for example, Gallego (2006) and Hsieh and Urquiola (2006); on Sweden, Bohlmark and Lindahl (2007); on the United Kingdom, Clark (2005); and on the United States, Hoxby (2000) and Rothstein (2006).

that more must be done to improve learning. This is not to say that choice did not raise aggregate welfare, but to point out that, for reasons we do not fully understand, its impact on test scores seems to have been smaller than expected.

Additionally, the Chilean and US evidence suggests that school choice can lead to stratification – in simple terms, the poor going to school with the poor and the rich with the rich. Without knowledge of the functional form of peer effects, it is not clear what to make of this. Nonetheless, Chile's government has concluded that it is of concern, and is promoting initiatives that might limit sorting, such as making the voucher worth more when used by poor children, and limiting schools' ability to select students (interestingly, the first of these seems to have clear support from the opposition parties as well).

The bottom line here is two-fold. First, much more than CCTs, "school choice" is not a clearly defined intervention – a Chilean and a Colombian educator, for instance, might understand it to entail different interventions that might have different results. For example, a smaller-scale "American-style" voucher program is unlikely to produce the stratification seen in Chile. Second, a broader look at the evidence on choice suggests that the specifics of these programs matter, and I would thus be wary of a blanket "most-promising" classification.

In closing, let me state two more points. First, I do not have comments on the first solution proposed by the chapter – nutrition programs for pre-school-aged children – except to say these indeed seem to be a promising option (for instance, as Glewwe and Jacoby (1995) have suggested, they may help ensure prompt entry into school and adequate learning readiness). Finally, as mentioned above, I fully share the authors' recommendation that more evaluation be undertaken in education in LAC.

Bibliography

Angrist, Joshua, Eric Bettinger, Erik Bloom, Elizabeth King, and Michael Kremer, 2002. "Vouchers for Private Schooling in Colombia: Evidence from a Randomized Natural Experiment." *American Economic Review* 92(5): 1535–58

Banerjee, A., S. Cole, and E. Duflo, 2007. "Remedying Education: Evidence from Two Randomized Experiments in India." *Quarterly Journal of Economics* 122(3): 1235–64

Barrera, F. and C. Domínguez, 2006. *Gratuidad en provision de educación básica*. Debates de coyuntura social, Noviembre, Número **19**, Fedesarrollo

Barrera, F., L. Linden, and M. Urquiola, 2006. "The Effects of User Fee Reductions on Enrollment: Evidence from a Quasi-Experiment." Columbia University, mimeo

Behrman, J., S. Parker, and P. Todd, 2006. "Do School Subsidy Programs Generate Lasting Benefits? A Five Year Follow-up of Oportunidades Participants." University of Pennsylvania, mimeo

Bohlmark, A. and M. Lindahl, 2007. "The Impact of School Choice on Pupil Achievement, Segregation, and Costs: Swedish Evidence." Stockholm University, mimeo

Chay, K., P. McEwan, and M. Urquiola, 2005. "The Central Role of Noise in Evaluating Interventions that use Test Scores to Rank Schools." *American Economic Review* **95**(4): 1237–58

Clark, D., 2005. "Politics, Markets and Schools: Quasi-Experimental Evidence on the Impact of Autonomy and Competition from Truly Revolutionary UK Reform." University of Florida, mimeo

Contreras, D., 2005. "Políticas educacionales en Chile: Vouchers, concentración, incentivos y rendimiento." In S. Cueto, ed., *Uso e impacto de la información educativa en América Latina*. Santiago: PREAL

Galiani, S., P. Gertler, and E. Schargrodsky, 2005. "School Decentralization: Helping the Good get Better, but Leaving the Poor Behind." Universidad de San Andrés, mimeo

Gallego, F., 2006. "Voucher–School Competition, Incentives, and Outcomes: Evidence from Chile." Universidad Católica de Chile, mimeo

Glewwe, P. and H. G. Jacoby, 1995. "An Economic Analysis of Released Primary School Enrollment in a Low Income Country: The Role of Early Childhood Nutrition." *Review of Economics and Statistics* **77**(1): 156–69

Greene, J., P. Peterson, and J. Du, 1997. "Effectiveness of School Choice: The Milwaukee Experiment." Harvard University, mimeo

Hoxby, C., 2000. "Does Competition among Public Schools Benefit Students and Taxpayers?" *American Economic Review* **90**(5): 1209–38

Hsieh, C.-T. and M. Urquiola, 2003. "When Schools Compete, How do they Compete? An Assessment of Chile's Nationwide School Voucher Program." NBER Working Paper **10008**

2006. "The Effects of Generalized School Choice on Achievement and Stratification: Evidence from Chile's School Voucher Program." *Journal of Public Economics* **90**(8–9): 1477–1503

Krueger, A. and P. Zhu, 2004. "Another Look at the New York City School Voucher Experiment." *American Behavioral Scientist*, January: 658–98

Mizala, A. and P. Romaguera, 2000. "School Performance and Choice: The Chilean Experience." *Journal of Human Resources* **35**(2): 392–417

Parker, S., P. Todd, and K. Wolpin, 2006. "The Impact of Oportunidades on Schooling in Mexico." University of Pennsylvania, mimeo

Peterson, P., D. Myers, and W. Howell, 1998. "An Evaluation of the New York School Choice Scholarships Program: The First Year." Mathematica Policy Research and Harvard University Program on Education Policy and Governance

Reimers, F., C. DeShano da Silva, and E. Trevino, 2006. "Where is the "Education" in Conditional Cash Transfers in Education?" UNESCO Institute for Statistics, Montreal, mimeo

Rothstein, J., 2006. "Good Principals or Good Press: Parental Valuation of School Characteristics. Trebout Equilibrium, and the Incentive Effects of Competition Among Jurisdictions." *American Economic Review* **96**(4): 1333–50

Rouse, C. E., 1998. "Private School Vouchers and Student Achievement: An Evaluation of the Milwaukee Parental Choice Program." *Quarterly Journal of Economics* **113**: 553–602

Schultz, T. P., 2004. "School Subsidies for the Poor: Evaluating the Mexican PROGRESA Poverty Program." *Journal of Development Economics* **74**(1): 199–250

Urquiola, M. and V. Calderón, 2006. "Apples and Oranges: Educational Enrollment and Attainment Across Countries in Latin America and the Caribbean." *International Journal of Educational Development* **26**: 572–90

Vegas, E. and J. Petrow, 2007. "Raising Student Learning in Latin America: The Challenge of the 21st Century." World Bank, mimeo

Witte, J., 1998. "The Milwaukee Voucher Experiment." *Educational Evaluation and Policy Analysis* **20**(4): 229–51

EMPLOYMENT AND SOCIAL SECURITY

3 | *Labor market reforms in the LAC region: consequences and costs*

ALEJANDRA COX EDWARDS*

1 Introduction

During the last few years the LAC region has reluctantly begun a process of market integration into the global economy. This process is likely to deepen in years to come, and workers in the region must have access to the opportunities that this global marketplace offers. While it is certainly a fact that global labor markets threaten individuals with the possibility of being replaced by other, perhaps cheaper or more productive workers in other countries, the same phenomenon brings about the opportunity to obtain a better job in a broader set of labor market offers. Globalization can potentially benefit all workers by changing the division of labor across countries. Yet, this new division of labor requires a fair degree of adaptability. The challenge is to seize the benefits from globalization, cognizant of the difficulties imposed by the need to adjust. To this end, policies should seek to improve the functional role of the labor market, encourage an effective response of the education and training markets, and ensure that minimum wage policies (geared towards improving the conditions of the working poor) do not discourage employment creation. As Kugler (2007) clearly puts it, a well-functioning labor market can better respond to the challenge of keeping income security for workers but reducing employers' disincentives to hire.

* This is a revised version of the paper with the same title prepared for the Copenhagen Consensus Center and the Inter-American Development Bank's roundtable Consulta de San José, 2007. I would like to thank Adriana Kugler for her insightful comments and members of the Expert panel for useful suggestions.

There has been a substantial body of work measuring the detrimental impact of current labor market regulation on employment creation, the extent of informality, and productivity (see, for example, Heckman and Pages 2004). Yet, labor market reforms seeking gains in efficiency have not been popular in the region, particularly because the original motivation for establishing these laws was to alter the distribution of labor incomes.

Botero *et al.* (2004) seek to explain differences in labor market regulations across countries. They examine labor market regulations in eighty-five countries through the lens of three broad theories of government regulation of labor. Efficiency theories hold that regulations evolve to address the problems of market failure. Political theories contend that political leaders put in place regulations that benefit themselves and their allies. Legal theories hold that the patterns of regulation are the result of legal tradition, which is largely determined by transplantation of a few legal systems across countries. The evidence provided is broadly consistent with the legal theory, according to which patterns of regulation across countries are shaped largely by transplanted legal structures. The fact is that in the LAC region most countries had a Labor Code by the 1930s and 1940s, motivated by the perceived need to protect the welfare of workers against the excessive power of employers and to insure workers against the risk of job loss and income security (Lindauer 1999).

We now have data that clearly point at the detrimental effects of current labor laws.[1] These labor laws can be revised to move them towards more efficient rules. Therefore, a way to respond to the challenges of employment creation and social security in the region is to re-regulate the labor market.

This chapter examines more efficient forms of regulating the labor market in the LAC region. To that aim, I first provide a simple framework for analyzing the effects of labor market re-regulation on wages, employment, earnings, and the return to capital. Second, I analyze, from a comparative perspective, the extent to which labor markets have been distorted and regulated in the region. In particular, I use indexes constructed by various organizations and scholars to evaluate whether the Latin American countries have a higher degree of labor market distortions than other regions and groups of countries. And,

---

[1] See, for example, Heckman and Pages (2004).

third, I use existing models and estimates on labor market behavior to provide computations of the costs and benefits of three specific (potential) labor market reforms in the region: (a) a *pension reform* that reduces the labor tax component of pay-as-you go regimes; (b) the elimination of restrictions on short-term contracts and the *replacement of current dismissal regulations* with an unemployment insurance account (UIA) system, and (c) the introduction of an earned income tax credit (Devolución de Impuestos a los Pobres, DIP) as an *alternative to a high minimum wage* and as an *instrument to formalize labor contracts and compensate the poor for the obligation to make contributions towards unemployment and pension benefits.* While this chapter will mainly address the cost and benefit of each solution, insights on the distributional impact of reforms become an important component in any attempts to make these solutions politically acceptable.

The rest of the chapter is organized as follows: in section 2 I present a model that captures some of the most salient features of labor markets in emerging economies such as LAC markets. The framework assumes an open economy that produces two types of goods – internationally tradable and non-tradable goods. There are labor market distortions – minimum wage, payroll taxes, costs of dismissal – that affect one of the sectors only; this sector is called the "formal" (or "protected") sector. Initially there is unemployment and labor market informality. In section 3 I summarize the existing data on labor market regulations and distortions in the region. In order to put things in perspective, I compare labor market policies in the region to four groups of countries: the Asian nations as a group; the so-called "Asian Tiger" countries; a group of Southern Mediterranean countries (Greece, Portugal, and Spain); and three advanced commodity-exporting countries (Canada, Australia, and New Zealand).[2] In section 4, I use the model to examine how the relaxation of distortions affects labor market outcomes. In spite of its simplicity, this model is very powerful, and illustrates the fact that labor market reforms imply significant redistributions of income. This, in turn, helps explain why there is so much resistance to labor reform: those groups whose income is reduced by the reforms – in particular, those employed in the "protected" sector – strongly oppose any change of legislation and regulations. I provide estimates of the

---

[2] I am aware, of course, that Portugal does not have a Mediterranean Sea coast.

costs and benefits of three types of labor market reform: (a) a pension reform, (b) a replacement of the minimum wage legislation with a program of public transfers to the working poor, and (c) a reform to the job security legislation. Section 5 contains conclusions.

Before proceeding a clarification is required: the computations presented in this chapter do not capture *all* the effects of a comprehensive and all-encompassing labor market reform. On the contrary, following the guidelines of the Copenhagen Consensus process, I have dealt with only three components of a potential labor market modernization reform. Readers interested in other elements of reform – including, for example, collective bargaining systems or public financing of workers' training systems, or the use of active labor market intermediation systems – should consult some of the works listed in the bibliography at the end of the chapter.

2 Labor market regulation: a conceptual framework

Labor markets in emerging economies in general – and in the LAC region in particular – have a number of institutional features that set them apart from labor markets in industrial nations. The most important among these features are:

- In emerging countries labor markets are usually characterized by a rather large "informal" segment. This segment is, *de facto*, not directly affected by labor market regulations, such as minimum wages, job security legislation, or social security contributions. The informal sector coexists with a "modern" sector, where labor market regulations are fully in effect.
- Labor market regulations take various forms, including payroll taxes, firing restrictions, limitations on the use of temporary contracts, and minimum wages, among others. Payroll taxes are typically earmarked to finance programs that benefit workers (pensions, health services, training, death and disability insurance), with rather weak links between individual contributions and benefits. The percentage of the contribution that is actually considered a pure tax depends on the nature of the social security system and, more specifically, on the perceived connection between contributions and benefits (Diamond and Valdés-Prieto 1994).

In this section, I develop a model of the labor market in an economy open to international trade that is characterized by the existence of a "formal" and "informal" labor market. Those employed in the formal sector are subject to social security contributions; those in the informal sector do not contribute to the social security system.[3] I also assume that the social security system is of a pay-as-you-go (PAYG) type. Although the model is stylized and does not incorporate every form of labor market intervention, it is quite powerful. In particular, it captures the most important effects of reforms on key variables, such as wages, earnings of capital, employment, and unemployment. More important, perhaps, the model clearly illustrates that a key consequence of labor market reform is to redistribute income across different economic actors.[4]

Formally, assume that, as is the case in many developing and transitional economies, the labor market is segmented. There is a "*modern*" or "*covered*" sector subject to a minimum wage and to social security coverage, and an "*informal*" or "*unprotected*" sector with no social security coverage, and competitively determined wages. With other things equal, workers will rather be employed in the "protected" sector. The problem, however, is that there are not enough jobs in that sector; individuals that apply for a job in the modern sector face a probability (p) of obtaining it, and a probability ($1 - p$) of being unemployed. In equilibrium, and under the assumption of risk neutrality, the wage rate obtained in the *informal* segment is equal to the expected (take-home) wage rate in the *protected* sector. I further assume that every period employment in the modern sector turns over fully, so that the probability of getting a job in that sector is equal to the ratio of openings to applicants.[5]

I also assume that prior workers in the *protected* sector are subject to a payroll tax – whose purpose is to fund the social security system (that is, to fund pension payments to the elderly) – equal to T_1. I assume there is no connection between social security contributions and individual benefits. More specifically, and as is usually the case in a PAYG system, I assume that social security contributions are considered by individuals to be fully a tax. Notice, however, that the

---

[3] Indeed, whether workers contribute to social security is often used as a way of defining labor market informality.
[4] The model is partially based on Edwards and Cox Edwards (2002).
[5] This mechanism is similar to the one considered in migration models of the Harris–Todaro type. In our model, however, there is no migration. The assumption of risk neutrality is not essential; all the results will follow if individuals have a constant degree of risk aversion.

analysis that follows would not be affected by the assumption that only a fraction of the contribution was considered to be a tax. Workers employed in the modern sector receive a "take-home" wage rate equal to the minimum wage (W_{min}). The cost of labor to firms operating in this sector is equal to the minimum wage plus the payroll tax.

A social security reform that replaces the PAYG system with an individual accounts-based system can lead to a reduction of the payroll tax as perceived by workers. There are two sources for this reduction: first, the reform itself may entail a reduction in the contribution (this, for instance, was the case in Chile's pension reform). Second, the replacement of the old PAYG system by individual retirement accounts increases the link between contributions and benefits, transforming the contribution towards pensions, or at least a portion of it, into a deferred compensation.

Equations (1)–(4) describe the wage determination process in this economy. Equation (1) establishes that in equilibrium the wage rate in the informal sector (W_I) is equal to the expected (net of taxes) wage rate in the modern sector $E(W_M^N)$. According to (2), and following the well-known Harris–Todaro model, the probability of finding a job in the modern sector is equal to the ratio of openings – that is, employment in that sector (L_M) – to applicants. The latter is given by the sum of openings (L_M) plus the total number of unemployed (U). It is assumed, for simplicity, that the unemployed received an income equal to S. Equation (3) says that the cost of labor in the modern sector is equal to the minimum wage inclusive of the payroll tax (T_1). In (4a) and (4b) I present the demand for labor equations in the modern and informal sectors. P_M and P_I are good prices in each sector, $f(\cdots)$ and $g(\cdots)$ are physical marginal productivity of labor functions, and K_M and K_I are the stock of capital used in the modern and informal sector, respectively.

$$W_I = E\left(W_M^N\right) = p\,W_{min} + (1 - p)S \tag{1}$$

$$p = \left(\frac{L_M}{L_M + U}\right) \tag{2}$$

$$W_M = W_{min}(1 + T_1) \tag{3}$$

$$W_M = P_M f(L_M, K_M) \tag{4a}$$

$$W_I = P_I g(L_I, K_I). \tag{4b}$$

Equation (5) is the resource constraint in the labor market, and establishes that employment in the modern sector, plus employment in the informal sector plus unemployment, has to be equal to total labor supply (L_S). According to (6), labor supply is a positive function of real wages; O represents "other" factors affecting the supply of labor.[6] Equation (7) defines the aggregate price index and the aggregate wage rate, as geometric means of sectoral prices and wages, respectively. In order to simplify the analysis, in (8) I have assumed that the modern sector corresponds to tradable goods and that, as a consequence, P_M is given by international prices (P_M^*).[7] Equation (9) establishes that product prices in the informal sector are a positive function of wages in that sector. We further assume that an increase in W_I will have a less than proportional effect on prices of goods produced in the informal sector:

$$L_M + L_I + U = L_S \tag{5}$$

$$L_S = h\left(\frac{W}{P}, O\right); h' > 0 \tag{6}$$

$$P = P_I^\beta P_M^{(1-\beta)};\ W = W_I^\theta W_M^{(1-\theta)} \tag{7}$$

$$P_M = P_M^* \tag{8}$$

$$P_I = z(W_I); z' > 0; d\log P_I < d\log W_I \tag{9}$$

Equation (10) is the resource constraint for capital, and says that the sum of capital used in each sector has to equal the total stock of capital. Equation (11) says that the allocation of the capital stock across sectors will depend on the relative product prices. Notice that in order to simplify the computations, and to focus on the issues at hand, I have assumed that there is no net investment

$$K_M + K_I = K \tag{10}$$

$$K_M = j\left(\frac{P_M}{P_I}\right);\ K_I = v\left(\frac{P_M}{P_I}\right) \tag{11}$$

The initial (pre-reform) labor market is depicted in figure 3.1, under the simplifying assumption that the unemployed get no assistance ($S = 0$). The distance O_M–O_I is total labor supply, the lines L_M and

---

[6] I abstracted from intertemporal issues. Although the results will still go through in an explicit intertemporal context, the computations would become significantly more complex.

[7] This simplification allows us to maintain product prices in the modern sector constant. An alternative assumption, and one that would not affect the basic aspect of the analysis, is that the modern sector comprises both tradable and non-tradable goods. In this case, we would need a product market-clearing condition for modern sector goods.

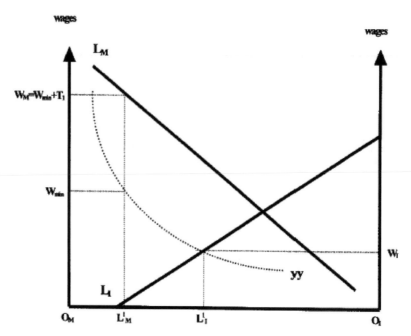

Figure 3.1 Costly labor market regulations reduce employment in the modern sector, depress wages in the informal sector, and create unemployment

L_I represent demand for labor schedules in the two sectors, and *yy* is a rectangular hyperbola, that satisfies the equilibrium condition in (1). The wage rate and the level of employment in the informal sector are determined by the intersection of the *yy* and L_I schedules. W_{min} is the minimum wage which, as stated above, is assumed to be set in net take-home bases. T_1 is the payroll tax and W_M is the cost of labor in the modern sector. W_I is the wage rate in the informal sector. The initial level of employment in the modern sector is given by the distance $O_M-L_M^1$; the distance $O_I-L_I^1$ depicts initial employment in the informal sector. The total number of unemployed is equal to the distance $L_M^1-L_I^1$.

3 Labor market regulations and distortions in the LAC region

Labor market distortions in the LAC region can be divided in two groups: (a) high payroll taxes and a binding minimum wage, and (b) high costs of adjustment (via restrictions to short-term contracts,

Table 3.1a *Labor regulation: LAC region, relative to other regions (Heckman and Pages 2004)*

	Advance notice	Indemnities for dismissal	Seniority pay	Social sec.	Share of soc. sec. total cost	Social sec. contrib. (% wage)
Latin America	0.78	2.69	5.84	33.00	0.79	0.25
Selected Latin America	0.64	2.64	3.50	27.82	0.81	0.22
Industrial	0.84	0.68	0.00	39.01	0.89	0.30
AU, NZ, CAN	0.52	0.39	0.00	6.84	0.50	0.05
Tigers	..	..	..	..	..	..
Scandinavian	1.43	0.00	0.00	30.97	0.96	0.24
East Europe	..	..	..	..	..	..
South Europe	0.59	2.41	0.00	48.33	0.94	0.37
LAC	0.64	2.64	3.50	27.82	0.81	0.22

Note: .. = Missing data.

high costs of dismissal, or variations in work schedule). While the two types of distortions represent an ultimate increase in labor costs, leading firms to substitute away from labor, the second type of distortion becomes particularly detrimental in an environment of change. Several researchers have examined the relative weight of labor regulations across regions and their overall assessment can be summarized as follows: (i) A comparison of the LAC region with OECD countries tells us that payroll taxes are higher in the OECD, but costs of adjustment are higher in the LAC region. (ii) LAC countries' regulations compare to those of Southern European and some Scandinavian countries. (iii) Anglo-Saxon countries have lighter labor regulations. (iv) "Asian Tigers" share with the LAC region the high dismissal costs, but they do not restrict short-term contracts nor do they over-regulate working hours leading to significantly lower costs of adjustment (see tables 3.1a, 3.1b, and 3.1c, which capture comparative analyses by Botero *et al.* 2004, Heckman and Pages 2004, and the World Bank (*Doing Business in 2007*)).

Social security programs in the region typically combine old-age, disability, and death, sickness and maternity, work injury, family allowances, and unemployment insurance benefits and are funded by

Table 3.1b *Labor regulation: LAC region, relative to other regions (World Bank, Doing Business in 2007); index values vary between 0 (low-cost) and 100 (high-cost)*

	Rank	Non-wage labor cost (% of salary)	Firing costs (weeks of wages)	Rigidity of employment index	Difficulty of hiring index	Rigidity of hours index	Difficulty of firing index
Latin America	104.61	15.83	63.71	41.94	46.28	46.67	32.78
Selected Latin America	95.33	22.32	50.72	39.83	46.33	43.33	30.00
Industrial	73.73	21.60	28.61	33.23	27.73	44.55	27.27
AU, NZ, CAN	10.67	11.97	10.67	4.67	7.33	0.00	6.67
Asian Tigers	55.17	10.33	65.07	16.83	16.67	23.33	10.00
Scandinavian	89.00	20.80	19.50	44.00	41.50	60.00	30.00
East Europe	86.23	28.50	22.91	41.41	30.68	56.36	36.82
South Europe	160.67	28.37	74.77	57.33	51.67	66.67	53.33
LAC	80.18	12.40	58.47	32.18	33.68	35.71	27.14
Caribbean	36.20	6.23	49.03	14.60	11.00	16.00	17.00

Note: Figures in **bold** type are averages of the subindicators shown to their right (see text).
Source: www.doingbusiness.org/documents/DoingBusiness2007_FullReport.pdf.

Table 3.1c *Labor regulation: LAC region, relative to other regions (Botero et al. 2004); index values vary between 0 (low-cost) and 1 (high-cost)*

	Employment laws index[a]	Cost of increasing hours worked[b]	Cost of firing workers[c]	Alternative employment contracts[d]	Dismissal procedures[e]
Latin America	0.50	0.24	0.56	0.80	0.38
Selected Latin America	0.48	0.26	0.53	0.71	0.39
Industrial	0.52	0.67	0.38	0.63	0.39
AU, NZ, CAN	0.26	0.15	0.19	0.50	0.19
Tigers	0.33	0.07	0.47	0.60	0.19
Scan	0.72	1.00	0.53	0.69	0.67
East Europe	0.60	0.76	0.55	0.58	0.53
South Europe	0.69	0.77	0.51	0.91	0.57
LAC	0.45	0.24	0.50	0.70	0.36
Caribbean	0.16	0.00	0.15	0.50	0.00

	Collective relations laws index[f]	Labor union power[g]	Collective disputes[h]
Latin America	0.49	0.49	0.49
Selected Latin America	0.49	0.46	0.51
Industrial	0.46	0.45	0.46
AU, NZ, CAN	0.27	0.14	0.40
Tigers	0.40	0.35	0.45
Scan	0.50	0.59	0.42
East Europe	0.50	0.48	0.52
South Europe	0.57	0.62	0.53
LAC	0.47	0.45	0.48
Caribbean	0.23	0.29	0.17

	Social security laws index[i]	Old age, disability, and death benefits[j]	Sickness and health benefits[k]	Unemployment benefits[l]
Latin America	0.67	0.57	0.79	0.65
Selected Latin America	0.61	0.54	0.81	0.49
Industrial	0.74	0.70	0.75	0.78
AU, NZ, CAN	0.76	0.80	0.79	0.70
Tigers	0.52	0.64	0.68	0.24

(*cont.*)

Table 3.1c *(cont.)*

	Social security laws index[i]	Old age, disability, and death benefits[j]	Sickness and health benefits[k]	Unemployment benefits[l]
Scan	**0.82**	0.77	0.87	0.82
East Europe	**0.69**	0.55	0.76	0.75
South Europe	**0.75**	0.68	0.75	0.82
LAC	**0.58**	0.54	0.74	0.45
Caribbean	**0.17**	0.50	0.00	0.00

Notes: Figures in **bold** type are averages of the subindicators shown to their right (see text).

[a] *Employment laws index* Measures the protection of labor and employment laws as the average of (1) Alternative employment contracts, (2) Cost of increasing hours worked, (3) Cost of firing workers, and (4) Dismissal procedures.

[b] *Cost of increasing hours worked* Measures the cost of increasing the number of hours worked. We start by calculating the maximum number of "normal" hours of work per year in each country (excluding overtime, vacations, holidays, etc.). Normal hours range from 1,758 in Denmark to 2,418 in Kenya. Then we assume that firms need to increase the hours worked by their employees from 1,758 to 2,418 hours during one year. A firm first increases the number of hours worked until it reaches the country's maximum normal hours of work, and then uses overtime. If existing employees are not allowed to increase the hours worked to 2,418 hours in a year, perhaps because overtime is capped, we assume that the firm doubles its workforce and each worker is paid 1,758 hours, doubling the wage bill of the firm. The cost of increasing hours worked is computed as the ratio of the final wage bill to the initial one.

[c] *Cost of firing workers* Measures the cost of firing 20% of the firm's workers (10% are fired for redundancy and 10% without cause). The cost of firing a worker is calculated as the sum of the notice period, severance pay, and any mandatory penalties established by law or mandatory collective agreements for a worker with three years of tenure with the firm. If dismissal is illegal, we set the cost of firing equal to the annual wage. The new wage bill incorporates the normal wage of the remaining workers and the cost of firing workers. The cost of firing workers is computed as the ratio of the new wage bill to the old one.

[d] *Alternative employment contracts* Measures the existence and cost of alternatives to the standard employment contract, computed as the average of (1) a dummy variable equal to 1 if part-time workers enjoy the mandatory benefits of full-time workers, (2) a dummy variable equal to 1 if terminating part-time workers is at least as costly as terminating full-time workers, (3) a dummy variable equal to 1 if fixed-term contracts are allowed only for fixed-term tasks, and (4) the normalized maximum duration of fixed-term contracts.

[e] *Dismissal procedures* Measures worker protection granted by law or mandatory collective agreements against dismissal. It is the average of the following seven dummy variables which equal one: (1) if the employer must notify a third party before dismissing more than one worker, (2) if the employer needs the approval of a third party prior to dismissing more than one worker, (3) if the employer must notify a third party before dismissing one redundant worker, (4) if the employer needs the approval of a third party to dismiss one redundant worker, (5) if the employer must provide relocation or retraining alternatives for redundant employees prior to dismissal, (6) if there are priority rules applying to dismissal or layoffs, and (7) if there are priority rules applying to reemployment.

[f] *Collective relations laws index* Measures the protection of collective relations laws as the average of (1) labor union power and (2) collective disputes.

[g] *Labor union power* Measures the statutory protection and power of unions as the average of the following seven dummy variables which equal one: (1) if employees have the right to unionize, (2) if employees have the right to collective bargaining, (3) if employees have the legal duty to bargain with unions, (4) if collective contracts are extended to third parties by law, (5) if the law allows closed shops, (6) if workers, or unions, or both, have a right to appoint members to the Boards of Directors, and (7) if workers' councils are mandated by law.

Table 3.1c *(cont.)*

[b] *Collective disputes* Measures the protection of workers during collective disputes as the average of the following eight dummy variables which equal one: (1) if employer lockouts are illegal, (2) if workers have the right to industrial action, (3) if wildcat, political, and sympathy/solidarity/secondary strikes are legal, (4) if there is no mandatory waiting period or notification requirement before strikes can occur, (5) if striking is legal even if there is a collective agreement in force, (6) if laws do not mandate conciliation procedures before a strike, (7) if third-party arbitration during a labor dispute is mandated by law, and (8) if it is illegal to fire or replace striking workers.

[i] *Social security laws index* Measures social security benefits as the average of (1) Old-age, disability, and death benefits, (2) Sickness and health benefits, and (3) Unemployment benefits.

[j] *Old-age, disability, and death benefits* Measures the level of old-age, disability, and death benefits as the average of the following four normalized variables: (1) the difference between retirement age and life expectancy at birth, (2) the number of months of contributions or employment required for normal retirement by law, (3) the percentage of the worker's monthly salary deducted by law to cover old-age, disability, and death benefits, and (4) the percentage of the net pre-retirement salary covered by the net old-age cash benefit pension.

[k] *Sickness and health benefits* Measures the level of sickness and health benefit as the average of the following four normalized variables: (1) the number of months of contributions or employment required to qualify for sickness benefits by law, (2) the percentage of the worker's monthly salary deducted by law to cover sickness and health benefits, (3) the waiting period for sickness benefits, and (4) the percentage of the net salary covered by the net sickness cash benefit for a two-month sickness spell.

[l] *Unemployment benefits* Measures the level of unemployment benefits as the average of the following four normalized variables: (1) the number of months of contributions or employment required to qualify for unemployment benefits by law, (2) the percentage of the worker's monthly salary deducted by law to cover unemployment benefits, (3) the waiting period for unemployment benefits, and (4) the percentage of the net salary covered by the net unemployment benefits in case of a one-year unemployment spell.

payroll taxation. The programs vary in terms of coverage and generosity of benefits, but in most countries there is a weak link between tax payments and value of program benefits. Estimates reported in Heckman and Pages (2004) place average social security taxes at 20% of wages in the LAC region.

Job-security regulations limit short-term contracts, mandate minimum advance notice periods, specify just cause for dismissal, and mandate severance pay in case of dismissal. The cost of job security is estimated to be one-fifth of that of social security when calculated as an up-front expected present value (Heckman and Pages 2004). Using this approximation, the combined impact of job-security and social security taxation adds up to 25% of wages for the LAC region. This estimate does not include the effects of current job-security legislation on the dynamics of the labor market, but rather reduces employment via higher costs. Several researchers have reported evidence on the impact of job security on labor market dynamics – see, for example, Caballero *et al.* (2004), Micco and Pages (2004). Theory predicts that mandated employment protections may reduce productivity by distorting production choices. Firms facing (non-Coasean) worker dismissal costs will curtail hiring below efficient levels and retain unproductive workers, both of which should affect productivity. Work by Autor, Kerr, and Kugler (2007) uses the adoption of wrongful-discharge protections by US state courts since the 1970s to evaluate the link between dismissal costs and productivity. Their estimates suggest that wrongful-discharge protections reduce employment flows and firm entry rates. Moreover, analysis of plant-level data provides evidence of capital deepening and a decline in total factor productivity (TFP) following the introduction of wrongful-discharge protections. This last result is potentially quite important, suggesting that mandated employment protections reduce productive efficiency, as theory would suggest. Following this idea, Adriana Kugler proposes a way to include these efficiency effects in this model.

Minimum wages are binding in LAC countries and have substantial effects on employment and wage distributions. Data on wage distributions examined by Maloney and Nuñez (2004) suggest that minimum wages are binding. Both formal and informal sectors respond to the minimum wage through some market mechanism. One possible mechanism is captured in the model presented in section 2 where, in equilibrium, the wage rate in the informal sector is equal to the expected (net of taxes) wage rate in the modern sector or the minimum wage. After a detailed examination of wage distributions and their patterns around the minimum wage, Maloney and Nuñez (2004) use Colombia data to examine the effect of an increase in the minimum wage on "wages around the minimum" and on "employment for those earning around the minimum." They find that about 90% of the increase in the minimum wage is communicated to wages, with the effect continuing to be significant up to 4 minimum wages, although much smaller.[8] On the other hand, an increase in the minimum wage has a significant impact on the probability of becoming unemployed for those earning around the minimum. The authors conclude that the minimum wage induces far-reaching rigidities in the labor market, and suggest that the region is paying a high price in reduced flexibility for possible small effects on poverty alleviation.

The papers published in the Heckman and Pages (2004) volume suggest that mandated benefits reduce employment and that job-security

---

[8] Their methodology parallels that of a study conducted for US data. While in the case of the United States the estimated effect at four minimum wages is of an increase of 0.06 times the change in the minimum, in the case of Colombia, at four minimum wages the effect was estimated at 0.38 times the change in the minimum.

regulations have a substantial impact on the distribution of employment and on turnover rates. Insiders and entrenched workers gain from regulation, but outsiders suffer. As a consequence, job-security regulations promote inequality among demographic groups, with the most adverse impact of regulation falling on youth, women, and unskilled workers. Most of the individual country studies demonstrate that regulations promoting job security reduce covered worker exit rates out of employment and out of unemployment, and on net reduce employment.

The challenge of labor market reform is to increase efficiency. As indicated before, payroll taxation provides funding for a number of programs with weak links between contributions and benefits. One of the great contradictions of labor market interventions in the LAC region is that they fail to help the poor. Thus, in rethinking these interventions it is reasonable to look for mechanisms whereby the beneficiaries of these programs pay for their costs, and those that are unlikely to receive any benefits are simply not taxed. Programs need to be *unbundled* and better designed in an effort to *reduce the effective tax component of each program*.

Policymakers willing to reform legislation to improve labor market efficiency must aim at reducing effective taxation. This requires designing a system of payments and benefits that is as actuarially fair as possible, and that offers benefits that are truly valued by the majority of the population.

Alternative regulations to address old-age pensions

An alternative approach towards provision of old-age pensions is for governments to mandate individuals to save towards old age in a "defined contributions" (DC) program. The key advantage of a DC program is that it can be designed to be actuarially fair, and thus significantly reduce the labor tax component, with its detrimental effect on employment. A number of countries in the LAC region have moved in this direction and there is evidence that these pension reforms have "removed distortions in the labor market improving workers' incentives to seek to participate in formal pension systems" (Gill, Packard, and Yermo 2004).[9]

---

[9] I do not discuss here the use of other policy instruments to address policy objectives, such as poverty in old age.

A system of contributions and benefits is actuarially fair if (1) upon retirement, the expected present value of payouts equals all contributions compounded by the market rate of return; (2) incremental contributions yield equivalent expected incremental lifetime benefits; and (3) expected incremental benefits from delaying the start of the pension equal the present value of the early benefits forgone. (For a more precise delineation of these and other dimensions of actuarial fairness see Disney, Queisser, and Whitehouse 2006). PV calculations implicit in these actuarially fair calculations are made using the market interest rate appropriate to the degree of investment risk for the system during the accumulation stage, a less-risky rate during the payout stage, and survival rates for the average member of the cohort covered. Viewed from a systemic perspective, the Chilean reformed system of old-age pensions satisfies these criteria for actuarial fairness.[10]

However, policies that mandate a change in behavior relative to individuals' preferences will continue to be considered taxing from the individual point of view, even if they are actuarially fair. In the case of a pension program, an individual worker uses his own subjective discount rate, risk preference, expected survival rate, and labor–leisure trade-off when evaluating the actuarial fairness of the system to him. To that extent, even when the Chilean system satisfies the actuarial fairness criteria, many Chilean workers do not perceive the system as actuarially fair at the individual level. This might occur because:

- A worker is forced by the mandate to save at a higher rate than she would prefer
- She wishes to start her pension sooner than the eligibility rules permit, because she has achieved her desired lifetime retirement accumulation
- She wishes to use her savings to cover emergency or other needs in the early years of retirement
- She prefers to invest in a different way than is permitted by the regulations

---

[10] Disney (2004) calculates the effective tax component of pension programs across a number of OECD countries and time periods. He then uses the measures in a cross-country panel analysis of the determinants of age- and gender-specific effects on labor force participation. He finds that when public pension program contributions are broken down into a tax component and a savings component, the tax component of the payroll contribution reduces labor force participation among women.

- Some workers might be in ill health, so the mortality table specified by the regulator does not apply to them and their own personal expected value is less than the market's estimate of expected value
- The pension program is bundled together with other government programs and regulations, and individuals are forced into an all-or-nothing choice.

Mandatory DC social security systems inevitably include restrictions on the minimum saving rate, and eligibility conditions for pensions, investments, and payouts. Yet, heterogeneity among workers implies varying willingness to save, risk–return preferences, tastes regarding mode and timing of pensions, and health conditions. Credit-constrained individuals who have little voluntary saving cannot make adjustments outside the system to compensate for deviations from optimality inside the system. A substantial tax component remains for this group, despite the actuarial fairness of the system as a whole.

Edwards and Cox Edwards (2002) assessed the labor market impact of mandated payroll contributions to individual saving accounts towards pensions, as opposed to traditional payroll contributions towards social security benefits. They hypothesize that under the new Chilean regime contributions would be seen (at least partially) as a deferred compensation scheme. For an individual employed in the formal sector, total labor compensation would be equal to her take-home (cash) salary plus a proportion of her contribution to the retirement system. If contributions are seen fully as deferred compensation, that proportion will be equal to one. If, on the other hand, contributions are seen fully as taxes, that proportion will be equal to zero, and the total compensation will be only equal to the take-home salary. Their estimates suggest that individuals consider little over half of their contribution to be a tax.

Alternative regulations on job security

The traditional labor market analysis placed a lot of emphasis on stock variables such as the labor force, total employment, total unemployment, and some key ratios such as labor force participation or the rate of unemployment. In the 1990s, a lot more emphasis was placed on the examination of the dynamics of the labor market, the number of jobs created and/or destroyed in a given period of time, and we currently have data on employment flows from a number of countries. The evidence points to a remarkable degree of similarity in gross job flows – the sum of job created plus the number of jobs destroyed as a percentage of total employment, measured by year. Annual gross job flows are between 20% and 30% in most countries (see, for example, Davis, Haltiwanger, and Schuh 1996; OECD Employment Outlook 1996; Kaplan, González, and Robertson 2003; Menezes-Fihlo *et al.* 2003; ILO 2004; Micco and Pagés 2004). Job flows are an integral part of the normal operation of labor markets, and they are relatively more important in some sectors (retail and construction, for example). Restrictions to job flows distort the normal function of the labor market and lead to a loss in TFP.

Consider a world in which employers and workers understand that labor contracts are likely to come to an end for multiple possible reasons. A regulation that establishes the obligation of employers to set aside a fund to be given to the employee in case of separation is likely to be appreciated by workers and employers. This fund will be built with monthly contributions, proportional to the employee's salary, and thus grow with tenure and productivity of employment. This mandated transfer from employers to workers in case of separation (severance payment) is likely to be internalized in the labor contract, rendering no real effects except for requiring the parties to agree on it. Lazear (1990) argued that if dismissal costs were paid in all separation cases, and if payments took the form of lump-sum or deferred payments, severance payments would have a well-defined counterpart in current salaries, and the contract could fully internalize the severance.

In contrast, most LAC countries have established severance payments that (a) are a multiple of the last salary, or the salary at the time of dismissal; (b) depend on the existence of just cause; (c) do not apply in the case of voluntary quits; and (d) apply to long-term contracts by default because of limitations on the use of short-term contracts. Therefore, the capacity to internalize the cost of severance is generally low. In addition, at the time of dismissal, firms may delay payments or may go bankrupt, leading to actual transfers to workers that can be significantly smaller than the ones established by law.

In recent years, some countries have moved closer to the Lazear (1990) conditions, or are considering reforms along those lines. For example, Bolivia and Brazil established severance in all separations, and Colombia replaced the traditional cost of dismissal with severance based on individual accounts. Prior to the 1990 labor market reform, the system of severance payments in Colombia resembled the traditional system in many countries, requiring employers to pay a multiple of the last wage at the time of dismissal. The reform established a monthly employer contribution rate of 8.3% (or 1/12 of salary) to an individual account, to be used in the event of unemployment. The idea is similar to the system of unemployment insurance savings accounts proposed by Feldstein and Altman (1998) to reduce the distortionary effects of unemployment insurance. In the case of Colombia, however, these new accounts replaced the system of severance pay. Firms' implicit liability was replaced by an explicit obligation to make monthly deposits to the worker's account. Kugler (2005) hypothesizes that in the context of savings accounts that guarantee severance payments and eliminate uncertainty, workers should be more willing to accept wage cuts to assume part of the costs of severance payments. In addition, the severance payment saving accounts (SPSAs) should reduce labor market distortions by partially neutralizing government-mandated severance with private transfers between firms and workers. Kugler's empirical analysis suggests that the introduction of SPSAs shifted between 60% and 80% of firms' contributions into the accounts towards workers as lower wages. This shifting of severance payments towards workers suggests that the reform facilitated an internalization of the cost by workers, who ultimately benefit from the transfers, reduce costs for employers as well as the job-security policy distortion to hiring and firing.[11]

---

[11] Anderson and Meyer (2000) studied the impact of a change in the unemployment insurance (UI) system in the state of Washington in the mid-1980s. At that time, the state moved from a flat UI tax rate to a variable rate or experience rated system, like all other states. In an experience rated system, the UI tax rate assigned to each employer is adjusted to take into account the use of UI benefits associated with that employer. Changes in subsequent years led tax rates to range from 0.36 to 5.40%. Employers, of course, noted these changes in both the cost of employing workers and of laying them off. It altered the way they dealt with layoffs and UI claims, just as economic theory would anticipate. Using UI data from Washington and some comparisons with similar data from Oregon and Idaho, the authors reach several conclusions. One is that employers passed on the higher tax to their workers in the form of lower wages. However, since a single firm faces price and wage competition in its specific market, it may not be able to pass on the extra tax cost fully to its workers through smaller pay raises.

Alternative regulations to meet the objectives of the minimum wage

While the goal of minimum wage legislation is to raise the labor incomes of the working poor, the reality is that it ultimately leaves the least skilled out of work. There are other policy instruments to help the working poor that are more effective than the minimum wage.[12] The US federal *Earned income tax credit* (EITC) is a refundable tax credit that reduces or eliminates the taxes that low-income working people pay (such as payroll taxes) and also frequently operates as a wage subsidy for low-income workers. Enacted in 1975, the then very small EITC was expanded in 1986, 1990, 1993, and 2001 with each major tax bill. Today, the EITC is one of the largest anti-poverty tools in the United States (despite the fact that income measures, including the poverty rate, generally do not account for the credit), and enjoys broad bipartisan support. Almost 21 million American families received more than $36 billion in refunds through the EITC in 2004. In addition to the federal EITC, as of 2006, 20 states (including Washington, DC) have their own EITCs. These state plans primarily mimic the federal EITC structure on a smaller scale, as individuals receive a state credit equal to a fixed percentage – between 15% and 30% depending on the state – of what they received from the Internal Revenue Service (IRS). Furthermore, small local EITCs have been enacted in New York City, Montgomery County in Maryland, and San Francisco.

Other countries with EITCs include Belgium, Canada, Denmark, Finland, France, Great Britain, Ireland, the Netherlands, and New Zealand. In some cases, these are small (the maximum EITC in Finland is 290 Euros), but others are even larger than the US EITC (the UK EITC is worth up to 6,150 Euros).

The size of the EITC, as its name suggests, is a function of how much earned income the individual claimant has accumulated, where "earned income" is a technical term defined by the IRS under guidance of the tax code. The main sources of income that count are wages, salaries, tips, and other taxable employee pay, net earnings from self-employment, and gross income received as a statutory employee.

The credit is also characterized by a unique three-stage structure that consists of a phase-in range in which the credit increases as

---

[12] See chapter 8 in Perry *et al.* (2007) for further discussion.

Table 3.2 *US EITC, tax year 2006*

Earned income (x)[a]	Stage[b,c]	Credit (2+ children)
$0–$11,340	phase in	40% * x
$11,340–$14,810	plateau	$4,536
$14,810–$36,348	phase out	$4,536 – 21.06% * (x – $14,810)
>= $36,348	no credit	$0

Earned income (x)	Stage	Credit (1 child)
$0–$8,080	phase in	34% * x
$8,080–$14,810	plateau	$2,747
$14,810–$32,001	phase out	$2,747 – 15.98% * (x – $14,810)
>= $32,001	no credit	$0

Earned income (x)	Stage	Credit (no children)
$0–$5,380	phase in	7.65% * x
$5,380–$6,740	plateau	$412
$6,740–$12,120	phase out	$412 – 7.65% * (x – $6,740)
>= $12,121	no credit	$0

Notes: [a] Household earned income.
[b] The no credit thresholds are above the poverty line. In 2006, the poverty line for a four-person family with two children was $20,444; a three-person family with one child was $13,89; a one-person family with no children was $10,488.
[c] In 2005, the mean income of the first quintile of the household income distribution was $10,655; $36,000 was the upper bound of the second quintile of income distribution among households.
Source: Urban Institute and US Census Bureau.

earnings increase, a plateau range in which the maximum credit has been reached and further earnings do not affect it, and a phase-out range in which the credit decreases as earnings increase. With a positive credit along a wide range of labor incomes, the program is attractive to a large fraction of the working poor. Table 3.2 describes the way in which the credit is calculated for a given family.

Consider a family with two dependent children in the tax year 2006. The credit is equal to 40% of the first $11,340 earned, plateaus at a maximum credit of $4,536, begins to phase-out when earnings increase beyond $14,810, and reaches zero when earnings pass $36,348. For filers using the Married Filing Jointly status, the phase-out thresholds are increased by $2,000. For a family with one dependent child, the structure is similar but has a phase-in rate of 34% and a maximum credit of $2,747.

For those filing without dependents, there is a small credit of 7.65% of earnings with a maximum of $412, which covers the employee's portion of the social security and medicare payroll taxes. Note how nicely this policy tool can be linked to an incentive to formalize employment for those that do not want to save for pensions. Workers without dependents must satisfy all of three additional criteria in order to qualify for the credit: (1) be at least age 25 but under 65 at the end of the year, (2) live in the United States for more than half the year, and (3) not qualify as a dependent of another person. All dollar amounts are indexed to inflation.[13]

Because of its structure, the EITC is effective at targeting assistance to low-income families. By contrast, only 30% of minimum wage workers live in families near or below the federal poverty line, as most are teenagers, young adults, students, or spouses supplementing their studies or family income. The EITC relies on a functioning tax system, and even in the United States is open to abuse through fraudulent tax credit claims. However, research shows that the EITC has boosted labor force participation, particularly by low-educated single mothers (see Hotz, Mullin, and Scholz, 2006).

Skeptics may argue that such a program cannot be implemented in the LAC region, one plagued by informality. The answer to them is that a Devolución de Impuestos a los Pobres (DIP) program can be designed precisely to entice the informal into the system. The goal of the program is to make gainful formal employment the key mechanism to gain access to government programs.

4 Cost and benefits of labor market reform

We consider three possible reforms. (1) A reduction in effective payroll taxes via redesign of the pension system; (2) a reduction in labor costs

---

[13] Many types of income that the IRS recognizes as such for other purposes do not count as "earned income." Things that do not count include (but are certainly not limited to) investment income, unemployment, and social security. In addition, not everyone whose income is in the range described below is eligible for the credit. For instance, if a person's earned income is in one of the qualifying ranges described below but her investment income is large enough ($2,800 for tax year 2006), then she cannot claim the credit.

via redesign of job security legislation; and (3) a replacement of binding minimum wages for an EITC (DIP).

Consider the case where reforms reduce the tax component of social security programs. That is, assume that as a result of reforms, T_1 is reduced to some lower level. If all programs currently bundled with pensions are transformed into defined contribution programs, the perceived tax would fall relatively more and if, in addition, they are made optional, the tax may fall to zero. This would unleash a series of effects, including a higher demand for labor in the modern sector, a change in aggregate labor supply, and changes in wages and in employment in the informal sector.

Social security reform

A social security reform that reduces the payroll tax will reduce labor costs and increase employment along the formal sector demand for labor. As a result there will be an increase in the wage rate in the informal sector I, the sector that is not covered by the social security system, and that prior to the reform had the lowest wage rate. Notice that, by construction, net (take-home) wages in the modern sector are not affected by the reform. This is because we have assumed that the minimum wage is set on a take-home basis, and that the reform does not affect it. However, the reform will change the composition of the net wage, substituting part of it into a savings account.

Formally, the model given by (1)–(11) can be solved to obtain the effects of this type of social security reform, on a number of variables, including informal sector wages (W_I), the volume of unemployment (U), and product prices in the informal sector (P_I). In order to simplify the exposition, we follow a long tradition in international trade theory – the Ricardo–Viner approach – and we assume that capital is fixed in its sector of origin. We begin with the effects of changes in the tax component of the social security contribution ($d \log T$) on informal sector wages ($d \log W_I$):

$$d \log W_I = \Delta^{-1} \left\{ -\left[\alpha_U \left(\frac{U}{L_M + U} \right) \left(\frac{1}{\eta_M} \right) \right] \right.$$
$$\left. - \left[\left(\frac{U}{L_M + U} \right) \alpha_M \left(\frac{1}{\eta_M} \right) \right] \right\} \left(\frac{T_1}{1 + T_1} \right) d \log T$$

$$(12)$$

where,

$$\Delta = -\alpha_U - \left[\alpha_I\left(\frac{U}{L_M + U}\right)\left(\frac{1}{\eta_I}\right)(\mu - 1)\right]$$
$$- \left[\left(\frac{U}{L_M + U}\right)\phi\left(\alpha_I + \mu\beta\right)\right] \tag{13}$$

α_I, α_M, and α_U are the shares of employment in the informal sector, employment in the modern sector, and unemployment in the labor resources constraint (5). η_I and η_M are the inverse of the elasticities of the demand for labor with respect to wages in the I and M sectors, respectively, and are negative.[14] φ is the supply elasticity of labor, and is positive. μ is the elasticity of the price of informal sector goods (P_I) with respect to the wage rate in that sector, and is greater than zero and smaller than one. It follows from (13), then, that Δ is negative. Consequently, according to (12), the following result holds:

$$\frac{d\log W_I}{d\log T} < 0$$

The effect of the reform on aggregate unemployment (U), is given by:

$$d\log U = \Delta^{-1}\left\{\left(\frac{\alpha_I}{\eta_I}\right) - \left[\alpha_I\left(\frac{U}{L_M + U}\right)\left(\frac{1}{\eta_I}\right)\left(\frac{1}{\eta_M}\right)(\mu - 1)\right]\right.$$
$$\left. - \left[\left(\frac{U}{L_M + U}\right)\phi\left(\alpha_I + \mu\beta\right)\left(\frac{1}{\eta_M}\right)\right]\right\}$$
$$\times \left(\frac{T_1}{1 + T_1}\right)d\log T \tag{14}$$

The sign of (14) is undetermined. It follows from this that within the framework developed in this chapter, a reduction in the payroll tax in the modern sector will have an ambiguous effect on the number of unemployed. Whether the level of unemployment will increase or decline will depend on two basic factors: the supply elasticity of labor in the economy – parameter φ in (14); and the elasticity of labor demand in the informal sector. The more elastic is the supply for labor and the more inelastic is the demand for labor in the informal sector,

[14] That is,

$$\eta_I = \frac{d\log W_I}{d\log L_I}.$$

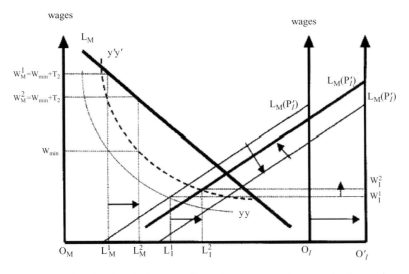

Figure 3.2 A reduction in the payroll tax increases employment in the modern sector, reduces informality, and improves wages in the informal sector

the more likely it is that the reform will result in an *increase* in the level of unemployment.

Equation (15) gives the effect of the reform on product prices in the informal sector, and is positive:

$$d \log P_I = \Delta^{-1}\left\{-\left[\left(\frac{U}{L_M+U}\right)\left(\frac{\alpha_M}{\eta_M}\right)\right]-\left[\alpha_U\left(\frac{U}{L_M+U}\right)\left(\frac{1}{\eta_M}\right)\right]\right\}$$
$$\times\left(\frac{T_1}{1+T_1}\right)d \log T \tag{15}$$

The working of the model is illustrated in figure 3.2, where it is assumed that the reform reduces the social security tax from T_1 to T_2. The new cost of labor in the modern sector is W_M^2. Distance O_I–O_I' is assumed to be equal to the increase in the amount of labor supplied to the economy. Because of this increase in aggregate labor supply, the original demand for labor in the informal sector has to be redrawn as L_I'. Since the product price of I has increased, the demand for labor in the informal sector shifts up, and is represented in figure 3.2 by L_I' (P_I'). The wage rate in the informal sector is now determined by the intersection of a new rectangular hyperbola $y'y'$ and a new demand for labor in sector I, and is given by W_I^2. Employment in the informal sector has changed from distance O_I–L_I^1 to distance O_I^1–L_I^2. Because of the reduction in W_M, employment in the modern sector has increased from L_M^1 to L_M^2. The new level of unemployment which, as indicated by (13), could be either higher or lower than the initial level of unemployment, is given by distance L_M^2–L_I^2.

The results in (12)–(15) assume that there is no change in the take-home wage in the modern sector.

Although the model developed here is simple, and has some limitations, it has enough structure to provide insights into some of the most important effects of a pension reform on labor markets.[15]

Benefits

As indicated in section 3, social security taxes add up to an average 20% of wages in the region. This 20% is earmarked to finance pension benefits and other programs. In addition as Heckman and Pages (2004) estimate, job-security legislation adds an additional 5% to labor costs on average, making the total tax increase rise to 25% of the net wage. In what follows, I consider a reform that does not change the nominal payroll tax, but isolates 10% of this tax and redirects it to individual saving accounts, transforming pension programs into DC systems in each country.

The key change introduced by this reform is that workers see part of this 10% contribution as deferred compensation. If workers valued the full 10% contribution towards their individual account as net compensation, the cost of labor in the formal sector would fall to $W_{min}(1.25 - 0.10)$. Based on evidence from Edwards and Cox Edwards (2002), I assume that workers value half of the 10% contribution towards pensions as a deferred payment, and that the reform will lead to a reduction of W_M from $W_{min}(1.25)$ to $W_{min}(1.20)$, a reduction of the overall distortion to the modern sector labor market from an average of 25% to 20%. Implicitly, I assume that the workers in the modern sector accept part of their pre-established net wage W_{min} in the form

---

[15] Some of the limitations of the model include the fact that it does not consider all the channels through which the reforms will feed back to the rest of the economy. Also, it does not consider explicitly the (possible) effect on the labor supply of the elimination of the expected future benefits of the entitlement component of the old system. This effect, however, is likely to be small and could be easily incorporated into the system by amending (6).

of a deferred compensation towards pension benefits, or that they see half of the 10% contribution as part of their net wage.[16]

The reduced deadweight loss (also known as excess burden or allocative inefficiency) can be measured by the triangle $\frac{1}{2}*0.05*dL_M$ per year. In addition, the reduction in labor costs will lead to an increase in formal employment. The change in employment in the formal sector can be calculated as $d\log L_M = \eta_M(-0.041)$, where η_M is the elasticity of demand for labor in the modern sector and -0.041 represents the reduction in labor costs in the modern sector.[17] Informal employment, on the other hand, will fall as follows: $d\log L_i = \eta_i d\log W_i$ where W_i is the wage in the informal sector. Since part of the newly employed in the formal sector will come from informal employment, the informal sector wage will increase. This change in the informal sector wage may be calculated using (12). If we denote by γ the proportion of employment in the formal sector, then the *change in total employment* will be:

$$d\log L = \gamma d\log L_M + (1 - \gamma)d\log L_i \qquad (16)$$

As shown in table 3.4, and given the assumptions regarding key parameters listed in table 3.3, employment is estimated to increase by 1% – in response to a 5% reduction in costs in the formal sector. This employment response estimate is consistent with results from a time-series analysis based on the case of Chile.[18] From the calculation above we compute the effect of reform on growth and output. A simple Cobb–Douglas aggregate production function:

$$Y = AL^\alpha K^{(1-\alpha)}$$

tells us that a reduction of payroll taxes that increases employment by a certain fraction relative to the baseline will lead to a higher output every year, relative to what would have been attained had the labor market distortion remained intact. The difference in output relative to the baseline output can be calculated as

$$d\log Y = \alpha^* d\log L \text{ (with } \alpha = 2/3)^{19}$$

---

[16] The assumptions made amount to a pre-setting of the cost of labor at 1.25 times the minimum wage pre-social security reform, and 1.20 times the minimum wage after the reform.

[17] $-0.041 = \log(1.20) - \log(1.25)$.   [18] See Edwards (2005).

[19] The share of national income earned by workers is based on Bernanke and Gükaynak (2002). The average share for their sample is 2/3. However, it is

Table 3.3 *Parameters for calculations in table 3.4*

	Parameter	% of labor force
Labor force	270 million	100
Modern sector employment	170 million	63
Informal employment	73 million	27
Unemployment	27 million	10
Initial payroll tax (% of W)	20%	
Initial cost of job security (% of W)	5%	
Elasticity of labor demand modern sector	0.4	
Elasticity of labor demand informal sector	0.5	
Sustainable GDP growth rate	3%	
Discount rate	5%	
Average wage/year	$5,400	
GNI (USAID)	US$2,000,000 million	
Population	570 million	

Note: W = Wage.
Sources: Population and Employment data: Cepal Anuario Estadistico GNI number; USAID LAC Databook (http://pdf.usaid.gov/pdf_docs/PNADG900.pdf).

The present value of that effect is

$$B = \frac{GDP_0}{r - g} * d \log Y$$

where GDP_0 is the level of GDP before the labor tax is reduced, r is the discount rate, and g is the rate of GDP growth that can be sustained in the long run.

Costs

In defined benefits (DB) programs the current generation of workers makes contributions to the program in the form of a tax taken out

---

easy to note that this number tends to be smaller, and with more variation around the mean for developing countries. Calculations of net benefits of reforms are sensitive to this number. For example, if the share of labor is reduced to 1/2, the estimated net benefits fall by 25 to 30%.

Table 3.4 *Estimated net benefits*

Policy option	Benefit 1 (B1) (reduced DWL) US$ million/ year	Estimated effect on labor costs dlogT^a	Estimated change in employment dlogL^a	Benefit 2 (B2); Estimated effect on GNI baseline dlogY^a	Estimated s(C) US$ million/year	NPV (B1 + B2 − C) US$ million
(1) Redesign of pension programs to make them actuarially fair (payroll tax falls from 25% to 20%)	$625	−0.041	0.010	0.006	$13,333	$380,834
(2) Redesign of job-security legislation into a UI account (payroll tax falls from 25% to 21%)	$498	−0.033	0.008	0.005	$4,000	$435,868
Combine Options (1) and (2) (payroll tax falls from 25% to 16%)	$1,143	−0.075	0.017	0.012	$17,333	$838,565
(3) Reduction of the minimum wage to make it not binding; and introduction of EITC-type transfers to the working poor (DIP)	$1,178	−0.077	0.018	0.012	$15,600	$909,340

Note: [a] Please refer to the model developed in section 3.

of every paycheck. In exchange for this tax, the government promises to pay the taxpayer an amount of benefits specified in the law when she retires. These programs are referred to as "pay-as-you-go" because governments "borrow" the payroll contributions of current workers to pay for the benefits of current retirees, without acknowledging the financial transaction in the budget. These programs are also unfunded because the first generation of beneficiaries receives benefits without having contributed, giving origin to the "legacy debt" or unfunded liability of these programs. As Diamond and Orzag (2004) clearly state, if a society decided to end this type of program, the existing generation who paid taxes to support the program would receive no benefits, and would be saddled with the legacy debt. A more precise statement however is that the legacy debt originates in the DB system disconnect between collected contributions and benefits paid: it may increase or decrease through generations, and societies begin to confront it when the systems fall into deficit.

Societies do not choose to end this type of program; they are typically driven to change it because it becomes unsustainable. As new generations are added to the system, the relative size of contributors and pension recipients changes, typically expanding the legacy debt. Legal changes that alter the indexation of benefits, the payroll contribution, or the minimum age of pension, among others, may also alter the legacy debt. The overwhelming trend of the twentieth century was population ageing, increasing the legacy debt of these systems and, at the same time, compromising the annual accounting balance of the system. Without population-related balancing mechanisms in sight, the actuarial balance of DB systems requires an increase in contributions, a reduction of benefits, or a combination of both. These remedies are met with resistance from pensioners who do not accept benefit reductions and taxpayers who try to avoid taxation. When countries get to a point where current tax collections towards social security are below pension benefit payments, the ensuing deficit is met with "explicit" government borrowing or other forms of taxation to pay the system's legacy debt. It turns out that societies start paying the legacy debt as soon as the systems move into accounting deficit, and governments start paying pension benefits using general tax collections or "explicit" borrowing.

Several countries have considered fundamental reforms, or a replacement of DB systems by DC systems. Two questions arise: First, "How does fundamental reform alter the legacy debt?" The answer is: It freezes it with the last generation of beneficiaries of the old system. Second, "Is there a social cost in transitioning from the old system to the new one?" A number of researchers have discussed and estimated the "cost of transition." For example, Edwards (1998), referring to the case of Chile, states: "From a fiscal point of view, the reform generated two major sources of public expenditures: (a) the servicing and payment of recognition bonds (to those that move to the new system), and (b) the payment of retirees in the old system." Feldstein and Samwick (1998) discuss alternative paths to move from an unfunded DB system to a DC system using US data. Kotlikoff (1998) uses a model to simulate the changes in taxation required to move from a DB to a DC system. These authors, however, ignore the fact that the liabilities of the public sector with contributors to the DB system exist with or without reform. In fact, a reform of a pension system from DB to DC does not create new sources of public expenditure; instead, it eliminates a source of funding for the already existing public liability – namely, the payroll contributions to the DB system. From the point of view of the economy as a whole, the resources that contributors would have paid to the government under the DB system are channeled to the financial system under the DC system. This redirection of financial resources is not an added cost of transition but rather a financial challenge for governments, who would have to "explicitly" borrow or find other sources to fund the pension benefits of the transition generation.

The fact that the government does not collect social security taxes any longer and must borrow or tax other sources to pay the pension benefits of the transition generation does not make this explicit borrowing or additional taxation a social cost of transition, because there are no resources taken out of the system. For this reason, I will not attempt to estimate the transition costs to be subtracted from the benefits of pension reform.

However, a system based on individual accounts will introduce a cost of managing the funds. These costs include capital costs incurred in the early years of a new system, record keeping and communication costs, investment costs, and marketing costs, all of which are sensitive to the system's design (see James, Smalhout, and Vittas 2001). Data published by the International Association of Pension Fund Supervisor Organizations (AIOS) indicate that administrative costs based on data for ten LAC countries have fluctuated between 10.5% and 10.9%

of contributions, and they have typically fallen through time within individual countries. I used an estimate of 10% of contributions as the cost of administrating individual accounts.

Reform to job-security regulation and its effect on the labor market

Benefits

The reform to job-security regulation transforms the extra labor cost associated with dismissals on a contribution towards an unemployment insurance account (UIA). Recall that, according to Heckman and Pages (2004) the effect of current job security is approximated to be equivalent to a 5% payroll tax. I assume a reform that eliminates the costs of dismissals and establishes a system whereby 5% of wages go to a UIA account. Labor costs fall under the assumption that workers value 80% of these UIA deposits as deferred compensation, leading the cost of labor to fall from $W_M(1.25)$ to $W_M(1.21)$. The change in employment in the formal sector can be calculated as $d \log L_M = \eta_M(-0.033)$.[20] The impact of this reform is parallel to that calculated above. If the reforms to pensions and job security are implemented at the same time, the tax reduction would be the combination of the two, and the change in employment in the formal sector can be calculated as $d \log L_M = \eta_M(-0.075)$.[21]

Costs

The economy will assume additional costs associated with the management of the UIAs. An estimate of this cost can be taken from the current experience in Chile, where management is financed with a 0.6% commission over deposits.[22]

Reform to minimum wage policy and its effect on the labor market

Consider a reform that lowers the minimum wage to the point where it no longer is binding, and introduces a transfer (DIP) to low-income

---

[20] $-0.033 = \log(1.21) - \log(1.25)$.   [21] $-0.075 = \log(1.16) - \log(1.25)$.
[22] Superintendencia de AFP. This is the regulatory agency that oversees the operation of private administrators of pension funds.

workers so that the overall labor supply remains unaltered. A reduction of the minimum wage in this model would lead to a decline in the
formal sector net wage, an increase in formal employment, the *elimination of the unemployment caused by the minimum wage*, and an
equalization of the net wage in both the formal sector and the informal
sector. At the same time, labor supply would tend to fall. However,
if low-income workers in the formal sector were given a transfer to
increase their net labor incomes, labor supply could be reinstated to
the original level.[23]

From (6),

$$L_S = h\left(\frac{W}{P}, O\right); h' > 0$$

labor supply is a positive function of real wages, and O represents
"other" factors affecting the supply of labor. A tax credit program
targeted to the working poor will increase the value of O, and it is
possible to find a value of O that offsets the effect of the reduction in
W/P, keeping labor supply constant. The equilibrium condition in the
market becomes:

$$W_i(1 + T) = W_m \tag{17}$$

Equation (17) replaces (1), (2), and (3) and indicates that after the
removal of the minimum wage, the labor market will be characterized
by the equalization of net wages across the two sectors and a differential in labor costs across sectors driven solely by T. In the presence of a
binding minimum wage, the wage differential across sectors is driven
by

$$\frac{(1 + T)}{p}$$

---

[23] Hotz, Mullin, and Scholz (2002) report that average annual disposable income
for single-parent welfare cases in their four-county California sample in 1998
was around $10,000. The average EITC differential for families with one and
two or more children in their sample was $439 in 1998: hence, the EITC
increased disposable income by roughly 4.4%. Employment rates for families
with two or more children in 1998 were around 60%, and the EITC expansion
increased employment of families with two or more children by 3.2 percentage
points, or 5.6% (3.2/(60 −3.2)). This implies an employment elasticity with
respect to disposable income of 1.3, which is at the upper end of the range of
such estimates for the previous studies of the employment effects of the EITC
discussed in Hotz and Scholz (2003).

While a labor market distortion remains, the elimination of "equilibrium unemployment" changes p to 1 and reduces the distortion proportionally. If one assumes that half of the unemployment in the region is explained by wage rigidities originated with the minimum wage, and given that we set

$$p = \frac{L_M}{L_M + U}$$

the starting value of p is 0.926; this reform will increase efficiency as a reduction in the payroll tax equivalent to:

$$\log(1 + T) - \log(1 + T)/0.926 = -0.077$$

As a result of this policy reform, there is a going to be an increase in output proportional to the increase in employment $d \log Y = \alpha^* d \log L$ where the change in L corresponds to the expansion of employment around the initial minimum wage level as a result of the reduction of the minimum wage. The present value of that effect is, as before,

$$B = \frac{GDP_0}{r - g} * d \log Y$$

where again, GDP_0 is the level of GDP before the labor tax is reduced, r is the discount rate, and g is the rate of GDP growth that can be sustained in the long run.

Costs

It is difficult to measure the cost of this type of program. For example, in the case of the EITC program in the United States, the cost to the federal government measured by direct tax transfers to beneficiaries was more than $36 billion in 2004.[24] At the same time, however, this cost may be at least partially offset by several factors such as: new taxes (such as payroll taxes paid by employers) generated by new workers drawn by the EITC into the labor force; reductions in entitlement spending that result from individuals being lifted out of poverty by the EITC; taxes generated on additional spending made by families receiving EITC; a potential reduction in crime and other more indirect factors.

I make a very rough assumption using a mean annual transfer of $600 per poor worker. I assume that 10% of workers (26 million)

[24] US GDP was approximately $12 trillion (US Department of Commerce).

qualify for this average transfer, generating a total annual transfer of $15.6 billion.[25]

Results

The baseline parameters used to calculate costs and benefits are indicated in table 3.3 (p. 130) and a summary of benefits and costs associated to each of these solutions is shown in table 3.4 (p. 131). The reforms proposed in this chapter are designed so that beneficiaries of programs pay for their costs and those unlikely to receive any benefits are not taxed. Each of these reforms would increase employment by 1–2% per year relative to current levels – that is 2.4–5 million jobs, generating an expansion in output of the order of 0.5 to 1 point relative to the baseline. These can yield high benefits and healthy BCRs, which are summarized below.

- *Option 1: redesign of pension programs to make them actuarially fair (effective payroll tax falls from 25 to 20%).* The PV of benefits is $647.5 billion; the PV of costs is $266.7bn. The cost-benefit ratio is 2.4. I should also add here that the BCR estimated for the social security reform is very sensitive to the assumption made regarding the individual valuation of contributions. In particular, the BCR increases by 0.5 points for every additional 0.01 of valuation assigned to the 0.10 contribution to social security.
- *Option 2: redesign of job security legislation into UIA (effective payroll tax falls from 25% to 21%).* The PV of benefits is $515.8bn; the PV of costs is $80bn. The cost-benefit ratio is 6.4.
- *Combine Options 2 and 3 (effective payroll tax falls from 25% to 16%).* The PV of benefits is $1,185bn; the PV of costs is $346.7bn. The cost-benefit ratio is 3.4.
- *Reduction of the minimum wage to make it not binding and introduction of EITC-type transfers to the working poor.* The PV of benefits is $1,221bn; the PV of costs is $312bn. The BCR is 3.9.

All these proposals have benefits much greater than their costs. Redesigning social security legislation comes last in quantitative terms,

---

[25] Based on the US$36 billion figure, the US program costs about US$120 *per capita* per year. The LAC program would cost about US$2.7 *per capita* per year. On a *per capita* income basis, the LAC program is about $\frac{1}{4}$ of the US program.

but would also create other economic benefits, particularly bringing solvency to the pensions system.

5 Summary and conclusions

The key challenge for LAC policymakers is to implement labor market reforms that reduce payroll taxes, ease job security regulations, and revise mandated benefits in an effort to improve the labor markets' capacity to generate employment and improve workers' compensation. Currently, payroll taxation provides funding for a number of programs with weak links between contributions and benefits. One of the great contradictions of labor market intervention in the region is that it fails to help the poor.

In rethinking these interventions it is reasonable to look for mechanisms whereby the beneficiaries of these programs pay for their costs, and those that are unlikely to receive any benefits are simply not taxed. Programs need to be *unbundled* and better designed in an effort to *reduce the effective tax component of each program*. This requires designing programs that offer benefits that are truly valued by the majority of the population, and a system of payments that is as actuarially fair as possible.

I use existing models and estimates on labor markets' behavior to provide computations of the costs and benefits of three specific (potential) labor market reforms in the region: (a) a *pension reform* that reduces the labor tax component of pay-as-you-go regimes; (b) the elimination of restrictions on short-term contracts and the *replacement of current dismissal regulations* with a UIA system; and (c) the introduction of an EITC/DIP as an *alternative to a high minimum wage* and as an *instrument to formalize labor contracts and compensate the poor for the obligation to make contributions towards unemployment and pension benefits*.

Calculations are based on relatively conservative assumptions regarding the welfare benefits of reforms by assuming that even actuarially fair programs create effective taxation. In other words, reforms towards efficiency do not remove labor market distortions, but they reduce them. In particular, it is assumed that a DC pension system based on mandated savings is seen by workers as partial deferred compensation and partial tax. Similarly, in the case of a reform to job-security legislation, it is assumed that part of the contributions to

Table 3.5 *BCRs*

Policy option	Estimated PV of benefits US$ million	Estimated PV of costs US$ million	BCR B/C
(1) Redesign of pension programs to make them actuarially fair (effective payroll tax falls from 25% to 20%)	647,500	266,667	2.4
(2) Redesign of job-security legislation into a UI account (effective payroll tax falls from 25% to 21%)	515,868	80,000	6.4
(3) Combine options (1) and (2) (effective payroll tax falls from 25% to 16%)	1,185,232	346,667	3.4
(4) Reduction of the minimum wage to make it not binding; and introduction of EITC-type transfers to the working poor (DIP)	1,221,340	312,000	3.9

the UIA is considered a tax, although the tax component in this case is assumed to be smaller than in the case of contributions towards pensions.

From the resulting CBA of the individual programs, the most effective of the proposed efforts is that of replacing minimum wage legislation with direct transfers. This program would lead to net benefits of the order of $1/2$ current gross national income (GNI) in the region. Efforts to redesign pension programs or job-security legislation would lead to net benefits of the order of $1/4$ current GNI.

The BCRs (table 3.5) place the redesign of job-security legislation solution at the top of the list with 6.4 dollars of benefit for each dollar of costs. This is a relatively low-cost solution that would greatly reduce labor market distortions in the region. The reform to the minimum wage solution ranks second, with a BCR of 3.9. The social security reform solution is a close third, with a BCR of 2.4. This solution, however, brings about other benefits to the economic systems that were not taken into account here, namely, solvency to the pension programs and its implications for macroeconomic stability and a deepening of financial intermediation.

Bibliography

Abowd, John, Francis Kramarz, Thomas Lemieux, and David Margolis, 2000. "Minimum Wages and Youth Employment in France and the United States." In David Blanchflower and Richard Freeman, eds., *Youth Employment and Joblessness in Advanced Countries*. Cambridge, MA: NBER

Abowd, John and Thomas Lemieux, 1993. "The Effects of Product Market Competition on Collective Bargaining Agreements: The Case of Foreign Competition in Canada." *Quarterly Journal of Economics* 108(4): 983–1014

Acemoglu, Daron and Robert Shimer. "Efficient Unemployment Insurance," *Journal of Political Economy* 107(5): 893–928

AIOS (Asociación Internacional de Organismos de Supervisión de Fondos de Pensiones), 2006. *Boletín Estadístico Número 16*, December

Anderson, Patricia and Bruce Meyer, 2000. "The Effects of the Unemployment Insurance Payroll Tax on Wages, Employment, Claims and Denials." *Journal of Public Economics* 78: 81–106

Angrist, Joshua and Daron Acemoglu, 2001. "Consequences of Employment Protection? The Case of the Americans with Disabilities Act." *Journal of Political Economy* 109(5): 915–57

Autor, David, 2000. "Outsourcing at Will: Unjust Dismissal Doctrine and the Growth of Temporary Help Employment." *Journal of Labor Economics* 21(1): 1–42

Autor, David, William Kerr, and Adriana Kugler, 2007. "Do Employment Protections Reduce Productivity? Evidence from US States." *Economic Journal* 117: 189–217

Bentolila, Samuel and Giuseppe Bertola, 1990. "Firing Cost and Labor Demand: How Bad is Eurosclerosis?" *Review of Economic Studies* 57(3): 381–402

Bentolila, Samuel and Gilles Saint-Paul, 1992. "The Macroeconomic Impact of Flexible Labor Contracts, with an Application to Spain." *European Economic Review* 36(5): 1013–147

Bernanke, Ben and Refer Gükaynak, 2002. "Is Growth Exogenous?: Taking Mankiw, Romer and Weil Seriously." *NBER Macroeconomics Annual 2001*, 16. Cambridge, MA: MIT Press

Blanchard, Olivier and Lawrence Summers, 1986. "Hysteresis and the European Unemployment Problem." *NBER Macroeconomics Annual 1986*

Botero, Juan C., S. Djankov, R. La Porta, F. Lopez de Silanes, and A. Shleifer, 2004. "The Regulation of Labor." *Quarterly Journal of Economics* **119**: 1339–82

Bronars, Stephen and Donald Deere, 1994. "Unionization and Profitability: Evidence of Spillover Effects." *Journal of Political Economy* **102**(6): 1281–8

Bronars, Stephen, Donald Deere, and Joseph Tracy, 1994. "The Effects of Unions on Firm Behavior: An Empirical Analysis Using Firm-Level Data." *Industrial Relations* **33**(4): 426–51

Caballero, Ricardo J., Kevin N. Cowan, Eduardo M.R.A. Engel, and Alejandro Micco, 2004. "Effective Labor Regulation and Microeconomic Flexibility." NBER Working Paper **10744**

Calmfors, Lars and John Driffill, 1988. "Macroeconomic Effects of Centralized Wage Setting." *Economic Policy* **6**: 13–61

Card, David, 1992. "Do Minimum Wages Reduce Employment? A Case Study of California 1987–89." *Industrial and Labor Relations Review* **46**(1): 38–54

Card, David and Alan Krueger, 1994. "Minimum Wages and Employment: A Case Study of the Fast-Food Industry in New Jersey and Pennsylvania." *American Economic Review* **84**(4): 772–93

CIEDESS (2005). *El Seguro de Desempleo en Chile: Evaluación y perspectives a dos años de su puesta en marcha*. Santiago: Alfabeta

Cunningham, Wendy, 2007. *Minimum Wages and Social Policy: Lessons from Developing Countries*. Washington, DC: World Bank

Davis, S., J. Haltiwanger, and S. Schuh, 1996. *Job Creation and Destruction*. Cambridge, MA: MIT Press

Diamond, Peter and Peter R. Orzagi, 2004. *Serving Social Security: A Balanced Approach*. Washington, DC: Brookings Institution

Diamond, Peter and Salvador Valdés-Prieto, 1994. "Social Security Reforms." In Barry Bosworth, Rudiger Dornbusch, and Raul Labán eds., *The Chilean Economy*. Washington, DC: Brookings Institution

Disney, Richard, 2004. "Are Contributions to Public Pension Programmes a Tax on Employment?" *Economic Policy* **19**(39): 267–311

Disney, Richard, Monica Queisser, and Edward Whitehouse, 2006. *Neutral, Fair or Something Else? A Taxonomy of Actuarial Concepts used in Pension-System Design*. Paris: OECD

Dolado, J.J., F. Kramarz, S. Machin, A. Manning, D. Margolis, and C. Teulings, 1996. "The Economic Impact of Minimum Wages in Europe." *Economic Policy* **11** (23): 319–72

Edwards, Alejandra Cox, 2005. "Pension Reforms and Employment." *International Economic Journal* **19**(2): 305–19

Edwards, S., 1998. "The Chilean Pension Reform: A Pioneering Program." Chapter 1 in Martin Feldstein, ed., *Privatizing Social Security*. Chicago:

University of Chicago for the National Bureau of Economic Research: 33–62

2002. "Social Security Reform and Labor Markets: The Case of Chile." *Economic Development and Cultural Change* 50(3): 465–89

Edwards, S. and A. Cox Edwards, 2000. "Economic Reforms and Labor Markets: Policy Issues and Lessons from Chile." *Economic Policy* 30: 183–229

Edwards, S. and N. Lustig, 1997. *Labor Markets in Latin America: Combining Social Protection with Market Flexibility*. Washington, DC: Brookings Institution

Employment Outlook, Chapter 2. Paris: OECD

Feldstein, Martin and Daniel Altman, 1998. "Unemployment Insurance Savings Accounts." NBER Working Paper **6860**

Feldstein, Martin and Andrew Samwick, 1998. "The Transition Path in Privatizing Social Security." Chapter 6 in Martin Feldstein, ed., *Privatizing Social Security*. Cambridge, MA: University of Chicago for the National Bureau of Economic Research: 215–64

Folster, Stefan, Gidehag, Robert, Orszag, Mike, and Snower, Dennis, 2002. "Assessing Welfare Accounts." In Torben Andersen and Per Molander, eds., *Alternatives for Welfare Policy: Coping with Internationalization and Demographic Change*. Cambridge: Cambridge University Press: 255–75

Gill, Indermit, Truman Packard, and Juan Yermo, 2004. *Keeping the Promise of Social Security in Latin America*. Washington, DC and Stanford, CA: World Bank and Stanford University Press

Gruber, Jonathan, 1994. "The Incidence of Mandated Maternity Benefits." *American Economic Review* 85(3): 622–41

1997a. "The Consumption Smoothing Benefits of Unemployment Insurance." *American Economic Review* 87(1): 192–205

1997b. "The Incidence of Payroll Taxation: Evidence from Chile." *Journal of Labor Economics* 15(3): S72–S101

Hamermesh, Daniel, 1993. *Labor Demand*. Princeton, NJ: Princeton University Press

Heckman, J. and C. Pages, 2004. *Law and Employment: Lessons from Latin America and the Caribbean*. Chicago: University of Chicago Press

Hopenhayn, Hugo and Richard Rogerson, 1993. "Job Turnover and Policy Evaluation: A General Equilibrium Analysis." *Journal of Political Economy* 101(5): 915–38

Hotz, V. Joseph, Charles H. Mullin, and John Karl Scholz, 2002. "The Effects of Welfare Reform on Employment and Income: Evidence from California," www.ssc.wisc.edu/~scholz/Research/CWPDP_paper_version6.pdf

2006. "Examining the Effect of the Earned Income Tax Credit on the Labor Market Participation of Families on Welfare." National Bureau of Economic Research Working Paper **11968**

Hotz, V. Joseph and John Karl Scholz, 2003. "The Earned Income Tax Credit." In Robert Moffitt, ed., *Means-Tested Transfer Programs in the United States*. Chicago: University of Chicago Press and NBER

Hunt, Jennifer, 1995. "The Effect of Unemployment Compensation on Unemployment Duration in Germany." *Journal of Labor Economics* **13**(1): 88–120

International Labor Organization (ILO), 2004. *Global Employment Trends.* Geneva: ILO

James, Estelle, J. Smalhout, and D. Vittas, 2001. "Administrative Costs and the Organization of Individual Account Systems: A Comparative Perspective." in R. Holzman and J. Stightz eds., *Ideas About Old Age Security*. Washington, DC: World Bank

Kaplan, D., M. González, and R. Robertson, 2003. "Worker- and Job-Flows in Mexico." Instituto Tecnológico Autónomo de México (ITAM), Instituto Mexicano del Seguro Social (IMSS) and Macalester College

Katz, Lawrence and Bruce Meyer, 1990. "Unemployment Insurance, Recall Expectations and Unemployment Outcomes." *Quarterly Journal of Economics* **105**(4): 973–1002

Kotlikoff, Lawrence, 1998. "Simulating the Privatization of Social Security in General Equilibrium." Chapter 7 in Martin Feldstein, ed., *Privatizing Social Security*. University of Chicago for the National Bureau of Economic Research: 265–312

Kugler, Adriana, 1999. "The Impact of Firing Costs on Turnover and Unemployment: Evidence from the Colombian Labour Market Reform." *International Tax and Public Finance Journal* **6**(3): 389–411

2005. "Wage Shifting Effects of Severance Payments Savings Accounts in Colombia." *Journal of Public Economics* **89**(2–3): 487–500

2007. Alternative view paper in this volume 3.1

Kugler, Adriana and Maurice Kugler, 2003. "Are the Effects of Payroll Taxes Asymmetric? Evidence from the Colombian Social Security Reform." CEPR Discussion Paper **4046**

Kugler, Adriana and Gilles Saint-Paul, 2003. "How do Firing Costs Affect Worker Flows in a World with Adverse Selection?" *Journal of Labor Economics* **22**(3): 553–84

Lazear, Edward, 1990. "Job Security Provisions and Employment." *Quarterly Journal of Economics* **105**(3): 699–726

Lindauer, David, 1999. "Labor Market Reforms and the Poor." Background paper for the *World Development Report, 2000*. New York: Oxford University Press

Machin, Steven and Sushil Wadhwani, 1991. "The Effects of Unions on Organisational Change and Employment." *Economic Journal* 101(407): 835–55

Maloney, William and Jairo Nuñez, 2004. "Measuring the Impact of Minimum Wages. Evidence from Latin America." Chapter 1 in James Heckman and Carmen Pages, eds., *Law and Employment in Latin America and the Caribbean.* Chicago: University of Chicago Press

Menezes, Fihlo., P. Medina, M. Meléndez, and K. Seim, 2003. "Productivity Dynamics of the Colombian Manufacturing Sector." Washington, DC: Banco Interamericano de Desarrollo

Meyer, Bruce, 1996. "What Have We Learned from the Illinois Reemployment Bonus Experiment?." *Journal of Labor Economics* 11(1): 26–51

Micco, Alejandro and Carmen Pages, 2004. "Employment Protection and Gross Job Flows." InterAmerican Development Bank Working Paper 508

Neumark, David and William Wascher, 1992. "Employment Effects of Minimum and Subminimum Wages: Panel Data on State Minimum Wage Laws." *Industrial and Labor Relations Review* 46(1): 55–81

Nickell, Stephen, 1997. "Unemployment and Labor Market Rigidities: Europe vs. North America." *Journal of Economic Perspectives* 11(3): 55–74

Organization for Economic Co-operation and Development (OECD), 1994a. *Jobs Study: Evidence, and Explanations. Part I: Labor Market Trends and Underlying Forces of Change.* Paris: Organization for Economic Co-operation and Development

1994b. *Jobs Study: Evidence, and Explanations. Part II: The Adjustment Potential of the Labor Market.* Paris: Organization for Economic Co-operation and Development

1996. *Employment Outlook 1996.* Paris: Organization for Economic Co-operation and Development

2004a. *Employment Protection Regulation and Labour Market Performance.* Paris: Organization for Economic Co-operation and Development

2004b. Wage-Setting Institutions and Outcomes. *Employment Outlook,* Chapter 3. Paris: Organization for Economic Co-operation and Development

Pencavel, J., 1999. "The Appropriate Design of Collective Bargaining Systems: Learning from the Experience of Britain, Australia, and New Zealand." *Comparative Labor Law and Policy Journal* 20(3): 447–81

Perry, Guillermo, W. Maloney, O. Arias, P. Fajnzylber, A. Mason, and J. Saavedra, 2007. *Informality: Exit and Exclusion.* Washington, DC: The World Bank

Sargeant, Thomas and Lars Ljundgvist, 1998. "The European Unemployment Dilemma." *Journal of Political Economy* **106**(3): 514–50

World Bank (2007) *Doing Business 2007, Creating Jobs.* Washington, DC: World Bank

3.1 Labor market reforms: an alternative view

ADRIANA KUGLER

1 The challenge and its solutions

Chapter 3 provides policy proposals to "the challenge [of] seizing the benefits from globalization, cognizant of the difficulties imposed by the need to adjust." While this challenge is very general, the chapter then narrows it down and explains that the challenge is one of "[creating] employment... and [providing] social security in the LAC region." The chapter proposes to re-regulate labor markets and provides three different solutions to this challenge. The solutions provided are very diverse and range from replacing social security taxes and dismissal costs with individual accounts to replacing the minimum wage with an income tax credit. All these solutions have in common that they respond to the challenge of keeping income security for workers but reducing inefficiencies in the labor market and, in particular, reducing employers' disincentives to hire. This challenge should be stated more clearly in the chapter.

The chapter proposes three specific responses to the challenge of keeping income security while reducing inefficiencies in the labor market. First, the chapter proposes to replace the current pay-as-you-go (PAYG) social security system, which exists in most LAC countries and around the world, with a fully-funded social security system. Second, it proposes to replace severance payments, which are paid to workers upon dismissal, with a system of severance payments savings accounts (SPSA). Finally, it proposes to eliminate minimum wages and replace them with a tax return for the poor or DIP, modeled after the earned income tax credit (EITC) in the United States and other developed countries.

This alternative view evaluates the policy proposals put forward in chapter 3 and provides new cost-benefit calculations based on alternative assumptions. These new calculations provide a different ranking from that provided in the chapter. In particular, my calculations rank the replacement of a PAYG system by a fully-funded system first while chapter 3 ranked this solution second. The replacement of severance payments for SPSAs ranked second according to my calculations, while it ranked last according to the chapter. Finally, the replacement of minimum wages for a tax refund for the poor ranked last according to my calculations but first according to the chapter.

Moreover, this alternative view puts forward a training program for disadvantaged youth as an alternative proposal for getting the disadvantaged back to work and increasing their earnings. Cost-benefit calculations of this program rank training for the disadvantaged above the three proposals in chapter 3.

2 Proposal 1: replacing a PAYG system by a fully-funded social security system

The first proposal of replacing a PAYG system by a fully-funded social security system has been implemented in a number of countries in the LAC region, including Chile. The idea behind this reform is that it transfers the cost of social security from the firm to the worker, thus reducing disincentives to hire in the formal sector. At the same time, workers are not left without retirement income during their old age. Chapter 3 presents a model showing the benefits assuming that half of the cost of social security contributions is transferred from employers to workers after the reform. The benefit comes from the reduced deadweight loss due to inefficiently low demand for labor and the subsequent increase in employment and GDP as a result of the elimination of a PAYG system. On the other hand, it assumes zero costs as a result of this re-regulation.

From the benefits side, the chapter may be under-estimate or over-estimate the gains of reform depending on what assumptions are made about how much of the cost of the social security contributions is passed on to workers before and after the reform. On the one hand, the chapter assumes that under the PAYG system, before the reform, all the social security contributions are paid by employers. That is, the model in the chapter assumes that prior to the reform there is no pass-through of the tax to workers. However, the theoretical literature on payroll taxes generally allows for the possibility that part of the payroll tax may be passed on to the worker as a lower wage if the worker values at least some of the benefits from the contributions and as long as labor demand is not perfectly elastic. The empirical literature has found various degrees of pass-through. For example, the studies by Gruber (1994) and Gruber and Krueger (1991) find that 100% of maternity leave costs and workers' compensation costs are passed on to workers. By contrast, in my own work for Colombia with Maurice Kugler (Kugler and Kugler 2009), we find instead that around a fifth of payroll taxes paid in this country are passed on to workers. The extreme assumption of zero pass-through in the chapter would maximize the gains from reform. On the other hand, the other extreme assumption of complete pass-through would imply no gain at all from replacing a PAYG by a fully-funded system. Moreover, while the chapter assumes that after the introduction of individual accounts with the fully-funded system workers value only 50% of these contributions, Gruber (1997) finds 100% pass-through after the privatization of the social security system in 1980. The assumption of 50% pass-through instead of full pass-through under-estimates the extent of the gains from reform.

Table 3.1.1 presents results of the cost-benefit calculations under different assumptions about the extent of pass-through before and after the reform. The first row presents the results under the same assumptions made in chapter 3 – i.e. no pass-through before the reform and 50% pass-through after the reform. The benefit, holding capital constant, as in chapter 3 is of $4,456,000 million, or about 4% of the present discounted value of GDP.[1] The second row reports similarly the gain from reform when there is no initial pass-through but allowing the pass-through to be 100% after the introduction of individual accounts as found by Gruber (1997). In this case, the gains from the reform more than double and these reach about 10% of the PDV of GDP. This means that not allowing for complete pass-through after the reform under-estimates the benefits from the replacement of PAYG by a fully-funded system. The third row now also allows for full shifting of taxes to workers even prior to reform, as has been found in some studies for the United States. If taxes are fully shifted to workers to

---

[1] These results are different from those in chapter 3, because it does not report the values of the parameters for the elasticity of labor supply, the elasticity of informal price with respect to the wage, and weights given to informal and formal goods in the CPI. I assume that the elasticity of labor supply is 0.3, the elasticity of the informal price with respect to its wage is 0.5, and the weights given to formal and informal goods are equal.

Table 3.1.1 *Cost-benefit calculations: proposal 1 under alternative assumptions*

Pre-post reform pass-through %	Fall in DWL [PDV] (1)	dlogT (2)	dlogL (3)	dlogY, fixed K [PDV] (4)	dlogK (5)	dlogY variable K [PDV] (6)	Net benefit, fixed K (7)	Net benefit, variable K (8)	Trans. costs (9)	Net ben. trans. costs (10)
0/50	0.001 [102,500]	−0.041	0.0635	0.042 [4,200,000]	−0.0529	0.0244 [2,436,111]	4,456,000	2,692,111	306,000	2,386,111
0/100	0.0022 [217,500]	−0.087	0.1358	0.0906 [9,055,000]	−0.1132	0.0528 [5,282,778]	10,142,500	4,195,278	306,000	3,889,278
100/100	0	0	0	0	0	0	0	0	306,000	−306,000
20/50	0	0	0	0	0	0	0	0	306,000	−306,000
20/100	0.0017 [172,000]	−0.043	0.0665	0.0444 [4,435,867]	−0.0554	0.0259 [2,592,778]	4,973,367	3,130,278	306,000	2,824,278

Notes: Column (1) reports the fall in the deadweight loss (DWL) after the reform. The numbers in square brackets transform the values in each column to their PDV. The net benefits and transitional costs are all reported as PDVs and are reported in million dollars.

begin with, then the taxes do not generate any disincentives in terms of hiring and there are no gains from replacing the taxes by individual accounts. Consequently, the gains are zero under this scenario and this implies that the chapter would over-estimate the gains from reform. The final two rows, examine the gains when a fifth of the taxes are passed on to workers and the pass-through with individual accounts is either 50% or 100%. Comparing the 20% pass-through with the zero pass-through before the reform assumed in chapter 3 shows that the gains from reform are substantially reduced even in this case of partial shifting. In the first case, when only 50% is passed on with individual accounts, the gains disappear altogether, while in the second case of full shifting with individual accounts, the gains exactly halve.

Another factor that could affect the calculation of benefits is the potential substitution away from capital and towards labor if the PAYG system is replaced by a fully-funded system. The reason is that the social security contributions under a PAYG system increase the costs of labor relative to capital and could distort the capital/labor ratio. When a fully-funded system is introduced, the cost of labor relative to capital falls and subsequently the stock of capital should fall while employment should increase. The chapter captures the latter effect of an increase in employment, but fails to account for the fall in the capital stock. This is because the model allows for capital stocks to differ in the formal and informal sectors, but the total capital stock is held fixed and the model imposes the Ricardo–Viner assumption that capital is fixed in its sector of origin (i.e. the informal sector), implying that the capital stock in the modern sector also remains fixed. Endogenizing capital stocks in the formal and informal sectors in the model would show precisely the decrease in capital stock in the formal sector as a result of the reform that I have just described. In particular, replacing a PAYG system by a fully-funded system would increase the probability of formal employment because of the reduction in the tax and of an increase the informal wage. This increase in the informal wage would then get passed on to prices in the informal sector, also increasing the return to capital in the informal relative to the formal sector, thus reducing the capital stock in the formal sector. Then, the effect of the reform on GDP would be over-estimated since the reduction in capital would have to be accounted for.

Table 3.1.1 reports results which allow the capital stock to remain fixed as in the chapter, and also results which allow the capital to respond to changes in the relative price of labor. In particular, I estimate the changes in capital implied by a change in employment. I allow for capital and labor to be substitutes. I use the mid-point of the estimates of the elasticity of employment with respect to capital, $\sigma_{EK} = -1.2$, reported by Hamermesh (1993). Thus, I estimate the change in capital as:

$$d \ln K = d \ln L / \sigma_{EK}$$

where the change in output then becomes:

$$d \ln Y = d \ln L / \sigma_{EK} + \alpha (1 - \sigma_{EK}) d \ln L / \sigma_{EK}$$

The change in GDP is then adjusted for the loss in capital stock, thus moderating the output gains from reform. For example, under chapter 3's preferred scenario the gain from reform is $2,692,111 million instead of $4,456,000 million, or about 40% less when labor substitutes capital. Similarly, under my preferred scenario of a 20% pass-through before the reform and full pass-through after the reform, the gain is $3,022,778 million instead of $4,005,867 million, or about 25% less when capital is allowed to vary.

Moreover, from the cost side, the chapter is likely to over-estimate the gains from the reform. The costs of introducing this program are assumed to be zero. The chapter explains the "transitional costs" involved in moving from one system to the other for the first generation transitioning to the new system and thus without their own individual accounts. However, it argues that these are costs that the government would have had to pay even without a reform. This is not clear, since the payroll taxes paid by the current generation under a PAYG system may be sufficient to cover the retiring generation (this all depends on the size of the cohort contributing and the size of the retiring cohort), even if there is an inefficiency being generated in the labor market in this case. By contrast, if the system gets replaced with individual accounts, the pensions for the generation retiring at that point in time will have to be covered by the government through another source of revenue. Table 3.1.1 includes an additional column with the transition costs. The calculation of these transitional costs assumes that 3% of workers employed in the formal sector retire every year, or about 5 million people, and that each of these employees is paid a pension of $1,200, which is the average *per capita* income in the LAC region. The total transitional costs in this case are \$306,000, which is still a modest amount under any of the scenarios presented above. Consequently, introducing transitional costs into our cost-benefit calculation does not affect the conclusion that the net benefit from the reform is still highly positive. Under the more realistic scenario where the pass-through is 20% before the reforms and 100% after the reforms and there are transitional costs, the BCR is 9.9.

The cost side also ignores the potential effect of payroll taxes on labor supply. Since the PAYG system pays pensions based on the last three years of contributions, individuals have little incentive to contribute to the system and pay taxes in the formal sector except for the three years prior to retirement. By contrast, under a fully-funded system benefits are directly linked to contributions so that individuals would have a greater incentive to participate in the labor force. This means that even though employment would increase on moving to a fully-funded system, unemployment may not necessarily fall and may even increase. This should be an additional cost to consider in the calculations.

3 Proposal 2: replacing severance payments with individual accounts

The second solution to the challenge of keeping income security while reducing inefficiencies in the labor market proposes to replace severance payments at the time of dismissal with SPSAs. This is a novel solution which has been introduced in only a handful of countries around the world, including in Colombia within the LAC region (see Kugler 2005 for an analysis of SPSA in Colombia). Chapter 3 suggests that the benefits of this reform would be very similar to those of replacing a PAYG by a fully-funded social security system, in the sense of increasing employment and reducing the deadweight loss and increasing GDP. The costs, on the other hand, are quantified as those involved in managing the individual accounts.

While this solution is clever, the model used to quantify the impact of this proposal is not the most appropriate. As well-known models of dismissal costs show, dismissal costs not only reduce dismissals but also hiring, with a resulting ambiguous effect on net employment (see Bentolila and Bertola 1990; Lazear 1990; Hopenhayn and Rogerson 1993). However, chapter 3 assumes that the reduction in dismissal costs as a result of the introduction of dismissal accounts will increase employment. Part of the problem is that the model in chapter 3 does not introduce costs of adjustment. In addition, jobs end exogenously after each period in this model, so that there is really no role for dismissal costs to affect turnover. However, the effect of a reduction in dismissal costs is ambiguous in terms of its effect on employment but clear in terms of an increase in turnover. In fact, the data reported in the chapter, as well as in other studies, do suggest lower turnover in the LAC region than in developed countries, potentially due to restricting regulations (Haltiwanger *et al.* 2004; Eslava *et al.* 2009). The elimination of dismissal costs may indeed be beneficial in the sense that it may generate efficiency-enhancing reallocation. In my work with M. Eslava, J. Haltiwanger, and M. Kugler (2009), we find that the reduction of adjustment costs on labor increases TFP by increasing the share of production of the most productive and shrinking the share of the least productive plants in Colombia. This would be captured in the model in chapter 3 by an increase in A and a subsequent increase in GDP. This is a much fruitful avenue to take in trying to quantify the benefits of this reform with the model proposed.

Table 3.1.2 presents the gains from a reform that replaces dismissal costs by individual accounts and thus increases turnover or churning in the labor market. The effect is captured by quantifying the gains in GDP implied by an increase in efficiency due to increased churning. I do this in two ways. First, I take the increase in TFP attributed to the labor reform estimated in Eslava *et al.* (2009) to estimate:

$$\mathrm{d}\ln Y = \mathrm{d}\ln A$$

I turn this into a present discounted value by using the values of initial GDP and the discount and growth rate used in chapter 3. Next, I estimate the increase in efficiency due to churning by estimating the change in output as:

$$\mathrm{d}\ln Y = \phi\,\mathrm{d}\ln C$$

where ϕ is the increase in productivity due to increased churning, and C indicates the churning or turnover rate. I get the increase in churning of a 6 log point increase from my analysis of the Colombian reform (Kugler 2004), and the increase in productivity due to increased churning of 2% comes from Autor *et al.* (2007).

Table 3.1.2 *Cost-benefit calculations: proposal 2 under*
alternative assumptions

Pass-through %	d log Y = d log A [PDV] (1)	d log Y = ϕ d log C [PDV] (2)	PDV of costs (3)	Net benefit (using (1)) (4)	Net benefit costs (using (2)) (5)
80	0.0008 [80,000]	0.00096 [96,000]	15,239	64,761	80,761
60	0.0006 [60,000]	0.00072 [72,000]	11,429	48,571	60,571

Notes: The numbers in square brackets transform the values in each column to their
PDV. The net benefits and costs of managing the individual accounts are all reported
as PDVs and are reported in million dollars.

As in chapter 3, the cost of this reform is estimated as the 0.5%
commission paid over the deposits made into the accounts. Since the
deposits are 8.3% of salaries for formal sector workers, we use the
average wage/year reported in chapter 3 as well as the 170 million
workers in the formal sector to estimate the costs of managing the
accounts.

In my previous analysis of the introduction of severance payments
savings accounts in Colombia (Kugler 2005), I find that the introduction of SPSA reduces costs to employers by between 60% and 80% by
passing the severance to the workers as lower wages. This implies that
this still leaves between 40% and 20% of the severance cost to the
employers, thus not eliminating totally the dismissal costs. Chapter 3
takes the upper bound of the pass-through I find in Kugler (2005) or
the lower of the remaining cost of 20%. The CBA in this alternative
view investigates the sensitivity of the results to this assumption.

Table 3.1.2 reports the benefits and costs of replacing severance
payments for SPSA. The first and second columns report the gains in
terms of efficiency-enhancing reallocation using two alternative methods. The results are similar and suggest gains of between $60,000
million and $96,000 million, depending on the pass-through assumed.
The costs range between 10% and 15% of the benefits, so that there
are positive net benefits regardless of the assumptions about shifting.
Under the best scenario, the gains from this reform are substantially

lower than under proposal 1 and are around 0.1% of the PDV of GDP. Under the preferred scenario of 20% of dismissal costs remaining for employers after the reform, the BCR is 6.6.

4 Proposal 3: replacing minimum wages by an EITC

The third solution to the challenge proposes to eliminate minimum wages altogether and instead introduce a tax return to the poor conditional on working. While minimum wages are often introduced with the idea of helping the poor reach a minimum income level, minimum wages also generate wage rigidities that reduce the demand for labor and may end up hurting precisely those that the policy is supposed to help. The proposal in chapter 3 is rather to introduce a tax return to the poor modeled on the EITC in the United States, which provides a tax return to those at the lower end of the distribution for every dollar earned at work. The EITC, and similar tax returns in other countries, have often replaced transfers to the unemployed and other welfare programs. The advantage of an EITC is that it generates income transfers to those who need them most, without generating disincentives to work.

Chapter 3 calculates the benefits to this proposal as the increased gain in terms of employment and the subsequent gain in GDP. It assumes that half of the unemployment in the region can be accounted for by the minimum wage. This may be a reasonable assumption for some countries, where the minimum wage appears to bind (e.g. see evidence by Maloney and Nuñez 2004 on Colombia). However, the assumption that the minimum wage will reduce half of the unemployment in all countries may not really hold for all countries. For example, the study by Bell (1997) finds evidence that the minimum wage reduces employment in Colombia but not in Mexico. To the extent that the minimum wage does not bind in all countries, then the benefits from eliminating this wage floor will be over-estimated. In particular, figure 3.1.1 which comes from Maloney and Nuñez (2004) shows six LAC countries having minimum wage:mean wage ratios above Colombia and five countries having ratios below Mexico, with Peru in between the two countries. In the CBA below I explore the alternative assumption that the minimum wage binds in half the countries but not in the other half.

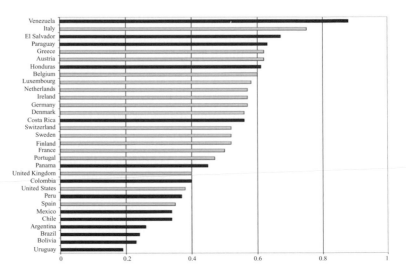

Figure 3.1.1 Ratio of minimum to mean wages: LAC region and around the world
Source: Maloney and Nuñez (2004)

The cost is then calculated on the basis that 10% of the population in the LAC region qualifies for the transfer and that there is an annual transfer of $600 per poor worker. It would be good to know more about where the 10% and $600 came from. In addition, as for proposal 1, I allow for capital–employment substitution and include the additional cost due to reduced GDP as a result of the fall in the capital stock.

Table 3.1.3 reports the benefits from eliminating minimum wages in terms of both the fall in deadweight loss and also in terms of increased output due to increased employment. The fall in the deadweight loss is close to a billion, assuming the minimum wage binds in all countries, and half a billion, assuming the minimum binds in only half the countries in the LAC region. This fall in the deadweight loss is about 10% larger than the fall seen under the preferred scenario in table 3.1.1 for the benefit calculation of the replacement of a PAYG by a fully-funded system. By contrast, the gain in GDP is 10% lower under the elimination of minimum wages than under the replacement of a PAYG for a fully-funded system. Similarly, the reduction in GDP due to the fall in the capital stock is also slightly smaller in this case

Table 3.1.3 *Cost-benefit calculations: proposal 3 under alternative assumptions*

Share of countries with binding MW %	Fall in DWL [PDV] (1)	dlogT (2)	dlogL (3)	dlogY, fixed K [PDV] (4)	dlogK (5)	dlogY variable K [PDV] (6)	Costs of DIP (7)	Net benefit, fixed K (8)	Net benefit, variable K (9)
100	0.0039 [385,000]	−0.077	0.1224	0.0816 [8,160,000]	−0.102	0.0476 [4,760,000]	780,000	7,380,000	3,980,000
50	0.0019 [192,500]	−0.077	0.0612	0.0408 [4,079,167]	−0.051	0.0238 [2,380,000]	780,000	3,299,167	1,600,000

Notes: Column (1) reports the fall in the DWL after the reform. The numbers in square brackets transform the values in each column to their PDV. The net benefits and costs are all reported as PDVs and are reported in million dollars.

than under proposal 1. However, the costs of introducing an EITC are a lot higher than the transitional costs of introducing a fully-funded system. This means that once all costs and benefits are taken into account, the net benefits of this proposal are somewhat smaller than the net benefits under the replacement of the social security system. In particular, the net gain from this reform is $2,081,250 or 2% of the PDV of GDP compared to about 3% in the case of the introduction of a fully-funded system. This result contrasts with the conclusion in chapter 3 which shows the elimination of the minimum wage as the dominant solution. Under the more realistic scenario that minimum wages account for only half the unemployment in the region, the BCR is 3.1.

5 Alternative proposal: replacing minimum wages with training for disadvantaged youth

Here we offer an alternative solution to provide income for those at the lower end of the distribution while eliminating the distortions introduced by the minimum wage. This is similar to the last proposal in chapter 3, except that instead of replacing minimum wages by an EITC, the proposal here replaces minimum wages by vocational training. While an EITC is an attractive way of encouraging individuals to work in countries where welfare benefits discourage individuals from working, this is not a big concern in Latin America. In fact, welfare benefits and unemployment insurance are very limited and even non-existent in many LAC countries. Instead, vocational training programs which combine classroom and on-the-job training have proven to be successful at getting disadvantaged workers back to work and increasing their earnings. This type of program has been introduced in several countries in the LAC region, including Chile, Colombia, Dominican Republic, Mexico, and Panama. Most of these studies show gains in terms of salaries and employment, especially for women.

A particularly convincing evaluation of a training program for disadvantaged youth is my work with Orazio Attanasio and Costas Meghir (Attanasio, Kugler, and Meghir 2008), which is based on a randomized trial. This program shows increases in overall and formal employment as well as increases in earnings for both women and men. The gains from the program are estimated as the rise in output due to increases in employment from eliminating the minimum wage and from increases

Table 3.1.4 *Cost-benefit calculations for alternative proposal under alternative assumptions*

Share of countries with binding MW %	Fall in DWL [PDV] (1)	dlog T (2)	dlog L (3)	dlog K (4)	dlog Y variable K [PDV] (5)	Costs of training (6)	Net benefit, variable K (7)
50	0.0019 [192,500]	−0.077	0.0612	−0.051	0.0556 [7,242,000]	685,125	6,556,875

Notes: Column (1) reports the fall in the DWL after the reform. The numbers in square brackets transform the values in each column to their PDV. The net benefits and costs are all reported as PDVs and are reported in million dollars.

in productivity assuming that the increase in wages that results from the training program is due to workers becoming more productive. As before, we allow for the possibility that labor substitutes for capital. On the other hand, the costs of the program are assumed to be the $875 per person that the program costs. Table 3.1.4 shows the benefits and costs under this assumption. This program generates a BCR of 10.6, which is higher than the effects of all other proposals in chapter 3.

6 Conclusion

Chapter 3 provides three possible alternatives to the challenge of maintaining income security while reducing labor market inefficiencies. The solutions propose to: (1) replace the current PAYG system existent in most countries by a fully-funded system, (2) replace severance payments by SPSAs, and (3) eliminate minimum wages and introduce an EITC-type transfer for the poor. All these proposals are right on target as payroll taxes, dismissal costs, and minimum wages have been found to be the most restrictive regulations in the Latin American context. By contrast, unions are not very strong in the LAC region and collective bargaining agreements do not exist at the country or even sectoral level in most countries. Similarly, disincentives generated by unemployment insurance systems are not as important in the LAC context as they are in Europe, because most countries have only a limited or no unemployment insurance system.

This alternative view has focused on re-calculating the costs and benefits of the various solutions based on alternative assumptions, which are more in line with other evidence. In particular, the cost-benefit calculations of replacing the PAYG by a fully-funded system and of eliminating minimum wages in chapter 3 ignored important costs due to the substitution of capital for labor and to transitional costs. More importantly, its calculation of dismissal costs was misleading as it was made under the assumption that the reduction in dismissal costs would increase employment levels as opposed to turnover. This alternative view offers another way of calculating the benefits from a reform that introduces SPSAs. This re-examination shows that these assumptions matter in terms of the ranking of the solutions. In particular, the re-design of the social security system now ranks as the top solution, with the replacement of severance payments by SPSAs ranking second, and the replacement of minimum wages for by EITC type program coming last. These results suggest that the introduction of fully-funded systems should remain a priority in those countries that still have not undertaken reforms of their social security systems. At the same time, the elimination of minimum wages and dismissal costs, while not as large, would also generate non-trivial gains. Most importantly, the replacement of minimum wages by training for disadvantaged youth ranks above all of these other priorities. This means that a good way to provide income support is by making young people more productive throughout the rest of their lives.

Bibliography

Attanasio, Orazio, Adriana Kugler, and Costas Meghir, 2008. "Training Disadvantaged Youth in Latin America: Evidence from a Randomized Trial." NBER Working Paper **13935**

Autor, David, William Kerr, and Adriana Kugler, 2007. "Do Employment Protections Reduce Productivity? Evidence from US States." *Economic Journal* **117**: F189–F217

Bell, Linda, 1997. "The Impact of Minimum Wages in Mexico and Colombia." *Journal of Labor Economics* **15**(3): S103–S135

Bentolila, Samuel and Giuseppe Bertola, 1990. "Firing Cost and Labor Demand: How Bad is Eurosclerosis?" *Review of Economic Studies* **57**(3): 381–402

Eslava, Marcela, John Haltiwanger, Adriana Kugler, and Maurice Kugler, 2004. "The Effect of Structural Reforms on Productivity and Profitability Enhancing Reallocation: Evidence from Colombia." *Journal of Development Economics* **75**(2): 333–71

   2009. "Factor Adjustments after Deregulation: Panel Evidence from Colombian Plants." *Review of Economics and Statistics*, forthcoming

Gruber, Jonathan, 1997. "The Incidence of Payroll Taxation: Evidence from Chile." *Journal of Labor Economics* **15**(3): S72–S101

Gruber, Jonathan and Alan Krueger, 1991. "The Incidence of Mandated Employer-Provided Insurance: Lessons from Workers' Compensation Insurance." In D. Bradford, ed., *Tax Policy and the Economy* **5**. Cambridge, MA: MIT Press

Haltiwanger, John, Adriana Kugler, Maurice Kugler, Alejandro Micco, and Carmen Pages, 2004. "Effects of Trade on Job Reallocation: Evidence from Latin America." *Journal of Policy Reform* **7**(4): 201–18

Hamermesh, Daniel, 1993. *Labor Demand*. Princeton, NJ: Princeton University Press

Hopenhayn, Hugo and Richard Rogerson, 1993. "Job Turnover and Policy Evaluation: A General Equilibrium Analysis." *Journal of Political Economy* **101**(5): 915–38

Kugler Adriana, 2004. "The Effect of Job Security Regulations on Labor Market Flexibility: Evidence from the Colombian Labor Market Reform." In J. Heckman and C. Pages, eds., *Law and Employment: Lessons from Latin America and the Caribbean.* Chicago: University of Chicago Press

   2005. "Wage-Shifting Effects of Severance Payments Savings Accounts in Colombia." *Journal of Public Economics* **89**(2–3): 487–500

Kugler, Adriana and Maurice Kugler, 2009. "The Labor Market Effects of Payroll Taxes in Developing Countries: Evidence from Colombia." *Economic Development and Cultural Change* **52**(2): 335–58

Lazear, Edward, 1990. "Job Security Provisions and Employment." *Quarterly Journal of Economics* **105**(3): 699–726

Maloney, William and Jairo Nuñez, 2004. "Measuring the Impact of Minimum Wages: Evidence from Latin America." in chapter 1 in J. Heckman and C. Pages, eds., *Law and Employment in Latin America and the Caribbean.* Chicago: University of Chicago Press

ENVIRONMENT

4 | *Forests, biodiversity, and avoided deforestation in the LAC region*

ROGER A. SEDJO AND JUHA SIIKAMÄKI

1 Introduction

The purpose of this chapter is to provide an overview of the benefits of forests and biodiversity in the LAC region and to move toward the selection of cost-effective solutions for the protection of these resources. It draws from the literature to describe the situation with forests and biodiversity, both generally and within the context of the region. The various techniques for estimating the value of biodiversity are particularly subtle and are developed at some length. The value of the benefits of forests and biodiversity and the costs of protection are identified and drawn from the literature. Utilizing these data, a number of CBAs are developed and some possible "solutions" posited. It is noted that the literature related to the costs and benefits of forests and biodiversity is poorly developed for many values and much of the world. Despite these limitations, the solutions are assessed, their strengths and weaknesses noted, and a preferred solution selected. Since some of the selections are built on contentious numbers from the literature and for cost systems that are not fully developed, the choice of solution considers questions of data reliability and completeness, as well as BCRs.

A rationale for the importance of Latin American biodiversity can be found in the Inter-American Development Bank's survey[1] that found "environment" one of the "challenges" facing the region. In the environment category, deforestation (81.5%) and loss of biodiversity (73.2%) were the top two concerns.

---

[1] www.iadb.org/res.ConsultaSanJose.

Forests and biodiversity often go hand-in-hand. Natural forests are the residence of much of the world's species and genetic biodiversity. The forest systems also provide a host of other useful outputs in the form of ecosystem services. These include erosion control, water management and purification, and wildlife and biodiversity habitats.

"Biological diversity" refers to all living things. Although biodiversity sometimes refers to the number of species in a geographical area, biodiversity also occurs at a number of levels of nature, including genetic variation among different individuals and populations of the same species. The range of ecosystems such as forests, agricultural areas, wetlands, mountains, lakes, and rivers and the differences between and within geographical landscapes, regions, countries, and continents also are important dimensions of biodiversity.

Many of the benefits of forest ecosystems and biodiversity are viewed as global public goods. "Public goods" are those where the benefits are such that their consumption by one individual does not diminish the amount available for others. This aspect makes the estimation of the value of public goods difficult, since they are not transacted in markets. The public good aspect is one reason that decisions with respect to these outputs usually are determined using the political process. This chapter discusses some methods for trying to assess the monetary value of the goods and services produced by biodiversity, and include various forms of contingent valuation. However, since estimates of value are usually for a single output, such as preventing the extinction of the spotted owl, the values usually do not represent the full array of biodiversity outputs.

Similar measurement problems hold for the goods and services produced by ecosystems. Often a host of ecosystem services is produced, many of which are public goods or for other reasons non-marketed, such as flood and erosion control or water retention for dry periods, as with mountain snows. Again, many of these outputs might be viewed as public goods, while others involve difficulties in establishing viable markets for various reasons. Thus, although estimates of the values of these ecosystem services have been made, they are often quite crude.

Forests may be viewed as providers of ecosystem services. Traditionally, forests have been viewed as providing both private goods, such as timber and private recreation, and public services and externalities, such as water flow control and erosion mitigation that may be largely

Table 4.1 *Forests, by major region, 2005 (million ha)*

Region	Forest area
Africa	655.6
Asia	566.6
Europe	988.1
North and Central America	707.5
Oceania	208.0
South America	852.8
World Total	3988.6

Source: Global Forest Resources Assessment (2005).

local. Thus, it has been argued that the decisions concerning these forests should be largely local. However, some aspects of forest ecosystem services can be viewed as a global public good. Avoided deforestation is often viewed as a global public good with substantial positive externalities that generate global benefits, such as being a repository of global genetic information and a non-atmospheric medium for the storage of carbon, large volumes of which are captured in the cells of trees and soils of the forests and if released would contribute substantially to global warming. Therefore, avoided deforestation has become an issue of serious global concern.

2 Forests and biodiversity

Forests

The UN Food and Agricultural Organization's (FAO) Global Forest Resources Assessment (2005) indicates that the globe's forest cover totaled 3.99 billion ha in 2000, or 29% of the land area (table 4.1). Forests are distributed among tropical forests (47%); subtropical forests (9%); temperate forests (11%), and boreal forests (33%). Forests are abundant on all continents except Antarctica.

In the LAC region, forests cover about 1,064 million ha; a large percentage of this area is tropical. The Global Forest Resources Assessment (FAO 2000) estimated the net loss of forest area at 9.4 million ha, with the tropics experiencing a decrease and the temperate region experiencing a modest increase in forest area.

Table 4.2 *Estimated number of species globally*

Kingdoms	Described worldwide	Estimated total worldwide
Bacteria	4,000	1,000,000
Protoctista (algae, protozoa, etc.)	80,000	600,000
Animals	1,320,000	10,600,000
Fungi	72,000	1,500,000
Plants	270,000	320,000
Total	1,746,000	ca. 14,000,000

Source: UNEP (1995), table 3.1–2: 118.

Biodiversity[2]

Biological diversity, as we have seen, refers to all living things; however, biodiversity often refers to the number of species in a geographical area. One estimate is that the total number of species globally is about 14 million, while the approximate number of identified (described) species is less than 2 million. Note that only somewhat more than 10% of the estimated species have been described. The species described for plants are more than half of the estimated global totals, while those described for bacteria and fungi are only a small fraction of the estimated total species (table 4.2).

Biodiversity definitions

Biodiversity typically is considered at three levels: species diversity, genetic diversity, and ecosystem diversity. "Species diversity" is the variety and abundance of species in a geographical area. Species are the central unit in biodiversity studies and conservation, at least in part because ecosystems are hard to delimit and genes until recently have been difficult to count and identify (Wilson 1999). However, each species consists of subspecies (i.e. geographical races), populations, and individuals that possess their own varying levels of genetic distinctiveness. A population is a geographically distinct group of individuals of a particular species. A biological community is defined as the

---

[2] This section draws heavily for its discussion of biodiversity on Siikamäki and Chow (2008).

collection of species populations that exist and interact in a particular location. An evolutionarily significant unit (ESU) is a population or group of populations that is substantially reproductively isolated and is genetically unique from other populations, making it an important evolutionary component of the species. Since a major goal of biodiversity conservation is to maintain the evolutionary potential of unique lines of descent, practical species management and conservation efforts often target ESUs rather than entire species.[3]

"Genetic diversity" refers to genetic variation within species, both among distinct populations and among the individuals within a population. Genes are the chromosomal units that code for specific proteins that generate the unique morphological and biochemical characteristics of an organism and are passed down along generations of organisms. Variation arises from mutations in genes, and natural selection of these characteristics within a population is the primary mechanism of biological evolution. In sexually reproducing species, genetic diversity also comes from the recombination that occurs when genes are exchanged. Genetic diversity within species populations helps to maintain reproductive vitality, disease resistance, and the ability of populations to adapt to changing environmental conditions. Biodiversity conservation methods sometimes include *in situ* efforts such as cross-breeding and translocation that help maintain the genetic diversity of wild populations. Germplasm repositories have also been established to store genetic diversity in the form of semen, embryos, and seeds *ex situ*.

"Ecosystem diversity" refers to the variation within and between communities and their associations with the physical environment. The richness of ecological systems within an area also is sometimes called "systems diversity." Species play different functions within their communities; some species are functionally substitutable, whereas others (keystone species) play determinant roles in the food web and cannot be removed from the system without fundamentally affecting the species composition of the community. Ecosystem diversity also relates to landscape diversity, which denotes the diversity and connectivity of ecosystems within large geographical areas.

---

[3] For example, Pacific salmon have more than fifty distinct ESUs, which are the basis for their management and conservation.

Biodiversity and ecosystem processes

Ecologists generally consider that species diversity increases ecosystem productivity, stability, and resiliency (e.g. McCann 2000). Results from long-term field experiments (e.g. Tilman and Downing 1994; Tilman *et al.* 2001) indicate that although species richness and the resulting interspecies competition may cause fluctuations in individual species populations, diversity tends to increase the productive stability of an ecosystem as a whole. This concept is similar to the portfolio theory in economics, which suggests that diversification of stock portfolios can effectively reduce stock-specific risks on returns. Like stocks, the returns (i.e. biomass) generated by different species are not perfectly correlated. Rather, changes in the biomass production by some species are associated with dissimilar changes in the biomass production by other species. In other words, a high number of species acts as a buffer against productivity reductions within any single species, and ecosystems with greater numbers of species experience fewer fluctuations in aggregate biomass production.

Diverse ecosystems generally have high rates of ecosystem processes, meaning that they produce more biomass than less diverse systems. However, increases in the rates of ecosystem processes seem to plateau at relatively low levels of species richness. Experimental analyses have also shown that what matters most is the diversity of functional groups, whereas species richness within functional groups may be less important (e.g. Holling *et al.* 1995; Knops *et al.* 1998).

Ecosystem resilience in ecology can be defined as the magnitude of disturbance that can be absorbed by the ecosystem before it changes to another equilibrium state. Robustness is the speed of return to equilibrium after a disturbance. Species, some of which may seem ecologically unimportant under current conditions, may play important roles in the resilience and robustness of ecosystems in the face of disturbances. For example, research has suggested that diverse communities may have a greater capacity to resist invasions by exotic, non-native species, which are major threats to biodiversity (e.g. Kennedy *et al.* 2002; Tilman 2004).[4]

---

[4] Exotic species that establish themselves in non-native habitats may displace native species through competition for natural resources, predate upon native species to extinction, or alter habitat to the point that native species can no longer persist.

Several components of species diversity determine its effects within actual ecosystems, including the number of species, the relative abundances of species, the particular species present, the interactions among the species present, and the spatial and temporal variations of these components. However, current knowledge about the consequences of biodiversity loss in actual ecosystems is limited, especially when considering large ecosystems and changes in biodiversity. Present information about how ecosystem functions relate to diversity comes mostly from simple ecosystems with only a few species. In addition, most scientific evidence relates to only small variations in species composition and relative abundance. Critics point out that real ecosystems may be structured quite differently and operate under different processes than those in experimental studies (e.g. Grime 1997); hence, the role of biodiversity within natural ecosystems remains problematic.

Measuring biodiversity

Biodiversity is typically characterized as the number of species, ecosystems, and genes. Ecological systems have three primary attributes – composition, structure, and function – that constitute biodiversity. Composition denotes the identity and variability of different elements such as species, genes, and ecosystems. Structure is the physical organization, pattern, and complexity of elements at different organizational scales (habitat, ecosystem, landscape). Function consists of ecological and evolutionary processes of elements, such as nutrient recycling, disturbance, or gene flow. Although each primary attribute of biodiversity is potentially important, interest in biodiversity concentrates around composition, especially species diversity (Noss 1990).

Two major approaches to the quantification of biodiversity have emerged. Economics literature has focused on measures of biodiversity that are based on joint dissimilarity among a set of species, whereas ecological literature has emphasized measures of biodiversity that are based on the relative abundance of species within ecological communities (Polasky, Costello, and Solow 2005).

The economics tradition of measuring biodiversity using the joint dissimilarity of species has its origins in Weitzman's work (1992). A phylogenetic tree describes the evolutionary inter-relationships among various organisms and their common ancestors. The phylogenetic tree can be used to determine joint dissimilarity of species from the branch lengths between different species on the tree. However, joint dissimilarity of species does not necessarily indicate the value of biodiversity. For example, Brock and Xepapadeas (2003) show that a slightly more diverse ecosystem can be much more valuable, although the increase in dissimilarity is almost zero.

Most conservation efforts, however, deal with habitat rather than species. Habitat-based measures of biodiversity are needed for assessing and designing alternative conservation strategies. In the ecological literature, the most common characterizations of biodiversity are based on the relative abundance of species within ecological communities. Mathematical indices of biodiversity quantify species diversity on three different geographical scales. Alpha diversity is the number of species in a certain community and can be used to compare the diversity of different locales or ecosystem types. Gamma diversity is the species richness of a wide geographical area that encompasses multiple ecosystems, such as a country or continent. Beta diversity measures the variability of species composition over an environmental or geographical gradient and is sometimes calculated as the ratio of gamma diversity to alpha diversity.

Diversity indices also are based on relative abundance in order to provide information about the rarity or commonness of species in a community. The Simpson index (Simpson 1949) and the Shannon–Weaver index (Shannon and Weaver 1949) are the most common indices based on the relative abundance of species. Simpson's index represents the probability that two randomly chosen individuals in a community belong to different species.[5] The Shannon–Weaver index measures the order or disorder of species composition.[6] In a more ordered system, the abundances of different species are similar and biodiversity is lower; in a less ordered system, the opposite is true.

Practical measurements of biodiversity often are based on a collection of biodiversity indicators – measures of ecological endpoints that are selected based on their perceived importance to biodiversity.

---

[5] Simpson's diversity index is calculated by taking the proportion of each species relative to the total number of species and then squaring and summing the proportions for all the species.

[6] The Shannon–Weaver diversity index is calculated from the proportion of each species relative to the total number of species, multiplied by the natural logarithm of this proportion. It is also known as the Shannon index and the Shannon–Weiner index.

Examples of such endpoints include species richness and the number of extinct, endangered, and threatened species within an ecological community or geographical area. Repeated measurements of different endpoints help evaluate how biodiversity is changing over time and how this relates to human activities.

Different indicators must be specified for particular ecosystems to reflect their unique characteristics. In the United States, the National Report on Sustainable Forests (USDA Forest Service 2004) has developed nine indicators for the conservation of biodiversity in forest ecosystems. Ecosystem diversity is addressed by five indicators, which measure the extent of forest fragmentation, different forest types, successional stages, and age classes in forests and protected areas. Other biodiversity indicators adopted by the Forest Service include the number of forest-dependent species, the percentage of forest-dependent species at risk of not maintaining viable populations, the number of forest-dependent species that occupy a small portion of their original range, and the population levels of representative species from diverse habitats monitored across their range. However, even in the United States, several of these indicators currently cannot be monitored due to insufficient data.

Status of biodiversity

Generally, biodiversity tends to be higher in southern areas and to decrease gradually toward the north. This pattern is especially true for flowering plants but it also emerges with the diversity of vertebrates. A similar longitudinal gradient can be observed in global biodiversity (Gaston 2000). However, many basic questions related to the current status of biodiversity remain unanswered. For instance, the total number of species in the world is unknown. Estimates vary from a few million species to more than 100 million species, with the current consensus around 14 million species (table 4.1). The species counts and their precision vary considerably across different taxonomic groups. Plant species are among the most completed inventories. It generally is accepted that approximately 300,000–500,000 plant species exist (Hammond 1995). For many groups of organisms, however, the precision of the estimated species counts is considered poor or moderate. The number of actually recognized and described species is fewer than 2 million.

The taxonomic group with the largest number of known species – about 1.3 million – is animals. Out of all known animal species, the vast majority (almost 1.1 million) are insects and other arthropods. In addition, animal species include about 45,000 known chordates and about 70,000 thousand mollusks. Sponges, jellyfish, corals, hydras, and other aquatic animals comprise approximately 20,000 known species. The rest of the known animal species mostly are worms of different kinds, such as flatworms, roundworms, or segmented worms (Hammond 1995).

Vertebrates and plants have been catalogued quite comprehensively, and their estimated numbers are not expected to change dramatically as more information is gathered over time. Viruses, bacteria, and fungi are the major groups of organisms with the largest estimated number of non-described species. New species are being identified in all taxonomic groups: every year, more than 10,000 completely new species are identified. This rate of more than 300 new species per day has stayed somewhat constant (UNEP 1995; Purvis and Hector 2000).[7]

Extinctions

A species becomes extinct when the last existing member of that species dies. However, extinction designations often are regionally specific – that is, applying to a state, region, or country. Global extinction, of course, refers to the species disappearance from the entire globe. When only a few individuals of species exist, a species may become functionally extinct, meaning that the reproduction and the survival of that species is not possible. A species becomes extinct in the wild when the only living individuals belonging to that species are maintained in unnatural environments, such as zoos.

Although extinctions are difficult to observe and verify, the World Conservation Union (IUCN) is widely recognized as the world's leading conservation network.[8] The IUCN provides an estimate of threatened

---

[7] Regardless of what the exact number of current species may be, scientists believe that it is more than at any other point in the Earth's history. The current species represent only a fraction of all species that have ever existed, which is estimated at around 5 billion.

[8] IUCN stands for the International Union for the Conservation of Nature and Natural Resources, the full name of the World Conservation Union. The IUCN

species based on its assessment of less than 3% of the world's 1.9 million described species (IUCN Red List 2004). The IUCN list contains 784 species worldwide that are documented to have gone extinct in the wild since 1500. Over the past twenty years, twenty-seven documented extinctions have occurred.

Extinctions can occur naturally. A key question, therefore, is how the current extinction rate compares to the natural or background extinction rate. Background extinction rates are determined by examining fossil records. Using these data, geologists have estimated that around 0.1–1 species per million species per year have gone extinct globally. During the last 400,000 years, approximately 400 invertebrate and 300–350 vertebrate species are known to have gone extinct globally. The number of plant extinctions is not well known, but it is believed to be several hundred. Among birds, mammals, and amphibians, the taxa for which extinction records are most reliable, the current average extinction rates are about 50–500 times the background extinction rate. If possible extinctions are included, the current extinction rates are about 100–1,000 times the geological extinction rates. These estimates generally are considered conservative. Consequently, the recent extinction rates seem to be at least one or two orders of magnitude higher than the background extinction rates (IUCN Red List 2004).

Although extinctions have become more common due to human activities, considerably fewer species have gone extinct than was predicted in some widely publicized – and criticized (e.g. Simon and Wildawsky 1984) – scenarios about twenty years ago. At the time, it was predicted that as many as 15–20% of all species on Earth would go extinct within the next twenty years (Global Report to the President 2000). This would have meant a loss of tens of thousands or even hundreds of thousands of species every year. As noted, now that more than twenty years have passed since these predictions, the *IUCN Red List* reports that worldwide twenty-seven species are known to have gone extinct during the last twenty years, so we have not witnessed the apocalyptic extinction rates once predicted. Nevertheless, even though extinction rates have remained relatively low, in many species groups

involves 82 states, 111 government agencies, and more than 800 non-governmental organizations (NGOs), and some 10,000 scientists and experts from 181 countries.

10–20% of all known species are endangered or threatened by extinction (*IUCN Red List 2004*).

Species endangerment

The IUCN characterizes endangered species as critically endangered, endangered, or vulnerable, depending on the estimated risk of extinction. Critically endangered, endangered, or vulnerable species are determined by the IUCN to be under extremely high, very high, or high risk of extinction, respectively. All species in these three threat categories depend on conservation measures for their continued existence. The degree of species endangerment is determined by using multiple criteria, including population size, population range, and the rates at which they are being decreased.

Threats to biodiversity

Major threats to biodiversity include habitat change, invasive alien species, pollution, and climate change. Almost certainly the primary cause of contemporary biodiversity decline is habitat destruction and the degradation that results from the expansion of human populations and activities. Habitat loss takes several forms: habitat can be completely lost (e.g. urban development), can be degraded (e.g. forest management, pollution of wetlands), or can become fragmented (e.g. urban sprawl).

Species loss due to habitat loss relates to the species–area relationship, which is a fundamental concept in ecology. Typically, smaller areas have fewer species than the larger ones. Ecologists view distinct areas of nature as islands, that can come in all sizes and differ in their connectivity with other islands. These islands are not necessary literal islands of land in an ocean or a lake; they refer to any relatively disconnected and distinct areas of habitat. So, for instance, parks within a city are islands, as are lakes within a continuum of land. The basic idea of island biogeography (MacArthur and Wilson 1967) is that the number of species in an area balances departures (extinctions) and arrivals of species. For example, the future number of species in a certain area will be determined by how many of its current species will persist and how many new species will immigrate there. Smaller islands tend to have fewer species than bigger ones, and the less connected these islands are, the fewer species they generally contain. Habitat loss tends both to create smaller islands and to decrease their connectivity.

After habitat loss, non-native species are the second leading cause of endangerment. Non-native species, which also are called invasive or alien species, are broadly distributed; their numbers vary and follow roughly the patterns of population density and transportation routes. The introduction of non-native species has important effects. Estimates of the economic losses due to non-native species are tentative, but Pimentel *et al.* (2000) suggest that the losses from invasive species may be more than $100 billion annually, although this estimate is generally considered speculative (Polasky, Costello, and Solow 2005).

In addition to habitat loss and non-native species, pollution, over-exploitation of species, and illnesses are among the causes of endangerment of several species.

Some researchers believe that in addition to current threats of extinction, climate change may become one of the greatest drivers of biodiversity loss in the long run. Although nature has a notable capacity to adapt to change, the relatively rapid climatic change that has been predicted may leave species without adequate opportunity to adjust their ranges, especially if combined with increased fragmentation and decreased connectivity of habitats that create additional barriers to adjustment (Thomas *et al.* 2004; Millennium Ecosystem Assessment 2005).

3 Costs and benefits of biodiversity: some estimates

Biodiversity losses

Extinctions are irreversible events that permanently remove a unique constituent of current biodiversity. How much of the evolutionary information passed on to the future is lost through extinctions? Since much of the evolutionary information (evolutionary history) is shared by other species, there is no one-to-one relationship between extinctions and the loss of evolutionary information. For example, if one in every ten species goes extinct, typically less than one-tenth of the total evolutionary information in all species is lost. Even in extreme mass extinctions, in which nearly all species would disappear, the majority of evolutionary information would be maintained by the surviving species (Nee and May 1997). This does not suggest that extinctions are somehow insignificant events; the idea is simply that species share significant amounts of evolutionary information and different species substitute as carriers of this information.

Alternative conservation strategies may be evaluated, based not only on the number of species they protect but also how effectively they preserve evolutionary history (e.g. Brooks, Mayden, and McLennan 1992; Mace, Gittleman, and Purvis 2003). For example, each species in the phylogenetic tree has some unique and some shared evolutionary history. Extinction of any one species leads to the loss of some unique evolutionary history, but not every species has the same amount of unique history.

Using preservation of evolutionary history for assessments of alternative conservation plans is intuitively appealing but difficult in practice because it requires currently lacking information on the evolutionary history of different species. Also, human ability to determine *ex ante* what evolutionary information is most valuable for preservation is problematic.

Values of biodiversity

The values of biodiversity can be divided into three types: biodiversity as a global public good (i.e. biodiversity that provides global public benefits); biodiversity that provides national or regional benefits, but involves externalities; and biodiversity that provides private goods absent externalities. The typical approach of economists is to argue that the private goods need no special policies outside that of the provision of appropriate and enforced property rights. For local and regional public goods, appropriate policies, such as tax or subsidy policies, are usually recommended. For global public goods, some mechanism to provide global policies and perhaps global funding are usually deemed appropriate. Specific values from biodiversity stem from different beneficial uses, functions, and purposes of biodiversity, ecosystems, and their different components.

Biological commodities, such as food, feed, wood, and other fiber materials, that are largely traded in markets, provide valuable goods and services. Biodiversity in breeding stocks adds to the long-term sustainability of the production of these commodities. Additionally, medicinal and pharmaceutical products and sources for biological control and remediation found in biodiversity are valuable assets to society. While the final products are traded in markets, the biological resources that are inputs are usually viewed as public goods (Sedjo 1992a).

Environmental services

Ecosystems, and especially forest ecosystems, provide a host of valuable environmental services. Many are largely non-market services, such as protection of water resources, nutrient storage and cycling, pollution breakdown and absorption, soil fertility and protection, climate stability, and recovery from disturbance of natural systems. In addition, forests and forest biodiversity generate benefits that are related to recreation and tourism, research and education, and culture and tradition. Many of these benefits are local or regional. Also, ecosystems provide a residence for unique plants and other organisms that have pharmaceutical potential.

Importantly, forest ecosystems also provide the ecological service of carbon sequestration. In the process of biological growth, carbon dioxide is taken into the plant, the carbon is captured into the cells of the plant, and the oxygen released back into the atmosphere. Forests, unlike many plants, accumulate large amounts of biomass over long periods of time. Within this biomass, huge volumes of carbon are held captive in forest ecosystems, including in the trees, litter, and forest soils. Unlike many ecosystem services, which are local in their benefits, the climate benefits of forests are not restricted to one locale but are truly global in nature.

Use and existence values of species: contingent valuation

The value of biodiversity, especially endangered and threatened species, is often not related to direct uses of those species but rather to the intrinsic worth of their existence. Such non-use values are difficult to estimate because they are not captured in market transactions. This has given rise to the development of a variety of non-market valuation methods that use surveys to elicit preferences for public goods, such as protection of threatened and endangered species. Because these methods are based on eliciting and examining stated rather than actual preferences, they also are broadly categorized as stated preference (SP) methods (e.g. Louviere *et al.* 2000). The contingent valuation (CV) method is the most commonly applied SP method for valuing biodiversity. The CV method requests people to state their approval or disapproval of specific policy programs for the protection of certain species or habitat. Because the proposed scenarios have specified costs that are varied across survey respondents, researchers can examine survey responses and estimate how much people are willing to pay for the protection of certain species. For a review of CV, see Carson and Hanemann (2005).

Not all economists agree that expressions of stated preferences are useful for economic valuation. For example, Diamond and Hausman (1994) argue that people simply do not have preferences for the types of goods CV studies deal with, and they note that the lack of experience in markets for environmental commodities make answering CV questions difficult. Hahnemann (1994) is more optimistic about CV and argues that, despite its challenges, the ability to place an economic value on environmental quality is essential for environmental policy and a cornerstone of the economic approach to the environment. SP methods are widely applied in other fields of research, such as marketing and transportation research and decision analysis (Louviere *et al.* 2000). In these fields, SP methods are regularly used for eliciting consumer preferences for new products, product alternatives, and transportation options, and to help their design and marketing.

Individual species

Although wild species are no longer essential for human survival, their direct uses continue through hunting, fishing, and gathering. Methods for the valuation of such benefits are quite well established; they are explained and reviewed by Phaneuf and Smith (2005). Values from recreational uses of nature can be substantial. For example, salmon fishing has been estimated to be worth from around $14 to more than $110 per day per angler, depending on location, and which type of salmon is fished. A day of hunting has been estimated to be worth between approximately $30 and $45 per hunter, depending on what game is targeted (Phaneuf and Smith 2005).

Willingness-to-pay (WTP) estimates suggest substantial variation in the WTP of the public for the protection of rare, threatened, and endangered species. Bell, Huppert, and Johnson (2003) estimate that the WTP for the protection of Coho salmon can surpass $100 per year per household. Giraud *et al.* (2002) and Giraud and Valcic (2004) predict that US households are willing to pay $69–99 for the protection of the Steller sea lion in Alaska, whereas the WTP of Wisconsin households for the protection of striped shiner (Boyle and Bishop 1987) and that of Massachusetts households for the protection of Atlantic salmon (Stevens *et al.* 1991) are both roughly $10. The finding that WTP varies between different species is not new. It is widely known that the preferences of both public and public officials vary across different species, often favoring charismatic megafauna over less magnificent yet equally or more vulnerable species.

Table 4.3 summarizes values for twenty-nine species for which values have been estimated by one or more CV studies. These studies estimate WTP for avoiding the loss of a species, or for an increase in population size or viability.

Four caveats should be kept in mind when interpreting these WTP results. First, they are for the United States and so are unlikely to be representative for many LAC countries. Second, since many animals are game animals, they are not representative for rare, threatened, or endangered species in general, where recreational values would be absent or quite different. Furthermore, most valuation efforts have focused on species of significant publicity – such as the bald eagle, spotted owl, pacific salmon, or whooping crane – and many less publicized yet susceptible species have not been valued by any studies. Third, sampled populations vary remarkably across different studies. Fourth, survey and estimation methods advance quite rapidly and not every study uses methods that are now considered state-of-the-art. While not necessarily representative, however, table 4.3 suggests that significant economic value is given to many very different individual species.

Natural habitat

Several studies, again largely in the United States, have estimated benefits from different types of natural habitat. The results of these analyses are summarized in table 4.5. Most of the benefits studied relate to water, and other ecosystem benefits are not considered. Also, most of these studies have estimated the value of specific resources in a specific geographic area. Thus, although many of the benefits are external to markets, they are largely confined to certain geographic areas. Where these areas are within one country, the public policy of that country should be able, in principle, to capture those benefits. And, indeed,

Table 4.3 *Estimates of WTP values, rare, threatened, or endangered species: United States ($2005)*

	Low ($)	High ($)	Avg. ($)	Reference(s)	Sample
Studies reporting annual WTP					
Striped shiner[a]			8	Boyle and Bishop (1987)	Wisconsin
Atlantic salmon[a]	10	11	10	Stevens et al. (1991)	Massachusetts
Florida manatee[a]			11	Solomon et al. (2004)	Citrus County, Florida
Squawfish[a]			11	Cummings, Ganderton, and McGuckin (1994)	New Mexico
Red-cockaded woodpecker	9	20	13	Reaves et al. (1994); Reaves et al. (1999)	Varies (South Carolina and United States)
Bighorn sheep	17	40	28	Brookshire, Eubanks, and Randall (1983); King et al. (1988)	Varies (Wyoming hunters, Arizona households)
Riverside fairy shrimp[a]	27	31	29	Stanley (2005)	Orange County, California
Gray whale	23	42	32	Loomis and Larson (1994)	California
Bald eagle[a]	21	44	32	Boyle and Bishop (1987); Stevens et al. (1991)	Varies (Wisconsin, New England)
Silvery minnow[a]	31	36	34	Berrens, Ganderton, and Silva (1996); Berrens et al. (2000)	New Mexico
Sea otter[a]			39	Hageman (1985)	California
Gray whale	31	47	39	Larson, Shaikh, and Layton (2004)	California
Grizzly bear			49	Brookshire, Eubanks, and Randall (1983)	Wyoming hunters
Mexican spotted owl[a]	49	58	53	Loomis and Eckstrand (1997); Giraud, Loomis, and Johnson (1999)	Varies (Arizona, Colorado, Utah, Northwest)

Whooping crane[a]	43	67	55	Bowker and Stall (1987)	Varies (Texas, United States)
Northern spotted owl[a]	30	128	64	Rubin et al. (1991); Hagen et al. (1992)	Varies (Washington, DC, United States)
Pacific salmon and steelhead	42	118	80	Olsen et al. (1991)	Pacific Northwest (anglers and households)
Steller sea lion	69	99	84	Giraud et al. (2002); Giraud and Valcic (2004)	United States
Coho salmon	23	137	87	Bell et al. (2003)	Oregon, Washington, DC
Studies reporting lump-sum WTP					
Sea turtle[a]			17	Whitehead (1991, 1992)	North Carolina
Cutthroat trout[a]			17	Duffield and Patterson (1992)	Visitors
Arctic grayling			23	Duffield and Patterson (1992)	Visitors
Peregrine falcon			35	Kotchen and Reiling (2000)	Maine
Shortnose sturgeon[a]			36	Kotchen and Reiling (2000)	Maine
Timber wolf	54	56	55	Heberlein et al. (2005)	Minnesota
Gray wolf	5	157	67	Duffield (1991, 1992); Duffield, Patterson, and Neher (1993); USDOI (1994); Chambers and Whitehead (2003)	Varies (Minnesota, United States, visitors)
Monk seal[a]			160	Samples and Hollyer (1989)	Hawaii
Humpback whale[a]			231	Samples and Hollyer (1989)	Hawaii
Bald eagle	239	341	290	Swanson (1993)	Washington, DC

Note: [a] Indicates that the study estimates WTP for avoiding the loss of species. Other studies typically estimate WTP for an increase in population size or chance of survival. Samples are typically households if not otherwise indicated.

Source: Siikamäki and Chow (2008), as adapted, expanded, and updated from Loomis and White (1996).

Table 4.4 *Estimates of the value of natural habitat: United States*

Author(s)	Study	Mean WTP estimates (per household) ($)
Holmes *et al.* (2004)	Riparian restoration along the Little Tennessee River in western North Carolina	0.69–40.89 per year
Loomis (1989)	Preservation of the Mono Lake, California	4–11
Silberman *et al.* (1992)	Protection of beach systems, New Jersey	9.26–15.1
Kealy and Turner (1993)	Preservation of the aquatic system in the Adirondacks region	12–18
Smith and Desvousges (1986)	Preservation of water quality in the Monongahela River Basin	21–58 (for users), 14–53 (for non-users)
Walsh *et al.* (1984)	Protection of wilderness areas, Colorado	32
Diamond *et al.* (1993)	Protection of wilderness areas in Colorado, Idaho, Montana, and Wyoming, United States	29–66
Boyle (1990)	Preservation of the Illinois Beach State Nature Reserve	37–41
Loomis, Gonzales-Caban, and Gregory (1994)	Fire management plan to reduce burning of old growth forests in California and Oregon	56 per year
Larson and Siikamäki (2006)	Removal of surface water quality impairment in California	67–133 per year
Loomis, Gonzales-Caban, and Gregory (1994)	Fire management plan to reduce burning of old growth forests in Oregon	90 per year
Hoehn and Loomis (1993)	Enhancing wetlands and habitat in San Joaquin Valley in California, United States	96–284 (single program)
Richer (1995)	Desert protection in California	101
Mitchell and Carson (1984)	Preservation of water quality for all rivers and lakes	242

Source: Siikamäki and Chow (2008), as adapted from Nunes and van den Bergh (2001).

Table 4.5 *Estimates of the value of selected ecosystem services: United States*

Author(s)	Study	Measurement method	Estimates ($)
Walker and Young (1986)	Value of soil erosion on (lost) agriculture revenue in the Palouse region	Production function	4 and 6 per acre
McClelland *et al.* (1992)	Protection of groundwater program, United States	Contingent valuation	7–22
Torell, Libbin, and Miller (1990)	Water in-storage on the high plains aquifer, United States	Production function	9.5–1.09 per acre-foot
Laughland *et al.* (1996)	Value of a water supply in Milesburg, Pennsylvania	Averting expenditures	14 and 36 per household
Heberlein *et al.* (2005)	Water quality in lakes of northern Wisconsin	Contingent valuation	107–260 per household
Abdalla, Roach, and Epp (1992)	Groundwater ecosystem in Perkasie, Pennsylvania	Averting expenditures	61,313–131,334
Holmes (1988)	Value of the impact of water turbidity due to soil erosion on the water treatment, United States	Replacement cost	35–661 million per year
Huszar (1989)	Value of wind erosion costs to households, New Mexico	Replacement cost	454 million per year
Ribaudo (1989a, 1989b)	Water quality benefits in ten regions, United States	Averting expenditures	4.4 billion per year

Source: Siikamäki and Chow (2008), as adapted from Nunes and van den Bergh (2001).

the projects undertaken reflect that objective. For example, Holmes *et al.* (2004) estimate the value of riparian restoration along the Little Tennessee River in western North Carolina; Kealy and Turner (1993) and Banzhaf *et al.* (2004) value the preservation of aquatic systems in the Adirondacks region; Smith and Desvousges (1986) estimate benefits from the preservation of water quality in the Monongahela River; and Hoehn and Loomis (1993) estimate the value of wetland and habitat in the San Joaquin Valley in California.

As an alternative to scrutinizing finely defined natural habitats, some studies have estimated values of broadly specified resources. For example, in a widely known study, Mitchell and Carson (1984) estimate the benefits from preserving water quality in all rivers and lakes of the United States at $242 per family per year. Given that there are somewhat over 100 million US families, the total annual value would be estimated at over $250 billion per year in water quality benefits. If extrapolated to the globe, the ecosystem water benefits would be very large. In another geographically broad study, Larson and Siikamäki (2006) estimate the WTP of California households for regional and state programs designed to improve surface water quality and remove the impairments of water quality that limit beneficial uses of surface water bodies. Although breaking down the value estimates of broadly defined resources – such as all water bodies in an entire region or state – can be difficult; using a broadly defined resource as the basis of valuation may help to estimate a WTP that better reflects actual WTP for an aggregate resource than can be estimated by summing up WTP estimates for its subcomponents.

Adding up results from separate studies, each of which is focused on valuing a single species or localized habitat, can lead to ignoring relevant substitutes, improper rescaling, and unrealistically high aggregate value estimates. For example, Brown and Shogren (1998) note that aggregating the estimates summarized in Loomis and White (1996) implies that the total WTP for less than 2% of endangered species exceeds 1% of GDP, which they consider suspiciously high.

Ecosystem services

A literature review of the valuation of ecosystem services is provided by Nunes and van den Bergh (2001). Ecosystem services are the economically valuable functions that ecosystems provide to humans. More broadly, natural capital consists not only of specific biophysical natural resources – such as minerals, energy, animals and trees – but their interaction within ecosystems (Heal *et al.* 2005). These functions can generate both marketed and non-marketed benefits. As discussed earlier, examples include water purification, oxygen creation, maintenance of soil productivity, waste decomposition, nutrient cycling, pest control, flood control, climatic control (climate moderation, carbon sequestration), pollination of crops and native vegetation, and provision of recreation opportunities. Valuation of ecosystem services can view the natural environment as a type of capital asset – natural capital – which generates returns in the form of ecosystem services. Biodiversity is considered an element of the natural capital and ecosystems are productive systems in which different elements serve different functions in the production of ecosystem services.

An example of ecosystem services is wetlands, which serve as flood barriers, soaking up excess water and slowing and preventing floodwaters from spreading uncontrollably. Wetlands help replenish groundwater and improve both groundwater and surface water quality, slowing down the flow of water, and absorbing and filtering out sediment and contaminants. Wetlands also provide spawning habitat for fish, supporting the regeneration of fisheries. Also, wetlands provide habitat for many species and support fishing, hunting, and recreation.

The National Academy of Sciences established a Committee on the Valuation of Ecosystem Services, which was given the task of evaluating methods for assessing ecosystem services and their associated economic value. The committee prepared a report, *Valuing Ecosystem Services* (Heal *et al.* 2005), which highlighted the central issues in valuing ecosystem services, especially those relating to aquatic ecosystems. The report noted that the key challenge in the valuation of ecosystem services was the successful integration of economy and ecology, required for "providing an explicit description and adequate assessment of the links between the structures and functions of natural systems, the benefits (i.e. goods and services), derived by humanity, and their subsequent values." The complexity of ecosystems makes the translation of ecosystem structure and function to ecosystem goods and services and their value especially difficult.

Table 4.5 summarizes a number of studies that have estimated values for ecosystem services that are related to water supplies, water quality, and soil-erosion control. These analyses have used a variety of methods, including CV (McClelland *et al.* 1992; Heberlein *et al.* 2005), averting expenditures (Ribaudo 1989a, 1989b; Abdalla, Roach, and Epp 1992; Laughland *et al.* 1996), replacement cost (Holmes 1988; Huszar 1989), and production function (Walker and Young 1986; Torell, Libbin, and Miller 1990). For different techniques of valuing the environment as a factor of production, including averting cost, replacement costs, and production function methods, see McConnell and Bockstael (2005).

An interesting example of ecosystem services valuation, not found in table 4.5, has to do with the Catskills Mountains, from where New York City obtains its water supply. For years, the Catskills watershed has provided New York City with water that is usable without additional filtering. By the end of the 1980s, changing land use patterns, urbanization, and agricultural practices in the Catskills degraded the quality of groundwater and left New York City evaluating different alternatives for securing the quality of its drinking water. Constructing and operating a filtration plant was estimated to cost approximately $8–$10 billion. Rather than making this expensive investment, New York City decided to invest in the preservation of the Catskills rural environment that had for so long provided the city with a high-quality water supply. The Catskills preservation program cost the city about $1.5 billion, generating considerable cost savings relative to constructing and operating a filtration plant. In this example, the cost savings from not having to construct and operate a filtration plant can be used as a value of ecosystem services of water filtration by the Catskills (Chichilnisky and Heal 1998). Using a replacement cost approach to the measurement of ecosystem services, however, requires the following three conditions to hold: (1) the replacement service is equivalent in quality and magnitude to the ecosystem service; (2) the replacement is the least-cost approach to replacing the service; and (3) people are willing to pay the replacement cost to obtain the services (Shabman and Batie 1978).

Carbon storage as an ecosystem service

A different approach to the evaluation of the benefits provided by the forest ecosystem has emerged from concerns about atmospheric carbon dioxide and climate change. The Intergovernmental Panel on

Climate Change (IPCC) *Third Assessment Report on Climate Change* noted that forests contain huge amounts of carbon and that controlling deforestation and establishing new forests could have a significant effect on net carbon emissions (Kauppi, Sedjo *et al.* 2001). Furthermore, more recent studies have suggested that forest carbon sequestration offers a low-cost approach to atmospheric carbon mitigation (Sohngen and Sedjo 2006). This has lead to a renewed interest in avoided deforestation, particularly in the tropics, as a tool to mitigate climate change.

4 Forests and biodiversity in Latin America

Much of the work on biodiversity has been done in cither a global context or, for studies of specific species or outputs, in North America. This section focuses on the very considerable biodiversity that is found largely in the tropical forests of the LAC region. LAC biodiversity is tied closely to its vast expanses of relatively undisturbed forests. However, this forest area is among the most threatened in the world: Brazil, for example, which has the world's largest area of tropical forests, is experiencing very rapid rates and absolute levels of deforestation (Kauppi *et al.* 2006). Similarly, fairly high rates of deforestation are being experienced in Venezuela, Argentina, and elsewhere in the region.

Forest losses

The FAO Global Forest Resources Assessment (2005) estimates total world forested area at 3.95 billion ha. It gives a global deforestation estimate of 13 million ha per year on average for 2000–5. Although the FAO does not give deforestation figures at the national level for all countries, it does note that Brazil leads the countries with a net annual loss of −3,103,000 ha and that Venezuela is tenth with net losses of −288,000 ha. South America has the largest continental net loss of forests, estimated at −7.3 million ha per year, but down from −8.9 million ha per year in the period 1990–2000. Central America has also experienced substantial losses.

An important ecosystem function of forests is the holding of large volumes of carbon in the tree cells, the dead wood and litter, and in the forest soils. South American forests hold roughly 90 billion tons of carbon directly in the forest biomass (about 32%) and another 70 billion tons (22%) in the dead wood, litter, and forest soils (FAO 2006).

LAC biodiversity

Although the region constitutes only 16% of the land area of the planet, it is home to 27% of the world's mammal species, 42% of known reptile species, 43% of known bird species, 47% of known amphibians, and 34% of known flowering plants (IUCN 1996, 1997).

Another measure of biodiversity and biodiversity challenges is that of biodiversity "hot spots"; IUCN estimates of conservation "hot spots" are given in figure 4.1. LAC biodiversity "hot spots" run geographically from northern Mexico along the Pacific coast of Colombia to parts of Chile and include forested areas along the Atlantic coast of Brazil. Although none of these areas is in the Amazon, parts of the Amazon also often are considered "hot spots." For example, high levels of unique biodiversity are found in the foothills of the Andes, which have a combination of wet tropical climatic conditions and large variations in elevation.

A second estimate of biodiversity "hot spots" is that of Conservation International. Conservation International identifies seven LAC regions in as biodiversity "hot spots" (figure 4.2). Again, these run geographically from northern Mexico to parts of Chile and include forested areas along most of the Pacific coast, and many of the forested regions along the Atlantic coastal regions of southern Brazil to parts of Argentina.

Threats to biodiversity in Latin America

The *IUCN Red List* (2004) contains 15,589 species threatened with extinction. Of these, some 10,823 are found in South America and 3,946 in Brazil. Roughly 60% of these are species that reside in forests. Mesoamerica accounts for 4,117 of the threatened species, with about half being forest species. Of these, Mexico accounts for 2,732 threatened species, more than 40% of which are forest species. While these lists may not be mutually exclusive, it is clear that the LAC region

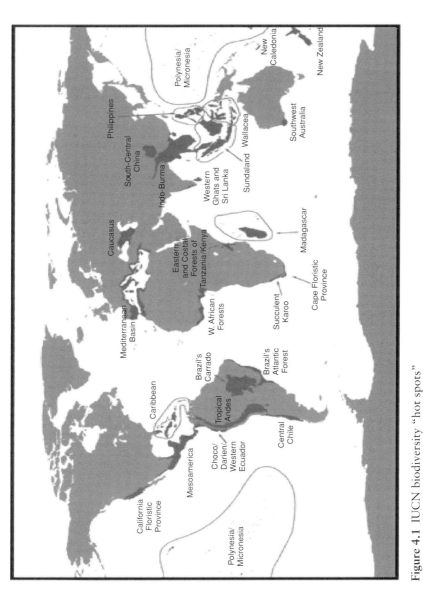

Figure 4.1 IUCN biodiversity "hot spots"

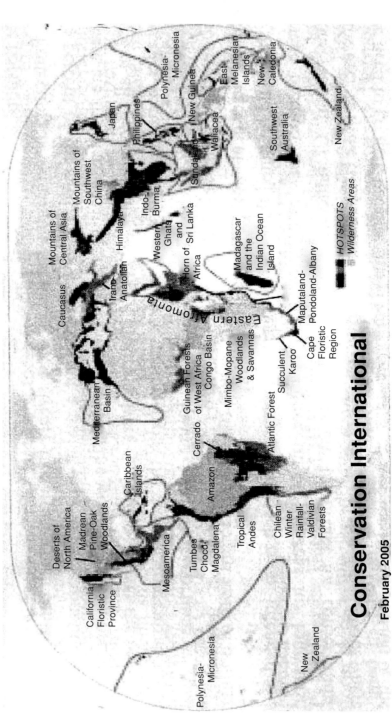

Figure 4.2 Conservation International's biodiversity "hot spots" and high biodiversity wilderness areas

Table 4.6 *Number of species threatened with extinction: LAC region[a]*

Habitat	South America	Brazil	Mesoamerica	Mexico	Caribbean	World
Total	10,823	3,946	4,117	2,732	2,072	15,589
Forest	6,065	2,157	1,913	1,151		

Note: [a] Note that there is a great deal of overlap in species across areas. While the total of species threatened globally is 15,589, the sum of threatened species by major region is almost 50,000.
Source: IUCN (2004), accessed February 6, 2007.

(South America and Mesoamerica) accounts for a very large portion of the world's total threatened species (table 4.6).

5 Valuation of benefits and costs of protection of global ecosystems and biodiversity

As demonstrated above, although there are a very large number of valuations of biodiversity and ecosystem services, most are quite specific to a region and an output. Typically, biodiversity has been addressed in a piecemeal and fragmented manner and there are a number of attempts to value various aspects of biodiversity and other non-market environmental services (tables 4.4 and 4.5). However, it is difficult to generalize these results more broadly. In this section, we look at the few attempts to examine the benefits associated with forest ecosystems and the costs associated with protecting forests for ecosystem outputs, including biodiversity and carbon sequestration functions and services.

The conception and technical problems in estimating the benefits and costs of forest and biodiversity are quite different. In many cases, the benefits are non-market final consumption goods. The question of what these are worth to consumers is not revealed in markets but must be estimated by a CV approach such as a hypothetical WTP. This question becomes increasingly difficult to answer as the outputs being evaluated expand from the value of a spotted owl (species), to the value of a specific forest or habitat, to the value of the global forest system.

Costs, by contrast, are typically less difficult to quantify, as they usually involve the expenditure of resources that are valued in the market. Thus, land set-asides for ecosystem purposes have an opportunity cost that the market recognizes and is relatively easy to estimate.

Not surprisingly, then, analysts often avoid trying to quantify both benefits and costs and focus on the least-cost way to achieve a desired (perhaps politically determined) environmental goal, such as the protection of the spotted owl. This reality is reflected in this study, which finds many more estimates of the costs of preserving global ecosystems than estimates of the benefits. Nevertheless, some estimates of both global benefits and costs do exist.

Global ecosystem services

There have been a limited number of broad ecosystem valuation attempts. Perhaps the grandest effort is that of Costanza *et al.* (1997) to evaluate the entire aggregate of global ecosystem services. They attempted to estimate the total value by deriving and summing up value estimates from the existing literature for a wide range of ecosystem services. The study, which estimates the likely range of the total value of global ecosystem services as $16–$54 trillion annually, was widely criticized on both the grounds that the global ecosystem values exceeded global GNP and also that estimating the total value of global ecosystem services is not meaningful because the global ecosystem is a necessity without which life would not be sustained. This latter argument is summed up by Toman (1998), who notes that the Costanza *et al.* (1997) estimate of the total value of global ecosystem services is "a serious underestimate of infinity." Although the Costanza *et al.* (1997) study has been influential and widely quoted, especially among scientists and environmentalists, it is considered by most economists fundamentally flawed, both conceptually and methodologically. For a critique of the Costanza *et al.* (1997) study see Toman (1998) or Bockstael *et al.* (2000).

Bioprospecting: pharmaceutical products

A major justification for preserving biodiversity has been its value as an input to medicinal and pharmaceutical products (table 4.7). Wilson (1992) argued that conserving species preserved an option value for the future since species might contain valuable compounds that would yield valuable pharmaceuticals in the future. The concept was developed that there might be large economic returns from bioprospecting – that is, collecting various wild plants (and perhaps animals) and developing commercially valuable products from them or their

Table 4.7 *Value of biodiversity for pharmaceuticals*

Unit	Value of benefits ($)	Authors and source
Biodiversity for pharmaceuticals	23.7 million per untested species (537 billion for 250,000 species)	Principe (1989)
Biodiversity for pharmaceuticals	44.00 per untested species (11 million)	Aylward *et al.* (1993)
Biodiversity for pharmaceuticals	As high as 9,431 for some species, or 20.63 per ha, but much lower for other species and lands	Simpson, Sedjo, and Reid (1996)
Biodiversity for pharmaceuticals	Land opportunity cost as bio-habitat as high as 9,177 per ha	Rausser and Small (2000)

constituents. Newman, Cragg, and Snader (2003) analyzed the origins of new drugs approved by the regulatory agencies over the period 1981–2002 and found that the majority of them had origins in nature.

Early studies estimated the value of conserving a species for pharmaceuticals use from $44 (Aylward *et al.* 1993) to $23.7 million (Principe 1989) per untested species. Besides the huge differences in estimates, the approach used – multiplying the probability of a successful product with its average revenue – was criticized in that it estimates the average value rather than the marginal value of an untested species. Because multiple species may contain the same compound and in this sense be redundant, marginal values are likely to be far less than average values. Simpson, Sedjo, and Reid (1996) developed a sequential search mode that takes redundancy into account. They demonstrated that when there is a large volume of biological material to search for valuable new products, the incremental value of one species is likely to be not very high. This is because when the total number of species is large and biological redundancy is common, different species may be close substitutes as sources of the useful biological constituent.

Nevertheless, in the 1990s bioprospecting was viewed as a vehicle by which developing countries could capture some of the rents that would accrue to their biodiversity. A famous project in the 1990s had Merck Pharmaceutical providing $1 million dollars to Costa Rica in return for 1,000 plants collected its forest. A Costa Rican organization was created to inventory and collect plants for possible use in the development of new pharmaceuticals (Sittenfeld and Gamez 1993). Although the Merck project has been successful in raising monies for Costa Rican biodiversity inventorying and research, few, if any, drugs were developed from the plants collected and the model has not been transferred readily to other countries.

The reason for the lack of commercial success was suggested by the work of Simpson, Sedjo, and Reid (1996). They solved for the probability that generates the maximum species values, using evidence to assign reasonable parameter values for revenues and costs. They found that the expected marginal value of a species may be as high as $9,431 in some locations. However, when estimating the economic returns from bioprospecting per ha of land, Simpson, Sedjo, and Reid found that the returns were modest – from $0.20 per ha in the California Floristic Province to $20.63 in Western Ecuador – even under assumptions likely to over-state the benefits and in regions that are known as global biodiversity "hot spots" and rich in endemic species. For this reason, Simpson, Sedjo, and Reid noted that the potential for new product development did not provide a compelling economic argument for protecting biodiversity "hot spots," and that bioprospecting alone likely would not provide incentives for private landowners or companies to protect land for its pharmaceutical biodiversity values.[9]

This result was challenged. Using a similar conceptual approach as Simpson, Sedjo, and Reid, Rausser and Small (2000) argued that if bioprospectors used prior information on the likelihood of product discovery, bioprospecting might in some cases result in considerable economic returns per ha of land. They estimated that the value of richest biodiversity "hot spots" land in Western Ecuador might be as high as $9,177 per ha (compared to the estimate of $20.63 per ha by Simpson, Sedjo, and Reid).

Costello and Ward (2006) resolved the conflict by showing that the difference between the results of Simpson, Sedjo, and Reid and Rausser and Small relate mostly to different underlying assumptions regarding the relevant real-world parameter values, such as the number of relevant species, development costs, and so forth. They show that, using

---

[9] Using the estimate of $122 per ha as the annual opportunity cost of the biodiversity "hot spots" in the LAC region would cost about 7.93 billion.

similar parameters, the alternative approaches by Simpson, Sedjo, and Reid and Rausser and Small give similar results. For example, the Rausser and Small value of a ha in Western Ecuador of $9,177 when conducting an optimal ordered search drops to $8,840 for a random search such as used by Simpson, Sedjo, and Reid. Thus, the differences are not a result of the different search methods but reflect the choice of different parameters. Furthermore, upon investigation, Costello and Ward conclude that the underlying assumptions of Simpson, Sedjo, and Reid comport substantially more closely with the estimated empirical values than those of Rausser and Small. An implication is that the marginal value of an average species or ha of land for bioprospecting is usually too small to cover the opportunity costs.

Regardless of the initial enthusiasm about benefit-sharing agreements and their use for biodiversity conservation, their success has been limited. One likely reason is that the economic returns from bioprospecting by themselves do not generate sufficient incentives to preserve biodiversity (Simpson, Sedjo, and Reid 1996; Polasky, Costello, and Solow 2005).[10] More relevant for this study is that, although global, the effort focused on only one use of biodiversity: as an input for pharmaceutical products. The results suggested that the benefits rarely exceeded the opportunity costs of the lands for other uses.

Carbon storage as an ecosystem service

Another aspect to the approach to evaluate the benefits provided by the forest ecosystem has emerged from concerns about atmospheric carbon dioxide and climate change. The IPPC *Third Assessment Report on Climate Change* (Kauppi, Sedjo *et al.* 2001) noted that forests contain huge amounts of carbon and that avoiding deforestation and establishing new forests could have a significant effect on net carbon emissions.

---

[10] Benefit-sharing agreement application has occurred in the United States in Yellowstone, the nation's oldest national park. Diversa Corporation, a biotech company, entered into a benefit-sharing contract in 1997 whereby Diversa compensates Yellowstone $175,000 for bioprospecting rights. In addition, the company pays to Yellowstone between 0.5–10% in royalties for products developed from biological material obtained from the park (Siikamäki and Chow 2008).

It is possible to estimate the value of a forest for sequestrating carbon. Market transactions in the European Climate Exchange have placed the value of carbon for atmospheric carbon reduction within a wide range, from $10 to $100 per ton of carbon.[11] While volatile, at least a market price is available.

The total LAC forest covers about 1 billion ha. The amount of carbon captured in a forest varies considerably, depending on the species, age, and density of the stand. Old primary, tropical forest may have 300 tons of carbon while young forests may have 100 tons.

An early effort to quantify the benefits and costs of using the forest ecosystem for carbon reduction was that of Pearce (1996). In quantifying the benefits, Pearce examined the relationship between land conversion in the tropics and the amount of carbon released. He related the carbon stored in the tropical forests to an estimate of the cost of carbon, which is an estimate of the damage associated with its net emission into the atmosphere, to obtain an estimate of the value of tropical forests in preventing a greater build-up of carbon in the atmosphere. Pearce used an average of about 100 tons of carbon per ha of forest and a price of $20 per ton of carbon. These figures provided estimated values for the services of ecosystems and forests as about $12 trillion, and are presented in table 4.8. This number is in the range estimated by Constanza *et al.* (1997).

Although these studies focus on the costs of the containment of carbon in the forest, the market approach for the cost of carbon provides some information on the benefits of containment. If a market for carbon credits is created, as in the European Union, the demand for carbon credits is determined by the severity of the constraints on emissions imposed by governments. One can infer from these constraints the value that governments place on containing carbon, which is an assessment of the benefits. Thus, the price per ton of carbon sequestered provides an estimate of the marginal damages believed to be forgone and an estimate of the market price of carbon times the quantity of carbon held captive as a result is an estimate of the benefits of this effort.

---

[11] The literature uses both carbon and carbon dioxide in its estimates of carbon storage and emissions. 1 ton of carbon dioxide is equal to 12/11 tons of carbon. The costs in this chapter are for carbon and range between $10 and $100 per ton. This is equivalent to $2.73 and $27.30 per ton of carbon dioxide.

Table 4.8 *Estimates of the value of global ecosystem and biodiversity benefits*

Unit	Value of Benefits ($)	Authors and sources
Global ecosystem services	Globally 16–54 trillion annually. Pro-rated to 3.2–11 trillion annually for Latin America[a]	Constanza *et al.* (1997)
Carbon capture globally for 4 billion ha	12 trillion net benefits	Extending Pearce's (1996) approach globally
Pharmaceutical values	0.20–20.63 per ha	Simpson, Sedjo, and Reid (1996)

Note: [a] The LAC region was assumed to be one-fifth of the world system, roughly based on land area. It would be smaller based on GDP or population. Based on threatened species, it might be as large as one-third.

Costs of protecting forests

As noted, a number of studies have looked at the costs of protecting very large areas or all tropical forests. These include Kindermann *et al.* (unpublished), Sedjo (1991, 1992a, 1992b), James *et al.* (2001), and Pearce (2006), or some fraction of the forest, e.g. Brumer *et al.* (2001), Pimm *et al.* (2001), and Greig-Gran (2006). These are discussed below and their pro-rated results applied to Latin America.

6 LAC benefit and cost estimates

Benefits from LAC forests and biodiversity

What are the benefits of LAC forests and biodiversity? As noted, the rationale for the importance of LAC biodiversity can be found in existing assessments of the challenges facing the region. The question of the benefits that the LAC region receives from forests and biodiversity, however, is complex. There often is confusion regarding biodiversity and ecosystem services and environmental damage. Environmental

Table 4.9 *Estimates of the value of LAC biodiversity benefits*

Unit	Value of benefits ($)	Authors and source
LAC ecosystem services	Pro-rated from global estimate to 3.2–11 trillion annually for Latin America[a]	Constanza *et al.* (1997)
Carbon captured in the LAC forest	3.4 trillion net benefits (carbon valued at $20/ton)[a]	Derived from Pearce (1996)
LAC ecosystem	Pharmaceutical value 20.63 per ha in Western Ecuador	Simpson, Sedjo, and Reid (1996)

Note: [a] The LAC region was assumed to be one-fifth of the world system, roughly based on land area. It would be smaller based on GDP or population. Based on threatened species, it might be as large as one-third.

damage can be large without any direct threat to biodiversity,[12] while biodiversity can be threatened with minimal other environmental damage.

Table 4.9 provides estimates of the benefit values of forest ecosystems derived from the sources discussed above. In the absence of any LAC-specific information, the value of forest ecosystems is simply a pro-rated value from the global estimates provided in table 4.8. Note that there are only three estimates of the value of benefits provided in the two tables: those derived from Constanza *et al.* (1997), Pearce (1996), and Simpson, Sedjo, and Reid (1996).

As already noted, Constanza *et al.* (1997) estimate the total value of all of the earth's ecosystem services. When pro-rated to the LAC region, this gives an estimate of the value of ecosystem services as $3.2–11.0 trillion annually. This study has been heavily criticized for various reasons. A different approach to estimating the value of forest/biodiversity

---

[12] A 2007 article has discussed environmental damage in "some of the world's most biodiverse rain forest." Although the article describes various types of environmental damage, it provides no discussion about threatened species or genetic resources, nor does it make any mention of threats to biodiversity as defined in this chapter. It does, however, imply concerns over future ecosystem services. See www.csmonitor.com/2007/0507/p04s01-woam.html.

systems in the region is to consider its value for carbon sequestration services, as done by Pearce (1996). This approach is straightforward in that the estimate is made from components that, at least in concept, are easily measurable – that is the value of carbon sequestered in forest systems. We have estimates of the value of sequestered carbon as transacted in markets; however, the prices are quite variable.

Pearce examined the various regions separately and thus provides some information specific to the LAC region. He concludes that "avoiding deforestation becomes a legitimate and potentially important means of reducing global warming rates" (1996: 31).

Using Pearce's average of 100 tons of carbon per ha for 1 billion ha of forest in the LAC region provides an estimate that about 100 billion tons of carbon would be sequestered by the forest. This estimate is consistent with that of the FAO (2006) for LAC forest carbon. Using a value of $20 per ton for sequestered carbon gives the estimate that the value of the ecosystem services provided by the region is about $2 trillion. If the value of the 70 billion tons of carbon in the dead wood, litter, and soils noted by the FAO is included (FAO 2006), the additional value is $1.4 trillion for a total value of $3.4 trillion.

Costs of protecting LAC forests and biodiversity

This section draws on the earlier sections estimating the global or near-global benefits and costs of forest ecosystems and adapting these to the LAC region. The approach is to pro-rate the global estimates to the region using a one-fifth factor, since it has roughly one-fifth of the earth's forest area.

An early study proposed a tradable systems approach for international forest protection (Sedjo 1991, 1992a, 1992b), with a major objective being to maintain biodiversity by preserving and protecting forest habitat. The study estimated the opportunity costs of closed-canopy forest land in other uses – that is, the costs of preventing forest conversion – and used this as an estimate of the cost necessary to keep the land in natural forest. The total opportunity cost of the world's 2.655 billion ha of closed-canopy forest was estimated at about $26.4 billion annually.[13] For South America, the average annual opportunity costs used were those estimated by Browder (1988), which are $183/ha

---

[13] With the use of a 10% real discount rate.

in 2005 dollars. At this land price, South and Central America's entire 670 million ha of closed forest was estimated to have a total opportunity cost of $12.3 billion annually (adjusted to 2005 dollars).[14]

It is sometimes suggested that most biodiversity could be preserved in a protected area of about 10% of the total ecosystem. In this case, the forest area to be preserved would be reduced to 67 million ha at an annual cost of around $1.23 billion. This estimate of land area necessary to preserve most biodiversity comports closely with Conservation International's estimate of LAC biodiversity "hot spots," which identifies seven regions and about 65 million ha there.[15]

In another global study of the costs of protecting global biodiversity, James *et al.* (2001) estimate that between 10% and 15% of global biodiversity could be protected for about $18–$27.5 billion per year. If one-fifth of the global total is pro-rated to the region, the amount would be roughly $3.5–5.5 billion annually.

Pearce (1996) also estimates the cost of preventing the forests from being converted to other uses in a similar manner to the studies above. He asks what level of compensation would be necessary to bid the land away from alternative uses and keep it in its current forested state. Using Schneider's (1992) estimate of the value of the cleared land at about $300 per ha, Pearce suggests that an average, one-time payment of $500 per ha could keep the land in forest. This is a cost estimate of about $500 billion to provide for the permanent protection of the entire 1 billion ha of LAC forests with their carbon sequestration services. Indeed, if Pearce had applied his approach to estimate the value of the entire global forest of 4 billion ha, table 4.8 summarizes this discussion of the costs and presents four very broad estimates of the costs of maintaining forest ecosystems to provide biodiversity and carbon sequestration services.

In another paper, Brumer *et al.* (2001) argued that 70% of global biodiversity (about 2% of the earth's terrestrial surface) could be protected at an additional cost of $19 billion above current expenditures, or about $29 billion annually. Pro-rating one-fifth to the region

---

[14] Browder's estimate, while dated, is similar to the much more recent estimates land opportunity cost estimates for Central America of $127 per ha and South America of $147 (cited in Chatham House Workshop, April 16–17, 2007, www.chathamhouse.org.uk/pdf/research/sdp/160407workshop.pdf).

[15] www.biodiversityhotspots.org/xp/Hotspots/.

provides an estimate of about $5.8 billion annually to protect 70% of LAC's biodiversity. For comparison, Simpson (2004) estimates current worldwide expenditures on biodiversity conservation at about $10 billion annually.

A more recent study by Grieg-Gran (2006) focuses on avoiding deforestation. The approach uses financial incentives to compensate owners for lost market value. The approach focused on eight countries that accounted for 6.2 million ha, or 46%, of global net deforestation from 2000 to 2005. The LAC countries included are Brazil and Bolivia. The goal of this study was not to protect the entire forest or even a fixed percentage of it. Rather, the study was designed to estimate the cost of preventing deforestation by compensating owners for keeping the land, which would have been deforested, in forest. The target was to offset the expected 6.2 million ha of annual deforestation, which has been the rate of deforestation in recent years. The causes of deforestation varied by region, with most deforestation in Brazil and Bolivia generated by conversion to pasturelands, while in Indonesia much of the conversion has been driven by land conversion to palm oil production. The study estimates the compensation costs at roughly $5 billion to permanently secure the 6.2 million ha in forest. Unlike most other studies, it explicitly included administrative and monitoring costs, which are estimated at $4–$15/ha per year and, thus, an additional $25–$93 million.[16] However, this payment would persist indefinitely and increase as additional lands were protected from deforestation.

In concept, the program would add an additional 6.2 million ha in protected forest in year 2 and subsequent years. If the program continued for ten years, the administrative and monitoring costs would be running at between $250 million and almost $1 billion per year. Also, since the concept involves monitoring and protection indefinitely, those costs of $250 million–$1 billion would continue indefinitely even if the basic program of adding new areas of forest were discontinued. However, the study notes that the actual costs are likely to be higher than programmed because of leakage[17] and administrative expenses.

---

[16] Measurement and monitoring promise to be substantial challenges to any attempt to protect topical forests. See Defries *et al.* (2007).

[17] "Leakage" refers to the shifting of deforestation within the country; that is, the situation where preventing deforestation in one location only deflects it to another forest.

Kindermann *et al.* (unpublished) use three economic models of global land use and management to analyze the potential contribution and cost of carbon credits to provide incentives for avoided deforestation activities to reduce greenhouse gas emissions. These models estimate the costs associated with a reduction of deforestation below the trend for 2030. The study finds that an average of about $3 per ton of CO_2, or about $0.4– $1.2 billion per year in 2030, would generate a 10% reduction in deforestation rates. The present value (PV) of the total costs using a 10% discount rate is roughly $4– $12 billion for the 10% reduction case. They estimate that a $20 per ton of CO_2 credit would reduce CO_2 deforestation emissions by 50%, or 1.5–3.4 Gt CO_2/year by 2030. This program would require $1.72–$2.80 billion per year through 2030 or a PV at 10% of $17.2–$28.0 billion for the 50% reduction case. However, the information cannot be used for this chapter since the study does not provide sufficient information to calculate the full costs of the project, nor does it report on deforestation avoided in the transitional thirty years.

Finally, Simpson, Sedjo, and Reid (1996), while not estimating costs specifically, find biodiversity values that are considerably below the opportunity costs of the land as reported in numerous other studies (e.g. Browder 1988; Schneider 1992).

These models are applied to the various tropical regions separately, including the LAC region. South and Central America have marginal costs similar to those for the rest of the globe, although the volume of carbon captured by avoided deforestation is a relatively large proportion: about three-eighths of the total, depending upon the price.

Note that the first three studies focus on the costs of establishing permanent forest reserves adequate to protect core biodiversity. The Grieg-Gran (2006) study, by contrast, estimates the cost of halting all deforestation in high-incidence countries with targeted (purchased) compensation each year for several years and with continuing monitoring. This study assumes that the remainder of the forest will provide its values without compensation. The Kindermann *et al.* (unpublished) study focuses on the costs of undertaking substantial investments gradually to reduce the rate of deforestation compared to the trend. The Pearce (1996) study focuses on the value of sequestered carbon and asks how much compensation would be required to all forest owners for not releasing the carbon through deforestation. Simpson, Sedjo,

Table 4.10 *Estimates of the costs of protection for LAC biodiversity*

Estimate (year)	% protected	Cost ($)
Sedjo (1992a, 1992b)	10% of closed forest (67 million ha) area, e.g. "hot spots"	1.23 billion annually (rental)
Chatham House (2007) James (2001)[a]	10–15% of forest land	3.5–5.5 billion annually (rental)
Pimm *et al.* (2001)[a]	1.4% of tropical forest	6.0 billion for land purchase
Brumer *et al.* (2001)[a]	2% of terrestrial area	5.8 billion annually
Pearce (1996)	100% of forest area,[a] LAC	500 billion one time, or 25 billion annually discounted at 5%
Grieg-Gran (2006)	6.2 million ha/year (1.5%) each year for indefinite period or an accumulation of about 1.5% of the global forest annually	5 billion purchase payment and 25–100 million each year for administration
Kindermann *et al.* (unpublished)	Reduce rate of deforestation from 10% to 50%	Cost is PV 4.0–12.0 billion for the period through 2030; for a 10% reduction case PV of costs 17.2–28.0 billion for the period through 2030 for the 50% reduction case
Simpson, Sedjo, and Reid (1996)	100%	Costs equal opportunity costs of the land at roughly 150–200/ha

Note: [a] Pro-rated from global estimates assuming the LAC region has one-fifth of the area and costs.

and Reid (1996) do not explicitly estimate the costs of protection. Rather, they implicitly use the market land price as an estimate of the cost. Table 4.10 summarizes these cost estimates for Latin American biodiversity.

Table 4.11 *BCRs for saving LAC forest/biodiversity*

Constanza *et al.*'s (1997) benefits (all ecosystem services) and Sedjo's (1992a, 1992b) (forest land costs)	Benefit-cost = 32,000–110,000/1.2 = 2,666–9,166 (Sedjo/Chatham House's low-cost estimate)
Constanza *et al.*'s (1997) benefits (all ecosystem services) and Brumer *et al.*'s (forest costs)	Benefit-cost = 32,000–110,000/5.8 = 572–1,896. (Brumer *et al.*'s 2001 high-cost estimate)
Pearce (1996) benefits (carbon storage) and costs (forest land values)	Benefit-cost = $2 trillion/$0.5 trillion = 4.0 (Pearce's 1996 cost and benefit estimates)
Carbon storage benefits derived from Pearce (1996) and Grieg-Gran (2006) avoided deforestation costs	Benefit-cost = $12.4 billion/$5.2 billion = 2.4 (carbon benefits and Grieg-Gran (2006) costs)
Benefits per ha (biodiversity for drugs) (Simpson, Sedjo, and Reid 1996)	Benefit-cost per ha = $20.63/$150 = 0.137 Costs per ha from selected land value estimates (Browder 1988, Schneider 1992)

7 Proposed solutions: benefits and costs

Benefits and costs

Four B/C calculations are reported in table 4.11. The first two use Constanza *et al.*'s high-benefit estimate with the low- and high-cost estimates from the literature. Although Constanza *et al.*'s estimates have been criticized, they are prominent in the literature. Also, they do provide the high-end boundary for benefits. The third benefit-cost (B/C) calculation is that implicated in Pearce's work, where the benefits are all derived from sequestered carbon conservatively valued. Finally, the fourth B/C calculation uses Pearce's benefits approach, calculating the carbon sequestration values of the forest protected in the Grieg-Gran study and matching it with their cost estimates.

The solutions using Constanza *et al.*'s benefits tend to generate massive BCRs, especially since these are placed against fairly modest cost estimates. The Pearce study has the advantage that both benefits and costs were addressed by the same researcher in a consistent manner.

The Pearce estimate of values is large, but so are his costs. The BCR of the fourth calculation appears reasonable, suggesting that forests provide a useful and relatively low-cost mechanism for addressing the damage associated with carbon emissions.

The final estimate focuses on the carbon benefits of preventing deforestation – a timely issue. The emissions avoided by avoiding deforestation are substantial, as is the associated damage that is avoided. The BCR of 2.4 is favorable. However, the research acknowledges that the costs of controlling leakage and monitoring are substantial, and continue indefinitely.

Results

These results indicate a range of BCRs from 0.134 to 9,166 using cost and benefit estimates from the literature. Benefit estimates are substantially more difficult to undertake and were done by only three researchers: Constanza, Pearce, and Simpson, Sedjo, and Reid. Few find Constanza *et al.*'s estimates creditable, due to both the nature of the methodology and the advocacy nature of the estimates. By contrast, Pearce's methodology is clear and sensible. Respectable estimates of benefits are obtained by looking at carbon capture – a service where market prices exist and where estimates of physical values are fairly straightforward. Although Pearce estimated the value for only one output – carbon storage services – this value appears to be large and important. Simpson, Sedjo, and Reid also provided useful estimates, but also for only one output – biodiversity for pharmaceuticals use. This value, while potentially large in the aggregate, is small compared to its cost, which is the opportunity cost of the land.

On the cost side, Grieg-Gran does the most comprehensive job of assessing costs. Details are included that examine the alternative uses of the forestland and develop opportunity costs accordingly. However, because the approach attempts to differentiate between lands that will be compensated and those that will not, substantial monitoring costs would be necessary and leakage is likely to be great and difficult to control.

A weakness of these aggregate results is that, in all of these cases but one, the costs and benefits were estimated independently by different groups of researchers. By far the most creditable estimates are those of Pearce since one researcher estimated both the costs and benefits in a consistent and creditable manner. Combining Pearce's benefits approach with the cost estimates of Grieg-Gran provides both a sensible combination of literature approaches and believable results.

Proposed solutions: overview of approach

The approach of this study is to examine the broad literature and several estimates of benefits and costs from these various sources and determine which of them have a scope and information that can be useful in the chapter's analysis.

The benefit side typically is more difficult to measure and the estimates more suspect. This is because benefits typically are not transacted in markets and, hence, are difficult to quantify. Approaches often use various CV techniques, typically survey approaches such as WTP. These approaches, and their application to specific examples, are discussed in some detail in this chapter. The benefit estimates of this approach remain somewhat controversial. Where the benefit outputs can be transacted in markets, however, as in the carbon sequestration services of forests, the estimates may be less controversial.

It should be noted that much of the existing literature deals with estimating the value of specific species, such as Alaskan salmon or the northern spotted owl, found in specific ecosystems or at specific locations. Typically, these studies are done in small and unique areas. For species, the focus usually is on a single activity, such as hunting or bird watching. For ecosystem outputs, the focus is also usually on one output, such as an aspect of water for a limited region. Upon investigation, these studies have been determined to be of limited usefulness for the current project of identifying solutions, because of their limited focus.

After reviewing the literature, this chapter moves to the identification of the few larger studies that take a continental or global perspective. First, regarding the value of biodiversity, only two studies were found that estimated the benefits value specifically of species biodiversity at the continental or global level (Simpson, Sedjo, and Reid 1996 and Rausser and Small 2000). These studies, which look at bioprospecting and estimate the value of the benefits of biodiversity as an input into pharmaceutical production, take a global perspective. However, they are limited to examining only one output – that of the value of biodiversity in the production of pharmaceuticals; other values are not addressed. The Simpson, Sedjo, and Reid study is used for some of the cost-benefit ratios.

Two other studies, Constanza *et al.* (1997) and Pearce (1996), esti-mate the values of the benefits of ecosystems and are used in our analysis. Constanza *et al.* develop an estimate of the aggregate value of global ecosystem services. Pearce derives an estimate of the value of the services of the forest in sequestering carbon. Although Pearce's study does not include all the outputs in its evaluation of benefits, it does demonstrate that the value of ecosystem services is quite large. In fact, Pearce's paper argues that the other values of ecosystem services are fairly modest. In this chapter, we adapt Pearce's carbon sequestration estimate, although admittedly conservative due to the absence of other outputs, as a component of our solutions analysis. The estimates of Constanza *et al.* and Pearce are utilized in our solutions-assessment process.

The cost-side estimates generally are less difficult to obtain and are viewed as more reliable. The approach often involves estimates of the opportunity costs of maintaining the land in habitat for environmen-tal and ecosystem uses rather than converting it to development or agricultural uses. Markets tend to provide information on opportunity costs of the land in the form of land market prices or land rents.

The costs are examined in seven cited studies. Three studies (Sedjo 1991, 1992a, 1992b, Brumer *et al.* 2001; and James *et al.* 2001) exam-ine the costs associated with preserving existing ecosystems and forests globally and provide information at the global or continental level. These studies are oriented to estimating the costs of protecting the ecosystem, and provide estimates of the portion of the global ecosystem that needs to be protected, such as 10% of the forests. Pearce's study is the only one that provides estimates of benefits and costs. His cost estimates are derived in a manner similar to Sedjo, in that he estimates the opportunity costs of the land by reference to average market prices. However, since his focus is on sequestration and not on simply protect-ing a representative sample of species biodiversity, he incurs the costs of protecting the entire forest, not just some fraction of it. Additionally, the studies of Grieg-Gran (2006) and Kindermann *et al.* (unpublished) provide estimates of the costs of preventing deforestation in areas of the world that currently are experiencing large-scale deforestation. How-ever, Kindermann *et al.*'s estimates are incomplete and are not used in this chapter's analysis. In these, as with the aforementioned studies,

Table 4.12 *Solution 1: BCR for saving LAC forest/biodiversity through the biodiversity values for drugs*

Benefits per ha (biodiversity for drugs) (Simpson, Sedjo, and Reid 1996)	BCR per ha = \$20.63/\$150 = 0.137 Costs per ha from selected land value estimates (Browder 1988, Schneider 1992)

costs are derived using land prices as a measure of opportunity costs. Although none of these studies provides estimates of the values of the benefits, their estimates of the costs are viewed as sensible, and are used in our solutions-assessment process. Finally, the Simpson, Sedjo, and Reid (1996) study provides estimates of the values of biodiversity for drug production as well as the basis for estimating the costs.

Some solutions

Four possible solutions are developed in the chapter, using our set of three benefit estimates and six cost estimates. The solutions use three of the benefit estimates and relate them to an appropriate cost estimate. Four possible solutions are proposed using several estimates of benefits and costs chosen selectively from these various sources. BCRs for each solution are developed. A discussion of each is presented and a preferred solution is chosen based on the BCR and other considerations.

Solution 1: protecting biodiversity for its value in drugs

For solution 1, the value of the land as a repository for biodiversity was estimated by Simpson, Sedjo, and Reid. The costs of protection are the opportunity costs of the land for other uses (table 4.12). The stated BCR of 0.134 suggests that even the lands most rich in biodiversity are unlikely to justify the repository status solely on the basis of the probability that the biodiversity may some day be useful for drugs and medicines.

Solution 2: protecting forests to prevent carbon emissions

Solution 2 combines Pearce's estimates of benefits with the cost approach of Grieg-Gran for restraining deforestation in regions with high recent rates of deforestation (table 4.13). This approach has the

Table 4.13 *Solution 2: BCR for saving LAC forest/biodiversity through payments for avoided deforestation*

Carbon benefits derived from Pearce (1996) and Grieg-Gran (2006) costs	BCR = \$12.4 billion/\$5.2 billion = 2.4 (carbon benefits and Grieg-Gran (2006) costs)

advantage of using the strongest estimates of benefits and costs available in the literature for large-scale projects of this type. The benefits side uses the estimated values of the ecosystem for keeping forest carbon from being released into the atmosphere – estimates that are based on the actual price experience in the EU carbon market. The cost approach is comprehensive, with the objective to avoid deforestation. The costs, as with most of the other studies, are based upon compensation based on the opportunity costs of keeping the land in forest. This approach also included estimates of administration and monitoring costs, something that is absent from all of the other cost estimates. A unique feature of this approach is that compensation is not provided for all forestlands, but only for those determined to be likely candidates for deforestation. This reduces overall costs but is susceptible to leakage problems, which the author acknowledges. The BCR of this solution is about 2.4.

For this estimate, the benefits are likely to be somewhat higher than listed because only carbon sequestration benefits were assessed; however, the carbon benefits may be somewhat lower because complete success in avoiding all deforestation is unlikely. However, the costs are also likely to be somewhat higher because some additional compensation may be required to prevent leakage. In addition, the likely administrative and monitoring costs have only crudely entered the B/C calculation.

Solution 3: protecting ecosystems for ecosystem services

Solution 3 justifies protecting forest and biodiversity on the basis of ecosystem services provided (table 4.14). The benefits are drawn from those estimated by Constanza *et al.* for the globe. Although these have been highly criticized, they are the only ecosystem benefit estimates available for very large, continental-size regions, and are estimated at \$11 trillion for the LAC region. Note that this estimate has been criticized for being both too high and too low (Toman 1998). However,

Table 4.14 *Solution 3: BCR for LAC ecosystem services*

Constanza *et al.*'s (1997) benefits and Sedjo's (1992a, 1992b) costs	BCR = 32,000–110,000/1.2 = 2,666–9,166 (Sedjo/Chatham House's low-cost estimate)
Constanza *et al.*'s (1997) benefits and Brumer *et al.*'s (2001) costs	BCR = 32,000–110,000/5.8 = 572–1,896 (Brumer *et al.*'s (2001) high-cost estimate)

Table 4.15 *Solution 4: BCR for saving LAC forest/biodiversity through payments for carbon sequestration*

Pearce (1996) benefits and costs	BCR = $2 trillion/$0.5 trillion = 4.0 (Pearce's cost and benefit estimates)

the value of the ecosystem for carbon storage is $3.4 trillion, so even without other values, Constanza *et al.*'s estimate is within an order of magnitude. Furthermore, if carbon prices escalate as expected, thereby raising Pearce's estimate, and other ecosystem service values are large, which seems reasonable, Constanza *et al.*'s estimate becomes even more within the range of being comparable. It may be that Constanza *et al.* is right for the wrong reason.

One reason why the costs tend to be low in the avoided deforestation at the marginal solutions is that there are some lands in which the forests would be the highest-value use and thus no payments would be necessary. Thus the average opportunity cost per ha would be drawn down by lands submarginal for non-forest use.

Solution 4: protecting forests for carbon values

Solution 4 is a different approach to estimating the value of forest/biodiversity systems in the region: considering its value for carbon sequestration services, as was done by Pearce (1996) (table 4.15). This approach is the most straightforward in that the estimate is made from components that, at least in concept, are easily measurable and include the carbon sequestered in forest systems and the value of sequestered carbon as transacted in markets.

With the advent of concern about global warming and the role of carbon and carbon dioxide in that warming, it is possible to estimate the value of a forest for sequestrating carbon. Market transactions in the EU Climate Exchange have placed the value of carbon for atmospheric carbon reduction within a wide range: from $10 to $100 per ton.[18] While volatile, at least a market price is available. The total LAC forest covers about 1 billion ha. The amount of carbon captured in a forest varies considerably, depending on the species, age, and density of the stand. Old, primary tropical forest may have 300 tons of carbon, while younger forests may have 100 tons. Using Pearce's average of 100 tons of carbon per ha for 1 billion ha of forest in the region provides an estimate that about 100 billion tons of carbon would be sequestered by the forest. This estimate is consistent with that of the FAO (2006) for LAC forest carbon. Using a value of $20 per ton for sequestered carbon provides the estimate that the value of the ecosystem services provided by the LAC forest is about $2 trillion. If the value of the 70 billion tons of carbon in the dead wood, litter, and soils of the forest noted by the FAO (FAO 2006) are included, the additional value is $1.4 trillion, for a total value of $3.4 trillion. Estimated global values for the services of ecosystems and forests are presented in table 4.7.

Extending Pearce's approach globally would result in global benefits valued at about $12 trillion. This number is not vastly different than that of Constanza *et al.* Pearce also estimates the costs of preventing the forests from being converted to other uses in a similar manner to the above studies. He asks what level of compensation would be necessary to bid the land away from alternative uses and keep it in its current forested state. Using Schneider's (1992) estimate of the value of the cleared land at about $300 per ha, Pearce suggests that an average, one-time payment of $500 per ha could keep the land in forest. This provides a cost estimate of about $500 billion to provide for the permanent protection of the entire 1 billion ha of LAC forests with their carbon sequestration services. Indeed, if Pearce had applied his approach to estimate the value of the entire global forest of 4 billion ha, table 4.8 summarizes this discussion of the costs and presents four very broad estimates for maintaining forest ecosystems to provide biodiversity and carbon sequestration services.

---

[18] This is equivalent to $2.73 and $27.30 per ton of carbon dioxide, respectively.

Choice of solution

Several authors have noted that most biodiversity could be saved by protecting only a relatively few "hot spots," and protecting them is estimated to require only relatively modest amounts of money. However, it is clear from the data presented above that the estimated benefits of protecting biodiversity alone have not been shown to justify the protection of massive amounts of forest. Furthermore, protecting "hot spots" only would not generate the very substantial estimated benefits associated with protecting forest areas for their carbon sequestration benefits. Thus, our choice of solution is driven largely by considerations of the benefits associated with forest carbon sequestration.

Solution 1, which addresses the protection of biodiversity for the purpose of maintaining biodiversity values for drugs and medicines, does not give a favorable BCR (only 0.134). A problem with this solution is that the benefits capture only the value of biodiversity as inputs to drugs, and ignore other values.

Solution 3 has the highest apparent BCR from the mid-100s to close to 10,000. However, as noted, the estimate of total ecosystem benefits has been highly criticized. Also, while all of the cost estimates cover forests, none of them appears to cover completely the full costs of maintaining the entire range of ecosystems. Instead, they are focused only on forest systems. So, the benefit estimates are suspect, while the cost estimates could be too low.

Solutions 2 and 4 seem the most reasonable and provide sensible and acceptable BCRs. Solution 2 has a BCR of 2.4, while solution 4 has a BCR of 4.0. These two solutions focus on the benefits from carbon storage associated with avoiding deforestation. Both of these are driven by the benefits associated with the value of forest carbon emissions avoided. Since other ecological benefits are not considered, the benefits are likely on the conservative side. Solution 2 focuses on avoiding deforestation at the margin, while solution 4 examines avoiding deforestation in the entire system. Solution 2 is more realistic in that it includes monitoring costs and recognizes that some benefits will be provided without costs to the project.

Table 4.16 presents the solutions ranking. I maintain that solution 2 is the desired solution; it has the advantage of working on the margin, where deforestation is high. Forests that are not about

Table 4.16 *Solutions ranking*

Ranking	Solution	Activity	BCR	Analysis source
First	2	Payments for avoided deforestation: Selected forests	2.4	Pearce (1996) and Grieg-Gran (2006)
Second	4	Payments for avoided deforestation: Large-scale	4.0	Pearce (1996)
Other	3	Forest set-aside	2,666 +	Constanza *et al.* (1997) Sedjo/Chatham House
Other	1	Protect for biodiversity values	0.134	Simpson, Sedjo, and Reid (1996), Browder (1988), Schneider (1992).

to be harvested need not receive compensation. Although in concept this is desirable, leakage will be a problem. However, the benefits are sufficiently large that some slippage can occur, perhaps associated with developing workable implementation systems, and the project still would still be economically viable by the cost–benefit calculus.

In the LAC context, areas of high deforestation could be identifiable at the national level and a compensation package could be applied at the country level. The country may then be given the task of implementing the policy domestically, with payment made upon successful performance. Periodic payments could be made for periodic performance, allowing for withholding payments from countries that are not successful.

The above discussion provides a range of general or average cost estimates that might be needed to protect LAC biodiversity. The costs are generic and are unrelated to any particular approach to protection. Rather, the costs reflect the market opportunity costs of the habitat to be protected and do not account for the costs of administering such a program. Of course, if the biodiversity values were private goods transacted in markets, a non-market-administered program would not be necessary. However, it is the externality aspect of biodiversity that makes an essentially non-market-oriented approach necessary.

8 Conclusions

The empirical evidence on the costs and benefits of protecting forest ecosystems and biodiversity is limited, particularly for large global or continental systems. Most of the considerable research on biodiversity benefits has focused on the value of individual species for a specific purpose or a confined ecosystem, often for only one of its multiple outputs.

There is more evidence for the costs of protecting species and ecosystems than for the benefits. The data on the costs of protecting individual species is very specific and narrow in focus. The information on protection of individual ecosystems is slightly more robust. Most studies apply to the United States, and deal with only one aspect of ecosystem services; even in the United States, there are only a few studies that look at forest ecosystems or biodiversity broadly and most focus on a single aspect, such as water or recreation.

Globally, there are a very few studies that look at the benefits of global or large regional ecosystems, or that look at the costs. Only two studies, Pearce (1996) and Simpson, Sedjo, and Reid (1996), have looked at both benefits and costs. Additionally, although no studies have been directed specifically at the LAC region, several of them have looked at this issue from a global perspective and have some regionally specific information or estimates.

This chapter estimated forest or ecosystem service benefits using information from Pearce (1996), Simpson, Sedjo, and Reid (1996), and Constanza *et al.* (1997). The range of costs used was found in six studies: Kindermann (unpublished), Sedjo (1992a, 1992b), Pearce (1996), Brumer *et al.* (2001), James (2001), and Grieg-Gran (2006). A preferred "solution" is suggested based on an estimate of the value of avoided deforestation for carbon sequestration derived from Pearce (1996) and a program to retard deforestation through compensation for retaining forests. A cost component of this approach involved that of monitoring the condition of the forest.

Bibliography

Abdalla, C.A., B.A. Roach, and D.J. Epp, 1992. "Valuing Environmental Groundwater Changes Using Averting Expenditures: An Application to Groundwater Contamination." *Land Economics* **68**: 163–9

Aylward, B.A., 1993. "A Case Study of Pharmaceutical Prospecting." In B.A. Alyward, J. Echeverria, L. Fendt, and E.B. Barbier, eds., *The Economic Value of Species Information and Its Role in Biodiversity Conservation: Case Studies of Costa Rica's National Biodiversity Institute and Pharmaceutical Prospecting.* London: Environmental Economics Centre

Baillie, J.E.M., C. Hilton-Taylor, and S.N. Stuart, eds., 2004. *2004 IUCN Red List of Threatened Species. A Global Species Assessment.* Gland, Switzerland and Cambridge: IUCN

Balmford, A., K. Gaston, S. Blyth, A. James, and V. Kapos, 2003. "Global Variation in Terrestrial Conservation Costs, Conservation Benefits, and Unmet Conservation Needs." *Proceedings of the National Academy of Sciences* **100**: 1046–50

Banzhaf, H.S., D. Burtraw, D. Evans, and A.J. Krupuick, 2006. "Valuation of Natural Resources in the Adirondacks." *Land Economics* **82**(3): 445–64

Bell, K. P., D. Huppert, and R. L. Johnson, 2003. "Willingness to Pay for Local Coho Salmon Enhancement in Coastal Communities." *Marine Resource Economics* **18**: 15–31

Berrens, R.P., P. Ganderton, and C.L. Silva, 1996. "Valuing the Protection of Minimum Instream Flows in New Mexico." *Journal of Agricultural and Resource Economics* **21**: 294–309

Berrens, R.P., A.K. Bohara, C.L. Silva, D. Brookshire, and M. McKee, 2000. "Contingent Values for New Mexico Instream Flows: With Tests of Scope, Group-Size Reminder and Temporal Reliability." *Journal of Environmental Management* **58**: 73–90

Bockstael, N., A.M. Freeman, R.J. Kopp, P.R. Portney, and V.K. Smith, 2000. "On Measuring Economic Values for Nature." *Environmental Science and Technology* **34**: 1384–9

Bowker, J.M. and J.R. Stoll, 1988. "Use of Dichotomous Choice Nonmarket Methods to Value the Whooping Crane Resource." *American Journal of Agricultural Economics* **70**: 372–81

Boyle, K.J., 1990. "Dichotomous Choice, Contingent Valuation Questions: Functional Form is Important." *Northeastern Journal of Agriculture and Resource Economics* **19**: 125–31

Boyle, K.J. and R.C. Bishop, 1987. "Valuing Wildlife in Benefit-Cost Analyses: A Case Study Involving Endangered Species." *Water Resources Research* **23**: 943–50

Brock W.A. and A. Xepapadeas, 2003. "Valuing Biodiversity from an Economic Perspective: A Unified Economic, Ecological, and Genetic Approach." *American Economic Review* **93**(5): 1597–1614

Brooks, D. R., R.L. Mayden, and D.A. McLennan, 1992. "Phylogeny and Biodiversity: Conserving our Evolutionary Legacy." *Trends in Ecology & Evolution* 7(2): 55–9

Brookshire, D., L. Eubanks, and A. Randall, 1983. "Estimating Option Prices and Existence Values for Wildlife Resources." *Land Economics* 59: 1–15

Browder, John O., 1988. "Public Policy and Deforestation in the Brazilian Amazon." In R. Repetto and M. Gillis, eds., *Public Policies and the Misuse of Forest Resources.* New York: Cambridge University Press

Brown, G.M., Jr. and J.F. Shogren, 1998 "The Economics of the Endangered Species Act." *Journal of Economic Perspectives* 12(3): 3–20

Brumer, Aaron, Richard E. Rice, and Gustavo da Fonseca, 2001. *Beyond Fences: Seeking Social Sustainability in Conservation.* Gland, Switzerland: IUCN

Carson, R.T. and M.W. Hanemann, 2005. "Contingent Valuation." In K.-G. Mäler and J. R. Vincent, eds., *Handbook of Environmental Economics,* 2. Amsterdam: Elsevier

Chambers, C.M. and J.C. Whitehead, 2003. "A Contingent Valuation Estimate of the Benefits of Wolves in Minnesota." *Environmental and Resource Economics* 26: 249–67

Chatham House 2007. Briefing paper, "Illegal 'Logging'," www.chathamhouse.org.onc/files/9384_bp0707illegallogging.pdf

Chichilnisky, G. and G. Heal, 1998. "Economic Returns from the Biosphere." *Nature* 391: 629–30

Convention on Biodiversity, 2007. www.biodiv.org/2010-target/focal.shtml, accessed February 2, 2007

Costanza, Robert, Ralph d'Arge, Rudolf de Groot, Stephen Farber, Monica Grasso, Bruce Hannon, Karin Limburg, Shahid Naeem, Robert V. O'Neill, José Paruelo, Robert G. Raskin, Paul Sutton, and Marjan van den Belt, 1997. "The Value of the World's Ecosystem Services and Natural Capital." *Nature* 387: 253–60

Costello, C. and M. Ward, 2006. "Search, Bioprospecting, and Biodiversity Conservation." *Journal of Environmental Economics and Management* 52(3): 615–26

Council on Environmental Quality, 1980. *Global 2000 Report to the President,* vol. 2. Washington, DC: Council on Environmental Quality

Cummings, R., P. Gandertow, and T. McGuckin, 1994. "Substitution Effects in CVM values." *American Journal of Agricultural Economics.* 76: 205–14

Daily, G.C., ed., 1997. *Nature's Services: Societal Dependence on Natural Ecosystems.* Washington, DC: Island Press

Dalton, R., 2004. "Bioprospects Less than Golden." *Nature* 249: 598–600

Defries, R., F. Achard, S. Brown, M. Herold, D. Murdiyarso, B. Schlamadinger, and C. de Souza, Jr., 2007. "Earth Observation for Estimating Greenhouse Gas Emissions from Deforestation in Developing Countries." *Environmental Sccience & Policy* 10: 385–94

Diamond, P.A. and J.A. Hausman, 1994. "Contingent Valuation: Is Some Number Better Than No Number?" *Journal of Economic Perspectives* 8(4): 45–64

Duffield, J. 1991. "Existence and Non-Consumptive Values for Wildlife: Application of Wolf Recovery in Yellowstone National Park." Western Regional Research Publication **W-133**. Western Regional Science Association Joint Session, Measuring Non-Market and Non-Use Values. Monterey, CA

1992. "An Economic Valuation of Wolf Recovery in Yellowstone: Park Visitor Attitudes And Values." In J. Varley and W. Brewster, eds., *Wolves for Yellowstone?* National Park Service, Yellowstone National Park

Duffield, J. and D. Patterson, 1992. "Field Testing Existence Values: Comparison of Hypothetical and Cash Transaction Values." Benefits and Costs in Natural Resource Planning, 5th Report. Western Regional Research Publication **W-133**, compiled by B. Rettig, Department of Agricultural and Resource Economics. Corvallis, OR: Oregon State University

Duffield, J., D. Patterson, and C. Neher, 1993. "Wolves and People in Yellowstone: A Case Study in the New Resource Economics." Report to Liz Claiborne and Art Ortenberg Foundation, Department of Economics. Missoula, MT: University of Montana

Food and Agriculture Organization (FAO), 2000

2005. "Global Forest Resources Assessment 2005: Progress Towards Sustainable Forest Management." FAO Forestry Paper **147**. Rome: FAO

2006. *The State of the World's Forests.* Rome: UNFAO

Gaston, K.G., 2000. "Global Patterns in Biodiversity." *Nature* **405**: 220–7

Giraud, K., B. Turcin, J. Loomis, and J. Cooper, 2002. "Economic Benefit of the Protection Program for the Steller Sea Lion." *Marine Policy* **26**: 451–8

Giraud, K.L., J.B. Loomis, and R.L. Johnson, 1999. "Internal and External Scope in Willingness-To-Pay Estimates for Threatened and Endangered Wildlife." *Journal of Environmental Management* **59**: 221–9

Giraud, K. and B. Valcic, 2004. "Willingness-to-Pay Estimates and Geographic Embedded Samples: Case Study of Alaskan Steller Sea Lion." *Journal of International Wildlife Law and Policy* 7: 57–72

Global Crop Diversity Trust, 2007. *Regional Strategies: Americas: 2007,* www.croptrust.org/main/regional.php?itemid=83, accessed March 2007

Greig-Gran, M. 2006. "The Costs of Avoiding Reforestation." Background Paper for the Stern Review of the Economics of Climate Change

Grime, J. P., 1997. "Biodiversity and Ecosystem Function: The Debate Deepens." *Science* **277**: 1260–1

Hageman, R., 1985. "Valuing Marine Mammal Populations: Benefit Valuations in a Multi-Species Ecosystem." Administrative Report LJ-85-22, Southwest Fisheries Center. La Jolla, CA: National Marine Fisheries Service

Hagen, D., J. Vincent, and P. Welle, 1992. "Benefits of Preserving Old-Growth Forests and the Spotted Owl." *Contemporary Policy Issues* **10**: 13–25

Hahnemann, W.M., 1994. "Valuing the Environment through Contingent Valuation." *Journal of Economics Perspectives* **8**(4): 19–43

Hammond, P., 1995. "The Current Magnitude of Biodiversity." In V.H. Heywood and R.T. Watson, eds., *Global Biodiversity Assessment.* Cambridge: Cambridge University Press: 113–38

Hanley, N., A. Konstantinos, D. Tinch, A. Davies, F. Watson, and E.B. Barbier, 2007. "What Drives Long-term Biodiversity Change?" Discussion Paper 07–23, Washington, DC: Resources for the Future

Heal, G.M., E.B. Barbier, K.J. Boyle, A.P. Covich, S.P. Gloss, C.H. Hershner, J.P. Hoehn, C.M. Pringle, S. Polasky, K. Segerson, and K. Shrader-Frechette, 2005. *Valuing Ecosystem Services: Toward Better Environmental Decision Making.* Washington, DC: National Academies Press

Heberlein, T.A., M.A. Wilson, R.C. Bishop, and N.C. Schaeffer, 2005. "Rethinking the Scope Test as a Criterion for Validity in Contingent Valuation." *Journal of Environmental Economics and Management* **50**: 1–22

Hoehn, J.P. and J.B. Loomis, 1993. "Substitution Effects in the Valuation of Multiple Environmental Programs." *Journal of Environmental Economics and Management* **25**: 56–75

Holling, C.S., D.W. Shindler, B.W. Walker, and J. Roughgarden, 1995. "Biodiversity in the Functioning of Ecosystems: An Ecological Synthesis." In C. Perrings, K.G. Mäler C. Folke, C.S. Holing, and B.O. Jansson, eds., *Biodiversity Loss: Economic and Ecological Issues.* Cambridge: Cambridge University Press.

Holmes, T.P., 1988. "The Offsite Impact of Soil Erosion on the Water Treatment Industry." *Land Economics* **64**: 356–66

Holmes, T.P., T.C. Bergstrom, E. Huszar, S.B. Kask, and F. Orr, III, 2004. "Contingent Valuation, Net Marginal Benefits, and the Scale of Riparian Ecosystem Restoration." *Ecological Economics* **49**: 19–3

Huszar, P.C., 1989. "Economics of Reducing Off-site Costs of Wind Erosion." *Land Economics* **65**: 333–40

International Union for the Conservation of Nature (IUCN), UN Environmental Program, and World Wildlife Fund, 1991. *World Conservation Strategy: Living Resource Conservation for Sustainable Development.* Gland, Switzerland: IUCN

1997. *United Nations List of Protected Areas.* Cambridge: IUCN

2004. *2004 IUCN Red List of Threatened Species,* www.iucn.org/themes/ssc/red_list_2004/gsaEXECSUMM_en.HTM, accessed February 7, 2007

James, Alexander N., Kevin J. Gaston, and Andrew Balmford, 2001. "Can We Afford to Conserve Biodiversity?" *BioScience* **51**: 43–52

Kauppi, P.E., J.H. Assubel, J. Fang, A. Mather, R.A. Sedjo, and P.E. Waggoner, 2006. "Returning Forests Analyzed with the Forest Identity." *Proceedings of the National Academy of Science* **103**(46): 17574–9

Kauppi, P.E., R.A., Sedjo, *et al.*, 2001. "Technological and Economic Potential of Options to Enhance, Maintain, and Manage Biological Carbon Reservoirs and Geo-Engineering." In B. Metz *et al.*, eds., *Climate Change 2001: Mitigation.* New York: Cambridge University Press: 303–53

Kealy, M.J. and R.W. Turner, 1993. "A Test of the Equality of the Close-Ended and the Open-Ended Contingent Valuation." *American Journal of Agricultural Economics* **75**: 311–31

Kennedy, T.A., S. Naeem, K.M. Howe, J.M.H. Knops, D. Tilman, and P. Reich, 2002. "Biodiversity as a Barrier to Ecological Invasion." *Nature* **417**: 636–8

Kindermann, G., M. Obersteiner, B. Sohngen, J.Sathaye, K. Andrasko, E. Rametsteiner, B. Schlamadinger, S. Wunder, and R. Beach, unpublished. "On the Economics of Avoiding Deforestation"

King, D., D. Flynn, and W. Shaw, 1988. "Total and Existence Values of a Herd of Desert Bighorn Sheep." Benefits and Costs in Natural Resource Planning, Interim Report. Western Regional Research Publication W-133. Davis, CA: University of California Press

Knops, J.M.H. *et al.*, 1998. "Effects of Plant Species Richness on Invasion Dynamics, Disease Outbreaks, Insect Abundance and Diversity." *Ecological Letters* **2**: 286–94

Kotchen, M.J. and S.D. Reiling, 2000. "Environmental Attitudes, Motivations, and Contingent Valuation of Nonuse Values: A Case Study Involving Endangered Species." *Ecological Economics* **32**: 93–107

Larson, D. and J. Siikamäki, 2006. "Valuing Surface Water Quality in California: A Mixed Panel Logit Model Using a $2\frac{1}{2}$-Bounded CVM." Paper contributed to the 3rd World Congress of Environmental and Resource Economics, July 3–7, Kyoto

Larson, D.M., S.L. Shaikh, and D.F. Layton, 2004. "Revealing Preferences for Leisure Time from Stated Preference Data." *American Journal of Agricultural Economics* **86**: 307–20

Laughland, A.S., W.N. Musser, J.S. Shortle, and L.M. Musser, 1996. "Construct Validity of Averting Cost Measures of Environmental Benefits." *Land Economics* **72**: 100–12

Loomis, J.B., 1989. "Test–Retest Reliability of the Contingent Valuation Method: A Comparison of General Population and Visitor Responses." *American Journal of Agriculture Economics* **71**: 76–81

Loomis, J. and E. Ekstrand, 1997. "Economic Benefits of Critical Habitat for the Mexican Spotted Owl: A Scope Test Using A Multiple-Bounded Contingent Valuation Survey." *Journal of Agricultural and Resource Economics* **22**: 356–66

Loomis, J.B., A. Gonzales-Caban, and R. Gregory, 1994. "Do Reminders of Substitutes and Budget Constraints Influence Contingent Valuation Estimates?" *Land Economics* **70**: 499–506

Loomis, J. and D. Larson, 1994. "Total Economic Values of Increasing Gray Whale Populations: Results from a Contingent Valuation Survey of Visitors and Households." *Marine Resource Economics* **9**: 275–86

Loomis, J.B. and D.S. White, 1996. "Economic Benefits of Rare and Endangered Species: Summary and Meta-Analysis." *Ecological Economics* **18**: 197–206

Louviere, J.J., D.A. Henscher, and J.S. Shwait, 2000. *Stated Choice Methods: Analysis and Application.* Cambridge: Cambridge University Press

MacArthur, R.H. and E.O. Wilson, 1967. *The Theory of Island Biogeography.* Princeton, NJ: Princeton University Press

Mace, G.M., J.L. Gittleman, and A. Purvis, 2003. "Preserving the Tree of Life." *Science* **300**: 1707–9

May, R.M., J.H. Lawton, and N.E. Stork, 1995. "Assessing Extinction Rates." In J.H. Lawton and R.M. May, eds., *Extinction Rates.* Oxford: Oxford University Press: 1–24

McCann, K.S., 2000. "The Diversity–Stability Debate." *Nature* **405**: 228–33

McClelland, G.H., W.D. Schultze, J.K. Lazo, D.M. Waldman, J.K. Doyle, S.R. Elliot, and J.R. Irwin, 1992. *Methods for Measuring the Non-Use Values: A Contingent Valuation Study of the Groundwater Cleanup.* Boulder, CO: Center for Economic Analysis, University of Colorado

McConnell, K.E. and N.E. Bockstael, 2005. "Valuing the Environment as a Factor of Production." In K.-G. Mäler and J.R. Vincent, eds., *Handbook of Environmental Economics* **2**. Amsterdam: Elsevier

Millennium Ecosystem Assessment, 2005. *Ecosystems and Human Well-Being: Synthesis.* Washington, DC: Island Press

Mitchell, R.C. and R.T. Carson, 1984. *Willingness to Pay for National Freshwater Improvements*. Washington, DC: Resources for the Future

National Oceanic and Atmospheric Administration, 2005. "Endangered and Threatened Species; Designation of Critical Habitat for Seven Evolutionarily Significant Units of Pacific Salmon and Steelhead in California: Final Rule." *Federal Register* **70**(170): 52488–586

NatureServe, 2003. *Ecological Systems Database*, version 1.02. Arlington, VA: NatureServe

Nee, S. and May, R.M., 1997. "Extinction and the Loss of Evolutionary History." *Science* **278**: 692–4

Newman, D.J., G.M. Cragg, and K.M. Snader, 2003. "Natural Products as Sources of New Drugs Over the Period 1981–2002." *Journal of Natural Products* **66**(7): 1022–37

Noss, R.F., 1990. "Indicators for Monitoring Biodiversity: A Hierarchical Approach." *Conservation Biology* **4**: 355–64

Nunes, P.A.L.D. and J.C.J.M. van den Bergh, 2001. "Economic Valuation of Biodiversity: Sense or Nonsense?" *Ecological Economics* **39**: 203–22

Olsen, D., J. Richards, and D. Scott, 1991. "Existence and Sport Values for Doubling the Size of Columbia River Basin Salmon and Steelhead Runs." *Rivers* **2**: 44–56

Pearce, D. 1996. "Global Environmental Value and the Tropical Forests: Demonstration and Capture." In W.L. Adamowicz, P.C. Boxall, M.K. Luckert, W.E. Phillips, and W.A. White, eds., *Forestry, Economics and the Environment*. Wallingford: CAB International: 11–48

Phaneuf, D.J. and V.K. Smith, 2005. "Recreation Demand Models." In K.-G. Mäler and J.R. Vincent, eds., *Handbook of Environmental Economics* **2**: Amsterdam: Elsevier

Pimentel, D., L. Lach, R. Zuniga, and D. Morrison, 2000. "Environmental and Economic Costs of Nonindigenous Species in the United States." *BioScience* **50**(1): 53–67

Pimentel, D., C. Wilson, C. McCullum, R. Huang, P. Dwen, J. Flack, Q. Tran, T. Saltman, and B. Cliff, 1997. "Economic and Environmental Benefits of Biodiversity." *BioScience* **47**(11): 747–57

Pimm, S.L., M. Ayers, A. Balmford, G. Branch, K., Brandon, T. Brooks, R. Bustamante, R. Costanza, R. Cowlings, L.M. Currna, A. Dobson, S. Fraber, G.A. B. da Fronseca, C. Gascon, R. Kitching, J. McNelly, T. Lovejoy, R.A. Mettermeier, N. Meyers, J.A. Patz, B. Raffle, D. Rapport, P. Raven, C. Roberts, J.P. Rodriguez, A. B. Rylands, C. Tucker, C. Safina, C. Samper, M.L.J. Stiassny, J. Supriatna, D.H. Hall, and D. Wilcove, 2001. "Environment – Can We Defy Nature's End?" *Science* **293**: 2207–8

Polasky, S., C. Costello, and A. Solow, 2005. "The Economics of Biodiversity." In K.-G. Mäler and J.R. Vincent, eds., *Handbook of Environmental Economics* 3. Amsterdam: Elsevier

Polasky, S., E. Nelson, E. Lonsdorf, P. Fackler, and A. Starfield, 2005. "Conserving Species in a Working Landscape: Land Use with Biological and Economic Objectives." *Ecological Applications* 15(4): 1387–1401

Principe, P., 1989. *The Economic Value of Biodiversity Among Medicinal Plants*. Paris: OECD

Purvis, A. and A. Hector, 2000. "Getting the Measure of Biodiversity." *Nature* 405: 212–19

Rausser, G. and A. Small, 2000. "Valuing Research Leads: Bioprospecting and the Conservation of Genetic Resources." *Journal of Political Economy* 108(1): 173–206

Reaves, D.W., R.A. Kramer, and T.P. Holmes, 1994. "Valuing the Endangered Red-Cockaded Woodpecker and its Habitat: A Comparison of Contingent Valuation Elicitation Techniques and a Test for Embedding." Contributed paper, American Association of Agricultural Economics annual meeting, San Diego, CA, August

1999. "Does Question Format Matter? Valuing an Endangered Species." *Environmental and Resource Economics* 14: 365–83

Redwood, III, John, 2002. "World Bank Approaches to the Brazilian Amazon." LCR Sustainable Development Working Paper 13. Washington, DC: World Bank

Ribaudo, M.O., 1989a. "Water Quality Benefits from the Conservation Reserve Program, Agricultural Economics Report." Washington, DC: Economic Research Service

1989b. "Targeting the Conservation Reserve Program to Maximize Water Quality Benefits." *Land Economics* 65: 320–32

Richer, J., 1995. "Willingness To Pay for Desert Protection." *Contemporary Economic Policy* 13: 93–104

Rubin, J., G. Helfand, and J. Loomis, 1991. "A Benefit-Cost Analysis of the Northern Spotted Owl." *Journal of Forestry* 89: 25–30

Samples, K. and J. Hollyer, 1989. "Contingent Valuation of Wildlife Resources in the Presence of Substitutes and Complement." In R. Johnson and G. Johnson, eds., *Economic Valuation of Natural Resources: Issues, Theory, and Application*. Boulder, CO: Westview Press

Schneider 1992. "An Economic Analysis of Environmental Problems in the Amazon." World Bank, Latin American Operation Division, Washington, DC

Sedjo, Roger A., 1991. "Toward a Worldwide System of Tradable Forest Protection and Management Obligations." Discussion Paper ENR91–16. Washington, DC: Resources for the Future

1992a. "Implications of a Tradable Obligations Approach to International Forest Protection," revised February 10. Washington, DC: Report for the EPA, Resources for the Future

1992b. "Property Rights, Genetic Resources, and Biotechnological Change." *Journal of Law and Economics* **35**(1): 00–00

2007. "An Overview of Changes in the Provision of Forest Ecosystem Services Through Forest Land Markets in the US". *Management and Environmental Quality* **18**(6): 00–00

Shabman, L. and S. Batie, 1978. "The Economic Value of Natural Coastal Wetlands: A Critique." *Coastal Zone Management Journal* **4**(3): 231–47

Shannon, C.E. and W. Weaver, 1949. *Mathematical Theory of Communication*. Urbana, IL: University of Illinois Press

Siikamäki, Juha and Jeffrey Chow, 2008. "Biodiversity." In R.A. Sedjo, ed., *Perspectives in Sustainable Resources in America*. Washington, DC: Resources for the Future

Siikamäki, Juha and David F. Layton, 2007. "Potential Cost-Effectiveness of Incentive Payment Programs for the Protection of Non-Industrial Private Forests." *Land Economics* **83**(4): 95–116

Silberman, J., D.A. Gerlowski, and N.A. Williams, 1992. "Estimating Existence Value for Users and Nonusers of New Jersey Beaches." *Land Economics* **68**: 225–36

Simon, J.L. and A. Wildawsky, 1984. "On Species Loss, the Absence of Data, and Risks to Humanity." In J.L. Simon and H. Kahn, eds., *The Resourceful Earth. A Response to "Global 2000"*. New York: Blackwell: 171–83

Simpson, E.H., 1949. "Measurement of Diversity." *Nature* **163**: 688

Simpson, R.D., 2000. "Economic Perspectives on Preservation of Biodiversity." In G.C. van Kooten, E.H. Bulte, and A.R.E. Sinclair. eds., *Conserving Nature's Diversity. Insights from Biology, Ethics, and Economics*. Aldershot Ashgate: 88–105

2004. "Conserving Biodiversity through Markets: A Better Approach." *PERC Special Issue* **32**, July, www.perc.org/printer-php?id=5168urc= perc.php?id

Simpson, R.D. and R.A. Sedjo, 1996. "Commercialization of Indigenous Genetic Resources." *Contemporary Economic Policy* **12**(4): 34–44

Simpson, R.D., R.A. Sedjo, and J. Reid, 1996. "Valuing Biodiversity for Use in Pharmaceutical Research." *Journal of Political Economy* **104**(1): 163–85

Sittenfeld, A. and R. Gamez, 1993. "Biodiversity Prospecting by INBio." In Walter V. Reid *et al.*, *Biodiversity Prospecting: Using Genetic Resources for Sustainable Development*. Washington, DC: World Resource Institute

Smith, V.K. and W.H. Desvousges, 1986. *Measuring Water Quality Benefits*. Dordrecht: Kluwer Nijhoff Publishing

Solomon B.D., C.M. Cory-Luse, and K.E. Halvorsen, 2004. "The Florida Manatee and Eco-Tourism: Toward a Safe Minimum Standard." *Ecological Economics* 50(1–2): 101–15

Sohngen, B. and R.A. Sedjo, 2006. "Carbon Sequestration in Global Forests Under Different Carbon Price Regimes." *The Energy Journal*, Special Issue, *Multi-Greenhouse Gas Mitigation and Climate Policy*: 109–62

Southgate, D., 1998. *Tropical Forest Conservation: An Economic Assessment of the Alternatives for Latin America*. Oxford: Oxford University Press

Stevens, T., J. Echeverria, R. Glass, T. Hager, and T. More, 1991. "Measuring the Existence Value of Wildlife: What do CVM Estimates Really Show?" *Land Economics* 67: 390–400

Stanley, D.L., 2005. "Local Perceptions of Public Goods: Recent Assessments of Willingness-To-Pay for Endangered Species." *Contemporary Economic Policy* 23: 165–79

Svalbard International Seed Vault, 2007. www.croptrust.org/main/articles.php, accessed February 2007

Swanson, C., 1993. "Economics of Non-Game Management: Bald Eagles on the Skagit River Bald Eagle Natural Area." PhD dissertation, Department of Agricultural Economics. Columbus, OH: Ohio State University

Terborgh, John, 2002. "Overcoming Impediments to Conservation." In John Terborgh, Carel van Schaik, Lisa Davenport, and Madhu Rao, eds., *Making Parks Work: Strategies for Preserving Tropical Nature*. Washington, DC: Island Press: 243–9

Thomas, C.D., A. Cameron, R.E. Green *et al.*, 2004. "Extinction Risk from Climate Change." *Nature* 427: 145–8

Tilman, D., 1996. "Biodiversity: Population versus Ecosystem Stability." *Ecology* 77(3): 350–63

    2004. "Niche Tradeoffs, Neutrality, and Community Structure: A Stochastic Theory of Resource Competition, Invasion, and Community Assembly." *Proceedings of the National Academy of Sciences* 101: 10854–61

Tilman, D. and J.A. Downing, 1994. "Biodiversity and Stability in Grasslands." *Nature* 367: 363–5

Tilman, D., P. B. Reich, J. Knops, D. Wedin, T. Mielke, and C. Lehman, 2001. "Diversity and Productivity in a Long-Term Grassland Experiment." *Science* 294: 843–5

Toman, M.A., 1998. "Why Not to Calculate the Value of the World's Ecosystem Services and Natural Capital." *Ecological Economics* 25: 61–5

Torell, L. A., J. D. Libbin, and M. D. Miller, 1990. "The Market Value of Water in the Ogalla Aquifer." *Land Economics* **66**: 163–75

UN Environmental Program (UNEP), 1995. *Global Biodiversity Assessment*. Washington, DC: UNEP

US Department of Agriculture, Forest Service (USDA), 2004. *National Report on Sustainable Forests – 2003*. Washington, DC: United States Department of Agriculture, Forest Service

US Department of Energy, 2007. "Natural and Accelerated Bioremedation Research." www.lbl.gov/NABIR/index.html, accessed March 2007

US Fish and Wildlife Service, 2002. *Candidate Conservation Agreements With Assurances for Non-Federal Property Owners*. Washington, DC: Department of the Interior, US Fish and Wildlife Service

USDOI, 1994. "The Reintroduction of Gray Wolves to Yellowstone National Park and Central Idahoe.' Final Environmental Impact Statement. Helena, MT: USDOI: 4.21–4.27

Walker, D.J. and D.L. Young, 1986. "The Effect of Technical Progress on Erosion Damage and Economic Incentives for Soil Conservation." *Land Economics* **62**: 83–93

Walsh, R.O., J.B. Loomis, and R.A. Gillman, 1984. "Valuing Option, Existence, and Bequest Demands For Wilderness." *Land Economics* **60**: 14–29

Weitzman, M., 1992. "On Diversity." *Quarterly Journal of Economics* **107**(2): 363–405

2000. "Economic Profit Versus Ecological Entropy." *Quarterly Journal of Economics* **115**(1): 237–63

Wells, M. and K.E. Brandon, 1992. "People and Parks: Linking Protected Area Management With Local Communities." Washington, DC: World Bank

Western, D., and R.M. Wright, eds., 1994. *Natural Connections: Perspectives in Community-based Conservation*. Washington, DC: Island Press

Whitehead, J., 1991. "Economic Values of Threatened and Endangered Wildlife: A Case Study of Coastal Nongame Wildlife." Transactions of the 57th North American Wildlife and Natural Resources Conference. Washington, DC: Wildlife Management Institute

1992. "Ex ante Willingness To Pay with Supply and Demand Uncertainty: Implications for Valuing a Sea Turtle Protection Programme." *Applied Economics* **24**: 981–88

Wilcove, D., D. Rothstein, J. Dubow, A. Phillips, and E. Losos, 1998. "Quantifying Threats to Imperiled Species in the United States." *BioScience* **48**: 607–15

Wilson, C. and C. Graham, 1983. *Exotic Plant Pests and North American Agriculture*. New York: Academic Press

Wilson, E.O., 1992. *The Diversity of Life*. New York: W.W. Norton
    1999. *The Diversity of Life*. New York: W.W. Norton
    ed., 1988. *BioDiversity*. Washington, DC: National Academy Press

World Conservation Monitoring Centre, 1992. *Global Biodiversity: Status of the Earth's Living Resources*. London: Chapman & Hall

World Resources Institute, United Nations Development Programme, UN Environment Program, and World Bank, 1998. *World Resources 1998–99*. New York: Oxford University Press

Wu, J. and W.G. Boggess, 1999. "The Optimal Allocation of Conservation Funds." *Journal of Environmental Economics and Management* **38**: 320–21

4.1 Forests and biodiversity: an alternative view

RANDALL A. KRAMER*

1 Introduction

The LAC region faces a number of major environmental challenges, including climate change, loss of biodiversity, provision of clean drinking water, deteriorating air quality in urban areas, and over-fishing of economically important fisheries. Roger Sedjo and Juha Siikamäki's study (2007) focuses on one of these issues – biodiversity in the region's forests. Fueled by population growth in the developing world and increased resource demands in both the developed and developing regions, the loss of forests and forest biodiversity has accelerated in many parts of the world. These issues are particularly acute in tropical forests, which also contain many of the world's biodiversity "hot spots." Forest fragmentation, deforestation, and over-utilization of residual forests have impacted the diversity of remaining species.

This has prompted international efforts to protect the remaining tropical forests, but conservation remains significantly under-funded. In the developing world, current expenditures have been estimated to be only a small fraction of what is needed to ensure the survival of representative species, habitats, and ecosystems (Balmford *et al.* 2003; Kramer 2007).

This alternative view provides a summary of some of the main points raised in chapter 4's assessment of LAC biodiversity issues and opportunities. Some additional economic information is introduced, and an alternative, more modest solution for addressing the region's biodiversity concerns is provided, based on an expansion of protected areas using international cost-sharing.

* The author thanks Yoanna Kraus Elsin for providing research assistance.

2 The context

Sedjo and Siikamäki have provided a thorough and balanced review of
the definition, measurement, and status of biodiversity. They note that
while the rate of species extinction is at least an order of magnitude
greater than background rates, IUCN has documented only twenty-
seven extinctions during the past twenty years. Thus, at the individual
species level, there is reason for concern but the predictions of two
decades ago that we would see thousands of extinctions by now have
fortunately not been realized. Some experts fear that climate change
may significantly increase rates of extinction since fast-moving climatic
shifts may leave behind some species that are unable to adapt their
range.

Sedjo and Siikamäki also review rates of forest and biodiversity loss
in the LAC region, noting that it accounts for a very large percentage
of the globe's total threatened species. Hence, the region is a location
where targeting of biodiversity conservation could generate significant
economic and social values.

Sedjo and Siikamäki rightfully acknowledge the dearth of information about the benefits and costs of biodiversity conservation. They
note that the most widely cited study of global ecosystem benefits by
Costanza *et al.* (1997) has been widely criticized by economists, but
they then go on to use the study's seemingly inflated benefits estimates
in some of their own analysis. Sedjo and Siikamäki search for other
benefit estimates and find several credible estimates of bioprospecting
benefits. For example, Simpson (2000) estimated the value to be as high
as \$9,431 for some species or \$21 per ha for some lands. However,
once one factors in the low probability of getting a commercial "hit"
from a particular species or tract of land, the bioprospecting benefits
are too low to justify much, if any, conservation.

Sedjo and Siikamäki are optimistic about the prospects of a global
market for carbon as a source of future revenue that could support
biodiversity conservation. They rely on a study by Pearce (1996) that
estimated a potential of 100 tons of carbon per ha and per ton price
of \$20 for carbon sequestered in forests. These numbers drive several
of the chapter's B/C calculations and proposed solutions.

One element that is missing from the chapter's analysis is the institutional changes that would be necessary to convince public and private forest owners to move from their current orientation to timber

production to one that emphasizes carbon storage and provision of other ecosystem services from all of the region's forests. Even if global carbon markets scaled up to the point of providing consistent demand for carbon at a level of \$20 per ton, would it be politically feasible to lock up all 1 billion ha of LAC forests for carbon sequestration? Would governments allow such a major structural change that would largely dry up local timber markets and cause large-scale job losses in wood manufacturing and sectors? While I agree that there are reasonably good prospects that substantial amounts of forests could be set aside for sequestration and the resulting biodiversity benefits would be important, I would expect such developments to occur on a smaller scale than Sedjo and Siikamäki suggest.

3 Measuring the non-use benefits of biodiversity conservation

It is inherently challenging to monetize the economic benefits of biodiversity conservation because of the array of services provided by biodiversity conservation (Pearce and Moran 1994). Sedjo and Siikamäki provide several different estimates of these benefits, primarily based on ecosystem services. While such services are an important part of the total economic value generated by forests, it is also appropriate to consider non-use values generated by biodiversity conservation. In some cases, the non-use values may well exceed the use values. In this section, I discuss two studies that have developed empirical estimates of the largely non-use, public good aspects of biodiversity conservation. Both employ the contingent valuation method (CVM), a stated preference (SP) approach that applies survey research methods to directly query respondents about their willingness to pay for a change in the provision of a public good such as biodiversity protection. The CVM approach permits the measurement of both use and non-use values. As Sedjo and Siikamäki observe, there are controversies surrounding the SP approach, but it is the only accepted empirical strategy for capturing non-use values (Carson *et al.* 2001).

Kramer and Mercer (1997) conducted a national CV survey of US residents to determine their preferences for protecting tropical rain forests. After focus groups, pre-testing, and expert review, a survey instrument was developed and sent to a random sample of 1,200 US residents. Respondents were asked several attitudinal questions about environmental and other social issues, awareness of tropical

Table 4.1.1 *US residents' WTP for global rainforest biodiversity conservation*

Measure	Estimated value ($1992)
Mean WTP/household	21
Total WTP all households	1.9 billion

Source: Kramer and Mercer (1997).

forest issues, socio-economic characteristics, and willingness to provide financial support to expand the protection of rain forests. When asked, "Should industrialized countries help developing countries pay for preserving their rain forests?" two-thirds of the respondents said "Yes." This finding has important implications for international financing of biodiversity conservation.

Respondents were presented with a CV scenario – would they be willing to contribute to a UN-managed fund to protect an additional 5% of the world's tropical forests? The mean response for a one-time payment was $21 per household (see table 4.1.1). If we aggregate across all US households, this results in a total WTP of nearly $2 billion in 1992 dollars. This shows a significant demand for biodiversity protection for its own sake – few of these respondents expected to enjoy use benefits from the protected forests.

Horton *et al.* (2003) conducted a similar study in Europe to see if these results could be replicated in a different cultural context. Their survey took a more narrow focus on forest conservation – the Brazilian Amazon. Interviews with 407 randomly selected individuals were conducted in Italy and the United Kingdom in 1999. Horton *et al.* (2003) found that 98% of their respondents were familiar with tropical rainforest issues, and some 93% believed that industrial nations should share in the cost of rainforest conservation. The mean WTP for protecting 5% more of the Brazilian Amazonia was $46 per household per year. Summing up over all households in the UK and Italy, this represents a WTP of $1.8 billion (1999 dollars). The authors' analysis of the survey data showed that the values held for the Amazonia rainforests were primarily due to non-use benefits (table 4.1.2).

Taken together, the results of these two studies show strong support in OECD countries for biodiversity conservation in the south. There is a large and measurable WTP for such conservation efforts. While these

Table 4.1.2. *European residents' WTP for forest biodiversity conservation: Amazonia*

Measure	Estimated value ($1999)
Mean WTP/household/year	$46
Total WTP all households in United Kingdom and Italy	$1.8 billion

measured values are likely approximations and not precise estimates, scaling up the household estimates suggests global non-use benefits in the billions of dollars from forest conservation.

4 Alternative solution: expanding or improving protected areas

Protected areas are a proven approach to conserving biodiversity. By restricting harvesting and most land disturbance, protected areas are one of the best ways to ensure that adequate amounts of representative ecosystems are in place to ensure stable biodiversity (Kramer and van Schaik 1997). Currently about 17% of LAC land is under some form of protection status (World Conservation Monitoring Centre 2007). However, much of the protection is on paper only, and many parks are woefully under-funded (Marquez 2003).

An alternative solution is presented here to add 5% more land to the protected area system. Alternatively, this approach can be viewed as providing adequate funding for an equivalent amount of land currently under legal protection but without effective conservation. Thus, one can interpret this solution as providing improved protection of biodiversity by placing more land under effective conservation regimes. Such a solution could be financed through existing conservation finance mechanisms such as the Global Environment Fund or Debt-for-Nature Swaps. Such international cost-sharing mechanisms transfer financial resources from beneficiaries in wealthy countries to those in less wealthy countries who bear the costs of conservation efforts.

The Horton *et al.* study estimated a non-use benefit from biodiversity conservation in the Amazon at $1.8 billion per year for protecting 5% of the remaining forest. This works out at a per ha benefit of $51 annually. The NPV of this non-use benefit is $1285 at a 4% discount

Table 4.1.3 *B/C analysis of expanded or improved protected areas:*
LAC region

Non-use benefits from Horton *et al.* (2003)	$1.8 billion per year for 5% of Amazonia or $51 per ha per year	$1285 NPV per ha
Cost estimates from Pearce (1996)	$500 one-time payment per ha	$500 per ha
BCR		2.5

rate. If we couple this benefit with the Pearce (1996) cost estimate of a one-time payment of $500 to take land out of production, the BCR is 2.5 (see table 4.1.3).

The B/C calculation buttresses Sedjo and Siikamäki's findings. There is a clear economic case for increased protection of biodiversity, whether one focuses on use or non-use benefits. In this case, only non-use benefits are employed on the benefit side, and only the amount of benefits that would accrue to residents of some European countries are included. Hence, if one expanded the range of beneficiaries to include national citizens in the countries where the conservation is practiced and included benefits to citizens in other wealthy nations outside the region, the BCR would increase considerably. While this analysis was done only for a 5% increase in protected area in the Brazilian Amazon, it is likely that a favorable BCR would be found for other LAC biodiversity "hot spots" as well.

5 Conclusions

The loss of biodiversity is one of the most pressing environmental issues in the LAC region. Sedjo and Siikamäki in chapter 4 have mounted substantial evidence to show that increased protection of the biodiversity in the region's forests will generate significant net social benefits. Their analysis hinges largely on the emergence of carbon markets that will provide sufficient use benefits to finance conservation. However, significant non-use benefits imply that it is economically feasible to increase the current level of biodiversity conservation even without the advent of large-scale carbon markets. To implement an expanded or improved biodiversity protection effort requires mobilizing the financial support from beneficiaries who are often geographically separated from those who bear the costs of biodiversity conservation (Kramer 2007). International cost-sharing mechanisms for capturing non-use benefits include the Global Environment Facility, Conservation International's Global Conservation Fund, and Debt-for-Nature Swaps. Of course, the emergence of ecosystem service markets such as those for carbon will only enhance these existing conservation finance tools and make it more politically feasible and economically attractive to reverse the decline in LAC's forest biodiversity.

Bibliography

Balmford A., K. Gaston, S. Blyth, A. James, and V. Kapos, 2003. "Global Variation in Terrestrial Conservation Costs, Conservation Benefits, and Unmet Conservation Needs." *Proceedings of the National Academy of Sciences* **100**: 1046–50

Carson, Richard T., Nicholas E. Flores, and Norman F. Meade, 2001. "Contingent Valuation: Controversies and Evidence." *Environmental and Resource Economics* **19**: 173–210

Costanza, Robert, Ralph d'Arge, Rudolf de Groot, Stephen Farber, Monica Grasso, Bruce Hannon, Karin Limburg, Shaeed Naeem, Robert d'Neill, José Paruclo, Robert G. Raskin, Paul Sutton, and Marjan van den Belt, 1997. "The Value of the World's Ecosystem Services and Natural Capital." *Nature* **387**: 253–60

Horton, B., G. Colarullo, I. Bateman, and C. Peres, 2003. "Evaluating Non-Users' Willingness to Pay for a Large-Scale Conservation Programme in Amazonia." *Environmental Conservation* **30**: 139–46

Kramer, Randall A., 2007. "International Financial Transfers for Biodiversity Conservation." Unpublished paper prepared for the OECD, March

Kramer, Randall A. and Evan Mercer, 1997. "Valuing a Global Environmental Good: US Residents' Willingness to Pay to Protect Tropical Rain Forests." *Land Economics* **73**: 196–210

Kramer, Raudall A. and C.P. van Schaik, 1997. "Preservation Paradigms and Tropical Rain Forests." Chapter 1 in R.A. Kramer, C. van Schaik, and J. Johnson, eds., *Last Stand: Protected Areas and the Defense of Tropical Biodiversity*. Oxford: Oxford University Press

Marquez, Huberto, 2003. "Environment – Latin America: Protected Nature – But On Paper Only." Global Information Network. New York: September 17: 1

Pearce, David, 1996. "Global Environmental Value and the Tropical Forests: Demonstration and Capture." Chapter 2 in W. L. Adamowicz, P.C.

Boxau, M.K. Luckeit, W.E. Phillips, and W.A. White, eds., *Forestry, Economics and the Environment*. Wallingford: CAB International

Pearce, David and D. Moran, 1994. *The Economic Value of Biodiversity*. London: Earthscan

Sedjo, Roger A. and Juha Siikamäki, 2007. "Forests, Biodiversity, and Avoided Deforestation in the LAC Region," chapter 4 in this volume

Simpson, R.D., 2000. "Economic Perspectives on Preservation of Biodiversity." In G.C. van Kooten *et al.* eds., *Conserving Nature's Diversity. Insights from Biology, Ethics, and Economics*. Aldershot: Ashgate: 88–105

World Conservation Monitoring Center, 2007. *World Database on Protected Areas*, www.unep-wcmc.org/protected_areas/UN_list/index.htm

5 | *Fiscal policy reforms in the LAC region*

MIGUEL BRAUN*

1 Introduction

The LAC region has historically been a fiscal basket case. Since the 1970s, debt crises, hyperinflations, and balance of payments crises have recurred, hampering growth prospects and affecting the welfare of low-income households the most.[1] Furthermore, public spending and the tax system are inefficient and regressive, and fiscal policy is procyclical, augmenting the already high macroeconomic volatility.

Although fiscal reforms in the 1990s combined with high growth and rising commodity prices significantly improved fiscal outcomes after 2004, it is not yet clear that a break with the past has occurred. High debt levels persist[2] and, as I shall show in the next section, an important part of the recent increases in revenue are transitory, while increases in expenditures tend to be permanent. This implies that the structural fiscal balance paints a less rosy picture than current figures, and that a downturn in economic activity could lead to a new bout of fiscal solvency problems.

---

* I wish to thank Robert Inman, who acted as academic supervisor for the Copenhagen Consensus Center process; Ernesto Stein; Eduardo Lora; Eduardo Cavallo; Carlos Scartascini; Gabriel Filc; Martín Ardanaz; Alexis Roitman and participants at the IDB research department seminar for very helpful discussions and suggestions. Ariel Dvoskin and Germán Feldman provided excellent research assistance.

[1] Poor households are more affected by inflation since they cannot use financial instruments to protect their assets and income, they tend to be employed in the informal sector and thus lack employment protection, and social spending tends to decline during crises.

[2] The average for the region is around 50%, and many analysts suggest that for countries with weak institutions, the recommended level is well below this figure (see section 4).

In this chapter I suggest four reforms to improve fiscal outcomes in the region, and attempt a quantification of the potential impact of these reforms based on the recent literature. The proposals are:

(1) Using contingent debt instruments to improve debt management
(2) Implementing fiscal rules, in particular, fiscal responsibility rules and structural balance rules
(3) Creating a regional public policy evaluation agency
(4) Tax reform, particularly eliminating distortionary taxes and replacing corporate taxes with personal income taxes.

The chapter is organized as follows. In section 2, I argue that the main challenge to be addressed in the region is consolidating fiscal solvency and making fiscal policy countercyclical. In section 3, I present specific proposals to contribute to solving the challenge and, in section 4, I attempt a quantification of the impact of these reforms. Section 5 draws some conclusions.

2 The challenge

The region's most important fiscal challenge is to consolidate the recent gains in fiscal solvency[3] and reduce the procyclicality of fiscal policy. The region has a history of fiscal profligacy, in which deficits were covered by printing money – resulting in high inflation and, in extreme cases, hyperinflation – or by tapping financial markets, leading to exploding debt ratios, often ending in debt crises.

In figure 5.1, I document primary fiscal outcomes from 1970 to the present.[4] The figure shows the well-known fact that until the early 1990s, the region suffered from systematic deficits.

The consequences of fiscal profligacy are shown in figure 5.2 and table 5.1. Average gross external debt surpassed 75% of GDP in 1987, when twenty years before it had been around 20%. The monetization of deficits following the 1982 debt crisis led to high inflation during the decade, and episodes of hyperinflation in Argentina, Bolivia, Brazil, Nicaragua, and Peru.

---

[3] It is, of course, also key to improve efficiency and equity of spending and tax systems. However, since other chapters in this volume deal more directly with these issues, I will focus mainly on the challenge of fiscal solvency.

[4] Unless otherwise specified, the sample of countries included for calculations is Argentina, Bolivia, Brazil, Chile, Colombia, Costa Rica, Ecuador, El Salvador, Guatemala, Honduras, Mexico, Nicaragua, Panama, Paraguay, Peru, Uruguay, and Venezuela.

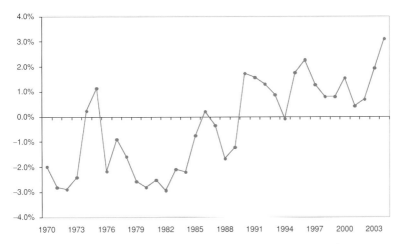

Figure 5.1 Primary fiscal balance: LAC region, 1970–2004 (% of GDP)
Source: World Development Indicators, World Bank

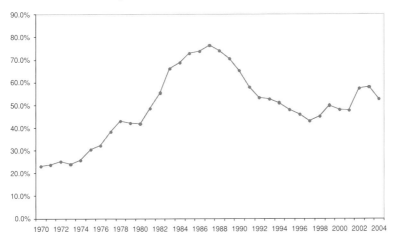

Figure 5.2 Gross external debt: LAC region, 1970–2004 (% of GDP, simple average)
Source: ECLAC (2005)

High debt levels and high inflation had a pernicious effect on growth, poverty, and income distribution in the LAC region. Fischer (1993), for instance, found that growth was negatively correlated with inflation and large budget deficits in a large sample of countries. Edwards (2007) shows that crises have cost the region up to 7% of GDP per decade since the 1970s, and that a significant contributor to the probability of facing a crisis is the fiscal balance.

Table 5.1 *Inflation: LAC region, by decade, 1980–2006*

	Annual variation in CPI		
	1980s (%)	1990s (%)	2000–6 (%)
Regional average[a]	333.7	148.3	8.0
Regional average (without hyperinflations)	26.4	21.4	8.0
Argentina	566.6	253.8	8.9
Bolivia	1368.1	10.5	3.5
Brazil	332.3	854.8	7.8
Chile	21.4	11.8	2.9
Colombia	23.4	22.1	6.6
Costa Rica	27.1	16.9	11.2
Ecuador	34.0	39.0	23.2
El Salvador	18.5	10.6	3.3
Guatemala	12.3	15.3	7.2
Honduras	7.4	19.7	8.4
Mexico	69.1	20.4	5.4
Nicaragua	2437.9	321.4	7.6
Panama	3.1	1.1	1.3
Paraguay	20.5	14.1	8.8
Peru	651.4	813.2	2.2
Uruguay	57.6	48.9	9.0
Venezuela	23.1	47.4	19.1

Note: [a] Simple average.
Source: Own calculations based on IMF–WEO.

Over the past fifteen years, and especially in the past five years, fiscal outcomes have improved dramatically in the region. Since the mid-1990s, high inflation has no longer been a problem, and debt ratios have improved. These results might suggest that fiscal solvency is no longer a serious challenge in the region. However, crises, in many cases motivated by sudden stops[5] in capital flows, are still a major risk, as witnessed by the Mexican peso crisis in 1994, the Brazilian devaluation in 1998, and more recently the Argentine collapse in 2001. As mentioned above, these crises are costly, and loose fiscal policy makes them more likely.

[5] See, for instance, Calvo (1998).

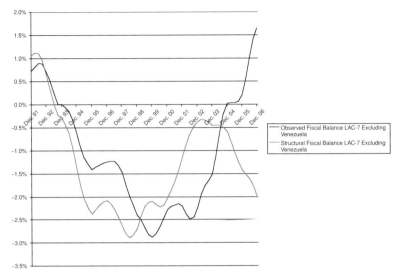

Figure 5.3 Observed and structural budget balance: LAC-7 countries excluding Venezuela (quarterly data, % of GDP)
Source: ECLAC (2005)

Furthermore, the recent favorable international context leads to an over-statement of the region's alleged fiscal virtue. The combination of favorable terms of trade and low interest rates has contributed to economic growth and therefore higher tax revenues, and to reduce debt payments. However, as shown by Talvi (2007), the recent improvements in revenues appear to be mostly transitory, whereas increases in expenditures are permanent. In other words, the structural budget balance for the region paints a less rosy scenario, and a reversal of fortunes could quickly lead to poor fiscal outcomes. In figure 5.3, I show the structural fiscal balance for the seven largest LAC economies[6] estimated by Talvi (2007). Whereas the observed fiscal balance for the fourth quarter of 2006 is 1.6% of GDP, the estimated structural balance is −2.0% of GDP.

The risk of a sudden stop, combined with the structural fragility of fiscal balances, lead me to argue that the region still faces a significant solvency challenge.

---

[6] Venezuela is excluded so as to avoid the large effect of its increased oil revenues. When Venezuela is included, the structural balance is −4.0% of GDP.

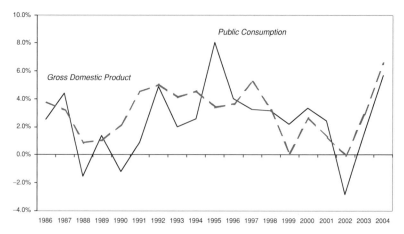

Figure 5.4 Procyclicality of government consumption: LAC region, 1985–
2004 (% change in real GDP and real government consumption)
Source: Perry *et al.* (2006)

In addition to solvency problems, fiscal policy in Latin America is
dramatically procyclical. Gavin and Perotti (1997) showed that, contrary to theoretical predictions[7] and the experience in developed countries, fiscal policy tends to be expansionary during economic expansions and contractionary during recessions in the region. Talvi and
Vegh (2000) showed that this was in fact true for a larger sample of
developing countries. Using a careful definition of procyclicality, focusing on policy instruments rather than endogenous outcomes, Kaminsky, Reinhart, and Vegh (2004) confirm that fiscal policy, in particular
government expenditure, is procyclical in the region.[8]

A first look at procyclicality is presented in figure 5.4, where I show
the similar pattern of changes in real GDP and real government consumption in the region.

In table 5.2, I present more rigorous results from Kaminsky, Reinhart, and Vegh (2004) for the correlation between the cyclical component of GDP and real government expenditure. Except for Colombia,

---

[7] Both Keynesian stabilization prescriptions and neoclassical tax-smoothing
arguments would lead to countercyclical fiscal policy (see Braun 2001).
[8] See also Alberola and Montero (2007) for an estimate of procyclicality in the
region that tries to separate structural from transitory factors in revenue
changes.

Table 5.2 *Procyclicality of government spending and amplitude of the spending cycle: LAC and other regions*

Country	Correlation between cyclical component of GDP and real central government expenditure	Amplitude of the cycle of central government expenditure level (percentage points)	Percentiles (%)
Argentina	0.25	5.35	17
Bolivia	0.09	3.43	11
Brazil	0.11	9.50	30
Chile	0.22	3.69	12
Colombia	−0.01	0.99	4
Guatemala	0.54	6.13	19
Honduras	0.17	4.62	15
Mexico	0.02	7.05	22
Nicaragua	0.40	15.92	50
Panama	0.10	7.06	22
Paraguay	0.57	4.97	16
Peru	0.59	5.12	16
Uruguay	0.58	10.98	34
Venezuela	0.46	8.67	27
LATAM average	*0.29*	*6.68*	*21*
OECD average	*0.13*	*−0.26*	*8*
Other developing	*0.34*	*7.19*	*21*

Note: The cyclical components of GDP and spending are obtained with a Hodrick–Prescott filter. The amplitude of the spending cycle is the difference between spending in good and bad times, where good (bad) times are defined as years of above (below) median growth.
Source: Kaminsky, Reinhart, and Vegh (2004).

all other countries in the region have a positive correlation, implying that government spending increases during good times, and falls during recessions. Compared to OECD countries, the average correlation is more than double. Furthermore, the amplitude of the fiscal cycle is significantly larger. Spending varies by almost 7 percentage points between good and bad times in the region, compared to almost zero for OECD countries (in fact, for OECD countries the difference is negative, meaning that expenditures are actually higher during bad times).

This means that fiscal policy amplifies the already high economic volatility in the region, negatively affecting growth.

In the current expansionary cycle, expenditures are rising, consistent with the historic tendency towards procyclicality. Therefore, I argue that combating the procyclicality of fiscal policy remains a significant challenge for LAC's development.

The determinants of insolvency and procyclicality

Recommendations for overcoming the challenge must of course start from an understanding of the cause of the problems. The recent literature has identified two types of causes for current fiscal policy problems: (1) economic volatility, caused in part by external shocks, combined with high levels of foreign currency debt (i.e. past fiscal problems), and (2) politico-institutional factors.

Volatility, sudden stops, and original sin

In a context of economic volatility, a country with high levels of foreign currency debt can quickly become insolvent. If a sudden stop or a rapid deterioration in terms of trade causes a recession and a devaluation, the dollar-denominated debt payments of the government – or the necessary bailout of the private sector – can cripple public finances and force a fiscal adjustment during bad times. This means that both insolvency and procyclicality can ensue.

Calvo and Talvi (2005) show that in the LAC region, GDP is highly correlated with financial flows. Following the Russian crisis in 1998, financial flows to all emerging markets plummeted, forcing macroeconomic adjustment in most, and causing a crisis in some. Calro and Talvi argue that, depending on the domestic financial structure, the exchange rate regime, and the fiscal stance, the impact of these sudden stops in capital flows will be different. They compare Chile and Argentina, and argue that the former did not suffer a crisis while the second did because, in Chile, the private and public sectors' liabilities were less dollarized, the exchange rate was flexible, and the fiscal position was more solid. Furthermore, more open economies require a smaller exchange rate adjustment to re-establish the current account balance following a sudden stop (see Calvo, Izquierdo, and

Talvi 2003). Therefore, more open economies suffer the impact of these sudden stops less.

One might argue that poor past fiscal policy outcomes lead to a high level of debt and low credibility, forcing governments to borrow in foreign currency. If this were the case, then proposals should focus exclusively on addressing the underlying causes of fiscal deficits (see below). However, Hausmann and Panizza (2003) find no significant correlation between debt/GDP or debt/revenue ratios and their measures of "original sin," i.e. the foreign currency fraction of debt.

This discussion leads us to identify economic volatility, debt dollarization (both in the private and public sectors), a closed economy, and a history of debt intolerance and low credibility as potential determinants of fiscal problems, both insolvency and procyclicality. In fact, IDB (2007) and Campos, Jaimovich, and Panizza (2006) calculate that 20% of the variation in public debt not explained by fiscal deficits is due to episodes of devaluation with highly dollarized debt and banking crises. At the same time, fiscal insolvency contributes to increasing the probability and impact of sudden stops, and leads to increases in the debt burden, creating a vicious cycle.

Proposals to address this source of fiscal problems should focus on limiting economic volatility, increasing the participation of local-currency debt, and improving credibility.[9]

Political economy

Turning to political economy considerations, since the costs of fiscal insolvency and procyclicality are so evident, it is hard to imagine a social planner with a reasonable social welfare function enacting these policies.[10] Recent research has pointed to underlying political causes for insolvency and procyclicality. I therefore turn to a discussion of the political economy determinants of fiscal policy.

The political problems identified in this literature as underlying poor fiscal behavior could be summarized in two categories: principal–agent

---

[9] We do not discuss proposals to open the economy further and make exchange rates more flexible, because these proposals would have multiple impacts whose quantification is beyond the scope of this chapter.

[10] However, see Talvi and Vegh (2000) for theoretical arguments opposing this view.

problems and cooperation problems.[11] By principal–agent problems we refer to the potential abuse that arises in the relationship between the citizens (principal) and their elected representatives (agent). Imprudent fiscal behavior is often the result of actions taken by public officers who are not maximizing the welfare of their constituencies, but rather pursuing private interests. The complexity of public policy decisions, the institutional framework of representative democracy,[12] and the free-rider problem faced by voters when deciding whether to invest time and resources to monitor government activity lead to asymmetric information and delegation of power. This is basically a variation of the classic principal–agent problem: if it were possible to limit policymakers' discretion by "contracting" clear rules, then the abuse of public office for personal or partisan gain would be limited. Furthermore, adequate transparency and accountability would allow voters to monitor and control their representatives more effectively. An example related directly to fiscal policy is when governments over-spend during an election year in order to stimulate the economy and convince voters that they are competent.[13]

By "cooperation," problems we refer to the game played by multiple political actors with heterogenous preferences that maximize objectives that, to some extent, include the welfare of their constituencies. A classic example of cooperation problems is the well-known common pool problem. In fiscal policy, this problem arises due to the following factors: (1) an important characteristic of many government programs is that while they tend to generate benefits that are concentrated, they are often financed from a common pool of resources, and (2) fiscal policy is not designed by a benevolent social planner but rather is the result of a collective decision process with several actors involved: the president, spending ministers, legislators, bureaucrats, pressure groups, etc.

Each of these actors represents specific interests, and faces diverse incentives with respect to fiscal solvency. For example, presidents and finance ministers have more incentives to internalize the aggregate, intertemporal government budget constraint *vis-à-vis* other political actors (legislators, spending ministers, governors). The president is elected in a single national constituency and cares about national issues

---

[11] See, for instance, Alesina and Perotti (1995), von Hagen (2006), and Eslava (2006) for surveys.
[12] See, Persson, Roland, and Tabellini (1997) for a model analyzing this problem.
[13] See Rogoff and Sibert (1988).

such as macroeconomic stability. Given that macroeconomic crises are blamed mainly on presidents, the executive is more likely to prioritize fiscal solvency as a policy objective than other political actors. In contrast, legislators, spending ministers, and subnational actors cater to specific constituencies in order to advance their political careers. For example, the constituencies of spending ministers are groups who benefit from government programs. As such, they do not internalize the aggregate costs of spending programs and have incentives to overspend.

As suggested by the discussion above, common pool and principal–agent problems with fiscal policy can vary across countries and over time due to variations in the underlying incentives faced by key players in the fiscal policymaking process (PMP). These incentives are in turn shaped by political and budget institutions. Thus, the political economy literature that will be reviewed in the following sections analyzes the contribution of institutions in aggravating or reducing common pool and principal–agent problems among voters and politicians, and thus, specifies the institutional sources of deficit biases and procyclicality in fiscal policy outcomes.

Common pool problems: on the consequences of fragmented fiscal PMPs

A general theme treated in the literature is the degree of fragmentation of the fiscal PMP (Velasco 2000). The basic proposition is that as the number of players drawing from a common pool of resources increases, the fiscal balance deteriorates. However, any procedure that forces the players to consider the full tax burden will reduce spending and budget deficits.

The problem of the commons has been studied in a variety of contexts. At the level of the legislature, Weingast, Shepsle, and Johnsen (1981) show how public expenditure can increase due to the common pool problem inherent in the political interaction between regions represented in Congress. Congressmen have an incentive to propose spending increases that accrue to their region, because resources are collected from the entire country, and thus the marginal benefit of an extra dollar of local spending is positive. At the level of the cabinet, Velasco (1999) illustrates how the common pool problem operates in a dynamic setting, resulting not only in higher spending, but also in higher deficits and debt accumulation.

As argued by von Hagen (2006), this tendency for excessive spending, deficits, and debt increases with the number of players drawing from the common pool. A key question is, then, what determines the degree of fragmentation and, hence, the size of the common pool problem in the fiscal PMP? The answer is institutional: electoral rules, government types, party systems, federalism, and budget institutions are among the key institutional variables affecting fiscal performance.

Electoral rules, government types, and the number of parties

Electoral systems refer to the set of rules under which members of legislatures and the executive are elected. The basic components of any electoral system are *district magnitude* (number of representatives elected per district) and *electoral formula* (plurality, PL, or proportional representation, PR). Under PL, all seats go the candidate/list winning the most votes. Under PR, seats are allocated in proportion to the votes received by each party list.

Another important consideration is whether legislators are elected from closed or open lists. In the first case, voters can choose only among party lists but they cannot choose among the candidates within a list. Therefore, the order in the list (established by party leaders) is the determinant for deciding which legislators win a seat to the legislature. In the second case, voters can choose individual candidates from the list according to their preferences. Seats are allocated first to parties, based on the sum of the votes of all the candidates of that party, and then the most-voted candidates from that party win those seats (Cox and McCubbins 2001).

The ballot structure has important implications, as it could affect electoral strategies, the degree of party discipline, and the link between voters and representatives (Carey and Shugart 1995). Assuming that party labels are meaningful, closed-list systems provide party leaders with the greatest control over rank-and-file legislators, encouraging party discipline (Mainwaring and Shugart 1997). As party leaders decide the order of the list, this may also weaken the nexus between legislators and voters.

By contrast, in open-list systems, as candidates of the same party compete against one another, they face incentives to form *factions* – that is, organized groups within parties that compete for control of valued resources. Thus, challenging the party line is less costly than in closed-list system where party leaders enjoy more carrots and sticks.

Summarizing, while closed-list systems encourage party votes, in open-list systems legislators face incentives to cultivate "personal votes" (Carey and Shugart 1995). Such personal votes encourage politicians to provide particularistic goods to specific groups to get reelected (Hallerberg and Marier 2004).

Electoral rules matter for fiscal performance as they affect the number of parties represented in legislatures, the type of government in place (single party or coalition, majority or minority), the likelihood that the executive enjoys a majority in Congress, and the extent to which legislators face incentives to consider the full or only a small part of the total tax burden. Thus, all these variables have an impact on the degree of fragmentation of the fiscal PMP, and as a result affect fiscal outcomes.

In a sample of twenty-six LAC countries for the period 1990–5, it has been found that countries with large district magnitude,[14] a large number of effective parties in the legislature, and weak support for the governing party in Congress tend to be associated with larger fiscal deficits (Stein, Talvi, and Grisanti 1998). In contrast, plurality systems lead to smaller government deficits (Persson and Tabellini 2003). The relationship[15] between legislative fragmentation and deficits is illustrated in figure 5.5.

Amorim Neto and Borsani (2004) find that a president enjoying strong legislative support and a stable team of ministers had a favorable impact on fiscal balance in a sample of ten LAC countries between 1980 and 1998. The fact that cabinet stability plays a role in determining budget outcomes points towards the importance of political actors' time horizons in the fiscal PMP: political instability, measured by frequency of government changes, appears to lead to larger deficits in both developed and developing countries (Roubini 1991).

Fiscal deficits are also the outcome of electoral rules that provide incentives for legislators to cultivate a personal vote[16] (Hallerberg and

---

[14] District magnitude is the size, in number of voters, of jurisdictions in which legislators are chosen. A large district magnitude will generally imply that there are many legislators per district, increasing the probability that multiple parties are represented in Congress.

[15] Legislative fragmentation is measured by IDB (2007) as the negative of the Herfindahl index for the fraction of seats held by different parties. The Herfindahl index takes a value of -1 if all seats are held by the same party and a value of 0 if there are as many seats as parties represented in parliament.

[16] By "personal vote," we understand the vote for an individual candidate rather than a party.

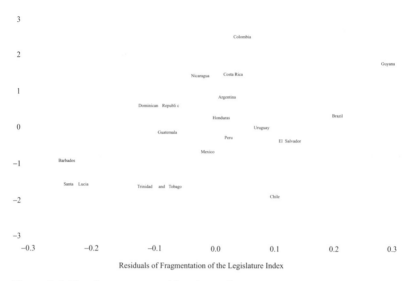

Figure 5.5 Fiscal outcomes and legislative fragmentation
Source: IADB (2007)

Marier 2004). This is consistent with the idea that common pool problems are exacerbated when politicians consider only a small fraction of the total tax burden and interact in fragmented settings. We now turn to a different set of institutions regulating the relationships between the central and subnational governments (federalism and decentralization) and examine their role in exacerbating the commons problem.

Regarding procyclicality, the number of actors has also been found to be a relevant determinant. Tornell and Lane (1999) present a model in which competition among powerful groups leads to an increase in over-spending of a common resource when this resource increases – for example, procyclical public spending. This pressure increases as the number of groups increases. Braun (2001) finds evidence consistent with this hypothesis for developing countries: as the number of political veto players increases, fiscal policy becomes more procyclical.

Federalism and decentralization

In this section, we analyze the incentives for fiscal discipline created by federal fiscal arrangements. In particular, we explore the potential of decentralization to aggravate the commons problem. These issues are of particular relevance not only for formally federal countries in the

LAC region (Argentina, Brazil, Mexico, Venezuela) but for the region as a whole: since the mid-1980s a wave of decentralization reforms has swept the continent, empowering regional politicians with more fiscal resources than in the past (Daughters and Harper 2007).

Federal fiscal arrangements define tax and expenditure assignments between different levels of government, the design of intergovernmental transfers, and the borrowing autonomy of subnational units (Stein 1999). In the LAC region, decentralization is typically much higher in the expenditure dimension than in the revenue sphere (IDB 1997). This asymmetry between expenditure responsibilities and revenue capacity at the subnational level generates a gap, known as "vertical fiscal imbalance," which is typically bridged through the use of transfers from the central government.

As should be clear by now, such institutions create an incentive for subnational governments to over-spend the common pool of resources, enjoying the full benefit of expenditures without internalizing the costs. This problem may become even more serious in cases where subnational governments have a large degree of borrowing autonomy, in particular if the central government finds it difficult to commit not to bail them out in case of financial trouble (Rodden 2002). In this case, bailout expectations and the commitment problem affect the behavior of subnational governments, and under certain configurations they will tend to over-borrow and over-spend, and then shift the burden onto the central government (Inman 2003; Rodden, Eskeland, and Litvak 2003). Under what conditions is this possible?

The degree of vertical imbalance and level of borrowing autonomy are key indicators of how soft or hard subnational budget constraints can be. If subnational actors face soft budget constraints, they would have the incentive to be fiscally irresponsible. On the contrary, hard budget constraints impose limits on fiscal profligacy. For example, Rodden (2002) shows that subnational governments tend to achieve balanced fiscal accounts when either the federal government imposes tight borrowing constraints or when subnational governments have wide-ranging taxing autonomy (a low level of common pool).

As a final point, one should also note that political federalism also plays a role in the fiscal PMP. In cases where electoral districts coincide with territorial units (e.g. states, provinces), the degree of "partisan harmony" (the extent of support for the president throughout the territorial units) affects fiscal policymaking. As shown by Rodden and

Wibbels (2002) a federation's capacity to control deficits increases as the share of subnational units controlled by the party of the chief executive increases.

Another key factor is the over-representation of smaller subnational units in the national legislature (malapportionment). Malapportionment strengthens the political power of the least-populated states relative to the most-populated units. It is interesting to note that malapportionment is not a unique feature of territorial chambers. In fact, several lower houses in federal systems show a certain degree of over-representation even in population-based lower chambers (Samuels and Snyder 2001).[17] As a consequence, over-represented units may skew the distribution of fiscal resources in their favor and typically receive higher resources *per capita* (Gibson, Calvo, and Falleti 2004).

Federal fiscal arrangements can also contribute to enhanced procyclicality. If federal transfers to subnational governments are a fixed percentage of federal tax collection, then transfers will increase automatically during expansions. If subnational governments have less incentives to save this increase than the federal government (for example, if they expect a bailout if problems arise down the line) then the procyclicality of spending will increase.

Budget institutions

In addition to the set of political institutions reviewed above, budget institutions are also considered key determinants of fiscal discipline. "Budget institutions" can be defined as all the rules and regulations according to which budgets are drafted, approved, and implemented (Alesina and Perotti 1996). One can identify three types of budget institutions: *fiscal rules*, which establish numerical restrictions on certain fiscal indicators (such as balanced budget laws); *procedural rules*, which determine the prerogatives of the actors involved in drafting, approving, and implementing the budget, as well as the rules of engagement throughout these phases; and *transparency rules*, which define the degree of comprehensiveness of the budget as well as the availability of information and *ex post* control of budget execution (Alesina *et al.* 1996; Filc and Scartascini 2007).

---

[17] This is a result of the existence of, among other things, lower and upper limits to the number of deputies that a certain region may have.

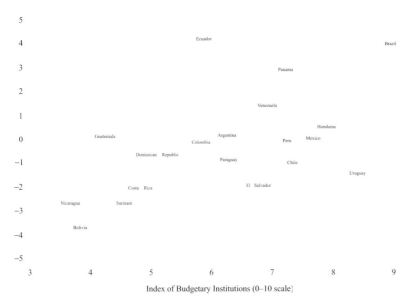

Figure 5.6 Budget institutions and fiscal outcomes
Source: IADB (2007)

Budget procedures have been classified along a "hierarchical–collegial" continuum (Alesina *et al.* 1996). Hierarchical procedures attribute strong prerogatives and powers to the finance minister in the budget preparation stage within the executive branch, and severely limit the prerogatives of the legislature in amending the budget. In contrast, collegial procedures emphasize the prerogatives of spending ministers *vis-à-vis* the treasury, and do not limit the extent of possible legislative amendments to the proposed budget.

Given that hierarchical procedures provide a leading role to the executive branch in the budget process, and that presidents and treasury ministers have more incentives to internalize the government intertemporal budget constraint, hierarchical rules should promote fiscal discipline.

In order to test this hypothesis in the LAC region,[18] Alesina *et al.* 1996 constructed a "budget institutions index" with several components which referred to all the stages of the budget-making process

[18] See Bohn and Inman (1996) for a test of the impact of fiscal rules in US states.

(preparation, approval, and implementation). Higher values of the index correspond to more hierarchical and transparent budget institutions. They find that countries that rank higher in the index have also lower deficits. Filc and Scartascini (2007) confirm these results for a larger time period and sample of countries (see figure 5.6).

So far, we have discussed coordination problems between policymakers (the common pool). We now turn to an example of a typical principal–agent problem found in fiscal policymaking: that of the political business cycle.

Principal–agent problems: the political business cycle

The literature on political business cycles deals with the incentives of policymakers to manipulate fiscal policy during election times. Classic studies argue that all governments increase spending and reduce taxes before elections, in order to increase their re-election prospects.[19] Thus, electoral opportunism may be another source of deficit bias in representative democracies.

However, recent empirical evidence shows that political budget cycles accrue only under certain specific circumstances. Given that these conditions are present in the region, we turn to the literature's main findings. First, Brender and Drazen (2005) find a political budget cycle in a large cross-section of countries, but this fact is driven by the experience of "new democracies" in the first few years after their transition to democratic regimes (see figure 5.7). The authors argue that, in these settings, fiscal manipulation may work because voters are inexperienced with electoral politics or may simply lack the information needed to evaluate the fiscal manipulation that is produced in more established democracies

Additionally, Shi and Svensson (2006) find that the size of political budget cycles is much larger in developing than in developed countries. To explain this difference they focus on two factors: politicians' rents from remaining in power (proxied by level of corruption) and the share of informed voters in the electorate (proxied by access to media data). Higher levels of corruption and a small share of informed voters imply larger deficit increases in election years for developing countries.

---

[19] See Drazen (2000) for a summary of the evidence on political budget cycles.

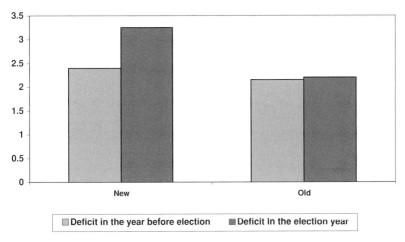

Figure 5.7 Average budget deficits: election year and previous year
Source: Brender and Drazen (2005)

The discussion above suggests that the ability of voters to monitor fiscal policy is a key determinant of fiscal outcomes. Lack of budget transparency and accountability provide incentives for opportunistic politicians to incur in fiscal deficits and debt accumulation. For example, Eslava (2006) shows for LAC countries that an accountability index[20] has a negative impact on the deficit (see figure 5.8).

Overall, there is evidence that political and budget institutions are key determinants of fiscal outcomes in general, and the budget balance and cyclical stance in particular. Fiscal discipline and stabilizing fiscal policy results when fragmentation of fiscal responsibility is limited and voters are able to monitor politicians' behavior. On the contrary, fiscal profligacy, debt accumulation, and procyclicality are the outcome of common pool and principal–agent problems in the fiscal PMP. These problems can be exacerbated by institutional arrangements that provide opportunities for politicians to ignore or shift the full tax burden of their fiscal decisions.

---

[20] This index draws from the World Bank's Governance indicators, measuring among other things, political rights, freedom of the press, and press development.

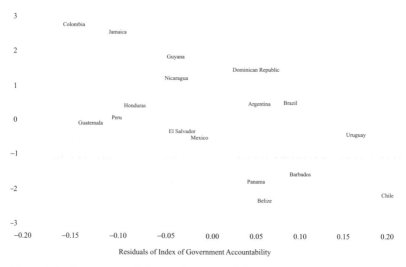

Figure 5.8 Government deficit and accountability
Source: IADB (2007)

In sum, rules such as electoral systems, federalism, or budget institutions shape the behavior of politicians in the fiscal PMP and,
hence, matter for understanding fiscal performance. The relevance
of political and fiscal institutions for fiscal solvency and procyclicality must therefore be taken into account for the design of specific
solutions.

3 The proposed solutions

If the determinants of insolvency and procyclicality are related to economic volatility caused by external shocks, high levels of foreign currency, external debt, and politico-economic factors, then proposals
should explicitly address these issues. I therefore propose three types
of solutions to the challenge of improving fiscal solvency and reducing
procyclicality. They are (1) improving debt management, (2) consolidating the budget process, and (3) improving the efficiency and equity
of taxes and expenditures.

I first briefly describe the reforms, then discuss the potential impact
they would have and, in section 4, attempt a quantification of this

impact based upon the empirical literature studying fiscal policy and growth.

Improve debt management

In section 2, we argued that one of the determinants of sudden fiscal solvency problems and sharp adjustments during bad times that lead to procyclical fiscal policy was the interaction of volatility with domestic balance sheet effects. In particular, the level of foreign currency debt appears as a relevant factor.

Of course, simply increasing the proportion of local-currency debt is not something countries can do by fiat, there has to be a demand for that debt. There are several proposals in the literature that seek to reduce the burden of foreign currency debt by using contingent contracts of different types (see IDB 2007 for a survey). For example, Eichengreen and Hausmann (2005) argue for a global initiative by International Financial Institutions (IFIs) and developed countries to create a market for local-currency debt by first creating a unit of account indexed to developing country inflation, and then having IFIs issue debt denominated in this unit, while lending to individual countries in inflation-indexed local currency. Borensztein and Mauro (2002) call for the use of GDP-linked bonds, that would essentially make bondholders partners in the economic success or failure of the borrowing country, reducing debt payments during bad times and increasing them during good times. Caballero and Kowan (2007) argue for the use of contingent contracts that are not linked to emerging-market instruments.

The proposal in this section, then, is for governments to take advantage of opportunities to use *contingent debt instruments* as part of their debt-management policies.

Using contingent debt would reduce the probability of a crisis, reduce the size of the fiscal adjustment necessary were a crisis to occur, and would therefore reduce the likelihood of sudden fiscal insolvency problems arising. At the same time, the forced procyclicality of fiscal policy would be reduced, since fiscal adjustments during bad times would be lower. Of course, these mechanisms have costs, since they perform the function of insurance. These costs must be paid up-front, with benefits accruing in the future, which often makes politicians wary of implementing these mechanisms.

Consolidate the budget process

The political economy roots of insolvency and procyclicality point us in the direction of modifying the rules and institutions by which fiscal policy is decided. In section 2, we identified electoral rules, federalism, and budget procedures as some of these key institutions. I hesitate in proposing changes in electoral rules and federal arrangements, since the consequences of these changes go well beyond fiscal[21] issues.[22] Furthermore, they often require constitutional changes or a special majority, since they reflect political equilibria regarding fundamental issues such as political representation and regional autonomy.

With this caveat in mind, I focus on proposals to improve budget procedures and transparency in the region. The region has already made progress in this aspect. Filc and Scartascini (2007) document the reforms made since 1990. They show that several countries have improved their procedural rules, making them more hierarchical, implemented numerical rules that limit deficits, spending and debt levels, and increased budget transparency.

However, there is still much that can be done. Several countries still lag in reforming the budget process. Filc and Scartascini (2007), following the methodology of Alesina *et al.* (1996), find that the difference in fiscal surplus between a country in the first and fourth quartiles of an index of fiscal institutions is 2.3% of GDP. Countries with more hierarchical budget procedures, numerical limits on deficits and spending, and more transparent fiscal policy, obtain better fiscal outcomes.

Specific proposals in this area include the following:

- **Implement fiscal responsibility laws** *(FRL)*
  These laws usually bundle together several of the desirable characteristics of budget procedures. They call for independent revenue estimates, limit the ability of legislatures and line ministries

---

[21] Also, most LAC countries are not federal, except for Mexico, Brazil, Argentina and Venezuela.

[22] See IDB (2006) for a deep analysis of political institutions in Latin America. The study warns about the risk implied in proposing reforms based on "partial equilibrium" analysis – that is, not considering the full effects of reforms.

to increase spending, impose numerical limits on deficits, spending, and debt, and include transparency clauses to improve the access to fiscal information by the public. The best example of a fiscal responsibility law in the region to date is Brazil (see, for example, Braun and di Gresia (2002) and Braun and Tommasi (2004) for analyses).

A well-designed fiscal responsibility law (FRL) will limit the common pool problem by limiting the pool of common resources to which agents have access (deficit and spending limits) and, by constraining the capacity of agents – especially subnational governments – of indirectly obtaining part of the common pool (e.g. borrowing constraints for subnational governments). Furthermore, it will limit the principal–agent problem by increasing transparency and accountability (e.g. independent revenue estimates, timely publication of fiscal information).[23]

- **Structural deficit rules**

  Chile has followed a policy of calculating its structural fiscal balance – i.e. the fiscal balance that would result absent cyclical fluctuations. The policy goal, first stated as an informal rule and then passed into law, was to maintain a structural surplus of 1% of GDP.[24] This means that during recessions, the country can run deficits as long as the structural surplus remains at 1% of GDP. This, of course, implies that during good times, the surplus must be higher than that which would simply result from cyclical increases in revenue (see Fiess 2002 for a discussion of the rule).

  The advantage of this kind of rule is that, in addition to limiting the overall deficit, just as well-enforced numerical rules would, it would also lead to countercyclical fiscal policy. The reason is that, during good times, when revenues increase, a higher surplus is demanded by the rule, since growth is above trend. During recessions, a deficit is allowed to the extent that income and revenues are below trend.

- **Create a Congressional Budget Office**

  A Congressional Budget Office (CBO) office of this kind would aim to increase the technical capability of parliaments in the region to analyze budgets and evaluate the impact of laws with fiscal

---

[23] See Lowry and Alt (2006) for a theoretical discussion of the different effects of transparency on fiscal policy.

[24] This limit has been reduced to 0.5% of GDP.

consequences.[25] It is important to note that this kind of office should have an informative function for Congress, not actual authority to influence the budget, so as to avoid the possibility of reducing the hierarchical nature of the budget process. Also, authorities should be selected following technical criteria so as to avoid simple capture by factions in Congress. This proposal should be considered as an integral part of an FRL, as a mechanism to increase transparency and accountability.

As a final note, it is worth emphasizing that a very important caveat in designing fiscal rules, both FRLs and structural surplus rules, is credibility and enforceability of reforms. In contexts in which laws and regulations are often violated by governments with no serious consequences ensuing – i.e. where enforcement of laws is weak – then fiscal rules will probably have little impact on fiscal outcomes, and in fact might even be counterproductive. Braun and Tommasi (2004) argue that, in weak institutional environments, fiscal rules do not significantly affect the incentives of policymakers in the fiscal policymaking process, and therefore, if the pre-rule equilibrium involved a deficit bias, fiscal outcomes would probably not comply with the limits set in the rule. Furthermore, the violation of the rule can actually further reduce policy credibility in the country, which could justify not passing the rule in the first place.[26]

Improve efficiency and equity of spending and taxes[27]

Although efficiency and equity of spending and taxes are not necessarily directly related to fiscal solvency and countercyclicality, given the pervasive problems in these areas I believe it is important to contribute suggestions.[28] Furthermore, even in the presence of poor fiscal

---

[25] See Braun, Diaz Frers, and Uña (2006) for discussions of CBOs in the LAC region.

[26] See Braun and Gadano (2007) for an example of this problem in Argentina.

[27] Note: in this section I have excluded sectoral reforms such as reforms to health and education spending, because these are addressed in chapters 2 and 6 of this volume, and their alternative view papers. I focused on reforms that one would expect to be implemented by the Economics Ministry.

[28] In fact, Berkman and Cavallo (2006) find that inefficiency of public spending, tax evasion, and inefficiency of the tax structure were the three highest-ranking fiscal problems in a survey of 308 regional public policy experts.

institutions, by finding good fiscal policies the negative impact on growth can be reduced.

Spending

- **Create an independent agency to provide rigorous and systematic evaluations and cost-benefit and distributive impact analysis for government programs**

  An agency of this kind, that should initially be regional in nature due to limited technical capabilities in several countries,[29] would perform evaluations, cost-benefit analysis, and distributive impact analysis of government programs, generate databases to monitor and evaluate social conditions and government programs over time, compare the impact of programs in different countries, and share information on effective policies. The existence of this kind of information and analysis should influence policymakers and the public to prioritize more effective programs.[30]

- **Increase the proportion of automatic stabilizers in the budget**

  Braun (2001) finds that almost 10% of the difference in the cyclical behavior between developed and developing countries can be accounted for by differences in the composition of their budgets. Developed countries have a stronger prevalence of transfers in their budgets, many of which act as automatic stabilizers. For example, well-functioning unemployment insurance programs automatically increase their spending during recessions as unemployment increases, and decrease their spending during expansions as jobs are created. Therefore, automatic stabilizers can actually help reduce the procyclicality of fiscal policy in the region.

  The risk, of course, is that if the problem of fragility of public finances in the face of sudden stops is not resolved, then automatic stabilizers would increase the size of the necessary fiscal adjustment in more flexible areas of the budget, probably making the fiscal adjustment politically more costly and therefore less likely, and increasing the probability of a full-blown crisis.

---

[29] See Galiani (2006).

[30] However, see Galiani (2006) for a discussion of the necessary conditions for impact evaluation to affect policy. Among others, Galiani suggests that a network of universities, think tanks, independent media, etc. that actually analyzes these evaluations is key.

Furthermore, it is not straightforward to implement a well-functioning unemployment insurance scheme in LAC countries, where a high percentage of workers are in the informal sector. Workfare programs are typical replacements, but it is often harder to reduce spending in these programs during good times, since recipients typically receive informal sector employment. This makes it difficult to detect the recipients that should be leaving the program during expansions.

Overall, automatic stabilizers should probably be used in moderation, and phased in only after financial risks are reduced and the extent of formal employment has increased sufficiently. For this reason, I believe that this proposal should not yet be considered as part of the solution package.

Tax reform

I focus on issues of tax policy, and purposely avoid tax administration, since these proposals would overlap with the administrative reform proposals in other chapters of this book, and because it is likely that many issues of tax administration will solve themselves to the extent that electronic transactions become more widespread.

- **Eliminate excessively distortionary taxes**

  Although the neutrality of tax systems in the region has improved significantly over the past fifteen years (see Lora 2007), there are still a number of excessively distortionary taxes that limit economic activity – for example, the financial transactions taxes which have become increasingly popular in the region. Coelho, Ebrill, and Summers (2001) document how, following economic crises in the late 1990s, six LAC countries adopted taxes on financial transactions. They argue that these taxes can have serious allocative efficiency problems. First, since the tax is levied on each financial transaction, it taxes the payments in each stage of a productive process, becoming a turnover tax with the well-known distortion of taxing activities with a larger number of stages more heavily. But more importantly for the LAC context, financial transactions taxes generate incentives to operate outside the financial system, contributing both to increasing informality in the economy and to reducing financial intermediation.

  In most cases, financial transactions taxes were put in place during fiscal crises, as a means to prop up revenues in the face of falling tax collection. However, they have not been removed during the recent expansion; instead, expenditures have increased, as shown above, making it difficult to remove them without negatively affecting the fiscal balance. Therefore, the elimination of these taxes should be gradual, and will require a commitment to moderate future spending increases.

- **Modify the income tax by (a) reducing corporate taxation and off-setting lost revenue by including dividends and capital gains in the personal income tax base, and (b) replacing complex personal income taxes with a constant marginal rate**

  Typically, corporations in the region pay corporate income taxes, but dividends and capital gains are exempt from personal income taxation. The problem with this arrangement is two-fold. First, given that LAC countries are generally small, open economies and that capital is significantly more mobile than labor, we can expect the incidence of corporate taxes to fall mainly on workers (see the classic study of Harberger 1962). Second, it limits incentives to re-invest profits.

  If instead re-invested profits were exempt of corporate income tax (as in Chile until the early 1990s, see Hsieh and Parker 2006) and dividends were included in the personal income tax base, there would be stronger incentives for companies to re-invest profits, leading to higher growth. Lost revenue would be recovered via dividend taxation and higher growth.

  Regarding simplification of the personal income tax schedule, this proposal is a classic in public finance (see, for example, Friedman 1962). Progressive income tax schedules have disincentive effects on work, especially by the most productive workers. (see Gruber and Saez 2002). Furthermore, the complexity of tax systems generates a compliance cost in terms of time that is not insignificant.[31] The main criticism against an income tax with a constant marginal rate would be that it would make the tax system less progressive. However, if there is an exemption, or a universal transfer, then even though the marginal rate is constant, the average tax rate will be progressive – i.e. people with higher income will pay a higher percentage of their income relative to low-income people.

---

[31] Hodge, Scott Moody, and Warcholik (2006) calculate the compliance cost for US federal taxes at $244 billion, or 24% of revenue.

4 The impact of the proposed solutions

In this section, I attempt a quantification of the impact of the reform
proposals, focusing on the impact of the proposals on economic
growth. For a full evaluation, one would also want to study distributive consequences, ideally mapping the impact of the reforms on
the distribution of individual income.[32] However, as will be evident
from the discussion below, even for the more straightforward connection between fiscal policies and growth, precise estimates are scarce
in the literature. The extra step of calculating the impact on individual income would compound the problem beyond what I believe is
productive.

Coming up with a precise number for the costs and benefits of
the proposed solutions, even when we focus on economic growth,
is a daunting task given the current state of knowledge. Fiscal policy affects the economy in numerous ways, and in general there is
no professional consensus on the magnitude – and sometimes even
on the sign – of the coefficients, even for broad issues such as the
size of taxation and spending. Domenech (2004) surveys the literature
that relates government spending and taxes with growth, and finds
highly variable results. For example, Engen and Skinner (1996) find
a negative correlation between a balanced budget increase in spending and taxes and economic growth, whereas Easterly and Rebelo
(1993) and Levine and Renelt (1992) find that the correlation between
size of government and growth is in general statistically insignificant.

This uncertainty increases even more when we consider reforms that
have only recently been attempted and for which insufficient time has
passed to have a precise evaluation, such as the implementation of
financial transactions taxes. The same happens for policies that have
been attempted in very few countries, such as the Chilean corporate
tax exemption for re-invested profits.

To add to the problem, in some of the cases we have to compound
estimates. For example, an FRL will affect growth indirectly through
its effect on fiscal solvency. To get an estimate of the final effect,
then, we need to first estimate the effect of the implementation of the

---

[32] In fact, one would ideally take this one step further and evaluate the impact on
individual welfare, and then evaluate this impact using a social welfare
function.

Table 5.3 *Summary of impact estimates*

Proposal	Potential impact
Contingent debt instruments	0.7%–0.8% of GDP per year
Fiscal rules	0.3%–0.6% of GDP per year
Policy evaluation agency	No available estimates
Tax reform	0.47%–1.82% of GDP per year

FRL on fiscal outcomes (not easy, since FRLs are recent and not too common in the region), and then multiply this by the effect of fiscal solvency on growth, a contentious issue in itself, at least in terms of magnitude.

Finally, as mentioned in section 3, since credibility and enforcement of reforms is a key issue, measuring what policies actually do is sometimes even more complex. The *de facto* impact of a reform may well be different from the *de jure* expectation in the context of weak institutions.

With these caveats in mind, I assess the existing empirical estimates to attempt an approximation of the possible impact of the proposed reforms.

In table 5.3, I present a summary of the results, and then develop the calculations below.

Improve debt management

Eichengreen (2004) makes a rough estimate of the benefit of eliminating currency crises at around 0.7% of GDP per year for developing countries. This number could be interpreted as an upper bound for the benefit of the proposal to incorporate contingent debt instruments in debt management policies since, at best, these policies would eliminate currency crises.

Caballero and Panageas (2008) calculate that, for a country like Chile, with good fundamentals, hedging the probability of suffering a sudden stop can be equivalent to a reduction in the stock of debt of 10 percentage points of GDP. However, IDB (2007) shows that the benefit of debt reduction varies by country, depending on the current stock of debt and the quality of policies and institutions. Caballero and Panageas (2008) show recent empirical estimates that have found a non-linear relationship between external debt levels and growth.[33] Low levels of debt appear to be beneficial for growth up to a point, and then the correlation turns negative. The problem is that estimates for this turning-point range between 10 and 60% of GDP! In addition, Imbs and Rancière (2005) find that the threshold level at which debt becomes negative for growth is higher for countries with better institutions.

To make an optimistic calculation, assume that Latin American countries are in the negative coefficient territory of the above non-linear relationship between debt and growth, so reducing debt would be beneficial – a not too unreasonable assumption, given an average level of external debt/GDP of almost 50% in 2004, excluding Argentina and Nicaragua that were above 110%. Following IDB (2007), this would mean that a 10 percentage point reduction in the debt/GDP ratio could generate a growth benefit of around 0.8 percentage points per year. However, the shakiness of this estimate cannot be stressed enough.[34]

Consolidate the budget process

To estimate the impact of the proposals to improve the budget process, we need first an estimate of the impact of fiscal rules on budget outcomes, and then an estimate of the impact of fiscal outcomes on economic growth.

For the first part of the calculation, we rely on Filc and Scartascini (2007), who replicate the cross-country estimates of Alesina *et al.* (1996) with newer information and a larger data set. Their dependent variable is the average fiscal balance between 2000 and 2002, and the relevant independent variable is an index of budget institutions measuring the degree of hierarchy and transparency of the budget process, and the existence of numerical limits to fiscal variables.[35]

---

[33] See, for example, Patillo, Poirson, and Ricci (2002), Clements, Bhattacharya, and Nguyen (2003), Cordella, Ricci, and Reciz-Arranz (2005), and Imbs and Ranciere (2005).

[34] First, it would mean extrapolating the 10% estimate of Caballero and Panageas (2008), which they already claim to be a very rough estimate, to the whole sample of LAC countries. Second, it would mean believing that an average of recent estimates, most of which have not been published in peer-reviewed journals, actually applies to Latin American countries today. Both of these assumptions are beyond heroic.

[35] The authors also control for the stock of debt, terms of trade shocks, and the dependency ratio.

They find that countries in the top quartile of the budget index have a fiscal result 2.3 percentage points of GDP better than countries in the bottom quartile.

This calculation has, of course, many problems. For starters, it is based on only nineteen observations for LAC countries. Second, it covers a short time period, and the true coefficients could be time-variant. Third, there is a fundamental problem of potential endogeneity in the estimates of the impact of fiscal rules that has not been addressed in the literature[36] – and is not addressed by Filc and Scartascini (2007): both good fiscal outcomes and solid fiscal institutions could be reflecting voter preferences rather than good institutions causing good outcomes. A final problem is posed by the fact that it is not clear how an FRL or structural balance rule would actually map into the index of fiscal institutions. Would it really be an increase from the bottom to the top quartile? It is far from obvious. This final problem is compounded by the fact that enforcement issues might severely limit the impact of the reform.

For the second part of the calculation, I take the estimated coefficients for the effect of fiscal surplus on growth from Fischer (1993), who estimates cross-section and panel growth regressions for a sample of ninety-four countries. These range from 0.133 for the cross-sectional estimates to 0.241 for panel estimates with standard controls. Compounding the impact of rules on the fiscal surplus with these coefficients would indicate that a successful fiscal rule, that could take a LAC country from the lowest to the highest quartile in the Filc–Scartascini index, could increase growth by 0.3–0.6% per year.[37]

Improve efficiency and equity of spending and taxes

Spending

Theoretical models of growth suggest that more efficient public spending, especially in human capital and infrastructure, can improve growth.[38] This has been confirmed by some empirical estimates. (see, for example, Baffes and Shah 1998). However, the impact of improved cost-benefit evaluation on public spending efficiency has

---

[36] See Braun and Tommasi (2004) for a critique.

[37] The growth coefficients, of course, could vary depending on time period selected, sample of countries, and estimation methodology, so that these results should also be considered very tentative.

[38] See, for instance, Lucas (1988) and de Long and Summers (1991)

not been estimated, to my knowledge, and in fact would be very hard to estimate, since isolating the effect of evaluation on program productivity would not be straightforward. For this reason, I believe it would be unreasonable to present even a rough estimate as with the other proposals to address the challenge presented in this chapter.

Tax reform

For the tax reform proposals, I will focus on the reform of income taxes, since the creation of financial transaction taxes in the LAC region is too recent to allow a serious quantification of their negative impact.

Taxes can affect growth in several ways. Heckman, Lochner, and Taber (1998) argue that a progressive income tax discourages investment in education, thus negatively affecting human capital. The recent economic growth literature emphasizes the importance of innovation and investment in research and development (R & D) for economic growth. Furthermore, it can be expected that entrepreneurship is linked to these drivers of growth. A burgeoning public finance literature based on US data shows a significant negative effect of corporate taxes and progressive personal income taxes on risktaking and innovation. For instance, Gentry and Hubbard (2000) show that a progressive personal income tax reduces risktaking, and Gordon (1998) shows that a low corporate tax rate relative to the personal income tax rate encourages risktaking. Cullen and Gordon (2002) show, using individual tax returns for the United States during 1964–93, that income taxation harms entrepreneurial activity.

Motivated by this literature, Lee and Gordon (2004) estimate the impact of personal income and corporate tax rates on growth in a panel of seventy countries for the period 1970–97. They find that GDP growth is negatively correlated with corporate tax rates, but find little effect for personal income taxes. Their estimates imply that a 10 percentage point decline in the tax rate leads to a 0.47–1.82 percentage point increase in the annual growth rate, depending on the controls included and the estimation strategy employed.

I take this calculation as the benchmark estimate for the impact of tax reform, since it is unlikely that a much larger decline in the tax rate than 10 percentage points can be politically feasible.

5 Conclusions

Despite the recent upswing in economic activity that has improved fiscal accounts throughout the LAC region, it still faces serious challenges in terms of fiscal solvency and procyclicality. These challenges are masked by the current favorable environment, but a deeper look at structural balances give us cause for concern.

Serious solutions to these problems must be based on a solid understanding of the underlying determinants of fiscal problems – namely, problems of volatility and debt structure and political economy issues.

In this chapter I have proposed policy measures based on the existing economic literature to address these challenges. These measures include improving debt management by using contingent debt instruments, the use of fiscal rules to overcome deficit bias problems and procyclicality, improving public spending efficiency by creating a regional policy evaluation agency, and tax reform to eliminate recently created distortionary taxes, reduce corporate taxes, and simplify and generalize personal income taxes.

I have attempted a rough quantification of the potential impact of these measures on economic growth based on the existing literature. A simple addition of these calculations leads to a potential benefit in terms of growth of up to 3 percentage points of GDP per year.[39] However, these estimates should be considered as extremely tentative, and any attempt to guide policy action based on them should apply the utmost caution. This work presents a challenge to the economics profession to come up with ever-better estimates of the impact of public policies to more successfully guide policy decision-making.

Bibliography

Alberola, Enrique and José Manuel Montero, 2007. "Debt Sustainability and Procyclical Fiscal Policies in Latin America." *Economía, Journal of the Latin American and Caribbean Association* 7(1): 157–93

Alesina, A., R. Hausmann, R. Hommes, and E. Stein, 1996. "Budget Institutions and Fiscal Performance in Latin America." NBER Working Paper **5586**

---

[39] Apart from the mentioned limitations of calculation, simple addition of these benefits is likely to be wrong, since there is probably important overlap in the benefit of the proposed solutions.

Alesina, A. and R. Perotti, 1995. "The Political Economy of Budget Deficits." IMF Staff Papers March: 1–31

1996. "Budget Deficits and Budget Institutions." NBER Working Paper 5556

Amorim Neto, O. and H. Borsani, 2004. "Presidents and Cabinets: The Political Determinants of Fiscal Behavior in Latin America." *Studies in Comparative International Development* 39(1): 3–27

Baffes, John and Anwar Shah, 1998. "Productivity of Public Spending, Sectoral Allocation Choices, and Economic Growth." *Economic Development and Cultural Change* 46(2): 291–303

Berkman, Heather and Eduardo Cavallo, 2006. "The Challenges in Latin America: Identifying what Latin Americans Believe to be the Main Problems Facing their Countries." IDB, mimeo

Bohn, Henning and Robert Inman, 1996. "Balanced Budget Rules and Public Deficits: Evidence from the US States." NBER Working Paper 5533

Borensztein, Ricardo and Paolo Mauro, 2002. "Reviving the Case of GDP Indexed Bonds." IMF Working Paper 02/10

Braun, Miguel, 2001. "Why is Fiscal Policy Procyclical in Developing Countries?" In Miguel Brown, *Three Essays on Economic Policy in Developing Countries*, PhD dissertation. Harvard University Economics Department

Braun, Miguel, Luciana Diaz Frers, and Gerardo Uña, eds., 2006. *Cada cual ¿atiende su juego? El rol del Congreso Nacional en el proceso presupuestario en la Argentina*. Buenos Aires: CIPPEC

Braun, Miguel and Nicolas Gadano, 2007. "¿Para qué sirven las reglas fiscales? Un análisis crítico de la experiencia argentina." Revista de la CEPAL 91

Braun, Miguel and Luciano di Gresia, 2002. "Towards Effective Social Insurance in Latin America: The Importance of Countercyclical Fiscal Policy." IDB Research Department Working Paper 487

Braun, Miguel and Mariano Tommasi, 2004. "Subnational Fiscal Rules: A Game Theoretic Approach." In George Kopits, ed., *Rules-Based Fiscal Policy in Emerging Markets: Background, Analysis and Prospects*. London: Macmillan

Brender, A. and A. Drazen, 2005. "Political Budget Cycles in New Versus Established Democracies." *Journal of Monetary Economics* 52(7): 1271–95

Caballero, Ricardo and Kevin Kowan, 2007. "Financial Integration Without the Volatility." World Bank, mimeo

Caballero, Ricardo and Stavros Panageas, 2008. "Hedging Sudden Stops and Precautionary Contractions." *Journal of Development Economics* 85: 28–57

Calvo, Guillermo, 1998. "Capital Flows and Capital-Market Crises: The Simple Economics of Sudden Stops." *Journal of Applied Economics* 1: 35–54

Calvo, Guillermo A., Alejandro Izquierdo, and Ernesto Talvi, 2003. "Sudden Stops, the Real Exchange Rate, and Fiscal Sustainability: Argentina's Lessons." NBER Working Paper **9828**

Calvo, Guillermo and Ernesto Talvi, 2005. "Sudden Stop, Financial Factors and Economic Collapse in Latin America: Learning From Argentina and Chile." NBER Working Paper **11153**

Campos, Camila F.S., Dany Jaimovich, and Ugo Panizza, 2006. "The Unexplained Part of Public Debt." *Emerging Markets Review* 7(3): 228–43

Carey, J. and M. Shugart, 1995. "Incentives to Cultivate a Personal Vote: A Rank Ordering of Electoral Formulas." *Electoral Studies* **14**(4): 417–39

Clements, Benedict, Rina Bhattacharya, and Toan Quoc Nguyen, 2003. "External Debt, Public Investment, and Growth in Low-Income Countries." IMF Working Paper **03/249**

Coelho, Isaias, Liam Ebrill, and Victoria Summers, 2001. "Bank Debit Taxes in Latin America – An Analysis of Recent Trends." IMF Working Paper **01/67**

Cordella, Tito, Luca A. Ricci, and Marta Ruiz-Arranz, 2005. "Debt Overhang or Debt Irrelevance? Revisiting the Debt–Growth Link." IMF Working Paper **05/223**

Cox, G. and M. McCubbins, 2001. "The Institutional Determinants of Economic Policy Outcomes." In S. Haggard and M. McCubbins, eds., *Presidents, Parliaments and Policy*. New York: Cambridge University Press

Cullen, Julie Berry and Roger H. Gordon, 2002. "Taxes and Entrepreneurial Activity: Theory and Evidence for the US." NBER Working Paper **9015**

Daughters, R. and L. Harper, 2007. "Fiscal and Political Decentralization Reforms." In E. Lora, ed., *The State of State Reform in Latin America*. Stanford, CA: Stanford University Press

de Long, J. Bradford and Lawrence H. Summers, 1991. "Equipment Investment and Economic Growth." *Quarterly Journal of Economics* **106**: 445–502

Domenech, Rafael, 2004. "Política Fiscal y Crecimiento Económico." Universidad de Valencia, mimeo

Drazen, A., 2000. "The Political Business Cycle after 25 Years." In B. Bernanke and K. Rogoff, eds., *NBER Macroeconomics Annual 2000*. Cambridge, MA: MIT Press

Easterly, W. and S. Rebelo, 1993. "Fiscal Policy and Economic Growth: An Empirical Investigation." *Journal of Monetary Economics* **39**(1): 417–58

Edwards, Sebastian, 2007. "Crises and Growth: A Latin American Perspective." NBER Working Paper **13019**

Eichengreen, Barry, 2004. "Financial Instability." Chapter 5 in Bjørn Lomborg, ed., *Global Crises, Global Solutions*, 1st edn. Cambridge: Cambridge University Press

Eichengreen, Barry and Ricardo Hausmann, eds., 2005. *Other People's Money: Debt Denomination and Financial Instability in Emerging Market Economies*. Chicago: University of Chicago Press

Engen, E. and J. Skinner, 1996. "Taxation and Economic Growth." *National Tax Journal* **49**(4): 617–42

Eslava, M., 2006. "The Political Economy of Fiscal Policy: Survey." IDB Working Paper **583**

Filc, G. and C. Scartascini, 2007. "Budgetary Institutions." In E. Lora, ed., *The State of State Reform in Latin America*. Stanford, CA: Stanford University Press

Fiess, Norman, 2002. "Chile's New Fiscal Rule." World Bank, mimeo

Fischer, Stanley, 1993. "The Role of Macroeconomic Factors in Growth." *Journal of Monetary Economics* **32**(3): 458–512

Friedman, Milton, 1962. *Capitalism and Freedom*. Chicago: University of Chicago Press

Galiani, Sebastian, 2006. "Políticas Sociales: Instituciones, información y conocimiento." Serie Políticas Sociales, CEPAL **116**

Gavin, Michael and Roberto Perotti, 1997. "Fiscal Policy in Latin America." NBER Macroeconomics Annual 1997. Cambridge, MA: MIT Press

Gentry, William M. and R. Glenn Hubbard, 2000. "Tax Policy and Entry into Entrepreneurship." *American Economic Review* **90**(2): 283–7

Gibson, E., E. Calvo, and T. Falleti, 2004. "Reallocative Federalism: Territorial Overrepresentation and Public Spending in the Western Hemisphere." In Edward L. Gibson, ed., *Federalism and Democracy in Latin America*. Baltimore, MD: Johns Hopkins University Press

Gordon, Roger, 1998. "Can High Personal Tax Rates Encourage Entrepreneurial Activity?" IMF Staff Papers March: 49–80

Gruber, J. and E. Saez, 2002. "The Elasticity of Taxable Income: Evidence and Implications." *Journal of Public Economics* **84**: 1–32

Hallerberg, M. and P. Marier, 2004. "Executive Authority, the Personal Vote, and Budget Discipline in Latin American and Caribbean Countries." *American Journal of Political Science* **48**(3): 571–87

Harberger, Arnold, 1962. "The Incidence of the Corporation Income Tax." *Journal of Political Economy* **70**: 215–40

Hausmann, Ricardo and Ugo Panizza, 2003. "On the Determinants of Original Sin: An Empirical Investigation." *Journal of International Money and Finance* **22**(7): 957–90

Heckman, J., L. Lochner, and C. Taber, 1998. "Tax Policy and Human Capital Formation." *American Economic Review* 88: 293–7

Hodge, Scott A., J. Scott Moody, and Wendy P. Warcholik, 2006. "The Rising Cost of Complying with the Federal Income Tax." Tax Foundation Special Report 138

Hsieh, Chang-Tai and Jonathan Parker, 2006. "Taxes and Growth in a Financially Underdeveloped Country: Evidence from the Chilean Investment Boom." NBER Working Paper W12104

IDB, 1997. *Latin America after a Decade of Reforms.* Economic and Social Progress Report. Washington, DC: InterAmerican Development Bank

2006. *The Politics of Policies.* Economic and Social Progress Report. Washington, DC: InterAmerican Development Bank

2007. *Living with Debt.* Economic and Social Progress Report. Washington, DC: InterAmerican Development Bank

Imbs, Jean M. and Romain Rancière, 2005. "The Overhang Hangover." World Bank Policy Research Working Paper 3673

Inman, Robert, 2003. "Local Fiscal Discipline in US Federalism." In Jonathan Rodden, Gunnar Eskeland, and Jennie Litvack, eds., *Decentralization and the Challenge of Hard Budget Constraints.* Cambridge, MA: MIT Press

Kaminsky, Graciela, Carmen Reinhart, and Carlos Vegh, 2004. "When it Rains, it Pours: Procyclical Capital Flows and Macroeconomic Policies." NBER Working Paper W10780

Lee, Young and Roger Gordon, 2004. "Tax Structure and Economic Growth." *Journal of Public Economics* 89(5–6): 1027–43

Levine, R. and D. Renelt, 1992. "A Sensitivity Analysis of Cross-Country Growth Regressions." *American Economic Review* 82(4): 942–63

Lindert, Peter, 2004. *Growing Public: Social Spending and Economic Growth since the Eighteenth Century.* Cambridge: Cambridge University Press

Lora, Eduardo, ed., 2007. *The State of State Reform in Latin America.* Washington, DC: IDB and Stanford University Press

Lowry, Robert and James Alt, 2006. "Transparency and Accountability in US States: Taking Ferejohn's model to data." Paper presented at the Annual Meeting of the Midwest Political Science Association, Chicago, April 20

Lucas, Robert E., 1988. "On the Mechanics of Economic Development." *Journal of Monetary Economics* 22: 3–42

Mainwaring, Scott and Matthew Shugart, 1997. *Presidentialism and Democracy in Latin America.* Cambridge: Cambridge University Press

Pattillo, Catherine, Hélène Koliane Poirson, and Luca A. Ricci, 2002. "External Debt and Growth." IMF Working Paper 02/69

Persson, T., G. Roland, and G. Tabellini, 1997. "Separation of Powers and Political Accountability." *Quarterly Journal of Economics* **112**: 1163–1202

Persson, T. and G. Tabellini, 2003. *The Economic Effects of Constitutions.* Cambridge, MA: MIT Press

Rodden, J., 2002. "The Dilemma of Fiscal Federalism: Grants and Fiscal Performance around the World." *American Journal of Political Science* **46**(3): 670–87

Rodden, J., G. Eskeland, and J. Litvack, 2003. *Fiscal Decentralization and the Challenge of Hard Budget Constraints.* Cambridge, MA: MIT Press

Rodden, J. and E. Wibbels, 2002. "Beyond the Fiction of Federalism: Macroeconomic Management in Multitiered Systems." *World Politics* **54**(4): 494–531

Rogoff, Kenneth and Anne Sibert, 1988. "Elections and Macroeconomic Policy Cycles." NBER Working Paper **1838**

Roubini, N., 1991. "Economic and Political Determinants of Budget Deficits in Developing Countries." *Journal of International Money and Finance* **10**: S49–S72

Samuels, D. and R. Snyder, 2001. "The Value of a Vote: Malapportionment in Comparative Perspective." *British Journal of Political Science* **31**(4): 651–71

Shi, M. and J. Svensson, 2006. "Political Budget Cycles: Do they Differ Across Countries and Why?" *Journal of Public Economics* **90**(8–9): 1367–89

Stein, E., 1999. "Fiscal Decentralization and Government Size in Latin America." *Journal of Applied Economics* **2**(2): 357–91

Stein, E., E. Talvi, and A. Grisanti, 1998. "Institutional Arrangements and Fiscal Performance: The Latin American Experience." NBER Working Paper **6358**

Talvi, Ernesto, 2007. "Latin American Macro Watch." Presentation at the IDB Research Department, May

Talvi, Ernesto and Carlos Vegh, 2000. "Tax Base Variability and Procyclical Fiscal Policy." NBER Working Paper **7499**

Tornell, Aaron and Philip Lane, 1999. "The Voracity Effect." *American Economic Review*, **89**(1): 22–46

Velasco, A., 1999. "A Model of Endogenous Fiscal Deficits and Delayed Fiscal Reforms." In J. Poterba and J. Von Hagen, eds., *Fiscal Institutions and Fiscal Performance.* Chicago: NBER and University of Chicago Press

  2000. "Debts and Deficits With Fragmented Fiscal Policymaking." *Journal of Public Economics* **76**: 105–25

Von Hagen, J., 2006. "Fiscal Institutions." In B. Weingast and D. Wittman, eds., *The Oxford Handbook of Political Economy*. Oxford: Oxford University Press

Weingast, B., K. Shepsle, and C. Johnsen, 1981. "The Political Economy of Benefits and Costs: A Neoclassical Approach to Distributive Politics." *Journal of Political Economy* **89**: 642–64

5.1 Fiscal policy reforms: an alternative view

MAX A. ALIER AND BENEDICT CLEMENTS*

1 Introduction

Miguel Braun's chapter 5 provides a strong case for his thesis that the principal fiscal challenge facing the LAC region is to build on recent gains in achieving fiscal solvency and reduce the procyclical tendency of fiscal policy. He rightly notes the negative consequences of fiscal insolvency and procyclicality on growth, poverty, and income distribution. He argues that there is no scope for complacency, as recent improvement in the region's fiscal position results, at least in part, from unusually favorable external conditions that have contributed to transitory increases in revenues and reduced borrowing costs. At the same time, he notes that public expenditure is rising during the economic expansion, in line with the region's legacy of procyclical fiscal policy.

Based on a broad review of the literature, the chapter argues that insolvency and procyclicality are the result of external shocks, high levels of foreign currency-denominated debt, and politico-institutional factors. It proposes four specific solutions to meet the challenge: issuance of contingent debt instruments, adopting fiscal rules, replacing corporate taxes with personal income taxes, and establishing a policy evaluation agency. It estimates the benefits of these solutions at up to 3 percentage points of GDP per year.

We find that we have much common ground with Braun regarding this assessment of the fiscal challenges facing the region. We especially share his concerns regarding the rapid growth of expenditures. Real non-interest public outlays rose by an average of 7.5% in 2005–6, with current spending accounting for the bulk of the increase. Expenditure/GDP ratios have also risen, reversing the declines realized during the early phases of the recovery. At the same time, we feel that he has

* The views expressed in this alternative view are those of the authors and do not necessarily represent those of the IMF or IMF policy.

described the challenges too narrowly. In what follows, we provide a broader, more comprehensive view of the challenges facing fiscal policy. Under our vision, the demands on the Ministry of Finance are even greater than those described by Braun, as we see fiscal policy as a key instrument for achieving high, sustainable, and equitable growth.

2 The challenge

In our view, LAC's main fiscal policy challenge is to address the region's immense social needs by helping create the conditions for sustained and equitable output growth. In this context, consolidating fiscal solvency and reducing procyclicality are necessary elements of any strategy to meet this broader challenge. However, we are less pessimistic than Braun regarding the progress made on these fronts in recent years. At the same time, we place greater emphasis than he does on the need to improve the efficiency and equity of taxation and spending. Although the chapter recognizes the relevance of tax policy and the need to strengthen the equity and efficiency of government outlays, we feel that it does not give these issues sufficient prominence.

Fiscal vulnerabilities have been reduced considerably during the recent economic upswing. Some, but not all, of this is the result of improvements in the external environment. For example, commodity-based revenues rose by an average of about 4.75 percentage points of GDP between 2002 and 2006, but non-commodity revenues also rose.[1] Revenue increases have outpaced the surge in spending, and primary surpluses climbed in 2006 for the fourth year in a row to over 3% of GDP. Stronger fiscal balances, in conjunction with solid economic growth, have reduced public debt burdens. On a weighted-average basis, public debt/GDP ratios have declined to about 52% of GDP, a drop of about 24 percentage points of GDP since 2002. Vulnerabilities have also been reduced by changes in the composition of public debt, with a sharp decline in the share of foreign currency-denominated liabilities. This has been facilitated by the ability of many countries in the region to issue debt in their own currencies, proving that "original sin" can, with sufficient redemption, be forgiven in international capital markets.

---

[1] This description of fiscal developments in the region draws heavily on IMF (2007).

Table 5.1.1 *Public investment: LAC and other regions,*
1995–2006 (% of GDP)

	1995–9	2000–4	2005–6
LAC[a]	5.8	5.1	5.1
Africa	7.6	7.4	8.0
Asia	8.6	8.4	8.6
Central and Eastern Europe	3.6	3.6	3.6

Note: [a] For LAC, data cover seventeen countries.
Sources: Authors' calculations, based on data from national
authorities, and the WEO database.

Although fiscal vulnerabilities have been reduced in recent years,
more progress would clearly be desirable. Continued solid performance in containing budget deficits and reducing debt burdens will
not, however, be enough to address one of the major shortcomings of
government in Latin America: the performance of the state in facilitating high and equitable economic growth. Economic growth in the
region still lags behind the developing country average, and social indicators, while improving, suggest a high level of unmet need and a high
degree of inequality. To achieve rapid progress on these fronts, it will
be essential that the state provide a more supportive role for economic
growth – including radical changes in tax and expenditure policy. In
what follows, we discuss some of these challenges:[2]

Reallocating public spending toward investment and raising the efficiency of these outlays

Public investment in the region lags that of other regions of the world
(see table 5.1.1). These outlays have been declining over time, and
have fallen as a share of total public spending. The increased role of
the private sector in providing infrastructure has helped compensate
for this decline. Nevertheless, low rates of public investment have most
likely contributed to lags in the region's infrastructure – as measured,
for example, by the quality of its road system.

---

[2] This section draws heavily on Clements, Faircloth, and Verhoeven (2007a,
2007b).

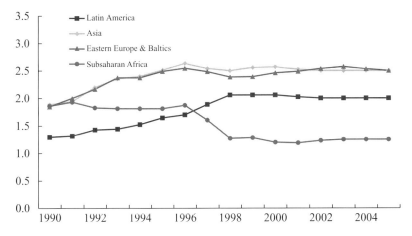

Figure 5.1.1 The quality of bureaucracy
Source: The International Country Risk Guide database

Inefficiencies in public investment spending may also be contributing to infrastructure shortfalls. The efficiency of these outlays – as measured by the relationship between public investment and improvements in infrastructure indicators – varies markedly across countries (Clements, Faircloth, and Verhoeven 2007a, 2007b). This suggests that there is scope for improvement, in particular by following the best practices in the region in project selection, evaluation, and monitoring (IMF 2005). Countries should also implement stable multi-year budgets for public investment and strengthen staff capacity and data for project evaluation (Aldunate 2007).

Improving the effectiveness of the civil service

The typical LAC country spends about 7% of GDP to compensate its public employees (excluding public enterprises), about average for developing regions. There is a wide variety in the quality of the civil service in the region, and most countries fall short in attracting sufficiently qualified staff at enforcing good performance (Echebarría and Cortázar 2006). The quality of government services in the region has stagnated since the late 1990s, and remains below that of other, more dynamic regions (figure 5.1.1).

There is ample evidence to suggest that greater value for money could be achieved in public wage bills in the region. Countries that more handsomely compensate their employees, for example, do not necessarily enjoy more productive bureaucracies (Clements, Faircloth, and Verhoeven 2007a). Achieving a more productive civil service will require deep-rooted changes in incentive systems and a need to address the key weaknesses of civil service systems noted in the comprehensive review of Echebarría and Cortázar (2006) – patronage in hiring and promotions, the absence of performance evaluation, and internal inequities in remuneration.

Increasing the efficiency and targeting of social spending

Social spending – defined as expenditure for education, health, pensions, social assistance, and housing – absorbs about half of non-interest government outlays (table 5.1.2). At 13% of GDP, these outlays are lower than in the OECD and Eastern Europe, but higher than in Emerging Asia. Education and health indicators in the LAC region are broadly in line with the region's level of development (ECLAC 2006), but still trail those of high-performing regions. Some of these lags reflect weaknesses in the quality of social spending, including in education. Repetition rates remain high, and performance on international examinations in mathematics, reading, and science indicates that the region fares poorly relative to other countries. As in the case of the civil service, improving the efficiency of education spending will require that countries address shortcomings in incentive systems and examine opportunities to improve the composition of spending, which remains heavily weighted toward salaries at the expense of other inputs (de Ferranti *et al.* 2003).

Reallocating social spending to programs that most benefit the poor will also be important for forging a more equitable society (table 5.1.3). The distributive incidence of social spending varies greatly across programs, with primary education and social assistance programs having the most favorable impact, while higher education and social insurance programs tend to benefit middle- and upper-income groups.[3] Because of the low share of spending in pro-poor programs – such as social assistance – the majority of social spending benefits accrue to those that are relatively well off.

---

[3] A study by Cubero and Vladkova-Hollar (2007) finds that this pattern holds also in Central America.

Table 5.1.2 *General government social spending: LAC and other regions, 2004 (% GDP)[a]*

	Education	Health	Social protection	Housing and community amenities	Total[b]
LAC[c]	**4.2**	**2.6**	**5.4**	**0.9**	**12.7**
Emerging Asia[d]	3.5	1.3	2.2	1.1	8.4
Eastern Europe and Central Asia	4.8	4.4	12.1	1.5	22.8
Middle East and North Africa[e]	4.2	2.0	1.8	1.1	9.1
SSA[f]	5.5	2.9	3.7	0.5	13.8
OECD	6.4	6.9	17.3	0.8	32.6

Notes: [a] 2004 or latest available year.

[b] Number of observations vary by category. Therefore, the total social spending regional averages may not necessarily equal the sum of the regional averages of the spending components.

[c] Unweighted averages for seventeen countries. 2004 data for Bolivia, Chile, Colombia, Peru, and Uruguay refer to 2003 data. 2004 data for Argentina are based on the national authorities and IMF staff estimates; for Honduras, 2002 and 2003 data are based on figures for 2001. For Peru, data for 2002–4 for education and social security refer to 2001 data. For Colombia and El Salvador, data were provided by the national authorities.

[d] The Emerging Asia sample includes Hong Kong SAR, Macao SAR, India, Korea, Singapore, Thailand, and Vietnam. Korea and Thailand refer to central government.

[e] Budgetary central government for eight countries.

[f] Central government for seven countries.

Sources: Government Financial Statistics, IMF; Social Indicators and Statistics database, ECLAC; national authorities; IMF staff estimates.

The region has demonstrated its capacity to develop efficient and well-targeted social assistance programs, such as Bolsa Familia in Brazil, Oportunidades in Mexico, and Familias en Accion in Colombia. Yet spending on these and other social assistance programs, for all their successes, reaches only about 1–1.5 of GDP – a modest share of total social spending. Beyond the expansion of these programs, it will also be necessary to undertake the difficult task of reallocating spending, over time, away from programs that primarily benefit upper-income groups. As suggested in Clements, Faircloth, and Verhoeven (2007a, 2007b), steps in this direction include further reform of public pension

Table 5.1.3 *LAC region: distribution of benefits from social spending to the top and bottom quintiles*[a]

	Poorest quintile	Richest quintile
Education	20.2	20.4
Primary	29.0	7.9
Secondary	13.2	18.3
Tertiary	1.9	52.1
Health	20.6	17.6
Social security	5.6	51.2
Total social spending	15.0	30.4
Memorandum item:		
Share of quintiles		
in primary income	3.6	56.4

Note: [a] Unweighted average. Country coverage varies by category. For total spending, total education, health, and social security spending, the number of countries covered is eight, thirteen, fourteen, and nine, respectively.
Source: Authors' calculations, based on ECLAC (2006).

systems to place them on an actuarially sound footing, while putting in place mechanisms to ensure adequate protection of living standards for the elderly poor; greater reliance on user fees in higher education, combined with more widespread access to scholarships for lower-income students; and improvements in the quality of secondary education to reduce repetition rates and increase access to higher education.

Moving towards a less regressive and less distortionary tax structure

There are very large differences in tax burdens across the region. They range from the low burdens of countries endowed with non-renewable resources such as Mexico and Venezuela (about 10% of GDP), to high levels in countries such as Brazil (36% of GDP).[4] Despite these differences, there are a number of common weaknesses in the tax

---

[4] Data refer to taxes collected by the federal government.

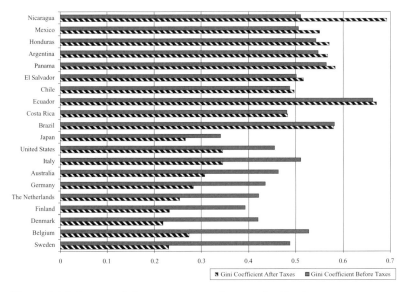

Figure 5.1.2 Impact of the tax system on income distribution
Source: Gomez Sabaini (2006)

systems across the region. First, there is heavy reliance on indirect and payroll taxes – representing about 75% of the total – which results in a regressive tax system. While in developed countries the tax system helps to reduce inequality, in the LAC region it exacerbates it (Gomez Sabaini, 2006) (figure 5.1.2). Second, the tax system is a source of significant distortions in resource allocation, and reduces the region's competitiveness relative to other fast-growing regions such as East Asia. For instance, numerous tax exemptions (especially for VATs) and various taxes on financial transactions are commonplace. More generally, the structure of the tax system does not appear to be based on efficiency criteria.

3 The root causes of the region's fiscal problems[5]

We are in broad agreement with Braun on the root causes behind the region's tendency for procyclical policy and periodic bouts of fiscal insolvency. We agree that these problems are related to economic volatility, which is the result of both external volatility and weaknesses

---

[5] This section draws heavily on Alier (2008).

in economic policies and strategies that have exacerbated, rather than mitigated, the impact of external shocks. These include a vulnerable structure of debt (with a high share denominated in foreign currency and at short maturities), a low degree of openness to trade, and a history of debt intolerance. While agreeing that these factors have been behind crises in earlier periods, it is important to note that the region has made great progress in reducing these vulnerabilities over the past few years.

We also agree that politico-institutional factors have played a key role in making fiscal policy procyclical and, in some instances, unsustainable. Institutional weaknesses in the region have prevented countries from ameliorating the common pool and principal–agent problems that characterize policymaking.

Chapter 5 proposes the creation of an independent agency to help improve the quality of public spending. We strongly support the idea that governments should provide rigorous and systematic evaluations of the cost-benefit and distributive impact of government projects and programs. However, it is not clear that an independent agency would need to be created, in all cases, to undertake such a task.

Budget rigidities

We believe that the chapter would have benefited from paying more attention to other causes underlying the poor quality of fiscal policy. In particular, we believe that the constraints imposed on fiscal management by budget rigidities deserve greater prominence.[6] Revenue earmarking and mandatory expenditure requirements together affect a significant share of governments' budgets, ranging from some 66% of primary revenue in Chile to about 85% in Brazil (figure 5.1.3). In our view, addressing the budget rigidities problem is a precondition to meeting the challenges identified in section 2.

---

[6] Budget rigidities stem from institutional arrangements that limit the budgetary authorities' ability to adjust the composition and size of the budget in the short run. A number of budget components are naturally inflexible – such as wages, pensions, and debt service. Other inflexibilities are rooted in the constitution, laws, or decrees that earmark revenues, set minimum spending requirements, or link spending to the evolution of certain macroeconomic variables – such as inflation, growth, or unemployment. Some expenditures are rigid for political reasons.

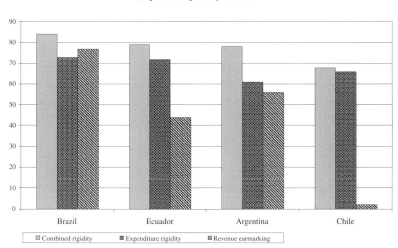

Figure 5.1.3 Budget rigidity: Selected LAC countries (% of primary revenue)

Some degree of budget rigidity can be justified on theoretical and practical grounds (see Alier 2008). But, on balance, the benefits of rigidities are outweighed by their significantly negative impact on budget management. Constraints to fiscal management introduced by budget rigidities reduce economic efficiency and lead to suboptimal outcomes. The negative consequences of budget rigidities stem from six main sources.

(1) *Limits to the reallocation of public spending in response to changing needs*

These limitations lead to overspending in some sectors at the expense of others. The resulting resource misallocation is likely to worsen over time as social preferences evolve and governments face limitations on shifting resources across sectors to equalize marginal benefits. LAC governments' difficulty in addressing emerging infrastructure gaps is a good example of the effect of budget rigidities on the allocation of public resources.

(2) *A built-in bias towards higher spending*

Mandatory spending requirements negatively affect the quality of fiscal adjustment, as the brunt of the spending retrenchment falls on a subset of budget items. Macroeconomic management and political economy reasons can provide reasonable explanations as to why it may be optimal first to cut capital spending in times of rapid fiscal retrenchment. However, after the initial tightening, budget rigidities limit the scope for governments to rebalance expenditure allocations to reflect tighter budget constraints. Budget rigidities also limit the government's capacity to reallocate resources towards social safety nets at times of economic crisis. Examples of this phenomenon can be found in numerous fiscal adjustment episodes in the region.

(3) *A built-in bias towards higher taxation*

Revenue earmarking also negatively affects the quality of fiscal adjustment by amplifying the contractionary effects of revenue-based fiscal adjustments. Because of requirements to spend at least part of the new revenues for designated purposes, revenue-based fiscal adjustments require sharper increases in taxes. Over the medium term, the additional public spending created during the tightening cycle is difficult to roll back, and governments face difficulties in cutting taxes back to pre-adjustment levels.

(4) *Distortions introduced in tax policy choices*

Tax policy decisions can be negatively affected by revenue-earmarking considerations. Earmarking arrangements introduce a bias for policymakers to favor revenues that are less earmarked, and governments may try to rebalance the tax burden in this direction. This bias is stronger when taxes are earmarked to expenditures executed by other spending agencies or levels of government, as is the case with revenue-sharing agreements in a federation. Examples of how earmarking provisions affected tax policy choices are abundant. In Brazil, the fiscal adjustment in 1999–2004 was largely achieved by increasing "social contributions," the revenues of which are earmarked but not shared with states and municipalities. In Argentina in 2001, the federal government introduced a bank credit and debit tax creditable against VAT and income tax obligations. The latter taxes were shared with the provinces and subject to extensive earmarking, while the newly created tax was not. Eventually, the government agreed to share 30% of the tax proceeds with the provinces.

(5) *Limits on the scope for countercyclical fiscal policy*

Extensive revenue earmarking limits governments' ability to implement an active countercyclical fiscal policy – that is, being able to generate surpluses in good times to offset deficits in bad times. In particular, expenditure requirements indexed to GDP and revenue earmarking limit the government's ability to commit to increase public saving during cyclical economic expansions.

(6) *Weak incentives to improve the efficiency of public spending*

Incentives to improve the efficiency of public spending are severely affected by the presence of budget rigidities, especially by mandated spending provisions. In an ideal budgetary process, spending agencies would compete for resources and the best-performing agencies (in terms of achieving the government's goals) would see their share of resources increase. Budget rigidities reduce these incentives as spending agencies can count on a guaranteed share of resources independent of their performance. Wasteful public spending may occur as governments are forced to fulfill mandatory spending requirements or comply with revenue-earmarking provisions.

The political process

Given that the economic costs of extensive budget rigidities outweigh their benefits, the rationale for their existence seems to be rooted in the political process. The literature in public choice economics provides a number of arguments to explain and justify the existence of budget rigidities.[7] These arguments include the use of budget rigidities as a means to mitigate or reduce four main problems.

(1) *Mitigate agency problems in the provision of public goods*

Buchanan (1963) explores the implications of revenue earmarking on tax and expenditure choices under majority voting. Davis and Hayes (1995) and Dhillon and Perroni (2001) show that tax earmarking can play a role in mitigating the agency problem in the provision of public goods. They argue that earmarking can reduce the free-riding problem in monitoring spending agencies and consequently increase their accountability to taxpayers. In countries that experience rapid decentralization (e.g. Argentina, Brazil, and Ecuador), mandatory spending provisions on health and education

---

[7] Most of the literature on the rationale for budget rigidities focuses on revenue earmarking. However, the conclusions typically also apply to expenditure requirements.

for subnational governments can play a role in ensuring the adequate provision of these goods while accountability mechanisms are developed.

(2) *Set limits on the voracity of "Leviathan governments"*

Tax earmarking has been proposed to limit the government's voracity and as a solution to certain externalities. Brennan and Buchanan (1978) argue that earmarking can be used to discipline a "Leviathan government" that seeks to maximize the surplus it extracts from taxpayers.

(3) *Reduce vertical and horizontal externalities in a federation when the tax base and expenditure responsibilities overlap*

Wrede (2000) argues that tax earmarking could be used to reduce vertical and horizontal externalities in a federation where the tax base and expenditure responsibilities of different levels of government overlap. In highly decentralized countries, minimum expenditure requirements in health and education for local governments can prevent a free-rider problem that would lead to under-spending in those sectors.

(4) *Garner support for tax initiatives*

Tax earmarking has also been proposed as a mechanism to garner support for tax initiatives. Brett and Keen (2000) argue that as voters become more cynical about politicians, the set of implementable taxes becomes more limited. In such circumstances, earmarking can serve as a mechanism to secure support for tax initiatives by earmarking the revenues to the provision of a good demanded by segments of the society that would have not supported the tax initiative otherwise. In Brazil, the introduction of the bank debit tax (CPMF) in the 1990s constitutes a good example. Political support for the CPMF was largely achieved by offering to earmark the tax to health spending.

Public debt

The literature on the political economy of public debt also provides three insights into the reasons underlying the existence of budget rigidities.[8]

---

[8] References include Buchanan and Wagner (1977) and Alesina and Perotti (1994) on theories of fiscal illusion; Alesina and Tabellini (1990) on using debt as a strategic variable; Alesina and Drazen (1991) on intra-generational conflict; and Veloso (2000) on the tragedy of the commons.

(1) *The fiscal illusion*

The fiscal illusion facilitates the emergence of budget rigidities. In such a scenario, different groups in society seek to obtain permanent benefits from public spending without fully internalizing the cost of their actions for themselves or society. At the same time, politicians eager to gain or maintain power (e.g. running for re-election) are willing to yield to pressures even when they are aware of the limited benefits for the economy as a whole. Echeverry, Fergusson, and Querubín (2005) show that budget rigidities can emerge when there is a common pool of budget resources that is allocated through a bargaining process in Congress.

(2) *Strategic considerations*

Under political uncertainty, incumbent politicians may use budget rigidities to constrain the behavior of their successors, who may have different preferences. Brett and Keen (2000) show that groups advocating particular policies (e.g. an environmental tax) favor earmarking if the efficiency loss of doing so is outweighed by the value of constraining subsequent policymakers' decisions. They conclude that politically weak politicians are the most likely to favor revenue earmarking. Another conclusion is that budget rigidities would be more prevalent in more polarized societies. A clear example of this is provided by Chile's Reserved Copper Law, which requires that 10% of the state-owned copper company's gross revenues be transferred to the armed forces for equipment purchase.

(3) *Inter- and intra-generational conflicts*

Such conflicts also provide explanations for the emergence of budget rigidities. Inter-generational conflict is largely at the heart of mechanisms that make it difficult for governments to reduce pension benefits. Such inflexibilities range from outright legal obstacles to modifying "acquired rights" to mechanisms that guarantee minimum periodical adjustments of benefits – for example, through indexation. On the other hand, intra-generational conflict occurs when different groups in society cannot agree on the burden-sharing of macroeconomic adjustment. These groups will try to introduce budget rigidities as a defense mechanism and to minimize the share of the adjustment costs that they have to bear. It is not surprising, then, that budget rigidities are more common in countries with a history of macroeconomic instability. For example, in Argentina and Brazil, the high degree of revenue earmarking is attributed by some as a legacy of the high-inflation years.

In sum, budget rigidities are the result of deep political conflict in the budget process. Consequently, a permanent solution to budget inflexibility would require a reform of budget institutions, with a view to reduce incentives and opportunities for new budget rigidities to emerge.

4 Proposed solutions and quantification of costs and benefits

The quantification of the costs and benefits of fiscal reforms is a difficult task. As a general caveat, we note that some of the solutions proposed by Braun may have a once-and-for-all impact on the level of GDP, and may not necessarily result in a permanent increase in the rate of growth. It is important to bear this possibility in mind and avoid over-estimating the benefits of the proposed solutions. We also need to make the following comments on chapter 5's specific solutions.

Improving debt management by using contingent instruments

We agree on the chapter's estimate of the benefits. However, non-standard debt instruments, for which there is little demand, can only be placed with a premium. This is a cost that Braun does not consider explicitly, and it can be sizeable. For example, in Brazil the government virtually eliminated all its external debt by replacing it with domestic debt. Although the benefits of this policy were clearly demonstrated during the international financial markets turmoil, there have been costs associated with this policy: (1) domestic debt was placed at a higher interest rate; (2) it was placed with shorter maturity (i.e. increasing vulnerabilities); and (3) the government lost the valuation gains associated with the appreciation of the *real*. Although evaluating the counterfactual is difficult, especially in regards to the latter appreciation, the cost of these balance sheet operations could be significant.

Consolidating the budget process by adopting fiscal rules

Estimates on the impact of fiscal rules may be too optimistic in the absence of details of the rules to be adopted. We believe that adequately designed macro-fiscal rules could play a useful role in mitigating procyclicality and solvency problems, especially if they focus on controlling expenditure growth during economic upswings. However, these rules should not introduce unnecessary rigidities in the budget process. It is also important to under-score, as Braun does, that fiscal rules would also need to be accompanied by credible enforcement, and rules cannot be seen as a substitute for political will.

Reducing budget rigidities, in our view, could be expected to generate benefits by improving the efficiency of public spending. As indicated in our earlier assessment, there is significant scope to improve the efficiency and equity of outlays for public investment, wages, and social spending. Budget rigidities undoubtedly contribute to some of these inefficiencies, and may be contributing to high levels of spending on current outlays.[9] The costs of this solution would be the compensation that needs to be given to those that benefit from present arrangements.

Bibliography

Aldunate, Eduardo, 2007. "Sistemas de Gestíon de Inversión Pública en América Latina." Paper presented at the 19th Annual Regional Seminar on Fiscal Policy, Economic Commission for Latin America and the Caribbean, Santiago

Alesina, A. and A. Drazen, 1991. "Why are Stabilizations Delayed?" *American Economic Review* **131**: 1170–88

Alesina, A. and R. Perotti, 1994. "The Political Economy of Budget Deficits." NBER Working Paper **4637**

Alesina, A. and G. Tabellini, 1996. "Budget Institutions and Fiscal Performance in Latin America." NBER Working Paper **5586**

Alier, Max, 2008. "Measuring Budget Rigidities in Latin America." IMF Working Paper, forthcoming

Apergis, Nicholas, Ioannis Filippidis, and Claire Economidou, 2007. "Financial Deepening and Economic Growth Linkages: A Panel Data Analysis." *Review of World Economics* **143**(1): 179–98

Barro, Robert, 1991. "Economic Growth in a Cross Section of Countries." *Quarterly Journal of Economics* **106**(2): 407–44

Barro, Robert and Xavier Sala-i-Martin, 1995. *Economic Growth*. Boston: McGraw-Hill

---

[9] As has been widely demonstrated in empirical studies, government consumption negatively affects long-term economic growth. See Barro (1991), Easterly and Rebelo (1993), Barro and Sala-i-Martin (1995), Apergis, Filippidis, and Economidou (2007), and, *more recently*, Edwards (2007)

Brennan, G. and J.M. Buchanan, 1978. "Tax Instruments as Constraints on the Disposition of Public Revenues." *Journal of Public Economies* 9(3): 301–18

Brett, C. and M. Keen, 2000. "Political Uncertainty and the Earmarking of Environmental Taxes." *Journal of Public Economics* 75: 315–40

Buchanan, J.M., 1963. "The Economics of Earmarked Taxes." *Journal of Political Economy* 71(5): 457–69

Buchanan, J.M. and R.E. Wagner, 1977. *Democracy in Deficit: The Political Legacy of Lord Keynes.* New York: Academic Press

Clements, Benedict, Christopher Faircloth, and Marijn Verhoeven, 2007a. "Getting Spending Right." *Finance and Development*, June: 50–2

   2007b. "Public Expenditure in Latin America: Trends and Key Issues." *CEPAL Review* 93: 37–60

Cubero, Rodrigo and Ivanna Vladkova-Hollar, 2007. "Equity and Fiscal Policy in Central America: Income Distribution Effects of Taxation and Government Spending." IMF

Davis, M.L. and K. Hayes, 1995. "The Demand for Good Government." *Review of Economics and Statistics* 75: 148–52

De Ferranti, David, Guillermo Perry, Indermit Gill, José Luis Guasch, William Maloney, Carolina Sanchez-Paramo, and Norbert Schady, 2003. *Closing the Gap in Education and Technology.* Washington, DC: World Bank

Dhillon, A. and C. Perroni, 2001. "Tax Earmarking and Grassroots Accountability." *Economic Letters* 72: 99–106

Easterly, William and Sergio Rebelo, 1993. "Fiscal Policy and Economic Growth. An Empirical Investigation." *Journal of Monetary Economics* 39(1): 417–58

Echebarría, Koldo and Juan Cortázar, 2006. "Public Administration and Public Employment Reform in Latin America." In Eduardo Lora, ed., *The State of State Reform in Latin America.* Washington, DC: Inter-American Development Bank

Echeverry, J.C., L. Fergusson, and P. Querubín, 2005. "Budget Inflexibility." Documento CEDE 2005–52, Universidad de los Andes, Bogota

Economic Commission on Latin America and the Caribbean (ECLAC), 2006. *Social Panorama of the Americas.* Santiago: United Nations

Edwards, Sebastian, 2007. "Crises and Growth: A Latin American Perspective." NBER Working Paper 13019

Gomez Sabaini, Juan, 2006. "Evolución y Situación Tributaria em América Latina: Una Serie de Temas para la Discusión." In Oscar Cetrángolo and Juan Gomez Sabaini, *Tributación em América Latina: En Busca de una Nueva Agenda de Reformas.* Santiago: United Nations

International Monetary Fund (IMF), 2005. *Public Investment and Fiscal Policy – Lessons from the Pilot Country Studies.* Washington, DC: IMF

   2007. *Regional Economic Outlook: Western Hemisphere.* Washington, DC: IMF

Veloso, A., 2000. "Debts and Deficits with Fragmented Policymaking." *Journal of Public Economics* **76**: 105–25

Wrede, M., 2000. "Shared Tax Sources and Public Expenditures." *International Tax and Public Finance* **7**(2): 7–163

6 | Challenges and solutions in health in the LAC region

PHILIP MUSGROVE[*]

1 Defining the challenges

The overall challenge can be expressed in one sentence: *People do not always get the healthcare they need.* Of course, to provide all the care that would ever do something to improve health, with no concern for cost, could use far more of society's resources than would make any sense. Spending too much on healthcare might actually worsen health outcomes, as resources were withdrawn from education, food, environmental protection, or other inputs to health. So the challenge or problem can be re-phrased as: *Of the interventions that society decides it can afford, people do not always get all those that they need.* "Intervention" is used in the sense of *Disease Control Priorities in Developing Countries*, 2nd edn. (Jamison *et al.* 2006, hereafter DCP2,

[*] I am extremely grateful to Rubén Suárez-Berenguela of the Pan American Health Organization (PAHO) for materials and advice on equity and on the interaction between access to care and knowledge of disease in Latin America; to Amanda Glassman and María Luisa Escobar of the Brookings Institution for providing much valuable material on the Colombian health reform of 1993; and to María Fernanda Merino Juárez for data on the Mexican Seguro Popular (even though I have not used it here). I have also to thank Anne Mills of the London School of Hygiene and Tropical Medicine for welcome support of the approach taken in this chapter, and Dean Jamison of Harvard University and the University of California, San Francisco, for sharing a draft of a related paper (Jamison 2007). Several staff members of the IDB offered suggestions, first on the outline for this analysis and then on an early draft. I particularly thank Eduardo Lora for advice and support at a crucial juncture. Sonja Thomsen and Maria Jacobsen of the Copenhagen Consensus Center helped with logistic details from the earliest discussion to the final draft. None of these helpful people is responsible for any of my errors of fact or interpretation.

The views expressed in this chapter are the author's own, and do not reflect those of the editorial staff of *Health Affairs* nor of Project HOPE, of which it is part.

chapter 15): actions are not limited to individual medical care but include public health measures. "Care" in this sense includes even the provision of information about health risks. If some people receive needed interventions more readily than others, the challenge is one of disparities.

One way to decompose the challenge ascribes the problem to four causes:

- *People don't realize that they need care* (that is, demand is lacking)
- *They lack access to care, for financial, physical, and cultural reasons* (health facilities are too costly to the patient, too distant, or impose cultural barriers to their use, such as language differences – these are supply deficiencies)
- *When care is accessible, it is provided inefficiently* (priorities are set badly or left to chance, resources are wasted through imbalances among inputs or operation at uneconomical scale, and so on) and
- *Even when care is accessible, its quality is often substandard* (so it does not protect or improve health as much as it could, because providers don't know what to do, or don't act on what they know).

The first and second of these challenges arise at the community and household level (Mills, Rashid, and Tollman 2006: 90). The third and fourth are characteristic of the level of health services delivery. All the challenges are affected by failings at the higher levels of health sector policy and strategic management, and public policies that cut across many sectors.

Figure 6.1 elaborates on these challenges and relates them to one another. Failure to recognize a need for care can result from ignorance of risk, under-estimation of severity, or not knowing that effective care exists. Lack of access, or failure to obtain care when the need for it is recognized, results from some combination of barriers of time, distance, money cost, and cultural obstacles. The first three of these factors interact, so that failure to get care cannot always be attributed to just one obstacle.

This way of defining the challenges differs from that primarily followed in the original Copenhagen Consensus volume (Lomborg 2004), which includes three chapters related to health: 2 (Communicable diseases), 7 (Malnutrition and hunger) and, to a lesser extent, 9 (Sanitation and access to clean water). The challenges the chapter authors proposed there are control of malaria and HIV/AIDS, reducing

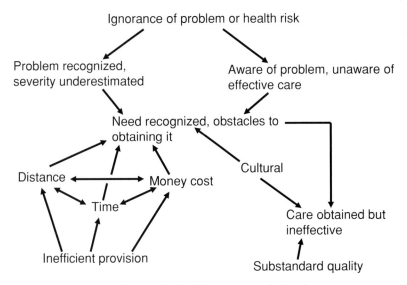

Figure 6.1 Reasons why needed healthcare is not obtained

the prevalence of low birthweight (LBW), improving infant and child nutrition and promoting exclusive breastfeeding, reducing the prevalence of micronutrient deficiencies; and community-managed water supply and sanitation. Jamison (2007), a paper for the Copenhagen Consensus meeting in 2008 that resulted in a 2nd edn. of the 2004 Lomborg volume (Lomborg 2009), also defines disease-specific challenges, including some related to chronic diseases or conditions.

Chapter 2 in Lomborg (2004) also defined "strengthening basic health services" as one of the challenges. The approach taken here is consistent with that, except that it is not limited to "basic" services, however those are defined. It is also consistent with an earlier effort to sketch what should be done in health in the LAC region to create a "new state" (Musgrove 2001). Several further reasons support the emphasis on health systems rather than specific diseases or conditions. First, when in 2006 two groups of UN ambassadors and senior diplomats were presented with the same exercise that the 2004 Expert panel had conducted, both groups moved scaled-up basic health services to the top of the list, ahead of the disease-specific proposals that the panel preferred (Copenhagen Consensus Center 2006). Putting improved basic services ahead of disease control efforts is also consistent with taking into account the need for functional institutions to

Table 6.1 *Deaths and disease burden, by cause: LAC region compared to low- and middle-income countries (LMIC) as a whole, 2001*

	LAC		LMIC	
	Deaths (000)	DALYs (000)	Deaths (000)	DALYs (000)
All causes	3,277	104,287	48,351	1,386,709
I Communicable diseases, maternal and perinatal conditions, and nutritional deficiencies	716 (21.8)	22,741 (21.8)	17,613 (36.4)	552,376 (39.8)
Tuberculosis	45 (1.4)	966 (0.9)	1,590 (3.3)	35,874 (2.6)
HIV/AIDS	83 (2.5)	2,354 (2.3)	2,552 (5.3)	70,796 (5.1)
Diarrheal diseases	55 (1.7)	2,362 (2.3)	1,777 (3.7)	58,697 (4.2)
Measles	0 (0.0)	0 (0.00)	762 (1.6)	23,091 (1.7)
Malaria	2 (<0.1)	111 (0.1)	1,207 (2.5)	39,961 (2.9)
Lower respiratory infections	157 (4.8)	3,043 (2.9)	3,408 (7.0)	83,606 (6.0)
Perinatal conditions	164 (5.0)	6,296 (6.0)	2,489 (5.1)	89,068 (6.4)
Protein-energy malnutrition	37 (1.1)	1,558 (1.5)	241 (0.5)	15,449 (1.1)
II Non-communicable diseases	2,187 (66.7)	67,815 (65.0)	26,023 (53.8)	678,483 (48.9)
Stomach cancers	57 (1.7)	735 (0.7)	696 (1.4)	9,616 (0.7)
Colon and rectum cancers	37 (1.1)	485 (0.5)	357 (0.7)	5,060 (0.4)
Liver cancer	21 (0.6)	277 (0.3)	505 (1.0)	7,945 (0.6)
Trachea, bronchus, and lung cancers	55 (1.7)	728 (0.7)	771 (1.6)	10,701 (0.8)
Diabetes mellitus	163 (5.0)	2,775 (2.7)	757 (1.6)	15,804 (1.1)
Unipolar depressive disorders	0 (0.0)	5,219 (5.0)	10 (<0.1)	43,427 (3.1)

Alcohol use disorders	17 (0.5)	2,883 (2.8)	62 (0.1)	11,007 (0.8)
Cataracts	0 (0.0)	1,813 (1.7)	0 (0.0)	28,150 (2.0)
Vision disorders, age-related	0 (0.0)	1,639 (1.6)	0 (0.0)	15,364 (1.1)
Hearing loss, adult onset	0 (0.0)	1,706 (1.6)	0 (0.0)	24,607 (1.8)
Hypertensive heart disease	87 (2.7)	1,052 (1.0)	760 (1.6)	9,969 (0.7)
Ischemic heart disease	358 (10.9)	4,328 (4.2)	5,699 (11.8)	71,882 (5.2)
Cerebrovascular disease	267 (8.1)	3,936 (3.8)	4,608 (9.5)	62,669 (4.5)
Chronic obstructive pulmonary disease	99 (3.0)	2,037 (2.0)	2,378 (4.9)	33,453 (2.4)
Cirrhosis of the liver	74 (2.3)	1,513 (1.5)	654 (1.4)	13,633 (1.0)
Nephritis and nephrosis	55 (1.7)	769 (0.7)	552 (1.1)	9,076 (0.7)
Osteoarthritis	1 (<0.1)	1,283 (1.2)	2 (<.01)	13,666 (1.0)
Congenital anomalies	47 (1.4)	2,460 (2.4)	477 (1.0)	23,533 (1.7)
Alzheimer and other dementias	14 (0.4)	1,215 (1.2)	173 (0.4)	9,640 (0.7)
III Injuries	**374 (11.4)**	**13,731 (13.2)**	**4,715 (9.8)**	**155,850 (11.2)**
Road traffic accidents	88 (2.7)	2,686 (2.6)	1,069 (2.2)	32,017 (2.3)
Falls	15 (0.5)	729 (0.7)	316 (0.7)	13,582 (1.0)
Self-inflicted injuries	30 (0.9)	711 (0.7)	749 (1.5)	17,674 (1.3)
Violence	130 (4.0)	5,154 (4.9)	532 (1.1)	18,132 (1.3)

Notes: Numbers in parentheses indicate percentages of column totals. Only selected causes are shown in each grouping I, II, and III, so group totals exceed the sum of the selected causes.

Source: Lopez *et al.* (2006, tables 1.1, 3.B.4 and 3.C.4).

carry out any solutions. Several members of the 2004 Expert panel emphasized in their rankings the requirements for institutional capacity, or criticized the solution papers in Lomborg (2004) for paying too little attention to this issue (Bhagwati 2004: 609; Frey 2004: 615; North 2004: 623).

Second, the LAC respondents to an IDB survey suggested that disparities in access to quality healthcare represented the highest priority challenge. Third, the disease burden in the LAC region is more diverse than it is in low- and middle-income countries generally, as table 6.1 shows. Non-communicable diseases (NCDs) account for 66.7% of deaths and 65.0% of disability adjusted life years (DALYs) in the LAC region, 13–16 percentage points higher than in other regions; and this category includes many more conditions that make significant contributions than occur for communicable diseases. Among the latter, malaria is much less important, and HIV/AIDS rather less important, in the LAC region than elsewhere. Defining the challenges by just a few diseases makes more sense for SSA and South Asia. The Expert panel's 2004 ranking was consistent with an emphasis on Africa (Bhagwati 2004: 608; Lin 2004: 619); and Jamison (2007) explicitly concentrates on the two poorest regions of the world. Where specific diseases are concerned, there is little new knowledge about the costs or benefits of meeting the challenges, except perhaps for HIV/AIDS.

Ignorance of need means lack of demand

The estimates of the global burden of disease, the most complete accounting for how sick or incapacitated the world's population is, necessarily count only incident cases of illness or injury (Lopez *et al.* 2006, hereafter GBD). Such estimates derive from contacts with the healthcare system (formal diagnoses and reports of cases), or population surveys. They include projections that often go beyond directly observed or reported cases – even for deaths – but they cannot easily find and count people who are sick but do not know it. Although that last phrase may seem an oxymoron, people who do not know their health status or the risks to it potentially constitute a major source of unmet need. This can arise for an early and asymptomatic stage of a disease, particularly a chronic condition such as diabetes or cardiovascular disease; or a current risk factor such as smoking, obesity, or exposure to toxic substances or pollution. For cases of incipient or early-stage disease, starting treatment earlier may be more cost-effective than when the disease is more advanced. DCP2 includes estimates of the costs and results of early detection for HIV infection that has not yet progressed to AIDS (chapter 18), several kinds of cancer (chapter 20), diabetes (chapter 30), hemoglobinopathies (chapter 34), and dental caries (chapter 38).

There are no estimates of the number of people who do not realize they already have one of these conditions, but two approaches show that unrecognized illness is important as an explanation for inadequate utilization of care. Detecting those cases when the patient is unaware of her condition through screening will vary greatly in cost-effectiveness depending on the prevalence of the condition, the target population, the frequency of screening or testing, and the cost of treating the previously undiagnosed cases. An analysis of the expected results of various cervical cancer screening programs in Brazil shows that either of two less expensive approaches could avert one death for every 100 women screened, while adding less than US$5.00 to lifetime costs per woman, compared to no screening and later treatment of cases.

A modeling exercise in Australia (Walker and Colaguiri 2008) looks at screening for diabetes, or high risk of the disease, among those aged 45+ with risk factors, and all those aged 55+, and treating or counseling those who need it. Fully half the prevalence of diabetes is estimated to be due to undiagnosed cases, even in a relatively well-educated population with adequate access to care. Screening would also be likely to find undiagnosed cases of heart disease and other risks.

No similar analysis has been conducted for any LAC country, but it is reasonable to presume that the share of undiagnosed cases is even higher and the potential savings comparable or better. Diabetes prevalence in the region is estimated at 6.0%, affecting 19 million people and causing the loss of nearly 3 million DALYs and economic losses of $4–9 billion (Narayan *et al.* 2006, table 30.1). Some risk factors, notably obesity, are as prevalent as in richer countries, and the costs of screening and lifestyle interventions should be lower.

An alternative indication of unrecognized disease, or under-estimated severity, comes from comparing how respondents in household surveys assess their health status with what they report in time lost to disability, or what epidemiological data show about mortality and morbidity, across income levels or socio-economic groups.

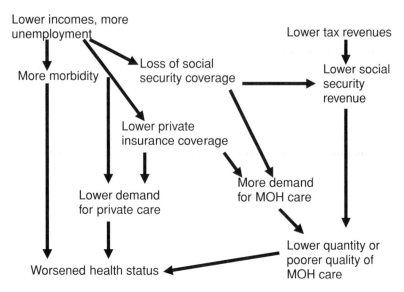

Figure 6.2 Health effects of economic contraction, when public spending (MOH and Social Security) is procyclical

Self-reported health improves with income, in surveys in Brazil, Ecuador, Guatemala, Jamaica, Mexico, and Peru, and reported illness decreases, as expected. But the differences by income or socioeconomic group in how people judge their health are smaller – the gradient is less steep – than for rates of mortality and morbidity or for time disabled by illness or injury (Suárez-Berenguela 2001, figures 6.1 and 6.2).

Comparisons after adjusting for age and sex "suggest that the poor may be less aware of chronic diseases. Lack of awareness of chronic conditions may be due to cultural or educational factors and to relatively low levels of access to or utilization of healthcare services" (Suárez-Berenguela 2001: 130). Ignorance of need may be even greater for preventive care, where inequity in utilization by income quintile is much greater than for chronic care. This motivates experiments with CCT programs, as discussed below. Curative care for acute conditions shows the least difference across income groups; ignorance of need is least likely in that case. These findings do not say how many people are in need without knowing it, or what it would cost to detect unrecognized illness and expand care, but they indicate that unrecognized need may be a major problem.

Impediments to obtaining wanted care

Once people recognize a need for care, several factors can interfere with their obtaining it. Financial difficulties appear to be the most important of these barriers for most of the population of the LAC region, but two other impediments – physical and cultural – also deserve mention.

Time and distance as barriers to care

Distance to a provider, and the time required to get there, can certainly deter people from using care. However, data on these variables are not systematically collected, and it is difficult to disentangle their effects. So far as the *cost* of travel is important, rather than the *time* taken, household surveys can ask for that information and add it to the cost of care. As a rule, "not having a provider available" is a much less important reason for not getting care than is cost. Data from Colombia in 1992, prior to the insurance reform discussed below, show that "no provider" explains 12% of the cases of forgoing care, in the poorest income quintile. This share shrinks as income rises, becoming insignificant in the richest quintile (Pinto and Hsiao 2007, figure 6.8).

Naturally, not having a (convenient) provider available is primarily a problem for rural dwellers, who are also often among the poorest. Distance is seldom a significant problem for urban residents; an extreme example, from Delhi, India, is that there are seventy providers within walking distance of every household (Das and Hammer 2007). Using Colombian data again, this time for 1997, the urban–rural difference in the probability of seeing a doctor for a health problem is about 12 percentage points for households with insurance and only 7–8 points for the uninsured. Since insurance lowers costs, this is consistent with cost being the dominant reason for not getting care. Distance – or, more to the point, time – can, of course, be crucial in emergencies. True emergencies, and not just the use of emergency facilities, are a small share of all medical consultations, but doubtless account for a higher share of preventable deaths and disabilities. There do not appear to be good estimates of these health losses attributable to physical access, as distinct from other problems such as poor quality of care.

Cultural barriers to effective care

Putting aside simple ignorance of non-symptomatic health problems, culture (or "social") barriers can be important in two ways. One is that people harbor mistaken and often dangerous beliefs about health risks and appropriate care. To continue with the example of diabetes – it seems both from casual observation and from the way the disease is often referred to as "sugar" that many diabetics and people at risk believe that by curbing sugar intake, but ignoring other carbohydrates, they can avoid the disease. The anthropological health literature is full of instances of similarly erroneous beliefs that can keep people from recognizing illness or from obtaining appropriate care for it. The other kind of cultural barrier arises when a person recognizes that care is needed, and consults a provider, but then does not understand or adhere to medical advice because of differences in language or ideas related to a particular culture or ethnic group. In the LAC region, this is chiefly a problem for indigenous peoples, especially when they do not speak the dominant language. Such patients sometimes suffer discrimination in the quality of care they receive, or get little benefit from information.

The household burden of financing healthcare

"Households in developing countries are exposed to high risks, with important consequences on their welfare" and "the costs related to these risks are much higher than a simple consideration of short term costs" (Dercon, Bold, and Calvo 2007). The risk of needing unafford-able care is among the commonest and most dangerous of these haz-ards, and provides a strong argument for protection against financial catastrophe.

It is well established that pre-payment (whether through taxes or insurance) accounts for a larger share of health financing as countries are richer (Musgrove, Carrin, and Zeramdini 2002). Out-of-pocket spending (OOP) is most important in poor countries, where there is also the greatest variation in the composition of health spending. Only OOP payments carry the risk of catastrophic or unaffordable levels of spending, so financial catastrophe is more common in poorer countries. Taxes and insurance obviously reduce what a household can spend on other items, but since both these kinds of financing are related to income and are relatively predictable, they do not threaten impoverishment.

In 2007, WHO analyzed 116 household surveys in 89 countries, including 13 LAC countries, to assess the extent of catastrophic OOP health spending (Xu *et al.* 2007). Since this effort did not involve new, uniform surveys, the data come from different years, sometimes more than a decade ago, and do not provide a snapshot of the region at one moment. Nor are they specifically timed to episodes of illness, as exit surveys from health facilities would be. The findings are out of date to the extent that improved economic conditions or deliberate programs to reduce financial risk have occurred since the survey in a particular country. Total OOP expenditure on health is a small share of total household spending, usually below 5%, as table 6.2 shows.

WHO defines "subsistence" spending as expenditure on food among households between the 45th and 55th percentiles of the distribution of the food share in total spending. This estimate is then adjusted for household size. (If a household spent less in total than its corresponding estimate of subsistence, *all* its expenditure is considered subsistence.) WHO defines "catastrophic" OOP health spending as expenditure exceeding 40% of non-subsistence spending.

The share of households suffering financial catastrophe may be as low as 1% or less in countries with more complete financial protection through publicly financed provision (Costa Rica, Guyana, Jamaica) or as high as 10% where such coverage is much less complete (Brazil, Nicaragua). Another comparison, between OOP health spending among the "catastrophic" households and the level of subsistence per capita, also appears in table 6.2. In ten of the surveys, and at least once in each of seven countries, those households spent more on health than the average for subsistence. A detailed study of health financing in Mexico, prior to the insurance reform discussed below, found that "each year between two and four million households either spent 30 percent or more of disposable income . . . or crossed the poverty line because of their health spending" (Knaul and Frenk 2005).

Although the households with catastrophic expenses account for only a small share of total household spending, they account for a much larger share of total OOP health spending, roughly half in Bolivia and more than a quarter in seven other surveys. This is consistent with those households having to use a large fraction of their total expenditure for health – nearly always more than a quarter.

These estimates, while illuminating, under-state the burden caused by inadequate financial protection and consequent reliance on OOP spending in at least three ways. First, they refer only to what households actually spent despite the high costs they faced. They say nothing about the care that people needed but failed to obtain because they

Table 6.2 *OOP and catastrophic health spending: selected LAC countries, ca. 1992–2002*

Country	Year	All households				Only households with catastrophic expenditure				
		OOP as % expenditure		Subsistence spending per capita (national currency)	OOP per capita	As % of all households		OOP as % total OOP in whole sample	OOP as % household spending	Catastrophic as % household spending
		Total	Non-subsistence			Mean	95% CI			
Argentina	1996–7	5.8	8.6	170	191	6.2	5.9–6.5	35.5	40.3	13.0
Bolivia	1999	3.2	5.3	294	562	4.7	3.9–5.4	55.8	39.9	13.6
Bolivia	2000	2.9	5.1	290	400	6.1	5.4–6.7	45.1	36.6	12.9
Bolivia	2001	3.6	6.5	313	90	3.4	3.0–3.9	49.1	34.1	11.4
Bolivia	2002	3.8	6.8	333	433	3.7	3.3–4.2	48.4	37.0	13.1
Brazil	1996	7.5	13.0	78	86	10.3	9.4–11.1	38.8	33.6	11.4
Colombia	1997	6.1	10.3	110,956	81,797	6.7	6.2–7.2	25.1	31.8	8.8
Costa Rica	1992	0.8	1.4	9,455	4,070	0.2	0.0–0.3	3.2	22.0	9.0
Guyana	1992	1.9	3.7	5,166	2,414	0.7	0.3–1.2	6.6	27.4	6.6
Jamaica	1997	2.3	5.0	4,818	1,526	1.1	0.6–1.5	7.6	25.3	6.3
Jamaica	2001	2.9	5.3	5,255	4,092	1.1	0.6–1.6	10.6	31.8	9.0
Mexico	1996	2.9	4.4	348	606	1.6	1.4–1.8	24.1	37.6	9.5
Nicaragua	1993	4.8	12.7	610	231	2.2	1.8–2.7	44.1	23.9	8.2
Nicaragua	1998	3.0	5.3	291	460	9.4	8.5–10.3	33.6	37.5	10.7
Panama	1997	3.6	6.3	111	82	2.8	2.3–3.2	18.2	32.9	12.8
Paraguay	1996	3.8	6.9	312,371	358,243	3.8	3.1–4.6	29.9	35.6	10.6
Paraguay	2000/1	5.0	9.7	240,220	164,928	3.2	2.5–3.9	19.1	30.1	9.0
Peru	1994	4.0	7.4	196	142	3.3	2.8–3.9	26.0	31.5	8.4
Peru	2000	2.9	5.0	266	361	3.8	3.2–4.4	46.6	36.1	11.8
Uruguay	1995	4.1	5.3	863	1,013	0.8	0.5–1.1	5.5	37.3	8.5

Source: Xu *et al.* (2007, appendix 1), and additional calculations in personal communications from Ke Xu, May 28 and 30, 2007. Survey identification is provided in the source.

Table 6.3 *Indicators (percentages) of medical attention for individuals reporting chronic health problems: Brazil, 1997*

	Income quintile					
Indicator of attention	1	2	3	4	5	Total
Consulted a professional	54.7	63.3	70.3	78.9	82.9	71.1
Among those who did consult:						
Follow-up visit with same professional	51.7	58.8	65.7	73.0	80.7	68.3
Periodic check-ups for the problem	60.9	65.3	70.3	77.6	82.5	73.1

Source: Campino *et al.* (2001, table 7).

couldn't afford it. What that care would have cost could easily be a large multiple of the cost of care that was obtained. Unfortunately, there is no easy way to estimate the cost that did not occur because it was judged to be catastrophic. People who do not seek care may be reacting to a combination of anticipated cost, distance to a facility, doubt as to whether care will be available and will actually solve their health problems, and ignorance or uncertainty as to what that problem is and what care it requires.

A second reason why such estimates under-rate the importance of financial barriers is that when the cost of care is catastrophic, it may matter greatly how it is financed – from savings, by borrowing, selling assets such as land, or taking children out of school and putting them to work. Both the long-run financial effects and those on future health will be worse if the household is permanently impoverished. Finally, household surveys usually inquire only after one recent episode of illness or injury. A high one-time cost relative to short-term ability to pay is considered catastrophic, but it may actually impose less of a burden than smaller but repeated costs required to treat a chronic condition. Table 6.3 provides data from Brazil showing that among individuals reporting a chronic health problem, the likelihood of consultation with a provider, of follow-up visits to that provider, and of periodic check-ups all rise monotonically with income. Accumulated cost may be a large part of the explanation. When LAC surveys ask about such chronic conditions, they concentrate on care and expense only in the last few weeks or, for hospitalizations, sometimes for the past year (Suárez-Berenguela 2001; Musgrove 2005). Since

some chronic conditions worsen if not treated, cost that keeps people from obtaining care early may imply greater cost or worse health
later. The catastrophic spending that actually occurs during a short
recall period is only a lower bound to the welfare loss associated with
the need for costly care.

If catastrophic spending C is defined as WHO does, as

$$OOP - 0.4NS$$

where NS is non-subsistence spending, the share of total household
spending E that is catastrophic – that exceeds the 40% share of NS –
can be estimated as

$$OOP/E - 0.4(NS/E) = OOP/E - 0.4/(OOP/E)/(POOP/NS)$$

This calculation appears in the last column of table 6.2; it is typically
about 10% of total expenditure by *those* households, which means that
it is a very small share of total spending by *all* households. In turn,
that means that "buying out" only that amount of spending through
more insurance coverage or public expenditure on health is clearly
affordable. However, indemnifying households *only for catastrophic
spending* would imply both high administrative costs and opportunities
for fraud, so it is not a feasible solution to the overall challenge of
financial access to care.

How might people react if what they had to pay for care were
sufficiently cheaper to protect them from catastrophe? Data from a
survey in rural Peru (Gertler and van der Gaag 1990) permit estimates of arc price elasticities for healthcare differentiated by income
quartile, age (adults vs. children), price level, and type of provider.
"Price" includes the attributed value of travel time, which is small
compared to monetary cost and reinforces the emphasis here on the
latter. The poorest quartile would increase the use of care almost proportionally to price decreases or even more, for both public and private
providers.

Going back to table 6.2, the Peruvian data on catastrophic spending
suggest that to eliminate altogether only that spending beyond 40%
of non-subsistence expenditure would require a reduction in cost to
households roughly equivalent to 10% of their total spending. That
would still leave them exposed to an OOP cost of about 20% of total
expenditure. Multiplying that price decline by the elasticities for the
lowest quartile, which range from –0.20 to -1.80, implies that the use
of healthcare would increase by an amount corresponding, in value,

to as little as 4% or as much as 36% of total spending among those households experiencing catastrophic costs. This exercise compares data from rural areas only in 1985–6 to countrywide information a decade or more later, so the calculation is approximate at best. Given the small share of households with catastrophic expenses in 1994 and 2001, these numbers suggest that capping costs at 40% of subsistence spending would imply an increase in healthcare utilization of only about 1% of the value of total household expenditure. However, a price reduction large enough to produce that effect would lead to a much larger increase in care-seeking, because it would also affect the non-catastrophic OOP health spending of all households, at least at lower incomes. The financial barriers to care are much higher overall than appears from examining only those households for which the impact is calamitous. The effects are surely larger where the share of catastrophic spending is higher.

This analysis concentrates on the effects of high OOP costs in impoverishing households or preventing them from getting needed care. But patients can get care, particularly if the costliest part of it is free or covered by insurance, and yet get little benefit from it because they still have to pay for drugs. A high OOP cost of drugs leads to reduced adherence to treatment and therefore less effective care. In one study, international differences in the cost to patients of drugs for kidney failure led to differences in compliance, with implications for the progression of disease and the need for dialysis or transplants (Hirth *et al.* 2008). This occurs to a significant degree even among high-income countries; the impact among poorer populations is surely greater. Financial protection that covers only some of the inputs to health interventions can prevent financial catastrophe and still expose people to serious health risks. Because patients very often have to pay for medication OOP, high drug costs can pose a financial barrier even if they represent only a fraction of the total cost of a service. The fact that patients are often willing to pay for drugs does not mean they get all the drugs, or all the care, that they need.

Inefficient provision

The provision of healthcare in the LAC region is widely criticized as inefficient, but it is hard to find good measures of wasted resources or excessive cost. Conceptually, it helps to distinguish four sources of inefficiency:

- *Health services deliver the wrong interventions, in particular providing less cost-effective care when more cost-effective alternatives
  exist.*

  This failure of allocative efficiency is the chief focus of the DCP2
  exercise and earlier such efforts (Jamison *et al.* 1993; World Bank
  1993) that analyze interventions offering the greatest health gains
  per dollar. No study has estimated how much cost could be reduced
  in one country by always choosing the most cost-effective intervention for each problem, although many specific choices can be
  shown to be cost-saving. It is worth noting, however, that while
  cost-effectiveness is a good criterion of efficiency for choosing among
  responses to a *given* health problem, as illustrated in table 6.2, it is
  somewhat more questionable for choices among different diseases
  or conditions, in part because different population groups may be
  affected. No fewer than nine criteria exist for choosing what to buy
  with public resources (Musgrove 2004a), and these can conflict with
  one another – particularly with equity considerations.

- *Inputs are provided in the wrong proportions, so that output is
  limited by the scarcest input and others are idle or under-utilized*

  This failure of technical efficiency typically arises as shortages of
  drugs or other supplies, or deteriorated capital, which makes human
  resources relatively superfluous and less effective than they could be.
  At the same time, drugs may be over-prescribed, with little attention
  to interactions among pharmaceuticals. Theft of supplies and other
  forms of corruption are one cause of this problem (Savedoff 2007;
  Lewis and Musgrove 2008), but imbalances occur even without
  crime, if budgets are rigid and are set inefficiently.

- *Facilities, especially hospitals, operate with diseconomies of scale or
  scope*

  This kind of inefficiency arises partly from misguided investment
  decisions in the public sector and partly from a poor distribution of
  responsibilities and capacities among the different levels of the health
  system. The various inefficiencies that plague hospitals in low- and
  middle-income countries generally are estimated to absorb as much
  as 10% of total health spending (Mills, Rasheed, and Tollman 2006:
  87). A study of hospital economics, including a sample in Colombia
  and some data for Argentina, Jamaica, Belize, and St. Lucia (Barnum
  and Kutzin 1993, especially chapter 3), includes cost functions and
  indications of economies of scale and scope, but none of the usual

measures of hospital operation – average cost per patient, average bed occupancy, bed turnover rate per year, and average length of stay – is by itself an indicator of efficiency. Using the latter three indicators together can suggest where excess bed capacity exists, some hospitalizations are likely to be ~~~~~~~~~~~~~~~age stay is longer than neede~~~~~~~~~~~~~~~~~~~~~~~~~~~~~e absence of information on ~~~~~~~

- *The health system* ~~is dynamically inefficient~~ *because public spending is procyclical and exacerbates rather than offsetting fluctuations in private employment, insurance coverage, and health expenditure*
  This was especially a problem in Latin America during the 1980s, when macroeconomic conditions were unstable (Musgrove 2004b). The share of families facing financial catastrophe is not a fixed feature of a country or its health system: surveys in different years in Bolivia, Nicaragua, Paraguay, and Peru show (in table 6.2) substantial variation as economic conditions change. Economic contraction raises the risk of financial catastrophe through various channels, as figure 6.2 shows (Musgrove 2004b, figure 20.1). Budget cuts can have a more than proportional effect on the availability of care, because they not only stop investment, including maintenance, but protect the staff and leave facilities without drugs and supplies, so that effectiveness and efficiency suffer (Petrera 1989). Under such conditions, stabilizing the macroeconomy may be the single most effective measure a government can take to improve health. Controversy continues over whether the stabilization measures promoted by the IMF are too rigid and constrain health expenditure needlessly (Center for Global Development 2007).

The dynamic inefficiency arising from the interaction of public and private financing and provision in health is arguably most severe when each subsector provides about half of healthcare spending. If the public share is very small, it simply cannot accommodate sizeable fluctuations in private expenditure or demand; whereas if it is much larger than half, the changes needed to compensate for private fluctuations are more easily managed. These problems are exacerbated by short-run political cycles and consequent myopic planning and lack of institutional memory. In good times, extra resources may be committed to investments that may not be maintained or operated adequately, or appropriated by public employees in the form of unsustainable higher wages. In lean times, investments can be stopped but not undone, and workers in the public sector tend to resist the changes, especially staff reductions, that may be needed to keep the system from becoming unbalanced and unproductive. The LAC region suffers more than other low- and middle-income regions from procyclical expenditure (Clements, Faircloth, and Verhoeven 2007: 12), making it particularly important to control this source of inefficiency.

Substandard quality

Quality of care, like efficiency in delivery, is commonly criticized as inadequate and also is difficult to measure satisfactorily. It is still harder to estimate how far substandard quality care contributes to poor health or excess mortality. In the extreme, failures of quality that can be classified as medical errors cost many lives – an estimated 44,000–98,000 preventable deaths in hospital annually in the United States, for example (IOM 2001). It would be surprising if medical mistakes did not occur at similar rates in Latin America and the Caribbean, but no such aggregate estimate exists. In the major countries of the region about sixty people per 1,000 population are hospitalized each year (PAHO 2007), for a total of slightly more than 30 million admissions, roughly equal to the 33.6 million in the United States from which the estimates of errors come. Assuming a comparable ratio of preventable deaths to hospitalizations – that is, from 1.3 to 2.9 per 1,000 admissions – would imply that poor-quality care in hospital kills at least 41,000 people every year in the region, and perhaps as many as 92,000. Differences in case mix between Latin America and the United States only add to the uncertainty of such estimates.

How much more health damage occurs due to mistakes in outpatient care is even less well known; but medical errors in both hospitals and ambulatory care are considered to be so common, worldwide, that WHO has developed, together with the Joint Commission and the Joint Commission International, a set of nine patient safety solutions (WHO Collaborating Centre 2007). These include such simple and well-known – but not always followed – procedures as correct identification of patients and frequent hand-washing, besides more sophisticated controls of medications, electrolyte solutions, and connections between catheters and tubes.

When a well-defined protocol exists for how to diagnose and treat patients presenting with specific symptoms (fever, cough, diarrhea, etc.) or for pre-natal care, it is possible to quantify either or both of two other measures of quality. These are (1) how well providers know what they should do ("competence"), as tested by questioning them with the aid of vignettes; and (2) how well providers actually do what the protocol calls for ("effort"), by observing encounters with patients or interviewing patients after a consultation. A study in rural Mexico (Barber, Bertozzi, and Gertler 2007) takes the second approach to judge the quality of pre-natal care, and a study in Paraguay (Das and Sohnesen 2007) uses direct clinical observation to assess "doctor effort" in a variety of patient encounters. These analyses, plus others in India, Indonesia, and Tanzania, are summarized by Das and Gertler (2007), who conclude that "Variations in practice quality are likely to explain a large fraction of the variance in outcomes, even in low-income settings". Similar failings in quality are documented in other developing countries (Peabody *et al.* 2006).

The Mexico study reports the percentage of times that providers in different subsectors performed each of fourteen standard pre-natal care procedures. As table 6.4 shows, the percentages, while often above 80%, sometimes fall below 50%. Four kinds of variation among providers and patients stand out:

- *Contrary to widespread belief, public providers often outperform private ones*
- *Doctors (with an MD-equivalent degree) perform better than those without a degree; the latter are more common in the private sector*
- *The poorest quartile of patients receive markedly worse care than the least poor quartile, in the private sector (but there is little difference in the public sector)*
- *Indigenous women receive less complete care in the private sector, with little difference in public institutions.*

In contrast to the discrimination by income and indigenous status in Mexico, the Paraguay study finds no differences in doctor effort according to patient characteristics – except for a tendency to devote *more* attention to poorer patients, giving them more time or asking more questions and performing more examinations. Controlling for doctor and patient characteristics and for symptoms, more effort always increases the probability of completing essential examinations and – to a lesser extent – of asking all the appropriate questions of a patient.

Table 6.4 *Percentage of pre-natal care procedures performed, by clinical setting: rural Mexico, 2003*

Procedure	Social security	IMSS Oportunidades	MOH, other public	Private sector	All settings
Asked about bleeding	82.24	78.26	74.40	57.01	72.28
Asked about discharge	85.34	80.71	75.71	60.36	74.44
Blood sample taken	61.21	44.02	46.12	31.79	45.23
Urine sample taken	68.79	49.46	50.27	34.36	49.73
Blood pressure taken	95.00	94.57	94.80	73.23	90.09
Weighed	97.93	98.10	97.98	75.16	92.99
Uterine height measured	90.00	89.95	88.24	61.78	82.92
Pelvic exam	51.21	42.93	48.80	35.26	45.62
Tetanus toxoid immunization	94.48	97.28	94.26	70.14	89.33
Iron supplements	90.52	88.86	85.12	65.89	82.18
Advised about lactation	92.21	92.93	91.30	71.04	87.19
Advised about family planning	90.17	91.85	85.72	55.21	80.41
Recorded information	80.00	83.15	77.08	43.24	70.79

Source: Barber, Bertozzi, and Gertler (2007, exhibit 2) (Sample size 3,553 women).

Studies limited to just two countries and a few conditions, and using different methods, are scant basis for generalization. Still, these results, together with those for the other countries, suggest several conclusions. First, quality is often unacceptably low, even for well-defined and uncomplicated situations. Second, both qualifications and effort matter – but competence does not guarantee a corresponding degree of good performance. Third, variation among providers, and discrimination among patients, can be substantial, but do not have to be.

2 Defining the solutions

When health challenges are defined in disease-specific terms, the corresponding solutions are specific interventions, as illustrated in Lomborg (2004) and elaborated in DCP2. Defining the challenges systemically means that the solutions must also be systemic, and often on a scale large enough to be called health sector *reform*. The larger the scale of the solutions, the harder it is to estimate their costs or potential outcomes. Questions of feasibility and of how to "get health reform right" also become more important (Roberts *et al.* 2004). The discussion here first characterizes the proposed solutions qualitatively, and then says something about what they might cost and what kind of benefits they could provide. In contrast to disease-specific solutions, which can often reduce the burden of one disease or condition without interaction with other health problems, the systemic solutions are synergistic: applying them all together would yield more than the sum of the benefits of each solution taken separately. Interactions among them are the norm.

Corresponding to the four challenges indicated above are four sets of measures to:

- *Increase access to care*
- *Raise quality*
- *Improve efficiency of delivery*
- *Reduce ignorance or misperceptions of needs.*

Measures to improve access to care are treated first because they appear to be the largest-scale solution and because only they directly attack the problem of financial risk, whereas all four kinds of solution aim to improve health status. (Improving quality and efficiency could also reduce financial risk, to the extent that they protect patients from the need to repeat care or to pay more than care should cost.) Raising quality is placed second because, together with better access, it matches the highest priority of respondents to the IDB survey. It also appears to be somewhat more straightforward to achieve, with fewer economic and political obstacles, than the third solution of improving efficiency of service delivery. Finally, while increasing understanding of health needs is undoubtedly important, it applies particularly to non-symptomatic conditions and risk factors. Progress on the other solutions would lead to more contacts with providers and would probably have the desirable side-effect of increasing public health knowledge.

Improving access to care

The Cuban health system provides close to universal, free access to care, and so could be a model for the rest of the LAC region. However, it was created only following a revolution; it excludes not only private insurance but also legal private practice by providers; and it requires a higher ratio of physicians to population than other countries have achieved or appear to aspire to. The discussion here considers experiences in countries characterized by mixed systems of both finance and provision, where efforts to extend access start from the status quo and differ according to each country's situation.

The solution needed is some kind of universal insurance coverage, with services to be delivered by qualified providers independently of their public or private, for-profit or non-profit status. That means competition among providers; and since insurance for the poor will have to be subsidized, it means using public funds to pay private providers, if that is not now done in a country's health system. It may, but need not, mean competition among insurers. Defining the solution this way means rejecting some other ideas, particularly that of simply expanding the network of public facilities. Insurance, and the inclusion of private providers, is consistent with the evidence that financial barriers to care are more significant than physical ones of time or distance, for most of the population. It is also consistent with the fact that private providers are often available in places lacking public facilities, and local residents need to be free to use them.

An extension of formal or explicit coverage to the entire population can take many forms; three examples, from Chile, Mexico, and Colombia, are briefly considered here. Many middle-income countries in other parts of the world are also extending coverage, sometimes by quite different models, leading to efforts to derive lessons for other such countries and for those still poorer (Mills 2007).

The Chilean model requires all wage and salary workers to contribute 7% of their pay either to the National Health Fund (FONASA) or to a private insurer (ISAPRE) of their choice. Higher-paid workers tend to buy private insurance and can pay OOP for more generous coverage; the lower-paid tend to register with FONASA and are classified into four groups by income. Which providers they can use depends on that classification; public facilities are, of course, available to all. The ISAPREs compete for clients; only at the margin, where the 7% contribution will buy a benefit package slightly better than what FONASA offers, do they compete with the public sector. This arrangement suffers the usual problems of a competitive private insurance (Fischer and Serra 1996), but it is saved from the worst failings of an inequitable two-tiered system by two features. First,

FONASA is also financed from general revenues, so that its enrollees obtain benefits costing more than their contributions, and the poorest are fully subsidized. This makes the system much more equitable than the health-specific financing alone would allow (Bitrán y Asociados 1999). Second, any medical intervention which the Ministry of Health guarantees to provide must also be provided by the ISAPREs. They are free to adjust their premiums accordingly, but not to deny care or to charge more for those interventions. Protection from financial risk is an explicit objective of the system, and is largely achieved (FONASA 2007).

The Seguro Popular in Mexico takes a different approach (Knaul and Frenk 2005). This is an insurance created in 2003 for those households (about half the population) not covered by either social security (Instituto Mexicano de Seguridad Social, IMSS, for wage and salaried workers) or the scheme for public employees (Instituto de Seguridad Social de los Trabajadores del Estado, ISSTE) and those too poor to afford private insurance, who were therefore dependent on services provided by the Ministry of Health. Enrollment is voluntary and is meant to expand gradually until 2010, with preference initially given to the poorest, who are fully subsidized. Households in the upper eight income deciles pay an income-dependent contribution of up to 5% of disposable income. Public financing comes from both the federal and state governments, with the shares varying according to the states' income levels. The Seguro Popular does not compete with the established schemes, in which enrollment and contribution are mandatory; it does promote competition among providers. There is a separate fund for public health measures, and another for catastrophically expensive care, to protect financing for those elements that might otherwise be neglected in a purely demand-side scheme. Fully subsidized households must participate in health promotion activities.

The third model is that of Colombia, which instead of a specific new insurance, as in Mexico, created the conditions for a new class of insurers to compete for clients and a new funding mechanism to finance them. The reform, launched by the Law 100 of 1993, also decentralizes public responsibilities for healthcare and splits the financing between a contributory regime and a subsidized one, with the latter receiving a less generous benefit package. The Sistema General de Seguridad Social en Salud (SGSSS) has been in operation for well over a decade, and is arguably the most far-reaching scheme of universal coverage, since it implies competition among all kinds of insurers and providers.

The Colombian reform has been extensively studied (Pinto and Hsiao 2007). As in Mexico, it has greatly expanded explicit insurance coverage. It has also illustrated the difficulties of making competition work, particularly in rural areas; in consequence, it has not been possible to shift entirely to demand-side financing without running the risk of putting public facilities out of business. Shifting public staff among facilities to match the new demands for care has also proved complicated, and political resistance has been strong enough to slow the expansion of coverage and probably to raise the costs somewhat.

These three approaches (four, counting Cuba) cover a range of possibilities for a solution to universal coverage. Each reflects something of the country's pre-existing health system, and none serves as the obviously preferable model. While each has been subject to some evaluation, they differ too much in how long they have been operating and in so many other features that it is impossible – or, at least, unwise – to rank them. In particular, the appropriate degree of competition, especially among insurers, is an open question. The six main points of this discussion are that:

- *Several paths to universal insurance* are already in use in LAC countries that formerly left large populations uninsured.
- *A serious attempt to enroll the uninsured can expand coverage rapidly*, despite obstacles. The Mexican scheme had enrolled 1.7 million families, 13% of the target population, by its second year of operation; the Colombian scheme had enrolled 13 million people (contributors and subsidized beneficiaries) within its first decade.
- *All these schemes aim primarily to finance demand for care* rather than its supply, but a mixed financing arrangement may be required by the limitations of competition among providers, including local monopoly situations in rural areas.
- *An explicit guarantee of coverage requires the definition of the package of care*, which establishes the rights of patients and the basis for rationing decisions. This can facilitate improvements in quality, as discussed below.
- *Any of these approaches is preferable to creating narrowly defined insurance* for specific groups, such as women or children, or only for specific diseases, or only for the most basic or primary care.

- *Although a two-tiered system is undesirable on ethical grounds, it may be the only feasible way to expand coverage significantly.* Moreover, the worst dangers of a two-tiered system can be avoided if beneficiaries have access to a wide range of providers and there is substantial subsidy from the better-off to the poor, either within the scheme, or through transfers of general revenues, or both.

Uruguay is currently developing its own model of a national health insurance, to proceed in stages – from expanding social security by the incorporation of 800,000 beneficiaries through the inclusion of spouses and minor children, to retirees, and eventually the whole population (Olesker 2007). The intention is to unify the various sources of finance for health in a single national health fund, somewhat on the Chilean model.

Raising quality of care

When people do not have access to care, its quality can hardly matter to them. Once they do have access, quality becomes paramount, because "better quality can improve health much more rapidly than can other drivers of health, such as economic growth, educational advancement, or new technology" (Peabody *et al.* 2006: 1293). The US Institute of Medicine treats quality as composed of six elements: safety, effectiveness, patient-centeredness, timeliness, efficiency, and equity (IOM 2001). Peabody *et al.* (2006) classify measures to improve quality in two categories: those affecting the whole health system, and those directly affecting the practice of individual providers or facilities. The former category includes legal mandates and their enforcement; accreditation and administrative regulation, which can keep out unqualified providers but otherwise have little impact on quality or its variation among providers; the development and use of clinical guidelines; targeted education; and organizational changes. The last of these can improve care substantially but implies sizeable investments of time to design, implement, and evaluate. The individual-level category includes peer review feedback in training staff, measures to assure that providers give a high volume of care, and rewards, both monetary and non-monetary, linked to measurable performance. Measuring quality in ways that are easily understood and resistant to manipulation is crucial to all efforts to improve care. Provider competence and effort are most closely associated with two of the IOM components – that care should be effective and should not pose needless risks to the patient.

Because many different approaches can be taken to improve quality, and the results will depend on the *ex ante* situation, it is difficult to specify just what should be done in any one country or facility, still less for the whole of the LAC region. The most important intervention to pursue is that of training with peer review for primary care – not only for childhood illnesses but for all complaints that are common and for which sound guidelines exist. A somewhat broader approach to training would allow for changes in the skill mix of providers or in the way different services are related (Preker *et al.* 2006). Substantial organizational changes may be desirable but are less urgent because they involve still more systemic reform, higher costs, and more uncertainty.

Improving efficiency

The two interventions already discussed – providing universal insurance coverage and improving quality – should both have the welcome side-effect of improving the *technical* efficiency with which care is delivered. Greater competition among providers, as private physicians and facilities are financed publicly, may improve efficiency, either by shifting care from less-efficient public providers to more-efficient private ones, or by forcing public providers to compete on quality and cost rather than, as traditionally, chiefly on price. Not too much should be expected from this approach, however. Private providers do not always use resources more economically, nor do they always deliver better quality; and the scope for competition is limited by the need to continue some supply-side financing, particularly in rural areas. Similarly, while an emphasis on quality may push providers toward greater efficiency, the outcome will depend on how performance is measured and rewarded. If better quality means doing more for patients, the cost of care will increase rather than decrease; it is important not to confuse efficiency simply with lower cost or expenditure.

There is no shortage of advice on how to make health facilities operate more efficiently by minimizing resource use for a given output. Much of this thinking centers on the concept of *new public management (NPM)*, implying a "rejection of traditional, hierarchic forms of public sector management" (Mills, Rasheed, and Tollman 2006:

92). Instead of rigid planning and control, what is wanted is more local autonomy, but also closer supervision, and more readiness to separate finance from provision of services, sometimes by contracts between public agencies and private providers. The three examples of expanded insurance coverage discussed above in Chile, Mexico, and Colombia all include such elements. Public funds pay for both private and public provision, and patients – with some exceptions, as in Chile – have free choice of providers. NPM is characterized, in the first place, by the recognition that health services *need to be managed*, that professional skill in management is as important to good health outcomes as the medical skills of practitioners (Preker *et al.* 2006: 1341).

Beyond these general ideas, there is evidence that "management strengthening" interventions have generally positive effects. However, there is little basis for uniform prescriptions, and efforts to improve technical efficiency often run into serious opposition from providers. The safest recommendation is that countries need to experiment with improvements in managing people, capital or physical assets, and drugs and other consumables. Making health service delivery more efficient is partly a technical problem, but it is also always a political problem.

The measures that promote better use of resources in the technical sense do not necessarily have any effect on *allocative* efficiency. Setting priorities for what health interventions to provide or finance is an even more political question than technical efficiency, since it often means making choices among patients. There is no ideal solution, but the single best recommendation is to make much more use of cost-effectiveness as a criterion to get the largest possible health gains from a given level of expenditure. The most striking such use is the Programa de Acceso Universal de Garantías Explícitas (AUGE) in Chile, which has added fifty-six treatments to the list of services the Ministry of Health guarantees to patients and therefore also requires private insurers to provide (Vargas and Poblete 2008). Another twenty-four treatments are under consideration. The decisions on interventions draw on research into the unit cost and required total expenditure on each service, and the likely effectiveness in healthy life years saved. For the most part, this information was not previously available, so the exercise has had the beneficial effect of requiring clinicians to study their outcomes and their use of resources in detail. The distinction between high-medium- and low-priority interventions also takes into account prevalence, the burden of disease, the financial burden on households, and public preferences among diseases, conditions, and age groups.

One other solution to the problem of efficiency looks less urgent today than it did twenty years ago, but still belongs among the valuable recommendations. That is to limit the dynamic inefficiency of the public system in health by reducing the volatility, and especially the natural procyclical character, of public expenditure for health. An expansion of publicly financed, explicit coverage obviously helps to dampen the interaction with the private sector and reduce the effects illustrated in figure 6.2 (p. 300).

Increasing public knowledge

The challenge is that people do not always know when they need healthcare, so the solution has to be to increase their understanding by supplying correct information about diseases, symptoms, and risk factors, and combating misperceptions that prevent people from obtaining care or from benefiting fully from it. Particularly where changes in diet and lifestyle are concerned, it is easy to say what behaviors are protective, but much harder to show that interventions to promote those behaviors are cost-effective, or – sometimes – even that they are effective at all (Willett *et al.* 2006).

The cheapest way to increase knowledge is through messages to the public via print and electronic media, without any face-to-face interactions. The next most expensive method is to offer face-to-face contact and counseling. The next costliest is to provide diagnostic tests such as those for blood pressure, anemia, glucose concentration, eyesight, and hearing, or antibodies to particular pathogens. Preventive interventions against HIV/AIDS employ all three methods, combining testing for HIV status with counseling (VCT). That approach makes sense for a particular, and particularly dangerous, communicable disease, when those infected may not be aware of it. It is less clear whether face-to-face transmission of information, with or without diagnostic tests, is worthwhile for health-related information in general.

Finally, the costliest way to increase knowledge of health needs and healthful behaviors is to pay people to attend educational sessions as part of a CCT program, in which they are also remunerated for attending pre-natal care, well-baby clinics or regular health center visits, or for having their children fully immunized and kept in school. Programs of this type in Brazil, Colombia, Honduras, Jamaica, Mexico, and Nicaragua have been subject to varying degrees of evaluation, and the findings synthesized (Glassman, Gaarder, and Todd 2006). These programs have a price effect, to the extent that beneficiaries would otherwise use, and have to pay for, the preventive and health-promoting services that are conditions of enrollment. The CCT program means there is also an income effect, which by itself may be enough to increase food consumption and improve diet, leading to the widely observed effect of reduced stunting among very young children. The CCT program also has the effect of compensating beneficiaries for the indirect costs of access to healthcare, particularly the cost of time lost from work.

CCT program design is based on nine assumptions, notably that the poor suffer not only from low incomes but also from insufficient knowledge of health, and that information induces desirable behavior change – but also that it is necessary to require attendance at health clinics for specific services. The natural targets for such programs are poor households with young children or pregnant women, who would especially benefit from greater use of preventive services. Regular check-ups may also lead to more treatment of acute conditions, and even to better detection and control of some chronic conditions such as hypertension and diabetes among adults.

Providing universal access to care is almost sure to lead more people to consult about symptoms, fears, or doubts, and therefore to detect more cases of disease or risks. The effect will be still greater if quality is simultaneously improved, so that diagnostic opportunities are not missed and people are adequately counseled about their health. How much more should be undertaken? The appropriate solution seems to be to start with population surveys to gauge public knowledge of important health problems. Questions about risk factors and diseases can be included in the health module of a standard household survey and need not be limited to questions to mothers about pregnancy and child care – as they often have been in the past (Musgrove 2005). Balancing that information about what people know with estimates of the undiagnosed prevalence of a condition can provide the basis for a judgment about screening for that condition. Prevalence, the state of public knowledge, and the cost of a screening program can determine how much effort to put into the program, and in particular whether to offer free screening to a particular population group. Certain tests – notably for blood pressure – of course can and should be part

of routine outpatient visits; here the solution is to train medical staff
not only to perform the test but to counsel the patient when the results
indicate it.

3 Costs of improving the utilization of good-quality care

Of the solutions discussed here, the extension of insurance coverage is
by far the most costly. It is also the only one for which approximate
estimates of cost are possible, since the interventions for improving
quality and efficiency and informing the public can usually be specified
only qualitatively. (A few exceptions are indicated below). What they
would cost to implement depends on their exact content, which can
be drawn from a wide range of alternatives. In some cases there is
evidence that the solutions would be cost-saving, which is equivalent
to providing monetary benefits alone in excess of costs.

It is not easy to estimate even the cost of extending coverage, since
reforms of the magnitude in operation in Chile and underway in Mexico and Colombia do not simply introduce new resources to apply to
the healthcare of people who formerly had no health expenses. Spending is redistributed on a large scale, as households reduce their own
OOP costs and financing shifts toward insurance premiums and tax
revenues. The net cost to society is less, possibly much less, than the
net cost to the public sector.

One important question is the cost of scaling up: what happens to
the marginal cost of including one more household as the number of
households is increased? The available data on costs of major reforms
do not answer this question, since over the years that it takes to enroll
millions of people, costs also change because of inflation, alterations
in the benefit package, or other modifications to the program, and the
exact way in which coverage is extended geographically. Extending
coverage does not necessarily start with the population easiest to reach
and climb an ascending marginal cost curve thereafter. If the object
is to protect the most vulnerable, notably the rural poor, the earliest
beneficiaries may be the most costly to incorporate, with cost declining
as coverage is extended to cities and to the less poor. It should also
be noted that the costs that vary with the extent of coverage are those
of identifying and recruiting beneficiaries and the other administrative
costs of the system, whether these are borne by government or by
insurance intermediaries. The premiums that contributing beneficiaries

pay and the payments to intermediaries do not vary with the scale of operation. The costs of healthcare will vary with scale only so far as people with different levels of utilization or more costly medical problems are enrolled at different stages of the expansion.

Data from Colombia are used here for rough estimates of cost; whether those costs are justified by the resulting benefits is considered in section 4. Relying on the experience of just one country is risky, but few other countries have undertaken so far-reaching an attempt to reach universal coverage. Colombia seems to offer as good a case study as there is of the magnitude of the challenge and the costs and potential benefits of meeting it. There are also recent detailed data on expenditures for the Seguro Popular, and for other public health spending, in Mexico. However, they cover a shorter period and have not been the subject of as much evaluation. Subsequent comparison with Chilean and Colombian experience may be of particular value since the new insurance in Mexico is a single-payer scheme and involves much less interaction with other forms of coverage, particularly private insurance, than in either Chile or Colombia.

Cost of expanding access in Colombia

The Colombian model is examined for a number of reasons:

- *It has been analyzed in considerable detail.* Some authors (Pinto and Hsiao 2007) state that "no actuarial studies of the real cost of providing the benefits package have been undertaken." A more recent set of studies has tried to estimate costs and outcomes more exactly (Escobar *et al.* 2007; Giedión *et al.* 2007; Glassman *et al.* 2007; and Tono *et al.* 2007).
- *There is an analysis of national health accounts for the decade 1993–2003* (Barón Leguizamón 2007).
- *The scheme attempts to promote efficiency through competition* among both providers and among insurers.
- *From 2003, the scheme includes regulations to measure quality and promote its improvement.*

Enrollment in the contributory part of the Colombian health system expanded from about 28% of the population in 1992, just before the reform, to a peak of almost 40% in 1998. It then declined, due to economic recession, until 2002, before rebounding in 2003. From

1998 to 2002, all the growth in total coverage came in the subsidized regime. This has limited further expansion, since the subsidized regime is designed to be financed partly by about one-eighth of the revenue of the contributory regime. For purposes of estimating cost, data are taken from 2002–3 only; whether this represents a stable estimate is uncertain. The redistributive effects come from comparing 2003 with 1993.

In 2002, the premium for the contributory regime was 300,684 Colombian pesos, or US$120 at the official exchange rate (and $413 in PPP). The premium for the subsidized regime was half that, corresponding to the less generous benefit package, or US$60–$61. With 5.3 million contributors and 8.0 million subsidized beneficiaries of the Solidarity and Guarantees Fund (SGF), the average premium was US$84. The SGF took in 4.74 billion pesos and paid out 4.59 billion, of which 3.99 billion was premium payments to the intermediaries that administer the insurance and another 0.24 billion was transferred to specific non-premium funds (Pinto and Hsiao 2007, tables 6.2, 6.5). If that were the whole cost, one could conclude that coverage could be extended for less than US$100 *per capita* per year if part of the population received a more limited benefit package, and for $120 if everyone got the full package.

Unfortunately, it is not that simple, because there is still substantial supply-side financing in the system – 27% of the total expenditure through the SGSSS in 2003 (Barón Leguizamón 2007, appendix A-11). Inflating the premium amounts accordingly suggests that the *per capita* cost of the scheme is about 37% higher than the premium amounts alone suggest, or about US$164 for coverage of the full package, or $83 for the fully subsidized coverage. This compares to *per capita* total health spending of US$136. As of 2007, the premiums paid to municipalities for coverage of their populations had risen to US$117 for subsidized beneficiaries and $208 for contributors, slightly below the monthly minimum wage of $223 (Escobar, private communication). The total population eligible for subsidy is estimated at 22 million, of whom only about 8.5 million were covered in 2003. Extending the subsidized package to the remaining 14 million people would cost, on these assumptions, about US$1.16 billion. However, those eligible may include about 9 million who would need the full subsidy, and another 5 million who would be partly subsidized and pay a small contribution

(Jaramillo Pérez 2007), so the public cost of universal coverage would be slightly less, around US$1 billion.

In 2003, expenditure by the SGSSS was 3.5% of GDP and 44.5% of total health spending. Full coverage by the subsidized regime would have required public spending of an additional 1% of GDP. Direct (non-social insurance) public expenditure on health had already risen by 0.8% of GDP since 1993, while social insurance expenditure rose from 1.6% to 4.3% of GDP. This increased insurance spending allowed private and OOP spending, mostly the latter, to fall dramatically, from 3.3% to 1.2% of GDP, so that total health spending rose only from 6.2% to 7.8%. As shares of national income, the redistributive effect is much larger than the effect on total spending. These changes accompanied an increase in coverage of the population from 23% to 63%, while the population itself grew by more than 7 million. In absolute numbers, then, the insured population increased by 19.5 million (Escobar *et al.* 2007, table 6.2). Some 16.5 million people remained uninsured.

Other costs of systemic improvement in Colombia

As discussed above, there is no good estimate of the additional costs that would be imposed in Colombia by the other solutions for raising quality and efficiency – but it seems safe to assume they would be small in comparison. Expenditure on health promotion and disease prevention has risen dramatically, from only 2.0% of total health spending in 1993 to 6% or more in most years since 1995, so there is probably ample funding for the informational activities needed. Training is still a small share, only 0.1% do in recent years (Barón Leguizamón 2007, tables 3.4, 3.5) and probably needs to increase in order to improve quality. When it comes to efficiency, the principal worry derives from the multiplicity of insurance intermediaries. Administering the system, including the private insurers outside the SGSSS, absorbs fully 15%–16% of total health spending, although strictly comparable data across all insurers do not exist (Escobar 2007, personal communication). Delivery of services takes only about two-thirds of expenditure, down from 80% in 1994–5. By coincidence, the administrative cost of about US$1.1 billion is roughly the same as the cost estimated above, for extending coverage to the rest of the population eligible for subsidy.

Other cost estimates

Quality improvements in general appear to provide large gains at relatively low cost, although exact cost estimates, or comparisons to outcomes and benefits for individual interventions, are hard to come by. The cost of applying such measures universally has not been estimated, but it is reasonable to suppose that the net effect would be cost-saving, or that monetary benefits alone would exceed costs. The principal component of cost would be training and supervision; relatively little investment is needed in supplies and equipment. The potential gains are very large. The hospital deaths in the United States that could be prevented by better quality control were estimated to cost the economy $17–$29 billion per year (IOM 2001), surely far in excess of what it would cost to avert many of those errors. Losses representing the same share of GDP would amount to $5–$10 billion in Latin America and the Caribbean, in PPP terms.

Modeling exercises have shown that training providers on specific protocols for diagnosing and treating common childhood illnesses – pneumonia and diarrhea – is very cost-effective when initial quality is low and disease incidence is high. Children's lives can be saved for as little as US$14, but more generally for US$100–$1,000.

Where increasing public knowledge is concerned, one option is to conduct large-scale screening for particular conditions. The cost-effectiveness of a screening program varies greatly with the prevalence of a condition and the frequency with which individuals are tested. For example, in the LAC region, screening for type 2 diabetes in the general population is estimated to cost US$8,550 per quality adjusted life year (QALY) gained, more than any of the other preventive or treatment interventions for the disease (Narayan *et al.* 2006, table 30.3). Cost-effectiveness ratios for clinical examination and mammography to detect breast cancer differ by a factor of more than three, depending on the type of screen, the age group examined, and the frequency of screening (Brown *et al.* 2006, table 29.5). Table 29.3 in Brown *et al.* (2006) shows even larger variation among forms of screening for cervical cancer. Whether such efforts would repay their cost in reduced medical treatment is uncertain; finding more cases could increase treatment.

CCT programs pursue several objectives; they are simultaneously a specific form of insurance and a means of educating beneficiaries, besides providing an income transfer. Such programs typically provide between 10% and 25% of households' pre-transfer consumption (Glassman, Gaarder, and Todd 2006, table 6.2), which limits their coverage. This substantial cost is roughly equivalent to the cost of catastrophic healthcare costs, as discussed above, if *all* the beneficiaries suffered financial catastrophe regularly. For this reason CCT programs can be a valuable adjunct to, but not a substitute for, universal coverage of a wide range of health services. The marginal cost of their educational component is, of course, much smaller, but that component would probably not be taken up, or would be relatively ineffective, if it were not accompanied by the income transfer and the free provision of care.

4 Benefits from the proposed solutions

One can distinguish at least three kinds of benefits as a consequence of expanded insurance coverage and improved knowledge, quality, and efficiency. These are better health status, higher incomes as a direct or indirect result of that status, and financial protection. The income effect is not considered here, but may be substantial – particularly in the long run, as better child health and a program to pay poor parents to keep their children in school translate into more schooling and eventual higher productivity. The shorter-run impacts on income from improved adult health are real enough, but data on health outcomes are generally too scarce and too difficult to attribute to specific solutions. (Health improvements leading to income gains can often be attributed to disease-specific health interventions, but not so readily to the more general solutions considered here.) Moreover, improvements beyond working age will have little or no effect on income.

Previous estimates of benefits, and their limitations

Defining health challenges and solutions in systemic rather than primarily in disease-specific terms has a cost. As the experience of the 2004 Copenhagen Consensus project shows, it is harder and more controversial to derive plausible, readily accepted estimates of the benefits from systemic changes. However, there are serious problems with the estimates of benefits, and therefore of BCR ratios, from the disease-specific solutions analyzed in that exercise. Two different approaches were used, but neither is an adequate representation of the monetary value of benefits, and in addition, the two methods are not comparable.

The analysis in chapter 2 of Lomborg (2004) took DCP2 estimates of the DALYs saved by the solution interventions, and then valued those life years at different arbitrary monetary amounts to convert them to estimated monetary benefits. The resulting BCR is simply the dollar value attributed to a DALY, divided by the cost-effectiveness ratio (CER):

$$Benefit/Cost = (\$Benefit/DALY)/(\$Cost/DALY) \qquad (1)$$

This approach makes the BCR inversely proportional to the CER, or strictly proportional to the number of DALYs that a given sum of money can buy. It does not add any real information to the cost-effectiveness estimates, since the value assigned to a DALY is not supported by any independent evidence but is simply taken to be a multiple of income *per capita*. The same technique is used to value the health benefits of safe water (chapter 9 in Lomborg 2004), and also by Jamison (2007) for several diseases. This amounts to comparing real apples with imaginary oranges.

In contrast, chapter 7 in Lomborg (2004) measures the benefits of better child nutrition only as subsequent increased income, directly as work effort or indirectly through schooling. One member of the Expert panel (Frey 2004: 615) noted that these two approaches are not comparable, and criticized estimates based on productivity for neglecting the utility or happiness component of better health. Self-reported health turns out to be the strongest determinant of happiness, across a sample of 15,209 survey respondents in Latin America (Graham 2008); income is only the second most important determinant. Another member of the Panel (Schelling 2004: 627) argued strongly against valuing life by productivity, or valuing healthy life years relative to income *per capita*. So although the Expert panel agreed on the ranking of solutions, one or another member dismissed as invalid both of the principal approaches to judging health benefits. Therefore neither method is accepted in the present discussion of benefits.

Discarding the calculation in (1) means that the findings and recommendations become impossible to compare to the benefits attributed to solving other, non-health challenges, as the Copenhagen Consensus process seeks to do. Techniques of evaluation that sometimes work reasonably well for setting priorities within one sector break down when applied across different sectors (Rivlin 1971). What follows is a discussion of two outcomes of the Colombian reform – increased financial protection and improved access to healthcare. The results are quantitative, but are not converted to monetary estimates of benefits to compare with the cost estimates in section 3.

Financial protection

The Colombian reform has dramatically changed the expenditure shares from households, enterprises, and the different levels of government, as table 6.5 shows. Households used to pay more than half the total cost of healthcare, and most of that (44%) was OOP. OOP spending has declined to only about one-quarter of the 1993 level, while total expenditure has risen by 50%. And the reform has succeeded in reaching the poorest households preferentially: insurance coverage, including private voluntary insurance, went from 9% to 48% in the lowest income quintile and from 60% to 81% in the top quintile, narrowing the disparities across the income distribution (Pinto and Hsiao 2007, figure 6.7). Coverage is still slightly worse in rural than in urban areas (by about 10 percentage points), but the subsidized regime accounts for a much larger share of beneficiaries in rural areas.

The declining share of health spending by households has been balanced by an increase in public spending, particularly a near-doubling of the national government's percentage contribution and a near-tripling in absolute amount. This has also relieved the departmental and municipal governments of some of their share, under rules designed to spread the geographic burden more equitably. Spending by enterprises has increased by 52%, keeping the share nearly constant. The other large shift is that "resources of the agents" – the intermediaries that operate the insurance – rose from 0.8% to 19.8% of the total. It is not entirely clear what this contribution represents (Jaramillo Pérez 2007).

This shift away from OOP financing has greatly reduced financial risk for households. When the reform was only a few years old, in 1997, the survey reported in table 6.2 showed 6.7% of households making catastrophic payments for health on the WHO definition (40% or more of disposable or non-subsistence income). The catastrophic part of these payments amounted to 8.8% of total expenditure among

Table 6.5 *Absolute amounts and percentage share of total health spending: Colombia, 1993 and 2003*

	1993		2003	
Source (payer)	Million constant 2000 pesos	%	Million constant 2000 pesos	%
Households	5,215,434	54.9	4,088,280	28.6
Voluntary insurance	344,184	3.6	749,144	5.2
Mandatory insurance	0	0	63,260	0.4
Social security tax	726,623	7.7	1,923,345	13.5
Copayments, etc.	0	0	127,653	0.9
OOP	4,144,626	43.7	1,071,964	7.5
Enterprises	2,150,734	22.7	3,268,302	22.9
Private insurance	355,143	3.7	205,917	1.4
Mandatory insurance	0	0	46,072	0.3
Social security tax	1,443,381	15.2	2,349,444	16.5
Other taxes	352,211	3.7	666,869	4.7
Public sector	2,046,476	21.6	4,080.276	28.6
National government	1,129,068	11.9	3,228,452	22.6
Departments	758,872	8.0	574,085	4.0
Municipalities	158,537	1.7	277,789	1.9
Total	9,494,096	100.0	14,270,063	100.0

Note: The item, "resources of the agents (insurance intermediaries)" is omitted but its value is included in the total.
Source: Barón Leguizamón (2007, table A.5).

those households. By 2003, only 3% of all households had to spend that much of their disposable income. Taking "catastrophic" to mean any share beyond 10% of non-subsistence spending, a high financial risk faced 10% of all households, or 28% of all those that actually had medical expenses, as table 6.6 shows. These data combine the insured with the uninsured: when those two groups are compared directly, in table 6.7, enrollment leads to consistently much lower likelihood of catastrophic spending. The most striking results are the relatively small difference for those enrolled in, or eligible for, the subsidized regime, and the much larger effect among the self-employed and informal workers in, or eligible for, the contributory regime. One might expect

Table 6.6 *Incidence of catastrophic expenditure, by income quintile: Colombia, 2003*

	% of households with catastrophic spending (threshold of 10% or more of disposable income)	
	---	---
Income quintile	All households	Only those that used services
1 (poorest)	12	41
2	12	38
3	9	25
4	7	19
5 (richest)	6	19
Total population	**10**	**28**

Source: Escobar *et al.* (2007, table 3).

Table 6.7 *Impact of insurance (difference in probability) on catastrophic spending and impoverishment: Colombia, 2003*

	Catastrophic spending		Impoverishment below national poverty line
	---	---	---
Insurance regime	10% threshold	40% threshold	
Subsidized	−21	−4	−4.00
Contributory			
Salaried (dependent) worker	−40	[a]	[a]
Self-employed, informal	−71	−8	−3.35

Note: [a] Not significantly different from zero.
Source: Escobar *et al.* (2007, table 4).

the reverse – that insurance would make the largest difference in the subsidized regime. That effect appears to be counterbalanced by the lower probability that a household eligible for that regime but not enrolled in it would actually use medical services at all. This is a reminder that catastrophic spending occurs only among those who actually obtain care. The deterrent effect of potentially catastrophic cost on utilization is not captured.

How should one value this massive redistribution of the financial burden? Clearly there is a welfare gain every time a peso that would have meant catastrophic spending for a household instead constitutes some form of pre-payment. If utility is assumed to be proportional to a power function of income or consumption beyond subsistence – $U \sim C^\beta$, where $\beta < 1.0$ – then a household with extra-subsistence consumption C that is relieved of OOP spending by the insurance sees its welfare rise from $(C\text{-}OOP)^\beta$ to C^β, quite aside from any long-term effects from how that spending is financed. Income of around US$1,000, leaving C at some US$200, and OOP spending of 10% of income or 40% of C (as is typical for catastrophic spending), with a value of $\beta = 0.5$, implies that the welfare gain is of the order of 12%. A taxpayer or contributor who pays a premium of 12% on an income closer to the national average of around US$2,000, and contributes 1 percentage point to the subsidized regime, suffers a loss of only US$20 (because the other 11% buys her own insurance). Her welfare loss, assuming the same subsistence cost of US$800, is then only 1% in purely monetary terms. Values of β closer to 1.0 reduce this difference, but do not eliminate it.

What these welfare assumptions are worth in monetary terms – that is, how welfare should be valued relative to income – is, of course, arbitrary. What is worth emphasizing is that on any assumption that welfare increases less than proportionally to income, and that the better-off contribute only a fraction of what they pay for health to subsidize the worse-off, the benefit of the redistribution may be quite large enough to compensate the extra social cost of expanding coverage. This simple exercise does not even take account of the welfare benefit both the contributor and the subsidized beneficiary obtain simply from knowing that they are protected from financial catastrophe.

Improved health access and outcomes

The expansion of health insurance in Colombia increased the monetary value of health services delivered by about 11%. Since this increase was concentrated among the poorest and the formerly unprotected, it is reasonable to suppose that the effect on health status was larger than if utilization had increased in that proportion across the whole population. Table 6.8 compares access and utilization in 2005 between the insured (including all those already insured before the 1993 reform)

Table 6.8 *Indicators of access and utilization by insurance status: Colombia, 2005 (%)*

Indicator, access, or utilization	Mean, uninsured	Mean, insured	Absolute difference	% difference
Received medical care when needed	54.3	73.9	19.6	+36
Not receiving care for supply reasons	13.2	30.4	17.2	+130
Not receiving care for financial reasons	56.9	23.8	−33.1	−58
Outpatient visit, last 12 months	46.2	68.2	22.0	+48
Child immunization complete	37.4	41.8	4.4	+12
Child taken to health facility with coughing	35.7	44.8	9.1	+26
Child taken to health facility with diarrhea	29.4	35.5	6.1	+21
Number of prenatal visits (not %)	5.19	5.39	0.2	+4
Birth in a health facility	83.2	85.8	2.5	+3
Birth attended by a professional	81.3	84.7	3.5	+4
Birth attended by a doctor	76.5	80.0	3.5	+5
Control after delivery	47.0	52.1	5.2	+11
Access to care for complications of delivery	42.3	48.8	6.5	+15

Source: Adapted from Giedión *et al.* (2007, table 1).

and the still uninsured. The former are better off by every measure but one, although the differences are small where coverage was already high, notably for attended births. The most striking differences occur for outpatient visits, including specifically for children with particular symptoms. Table 6.9 shows how several indicators of utilization have changed since 1995, in both urban and rural areas. With one exception, improvements have been larger in rural areas, since that is where the uninsured were a larger share of the population. The insured appear worse off only because their increased demand meant

Table 6.9 *Changes in percentage utilization: Colombia, 1999–2005*

Utilization variable	National	Urban	Rural
Child immunization complete	6.1	4.1	11.8
Child taken to health facility with coughing	10.7	9.0	7.8
Child taken to health facility with diarrhea	7.4	9.9	15.1
Number of prenatal visits (not %)	*0.42*	*0.17*	*0.39*
Birth in a health facility	4.3	0.9	4.7
Birth attended by a professional	5.1	0.7	4.4
Birth attended by a doctor	5.7	0.8	6.2

Source: Adapted from Giedión *et al.* (2007, table 2).

that they more often failed to get care because of supply constraints. Simply increasing demand without guaranteeing an adequate supply response can endanger the quality of care and discourage patients. This is a major issue for CCT programs, which sometimes incorporate specific measures to bolster supply or capacity before enrolling beneficiaries.

It is much easier to measure what happened to utilization than to translate those changes into reduced mortality, illness, or disability. It would be possible, however, to estimate the likely health improvement from several of the indicators of services use, if these were combined with estimates of risk from not getting care. For example, complete immunization coverage increased slightly, and that must have prevented some cases of disease, particularly since immunization levels are far from high enough to provide herd immunity. The effect is reduced by the elimination of polio and the sharp reduction in measles incidence throughout the LAC region during the same period that the reform was implemented. Immunization only against measles, mumps, and rubella (MMR) increased from 82% to 89% between 1990 and 2006, and several other indicators improved markedly, as table 6.10 shows. These data do not say what share of the improvement can be attributed to the expansion of coverage, but so much change is implausible in the absence of increased access and reduced financial burden.

The various CCT programs in Latin America, including that in Colombia, have been subjected to fairly detailed evaluation, so the impact on utilization can be attributed with more confidence to the

Table 6.10 *Public health indicators before and after reform: Colombia, 1990–2006*

Indicator	ca. 1990	ca. 2006
Unmet basic needs (% of population lacking at least one of clean water, sewerage, etc.)	35.8	27.6
Life expectancy at birth (years)	68.3	72.8
Infant mortality rate (per 1,000 live births)	26.3	17.2
Under-five mortality rate (per 1,000)	34.7	21.4
Births attended by a professional	81.8	96.4
MMR immunization (children aged 12–23 months)	82.0	89.0

Source: Glassman *et al.* (2007, table 1).

program. Visits to public clinics for children under the age of 2 increased by 30% among beneficiaries; in the age group 2–4, the increase was 50% (Glassman, Gaarder, and Todd 2006, table 6.5). These changes are larger than the differences between the insured and uninsured in table 6.9 – but the CCT beneficiaries may be drawn predominantly from the newly insured, and the age group for the latter is not specified. It appears that impacts have been systematically greater among those initially worse off, as might be expected.

This analysis does not try to put a dollar value on these gains, but an extension of life expectancy by 4.5 years would, on any reasonable valuation of an extra year of life, be worth a great deal. This effect, plus the benefits of the dramatic increase in financial protection that result from expanded coverage, appear quite large enough to justify the costs involved. Generalization to other countries that are farther from achieving universal coverage would require calculation of their own costs and probable benefits, and might show better or worse results. The qualitative conclusion that these solutions offer benefits in excess of their costs is likely to remain valid.

5 Conclusions

The crucial solution to the health challenges of the LAC region is to extend insurance coverage to the whole population where that is not already the case, with a benefit package that includes catastrophic care and allows considerable choice of provider, and with financing that implies affordable premiums for some beneficiaries and complete subsidy for others, on the basis of income rather than any demographic characteristic. A reform of that sort, of whatever specific model, does not guarantee higher quality or efficiency in the delivery of healthcare, but it probably facilitates simultaneous reforms pursuing those ends. It most definitely will improve access, particularly by removing financial barriers – and, to a lesser extent, also physical barriers of time and distance. Including a CCT program to boost demand for care among the poor may complement the general extension of coverage, particularly for the preventive services for which such programs are best suited, and for which the income gradient in utilization is steepest.

This way of posing the challenges and suggesting solutions does not lead to clear benefit-cost comparisons. However, there is no conflict between this way of stating and confronting challenges to health, and the way followed in the previous Copenhagen Consensus process. One approach looks at what changes are needed in the health system so that it can deliver quality care to the whole population. The other looks at what diseases, conditions, and risk factors the system should try especially to control. Without a well-functioning system, efforts against specific health problems will be less effective than they could be; without sensible priorities, even a well-run system will waste resources and opportunities. Where the two approaches meet is in the definition of an affordable, cost-effective package of benefits for the system to deliver, and a mechanism to assure that the package reaches as much of the population as possible.

Bibliography

Akin, J., D. K. Guilkey, C. C. Griffin, and B. M. Popkin, 1985. *The Demand for Primary Health Services in the Third World.* Totowa, NJ: Rowman & Allanheld

Barber, S. L., S. M. Bertozzi, and P. J. Gertler, 2007. "Variations in Prenatal Care Quality for the Rural Poor in Mexico." *Health Affairs* **26**(3): w310–w323, published online March 27

Barnum, H. and J. Kutzin,1993. *Public Hospitals in Developing Countries: Resource Use, Cost, Financing.* Baltimore, MD: Johns Hopkins University Press for the World Bank

Barón Leguizamón, G., 2007. *Cuentas de Salud de Colombia 1993–2003: El Gasto Nacional en Salud y su Financiamiento.* Ministerio de la Protección Social, Bogotá

Bhagwati, J., 2004. "Individual Ranking." In Lomborg (2004): 608–12

Bitrán y Asociados, 1999. "Equidad en el Financiamienot de al Seguridad Social para la Salud en Chile." Chapter 8 of *Focalización y Paquetes de Beneficios*. Washington, DC: World Bank, World Bank Institute Flagship Program in Health Sector Reform and Sustainable Financing

Brown, M. L., S. J. Goldie, G. Draisma, J. Harford, and J. Lipscomb, 2006. "Health Service Interventions for Cancer Control in Developing Countries." Chapter 29 in DCP2

Campino, A. C., C. M. D. M. Diaz, L. M. Paulani, R. G. de Oliveira, S. Piola, and A. Nunes, 2001. "Health System Inequalities and Poverty in Brazil." In Pan American Health Organization, *Investment in Health: Social and Economic Returns*, Scientific and Technical Publication 582. Washington, DC: Pan American Health Organization

Center for Global Development (CGD) Working Group on IMF-Supported Programs and Health Spending, 2007. *Does the IMF Constrain Health Spending in Poor Countries? Evidence and an Agenda For Action.* Washington, DC: CGD

Clements, B., C. Faircloth, and M. Verhoeven, 2007. "Public Expenditure in Latin America: Trends and Key Policy Issues." International Monetary Fund Working Paper 07/21

Copenhagen Consensus Center, 2006. "Copenhagen Consensus 2006 – A United Nations Perspective," available online at www.copenhagenconsensus.com/Default.aspx?ID=770, accessed May 9, 2007

Das, J. and P. J. Gertler, 2007. "Variations in Practice Quality in Five Low-Income Countries: A Conceptual Overview." *Health Affairs* 26(3): w296–w309, published online, March 27

Das, J. and J. Hammer, 2007. "Location, Location, Location: Residence, Wealth, and the Quality of Medical Care in Delhi, India." *Health Affairs* 26(3): w338–w351, published online, March 27

Das, J., and T. P. Sohnesen, 2007. "Variations in Doctor Effort: Evidence from Paraguay." *Health Affairs* 26(3): w324–w337, published online, March 27

Dercon, S., T. Bold, and C. Calvo, 2007. "Insurance for the poor?" Economic and Social Research Council Global Poverty Research Group, GPRG–WPS–073. Oxford: University of Oxford, available online at www.gprg.org/pubs/workingpapers/pdfs/gprg-wps-073.pdf

Escobar, M. L., U. Giedion, O.-L. Acosta, R. Castaño, D. Pinto, and F. Ruiz, 2007. "Ten Years of Health System Reform: Health Care Financing Lessons from Colombia." Washington, DC: Global Health Financing Initiative, Brookings Institution

Fischer, R. and P. Serra, 1996. "Análisis económico del sistema de seguros de salud en Chile." *Revista de Análisis Económico* 11(2): 187–217

Fondo Nacional de Salud (FONASA), 2007. *Protección Social en Salud en Chile.* FONASA, Santiago, available online at www.fonasa.cl/prontus_fonasa/site/artic/20070413/asocfile/libro_proteccion_social_en_salud_en_chile.pdf

Frey, B. S., 2004. "Individual Ranking." In Lomborg (2004): 614–18

Gertler, P. and J. van der Gaag, 1990. *The Willingness to Pay for Medical Care: Evidence from Two Developing Countries.* Baltimore, MD: Johns Hopkins University Press for the World Bank

Giedion, U., Y. Díaz, E. A. Alfonso, and W. D. Savedoff, 2007. "The Impact of Subsidized Health Insurance on Access, Utilization and Health Status in Colombia." Washington, DC: Global Health Financing Initiative. Brookings Institution

Glassman, A., M. Gaarder, and J. Todd, 2006. "Demand-Side Incentives for Better Health for the Poor: Conditional Cash Transfer Programs in Latin America and the Caribbean." Report RE2-06-033, Economic and Sector Study Series, Region IV. Washington, DC: Inter-American Development Bank

Glassman, A., D. Pinto, L. F. Stone, J. G. López, and M. Velandia, 2007. "After a Decade of Reform in the Health Sector." Washington, DC: Global Health Financing Initiative, Brookings Institution

Graham, C., 2008. "Happiness and Health: Lessons – and Questions – for Public Policy." *Health Affairs* 27(1): 72–87

Hirth, R. A. *et al.*, 2008. "Out-of-Pocket Costs and Medication Adherence in an International Sample of Patients with Kidney Failure." *Health Affairs* 27(1): 89–102

Institute of Medicine (IOM), 2001. *Crossing the Quality Chasm.* Washington, DC: National Academy Press

Jamison, D. T., 2007. "Disease Control: Paper prepared for the Copenhagen Consensus," 2008

Jamison, D. T., J. G. Breman, A. R. Measham, G. Alleyne, M. Claeson, D. B. Evans, P. Jha, A. Mills, and P. Musgrove, eds., 2006. *Disease Control Priorities in Developing Countries*, 2nd edn. Oxford and New York: Oxford University Press

Jaramillo Pérez, I., 2007. "El Libro de Gilberto Barón: ¿En Dónde Está el Dinero de la Salud?" Personal communication by Amanda Glassman, July 18

Knaul, F. M. and J. Frenk, 2005. "Health Insurance in Mexico: Achieving Universal Coverage Through Structural Reform." *Health Affairs* 24(6): 1467–76

Lewis, M. and P. Musgrove, 2008. "Governance Issues in Health Financing." In H. K. Heggenhougen, ed., *Encyclopedia of Public Health*. San Diego, CA. Elsevier: 81–8

Lin, J. Y., 2004. "Individual Ranking." In Lomborg (2004): 618–22

Lomborg, B., 2004. *Global Crises, Global Solutions*, 1st edn. Cambridge: Cambridge University Press

2009. *Global Crises, Global Solutions*, 2nd edn. Cambridge: Cambridge University Press

Lopez, A. D., C. D. Mathers, M. Ezzati, D. T. Jamison, and C. J. L. Murray, eds., 2006. *Global Burden of Disease and Risk Factors*. Oxford and New York: Oxford University Press

Mills, A., 2007. "Strategies to Achieve Universal Coverage: Are There Lessons from Middle Income Countries?" A literature review commissioned by the Health Systems Knowledge Network, Health Economics and Financing Programme. London: London School of Hygiene and Tropical Medicine

Mills, A., F. Rasheed, and S. Tollman, 2006: "Strengthening Health Systems." Chapter 3 in DCP2

Musgrove, P., 2001. "*Salud.*" In Grupo Columbus, *Hacia un Nuevo Estado en América Latina*. Buenos Aires: Centro de Implementación de Políticas Públicas para la Equidad y el Crecimiento

2004a. "Criteria for Public Spending in Health Care." Chapter 9 in P. Musgrove, ed., *Health Economics in Development*. Washington, DC: World Bank

2004b. "Economic Crisis and Health Policy Response." Chapter 20 in P. Musgrove, ed., *Health Economics in Development*. Washington, DC: World Bank

2005. "Social Protection and Equity in Health Care: What Can We Learn From Household Surveys?" Paper prepared for the Inter-American Development Bank

Musgrove, P., G. Carrin, and R. Zeramdini, 2002. "Patterns of National Health Expenditure." *Bulletin of the World Health Organization*, 80(2): 134–46

Narayan, K. V., P. Zhang, A. M. Kanaya, D. E. Williams, M. M. Engelgau, G. Imperatore, and A. Ramachandran, 2006. "Diabetes: the Pandemic and Potential Solutions." Chapter 30 in DCP2

North, D., 2004. "Individual Ranking." In Lomborg (2004): 623–6

Olesker, D., 2007. "Seguro Nacional de Salud." Presentation at the International Seminar on Priorities in Health, Santiago, April 10–11

Pan American Health Organization (PAHO), 2007. "Regional Core Health Data Initiative," available online at www.paho.org/english/dd/ais/coredata.htm, accessed July 23, 2007

Peabody, J. W., M. M. Taguiwalo, D. A. Robalino, and J. Frenk, 2006. "Improving the Quality of Care in Developing Countries." Chapter 70 in DCP2

Petrera, M., 1989. "Effectiveness and Efficiency of Social Security in the Economic Cycle: The Peruvian Case." In P. Musgrove, ed., *Health Economics: Latin American Perspectives.* Washington, DC: Pan American Health Organization

Pinto, D. and W. C. Hsiao, 2007. "Colombia: Social Health Insurance with Managed Competition to Improve Health Care Delivery." In W. C. Hsiao, and R. P. Shaw, eds., *Social Health Insurance for Developing Nations.* Washington, DC: World Bank, WBI Development Studies

Preker, A. S., M. McKee, A. Mitchell, and S. Wilbulpolprasert, 2006. "Strategic Management of Clinical Services." Chapter 73 in DCP2

Rivlin, A., 1971. *Systematic Thinking for Social Action.* Washington, DC: Brookings Institution

Roberts, M. J., W. Hsiao, P. Berman, and M. R. Reich, 2004. *Getting Health Reform Right: A Guide to Improving Performance and Equity.* New York: Oxford University Press

Savedoff, W., 2007. "Transparency and Corruption in the Health Sector: A Conceptual Framework and Ideas for Action in Latin America and the Caribbean." Health Technical Note **03/2007**. Washington, DC: Sustainable Development Department, Inter-American Development Bank

Schelling, T. C., 2004. "Individual Ranking." In Lomborg (2004): 627–30

Suárez-Berenguela, R., 2001. "Health System Inequalities and Inequities in Latin America and the Caribbean: Findings and Policy Implications." In Pan American Health Organization, *Investment in Health: Social and Economic Returns*, Scientific and Technical Publication **582**. Washington, DC: Pan American Health Organization

Tono, T. M., E. Cueto, A. Giuffruida, and C. H. Arango, 2007. "Public Hospitals and Healthcare Reform in Colombia." Washington, DC: Global Health Financing Initiative, Brookings Institution

Vargas, V. and S. Poblete, 2008. "Health Prioritization: the Case of Chile." *Health Affairs* **27**(3): 782–92

Walker, A. and S. Colaguiri, 2007. "Using an Economic Model for Diabetes to Evaluate Prevention and Care Strategies in Australia." *Health Affairs* **27**(1): 256–68

Willett, W.C., J. P. Koplan, R. Nugent, C. Dusenbury, P. Puska, and T. A. Gaziano, 2006. "Prevention of Chronic Disease by Means of Diet and Lifestyle Changes." Chapter 44 in DCP2

World Bank, 1993. *Investing in Health: World Development Report 1993.* New York: Oxford University Press for the World Bank

World Health Organization Collaborating Centre for Patient Safety Solutions, 2007. "Aides-Memoires for Nine Patient Safety Solutions." Geneva: WHO, May 2

Xu, K., D. Evans, G. Carrin, A. M. Aguilar-Rivera, P. Musgrove, and T. Evans, 2007. "Protecting Households from Catastrophic Health Spending." *Health Affairs,* **26**(4): 972–83

6.1 | *Challenges and solutions in health: an alternative view*

WILLIAM D. SAVEDOFF

This alternative view presents a comment on Philip Musgrove's chapter 6 in this volume. I essentially reaffirm Musgrove's proposal for four priority interventions: improving healthcare access, healthcare quality, healthcare efficiency, and healthcare-seeking behaviors. However, I both depart from and complement the chapter in four ways:

- First, shifting the solution from the disease-specific focus of the 2004 Copenhagen Consensus process to the system focus of the Consulta de San José 2007 is justified by the specific epidemiology and resources of the region.
- Second, increasing health insurance coverage is not the only or best way to expand access to healthcare in the region. The public sector may be able to expand coverage through other demand-side alternatives, such as public purchasing of healthcare for the population. Furthermore, some governments have successfully expanded publicly provided services – usually with innovative payment mechanisms – in supply-side approaches which may be feasible and less costly.
- Third, while Musgrove correctly rejects calculating a specific BCR on firm technical and ethical grounds, there are competing ethical concerns *for this specific process* that call for such calculations, despite the shaky empirical foundations.
- Finally, additional solutions that require actions *outside* the healthcare sector, such as addressing alcohol abuse and tobacco addiction, should not be forgotten.

1 Why a system approach?

In the 2004 Copenhagen Consultation Process, the "health challenge" was taken to mean improving population health status, and attention was focused on public health and medical interventions for high-priority diseases. For the purposes of the 2008 Consultation, a background paper (Jamison 2007) followed a similar approach, proposing a modified list of priority interventions and recognizing the need for some kind of "health system capacity" to implement them.[1]

Chapter 6 similarly focuses on improving population health status, but expands its attention to include two other aspects of the health system that are valued by society – increased productivity and financial protection. Musgrove's major departure from the previously cited works is to argue that the priority "solution" for improving health in the LAC region is to improve access to medical care. In order of importance, he adds improving the quality of healthcare, the efficiency of healthcare, and, finally, educating people to better recognize their own healthcare needs.

Musgrove's argument in favor of this "system approach" (in contrast to the earlier "disease-specific approaches") is made on both technical and socio-political grounds. He notes that several Expert panelists in the Process (Lomborg 2004) rejected the main approaches to measuring health benefits (putting a dollar value on life and measuring health benefits by increased productivity) that were used to calculate BCRs. He then notes that politicians (UN Ambassadors and senior diplomats) considered access to health services to be of higher priority than the technical experts, postulating that the technical experts gave greater weight to rigor of evidence. Furthermore, LAC respondents to the IDB survey (see chapter 6 in this volume) demonstrated a strong interest in addressing disparities in access to quality healthcare – drawing attention not only to improving physical and financial access to such care, but also valuing improved equity and quality.

Musgrove's decision to focus on systemic issues rather than disease-specific interventions is correct for yet another reason, which he mentions briefly. Chapter 2 in Lomborg (2004) was strongly influenced by concern over the dire health conditions of SSA – a region which is experiencing *declining* life expectancy and has a large disease burden

---

[1] "Health system" has been defined as all the activities that have as their primary purpose the improvement of health (WHO 2000). With this definition, improving air quality and research for new drugs would be included, but not other things such as schooling and safe transport, since they are not primarily undertaken to improve health. This alternative view will follow this definition, though it should be noted that the large cost of medical care relative to many important public health interventions will tend to occupy greater attention.

from infectious and parasitic diseases for which low cost, cost-effective solutions are available (DPT vaccines, treatment for respiratory infections, ORT, etc.). The LAC region as a whole presents a very different picture. First, average life expectancy in the region is over 71 years at birth, a full 10 years higher than it was in the early 1970s (Dorling, Shaw, and Davey Smith 2006). Second, all infectious and parasitic diseases account for about 15% of all deaths in the region, compared to 63% in SSA. Furthermore, countries in the LAC region have much greater resources available to address their health problems. Average income in the region is US$4,767 per capita, 5.5 times higher than SSA. With higher income, the region is able to spend an average of US$334 per person on healthcare services compared to less than an average of US$60 per person in the countries of SSA (if Botswana, South Africa, and Seychelles are excluded, the average falls to US$37 per person).

The literature demonstrates that both system approaches and disease-specific approaches can contribute to improved health status (see, for example, Soares 2007); however, disease-specific interventions that can be implemented without strong system capacity, such as vaccination campaigns, are much less important in countries that have largely addressed and controlled these diseases. By contrast, diseases that are of greatest concern to the people of the LAC region – increasingly non-communicable in nature – are ones for which even disease-specific interventions require a broader range of healthcare services – screening, counseling, diagnostic testing, surgery, public education campaigns, etc.

In effect, the countries of the LAC region as a whole are in a fairly advanced stage of what has been called the "health transition"[2] – prevention and treatment for most infectious diseases are fairly widespread, and interventions for non-communicable diseases (NCD)

---

[2] Note, the "health transition" (Frenk *et al.* 1991) is a model that overlaps with but differs in important ways from the "epidemiological transition" (Omran 1971). The "health transition" posits that the shifting profile of illnesses in countries reflects the extent to which different health technologies have been adopted. These health technologies can be grouped into basic treatments and prevention of infectious diseases, treatments and prevention for cardiovascular illnesses, and treatments for ageing. While the United States and other wealthy countries adopted these technologies in a sequence that paralleled shifts in their disease burden, developing countries are experiencing the simultaneous adoption of all three kinds of technologies, unevenly through their population.

are becoming generalized. Having reached this point, the LAC region's countries have mostly demonstrated that they *can* provide essential health services – even for NCD – to significant shares of their population. Assuring that these essential health services are available to *everyone* is not only possible, but is probably cost-effective and certainly addresses the publicly voiced concerns over equity and financial protection.

One important caveat is necessary. The region has large geographic disparities and some places are still greatly in need of the disease-specific interventions highlighted in Jamison (2007), whether addressed through campaigns or system approaches. In Haiti and among marginalized rural populations throughout the region, disease-specific campaigns might still be the most effective approach.[3] However, most national governments have demonstrated the capacity to address the prevalent diseases among the poor by expanding access to the health system rather than through isolated and parallel campaigns. This reinforces the argument in favor of systemic approaches.

An additional argument for addressing health through a system approach is the revealed preferences of the population. As incomes have risen in the region, people are spending more and more money on healthcare – through OOP payments or private health insurance premiums. The large share of private spending, more than half of all health expenditure in the region, partially explains the demand for financial protection. It also demonstrates the extent to which people feel that public programs are inaccessible or of poor quality. Considering that most LAC countries subscribe to concepts of "solidarity," "universality," and "equity," along Western European lines and seek to emulate those health systems, progress requires assuring that sufficient public funding is effectively used to provide universal access to quality services.[4] To the extent that countries approach this ideal, the private share of health spending, and the share of OOP spending in particular, is almost certain to decline.

---

[3] Even in Haiti, NGOs have demonstrated that establishing healthcare networks can be an effective strategy for addressing infectious disease.

[4] A review at the IDB in 1996 found that seventeen out of twenty-six member countries in the LAC region had provisions in their constitutions making access to healthcare a right of citizenship.

2 Solution: increase access to healthcare services

There are many different ways to improve access to healthcare services, and this choice of strategy is itself a subject of vociferous debates in the LAC region. Many countries in the Caribbean that inherited publicly provided healthcare systems from their colonial periods are currently seeking to introduce national health insurance systems based on payroll taxes at the same time that many LAC countries are seeking to replace their social insurance schemes with systems funded out of general tax revenues.[5] Other strategies that have been promoted include changing the "medical model of attention," decentralizing responsibility to municipalities, contracting from private providers, and introducing competitive mandatory health insurance, to name just a few.

Chapter 6 cuts through this range of strategies to propose simply that countries increase access to healthcare services by agreeing to pay providers for those services (i.e. demand-side reforms). In its support, two of the most rapid expansions of access to healthcare in the region since the 1990s used such strategies – Guatemala extended basic healthcare to an additional 3.4 million by contracting NGOs; Colombia implemented a subsidized scheme that increased coverage to an additional 13 million people from 1993 to 2004 (raising insurance coverage from 6% to 43% in the poorest quintile over the same period). Efforts that have relied exclusively on extending coverage through publicly provided and owned healthcare facilities are less well documented. The most successful examples – Costa Rica and Chile – built their effective networks of public healthcare provision prior to 1980, in periods with lower incomes and lower expectations because medical technology was much less advanced.

The advantages of working through the "demand side" are many. The allocation of resources across regions, gender, ethnicity, and income becomes much more transparent and usually more equitable when funds are allocated to the person rather than the provider. By financing through the demand side, countries (and individuals) can

---

[5] For example, Brazil eliminated its social security system in 1986 and replaced it with the Sistema Única da Saúde. In Mexico, the Instituto Mexicano de Seguridad Social (IMSS) was originally financed largely through payroll taxes, but in recent years has come to rely on substantial subsidies out of general revenues. By contrast, Belize and Jamaica had national health services modeled on the British system but created national health insurance funds in 2001.

potentially extend access more rapidly by taking advantage of the existing capacity of private providers. Depending on the exact form of reimbursement and supervision of contracts, countries can use the "power of the payer" to promote better quality and efficiency.

Nevertheless, in some cases a "supply-side" approach can be implemented and – when it is successful (a very important caveat) – be less costly and more effective than demand-side programs. One possible example can be found in Brazil's Programa da Saúde da Família, which contracts public sector workers to form healthcare teams that are responsible for serving a defined community.[6] There is some evidence that the program has a positive impact on health status (Macinko, Guanais, and de Souza 2006) and that its costs are modest (World Bank 2006). But this success has to be contextualized. The program builds on decades of earlier experience with community health initiatives, dating back to the early 1970s; it is being implemented in a country which has demonstrated considerable capacity to implement public programs; and it relies on financial incentives to motivate municipalities to adopt the program and healthcare workers to sign up.

In sum, Musgrove's proposal to increase access to healthcare services, and simultaneously reduce financial risk, through demand-side programs in which governments buy healthcare services for their citizens, is a proposal that is well grounded in the region's reform experiences. This alternative view qualifies this solution by noting that health *insurance* is only one of many effective demand-side approaches *and* the region's diversity suggests that there may be situations where either a supply-side approach or disease-specific approach might be preferred. For the region as a whole, however, the emphasis on demand-side programs is sound.

3 Is it cost-effective? Do benefits exceed costs?

Musgrove chooses not to provide a BCR for his proposed solution, for sound reasons. There is substantial debate about how to measure

---

[6] Even though the Programa da Saúde da Família (PSF) covers almost 25% of the population, it is still only one of many public programs encompassed by Brazil's Sistema Única da Saúde (SUS). The author was unable to find a comprehensive evaluation of the SUS, which represents the largest most comprehensive effort to undertake a supply-side expansion of guaranteed public healthcare provision in Latin America in recent decades.

the benefits of "access to healthcare." Are these benefits primarily the impact on health status? If so, are the health benefits to be valued intrinsically through some hedonic or contingent valuation (CV) method or by calculating the implicit value of a statistical life from compensating differentials across occupational risks? Or should it be valued extrinsically by calculating increased productivity and incomes? Each one of these approaches has ethical, epistemological, and practical drawbacks.

This alternative view, however, does provide benefit and cost estimates, for both practical and ethical reasons. First, policymakers are uncomfortable with expert advice that is based on precise but relatively narrow evidence. Since policymakers, and not technical experts, are ultimately the ones who will implement these solutions, it is appropriate to apply the standards of evidence that they would accept. This does *not* mean that any evidence can be slapped together to make an argument. The technical analysis still has to be conducted with integrity and represent the analyst's best effort to marshal the available evidence impartially. Furthermore, the effort has to be transparent so that other technical analysts can pick it apart and policymakers can judge the plausibility of its assumptions.

Second, *in the context of chapter 6*, refusing to provide a best-guess of the BCRs would probably lead to a lower ranking for this solution than might be merited because other solutions would, by contrast, appear more assured and certain. For these two reasons, and at the risk of the author's reputation,[7] this alternative view presents rough calculations of the BCR of increasing access to healthcare in the LAC region. Two different approaches will be taken. Approach 1 derives the BCR from information in the Disease Control Priorities Project. Approach 2 derives the benefit-cost ratio by extrapolating from the Colombian experience with extending subsidized health insurance.

Musgrove notes that there are at least two other benefits from introducing universal access to healthcare services: the value people ascribe to financial protection, and higher productivity. The calculations below are focused exclusively on the intrinsic benefits of improving health status. To the extent that financial protection and productivity also

---

[7] If necessary, the author accepts the risk of losing his membership in the American Economic Association.

Table 6.1.1 *Calculations for "basic package approach"*

Total DALYs lost to communicable, maternal, perinatal, and nutritional deficiencies		26,500,000
Regional GNI *per capita* (US$)		4,767
Cost per DALY (US$)		168
Value of each DALY (US$)	1,000	14,301
BCR	6.0	85.1
Infectious disease, maternal, and neonatal conditions reduced by (%)	50	25
Total disease burden reduced by (%)	7	3.5
Total disease burden reduced by (DALYs)	13,250,000	6,625,000
Total cost (US$)	2,226,000,000	1,113,000,000

Sources: Author's calculations using data from WHO, World Bank, and Jamison *et al.* (2006).

improve, the BCRs calculated below should be considered conservative estimates.

4 Approach 1: extension of basic services identified in the Disease Control Priorities Project

Following a common line of analysis in the international health field, the Disease Control Priorities Project (DCPP) identified a package of cost-effective interventions that includes expanded immunization programs, HIV/AIDS prevention, vector control, TB treatment, integrated management of childhood illnesses, family planning, pre-natal care, assisted delivery, and limited treatment for trauma (Tollman, Doherty, and Mulligan 2006). For a middle income country, the authors estimate that providing these services to a community would avoid one lost DALY for every US$168.

Calculating a BCR from this information requires assigning a monetary benefit to each DALY. Despite the ethical and conceptual problems with assigning a monetary value to reducing a DALY, researchers have estimated such a value for a variety of reasons and purposes. Some examples include Viscusi (1993); Liu, Hammitt, and Liu (1997);

Mrozek and Taylor (2002); Evans (2004); and Mills and Shillcutt (2004). In no case are DALYs valued below US$1,000 – fully five times larger than the cost estimate for this service package. Table 6.1.1 illustrates the range of BCRs that would result from assuming that each DALY is worth US$1,000 for a lower bound and three times the region's average gross national income (GNI) for an upper bound. The resulting BCRs would be extremely favorable, ranging from 6.0 to 85.1.

Calculating the total cost of this solution requires information about how many DALYs would be avoided by the program. WHO estimates that people in the region lose approximately 26.5 million DALYs each year to communicable, maternal, perinatal, and nutritional deficiency conditions – the categories that are most directly addressed by this basic package of services and which represent about 14% of all DALYs lost to disease and injuries each year. Under numerous assumptions (e.g. marginal costs are equal to average costs), cutting the loss of DALYs from these diseases and conditions by half (i.e. 13.25 million DALYs or 7% of the total DALYs) would cost about US$2.3 billion each year.

5 Approach 2: extrapolation from Colombia's subsidized insurance

Approach 1 approximates the idea of extending basic healthcare services to all, but provides a much more limited set of services than are envisioned by the solution proposed in chapter 6. A more appropriate approach might rely on empirical evidence from a program that has demonstrable achievements. The Colombian reform of 1993 provides such an opportunity because the demand-side guarantee of access to healthcare services expanded rapidly and *some* data is available to analyze costs and benefits.

Chapter 6 reports the annual cost of the Colombian subsidized health insurance package at about US$164 per person. If we take three times gross national income as the value of avoiding a single lost DALY (approx. $14,300) and assume that health insurance is extended to an additional one-third of the regional population (284 million people), the only missing information is how many DALYs can actually be reduced. Though several studies have used the available data to assess the impact of subsidized insurance on healthcare utilization and

Table 6.1.2 *Calculations for demand-side approach to expanding access to healthcare*

Cost/person (US$)	164	
Affected pop. (1/3)	284 million	
Benefit/DALY (US$)	14,301	
Total annual cost (US$)	46.6 billion	
Cost per capita (US$)	55	
Share of GNI per capita	1.1%	
Assumed benefits	**Low**	**High**
Reduction in DALYs (%)	5%	10%
Reduction in DALYs	7.25 million	14.5 million
BCR	2.2	4.5

Sources: Author's calculations using data from WHO, World Bank, and chapter 6 in this volume.

financial protection, no surveys have collected adequate information on health status with which such a calculation could be made.[8]

One way of obtaining an idea of the health benefits of a commitment to purchase healthcare services for all citizens as Colombia has done would be to compare it with other countries. A full statistical analysis is beyond the scope of this alternative view, but in order to get an idea of the potential order of magnitude, it is useful to compare Colombia with Peru – a neighboring country that shares many common characteristics but which has far from universal access to healthcare services. The Age-Standardized DALYs lost per person are almost identical – about 0.19; however, Colombia loses twice as many DALYs to injuries due to high levels of violence. Focusing just on communicable and non-communicable conditions by excluding injuries, Peru has a 23% higher disease burden per person. For this exercise, then, the BCR is calculated by assuming that a demand-side program to extend access to healthcare could account for about half of this difference, between 5% and 10%. The resulting BCRs, then, range from 2.2 to 4.5 (table 6.1.2).

The total cost of such an approach, US$46.6 billion, is significantly higher than Approach 1 by a full order of magnitude, but it "buys"

---

[8] See, for example, Castano *et al.* (2002); Gaviria *et al.* (2006); Giedion *et al.* (2007).

much more. This estimate encompasses many more healthcare services than the basic package of cost-effective measures used in Approach 1. Furthermore, this exercise uses the "real" cost of healthcare services in Colombia, including whatever inefficiencies and problems may arise in a real situation.

In sum, both these approaches propose that the BCR for extending universal access to healthcare in the LAC region through a demand-side approach could be as low as 2.2 and as high as 85.1, even without considering non-health benefits. The lowest ratio corresponds to extending a full range of healthcare services, with all the inefficiencies and problems that plague such systems in the real world. The highest ratio corresponds to extending a focused set of cost-effective healthcare services in a reasonably efficient way. The corresponding range of costs ranges from US$2.2 billion to as high as $46.6 billion per year.

In a sense, the contrast between these two approaches hints at something that was already pointed out by Van der Gaag (2004) in the 2004 Copenhagen Consensus process – it is no accident that health systems are inequitable, inefficient, and limited. There are real political and economic factors that undermine health systems and obstruct progress toward universal access. Making progress in such circumstances requires more than "political will" or technical information. It requires imagination, innovation, and effective political strategies. This is one of the reasons that countries that lack a universal health coverage would be well advised to consider trying a demand-side strategy.

Demand-side approaches are not without their problems, however. Experience shows, in particular, that systems with a third-party payer(s) and that reimburse providers in relation to the volume of services tend to produce more services at increasing cost. In countries with under-provision, these features are precisely why health insurance is attractive. In the long run, however, these tendencies will have to be contained, as shown by the experiences of countries in Western Europe today.

The harder road is to make a supply-side initiative expand rapidly and efficiently. Very few countries have successfully established universal access to quality healthcare with such an approach.[9] To be successful, however, even this more traditional approach has to

---

[9] The few exceptions might include Chile, Costa Rica, Cuba, and Malaysia.

incorporate innovations that involve incentives and modern forms of public administration.

6 An additional solution: taxes and restrictions on alcohol and tobacco

In the LAC region, a large and growing share of the disease burden is due to non-communicable causes, 67% of all deaths and 61% of all DALYs. Many interventions for preventing these diseases require actions that have little to do with healthcare services. For most of the region's countries,[10] the three highest risk factors, measured by their contribution to lost DALYs, are alcohol (8.7%), high blood pressure (5.1%), and tobacco use (3.8%) (Lopez *et al.* 2006). Recent studies have shown several interventions, outside the healthcare sector, that are highly cost-effective in addressing the risks of alcohol and tobacco abuse – namely, raising taxes, banning advertising, and restricting access.

Alcohol abuse in the region contributes to an estimated 3% of all DALYs lost through intentional and unintentional injuries; another 3% from neuropsychiatric disorders; and an additional 2% from cardiovascular and other NCDs. As much as half of the 89,000 annual road traffic fatalities may be attributable to alcohol abuse alone. Among the most cost-effective interventions are raising excise taxes by 50% (US$184/DALY); reducing hours of sale at retail establishments (US$340/DALY); and comprehensive bans on advertising (US$380/DALY). The associated BCRs, assuming conservatively that each DALY is valued at US$1,000, are 5.4, 2.9, and 2.6, respectively. If DALYs are valued at 3 times GNI, then the BCRs are 77.7, 42.1, and 37.6, respectively. The total cost to the region of these three programs would be US$110 million, US$85.2 million, and US$76.7 million, respectively (Rehm *et al.* 2006).

Tobacco use significantly increases the risk of death and disability from a wide range of cardiovascular diseases and cancers and is

---

[10] The estimates provided by WHO group countries by income level and mortality rate and the ranking reported here applies to a category that contains all but five of the IDB's borrowing members (Bolivia, Ecuador, Guatemala, Nicaragua, and Peru). The category that contains these other countries faces larger health risks from malnourishment, unsafe sex, and unsafe water. The differences only demonstrate the need to look at each country's specific profile when setting priorities, rather than relying on group averages.

responsible for about 260,000 deaths in the LAC region each year. Among those who were smoking in the year 2000, tobacco will cause premature deaths for 40 million of them – reducing each lifetime by an average of 20–25 years. A 30% increase in taxes on cigarettes would reduce this number by somewhere between 2.3 and 6.7 million at a cost of between US$6 and US$85 per DALY. If each DALY is estimated to be worth US$1,000, then the BCR would be between 11.8 and 167; valued at US$14,300, the BCR would be between 168 and 2,383! The total cost of such a program in the entire region would be between US$335 million and US$836 million (Jha *et al.* 2006).

7 Summary of solutions

The primary focus of public policy in the LAC region should be on a systems approach to improving equitable access to high-quality healthcare services. Reforms that make a public commitment to purchase healthcare services for everyone are probably the best solution for most of the region's countries and provide benefits well in excess of costs.

While improving the system that provides healthcare *services* is necessary for both preventing and treating many health conditions, the public sector should not ignore the interventions *outside the health sector* that can lead to dramatic reductions in deaths, illnesses, and disabilities – such as efforts to combat alcohol abuse and tobacco addiction.

However, beware of easy answers. This alternative view provides BCR estimates for use in this specific Consultation because the author judges that they are needed for the debate. But providing such numbers raises the risk that decisions will be made simplistically and without regard to the full context of the argument. Some of the factors that must be kept in mind when using the estimates are:

- These are averages, and by definition are not going to be correct for any particular country or area.
- The estimates assume that marginal and average costs are comparable.
- The estimates are highly sensitive to the value ascribed to health status and the predicted reductions in disease, both of which are subject to substantial error.

Table 6.1.3 *Estimated benefits and costs of solutions*

Solution	BCR estimates		Total cost (US$ million)	Reduction in regional disease burden (%)
	Low	High[a]		
Purchasing universal access to healthcare via a "basic package"	7.1	85.1	2,200	3.5–7
Purchasing universal access to healthcare via a "complete package"[b]	2.2	4.5	46,600	5–10
Tobacco excise tax	11.8	2,383	586[c]	4.1
Alcohol excise tax	5.4	77.7	110	0.6
Restrict hours of alcohol sales	2.9	42.1	85.2	0.2
Ban alcohol advertising	2.6	37.6	76.7	0.2

Notes:
[a] High estimates include only intrinsic value ascribed to improved health status, excluding the value of reduced exposure to financial risks and increased productivity.
[b] Equivalent to services included in the Colombian Subsidized Regime.
[c] Average of high and low estimates in Jha *et al.* (2006).

- One of the key sources of error in predicting reductions of disease is whether funds will be applied as efficiently as in the interventions used in the analysis.
- The estimates do not provide information about the distributional consequences of the solution.

Furthermore, the BCRs have to be considered in the context of both the total cost and the total benefits. Interventions to address alcohol abuse have reasonably reliable estimates of very high BCRs, suggesting that they should be priorities. However, when all three are combined they affect about 1% of the total disease burden. By contrast, extending access to healthcare services by committing the public sector to purchase them has a lower BCR but is likely to address a much larger share of the disease burden, as well as provide additional benefits such as protection from financial risks and increased incomes (table 6.1.3).

In sum, the information here should be viewed as a "hard" answer, complementing the nuanced argument provided by Musgrove in chapter 6.

Bibliography

Castaño, Ramón A., José J. Arbelaez, Ursula B. Giedion, and Luis G. Morales, 2002. "Equitable Financing, Out-of-Pocket Payments and the Role of Health Care Reform in Colombia." *Health Policy and Planning* 17(Suppl 1): 5–11

Dorling D., M. Shaw, and G. Davey Smith, 2006. "Global Inequality of Life Expectancy Due to AIDS." *British Medical Journal* 332: 662–4

Evans, David B. 2004. "Alternative Perspectives." Paper in Lomborg (2004) *Global Cases, Global Solution*, 1st edn. Cambridge, Cambridge University Press

Frenk, Julio, José Luís Bobadilla, Claudio Stern, Tomas Frejka, and Rafael Lozano, 1991. "Elements for a Theory of the Health Transition." *Health TransitionReview* 1(1): 21–38

Gaviria, Alejandro, Carlos Medina, and Carolina Mejía, 2006. "Evaluating the Impact of Health Care Reform in Colombia: From Theory to Practice." Working Paper CEDE **2006–06**. Colombia: CEDE

Giedion, Ursula, Yadira Díaz, Eduardo Andres Alfonso, and William D. Savedoff, 2007. "The Impact of Subsidized Health Insurance on Access, Utilization and Health Status in Colombia." Washington, DC: Global Health Financing Initiative

Jamison, Dean T., 2007. "Disease Control." Paper prepared for the Copenhagen Consensus 2008. Brookings Institution

Jamison, Dean T., Joseph G. Breman, Anthony R. Measham, George Alleyne, Mariam Claeson, David B. Evans, Prabhat Jha, Anne Mills, and Philip Musgrove, eds., 2006. *Disease Control Priorities in Developing Countries*, 2nd edn. (DCP2). Oxford and New York: Oxford University Press

Jha, Prabhat, Frank J. Chaloupka, James Moore, Vendhan Gajalakshmi, Prakash C. Gupta, Richard Peck, Samira Asma, and Witold Zatonski, 2006. "Tobacco Addiction." Chapter 46 in DCP2

Liu, Jin-Tan, James K. Hammitt, and Jin-Long Liu, 1997. "Estimated Hedonic Wage Function and Value of Life in a Developing Country." *Economics Letters* 57(3): 353–8

Lomborg, Bjørn, 2004. *Global Cases, Global Solution*, 1st edn. Cambridge, Cambridge University Press

Lopez, Alan D., Colin D. Mathers, Majid Ezzati, Dean T. Jamison, and Christopher J. C. Murray, eds., 2006. *Global Burden of Disease and Risk Factors*. Oxford and New York: Oxford University Press

Macinko, James, Frederico C. Guanais, and Maria de Fátima Marinho de Souza, 2006. "Evaluation of the Impact of the Family Health Program on Infant Mortality in Brazil, 1990–2002." *Journal of Epidemiology and Community Health* 60: 13–19

Mills, Anne J. and Sam Shillcut, 2004. "Challenge Paper on Communicable Diseases." Copenhagen Consensus

Mrozek, Janusz and Laura Taylor, 2002. "What Determines the Value of Life? A Meta Analysis." *Journal of Policy Analysis and Management* 21(2): 253–70

Musgrove, Philip, 2007. "Challenges and Solutions in Health in the LAC region." Chapter 6 in this volume

Omran, Abdel, 1971. "The Epidemiological Transition: A Theory of the Epidemiology of Population Change." *Milbank Memorial Fund Quarterly* 49: 509–38

Rehm, Jürgen, Dan Chisholm, Robin Room, and Alan D. Lopez, 2006. "Alcohol." Chapter 47 in DCP2

Soares, Rodrigo R., 2007. "On the Determinants of Mortality Reductions in the Developing World." NBER working Paper 12837, available online at www.nber.org/papers/w12837

Tollman, Stephen, Jane Doherty, and Jo-Ann Mulligan, 2006. "General Primary Care." Chapter 64 in DCP2

Vallin, Jacques and France Meslé, 2004. "Convergences and Divergences in Mortality: A New Approach to Health Transition." *Demographic Research*, Special Collection 2, article 2: 11–43

Van der Gaag, Jacques, 2004. "Alternative Perspectives." Paper in Lomborg (2004) *Global Cases, Global Solution*, 1st edn. Cambridge, Cambridge University Press

Victora, César G., Taghreed Adam, Jennifer Bryce, and David B. Evans, 2006. "Integrated Management of the Sick Child." Chapter 63 in DCP2

Viscusi, W. Kip, 1993. "The Value of Risks to Life and Health." *Journal of Economic Literature* 31(4): 1912–46

World Health Organization (WHO), 2000. *The World Health Report 2000: Health Systems, Improving Performance*. Geneva: WHO

World Bank, 2006. "Brazil: Improving the Quality of Health Spending Resource Management in Brazil's Unified Health System (SUS)." Report 36601-BR, November

7 | *High logistics costs and poor infrastructure for merchandise transportation in the LAC region*

JULIO A. GONZALEZ, JOSÉ LUIS GUASCH,
AND TOMAS SEREBRISKY*

1 Introduction

Access to basic infrastructure services – roads, electricity, water, sanitation – and the efficient provision of the service, still remains as a key challenge in the fight against poverty in the LAC region and in the elusive search for sustainable growth. These services provide not only direct and fundamental benefits but also have important indirect effects on the living conditions of the population and are key ingredients for productive development and the enhancement of competitiveness.

Infrastructure services are central to individual and firm productivity and the opportunity for advancement. While this is intuitive for water, electricity, and telecommunication services, which bring with them the promise of connectivity and higher productivity, it is also true for roads and transport services. Access to markets, jobs, healthcare, and education is still an issue for the poor. Many of the poor (and particularly the extreme poor) in rural communities in the LAC region live on average 5 km or more from the nearest paved road, which is almost twice as far as non-poor rural households, limiting their access to all those services and opportunities.

* The findings, interpretations, and conclusions expressed in this chapter are entirely those of the authors and should not be attributed in any manner to the World Bank, its affiliated organizations, members of its Board of Executive Directors, or the countries they represent.

Since 1990, infrastructure coverage and quality have increased in most LAC sectors and countries. There have been major improvements in access to water, sanitation, electricity, telecommunications, ports, and airports. Only in roads has coverage not changed much, but efforts and resources have still been invested to improve the quality of road networks.

This chapter focuses on the main determinants of logistics costs and physical access to services and, whenever possible, provides evidence on the effects of these determinants and their impact on competitiveness and the growth and poverty of LAC economies. It shows the impact of improving infrastructure and logistic costs on three fronts: the macro front, showing the impact on growth; the micro front, showing the impact on productivity at the firm level; and the poverty front, showing the impact on the earnings of poor/rural people. In addition, this chapter provides recommendations/solutions that encompass a series of policies to reduce the prevalent high logistics costs and limited access to services in the LAC region. The recommendations rely on applied economic analysis on logistics and trade facilitation. All the recommendations were elaborated under the main premise of the feasibility of implementation.

Although it is difficult to do justice to the tremendous diversity of the LAC region – which is home to both Caribbean islands with fewer than 100,000 inhabitants as well as Brazil with close to 180 million, and with annual *per capita* income ranging from $467 in Haiti to more than $6,000 in Mexico – the recommendations emanating from this chapter apply to most countries, though the best ways to implement them may vary according to country conditions.

This chapter is organized as follows: section 2 provides a brief overview of the recent literature on the effects of infrastructure on productivity and growth. Section 3 presents the challenge, understood as the need to reduce high logistics cost in the LAC region (with its direct impact on improving competitiveness). Section 4 aims at identifying the impact of the quantity of infrastructure on growth. Section 5 presents an assessment of the levels and determinants of inventory costs and their impact on competitiveness. Section 6 evaluates the potential benefits of trade facilitation on competitiveness. Section 7 shows the impact of increased and bundled access to infrastructure services on the earnings of poor/rural people. Finally, section 8 presents a set of solutions/recommendations to meet the challenge.

2 Brief literature review on the impact of infrastructure on growth and logistics costs

This section provides a rapid overview of the recent empirical literature on the effects of infrastructure on productivity and growth. For the sake of brevity, the discussion is selective rather than exhaustive.

A number of empirical studies have found that infrastructure has a positive effect on output, especially in developing countries. Returns on infrastructure investments are generally highest during the early stages of development, when infrastructure is scarce and basic networks have not been completed. However, returns tend to fall with development, sometimes sharply. Indeed, some US studies have found that infrastructure investment has negative effects on total output (Briceño-Garmendia, Estache, and Shafik 2004).

In his paper "Is Public Expenditure Productive?" Aschauer (1989) found that the stock of public infrastructure is a significant determinant of aggregate TFP. However, the economic significance of these results was found to be implausibly large and not robust when more sophisticated econometric techniques are used (Baltagi and Pinnoi 1995; Cashin 1995; Holtz-Eakin 1994). Gramlich (1994) provides an overview of this literature.

The more recent empirical literature, relying on cross-country panel data, confirms that infrastructure makes a significant contribution to output. Such analysis relies on increasingly sophisticated econometric techniques to address reverse causation; infrastructure may cause growth, but growth may lead to a higher demand of infrastructure. Failure to take this endogeneity problem into account would result in an over-estimation of infrastructure's contribution to growth. Notable papers on this line include Canning (1999), which uses panel data for a large number of countries, and Demetriades and Mamuneas (2007), which uses data for OECD countries. Röller and Waverman (2001), using a framework that controls for the possible endogeneity of infrastructure accumulation, find that telecommunications infrastructure has large output effects. Similar results for roads are reported by Fernald (1999), using data on US industry. Calderón and

Servén (2003a) present a similar empirical analysis focused on Latin America. They find positive and significant output contributions from three types of infrastructure: telecommunications, transport, and energy.

A few papers go beyond measures of infrastructure spending and stock and consider infrastructure efficiency or quality. Hulten (1996) finds that differences in effective use of infrastructure explain 25% of the growth difference between Africa and East Asia, and more than 40% of the difference between low- and high-growth countries. Using a large panel data set, Esfahani and Ramirez (2002) report that infrastructure has significant growth effects, but that its contribution is affected by institutional factors. Finally, Calderón and Servén (2004b) find that infrastructure quantity and quality both have a robust impact on economic growth and income distribution. The authors use a large panel data set covering more than 100 countries and spanning the period 1960–2000, and conduct a variety of specification tests to ensure that the results capture the causal impacts of infrastructure quantity and quality on growth and inequality.

The relevance of infrastructure as determinant of logistics costs is enormous. Logistics costs, defined as the costs incurred to take a given good from the producer to the consumer, are heavily determined by the availability and quality of infrastructure. Infrastructure influences directly transport costs and indirectly the level of inventories and consequently financial costs, the main components of logistics costs. A variety of studies (World Bank 2006a, 2006b) emphasize the fact that infrastructure stock and quality, by lowering logistics costs, has a significant impact on countries' competitiveness.

It has been widely shown that poor infrastructure contributes to LAC's low rankings on competitiveness indexes. Several indexes, aggregating infrastructure variables, have been developed. These include the World Economic Forum's Growth and Business Competitiveness index and the International Institute for Management Development's *World Competitiveness Yearbook*.[1] These indexes use data and firm surveys to rank countries' ability to create and maintain an environment that sustains enterprise competitiveness. The World Bank's investment climate assessments survey firms about the

---

[1] See www.webforum.org/ for the World Economic Forum's indexes and www02.imd.ch/wcc/yearbook/ for the *World Competitiveness Yearbook*.

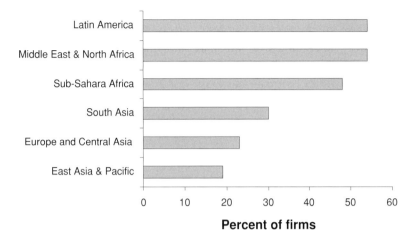

Figure 7.1 Businesses that consider infrastructure a serious problem, by region
Source: World Bank (2005a)

environments in which they operate, including the performance of infrastructure. More than half of the respondents in Latin America consider infrastructure to be a major or severe obstacle to the operation and growth of their business (figure 7.1).

3 The challenge: reducing current high logistics costs in the LAC region

A complex logistics system, composed of transport infrastructure and services, business logistics practices, and trade facilitation procedures, is responsible for the physical flows of goods. Several studies have analyzed the link between competitiveness and the physical flow of goods (World Bank 2005a, 2005b, 2006a, 2006b, 2007), concluding that three major areas have to be dealt with in order to optimize the flow of goods throughout the logistics chains: (a) transportation, (b) business logistics, and (c) trade facilitation. This conceptualization of the factors involved in the flow of goods makes clear that the analysis and policy options should not be limited exclusively to infrastructure bottlenecks (infrastructure being considered the "hard" component of logistics) but should also consider the rules and procedures regulating the services (the "soft" component). Thus, the performance of a country's logistics system depends on the activities of both the

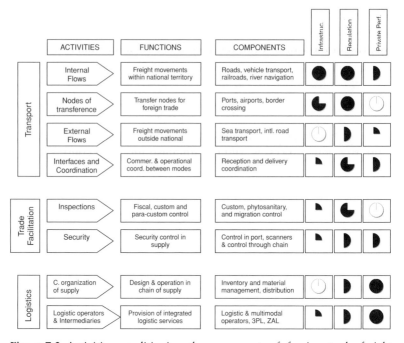

Figure 7.2 Activities conditioning the movement of foreign trade freight
Note: Full circle indicates high relevance, an empty circle indicates minimum relevance
Source: World Bank (2006b)

public and the private sectors. Figure 7.2 shows the impact that the supply of infrastructure, rules and regulations, and the performance of the private sector have on each of the activities defined. It also makes it possible to appreciate the diversity of instruments, both public and private, that converge to define the efficiency of the logistics system.

Relevance of the physical movement of goods and available measures of logistics costs

In recent decades there has been a profound change in the way that companies organize their physical flow of goods, with the development of modern business logistics that integrate movements over distance (transport) and time (storage), from supply to distribution. The process of change in the organization of the physical flows of goods began in the more developed economies, and has been extending gradually into the rest of the world. Until the 1980s, companies managed the transport of their inputs, distribution of final products, and storage systems in a relatively independent manner. Companies then began to integrate the processes, considering logistics to be the complete cycle of materials, documentation, and information, from purchase to final delivery to the consumer, covering transport, storage, inventory management and packaging processes, and the administration and control of these flows.

For most countries, logistics costs are a more important component of total trade costs than tariff barriers.[2] The gradual unilateral tariff reduction implemented in recent years by a large number of countries, together with free-trade agreements (FTAs), brought about an increase in the relative share of logistics costs in total trade costs. This motivated several public policy initiatives aimed at improving the performance of the components making up logistics costs. One example is the trend towards the signing of "open skies" agreements. Empirical evidence (Micco and Serebrisky 2006) indicates that import-related transport costs fall by up to 9% five years after the signing of an "open skies" agreement.

Definition and estimation of logistics costs

There is no agreement on a precise definition of logistics costs, and a review of the literature shows significant discrepancies regarding the activities that should be included in the definition. In this chapter, we consider logistics costs to include: transaction costs (those related to transport and trade-processing of permits, customs, or standards), financial costs (inventory, storage, security), and non-financial costs (insurance).

Lacking a uniform definition, international logistics cost comparisons tend not to be precise. In addition to the difficulties common to any survey carried out across countries, the lack of a precise definition of logistics costs, on the components that form them, and how to measure them, adds to the complexity of comparison. For this reason,

---

[2] For example, in the LAC region, average tariffs were lowered from 40% in the 1980s to 10% in the early 2000s.

Table 7.1 *Doing Business in 2007: trading among borders*

Region or economy	Documents for export (no.)	Time for export (days)	Cost to export (US$ per container)	Documents for import (no.)	Time for import (days)	Cost to import (US$ per container)
East Asia and Pacific	6.9	23.9	884.8	9.3	25.9	1,037.1
Europe and Central Asia	7.4	29.2	1,450.2	10.0	37.1	1,589.3
LAC	7.3	22.2	1,067.5	9.5	27.9	1,225.5
Middle East and North Africa	7.1	27.1	923.9	10.3	35.4	1,182.8
OECD	4.8	10.5	811.0	5.9	12.2	882.6
South Asia	8.1	34.4	1,236.0	12.5	41.5	1,494.9
SSA	8.2	40.0	1,561.1	12.2	51.5	1,946.9
USA	6	9	625	5	9	625
Argentina	6	16	1,470	7	21	1,750
Brazil	7	18	895	6	24	1,145
Chile	7	20	510	9	24	510
Colombia	6	34	1,745	11	35	1,773
Costa Rica	7	36	660	13	42	660
Mexico	6	17	1,049	8	26	2,152
Peru	7	24	800	13	31	820
Uruguay	9	22	552	9	25	666

Source: World Bank (2007).

much care is necessary when concluding that one country has higher or lower logistics costs than another based on international comparisons that use different methodologies, heterogenous databases, and were conducted in different years for each country that is part of the comparison.

Various studies have been carried out with the aim of making international comparisons of logistics costs. Taking into account the limitations detailed in the previous paragraph, estimates and international comparisons can provide valuable information. The added value of international comparisons lies basically in the relative ranking of the countries (or regions, if that is the way the grouping has been made) and less in the percentage difference of the cost indicator used. Below are the results of the principal studies that include LAC countries within their sample:

- **World Bank: Doing Business, analysis of regulations**

  The Doing Business database provides measurements of trade regulations and their application. Doing Business indicators make it possible to compare 155 economies, and can be used to analyze concrete regulations that favor or restrict investment, productivity, and growth. The database contains a category denominated "Trade Among Borders" that provides information on aspects of trade facilitation that have a direct impact on transaction costs, one of the components of logistics costs.

Compared with other regions in the world, the LAC region shows an acceptable performance on the indicators of official procedures and time necessary for foreign trade (table 7.1). Nevertheless, if its performance is compared with that achieved by OECD countries, it can be seen that the LAC region has significant room for improvement. As the time taken for customs and fiscal processing has a direct financial impact on the economic agents participating in the tradable sector of the economy, the "extra" days that the goods are delayed in the LAC region have a negative effect on its competitiveness. By calculating an average for the indicator, a ranking can be made of the various economies. It can be seen that although Argentina, Chile, and Mexico have much to do, other countries in the region, such as Brazil (in 107th place in the ranking) and Peru (93rd) need to make reforms far more urgently.

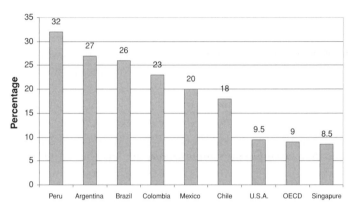

Figure 7.3 Logistic cost as a percentage of product value, 2004
Source: Guasch and Kogan (2006)

- **World Bank, estimate of logistics costs as a proportion of GDP**
  In an estimate made for various countries in the LAC region in 2001
  (Guasch 2004b) logistics costs were calculated as a percentage of the
  sale value of the products. The results show that all LAC countries
  face logistics costs that are significantly higher than those in the
  OECD and the United States (figure 7.3).[3]

- **World Bank, Logistics Perception Index**
  The World Bank has developed an innovative questionnaire to be
  distributed to shippers and logistics operators with the aim of identifying the areas that require immediate intervention if costs are
  to be lowered. Those receiving the questionnaire have to assign
  points to each question, on topics that include: effectiveness and
  efficiency of the cargo shipment process, available infrastructure for
  logistics operations, and the quality of infrastructure in use for logistics operations. In a preliminary round of this questionnaire,[4] the
  Netherlands was in 1st place, the United States 19th, South Korea
  25th, while in the LAC region Chile was 29th and Argentina was
  40th, followed by Mexico 45th. Ecuador was 46th, Brazil 51st, and
  Peru 55th, among 70 countries included in the sample.

---

[3] The estimation of logistics costs for Argentina was updated in a recent World
Bank report (World Bank 2006b). Logistics costs, in part as a result of the
devaluation of the domestic currency and the improvement in the terms of trade
account for 16% of product value.
[4] www.gfptt.org/uploadedEditorImages/00000325.pdf.

Role of inventories and other determinants of logistics costs

Inventory levels are usually studied to assess the reliability of infrastructure services – in particular, transport. When a country has poor transport infrastructure, firms need to have high levels of inventories to account for contingencies. Maintaining such levels is expensive because it ties up capital, which has a high cost in the region. This significantly increases unit costs, lowering competitiveness and productivity. Estimates show that, assuming an interest rate of 15–20%, additional inventory holdings made necessary by poor logistics systems cost LAC economies more than 2% of GDP (Guasch and Kogan 2001, 2006).

Whereas US businesses hold inventories equal to about 15% of GDP, inventories in LAC and other developing regions are often twice that amount (Guasch and Kogan 2006) (table 7.2).

Other determinants of logistics costs, such as loss in sales due to transport interruptions, or average time to clear customs, have a direct impact on productivity in the LAC region. Investment climate surveys in Brazil, Ecuador, El Salvador, Guatemala, Honduras, and Nicaragua confirm that most entrepreneurs consider inadequate infrastructure to be a serious issue. An analysis of these surveys plus Indonesia, conducted for the publication by Fay and Morrison (2007), supports this finding (figure 7.4).

In section 4, we will expand the analysis of the three areas that have the largest impact on logistics costs: (i) infrastructure and transport services, (ii) company logistics organization, and (iii) the organization of the public sector in trade facilitation of the flow of foreign trade. For each of the areas, we will then present empirical evaluations of the impact of (i) infrastructure quantity and quality on growth (section 4), (ii) the impact of inventory levels on logistics costs (section 5), and (iii) improvements in trade facilitation and their impact on growth (section 6).

4 Analysis (i): the impact of infrastructure on growth

This section, that relies heavily on Calderón and Servén (2004b), aims at identifying the impact of the quantity of infrastructure on growth. To assess the impact of infrastructure on growth, Calderón and Servén use a large panel data set comprising 121 countries and spanning the years 1960–2000. Using this data set, they estimate empirical growth

Table 7.2 LAC: ratios to US inventories (all industries)

	Chile	Venezuela	Peru	Bolivia	Colombia	Ecuador	Mexico	Brazil
	Raw material inventory level ratios: ratio to US level, by industry (average of all available data for 1990s)							
Mean	2.17	2.82	4.19	4.20	2.22	5.06	1.58	2.98
Minimum	0.00	0.30	0.10	0.11	0.52	0.86	0.42	0.8
1st quartile	0.36	1.87	1.25	1.39	1.45	2.55	1.06	1.6
Median	1.28	2.61	2.30	2.90	1.80	3.80	1.36	2.00
3rd quartile	2.66	3.12	3.90	4.49	2.52	5.64	2.06	3.1
Maximum	68.92	7.21	31.1	34.97	13.59	20.61	3.26	7.1
	Final goods inventory levels: ratio to US level, by industry (average of all available data for 1990s)							
Mean	1.76	1.63	1.65	2.74	1.38	2.57	1.46	1.98
Minimum	0.01	0.10	0.39	0.11	0.19	0.67	0.35	0.75
1st quartile	0.17	0.87	1.17	1.13	1.05	1.67	0.82	1.1
Median	0.72	1.60	1.54	2.02	1.28	1.98	1.36	1.60
3rd quartile	1.38	2.14	2.11	3.18	1.63	2.86	2.14	2.00
Maximum	31.61	5.29	3.87	21.31	5.31	7.94	4.91	5.2

Source: Guasch and Kogan (2001)

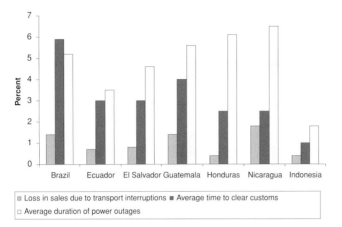

Figure 7.4 Productivity gains from a 20% improvement in selected investment climate variables: various LAC countries and Indonesia
Sources: Escribano *et al.* (2005); Fay and Morrison (2007)

equations including a standard set of control variables augmented by infrastructure quantity measures, and controlling for the potential endogeneity of infrastructure indicators.

Econometric methodology

Assessing empirically the impact of infrastructure on growth in the panel data set poses some econometric issues that can be illustrated in the context of a simple dynamic equation:

$$
\begin{aligned}
y_{it} - y_{it-1} &= \alpha y_{it-1} + \phi' K_{it} + \gamma' Z_{it} + \mu_t + \eta_i + \varepsilon_{it} \\
&= \alpha y_{it-1} + \beta' X_{it} + \mu_t + \eta_i + \varepsilon_{it}
\end{aligned}
\tag{1}
$$

In (1) K is a set of standard growth determinants, and Z is a vector of infrastructure-related measures. The terms μ_t and η_i, respectively, denote an unobserved common factor affecting all countries, and a country effect capturing unobserved country characteristics. The second equality follows from defining $X_{it} = (K'_{it}, Z'_{it})'$ and $\beta = (\phi', \gamma')'$. y denotes (log) *per capita* GDP.

Estimation of (1) faces the potential problem of endogeneity of the regressors. In principle, this affects both the standard determinants of growth in K (e.g. variables such as inflation, financial depth, and so on, commonly included in growth regressions) as well as the infrastructure measures in Z, since it can be argued that these are jointly determined with the rest of the economy's endogenous variables. Furthermore, in the growth equation the lagged dependent variable y_{it} is also endogenous due to the presence of the country-specific effect.

Therefore, suitable instruments are needed to deal with endogeneity. However, apart from the terms of trade, which shall be assumed strictly exogenous, there are no obviously exogenous variables at hand to construct them, and therefore we shall rely primarily on internal instruments, provided by taking first differences.

Empirical results

As noted, the strategy involves estimation of an infrastructure-augmented growth regression. The analysis includes the following standard (i.e. non-infrastructure) growth determinants: indicators of human capital, financial depth, trade openness, government burden, governance, inflation and real exchange rate over-valuation, and terms of trade shocks. In addition, the set of explanatory variables includes indices of infrastructure quantity. The empirical experiments use an unbalanced panel data set of five-year averages over the 1960–2000 period, with a total number of observations exceeding 400.

Growth and infrastructure stock

Table 7.3 presents the results. According to the best estimate – column (6), which is the specification that includes best-possible instruments – the coefficient of infrastructure stock is positive and significant, pointing to a positive contribution of infrastructure to growth. To contextualize the importance of this effect, let us consider a 1 standard deviation increase in the aggregate index of infrastructure; this amounts to an increase of 1.3 in the global index, which represents an improvement of the aggregate infrastructure stock from 0.4 (the level exhibited by Ecuador and Colombia in the 1996–2000 period) to 1.7 (the level displayed by Korea and New Zealand in the same period).[5] The coefficient estimate in column (6) implies that, other things equal, such an

---

[5] Such increase in infrastructure stocks was in fact achieved between 1976–80 and 1996–2000 by countries such as China, Indonesia, Korea, Malaysia, and Turkey.

Table 7.3 *Infrastructure stocks and economic growth: panel regression analysis using different estimation techniques*

Dependent variable: growth in GDP per capita
Sample of 121 countries, 1960–2000 (5-year averaged rate)

Variable	Pooled OLS (1)	Country effects (2)	Time effects (3)	GMM-IV (D) (4)	GMM-IV System Estimator[a] (5)	(6)
Constant	0.1527**		0.1712**	0.2214**	0.2956**	0.3064**
	(0.03)		(0.03)	(0.02)	(0.04)	(0.06)
Output *per capita* (in logs)	−0.0147**	−0.0663**	−0.0145**	−0.0143**	−0.325**	−0.0381**
	(0.00)	(0.01)	(0.00)	(0.00)	(0.01)	(0.01)
Human capital	0.0020	−0.0045	0.0059**	0.0079**	0.0081*	0.0059
	(0.00)	(0.00)	(0.00)	(0.00)	(0.00)	(0.01)
Financial depth	0.0024*	0.0057**	0.030**	0.0036**	0.0026**	0.0020*
	(0.00)	(0.00)	(0.00)	(0.00)	(0.00)	(0.00)
Government burden	−0.0102**	−0.0190**	−0.0091**	0.0016	−0.0128**	−0.0172**
	(0.00)	(0.01)	(0.00)	(0.00)	(0.01)	(0.01)
Trade openness	−0.0051	0.0276**	0.0007	−0.0046*	0.0267**	0.0215**
	(0.00)	(0.01)	(0.00)	(0.00)	(0.01)	(0.01)
Governance	0.0038**	0.011	0.0030**	0.0005	0.0027**	0.0039**
	(0.00)	(0.00)	(0.00)	(0.00)	(0.00)	(0.00)
Inflation	−0.0190**	−0.0177**	−0.0166**	−0.0204**	−0.0236**	−0.0214**
	(0.00)	(0.00)	(0.00)	(0.00)	(0.00)	(0.00)
RER Overvaluation	−0.0053*	0.0035	−0.0064**	−0.0131**	−0.0046**	0.0017
	(0.00)	(0.00)	(0.00)	(0.00)	(0.00)	(0.00)

(cont.)

Table 7.3 (cont.)

Dependent variable: growth in GDP per capita
Sample of 121 countries, 1960–2000 (5-year averaged rate)

Variable	Pooled OLS (1)	Country effects (2)	Time effects (3)	GMM-IV (D) (4)	GMM-IV System Estimator[a] (5)	(6)
Terms of trade shocks	0.0251	0.0221	0.0140	0.0733**	0.0391**	0.0464**
	(0.03)	(0.02)	(0.03)	(0.01)	(0.02)	(0.02)
Infrastructure stock[b]	0.0072**	0.0195**	0.0059**	0.0043**	0.0207**	0.0226**
	(0.00)	90.010	(0.00)	(0.00)	(0.01)	(0.01)
Observation	399	331	399	331	331	331
R^2	0.199	0.346	0.0274	0.0219	0.409	0.407
Specification test (p-value)						
– Sargan test				(0.52)	(0.71)	(0.81)
– Second-order correlation	(0.01)	(0.84)	(0.11)	(0.9)	(0.78)	(0.81)

Notes: Number in parenthesis below the coefficient estimates are standard errors. *(**) implies that the variable is significant at the 10(5)% level.
[a] The GMM-IV System estimations presented in columns (5) and (6) differ in the set of instruments used. In (5) the analysis used only internal instruments (lagged levels and lagged differences of all the explanatory variables in the regression). In (6) we use internal instruments for the growth determinants except for the infrastructure variable. For the variable of interest (infrastructure), actual and lagged levels are used as well as lagged differences of demographic variables such as urban population, size of labor force and population, size of labor force and population density.
[b] The aggregate infrastructure stock is the first principal component of the following normalized variables: main telephone lines per 1,000 workers, energy-generating capacity (GW per worker), and roads (km per km²).
Source: Calderón and Servén (2004b).

increase in the index of infrastructure stocks would raise the growth rate of the economy by 3 percentage points – a fairly substantial effect.

Among LAC countries, we find that if the infrastructure levels in Peru (located in the 25th percentile of the region) were to rise to the levels of Chile (in the 75th percentile of the region) during the 1996–2000 period, Peru's growth rate would rise by 1.7 percentage points. Note that these growth benefits imply a very significant expansion of the infrastructure network. According to the figures for the 1996–2000 period, an improvement in the infrastructure of Peru to the levels exhibited by Costa Rica (the leader in the LAC region) implies an increase in: (a) main lines (per 1,000 workers) from 164 to 457, (b) electricity generating capacity (per 1,000 workers) from 0.5 to 0.9, and (c) roads (in km per km^2) from 0.06 to 0.70.

The impact of different categories of infrastructure

Table 7.4 presents the estimates of the growth regression using the different categories of infrastructure – telecommunications, power, and transportation – individually or jointly.

In columns (1)–(5) of table 7.4, one infrastructure indicator at a time is used. The analysis evaluates the impact on growth of main telephone lines, main lines and cellular phones, power-generating capacity, length of the road network, and length of the road and railways network. Results show that two indicators of telecommunications – main telephone lines and total lines per 1,000 workers – have a positive and significant coefficient, and the latter measure has a larger effect on growth than the former. Power-generating capacity also has a positive and significant coefficient, but smaller than the growth effects of an expansion in telecommunications. Finally, an expansion in the transportation network – measured by either the length of the road network or the length of the road and railways network – has a positive and statistically significant effect. It is important to note that the impact of roads and rails is slightly larger than the impact of roads alone.

From these point estimates, the following three conclusions can be deduced:

- A 1 standard deviation increase in either main telephone lines (1.65) or total lines (1.69) raises the growth rate of the economy between 2.6 and 3.1 percentage points. Such an increase implies a surge in the number of lines from the levels of Indonesia (located in the bottom

Table 7.4 Infrastructure stocks and economic growth: panel regression analysis using different categories of infrastructure

Dependent variable: growth in GDP per capita
Estimation technique: GMM-IV system estimator
Sample of 121 countries, 1960–2000 (5-year averaged rate)

Variable	(1)	(2)	(3)	(4)	(5)	(6)	(7)	(8)	(9)
Constant	0.2000**	0.2291**	0.1844*	0.1430**	0.1854**	0.2905**	0.2767**	0.3278**	0.3326**
	(0.06)	(0.07)	(0.05)	(0.06)	(0.06)	(0.06)	(0.07)	(0.07)	(0.07)
Output per capita (in logs)	−0.0300**	−0.0355**	−0.0232**	−0.0194**	−0.0203**	−0.04121**	−0.0405**	−0.441**	−0.0460**
	(0.01)	(0.01)	(0.01)	(0.01)	(0.01)	(0.01)	(0.01)	(0.01)	(0.01)
Human capital	0.0111*	0.0093*	0.0098	0.0124**	0.0118**	0.0083	0.0062	0.0050	0.0019
	(0.01)	(0.01)	(0.01)	(0.00)	(0.01)	(0.01)	(0.01)	(0.01)	(0.01)
Financial depth	0.0040*	0.0046*	0.0032*	0.0004	0.0001	0.0026*	0.0029*	0.0023	0.0020
	(0.00)	(0.00)	(0.00)	(0.00)	(0.00)	(0.00)	(0.00)	(0.00)	(0.00)
Government burden	−0.0221**	−0.0208*	−0.0262**	−0.0205**	−0.0218**	−0.0231**	−0.0257**	−0.0199**	−0.0219**
	(0.01)	(0.01)	(0.01)	(0.01)	(0.01)	(0.01)	(0.01)	(0.01)	(0.01)
Trade openness	0.0170	0.0135	0.0137	0.0240**	0.0269**	0.0187*	0.0192	0.0279**	0.0262*
	(0.01)	(0.01)	(0.01)	(0.01)	(0.01)	(0.01)	(0.01)	(0.01)	(0.01)
Governance	0.0035**	0.0041**	0.0040**	0.0041	0.0028**	0.0044**	0.0041**	0.0023**	0.0028**
	(0.00)	(0.00)	(0.00)	(0.00)	(0.00)	(0.00)	(0.00)	(0.00)	(0.00)
Inflation	−0.0232**	−0.0240**	−0.0250**	−0.0229**	−0.0192**	−0.0242**	−0.0271**	−0.0207**	−0.0234**
	(0.00)	(0.00)	(0.00)	(0.00)	(0.00)	(0.00)	(0.01)	(0.00)	(0.00)
RER overvaluation	−0.0013*	0.0008	−0.0010**	0.0031	0.0030	−0.0033	0.0033	−0.0014	−0.0413**
	(0.00)	(0.00)	(0.00)	(0.00)	(0.00)	(0.00)	(0.00)	(90.00)	(0.02)

Terms of trade shocks	0.0219	0.0229	0.0428**	0.0353**	0.0424**	0.0457**	0.0429**	0.0497**	0.0164**
	(0.02)	(0.02)	(0.02)	(0.02)	(0.02)	(0.02)	(0.02)	(0.01)	(0.01)
Main lines	0.0157**								
	(0.01)								
Main lines + cell		0.0187**				0.0130**	0.0153**		0.0082
		(0.01)				(0.00)	(0.01)		(0.01)
Power			0.0120*			0.0102	0.0129*	0.0095	
			(0.01)			(0.01)	(0.01)	(0.00)	
Roads				0.0070**		0.0084**	0.0093**	0.0072**	0.0077**
				(0.00)		(0.00)	(0.00)	(0.00)	(0.00)
Roads + rails					0.0077**				
					(0.00)				
Observation	338	332	334	335	326	331	325	322	316
R^2	0.417	0.411	0.415	0.393	0.396	0.387	0.39	0.413	0.411
Specification Test (p-value)									
– Sargan test	(0.45)	(0.33)	(0.49)	(0.72)	(0.73)	(0.63)	(0.44)	(0.62)	(0.62)
– Second-order correlation	(0.50)	(0.38)	(0.54)	(0.78)	(0.83)	(0.79)	(0.63)	(0.66)	(0.72)

Notes: Number in parenthesis below the coefficient estimates are standard errors. *(**) implies that the variable is significant at the 10(5)% level.

Source: Calderón and Servén (2004b).

quintile of the distribution, with 51 main lines per 1,000 workers) to the levels of Japan (in the top quintile of the distribution, with 977 main lines per 1,000 workers) in the 1996–2000 period.

- An increase of 1 standard deviation in power-generating capacity (1.43) – that is, from the levels exhibited in India (with 0.7 GW per 1,000 workers, at the bottom quintile of the distribution) to the levels in Israel and Hong Kong (with 2.8–2.9 GW per 1,000 workers, at the top quintile of the distribution) during the 1996–2000 period – will enhance the growth rate of income *per capita* by 1.7 percentage points.

- Finally, if the road and railways system expands by 1 standard deviation (1.88) – which implies an increase from the levels displayed in Argentina (with 0.6 km per km^2 of surface area at the bottom quintile of the distribution) to levels in Korea and Taiwan (with 3 km per km^2 of surface area at the top quintile of the distribution) – growth will be higher by 1.4 percentage points.

Conclusions (i)

The main results of the work done by Calderón and Servén (2004b) indicate that the volume of infrastructure stocks has a significant positive effect on long-run economic growth. This conclusion is robust to changes in the infrastructure measure used as well as the estimation technique applied. Illustrative experiments show that the empirical findings are significant not only statistically but also economically. For example, if all LAC countries were to catch up with the region's leader in terms of infrastructure quantity, their long-term *per capita* growth gains would range between 1.1% and 4.8% per annum. Catching up with the East Asian median country would involve even larger gains, ranging from 3.2% to 6.3% extra growth. It is important to note, however, that these catch-up scenarios implicitly assume potentially very large investment efforts in the transition toward the increased levels of infrastructure development.

Finally, and perhaps most importantly, the conclusion that infrastructure raises growth implies that infrastructure development may be a key win–win ingredient for poverty reduction. In addition to raising society's overall level of income, it would help raise the income of the poor more than proportionately. This suggests that infrastructure development should rank at the top of the poverty reduction agenda.

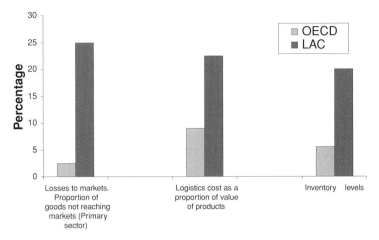

Figure 7.5 Deteriorating and insufficient infrastructure contributes to uncompetitive industries, 2004
Source: Guasch and Kogan (2006)

5 Analysis (ii): logistics costs, inventories, and their influence on competitiveness and growth

As mentioned in section 3, the second of the three major groups that condition the physical movement of goods – and, consequently, have a significant effect on logistics costs – refers to the logistics organization of firms. In particular, we consider the role of inventories, a key aspect of how firms organize their production and distribution processes. Large inventories are, in general, the consequence of unreliable infrastructure and logistics services. By measuring them, we can obtain an estimate of avoidable logistics costs and their overall impact on growth. To assess the potential benefits of reducing the cost inventories on growth and competitiveness, we will draw on the work done by Guasch and Kogan (2001, 2003, 2006).

Figure 7.5 provides a comparison of average inventory levels in the LAC region and the OECD. If we consider that inventories have an associated financial cost, the fact that inventory levels in the LAC region are three times higher than in the OECD translates into a significant competitive disadvantage. The need to have more inventories is in part explained in the first column of figure 7.5. The proportion of goods not reaching markets, due to poor infrastructure and business logistics, forces firms to hold more inventories.

In this section we present an assessment of the levels and determinants of inventory costs so as to facilitate appropriate government interventions to reduce them and, in doing so, improve competitiveness.

Inventories

At present, the logistics industry is a global hub-and-spoke network designed to link hundreds of towns and cities with an overnight communication infrastructure that keeps the world's 'just-in-time' (JIT) supply chain taut. In developed markets such as the United States, the ability to guarantee overnight shipment of parts and finished goods has allowed companies to reduce average inventory levels by a fifth since 1995 and is thought to have played a significant role in improving productivity across the economy.

In developing markets, however, the evidence shows large inventory holdings. While it is well known from anecdotal evidence that inventories are higher in developing countries, there are no systematic studies that attempt to explain this phenomenon, or even to quantify the difference. Guasch and Kogan (2001) assembled data for fifty-two countries from the 1970s and 1980s to draw out some stylized facts about the pattern of inventory holdings. More recent data in LAC countries, for the 1990s, show that the problem persists.

US businesses typically hold inventories equal to 15% of GDP, while inventory levels in many developing countries are often twice as large, and for raw materials three times as large. If the private sector interest rate for financing inventory holdings is 15%–20%, a conservative estimate in most developing countries, then the cost to the economy of the additional inventory holdings is greater than 2% of GDP.

Suppose that firms in developing countries keep high levels of inventories in response to poor infrastructure and logistic services. Then, as an example, consider that the total transport infrastructure stock in Bangladesh is about 2% of GDP[6] (Guasch and Kogan, 2001) while this figure is above 12% in the United States.[7] One year's worth of savings

---

[6] Rough calculation, based on graphs of infrastructure stock *per capita* and composition of Infrastructure. See World Bank (1994), figures 1 and 2.

[7] Non-military, non-residential net public stocks of highways and streets.

Table 7.5 *Inventory carrying costs as percentage of product value*

Element	Average (%)	Ranges (%)
Capital cost	15.00	8–40
Taxes	1.00	0.35–1.52
Insurance	0.05	0.01–0.25
Obsolescence	1.20	0.5–3
Storage	2.00	0–4
Totals	19.25	9–50

Source: Guasch and Kogan (2006), various studies.

in inventory holding costs would be enough to double Bangladesh's infrastructure stock; infrastructure improvement could pay for itself. At the firm level, the impact of these high levels of inventories is also enormous. Given the high cost of capital in many developing countries, cutting inventory levels in half could reduce unit costs by over 20%, with a significant impact on competitiveness, aggregate demand, and employment.

These calculations are merely a lower bound on the cost of additional inventories. First, there are certain transactions that would have been worthwhile were it not for the high level of inventory holdings necessary to complete them effectively. It is difficult to estimate the size of these lost transactions. Second, firms in developing countries will take costly steps to mitigate the institutional or structural factors creating a need for high inventories. Suppose that for a particular firm, thirty days' inventory are sufficient when transportation networks are well developed, but ninety days' inventory are required when transportation networks are poor. The firm might choose to reduce these ninety days to sixty days by requiring suppliers to locate nearby. Additional costs due to poor infrastructure, as measured by increased inventory levels, would be thirty days while the actual costs are higher. Third, high inventories can obscure efficiency problems. Current thinking in the manufacturing and operations research (OR) fields suggests that low inventories make it easier to trace problems in the production processes.

The direct impact of inventory costs is quite large, as table 7.5 shows. Given the high levels of cost of capital, they can on average reach about 19% of product value. If countries could rely on near-JIT strategies, those costs could be cut in half, with significant impacts on competitiveness and export growth.

The analysis carried out by Guasch and Kogan (2001) explains the magnitude and the determinants of the inventory holdings and the potential cost to the economy and the benefits for competitiveness. The following regression is estimated to explain the determinants of inventory levels:

$$\text{Inventory level}_{I,C}$$
$$= \sum_i \beta_i \cdot \text{Industry dummy}_i + \sum_x \lambda_x \cdot \text{Country characteristic}_x + \varepsilon_{I,C}$$

It is difficult to obtain consistent time-series data on inventory holdings for developing countries. The aggregate data reported in the national accounts is the change in inventories rather than the stock of inventories; often, this data is based not on an inventory survey but on the difference between production and sales, which can lead to highly inaccurate data.[8] Most national statistics agencies do have inventory stock data, but they do not publish them. In order to report the size of the country's industrial production, the statistics agency typically carries out a firm survey or census, which asks about total inventory holdings at the beginning or end of the year. More detailed surveys break down inventories into three or more categories: raw materials inventory, goods-in-process inventory, and finished goods inventory.

Regressions (1), (2), and (3) of table 7.6 present the results of regressing raw materials inventory on infrastructure and the presence of a free market, as well as some control variables. The analysis uses two proxies for infrastructure – telephone mainlines per person and BERI's infrastructure quality index which, although more comprehensive, is available for fewer countries. These proxies for infrastructure are significant at the 1% or 5% level; the coefficients suggest that a 1 standard deviation worsening in infrastructure increases inventories by 27%–47% relative to US levels. The proxy for the lack of a free market is transfers and subsidies to private and public enterprises expressed as a fraction of GDP. A 1 standard deviation restriction on the free market increases raw materials inventories by 19%–30%.

---

[8] However, it is worth pointing out that the initial results of the research, using the aggregate inventory levels computed from the National Accounts data, were not inconsistent with the stylized observation that developing countries hold more inventory than developed countries.

Table 7.6 Regressions

Dependent variable	Raw materials (1)	Raw materials (2)	Raw materials (3)	Upstream inventories (4)	Upstream inventories (5)	Upstream inventories (6)	Raw as % of raw + upstream (7)	Raw as % of raw + upstream (8)
Log real PPP GDP/per capita	-0.0229 (0.0186)	0.0010 (0.0285)	-0.0304* (0.0171)	-0.0328*** (0.0950)	-0.0193** (0.0103)	-0.0320*** (0.0077)	0.0444* (0.0227)	0.0523* (0.0274)
Telephone mainlines per person	-0.2934*** (0.0948)		-0.1968** (0.0928)	0.0950* (0.0539)		-0.0926** (0.0549)	54.17*** (0.1695)	
Infrastructure quality		-0.0300*** (0.0086)			0.00021 (0.0044)			-0.0374*** (0.0076)
Transfers and subsidies/GDP	0.7427*** (0.2226)	0.4105** (0.1947)	0.6453** (0.3128)	0.2136* (0.1202)	0.3098** (0.1235)	0.6608*** (0.1238)	0.4385 (0.4809)	-0.3475 (0.4063)
Imports/GDP	0.0290* (0.0166)	0.0372*** (0.0124)	0.0449 (0.0296)				-0.1765 (0.1798)	0.1615 (0.1596)
Exports/GDP				-0.0157 (0.0108)	-0.0151 (0.0111)	0.0158* (0.0110)	0.2721 (0.1798)	-0.0767 (0.1856)
Lending interest rate (real)			-0.0317 (0.0368)			-0.0442*** (0.0149)		
GDP growth			-0.0113 (0.0073)			-0.0038** (0.0016)		

(cont.)

Table 7.6 (cont.)

Dependent variable	Raw materials (1)	Raw materials (2)	Raw materials (3)	Upstream inventories (4)	Upstream inventories (5)	Upstream inventories (6)	Raw as % of raw + upstream (7)	Raw as % of raw + upstream (8)
GPD growth standard deviation		0.0108 (0.0075)		−0.0066** (0.0019)				
(24 industry dummy variables)	Included	Included	Included	Included	Included	Included	Included	Included
No. of clusters (countries)	42	29	31	44	30	32	41	29
R^2	0.2528	0.2897	0.2846	0.3893	0.4291	0.4549	0.3234	0.3518
No. of observations	2,086	1,627	1,408	1,962	1,642	1,271	1,554	1,307

Notes: Robust standard errors corrected for clustering at the country level are in parentheses.

* (**, ***) implies that the variable is significant at the 10(5, 1) level.

Inventories greater than 0.5 have been dropped for these regressions.

Coefficients in regressions (1)–(6) represent the effect of an absolute change in the explanatory variable on inventory level expressed as fraction of a year. For example, if telephone mainlines per person increased from 0.5 to 0.6 in regression (1), inventories would fall by 0.2934 of a year, or about 12 days.

Coefficients in regressions (7)–(8) represent the effect of an absolute change in the explanatory variable on the percentage of inventories held as raw materials. For example, if telephone use increased from 0.5 to 0.6 in regression (7), 0.5417% of inventories more will be held as raw materials. In the United States, the median industry holds 57% of inventories as raw materials so that the 0.1 in telephone mainlines leads to a 9% change in holdings.

Conclusions (ii)

The work done by Guasch and Kogan (2001) introduced a new cross-country data set on inventories at the industry level into the literature documenting the determinants of inventory levels in developing countries. Given the high costs of capital in developing countries, usually in the 15%–30% range, the impact on unit costs of holding inventories is enormous. Their analysis explores some broad causes of high raw materials inventory levels across countries in the 1970s and 1980s, and confirms the validity of the two causes – infrastructure and poor markets – which have been suggested in case studies.

Since high inventories are a problem today in many developing countries, this chapter should be useful in understanding one type of obstacle faced by manufacturing firms in LAC countries – and, from a policy standpoint, it indicates the direction to take to address the problem.

The policy implications are clear: improvements in infrastructure (roads, ports, and telecommunications) can have a significant impact in reducing inventory levels, particularly when accompanied by appropriate and effective regulation. Likewise, the development and deregulation of associated markets can also have a significant impact on inventory levels and consequently on reducing the costs of doing business.

6 Analysis (iii): potential benefits of trade facilitation and its impact on competitiveness and growth

The last of the three major groups of factors that condition the physical movement of goods is the organization of the public sector is trade facilitation and security. To assess the potential benefits of trade facilitation on competitiveness, we will mainly draw on the work done by Wilson, Mann, and Otsuki (2003, 2004).

The relationship between trade facilitation and trade flows is complex, and empirically challenging to assess. Wilson, Mann, and Otsuki (2004) measure and estimate the relationship between trade facilitation and trade flows for manufactured goods for the period 2000–1. Four indicators of trade facilitation are developed: (1) Port efficiency, designed to measure the quality of infrastructure of maritime and air ports; (2) Customs environment, designed to measure direct customs costs as well as administrative transparency of customs and border crossings; (3) Regulatory environment, designed to measure the economy's approach to regulations; and (4) Service sector infrastructure, designed to measure the extent to which an economy has the necessary domestic infrastructure (such as telecommunications, financial intermediaries, and logistics firms) and is using networked information to improve efficiency and to transform activities to enhance economic activities. We present the results obtained with a gravity model and those obtained with a simulation exercise that offers more information about what type of trade facilitation efforts might provide the largest gains in terms of increasing trade flows.

There is no standard definition of trade facilitation in public policy discourse. In a narrow sense, trade facilitation efforts simply address the physical and paper (customs-related documentation) logistics of cross-border trade (Wilson, Mann, and Otsuki 2003). In recent years, the definition has been broadened to include the environment in which trade transactions take place, including transparency and professionalism of customs, regulatory environments, as well as harmonization of standards and conformance to international or regional regulations. In addition, the rapid integration of networked information technology into trade means that modern definitions of trade facilitation need to encompass technological concepts as well (Wilson, Mann, and Otsuki 2004). In light of this broadening definition of trade facilitation, the definition used here incorporates relatively concrete "border" elements (port efficiency and customs administration) and "inside-the-border" elements (domestic regulatory environment and the infrastructure to enable e-business usage).

Wilson, Mann, and Otsuki (2004) rely on three data sources – World Economic Forum Global Competitiveness Report 2001–2 (hereafter, GCR), IMD Lausanne, World Competitiveness Yearbook 2002 (hereafter, WCY), and Kaufmann, Kraay, and Zoido-Lobatón (2002) (hereafter, KKZ). See Wilson, Mann, and Otsuki (2004) for a more complete description of the sources and each of their methodologies used to estimate the gravity model.[9] In this chapter, we summarize the main results:

- Port efficiency for each country is the average of two indexed inputs from GCR:
  - Port facilities and inland waterways
  - Air transport.

[9] The gravity model of international trade flows is a common approach to modeling bilateral trade flows. The standard gravity formulation includes various measures of market size (GDP, population, GDP *per capita* to account

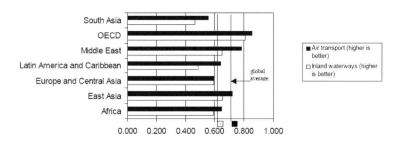

Figure 7.6 Two indexed inputs to port efficiency
Source: Wilson *et al.* (2004)

- Customs environment for each country is the average of two indexed inputs from GCR:
  – Hidden import barriers
  – Irregular extra payments and bribes.
- Regulatory environment for each country is constructed as the average of indexed inputs from WCY and KKZ:
  – Transparency of government policy is satisfactory (WCY)
  – Control of corruption (KKZ).
- Service sector infrastructure for each country is from GCR:
  – Speed and cost of internet access
  – Effect of internet on business.

Figures 7.6–7.9 (pp. 387–8) report information about these indicators. The figures show the indexed inputs for regional groups of countries for each specific trade facilitation indicator.[10] Each indexed input is represented by a horizontal bar. The longer the bar extends to the right toward the maximum of 1.0, the higher-ranked the region is in the category of trade facilitation. A vertical line is drawn at the average value. If a bar extends beyond the average for the particular trade facilitation measure, that indexed input for that region represents a condition superior to the average for all countries. For example,

for intra-industry trade effects that may be associated with countries of similar incomes but varied tastes), measures of remoteness (distance and adjacency), and measures of kinship (regional trade arrangements and language/ethnic similarities). To this basic formulation, Wilson, Mann, and Otsuki (2004) add tariffs as well as trade facilitation indicators and some additional factors.

[10] These regional indicators use simple average of the region. An average weighted by trade or GDP would no doubt yield somewhat different results. There is no clear interpretation of alternative weighted averages. Moreover, these regional indexes are not used in estimation.

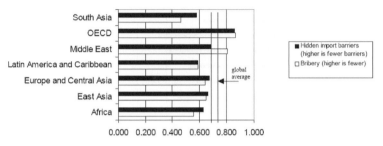

Figure 7.7 Two indexed inputs to customs environment
Source: Wilson *et al.* (2004)

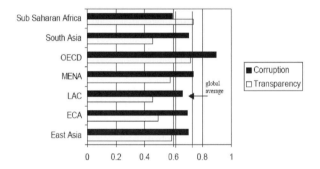

Figure 7.8 Two indexed inputs to regulatory environment
Source: Wilson *et al.* (2004)

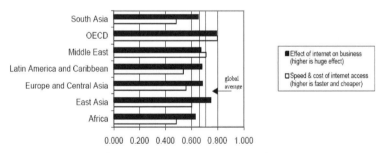

Figure 7.9 Two indexed inputs to service sector infrastructure
Source: Wilson *et al.* (2004)

figure 7.6 shows that OECD, Middle East and North Africa (MENA),[11] and East Asia regions are above the global average in terms of the two indexed inputs used for port efficiency.

Regression results

The approach used by Wilson, Mann, and Otsuki (2004), which constructs a set of distinct trade facilitation indicators and deploys them in a gravity model of trade, is generally successful. Table 7.7 displays regression results. Model (1) includes the estimated coefficients and standard errors for the basic gravity model specification. Model (2) includes those for a specification that measures the effect of FTAs and language dummies (i.e. membership of any FTA, or any common language). The model was run using ordinary least squares (OLS). The coefficients for the four trade facilitation measures are statistically significant and the estimated coefficients differ for the different trade facilitation indicators.

Before considering the trade facilitation indicators, it is worthwhile to consider *tariffs*. Higher tariffs have a significant and the expected negative effect (with a -1.2 coefficient) on trade. The coefficient on tariffs is similar to that of distance. In *ad valorem* terms, the elasticity of tariff is -1.1 at the global average level of tariff rates – i.e. a 1% reduction in *ad valorem* tariff from the global average (from 8.5 to 7.5%) will increase the trade flow by 1.1% and a 1% reduction in distance (80 km from the global average) would yield a 1.3% increase in trade flow. These figures are useful benchmarks against which to compare the coefficients on the trade facilitation indicators.

Port efficiency of both the importer and the exporter is positively associated with trade – that is, an improvement in the indicator toward best practice is associated with an increase in trade flows. Comparing the effect of port efficiency on imports vs. exports, it is noticeable that the coefficient is higher for exporters than importers, which implies that global trade flows get a bigger boost when the exporters' port efficiency improves. So for countries and regions that are well below the global best practice, such as the LAC region, there is great potential for improvement in terms of port efficiency. Moreover, the range of

---

[11] Data are available only for Egypt, Israel, and Jordan.

Table 7.7 *Regression results*

	Model (1)		Model (2)	
	Coef.	Std err.	Coef.	Std err.
Constant	−10.641***	1.558	−10.771***	1.549
Tariff rates	−1.155***	0.318	−1.163***	0.318
Port efficiency of importer	0.307*	0.163	0.338*	0.160
Port efficiency of exporter	0.924***	0.148	0.938***	0.146
Customs environment of importer	0.472**	0.199	0.486*	0.199
Regulatory environment of importer	0.281*	0.144	0.264	0.144
Regulatory environment of exporter	0.620***	0.132	0.580***	0.131
Service sector infrastructure of importer	0.729***	0.224	0.657**	0.224
Service sector infrastructure of exporter	1.943***	0.216	1.943***	0.217
GNP of importer	0.915***	0.014	0.915***	0.014
Per capita GNP of importer	−0.182***	0.037	−0.210***	0.037
GNP of exporter	1.246***	0.014	1.241***	0.014
Per capita GNP of exporter	−0.226***	0.029	−0.251***	0.029
Geographical distance	−1.258***	0.025	−1.225***	0.025
Adjacency dummy	0.336***	0.114	0.426***	0.108
Membership dummy for any FTA			−0.021	0.078
ASEAN membership dummy	0.509***	0.190		
NAFTA membership dummy	−0.645	0.501		
LAIA membership dummy	0.593***	0.154		
AUNZ membership dummy	1.118	0.858		
MERCOSUR membership dummy	0.229	0.302		
EU membership dummy	−0.515***	0.106		

Table 7.7 *(cont.)*

	Model (1)		Model (2)	
	Coef.	Std err.	Coef.	Std err.
Dummy for any common language			0.823***	0.061
English-language dummy	0.808***	0.089		
French-language dummy	−1.413***	0.500		
Spanish-language dummy	0.598***	0.098		
Arabic-language dummy	−1.223	0.992		
Chinese-language dummy	1.747***	0.406		
German-language dummy	−0.826	0.505		
Portuguese-language dummy	0.569	0.986		
Russian-language dummy	2.026***	0.362		
Year 2000 dummy	−0.031	0.039	−0.038	0.039
Adjusted R^2	0.758		0.755	
No. of observations	7,904		7,904	

Note: ∗ (∗∗, ∗∗∗) implies that the variable is significant at the 10(5, 1) level.
Source: Wilson, Mann, and Otsuki (2004).

performance on this measure of trade facilitation is the largest among the trade facilitation indicators.

Customs environment also has a significantly positive effect on the trade of the importing country with an elasticity of 0.47, which is smaller than that for tariffs. Trade facilitation is a possible avenue for reducing the cost of imports through customs improvements even if tariffs remain where they are.

Improving the *regulatory environment* of the importer and exporter has a positive and significant association with trade, with coefficients of 0.28 and 0.62, respectively. As with ports, the magnitude of the coefficient is larger for exporters than for importers. Regulatory transparency and control of corruption (the two inputs) reduce unnecessary transaction costs of trading and reduce barriers to private business.

Improving indicators of *service sector infrastructure* are positive and significantly associated with trade among the countries in the sample. Similar to port efficiency and regulatory environment, service sector infrastructure has a more significant positive effect on exporters than on importers. The elasticity of the exporters' service sector infrastructure is the highest among all the trade facilitation measures (1.94).

Potential benefits from trade facilitation

In this section we present the results of several simulation exercises conducted by Wilson, Mann, and Otsuki (2003). These simulations use a formula that brings the below-average countries in the group half-way to the average for the entire set of countries. Special attention is devoted to the below-average country, on the grounds that donor attention and capacity building efforts should be extended to this group. An improvement of 'half-way' to the average is chosen because there are limited development resources, and improvements take time. Dramatic improvements are possible, but it is not realistic to presume a scenario whereby all countries in the sample are assumed to achieve best practice as measured by the nation with the highest score on a particular measure of trade facilitation.

From the standpoint of a specific country, improvement in port efficiency should increase its own imports and exports. The same can be expected for the regulatory environment, and service sector infrastructure, as well as customs on the import side. But a country will export more not only from its own reforms, but also because of reforms undertaken by its trading partners as importers. Thus, export gains are the sum of the simulated effect on exports of unilateral reform and of import reforms undertaken by the country's trading partners. On the import side, a country's imports increase first on account of its unilateral import reforms, and secondarily on account of the reforms undertaken by its trading partners as exporters. Examining the relative gains to trade from unilateral reforms as compared to partner's reforms, and on exports vs. imports, and across trade facilitation indicators, offers three dimensions of potential insight to policymakers, donors, and the private sector.

Table 7.8 summarizes the results for the simulations and presents the results for the seventy-five countries as a whole. In total, the collection of simulations on the four trade facilitation indicators yields an increase in trade among the seventy-five countries worth about $377 billion, representing an increase of about 9.7% in total trade among these countries. About $107 billion of the total gain comes from the improvement in port efficiency and about $33 billion from

Table 7.8 *Overview of simulation: bring below-average members half-way up to the global average (change in trade flow, $ billion)*

	Importer's change in trade facilitation	Exporter's change in trade facilitation	Total
"Border" measures			
Port efficiency	23.40 (0.6%)	84.53 (2.2%)	106.93 (2.8%)
Customs environment	32.87 (0.8%)		32.87 (0.8%)
"Inside-the-Border" measures			
Service sector infrastructure	36.64 (0.9%)	117.38 (3.0%)	154.02 (4.0%)
Regulatory environment	24.39 (0.6%)	58.86 (1.5%)	83.25 (2.1%)
Grand total	**117.30 (3.0%)**	**259.77 (6.7%)**	**377.06 (9.7%)**

Source: Wilson, Mann, and Otsuki (2004).

the improvement in the customs environment. The gain from the improvement in the regulatory environment is $83 billion. The largest gain comes from the improvement in service sector infrastructure ($154 billion), which is consistent with the broad concept of services infrastructure that this variable is designed to capture.

Table 7.9 summarizes the change in trade flow, by region, by trade facilitation indicators, and by own vs. trading partners' reforms. These results can be combined in several ways to give different perspectives on which regions gain the most, and why. One cut, exports by region and by trade facilitation indicator, is shown in figure 7.10.

On the whole, as table 7.9 shows, from improvement in all trade facilitation measures the highest export gain is attained by South Asia (40.3%). The LAC region is in fourth place (20%), after East Europe and Central Asia (30.0%) and East Asia (24%). The high gains for South Asia emanate from high export gains due to improvements in port efficiency and service sector infrastructure. Likewise, the LAC region's gains in its exports come mainly from reforms in port efficiency and service sector infrastructure. In both cases, the gains are generated from own improvements, rather than from improvements by

Table 7.9 Details of simulation results

Experience of exporters

Region	Initial trade	Port efficiency			Customs environment	Regulatory environment			Service sector infrastructure			Combined effect
		Importer change, %	Exporter change, %	Total change, %	Total change, %	Importer change, %	Exporter change, %	Total change, %	Importer change, %	Exporter change, %	Total change, %	Total change, %
East Asia	753	0.5	7.0	7.6	0.8	0.6	3.3	3.9	0.9	10.8	11.7	24.0
ECA	139	0.8	8.7	9.5	0.9	0.7	5.5	6.1	1.4	12.1	13.5	30.0
LAC	179	0.6	7.3	7.9	0.9	0.8	3.6	4.4	0.8	6.0	6.8	20.0
MENA	26	0.4	0.2	0.6	0.7	0.5	0.1	0.6	0.7	0.7	1.4	3.3
OECD	2,735	0.6	0.0	0.7	0.8	0.6	0.6	1.3	1.0	0.0	1.0	3.8
South Asia	36	0.4	11.7	12.1	0.8	0.5	6.9	7.4	0.7	19.2	20.0	40.3
SSA	12	0.4	1.1	1.4	0.6	0.5	2.8	3.3	0.8	4.8	5.6	10.9
Total	3,879	0.6	2.2	2.8	0.8	0.6	1.5	2.1	0.9	3.0	4.0	9.7

Experience of Importers

Region	Initial trade	Port efficiency			Customs environment	Regulatory environment			Service sector infrastructure			Combined effect
		Importer change, %	Exporter change, %	Total change, %	Total change, %	Importer change, %	Exporter change, %	Total change, %	Importer change, %	Exporter change, %	Total change, %	Total change, %
East Asia	620	1.5	2.7	4.2	2.2	1.1	2.1	3.3	2.7	4.4	7.0	16.7
ECA	165	3.1	1.8	4.9	3.2	2.7	1.3	4.0	5.3	2.4	7.7	19.8
LAC	260	2.9	1.3	4.2	3.4	2.4	1.4	3.8	2.9	1.8	4.7	16.1
MENA	32	0.2	1.0	1.3	1.3	0.1	1.1	1.2	0.7	2.1	2.8	6.6
OECD	2,761	0.0	2.2	2.2	0.1	0.2	1.4	1.6	0.1	2.9	3.0	6.9
South Asia	21	3.1	1.4	4.5	5.8	3.3	1.5	4.8	6.8	2.5	9.3	24.4
SSA	20	1.5	1.5	3.0	3.0	1.8	1.3	3.1	3.5	2.6	6.1	15.2
Total	3,879	0.6	2.2	2.8	0.8	0.6	1.5	2.1	0.9	3.0	4.0	9.7

Notes: ECA: East Europe and Central Asia
LAC: Latin America and the Caribbean
MENA: Middle East and North Africa
OECD region
SSA: Sub-Saharan Africa
Source: Wilson, Mann, and Otsuki (2004).

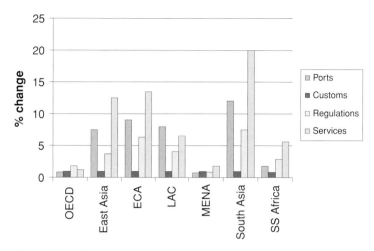

Figure 7.10 Change in exports, by region
Source: Wilson *et al.* (2004)

trading partners. In the LAC region, Mexico garners an export gain of $17.3 billion (i.e. the highest in the region) and Paraguay 74.8%. Mexico and Paraguay's high gains again come from the improvement in ports and service sector infrastructure.

Conclusions (iii)

In conclusion, the results from this section suggest that the scope and benefit of unilateral trade facilitation reforms are very large and that the gains fall disproportionately on exports. Some of the policies required to improve the four trade facilitation indicators are easier to adopt than others. But the message is clear: there are significant gains to be made from improving the components of trade facilitation, even if the improvements are unilateral.

7 The impact of poverty

The recent expansion of infrastructure coverage has generally tended to benefit the poor. As the poor, particularly in remote rural areas, are usually the last to be connected, the gradual recent expansion of services in the LAC region can be expected to have benefited them more than the better-off. But country data present a mixed picture (Estache,

Foster, and Wodon 2002). For example, Brazil made great progress in providing water access to the lowest urban income decile between 1989 and 1996. The proportion of this group with access jumped from 53% to 74%, against a rise from 92% to 97% for the seventh decile. But in rural areas, absolute increases benefited the seventh decile more than the poorest (Fay and Morrison 2007).

Infrastructure access is critical for improving economic opportunities for the poor. When poor individuals and under-developed areas become connected to core economic activities, it enables them to access additional productive opportunities (Estache 2004). Likewise, infrastructure development in poor regions contributes to the reduction of production and transaction costs (Gannon and Liu 1997). For example, in poor rural areas infrastructure expands job opportunities for the less advantaged by reducing the costs of accessing product and factor markets. Infrastructure access can also raise the value of the assets of the poor. Recent research links the asset value of poor farm areas – as proxied by the NPV of the profits generated by their crops – to the distance to agricultural markets (Smith *et al.* 2001). Improvements in communication and road services also imply capital gains for these poor farmers (Jacoby 2002).

Improved infrastructure also affects the health and education levels of the poor. Several impact evaluations have demonstrated the causality between higher access to basic services and human development indicators (HDIs). For instance, in Argentina, Galiani, Gertler, and Schargrodsky (2005) find that child mortality fell by 8% in areas which had privatized water utilities (and hence experienced improved coverage and quality), with most of the reduction occurring in low-income areas where the water network expanded the most. More generally, Fay *et al.* (2005) find that providing the poorest quintile in developing countries the same access to basic services as the richest would reduce child mortality by 8% and stunting by 14%. There are other, less obvious, linkages (explored in Brenneman 2002), such as improved transport facilitates access to healthcare, as well as easier staffing and operation of clinics. A stronger transportation system and a safer road network help raise school attendance. For girls, enrollment is also helped by greater access to piped water, which would otherwise have to be fetched. Electricity also allows more time for study, while the positive health impacts of clean water allow more time in the classroom (Fay and Morrison 2007).

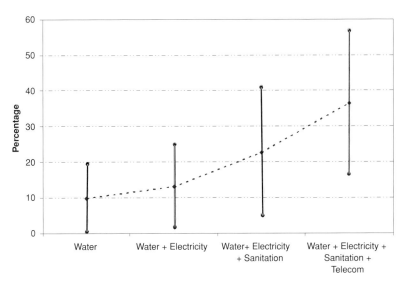

Figure 7.11 Increase in household earnings for access to infrastructure public services, three years after securing access to services (% earnings)
Source: Escobal and Torero (2004)

With regard to *new* consumers, the initial access entails major positive welfare effects due to having access to the service. In relation to the *existing* consumers, the welfare effect also appears positive due to better quality of service. While the price effect on those consumers with mixed tariffs increased in some countries and sectors while they diminished in others, the quality of service improved significantly, and that appears to more than compensate the increases in tariffs. But perhaps the most dramatic effects are seen in the impact on new consumers. To illustrate the magnitude of the impact, a study in Peru (Escobal and Torero 2004) analyzed the impact on household earnings due to access to services, three years after securing access, and the numbers are quite large, as seen in figure 7.11. Having access to water and electricity increases earnings by 13%; having access to water, electricity, and sanitation increases earnings by 23%; having access to water electricity, sanitation, and telecoms increases earnings by 36%; and having market access through rehabilitated roads increases earnings by 35% (figure 7.12).

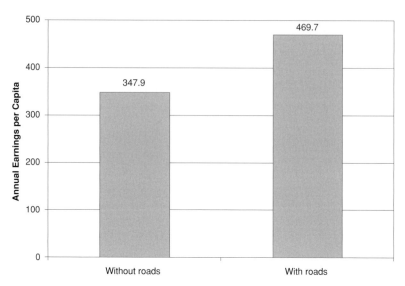

Figure 7.12 Increase in household earnings from access to market through rehabilitated rural roads (US$ annual)
Source: INEI (2004–6)

8 Solutions and recommendations

In this chapter, we presented the three areas that have the largest impact on logistics costs, and consequently on competitiveness: (i) transport infrastructure, (ii) company logistics organization, and (iii) the organization, rules, and regulations that affect trade facilitation.

The recommendations follow the progression developed in the paper. Some of the recommendations can be assessed following a standard CBA. Others, however, can not. Such is the case of company logistics organization: a well-developed market for business logistics providers can have a tremendous impact on aggregated logistics costs. The problem is that the performance of service logistics providers depends on a wide variety of factors, most of them related to investment climate (taxation, standards, and quality regulation, among others). Coming up with a cost-benefit estimate for the measures aimed at improving the productivity of service logistics providers or to facilitate trade is very difficult. This is clearly not the case of infrastructure investments (road, railways, etc.) because their costs and benefits can be measured with more accuracy.

Recommendation 1: the LAC region needs to spend more and better on infrastructure

- **The LAC region needs to spend "more" on infrastructure**
  On average, countries in the region spend less than 2% of GDP on infrastructure, while 3%–6% is needed to keep pace with other countries such as China or Korea.[12] Regardless of the source of financing, infrastructure investment costs (including operation and maintenance costs) are ultimately borne by users or taxpayers. So if infrastructure investment is to increase, users must cover a higher share of the costs. This requires changing the payment culture, as well as protecting users who cannot afford to pay by creating safety net programs.

- **The LAC region needs to spend "better", including better project selection and much more emphasis on investments in maintenance**
  Resources should be better allocated between investment and maintenance. Very little has been invested in maintenance, when the rates of returns there can be enormous. The temptation to build "white elephants" should be avoided; countries in the LAC region ought to conduct a careful analysis of investment needs, eliminating biases towards investment in operation and maintenance of infrastructure. A much better selection of projects is needed, with units that provide careful analysis of the costs and benefits of projects. New investments must focus on increasing productivity and competitiveness, though that does not need to be at the expense of social goals, since universal coverage of water, sanitation, and electricity could be achieved within ten years for less than 0.25% of GDP a year. Subsidies must be better targeted to those who need them. The most important concern when it comes to infrastructure investment in the LAC region is project selection. The vast majority of countries lack the institutional set-up to prioritize investment according to sound processes and cost-benefit criteria. Moreover, few countries have the institutions and technical skills to monitor the achievement of the outcomes sought by infrastructure projects. In summary, in order to increase the quality of their infrastructure, LAC countries need to set up institutions capable of conducting adequate planning, CBA, and monitoring and evaluation.

[12] A World Bank study, *Argentina: Infrastructure for Growth and Poverty Alleviation* (World Bank 2006c), indicates that Argentina would need to invest between 2.5%–4% of GDP to cover its investment needs in the next five years.

- **The LAC region needs to leverage its scarce public funds through increased use of public–private partnerships (PPPs)**
  The private financing of infrastructure projects, along with better know-how and faster turn-around is essential to bridge the large financial needs and improved efficiency of service delivery. At the same time, a better regulatory and oversight framework, as well as improved communications and transparency of processes, are needed to avoid the problems and conflicts of the past, that led to a generic backlash against private participation. We should always account for the possible adverse social effects, through social tariffs and connection to the service, subsidy programs when applicable.

As an illustration of a CBA, we present two cases prepared to secure World Bank investment loans. The rates of returns and NPVs obtained from these investments are quite high, in both cases above 25%.[13] Both projects finance investment in maintenance of roads and aim to improve the quality of transport infrastructure.

The economic analysis of both cases was carried on using the High-way Design and Maintenance Standard Model (HDM-III), which simulates the deterioration of the road on the basis of existing conditions and the traffic on the road, and measures the incremental benefits to the road users from a base "without-project" alternative. A sensitivity analysis[14] was also carried out in both cases.

CBA case 1: Bolivia's road rehabilitation and maintenance project
An economic analysis was undertaken as part of project preparation. The investment component includes the rehabilitation of the Calamarca–San Pedro and the Boyuibe–Yacuiba road segments. Table 7.10 summarizes the results of the analysis of the rehabilitation component. The present value of the economic and financial benefits has been calculated using a 12% discount rate.

The summary of benefits and costs suggests that the proposed project would reduce road-user transport costs by (a) lowering vehicle

---

[13] It should be highlighted that the CBA presented is *ex ante*; no *ex post* information is available to test whether the estimated benefits differ from actual benefits.

[14] Analysis of how sensitive outcomes are to changes in the assumptions. The assumptions that deserve the most attention should depend largely on the dominant benefit and cost elements and the areas of greatest uncertainty of the program or process being analyzed.

Table 7.10 *Bolivia case: summary of economic analysis*

	PV of flows Economic analysis	Fiscal impact Financial analysis	Taxes	Subsidies
Benefits: US$ million	45.16	60.99	15.83	–
Costs: US$ million	23.40	27.51	4.11	–
Net benefit (NPV): US$ million	21.76	33.48	11.72	–
IRR (%)	27.0	31.0		

Source: World Bank (2001).

Table 7.11 *Bolivia case: sensitivity analysis*

		Increase in costs 0%		20%	
		NPV (US$ million)	IRR (%)	NPV (US$ million)	IRR (%)
Decrease in benefits	0%	21.76	27.0	17.08	22.2
	−20%	12.73	21.2	8.05	16.9

Source: World Bank (2001).

operation, accident, and travel time costs, (b) removing physical constraints to road transport of goods and people within Bolivia and from Bolivia to the neighboring countries of Argentina and Chile, and (c) allowing the provision of more reliable and safer transport services.

The sensitivity analysis shows that both subprojects will continue to show rates of return above a cutoff of 12%[15] (rate most commonly used in World Bank projects) in the event of a 20% increase in the investment cost, a 20% decrease in the benefits, or a combination of the two. In these latter events, the rate of return is 16.9% (table 7.11).

Switching values were calculated for the increase in costs or the reduction in benefits. In the case of the Calamarca–San Pedro subproject, costs would have to increase by more than 72% or benefits reduce by more than 42% for the subproject to yield a rate of return

[15] The World Bank adopted a 12% discount rate for all its investment projects. This discount rate has been applied to all CBAs in investment projects since 2000.

Table 7.12 *Mexico case: summary of economic analysis*

PV of flow	Rehab. and maint. program	Comprehensive maint. program	Bridge maint. program	All programs
Benefits: US$ million	304	77	231	612
Costs: US$ million	54	12	11	77
Net benefits (NPV): US$ million	250	65	220	535
IRR (%)	114	140	68	111
MIRR (%)	36	38	57	40

Source: World Bank (2000).

lower than 12%. In the case of the Boyuibe–Yacuiba subproject, costs would have to increase more than 1.5 times, or benefits reduce by more than 61% for the project to become not economically feasible. These results show the robustness of the economic worth of such rehabilitation investments.

CBA case 2: Mexico's federal highway maintenance project
The main objective of this project is the reduction of road transport costs and the preservation of the road network in an efficient and sustainable manner. The proposed investments would reduce road-user transport costs by lowering vehicle operating and travel time costs. An economic analysis was done for the civil works program under the project consisting of: (i) a rehabilitation and maintenance program (85% of civil works); (ii) a comprehensive maintenance by contract program (7% of civil works); and (iii) a bridge rehabilitation program (8% of civil works).

Table 7.12 summarizes the NPV, internal rate of return (IRR), and modified internal rate of return (MIRR) of the programs.

The Ministry of Communications and Transports of Mexico (SCT) estimated maintenance and rehabilitation costs in financial and economic terms (net of taxes), economic costs being on average 85% of financial costs; and defined vehicle fleet characteristics and unit costs for five vehicle classes. Traffic growth rate was set to 3%, based on

Table 7.13 *Mexico case: sensitivity analysis*

		Increase in agency costs			
		0%		20%	
		IRR (%)	MIRR (%)	IRR (%)	MIRR (%)
Decrease in traffic	0%	114	36	97	33
	−20%	91	32	77	30

Source: World Bank (2000).

past trends for the duration of the analysis period. The discount rate was set to 12%.

An analysis of the road conditions in 2001 indicated that 23% of the network was in good condition, 34% in fair condition (requiring seals or thin overlays), 19% in poor condition (requiring overlays), and 24% in very poor condition (requiring thick overlays or reconstruction). By 2004, the successful implementation of the program resulted in roads in a good and fair condition accounting for 75% of the total.

The sensitivity analysis shows that the first-year rehabilitation and maintenance program IRR was 114% and the MIRR 36%. Assuming there was an increase of 20% in agency costs, the IRR decreases to 97% and the MIRR to 33%. A 20% decrease in traffic decreases the IRR to 91% and the MIRR to 32%. A combination of increased agency costs by 20% and decreased traffic by 20% decreases the IRR to 77% and the MIRR to 30% (table 7.13).

To have a NPV equal to zero, agency costs have to be 560% higher than the estimated costs or traffic levels reduced to only 18% of the estimated traffic. These events have a very low probability of occurrence, indicating that the project's economic viability was very robust.

Recommendation 2: the LAC region needs to bundle infrastructure investments with the adoption of policies aimed at improving the development and efficiency of logistics service providers

Previous sections showed that firms in the LAC region need to have high levels of inventories. This responds to the lack of good-quality infrastructure and unreliable service providers. For instance, it has been

Table 7.14 *Impact of reduction in logistics costs from 34% to 20%*

Sector	Increase in demand (%)	Increase in employment (%)
Agro-industry	12	6
Wood and furniture	14	16
Textiles	8	9
Leather-shoes	18	15
Mining industry	10	2.5

Source: Guasch (2004a).

shown that the trucking industry in Colombia has very low standards of quality, imposing high costs for export oriented firms.[16]

The policies required to reduce high inventory levels are clear: improvements in transport infrastructure have to be accompanied by appropriate and effective regulation – for instance, a good framework for the development of multimodal operators. Likewise the deregulation of associated markets can also have a significant impact on inventory levels and then reducing the costs of doing business. The ultimate goal of better regulation is to foster private sector investment to provide a menu of efficient logistics services, including among other things dry ports and multimodal distribution centers.

Policy reforms aimed at improving sector regulation are not costly, as they require changes in laws and other norms and regulations. However, even if the monetary costs are low, political costs could be quite high and a *de facto* barrier to change. The challenge, then, is to find out how countries in the LAC region can generate the political consensus needed to adopt the optimal policies to reduce logistics costs.

Table 7.14 shows the results of an exercise conducted by Guasch (2004) that estimates the effect of reducing logistics costs from 34% of product value to 20% in Peru. The results are impressive. To achieve the reduction of logistics costs presented by Guasch, it is necessary to combine investments in infrastructure and changes in regulations. Thus, the monetary cost is difficult to estimate, but the potential

[16] World Bank (2006a).

benefit is huge. Assuming the increase in demand and employment presented in table 7.14 fosters the rate of growth just 1%, Peruvian GDP would grow US$800 million per year (the nominal 2005 GDP was US$79 billion). This growth would generate additional fiscal space to fund the investment required to address infrastructure bottlenecks.

Recommendation 3: Latin American countries need to adopt policies to improve trade facilitation. In particular, they need to (i) strengthen the institutions that promote trade facilitation; (ii) support the internationalization of national firms, which implies helping national firms open new markets and adopt the technologies and quality standards required to compete in the global economy; (iii) the implementation of effective multimodality laws, providing in particular insurance across modes and the use of a single bill of lading; (iv) the improvement of access areas to ports and connections to the other transport modes; and (v) the facilitation of the development and supply of associated services such as transport services, testing, cooling services, and logistic terminals/dry ports

In the LAC region, recent studies (Soloaga, Wilson, and Mejia 2007) show that the main reforms on trade facilitation are of relatively low cost, as they relate to regulatory and policy reforms and not to hard infrastructure. Thus, it can be expected that the benefits from reform will most likely outweigh the costs.

The areas that would benefit from a better policy design and implementation and a capacity-building program to strengthen trade promotion institutions are:

- **A country strategy for capacity building in trade facilitation**
  This includes the creation (or strengthening) of an export development corporation to promote international trade. National governments should aim at reducing administrative costs through better regulation. Finally, it also incorporates the "building connections" component fostering the access and flow of information needed to achieve access to new markets or expand the share in international markets where local firms are present.

- Support the modernization of local firms' processes related to international trade
  International competition will make firms more efficient, innovative, and therefore competitive. It has been observed that firms that "go global" tend to subsist, while firms that "stay local" tend to disappear over time. LAC firms need to insert themselves in the new international economy. Accordingly, firms need to create their own trade facilitation strategies.

- Creation of a national logistics council
  This will need the participation of the public bodies responsible for providing services (transportation, public works, customs), and fundamentally those representing users (Foreign trade, industry, agriculture, small and medium-sized enterprises (SMEs), and other representatives of the private sector (chambers of commerce). Its aim would be to define an agenda of actions to reduce logistics costs, establish measurement and control procedures, develop a control panel of logistics actions, and conduct regular follow-up of its progress. It has increasingly been recognized that achievement of real operational improvement depends crucially on better communication among private traders and freight forwarders, transport providers, and the government services that regulate and control movements across borders.

- A central focus on modernization and simplification of custom procedures
  This will involve the introduction of computer applications to make processes more efficient and transparent, special lines for reliable clients, and randomized testing and improvement in human resource management (HRM), all as instruments that will gradually shift the basic orientation of the customs services from obstructing the easy flow of private international trade to actively facilitating it. Performance indicators may be collected monthly and published on the internet, which will help to stimulate action towards further improvement.

- Special emphasis on the development of multimodality and access to essential facilities, particularly ports
  Very few countries have adopted a comprehensive multimodality law that permits the use of a single bill of lading and provides insurance across modes. Similarly, most countries fail to have well-integrated and connected access to ports, leading to congestion and

Table 7.15 *Summary table with qualitative BCRs*

Solutions/ Recommendation	Quantitative range of IRR	Qualitative ranking[a]
More and better investment in: (i) infrastructure and (ii) maintenance	Infrastructure: between 25 and 50% (World Bank investment projects) Maintenance: between 85 and 150%	Medium/high
Policies aimed at improving the efficiency of logistics service providers	Higher than 50% (due to very low monetary cost of implementation and enforcement): costs significantly lower than investment in infrastructure	High
Policies to improve trade facilitation	Higher than 50% (due to very low monetary cost of implementation and enforcement): costs significantly lower than investment in infrastructure	Very high

Note: [a] Qualitative ranking: given current political constraints and difficulties associated with planning, design, and implementation of infrastructure projects, 'Very high' means that BCRs from adopting this solution are the highest but are the least likely to be implemented given the political economy behind these policies. Despite having a lower qualitative ranking, traditional investment in infrastructure has proven easier to carry out.

urban chaos around the port areas. A plan for an effective logistic park near the port is critical.

- **Heavier emphasis on a comprehensive and coherent supply of associated logistic services**
  In particular, assuring the supply of effective transport services includes treatment of cool, testing, and certification, logistic terminals and dry ports, and adoption of quality standards.
- **Creation of regional trade facilitation committees**
  The main role of these committees would be to recommend policies and procedures to improve border crossings and regional facilities so that merchandise does not need to pass through the capital, as is usually the case in most LAC countries, and to make the regions

engines of growth. As part of the tasks of these committees, a common regional website could be developed to promote trade facilitation, provide up-to-date information on procedures for crossing the various border points and on delay times, and to convey distance-learning programs in transport and logistics management, assisted by international associations.

Table 7.15 is a summary table with qualitative BCRs. We can only provide a quantitative range for BCRs, expressed as an IRR. The other two solutions involve institutional reforms that have a very low monetary cost but are seldom implemented due to political difficulties. Accordingly, table 7.15 presents two criteria to the rank the solutions.

Bibliography

Aschauer, D., 1989. "Is Public Expenditure Productive?" *Journal of Monetary Economics* 23: 177–200

Baltagi, H. and N. Pinnoi, 1995. "Public Capital Stock and State Productivity Growth: Further Evidence from an Error Components Model." *Empirical Economics* 20: 351–9

Brenneman, A., 2002. "Infrastructure and Poverty Linkages, a Literature Review." Washington, DC: World Bank, mimeo

Briceño-Garmendia, C., A. Estache, and N. Shafik, 2004. "Infrastructure Services in Developing Countries: Access, Quality, Costs and Policy Reform." World Bank Policy Research Working Paper 3468

Canning, D., 1999. "The Contribution of Infrastructure to Aggregate Output." World Bank Policy Research Working Paper 2246

Calderón, C. and L. Servén, 2003a. "The Output Cost of Latin America's Infrastructure Gap." In W. Easterly and L. Servén, eds., *The Limits of Stabilization: Infrastructure, Public Deficit and Growth in Latin America*. Palo Alto, CA and Washington, DC: Stanford University Press and the World Bank

2003b. "Macroeconomic Dimensions of Infrastructure in Latin America." Paper presented at the Fourth Annual Stanford Conference on Latin American Economic Development, November: 13–15

2004a. "Trends in Infrastructure in Latin America, 1980–2001." World Bank Policy Research Working Paper 3401

2004b. "The Effects of Infrastructure Development on Growth and Income Distribution." World Bank Policy Research Working Paper 3400

2006: "Is Infrastructure Capital Productive?" Washington, DC: World Bank, mimeo

Cashin, P., 1995. "Government Spending, Taxes, and Economic Growth." IMF Staff Papers **42**(2): 237–69

Demetriades, P. and T. Mamuneas, 2007. "Intertemporal Output and Employment Effects of Public Infrastructure Capital: Evidence from 12 OECD Economies." *The Economic Journal* **110**: 687–712

Escobal, J. and M. Torero, 2004. "Análisis de los Servicios de Infraestructura Rural y las Condiciones de Vida en las Zonas Rurales de Perú." Grupo de Análisis para el Desarrollo (GRADE), Lima

Escribano, A., N. Peltier-Thiberge, L. Garrido, and H. Singh, 2005. "The Impact of Infrastructure on Competitiveness in Latin America: A Firm Level Analysis Based on Investment Climate Assessment." Washington, DC: World Bank

Esfahani, H. and M. T. Ramirez, 2002. "Institutions, Infrastructure and Economic Growth." *Journal of Development Economics* **70**: 443–77

Estache, A., 2004. "Emerging Infrastructure Policy Issues in Developing Countries: A Survey of Recent Economic Literature." Background Paper for the October 2004 Berlin meeting of the POVNET Infrastructure Working Group. Washington, DC: World Bank, mimeo

Estache, A., V. Foster, and Q. Wodon, 2002. "Accounting for Poverty in Infrastructure Reform: Learning from Latin America's Experience." World Bank Institute Development Studies, Washington, DC: World Bank

Fay, M., D. Leipziger, Q. Wodon, and T. Yepes, 2005. "Achieving Child Health-Related Millennium Development Goals: The Role of Infrastructure." *World Development* **33**(8): 36–56

Fay, M. and M. Morrison, 2007. "Infrastructure in Latin America and the Caribbean. Recent Developments and Key Challenges." Directions in Development Infrastructure, Washington, DC: World Bank

Fernald, J.G., 1999. "Roads to Prosperity? Assessing the Link between Public Capital and Productivity." *American Economic Review* **89**: 619–38

Galiani, S., P. Gertler, and E. Schargrodsky, 2005. "Water for Life: The Impact of the Privatization of Water Services on Child Mortality." *Journal of Political Economy* **113**: 83–120

Gannon, C. and Z. Liu, 1997. "Poverty and Transport." TWU Discussion Paper **30**, Washington, DC: World Bank

Gramlich, E., 1994. "Infrastructure Investment: A Review Essay." *Journal of Economic Literature* **32**: 1176–96

Guasch, J.L., 2004a. "Presentación: Elementos de Una Estrategia de Desarrollo de la Competitividad en un Entorno Descentralizado." Washington, DC: World Bank, mimeo

2004b. " Granting and Renegotiating Concessions: Do it Right." Washington, DC: World Bank, WBI

Guasch, J.L. and M. Fay, 2003. "Economic Activity, Agglomerations and Logistics in the Mexican Southern States." In *Mexico: Southern States Development Strategy*. Washington, DC: World Bank

Guasch, J.L. and J. Kogan, 2001. "Inventories in Developing Countries: Levels and Determinants – A Red Flag for Competitiveness and Growth." World Bank Policy Research Working Paper 2552

2003. "Just-in-Case Inventories: A Cross Country Analysis." In World Bank Policy Research Working Paper 3012

2006. "Inventories and Logistic Costs in Developing Countries: Levels and Determinants – A Red Flag for Competitiveness and Growth." *Revista de la Competencia y de la Propiedad Intelectual*, Lima

Hausman, W.H., H.L. Lee, and U. Subramanian, 2005. "Global Logistics Indicators, Supply Chain Metrics and Bilateral Trade Patterns. Washington, DC: World Bank, mimeo

Heston, A., R. Summers, and B. Aten, 2002. "Penn World Table Version 6.1." Center for International Comparisons at the University of Pennsylvania, October

Holtz-Eakin, D., 1994. "Public Sector Capital and the Productivity Puzzle." *Review of Economics and Statistics* 76(1): 12–21

Hulten, C., 1996. "Infrastructure Capital and Economic Growth: How Well You Use It May Be More Important than How Much You Have." NBER Working Paper 5847

Jacoby, H., 2002. "Access to Rural Markets and the Benefit of Rural Roads." *The Economics Journal* 110: 713–37

Kaufmann, D., A. Kraay, and P. Zoido-Lobatón, 2002. "Governance Matters." World Bank Policy Research Working Paper 2196

Micco, A. and T. Serebrisky, 2006. "Competition Regimes and Air Transport Costs: The Effects of Open Skies Agreements." *Journal of International Economics* 20: 25–51

Rodrigues, M.A., D.J. Bowersox, and R.J. Calantone, 2005. "Estimation of Global and National Logistics Expenditures: 2002 Data Update." *Journal of Business Logistics* 26(2): 1–16

Röller, L. and L. Waverman, 2001. "Telecommunications Infrastructure and Economic Development: A Simultaneous Approach." *American Economic Review* 91: 9009–23

Smith, D., A. Gordon, K. Meadows, and K. Zwick, 2001. "Livelihood Diversification in Uganda: Patterns and Determinants of Change Across Two Rural Districts." *Food Policy* 26: 421–35

Soloaga, I., J.S. Wilson, and A. Mejia, 2007. "Moving Forward Faster: Trade Facilitation Reforms and Mexican Competitiveness." World Bank Policy Research Working Paper **3953**

Wilson, J.S., C.L. Mann, and T. Otsuki, 2003. "Trade Facilitation and Economic Development: Measuring the Impact." World Bank Policy Research Working Paper **2988**

    2004. "Assessing the Potential Benefit of Trade Facilitation: A Global Perspective." World Bank Policy Research Working Paper **3224**

World Bank, 1994. *World Development Report 1994: Infrastructure for Development*. New York: Oxford University Press

    2000. Project Appraisal Document **P065779**. *Mexico, Federal Highway Maintenance Project*. Washington, DC: World Bank

    2001. Project Appraisal Document **P068968**. *Bolivia, Road Rehabilitation & Maintenance Project*. Washington, DC: World Bank

    2002. Report **22803-AR**. *Small and Medium-Sized Enterprises in Argentina. A Potential Engine for Economic Growth and Employment*. Washington, DC: World Bank

    2005a. *World Development Report 2005: A Better Investment Climate for Everyone*. New York: Oxford University Press for the World Bank

    2005b. Informe Estratégico (REDI-SR). *El Salvador: Desarrollos Económicos Recientes en Infraestructura*. Washington, DC: World Bank

    2006a. Reporte No. 35061-CO. *Infraestructura Logística de Calidad para la Competitividad de Colombia*. Washington, DC: World Bank

    2006b. Informe No. 36606-AR. *Argentina: El Desafío de Reducir los Costos Logísticos ante el Crecimiento del Comercio Exterior*. Washington, DC: World Bank

    2006c. Argentina: *Infrastructure for Growth and Poverty Alleviation*. Washington, DC: World Bank

    2007. *Doing Business Report 2007: How to Reform*. Washington, DC: World Bank

7.1 | High logistics costs and poor infrastructure for merchandise transportation: an alternative view

RONALD FISCHER

This alternative view is meant to provide critical comments on Gonzalez, Guasch, and Serebrisky's chapter 7. I shall argue that the chapter does a good job of describing the challenge and providing suggestions to improve on the present situation. Since the authors are unable to evaluate the social return of their proposals, they present simulation exercises using the best available data to gauge the size of the returns on their policy recommendations, which I believe is appropriate in this case. Except for some points of emphasis, I do not find any important omissions in the chapter's assessments, but believe there are conceptual problems in terms of the organization of the chapter. I would like to add some additional details, change the emphasis of some recommendations, and provide some comments.

1 General assesment

Gonzalez, Guasch, and Serebrisky's chapter 7 defines their challenge as that of reducing logistic costs in the LAC region. They acknowledge that there are three aspects to these high logistic costs: (1) access to basic infrastructure services; (2) logistic costs and inventories; and (3) trade facilitation. It is clear that access to basic infrastructure services is a key challenge in the fight against poverty in the LAC region, especially because of its contribution to sustainable growth. The authors point out that better access provides direct benefits to the population and, by reducing logistic costs, are key ingredients in development and competitiveness.

The authors provide data that show the principal determinants of the relatively high logistic costs in the LAC region, and their effects on competitiveness and growth in the continent. There is no question, given the data provided by the authors, that logistic costs are higher in the LAC region than in South Asia. Moreover, they show how the lack of reliable infrastructure services affects development not only directly, but also indirectly, by increasing the fraction of goods not reaching the market, and by increasing the inventory requirements as compared to the average for OECD countries. Moreover, they quote studies showing that lack of infrastructure substantially reduces the growth rate (Calderón and Servén 2006). Even though I am convinced the effect exists, I have some doubts about its size, since it seems to me that the impacts are excessive. According to the calculations cited by the authors, simultaneously raising the density of main telephone lines, power-generating capacity, and the road and railways system from the bottom quintile to the top quintile of the world distribution should increase growth by 5.7% annually, independently of any other changes to the country's economy. But does it make sense, and would it be productive, to increase the road infrastructure levels of Argentina, a sparsely populated country, to those of a densely populated country such as Korea (in the example cited by the authors)?

The authors go on to describe the impact of inventory costs and of poor business logistics. The question here is whether logistic costs and inventories are independent factors, or are caused by lack of infrastructure and barriers to trade (plus excessive and inefficient regulation, which the authors mention elsewhere). In that sense, inventories and firms' logistic costs are a derived feature of lack of infrastructure, poor regulations (and perhaps deficiencies in contract compliance, a problem of the judicial system), lack of competition, impediments to trade, and excessive regulations.

Nevertheless, they show that costs that may be classified as logistic are substantial. In particular, these problems lead to higher inventory levels, and since inventories tend to be costlier in developing countries (higher capital costs, storage-quality problems), this overhead can reach almost 20% of product value. It is difficult to believe that, under competitive conditions, a firm can survive in the long run if it is inefficient given the prevailing conditions, so it might be that these additional costs are an efficient response to the economic environment. Under this interpretation, the section of the chapter dedicated to the analysis of these costs is really an exploratory analysis of the mechanisms by which infrastructure deficits, inefficient regulations, trade impediments, and lack of competition lead to increased costs.

Finally, the authors study the effects of trade impediments. In order to perform the analysis they classify them into four categories: (i) port efficiency, (ii) customs efficiency, (iii) regulatory inefficiency (which I believe should appear in its own category, instead of under logistic costs), and (iv) service sector infrastructure (again, this is already included). They proceed to estimate the importance of these costs by regression. Next, they simulate the effects of having countries with trade impediments reduce these barriers to the average level of the seventy-five countries in their sample, showing that this improvement leads to increases of 9.7% in their trade, on average. For LAC countries, the positive effects of trade facilitation policies would be much larger, with a 20% increase in exports and 16.1% increase in imports.

On the basis of the evidence they present, the authors provide a set of solutions:

(1) Spending more and more efficiently in infrastructure
(2) Bundling infrastructure investments with policies aimed at improving efficiency of service logistic providers
(3) Adopting policies to improve trade facilitation.

All of these are reasonable, and I analyze them in more detail below. The chapter does not provide an overall estimate of the benefits of these policies but this makes sense, given the scope of the policies and the diffuseness of their effects.

2 Additional aspects

In this section, I review in more detail chapter 7's various recommendations, extending the analysis and using additional evidence from the literature.

Infrastructure recommendations

A magnificent high-road cannot be made through a desert country, where there is little or no commerce, or merely because it happens to lead to the country villa of the intendant of the province, or to that of some great lord, to whom the intendant finds it convenient to make his court. A great bridge cannot be thrown over a river at a place where nobody passes, or merely to embellish the view from the windows of a neighbouring palace; things which sometimes happen in countries, where works of this kind are carried on by any other revenue than that which they themselves are capable of affording. (Adam Smith, *Wealth of Nations*)

For this issue, the detailed recommendations of the authors are:

(i) Increase spending in infrastructure
(ii) Users must pay a higher fraction of infrastructure costs, creating safety nets for those unable to pay
(iii) Spending must improve, with a better allocation of resources to maintenance and no building of "white elephants"
(iv) Institutions must be developed for project selection.

There is very little to quarrel with in these recommendations, and I only miss a proposal regarding the role of local and regional interests in infrastructure proposals. But perhaps this can be achieved as a consequence of the proposal of direct payments for a larger fraction of the services of infrastructure (including, presumably tolling of roads, true costs of water supply, etc.). Though these payments are usually unpopular, and are often accused of discriminating against the poor, they can be very effective in delivering good services. In a report of the Asian Development Bank (Cook *et al.* 2004) which reviews the literature and various country studies of the impact of transport and energy infrastructure on poverty reduction, they conclude, among other things, that whether these investments provide benefits to the poor depends on the quality of the services offered. Similarly, in a paper reviewed by the authors of the present alternative view (Briceño-Garmendia, Estache, and Shafik 2004), which reviews the literature, they cite Rioja (1999, 2003), who claims that there is a misallocation of resources in infrastructure investment, with just one-third of investment dedicated to maintenance. This has a large cost in terms of long-run GDP. More specifically, public infrastructure is only 74% as effective in LAC countries as in industrial countries. In the case of Uganda, Reinikka and Svensson (1999) show that the poor public supply of electricity leads to less productive investment.

The evidence is therefore consistent with the fact that the allocation of resources to public infrastructure is not only insufficient, but is inefficient. One source of inefficiency, identified already by Adam Smith, is that centralized funding and direction does not necessarily lead to useful projects. It is also clear that the private sector can be a very efficient provider of infrastructure services under competition, as shown by the example of the cellphone industry in under-developed countries.

In the case of transportation, perhaps the best option is, in the case of major roads, to have users pay fees that at least cover the maintenance costs of the project. This provides the following benefits: local and central pressures on the operator if she does not provide sufficient maintenance, a test of sorts for the social value of investment, since the private value is usually smaller than the social value (especially given that the "poor are relatively unconcerned about the potential environmental impacts of transport or energy infrastructure" (Cook *et al.* 2004). This reduces the possibility of "white elephants," at least in maintenance projects. Moreover the central funds that are released from these obligations can be used to improve the quality of those roads that do not generate enough income to even collect user fees, but that can be economically very important, and can alleviate rural isolation.[1]

The authors fail to mention PPPs as an alternative approach to financing infrastructure, especially for roads and highways, or even for financing their maintenance. This lack is surprising, because Guasch has written often about PPPs, their advantages and their problems (Guasch 2001; Guasch, Laffont, and Straub 2002; Sirtaine *et al.* 2004, for example). While PPPs have clear problems (see below), they are often an improvement on other types of financing of projects (Engel, Fischer, and Galetovic 2003, 2006), where we show that even though

---

[1] In order to avoid the following observation of Adam Smith:

> In France, however, the great post-roads, the roads which make the communication between the principal towns of the kingdom, are in general kept in good order; and, in some provinces, are even a good deal superior to the greater part of the turnpike roads of England. But what we call the cross roads, that is, the far greater part of the roads in the country, are entirely neglected, and are in many places absolutely impassable for any heavy carriage. The proud minister of an ostentatious court, may frequently take pleasure in executing a work of splendour and magnificence, such as a great highway, which is frequently seen by the principal nobility, whose applauses not only flatter his vanity, but even contribute to support his interest at court. But to execute a great number of little works, in which nothing that can be done can make any great appearance, or excite the smallest degree of admiration in any traveller, and which, in short, have nothing to recommend them but their extreme utility, is a business which appears, in every respect, too mean and paltry to merit the attention of so great a magistrate. Under such an administration therefore, such works are almost always entirely neglected.

PPPs in highway projects suffer from many problems, they are preferable to public provision because they are implemented faster and usually at lower cost (notwithstanding the example of Mexico during the early 1990s). This does not mean that PPPs should be used to alleviate the government's budget constraints, since these projects usually do impose intertemporal obligations on the government (Engel, Fischer, and Galetovic 2007).

Another important source of logistic costs is port inefficiency. Clark, Dollar, and Micco (2004), show that improving port efficiency from the 25th to the 75th percentile reduces shipping costs by 12% and that inefficient ports are comparable to an increase in costs equivalent to being 60% farther away from markets, for the average country. Inefficient ports also increase handling costs, which are one of the components of shipping costs. Finally, they show that reductions in country inefficiencies, associated with transport costs, from the 25th to 75th percentiles imply an increase in bilateral trade of around 25%.

Ports can improve substantially under private management. In the case of Chile, the effect of changing from a state-run operation to having private operators in ports led to large improvements in productivity, and further progress arrived when port terminals were concessioned to single companies (Fischer and Serra 2005). The results were substantial reductions in port costs due to increased throughput (table 7.1.1).

Table 7.1.2 shows a comparison between port costs in different countries, which demonstrates the benefits of the Chilean program of port franchising.

With regard to problems that could appear from following the authors' recommendations, rapidly increased spending in infrastructure can lead to serious difficulties. A large increase in spending may overwhelm the ability of the public works bureaucracy, leading to projects that are badly designed and need extensive renegotiation of construction contracts. This, in turn, may lead to increased corruption.

Another danger, in the case where public works such as roads are franchised to private operators, as in PPPs, is that the government may use the procedure to expand expenditure without being subject to the usual budgetary constraints, so they can be used to gain electoral advantage with a public which does not perceive the future costs of the policy, again leading to badly designed projects and "white elephants" (Engel, Fischer, and Galetovic 2006).

Table 7.1.1 *Throughput (boxes/hour/ship): Chilean ports*

Terminal	1999	2003
Mono, Valparaíso	26	75
Mono, San Antonio	25	75
Multi, Valparaíso	18	36
Multi, San Antonio	18	36

Note: One terminal at each port continued to operate in the original "multioperator" scheme, while the other was franchised to a "monoperator."
Source: Sistema Portuario de Chile (2005).

Table 7.1.2 *Cost of transferring a 20 ft in the port*

Region	Cost $
USA	312
Africa	256
LAC	174
Far East	164
East Europe	144
Australasia	130
Northern Europe	120
Southern Europe	113
Middle East/South Asia	106
Southeast Asia	92
Chile	85

Source: Drewry Shipping Consultants (October 2002).

In any case, the authors showcase simulations that help them estimate the benefits that could result from following their recommendations. The effects can be substantial, with a return of over 25% in their examples. It is not clear that all infrastructure improvements will be that productive, given some of the problems detailed above, but there is certainly a large potential for improvement in infrastructure provision which lowers logistic costs.

I would like to emphasize the important role of the recommendation for the creation of institutions or organisms for project selection (even in the case of PPPs). Public works are a favorite resort of governments for political purposes, and the cost of misallocated resources in poor countries can be important. Thus, a call for increased infrastructure investment requires an institution that insures that public investment satisfies social cost-benefit criteria.[2]

Logistic cost recommendations

As already mentioned, I have certain qualms about the existence of an issue with the inefficient logistics at the level of the firm. Under competition, firms cannot afford to be inefficient, and perhaps some forms of observed inefficiency are the appropriate response to some other problem, such as regulatory failure, cartelized or monopolized provision of services (truck services in Colombia, for example), or if there is low or no access to infrastructure services.

The proposals in this section consist of improving sector regulation and deregulating where appropriate. There is no question that these proposals are correct and point in the right direction. However, their level of generality makes them difficult to evaluate, especially given the potential for opposition by entrenched groups. This is perhaps the weakest part of the chapter, because this type of recommendation has been provided to LAC governments for the last twenty years (at least). While there have been some successes, the recommendation continues to be applicable, indicating the difficulties in implementing a solution. The main example of the gains is a simulation of a reduction in the logistic costs of Peru (table 7.1.1). It shows the extent of the potential benefits, but not how to achieve them and if in fact if they are possible (orographic conditions may make it impossible to have a reduction of logistic costs of that magnitude in Peru).

Trade facilitation recommendations

In this case, the recommendation consists of various limited proposals: (i) creating an export development agency to promote trade, (ii) supporting the modernization of local firms, (iii) creating a national

---

[2] From the middle 1970s to the late 1990s, Chile had a successful system of this type. Even there, the pressure of short-term politics managed to coopt the system, which now approves projects according to the whims of government.

logistics council, (iv) modernization and simplification of customs procedures, (v) multimodality law and improved access to ports, (vi) more
emphasis on the supply of required logistical services, and (vii) the
creation of regional trade facilitation committees. All of these recommendations are commendable, and none requires large expenditures,
so I agree with all of them without qualification.

The example of Chile is interesting in this regard, given that it has
overcome its geographical disadvantages and become an extremely
open economy. Chile has achieved respectable progress on points
(i), since a trade facilitation agency has existed for almost three
decades, (v), with port franchises and new private ports, which have
improved efficiency and reduced waiting times for shipments, (vi), in
part provided by the private sector in response to demand (cooling
reefers, testing and certification) and via PPPs, in the case of logistic
terminals and dry ports; these have been very successful, which may
explain why, even though Chile is farther away from demand centers than most LAC countries, and has a rugged geography, it has the
lowest logistic costs in the sample of LAC countries provided by the
authors. Chile has not been quite as successful in the modernization
of custom procedures, apparently due to leadership deficiencies at the
customs office. As regards supporting the modernization of local firms,
the most successful effort has been driven by the tax office, which has
begun to require companies to deliver their tax information to its web
site, thus pressing for the adoption of information technologies.

3 Conclusions

Chapter 7 provides a fairly complete answer to the challenge of reducing logistic costs in the LAC region in order to encourage growth. I have
some differences in terms of the organization of the chapter, but these
are minor complaints. The authors have assembled a large collection
of difficult to obtain data (the size of the inventory costs is especially
convincing) and use them to great effect, showing the importance of
logistic costs to growth and development. Their recommendations are
reasonable, and one could find fault only with the degree of generality in the case of the second. The objectives put forward are not
easy to achieve, because in many cases they go against vested interests
which would prefer the current situation. The measures are also technocratic and liberal, and they may face opposition in countries that

have been disappointed by the failures of the 1990s experiments in liberalism. However, the example of Chile, which has gone the farthest in implementing these measures, shows that they can be effective and that it is possible to design a protection network for the poorest sections of society, while growing quickly.

Bibliography

Briceño-Garmendia, C., A. Estache, and N. Shafik, 2004. "Infrastructure Services in Developing Countries: Access, Quality, Costs and Policy Reform." World Bank Policy Research Working Paper **3468**

Calderón, César and Luis Servén, 2006. "The Effects of Infrastructure Development on Growth and Income Distribution." Central Bank of Chile Working Papers **270**

Canning, David and Esra Bennathan, 1999. "The Social Rate of Return on Infrastructure Investments."

Clark, X., D. Dollar, and A. Micco, 2004. Port Efficiency, Maritime Transport Costs, and Bilateral Trade. *Journal of Development Economics* **75**(2): 417–50

Cook, Cynthia C., Tyrrell Duncan, Somchai Jitsuchon, Anil K. Sharma, and Wu Guobao, 2004. "Assessing the Impact of Transport and Energy Infrastructure on Poverty Reduction – Reta 5947." New York: Asian Development Bank, June

Engel, E., R. Fischer, and A. Galetovic, 2003. "Franchising Highways in Latin America." *Economia* (**4**)1: 129–64

 2006a. "Privatizing Highways in the United States." *Review of Industrial Organization* **29**(1): 27–53

 2006b. "Renegotiation Without Holdup: Anticipating Spending and Infrastructure Concessions." NBER Working Paper **12399**

 2007. "The Basic Public Finance of Public-Private Partnerships." NBER

Fischer, R. and D. Serra, 2004. "Efectos de la privatización de servicios públicos en Chile, Casos Sanitario, Electricidad y Telecomunicaciones." Serie de estudios económicos y sociales **R1-04-017**, BID

Gonzalez, J., J. L. Guasch, and T. Serebrisky, 2007. "High Logistics Costs and Poor Infrastructure for Merchandise Transportation." Chapter 7 in this volume

Guasch, J.L., 2001. "Concessions and Regulatory Design: Determinants of Performance – Fifteen Years of Evidence." Washington, DC: World Bank

Guasch, J., J. Laffont, and S. Straub, 2002. "Renegotiation of Concession Contracts in Latin America." World Bank Policy Research Paper **3011**

Reinikka, Ritva and Jakob Svensson, 1999. "How Inadequate Provision of Public Infrastructure and Services Affects Private Investment." Washington, DC: World Bank

Rioja, Felix, 1999. "Productiveness and Welfare Implications of Public Infrastructure: A Dynamic Two-Sector General Equilibrium Analysis." *Journal of Development Economics* 58(2): 387–404

2003. "Filling Potholes: Macroeconomic Effects of Maintenance vs. New Investments in Public Infrastructure." *Journal of Public Economics* 87(9–10): 2281–2304

Sirtaine, Sophie, Maria Elena Pinglo, J. Luis Guasch, and Vivien Foster, 2004. "How Profitable are Infrastructure Concessions in Latin America? Empirical Evidence and Regulatory Implications." WB Group, August

Sistema Portuario de Chile, 2005

8 | Reducing poverty in the LAC region

SEBASTIAN GALIANI[*]

1 Introduction

Poverty still is one of the central problems in the LAC region. As measured by international poverty lines, approximately one out of every five people in the region is poor. The elimination of poverty thus continues to be one of the main challenges facing the region and remains at the top of its policy agenda.

Clearly, one way to reduce absolute poverty is by stimulating economic growth. In reality, it is unlikely that poverty can be reduced to any significant degree without persistent economic growth. Ultimately, an economy that grows on a sustained basis is an economy in which wages will be rising, thereby lifting households out of poverty. In the LAC region, Chile is an impressive success story in terms of poverty reduction. Between 1987 and 1998, real *per capita* income increased at an annual rate of 5.7% while the poverty rate dropped by 60%.

Even though growth is fundamental in the battle against poverty, it is unlikely to be enough, even when growth is very rapid. This is especially true in the presence of high levels of inequality such as those existing in the LAC region (Besley and Burgess 2003). Cost-effective redistribution is also needed to succeed in eliminating poverty.

The standard framework within which economists and policy-makers have traditionally thought about redistribution is that of an

* I gratefully acknowledge the research assistance of Maximiliano Appendino, Gabriela Farfan, and Paulo Somaini. I have also benefited greatly from conversations about this project with G. Cruces, F. Ferreira, P. Gertler, and M. Torero. G. Cruces and S. Younger provided me with very valuable comments. Paulo Somaini also contributed excellent comments and suggestions.

equity/efficiency trade off in which society's redistributive goals must be weighed against the supply-side distortions that taxes and transfers create in the economy. However, recognition that the earning capabilities of households are not fixed, but can instead be altered by investments, and taking into account the role of missing and imperfect markets, the importance of this trade off fades. Indeed, in many cases, redistribution is actually found to be efficient (Mookherjee 2006).

Poverty is an intrinsically dynamic phenomenon. Poor people are locked into a low-level asset (or capability) trap that results in their exclusion from participating in social and economic affairs on an equal footing with the rest of society. Hence, poverty reduction efforts, in the long run, must seek to provide incentives that will encourage the poor to acquire capabilities and assets that will enable poor households to escape poverty in the future.

Thus, at the micro level, we favor interventions that, via redistribution, increase the current consumption of the poor, alleviating poverty. In fact, redistribution is a critical component of an effective welfare state that is missing in the LAC region. We also favor interventions that cause investments in human capital that in the future would help pull poor households out of the actual asset trap in which they are caught. These interventions, by improving the current and future consumption of the poorest members of society, will also reduce inequality in the region.

2 Poverty in the LAC region

Although many authors have expressed serious doubts about whether there is some degree of discontinuity in the distribution of welfare, with poverty on one side and an absence of poverty on the other (see Deaton 1997), the poverty count is clearly a useful statistic, and it is difficult to imagine engaging in discussions about poverty without it.

In table 8.1, we summarize the most recent international comparisons of absolute poverty conducted by Chen and Ravallion (2007). The World Bank currently defines the extremely poor population as being composed of those individuals who are living on no more than US$1.08 per person per day, as measured by the 1993 PPP exchange rate. This poverty line is based on a deliberately conservative definition of poverty and is on par with the poverty lines typical of low-income countries (World Bank 1990; Ravallion, Datt, and van de Walle 1991). Alternatively, Chen and Ravallion (2007) also calculate poverty rates

Table 8.1 *Poverty around the world, 1981–2004 (%)*

Region	Extreme poverty rates (US$1.08 per day)		Poverty rates (US$2.15 per day)	
	1981	2004	1981	2004
LAC	10.77	8.64	28.45	22.17
Total	**40.14**	**18.09**	**66.96**	**47.55**
East Asia and the Pacific	57.73	9.05	84.80	36.58
Eastern Europe and Central Asia	0.70	0.94	4.60	9.79
Middle East and North Africa	5.08	1.47	29.16	19.70
South Asia	51.75	34.33	88.53	77.12
Sub-Saharan Africa	42.26	41.10	74.52	71.97

Sources: Chen and Ravallion (2007).

by region using a US$2.15 poverty line. This provides a more meaningful measure of poverty in middle-income countries and, as such, is better suited to the LAC region.

Although these international poverty lines have been criticized by many, their simplicity, and the lack of a better alternative, have made them the standard for international poverty comparisons. Nevertheless, before we move on to analyze the data presented in table 8.1, it must be noted that PPP exchange rates, although an essential means of harmonizing poverty lines across countries and time, are an infrequently updated tool that is an unsuitable yardstick for gauging the consumption levels of the extremely poor (see Deaton 2006). Additionally, because prices are higher in urban than in rural areas, adjustments in these lines are desirable.[1] Unfortunately, not all countries have the necessary micro-data on household expenditure or consumption. Household income is used when data on consumption are not available, but this is clearly a poorer measurement of welfare at the individual level (see Deaton and Zaidi 2002) and makes the discernment of cross-section contrasts more difficult. Finally, and inevitably, there are differences across surveys in terms of the way in which income and consumption are captured.

---

[1] Indeed, Chen and Ravallion (2007) also present poverty rates for rural and urban areas separately using a subsample of countries for which this division is possible.

Bearing these caveats in mind, the reader will see that, as shown in table 8.1, extreme poverty, when aggregated across regions, declined dramatically between 1981 and 2004. The overall poverty count, in the aggregate, is heavily influenced by what has happened in India and China, where very strong growth has led to a large drop in the share of the population living in extreme poverty. Even so, almost one out of every five people in the developing world is extremely poor.

There was also a large drop in the poverty rate during the same period, although the decline was proportionally smaller than the decrease in the extreme poverty rate. This, to some extent, reflects the fact that many of the people who succeeded in lifting themselves out of extreme poverty have not yet managed to raise their income levels above the poverty line.

These data appear to indicate that extreme poverty is not that widespread in the LAC region, but that poverty still is. Poverty did not decrease a great deal in the region during this period, although it did remain on a downward trend (particularly as measured by the poverty rate). Additionally, the LAC region displays historically high levels of income inequality. In fact, at least since the 1960s, inequality in the LAC countries has been higher than in any other region of the world. With the exception of countries in SSA, the differences in terms of the Gini coefficient of inequality between the LAC and other regions are large (see, among others, Gasparini 2004).

In table 8.2 we present the latest available estimates of the LAC region's poverty rates, by country. On average, these statistics are quite similar to those presented in table 8.1. Clearly, poverty rates are much higher in rural areas than in urban ones. The extreme poverty rate for rural areas is approximately three times higher than the corresponding urban rate, while the rural poverty rate is slightly greater than two and half times the urban rate. Nonetheless, the number of poor people is more or less evenly distributed between rural and urban areas, since the ratio of urban to rural population in the LAC region (slightly above 3:1) offsets these differences in poverty rates. As in all other regions, poverty tends to be concentrated among young people. The average poverty rate for children under 6 years of age in the region as a whole is about 1.9 higher than the rate for adults.

Poverty is also concentrated among the indigenous population. For fifteen countries for which data on ethnicity are available, the ratio

Table 8.2 *LAC poverty rates (%)*

Country	Survey Year	International extreme poverty line			International poverty line		
		Urban	Rural	National	Urban	Rural	National
Argentina[a]	2005	3.9	n.a.	3.9	11.6	n.a.	11.6
Bolivia	2002	7.7	51.6	23.7	26.2	72.6	43.1
Brazil	2004	5.9	12.2	6.9	14.8	31.9	17.7
Chile	2003	1.4	1.7	1.4	4.7	8.0	5.1
Colombia	2004	12.5	21.2	14.8	20.9	40.8	26.2
Costa Rica	2004	2.5	5.6	3.8	5.5	12.6	8.5
Dominican Republic	2005	1.6	3.4	2.2	9.2	13.7	10.8
Ecuador	2003	9.1	20.2	12.9	25.5	47.6	33.1
El Salvador	2004	8.3	28.3	16.3	26.4	56.9	38.7
Guatemala	2004	8.0	16.8	12.8	23.1	44.7	34.9
Honduras	2005	7.0	35.1	19.8	21.2	59.6	38.7
Mexico	2004	3.5	17.3	6.7	11.7	36.8	17.5
Nicaragua	2001	10.7	27.6	17.6	35.7	59.9	45.6
Panama	2004	2.2	12.6	6.1	6.2	32.2	15.8
Paraguay	2004	4.0	18.4	10.2	14.8	40.6	26.0
Peru	2003	3.5	20.9	9.7	13.9	59.8	30.3
Uruguay[a]	2005	0.6	n.a.	0.6	6.0	n.a.	6.0
Venezuela[a]	2004	16.2	n.a.	16.2	38.7	n.a.	38.7
Average		6.2	17.5	8.6	16.1	39.2	21.1

Notes: [a] Poverty rates are estimated using a constructed homogenous *per capita* household income that varies across countries and includes all the typical sources of current income (see www.depeco.economo.umlp.edu.ar/cedlas/sedlac). It is well known that household consumption is a better proxy for wellbeing than household income. However, only a few countries in the LAC region routinely conduct national household surveys that collect information on expenditures. Household income has been adjusted by imputing implicit rents from home-ownership and by area (rural/urban) of residence (see Gasparini 2007). See also Gasparini (2007) for a discussion of the treatment of missing incomes.

We use the urban rates to approximate the national rates. In the case of Argentina and Uruguay, most of the population resides in urban areas.

Source: The statistics shown in this table were obtained by processing microdata from household surveys and the constitute part of the Socio-Economic Database for Latin America and the Caribbean (SEDLAC) developed by the Center for Distributive, Labor, and Social Research (CEDLAS).

Table 8.3 *Poverty and education*

Country	25 years						25–59 years					
	Average years of schooling			At least complete Secondary school (%)			Average years of schooling			At least complete Secondary school (%)		
	Poor	Non-poor	All	Poor	Non-poor	All	Poor	Non-poor	All	Poor	Non-poor	All
Argentina	9.0	11.7	11.4	26	63	59	7.6	10.8	10.5	15	52	49
Bolivia	5.9	10.7	9.1	17	57	44	4.7	9.2	7.5	9	41	29
Brazil	5.3	8.9	8.4	14	51	45	4.0	7.5	7.1	9	37	33
Chile	9.0	12.4	12.3	22	73	71	8.2	10.9	10.8	22	54	53
Colombia	7.7	9.7	9.4	41	59	56	5.8	8.4	7.8	23	44	39
Costa Rica	6.1	9.3	9.2	18	40	39	5.5	8.4	8.2	9	34	32
Dominican Republic	8.8	9.9	9.8	32	48	46	5.4	8.4	8.1	11	32	30
Ecuador	7.2	10.3	9.5	19	50	42	6.2	9.6	8.6	15	44	36
El Salvador	5.9	9.8	8.6	18	50	40	4.2	8.2	6.9	10	36	28
Guatemala	3.3	6.6	5.8	6	29	24	2.2	5.4	4.5	2	22	16
Honduras	4.3	7.6	6.5	3	19	14	3.4	7.4	6.0	3	24	17
Mexico	6.1	10.2	9.8	12	37	35	4.9	8.8	8.3	6	31	27
Nicaragua	4.9	7.5	6.5	9	29	22	3.6	6.7	5.5	6	24	17
Panama	6.0	11.0	10.2	12	57	50	5.6	10.2	9.7	11	48	44
Paraguay	6.3	10.0	9.2	15	43	38	4.9	8.1	7.5	5	29	24
Peru	6.2	10.7	9.7	22	72	62	4.5	9.5	8.3	14	60	49
Uruguay	7.2	11.0	10.8	4[a]	45	43	6.8	10.1	9.9	3[a]	40	38
Venezuela	8.0	10.5	9.7	12	32	25	6.7	9.5	8.6	7	25	20
Average	6.1	9.7	9.1	16	49	44	4.8	8.4	7.9	10	37	33

Notes: Survey years are the same as those shown in table 8.1.

[a] Sample sizes are very small and we should not give much confidence to these point estimates.

Source: The statistics shown in this table were obtained by processing microdata from household surveys and constitute part of the Socio-Economic Database for Latin America and the Caribbean (SEDLAC) developed by the Center for Distributive, Labor, and Social Research (CEDLAS).

of the poverty rates for Caucasians and non-Caucasians is, on average (unweighted across countries), 2.4 (see Busso, Cicowiez, and Gasparini 2005). This should not be surprising, since a majority of the indigenous people in the LAC region still live in rural areas (Busso, Cicowiez, and Gasparini 2005).

Education and fertility

Education is the most important dimension of human capital and, hence, plays a salient role in the determination of income. In table 8.3 we present the average years of schooling for both the adult population at large and individuals at the lower limit of that age group (i.e. 25-year-olds). The statistics are then further divided into poor and non-poor populations (using the US$2.15 poverty line as the discriminator).

Education levels in the LAC region are still low. The adult population at large has completed an average of only 7.9 years of schooling, which is roughly equivalent to a complete primary school education. Young cohorts have completed more years of schooling and, at the margin, have finished an estimated 9.1 years of instruction, which is still well below the 12 years of schooling needed to acquire a secondary education. Among the poor, school attainment is substantially lower: the overall population has had only 4.8 years of schooling, while 25-year-olds have completed 6.1 years of education.

The proportion of people who have a secondary or higher education is also low. At the margin, it is estimated to be 44%. However, among the poor, only 16% of the young population has at least completed secondary school. Indeed, education has lagged behind international standards in the LAC region ever since its countries won their independence (see Mariscal and Sokoloff 2000).

In addition, there still are large racial differences in educational attainment through the region. In contrast, with respect to gender women have made significant advances relative to men. Among younger cohorts in most countries, women are at an educational advantage, at least with respect to years of education attained (see Duryea *et al.* 2007).

A related issue is child labor. Unfortunately, in some countries (mainly in rural areas), a large percentage of children still work. On average, 10% of children between 10 and 14 years of age work in the LAC region and, in rural areas, the rate rises to 23%.

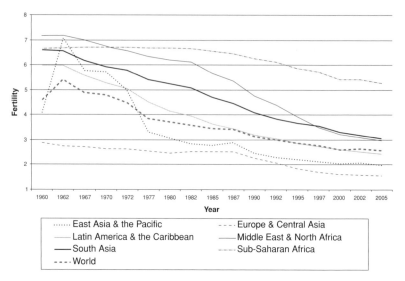

Figure 8.1 Fertility levels, by region
Source: IMF-World Economic Outlook

Fertility is strongly related to education and child labor. It tends to be higher among poor households within a society and, across countries, households with higher average fertility rates tend to have lower average incomes. In the aftermath of the Second World War, age-specific mortality rates declined, and population growth consequently increased in most low-income countries. The continuing decline in infant and child mortality in the 1960s caused the proportion of children in these low-income populations to increase. After a half-century, the empirical record shows that birth rates have declined rapidly in most parts of the low-income world since the 1960s, with the number of children born per woman falling by at least half in most countries (see figure 8.1). The LAC region, in particular, has witnessed an impressive drop in fertility rates since that decade and now has one of the lowest fertility rates of all developing regions. Fertility still varies substantially across countries, however, as well as within countries by education and income levels.

Child health

Health is another important dimension of human capital. Infant and child mortality indicators have evolved satisfactorily in the LAC region

Table 8.4 *Infant and child mortality rates, 1960–2005 (%)*

Country	Under-5 mortality rate					Infant mortality rate				
	1960	1980	1990	2000	2005	1960	1980	1990	2000	2005
Argentina	73	41	29	19	18	61	36	26	17	15
Bolivia	255	175	125	84	65	152	115	89	63	52
Brazil	177	86	60	39	33	115	67	50	35	31
Chile	155	45	21	11	10	118	35	18	10	8
Colombia	122	51	35	26	21	77	37	26	20	17
Costa Rica	123	31	18	14	12	87	26	16	13	11
Dominican Republic	149	92	65	40	31	102	71	50	33	26
Ecuador	178	98	57	32	25	107	64	43	27	22
El Salvador	191	118	60	35	27	129	84	47	29	23
Honduras	204	103	59	43	40	137	75	44	33	31
Jamaica	74	34	20	20	20	56	28	17	17	17
Mexico	134	74	46	30	27	94	56	37	25	22
Nicaragua	193	113	68	43	37	130	82	52	34	30
Panama	88	46	34	26	24	58	34	27	20	19
Paraguay	94	61	41	27	23	68	46	33	23	20
Peru	239	121	78	41	27	160	86	58	33	23
Uruguay	55	42	23	15	15	47	37	21	14	14
Venezuela	79	46	33	25	21	59	37	27	21	18
Unweighted average	144	77	48	32	26	98	56	38	26	22

Source: UNICEF web page, www.unicef.ore.

since the 1960s. Even in the 1980s there was a large drop in both rates. Not only did average mortality rates decline, but the variance across countries was substantially reduced as well (see table 8.4). For example, between 1960 and 2005, the infant mortality rate decreased by 77%, on average, while the standard deviation of the rates across countries declined by 71%. Notwithstanding, the actual levels are still high and should be reduced further.

Let us now consider the nutritional situation in the LAC region. Under-nutrition and micronutrient deficiencies contribute substantially to the global burden of disease. Under-nutrition and infectious diseases exist in a threatening synergy. They further exacerbate poverty

Table 8.5 *Nutrition indicators, 2005 (%)*

Region	Prevalence of LBW[a] infants, by region (1)	Estimated prevalence of under-weight[b] children age 0–4 years (2)	Estimated prevalence of stunted[c] children age 0–4 years (3)	Estimated prevalence of wasted[d] children age 0–4 years (4)
LAC	10	5	11.8	1.5
Developing countries	17	22.7	26.5	8.3
Africa	15	24.5	34.5	9.5
Asia	19	24.8	25.7	8.9

Notes: [a] LBW is defined as under 2,500 grams.
[b] "Underweight" is defined as $z < 2$ standard deviations of the weight-for-age median value of the NCHS/WHO international reference data. For further details, see annex 4 of UN (2005).
[c] "Stunted" is defined as $z < 2$ standard deviations of the height-for-age median value of the NCHS/WHO international reference data. For further details, see annex 4 of UN (2005).
[d] "Wasted" is defined as $z < 2$ standard deviations of the weight-for-height median value of the NCHS/WHO international reference data. For further details, see annex 4 of UN (2005).
Source: UN (2005).

through lost wages, increased health costs and – most insidiously – impaired intellectual development that can significantly reduce the future earning potential of the poor.

Nutrients provided by food combine with other factors, including the health of each person, to produce each individual's nutritional status. Many poor nutritional outcomes begin in utero. A number of maternal factors have been shown to be significant determinants of intrauterine growth retardation (IUGR). IUGR is measured as the prevalence of newborns falling below the 10th percentile for weight, taking their gestational age into account. Since gestational age is rarely known, IUGR is often proxied by low birth weight (LBW) (the percentage of newborns who weigh less than 2,500 grams). Column (1) in table 8.5 indicates that the situation in the LAC region is far from satisfactory since, although the prevalence of LBW infants is substantially below the average for developing countries, it is still 10%.

The nutritional status of children is often characterized by comparing the weights or heights at a specific age and sex with the distribution of observed weights or heights in a reference population of presumed healthy children of the same age and sex. Three indicators are widely used: standardized weight-for-age, standardized height-for-age, and standardized weight-for-height. The first indicator captures the current nutritional status of the children, while the other two reflect their chronic nutritional status. Columns (2), (3), and (4) in table 8.5 show these statistics. On average, the LAC region is also doing substantially better in terms of these statistics than the rest of the developing world. Still, there are signs of nutritional problems. The percentage of under-weight children still is 5%. Fishman *et al.* (2004) report a prevalence of under-weight for the LAC region of 6%, which compares with a prevalence of just 2% in high-income countries. When including in the category of under-weight those children with z-scores below 1 standard deviation (instead of 2 standard deviations), the prevalence rate in the region goes up to 29% while in high-income countries it rises to 16%. Using data from ECLAC (2005), where the prevalence of under-weight for the LAC region is estimated at 7.5%, we also see substantial differences across countries. The range of under-weight rates varies from 0.8% in Chile to 24.2% in Guatemala (see figure 8.2). Additionally, the region still has a significant share of stunted children (11.8%). Again, there are substantial differences across countries. The range of prevalence rates for stunted children varies from 1.5% in Chile to 46.4% in Guatemala (see figure 8.3).

Finally, table 8.6 presents prevalence rates of vitamin A deficiency, anemia (Iron deficiency), and zinc deficiency. Vitamin A deficiency is a common cause of preventable blindness and a risk factor for increased severity of infectious disease and mortality. Iron deficiency is the main cause of anemia. Anemia is one of the world's most widespread health problems, especially among children. In particular, iron deficiency anemia leads to weakness, poor physical growth, and a compromised immune system, and is also thought to impair cognitive performance and delay psychomotor development. Zinc is vital to protein synthesis, cellular growth, and cellular differentiation. Its deficiency in children

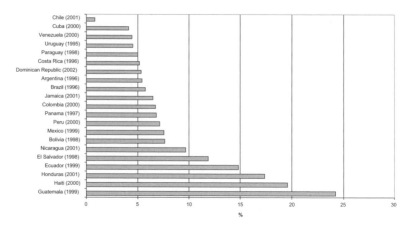

Figure 8.2 Distribution of underweight prevalence, by country
Source: World Bank – World Development Indicators

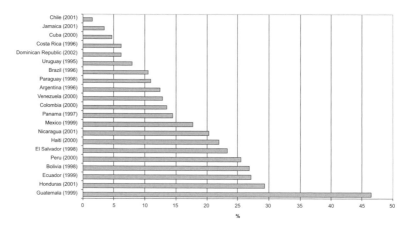

Figure 8.3 Distribution of prevalence of stunted children, by country
Source: Talvi (2007)
Note: LAC-7 refers to Argentina, Brazil, Chile, Colombia, Mexico, Peru, and
Venezuela
The Structural Fiscal Balance is calculated by replicating Chile's structural
balance calculation for LAC-7 countries. (see Talvi 2007 for details)

is also responsible for deficient growth and development. The LAC
region performs relatively worse in terms of these indicators than in
terms of the anthropometric indicators presented in table 8.5. The
prevalence of iron deficiency anemia and zinc deficiency are both particularly high.

Table 8.6 *Prevalence of selected nutritional deficiencies in children age 0–4 (%)*

Region	Vitamin A deficiency (1)	Iron deficiency anemia (2)	Zinc deficiency (3)
LAC	15	46	33
East Asia and the Pacific	11	40	7
Eastern Europe and Central Asia	1	22	10
Middle East and North Africa	18	63	46
South Asia	40	76	79
SSA	32	60	50
High-income countries	0	7	5

Source: Caulfield *et al.* (2006).

3 Reducing poverty in the LAC region

Economic growth appears to be, *a priori*, a powerful instrument for reducing absolute poverty. Bourguignon and Morrison (2002) show that the world extreme poverty rate decreased from 84% to 24% between 1820 and 1992. In the long run, wages are cointegrated with labor productivity and will therefore tend to rise as an economy grows.

In the LAC region, Chile is an impressive success story in terms of poverty reduction. Between 1987 and 1998, real *per capita* income increased at an annual rate of 5.7%, while the poverty rate dropped by 60%. Regressing poverty on *per capita* GNI and the Gini coefficient of income inequality, the World Bank (2001) reports the *per capita* income elasticity of poverty for Chile during this period to be 1.26. This suggests just how powerful economic growth can be in reducing poverty.

However, growth is not always so effective, at least in the short and medium terms. In the United States, poverty plummeted between 1959 and 1962, which was a period of rapid economic growth. It has remained relatively stable since then, however, even though the economy has continued to grow and has in fact expanded quite swiftly from the late 1980s on. This change in trend is mainly accounted for by the increase in income inequality that has taken place during this latter period.

As is well known, a change in the distribution of income can be decomposed into two effects. First, there is the effect of a proportional change in all incomes that leaves the distribution of relative income unchanged (i.e. growth effect). Second, there is the effect of a change in the distribution of relative incomes which, by definition, is independent of the mean (i.e. distributional effect) (see Datt and Ravallion, 1992). Kraay (2006) provides the most up-to-date exploration of these issues. Using a data-set comprising eighty-five countries for which there are at least two estimates for extreme poverty rates at different points in time (mainly in the 1990s), he finds that most of the variation in poverty levels is due to growth in average incomes. In contrast, changes in relative incomes account for only 30% of the variance in the headcount measure of poverty in the short run and only 3% in the long run.

Wodon (2000) presents estimates based on a panel data model of the change in the logarithm of poverty as compared to the change in the logarithm of *per capita* income and the change in the logarithm for the Gini coefficient using data for twelve countries in the LAC region for which he has six observations from the mid-1980s to the mid-1990s. He reports elasticities for both an extreme poverty measure and a poverty measure but uses regional poverty lines instead of the international poverty lines employed in this chapter. He finds a *per capita* income elasticity of poverty equal to −1.27 (−0.93 for extreme poverty) and an inequality elasticity of poverty equal to 1.46 (0.74 for extreme poverty). All these elasticities are statistically different from zero at conventional levels of statistical significance.[2]

Based on these estimates and noting that the annualized *per capita* growth rate of the region between 1990 and 2005 was around 1.7%, growth alone would reduce poverty by 20% in ten years. In order to halve poverty in ten years, *ceteris paribus*, *per capita* growth would need to accelerate to at least 3.5% per year, which is not only well above the region's historical average for the last forty years, but is also higher than the levels achieved during the last decade. Of course, these exercises should be interpreted cautiously, since the estimated elasticities may be biased by the occurrence of omitted variables and measurement error in the regressors. However, we believe they are still suggestive of the important role that economic growth should play in poverty-reduction strategies in the LAC region. Additionally, they

[2] Gasparini, Gutiérrez, and Tornarolli (2007) also present estimates of the *per capita* income elasticity of poverty for eighteen countries in the LAC region for a period starting in the late 1980s and ending in the early 2000s. They report this elasticity to be around 1.5.

underscore the importance of finding ways to increase long-run growth in order to reduce poverty. Indeed, we believe that it is possible for the LAC region to grow at between 3–4% *per capita* over the next decade if the reform process initiated twenty years ago is invigorated and enhanced instead of depleted.

The main sources of economic growth are the accumulation of human and physical capital and productivity gains. The latter is driven primarily by the rate of technological innovation in the form of new products, new processes, and new ways of organizing production, all of which involve risky experimentation and learning. The recent history of the LAC region has clearly not been conducive to growth. The region still exhibits a highly unreliable business environment, which discourages investment and innovation.

To accelerate economic growth, it is of key importance for the region to create an environment that reduces the distortions between the private and social returns to investments, thereby allowing entrepreneurs to appropriate a significant portion of the revenues generated by their investments and innovative projects.

A vast amount of evidence for developing countries suggests that growth accelerations are feasible with minimal institutional changes (see Hausmann, Pritchett, and Rodrik 2004; Rodrik 2005). However, in order to achieve and maintain sustained growth and convergence toward the income levels of developed countries, an institutional scheme needs to be devised that provides investment and innovation incentives for a broad segment of the population, rather than only for elite groups (see, among others, Acemoglu, Johnson, and Robinson 2005).

Adaptive, as well as allocative, efficiency influences economic performance. Successful economic systems have evolved flexible institutional structures that can survive the shocks and changes that are an intrinsic part of the process of economic development. But these systems are the product of a long gestation period, rather than being the outcome of an overnight transformation (see North 1990).

Macroeconomic stability also tends to foster long-term productivity growth, as it reduces interest rates and therefore increases the present (discounted) value of rents for successful innovators (see Aghion *et al.* 2004a).

Markets in Latin America are not that competitive. This is the result of a long history of trade protection, regulations benefiting incumbents, and critical factor market failures. Then again, fiercer competition among incumbent firms and/or a higher entry threat would also tend to encourage innovations by incumbent firms aimed at escaping competition or blocking entry by potential rivals (see Aghion *et al.* 2004b).

Having an effective education system is also a fundamental factor in speeding up economic growth in the region. Benhabib and Spiegel (1994) and Krueger and Lindahl (2001) show that a larger stock of human capital increases innovation and promotes the adoption and imitation of technological advances, which in turn fosters economic growth.

Finally, there are significant market imperfections in low-income environments that hinder investment and innovation in non-traditional activities. These imperfections may be typified as being the result of the existence of non-pecuniary and market-size externalities. Removing these distortions may require the crowding in of private investment through subsidies (see Rodrik 2005). This, in turn, calls for competent and non-corrupt governments, but unfortunately only a few countries in the region have made progress toward this goal.

Inequality, *per se*, may also be detrimental for economic growth. When markets are missing or imperfect, the distribution of wealth and power affects the allocation of investment opportunities and thus detracts from the economy's efficiency (see, among others, Banerjee and Newman, 1993; Galor and Zeira, 1993; and Aghion and Bolton, 1997). Additionally, high levels of economic and political inequality tend to give rise to economic and political institutions that systematically favor the interests of the most influential groups (see Acemoglu, Johnson, and Robinson 2005; Acemoglu *et al.* 2007). This in turn can lead to inefficient economic outcomes (see, among others, Alesina and Rodrik 1994).

Clearly, there are grounds for arguing that the high levels of inequality prevalent in the LAC region generate an excess burden of poverty over and above what would be expected given the region's level of development. Taking the inequality elasticity of poverty estimated by Wodon (2000), we see that reducing inequality is another powerful strategy for reducing poverty in the region. Taken at face value, the estimate of 1.46 implies that a reduction in inequality of 20% would induce a 30% drop in the poverty rate. This seems, admittedly, very difficult to achieve in the short-run in view of the region's history of

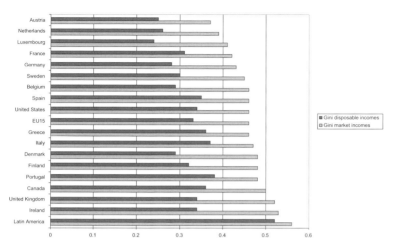

Figure 8.4 Gini coefficients for market and disposable incomes
Source: IMF-WEO

high and stable levels of inequality. However, there is no reason to think that it should not be a medium-term objective. One striking feature in the region is how little redistribution is carried out. Comparing income inequality between members of the OECD and the LAC region countries, Perry *et al.* (2006) show that roughly half of all sharp income inequalities stem from differences in returns to factors of production, while the other half are the result of the more progressive taxation and transfer systems in existence in the OECD area (see figure 8.4).

A review of quantitative studies of tax incidence in developing countries finds that taxes generally have little redistributive effect in the LAC region, largely because most of the countries rely heavily on indirect taxes (Chu, Davoodi, and Gupta, 2000). Indeed, in a very carefully prepared study, Engel, Galetovic, and Raddatz (1998) find Chile's tax system to be slightly regressive, despite the fact that it is the most effective system of taxation in the region, collects the most from personal income taxes, and has the highest marginal rates.

Revenues from personal income taxes are low in the LAC region, even when compared with receipts in countries with similar income levels (see Coady *et al.* 2004). This suggests that there is scope for increasing such revenues in order to improve the after-tax distribution of income. Property taxes are also currently under-utilized and could be used to increase redistribution in the region (see Coady *et al.* 2004). Nevertheless, the potential for achieving greater redistribution only via taxation is to some extent limited in developing countries by the fact that their tax systems rely heavily on indirect taxes (Burgess and Stern 1993).

An effective tax system is an instrument of power. Building such an organization is a long-term investment that will provide a greater measure of control over resources for a long time to come. High-income groups in unequal societies may well see this potential power as a threat. Elites often refuse to support the creation of practical revenue-raising machinery that could fall under the control of other groups in the future because they fear that it could be turned into an instrument for use by a "predatory state" (see Heymann, Navajas, and Warnes 1991).

Additionally, in most developing countries, and certainly in the LAC region, the poor operate primarily in the informal economy and are therefore beyond the reach of conventional tax and transfer mechanisms.[3] Not only that, but a broad range of labor market policies dealing with such matters as minimum wages and wage subsidies for unskilled workers, although used in developed countries to affect the income levels of the working poor, are unlikely to be effective in most of the countries in the LAC region. This fact represents a constraint for any strategy aimed at reducing poverty and inequality.

Given the high levels of inequality prevalent in the region and the deficient capacity that exists for redistribution through conventional tax and transfer mechanisms, a package of cost-effective policies targeting poor households is needed to build up the present and future income-generation capacity of the poor. These interventions need to be directed toward remedying the shortage of appropriate (legal, financial, human, physical, and social) assets that results in the exclusion of the poor from productive participation in formal sector economic activity, which in turn leads to the perpetuation of poverty and inequality within and across generations. Our focus will be on well-defined

---

[3] In the LAC region, approximately 50% of all salaried employees work informally. Galiani and Weinschelbaum (2007) report the following stylized facts for the region: (1) small firms tend to operate informally while large firms tend to operate formally; (2) unskilled workers tend to be informal while skilled ones generally have formal sector jobs; and (3) *ceteris paribus*, secondary workers are less likely to operate formally than primary workers.

intervention programs that are accepted to be effective in affecting the earnings and wellbeing of the poor. We will abstract from discussing general economy-wide interventions. In particular, we will abstract from discussing labor market reforms and, more generally, reforms to the welfare systems in the LAC region, even though such interventions could play an important role in reducing poverty (see Galiani 2007a).

4 Cost-effective interventions

In this section we will present a set of redistributive interventions that have proven to be cost-effective in reducing poverty and inequality in the LAC region. These interventions are targeted (or can be targeted) at the poor and have been found to generate present and future benefits which, properly discounted, are worth the cost of the intervention. The interventions evaluated from this perspective are mainly directed at enhancing the human capital of the poor early in life. In other words, they seek to foster the accumulation of human capital among poor children by improving education, health, and nutritional conditions in poor households.

A frequent, often justified, criticism of cost-effectiveness analyses is that they address only one of many criteria that could be used to evaluate interventions. Asking policymakers to make a binary choice between interventions may be misleading. Instead, cost-effectiveness plays the more useful function of informing trade-offs that policymakers are forced to undertake when investing in a portfolio of interventions.

Additionally, cost-effectiveness analysis is certainly not an exact science. As such, all the BCR estimates presented in this section should be regarded simply as first-order approximations to the true cost-effectiveness of the relevant interventions. In the absence of long-term impact evaluations, all long-run estimates of benefits are projections that have been arrived at by compounding parameter estimates from different evaluations. In order to minimize the build-up of uncertainties, we restrict the analysis to the direct benefits for treated individuals. We also assume the earnings-generating process to be stationary. Thus, interventions that affect the stock of human capital of the poor would likely end up being more cost-effective that we estimate under this assumption. Additionally, not all benefits and costs are easily incorporated into the analysis. This tends to have a more significant effect in terms of the indirect benefits of such interventions, but it is also a factor in the case of direct benefits whose future expected market value is very difficult to assess.

Moreover, as in any econometric project, there are questions of internal and external validity. Regarding the first issue, we report only BCRs for interventions for which we could obtain parameter estimates from experimental or quasi-experimental designs. In relation to the second issue, we have made an effort to rely only on evaluations conducted in the LAC region. However, in the case of nutrition interventions, we also relied on estimates for other regions. Therefore, these estimates should be taken even more cautiously than all the others we present in this section. Finally, throughout the analysis presented in this section, we have assumed that there are no significant externalities or general equilibrium effects; accordingly, this analysis is valid only to the extent that this assumption is plausible.

In the LAC region, there is an inexcusable lack of long-term experimental evidence upon which to base advice for policymakers as to the best way to put taxpayers' money to use. Clearly, given this level of under-investment in knowledge, more well-designed evaluations are needed as inputs for poverty-reduction efforts in the region. In the case of the CCT programs discussed below, we have already accumulated a great deal of knowledge, and the need of further evaluations (with the exception, perhaps, of assessments of some long-term impacts) is therefore less pressing. Well-designed evaluations will be essential, however, for the implementation of a wide array of other types of policy interventions. However, we should not only devote more resources to obtain more accurate impact evaluations of programs and policies, but we also need to assign substantially more effort to gathering precise information on the cost function of these programs and interventions. Surprisingly, there is better information on program impact than on costs structures.

All interventions considered here can be effectively targeted to the poor. The available evidence suggests that, among other program design considerations, the use of targeting methods to identify the poor is associated with greater anti-poverty impacts. Using a sample of 122 intervention programs in 48 countries, Coady, Grosh, and Hoddinott (2004) analyze the targeting performance of different methods, defining "targeting performance" as the proportion of transfers accruing to the target poor population. Although various considerations prevent them from establishing a strict ranking, they find that some targeting procedures, such as means or geographic targeting, are systematically associated with better targeting performance, while proxy-means testing and demographic targeting of children yield good but highly variable results (see also De Watcher and Galiani, 2006). Another result found by these authors is that, in general, the use of more than one targeting method is associated with better targeting performance (each additional method is associated with an increase in targeting performance of about 15%).

Most economists would highlight the primacy of human capital in the battle against poverty. This belief stems both from the fundamental role that human capital plays in income generation and from the many other ways in which human capital is thought to promote and sustain development.

A compelling economic case for public investments early in individuals' life cycles has been made by a number of authors. Carneiro and Heckman (2003) argue for early child development (ECD) investments on two grounds. First, all else being equal, returns to investments in early childhood will be higher than returns to investments made later in life simply because beneficiaries have a longer time to reap the rewards from these investments. Second, investments in human capital have dynamic complementarities, so that learning begets learning. Carneiro and Heckman argue that, at least for the United States, at current levels of investment, returns to investments in early childhood are high, whereas returns to investments in the old are low. Heckman and Masterov (2007) summarize the most recent evidence supporting this view (see also Schady 2006 for a review of ECD interventions in the LAC region).

Currie (2001) makes a number of complementary arguments for ECD investments. She contends that it may be more effective for a government concerned with equity to equalize initial endowments through ECD programs than to compensate for differences in outcomes later in life – both because ECD investments may be more cost-effective and because they avoid many of the moral hazard problems inherent in programs that seek to equalize outcomes in adulthood. She also asserts that there may be a variety of market failures, including liquidity constraints, information failures, and externalities, all of which lead to under-investment in early childhood.

Huggett, Ventura, and Yaron (2007) explore this issue within a model that features idiosyncratic shocks to human capital, estimated directly from the relevant data, as well as heterogeneity in levels of ability to learn, initial human capital, and initial wealth, all chosen to match observed properties of earnings dynamics by cohorts. They find that, as of age 20, differences in initial conditions account for more of the variation in lifetime earnings and lifetime wealth. Among initial conditions, differences in human capital are substantially more influential than variations in learning ability or initial wealth.

Nutrition interventions[4]

Many nutritional outcomes are the consequence of cumulative life cycle processes. There is evidence indicating that growth lost in early years is never (or only partially) recovered later in life (Martorell, Khan, and Schroeder 1994). Indeed, the nutritional status of adults reflects, to a substantial degree, their nutritional experience since conception.

Moreover, severe malnutrition in early childhood often leads to deficits in cognitive development (Pollitt 1990; Grantham-McGregor, Fernald, and Sethuraman 1999a). Micronutrient deficiencies, particularly of iodine and iron, are strongly implicated in impaired cognitive development. A meta-analysis indicates that the IQs of individuals with an iodine deficiency were, on average, 13.5 points lower than those of comparison groups (Grantham-McGregor, Fernald, and Sethuraman, 1999b).

Behrman *et al.* (2003) investigate the impact of community-level experimental nutritional interventions in rural Guatemala on a number of aspects of education, using the INCAP longitudinal data set dating back to the initial intervention in 1969–77 (when the subjects were 0–15 years of age) by comparing their results with the most recent information collected in 2002–3 (when the subjects were 25–40 years of age). They find that being exposed to a randomly available nutritional supplement when 6–24 months of age had significantly positive and fairly substantial effects on the probability of attending school and of passing the first grade, the grade attained by age 13 (through a combination of increasing the probability of ever enrolling,

---

[4] This section is based on Behrman, Alderman, and Hoddinott (2004).

reducing the age of enrolling, increasing the grade completion rate per year in schooling, and reducing the drop-out rate), completed schooling attainment, adult achievement test scores, and adult Raven's test scores.

One significant cost of malnutrition is higher mortality (see, among others, Ashworth 1998). Experimental evidence on the use of micronutrient supplements provides unambiguous evidence concerning the relationship between mortality and vitamin intakes in many environments, including those that exhibit few clinical symptoms of deficiencies. The potential to reduce child deaths by distributing vitamin A on a semi-annual basis is dramatic; meta-analysis of field trials indicates that the provision of vitamin A can reduce overall child mortality by 25%–35% (Beaton, Martorell, and Aronson 1993).

Iron deficiency is another important nutritional problem, as over a fifth of maternal deaths are associated with anemia (Ross and Thomas, 1996; Brabin, Hakimi, and Pelletier 2001). Anemia is also among the most widespread health problems for children in developing countries. As we saw in section 2, the prevalence of iron deficiency anemia is still extremely high among children in the LAC region. Iron deficiency anemia leads to weakness, poor physical growth, and a compromised immune system, and is also thought to impair cognitive performance and delay psychomotor development. Deficient growth development ultimately impinges on the formation of human capital of children, and on their productivity as workers.

There is, indeed, evidence of direct links between nutrition and productivity. Behrman and Deolalikar (1988), Deolalikar (1988), Behrman (1993), Foster and Rosenzweig (1993), Schultz (1997), Thomas and Strauss (1997), and Strauss and Thomas (1998) all find that, after controlling for a variety of characteristics, lower adult height (a consequence, in part, of poor nutrition in childhood) is associated with reduced earnings as an adult. Thomas and Strauss (1997) estimate the direct impact of adult height on wages in urban areas of Brazil. While the elasticity varies somewhat according to gender and other specifications, for both men and women who work in the market sector, a 1% increase in height leads to a 2%–2.4% increase in wages or earnings.

Multiple strategies exist for preventing malnutrition in young children in the short and long term. Caulfield *et al.* (2006) and Behrman, Alderman, and Hoddinott (2004) present surveys on interventions that, properly targeted, appear to be cost-effective. Behrman, Alderman, and Hoddinott (2004) focus on: (a) reducing the prevalence of LBW, (b) infant and child nutrition and exclusive breastfeeding promotion, and (c) reducing the prevalence of iron-deficiency anemia and vitamin A, iodine, and zinc deficiencies.

A cost-effective opportunity for the LAC region is directed toward improving the nutrition of infants and young children through, for example, breastfeeding promotion and improved knowledge about the timing and composition of weaning foods. Horton *et al.* (1996) have calculated the effect of breastfeeding promotion in hospital settings in the LAC region, and provides an estimate of the costs of this intervention. On the benefit side, however, the study accounts only for the benefits per death averted and the benefits for reduced cost of child illness. Productivity gains from reduced stunting and increased ability are not accounted for. Behrman, Alderman, and Hoddinott (2004) calculate that, if the proportional value of these other gains relative to measured mortality and infant/child illness gains are the same as those they estimated for interventions directed toward reducing LBW, then discounting future benefits at 5% per year yields a BCR equal to 4.8 while, with a discount rate of 3%, it equals 7.35.

Reducing the prevalence of iron-deficiency anemia and vitamin A, iodine, and zinc deficiencies are also cost-effective interventions that could have positive impacts in the LAC region. There is evidence that suggests that socially profitable interventions can be implemented to reduce micronutrient deficiencies, although this is limited to areas in which the prevalence of such deficiencies is high (see Behrman, Alderman, and Hoddinott 2004). This point is important since it implies that we cannot easily extrapolate these estimates to places where the prevalence of these nutritional deficiencies is low.[5] Thus, the proper target of these interventions is very important in order to get the most from them.

Approaches for reducing micronutrient deficiencies are classified as either supplementation or food-based programs. The latter are further divided into fortification of foods commonly consumed and encouragement of increased consumption of micronutrient-rich foods, through either social marketing or horticulture or both.

---

[5] Needless to say, this does not mean that these interventions are not also cost-effective in low-prevalence environments.

Table 8.7 *BCRs for reducing micronutrient deficiencies*

	Discount rate (%)	
Intervention	3	5
Iodine (per woman of childbearing age)	15	520
Vitamin A (pre-school children under age 6)	4.3	43
Iron (*per capita*)	176	200
Iron (pregnant women)	6.1	14

Source: Behrman, Alderman, and Hoddinott (2004).

Behrman, Alderman, and Hoddinott (2004) discuss several studies evaluating interventions aimed at reducing micronutrients deficiencies. Since outcomes are so sensitive to intervention details and population conditions, BCRs vary widely between and within interventions. Based on these authors' findings, we show the range of such variations in table 8.7.

Conditional cash transfers (CCTs)

CCTs have been extensively adopted since the mid-1990s in developing countries. These programs are aimed at dealing simultaneously with current and permanent poverty reduction. They provide cash transfers to finance current consumption, subject to the "attainment" of certain conditions that foster human capital investments. They are referred to as "conditional" because transfers are conditional upon certain behaviors (such as school enrollment of children, or regular use of primary health services, especially by pre-school children and by pregnant women and nursing mothers).

In this section, we present BCR estimates for a pioneering CCT program being implemented in Mexico, the Programa Nacional de Educación, Salud y Alimentación (National Education, Health, and Nutritional Program, Progresa), renamed Oportunidades in 2002. Before presenting these estimates, we will discuss the evidence on the effects that this kind of intervention has had in four countries in the LAC region between 1997 and 2003; in each of these cases, the evaluation of the program was based on an experimental design.

In addition to Progresa, we present results concerning the Programa de Asignación Familiar (Family Allowance Program, PRAF) in Honduras,[6] Red de Protección Social (Social Safety Net, RPS) in Nicaragua,[7] and the Bono de Desarrollo Humano (Human Development Bond, BDH) in Ecuador.[8] All of these programs cover mostly rural households but there is a great deal of variation in program size. Progresa is a national program, covering 20% of the Mexican population as of 2002, and delivers monthly transfers that represent, on average, 20% of beneficiaries' total household expenditures and 25% of household consumption. PRAF covers one-sixth of the Honduran population and delivers transfers that are much smaller than those of the Mexican program, representing just 10% of household consumption. RPS is a pilot program and therefore has a more limited coverage (21,619 families as of 2005), although it delivers cash transfers that are similar to Progresa's (20% of household consumption). Finally, BDH is also a national program that was designed to cover the poorest 40% of households; due to budget restrictions, however, the program's expansion has been gradual. Monthly transfers account for approximately 7% of pre-transfer household expenditures.

With the exception of BDH, the programs have relied on randomization applied at the community rather than at the household level, primarily due to the broader geographic coverage of some benefits and to the difficulties that could arise in implementing the program when control and treatment households reside in the same communities. In Progresa, participating communities were selected based on a marginality index that was designed to identify the poorer communities. Afterwards, a random procedure was implemented to assign each community to a treatment or control group. The PRAF operates in seventy of the poorest municipalities in Honduras, which were randomly assigned to four different groups: twenty municipalities received only demand-side interventions and ten only supply-side interventions, another twenty received both, and the last ten did not receive any (the control group). In Nicaragua, both poverty levels and capacity to implement the programs were considered in selecting two departments and six municipalities within these departments. A marginality index was then used to identify the forty-two most impoverished rural

---

[6] PRAF was actually established in 1991 but started as a CCT program in 1998. Most studies refer to the second phase of the program as PRAF II.

[7] The RPS started as a pilot program that was designed to last three years.

[8] The BDH is slightly different from the other programs since, although it was designed as a CCT program, the conditions were never enforced or monitored.

comarcas, of which twenty-one were randomly assigned to the treatment group, leaving the other twenty-one to form the control group. Finally, the BDH chose four provinces in the same geographic region of the country, and parishes as well as households within parishes were randomly selected. Half of the households selected were further assigned to the treatment group whereas the rest were assigned to the control group.

All of the programs share a common view as regards their poverty alleviation strategies, which take an integrated approach focusing on various dimensions of human capital, including education, healthcare, and nutritional status. Education grants are targeted to children between 6 and 13 years of age who attend primary school. Progresa also includes older children (until the age of 18) enrolled in secondary school.[9] Healthcare services and nutritional supplements are generally targeted at pregnant women, nursing mothers, and children under 5. Progresa also provides for annual health check-ups for the other household members. Fixed family-level transfers are also delivered, and health and nutritional education components are usually included. Besides demand-side interventions, most of the programs involve some supply-side interventions in anticipation of demand increases brought about by the program.

CCT programs are found to have had significant positive impacts on a wide range of outcomes such as consumption, education, health, nutrition, and labor participation. We summarize these in table 8.8.

As regards household consumption, CCT beneficiaries seem not only to increase the levels but also to improve the quality of food consumed. There is evidence of higher caloric acquisition levels and better dietary diversity among program participants. On a longer-term basis, in Mexico it was found that program participation might have increased permanent household consumption. The positive effect on savings as well as the increased participation in micro enterprise activities and investments in agricultural production activities is expected to have long-lasting effects on treated households.

A large number of measures were used to evaluate the impact of CCT programs on education. They included: enrollment rates, attendance

---

[9] In 2001, the program extended the transfers to cover upper-secondary school grades, and introduced households located in marginal urban areas in 2002.

Table 8.8 *CCT impacts*

	PROGRESA (Mexico)		PRAF (Honduras)		BDH (Ecuador)		RPS (Nicaragua)	
	Program impact	Comments	Program impact	Comments	Program impact	Comments	Program impact	Comments
Education[a]	8.7%–9.4% all	Transition from primary to secondary school.	3.30%		8.6% across all grades 17.8% for 6th grade	Results based on IV estimation methods because of low take-up rates. "Lottery" effects are smaller	13%–22%	Impacts highly concentrated among the poor: 25%–30% for the extremely poor and 5%–6% for the non-poor
Enrollment rates	10%–12% girls 7%–8% boys	Although smaller, significant positive impacts for all the other grades as well		There is evidence of greater impacts among the poor				

Attendance rates	No sig. impact		4.60%	From a base-line rate of 91%	13%–26%	33%–36% for the extremely poor
Progression rates	8%–11%	6–10-year-old children	12.30%	Transition from primary to secondary school		
Grade repetition	(–) 7%–12%	6–10-year-old children				
Drop-out rates	0.9%	11-year-old children				
Achievement	No sig. impact					
Preventive healthcare and health status[b]						
Health check-ups	Positive impact	Visits at public clinics. Effect at the family level	Positive effect	0–3-year-old children		

(*cont.*)

Table 8.8 (*cont.*)

	PROGRESA (Mexico)		PRAF (Honduras)		BDH (Ecuador)		RPS (Nicaragua)	
	Program impact	Comments	Program impact	Comments	Program impact	Comments	Program impact	Comments
Nutritional monitoring visits	30%–60%	0–2-year-old children				Positive effect on parasite treatment, especially on the poorer		
	25%–45%	3–5-year-old children			No sig. impact		Positive effect	0–3-year-old children
Hospital visits	Reduction	0–2-year-old children						
	Reduction	Adults over 50						
Pre-natal care visits	Increase	1st trimester of pregnancy						
	Reduction	Other trimester						

Vaccination rates	12% lower	0–5-year-old children	30% increase in both treatment and control areas when decreased in other rural areas (children aged 12–13 months)
Illness rates	25.3% lower 22.3% lower	Newborns 0–3-year-old children Rural rates	
Infant mortality rates	11% lower	Municipality level	
Days of difficulty with daily activities	19%	Difficulties due to illness Adults older than 18	

(cont.)

Table 8.8 (cont.)

	PROGRESA (Mexico)		PRAF (Honduras)		BDH (Ecuador)		RPS (Nicaragua)	
	Program impact	Comments	Program impact	Comments	Program impact	Comments	Program impact	Comments
No. of km walked without getting tired	7%	Adults older than 18. Incapacitation due to illness						
Days of incapacitation	(–)17%	Adults older than 50. Due to illness						
Days in bed	(–)22%	Adults older than 50						
Nutritional status[c]								
Probability of stunting	Decreased	Children aged 12–36 months. Impact greater on poorer					(–)5%	0–5-year-old children

Child growth	0.96–1 cm taller households and poorer communities	Positive impact	Although quite small
Motor skills	Positive impact	Positive impact	
Emotional problems	Positive impact		Positive impact on 1 out of 5 measures
Cognitive development measures	No sig. impact	Modest impact	Greater impact on poorer households
Hemoglobin levels	Positive impact		Positive impact On poorer households	No sig. impact

(*cont.*)

Table 8.8 (cont.)

	PROGRESA (Mexico)		PRAF (Honduras)		BDH (Ecuador)		RPS (Nicaragua)	
	Program impact	Comments	Program impact	Comments	Program impact	Comments	Program impact	Comments
Consumption and investment[a]								
	2% 1-year impact	Impact on the median household Greater impact on the poorer						
Value of food consumption (per person per month)	10% 2-year impact	Increase of 13.5% at the 25th percentile after 2 years						
Share of food expenditure							4.7% 1-year impact 4.5% 2-year impact	Similar positive impacts on *per capita* annual total expenditures

			Positive effect	Improvement on the nutritional value of food consumed
Caloric acquisition/ dietary diversity	6.40%	Household caloric acquisition Median caloric		
	7.10%	intake per person per day		
Permanent consumption	34%	After 5 years of program		
Savings	12 cents for every peso transferred			
Investment	Increased participation in microenter- prise activities			

(*cont.*)

Table 8.8 (cont.)

	PROGRESA (Mexico)		PRAF (Honduras)		BDH (Ecuador)		RPS (Nicaragua)	
	Program impact	Comments	Program impact	Comments	Program impact	Comments	Program impact	Comments
Child labor and time allocation[e]								
Probability of working	(–)15–25%	Impact concentrating on children 12–15 years old	No sig. impact		(–)5–6%/ 17%	Lottery effect	(–)5%	7–13-year-old children Impact on boys twice as large as that for girls
					(–)17%	Treatment effect	(–)9%	10–13-year-old children Impact on boys twice as large as that for girls
Probability of starting to work					(–)6–8%	Lottery effect		
					(–)25%	Treatment effect		

		2.5 hours less	Per week	10 hours less	Per week
Hours of work	No sig. impact.				
Adult labor participation and time allocation[f]					
Labor market participation	No sig. impact.	No sig. impact		No sig. impact	
Leisure time	No sig. impact.				
Time on childrearing activities				Positive effect	
Change in working patterns					More time working on own farms or work nearer households
Other effects[g]					
Fertility rates	No sig. impact.				

(*cont.*)

Table 8.8 (*cont.*)

	PROGRESA (Mexico)		PRAF (Honduras)		BDH (Ecuador)		RPS (Nicaragua)	
	Program impact	Comments	Program impact	Comments	Program impact	Comments	Program impact	Comments
Private inter-household transfers	No crowding-out effect							
Women's empowerment	Positive impact							

Notes:

[a] Results reported are based on: Behrman, Sengupta, and Todd (2000, 2001); Schultz (2000a, 2000b, 2000c, 2001, 2004); Behrman, Parker, and Todd (2004, 2006, 2007); Coady (2000) for Progresa; Schady and Araujo (2006) for BDH; Maluccio (2004), Maluccio and Flores (2005), and Maluccio *et al.* (2005) for RPS; and Glewwe, Olinto and Souza (2003) and Glewwe and Olinto (2004) for PRAF.

[b] Results based on: Gertler (2000, 2004) and Barhman (2005) for Progresa; Maluccio and Flores (2005) and Maluccio *et al.* (2005) for RPS; and Paxson and Schady (2007) for BDH.

[c] Results based on: Behrman and Hoddinott (2000), Gertler (2004), Gertler and Fernald (2004), Rivera *et al.* (2004), for Progresa; Maluccio (2004), Maluccio and Flores (2005) for RPS; Paxson and Schady (2007) for BDH.

[d] Hoddinott, Skoufias, and Washburn (2000), Hoddinott and Skoufias (2004), Gertler, Martinez, and Rubio (2006) for Progresa; Maluccio *et al.* (2005) for RPS.

[e–f] Results based on Parker and Skoufias (2000) and Behrman, Parker, and Todd (2007) for Progresa; Maluccio (2004), Maluccio and Flores (2005), and Maluccio *et al.* (2005) for RPS; Glewwe, Olinto, and Souza (2003) for PRAF; Schady and Araujo (2006) for BDH.

[g] Schultz (2004); Teruel and Davis (2000); Adato (2000).

rates, progression or continuation rates, drop-out rates, and achieve-ment. Results in general are encouraging, although not on all of the dimensions considered. Most of the programs have had positive effects on enrollment rates, drop-out rates, and progression rates; results for attendance rates are mixed, and there is barely any evidence of posi-tive impacts on achievement. Impacts on enrollment rates are generally larger on those groups who have lower base-line enrollment rates: the transition grade from primary to secondary school, girls, or poorer households. The evidence from Progresa suggests that the greatest and more permanent impact on enrollment rates is generated by children who were already enrolled in school (continuation rates), rather than by those who were out of school (return rates).

In Mexico, medium-term impacts after $5\frac{1}{2}$ years of exposure to the program are also available.[10] The relevant studies report reductions in the "age at starting school," improvements in "grade progression on time," and grades of school completed. It is worth mentioning that these effects are found not only in children who benefit from school transfers, but also in children who benefit only from the infant nutritional supplement and health check-ups, or even just from health check-ups. Although limited, this can be taken as preliminary evidence of synergies between the health and school components of the program.

Overall, there is evidence of improvement in the use of preventive healthcare services, such as more frequent health check-ups, nutritional or growth-monitoring visits, and pre-natal care visits. The reduction in hospital visits in Mexico is taken as an indicator of a positive impact on health status, since those visits are equated with the utilization of health facilities for curative purposes. In Mexico, children's health status improves, as measured by the reduction in illness and mortality rates, as well as adult health status, measured by fewer days of difficulty with daily activities, days of incapacitation, or days in bed due to illness and the ability to walk more km without getting tired.

Nutritional supplements seem to have significant effects, even though some evidence indicates that, in many cases, they were not fully consumed or not received regularly. The programs seem success-ful in reducing the probability of stunting among beneficiaries, and

---

[10] These impacts no longer rely on the experimental design of the program, since by the time they were measured, the original control households had been included in the program.

two of them show improvements in motor skills. Some positive effects are also found on emotional problems, cognitive and behavioral development measures, and hemoglobin levels, although the evidence is not that conclusive.

There is no evidence that programs affect labor market participation among adults. There is no evidence of significant changes in fertility rates, which in turn suggests that there has been no change in demographic incentives. There do not seem to be any crowding-out effects of Progresa transfers over private inter-household transfers, either. Finally, there is some evidence of positive effects on empowerment among Mexican beneficiary women and on the recognition of woman's responsibilities by men and the community in general.

Comparing benefit and cost

The main cost of the program is the cash transferred to households. There are also costs associated with the selection of localities, identification of beneficiary families, certification of fulfillment of co-responsibility actions, delivery of cash transfers, and servicing. In addition, there are private costs that are borne by beneficiary households in terms of money and reduced leisure. We will treat these private costs as negative benefits to maintain the idea that the BCR estimates the return to $1 invested in the project by the government. Of course, treating some costs as negative benefits does not affect other profitability indicators, such as the NPV. The benefits of the program are better nutrition and health status and higher current consumption for targeted households, as well as better levels of school achievement for school-age children. For the purposes of this exercise, our analysis of the Progresa program focuses on a group of 100 households that are assumed to be exposed to the program for 2 years. All monetary flows are deflated to 1996 Mexican pesos.

Costs of the project

Skoufias (2005) estimated that, on average, a household received 197 pesos (as of November 1998) per month during the period from November 1998 to October 1999. Deflated to 1996 pesos and multiplied by 100 households, this amounts to a total monthly transfer of 13,311 pesos. Coady (2000) estimates that the sum of all other costs associated with the program and borne by the government represent between 8.9% and 9.5% of the total transfers. Thus, we estimate the monthly operational costs of the project analyzed as 1,231 pesos. Monthly costs to be paid by the government then add up to 14,542 pesos.

The private costs (or negative private benefits) were estimated by Coady (2000) to be around 2.44% of the total transfers: 325 pesos per month. He focused exclusively on the financial cost of traveling to comply with health requirements, attend school, and collect the cash transfers. Parker and Skoufias (2000) found some evidence that adults' leisure time was reduced, particularly in the case of men aged 18–24. However, the effects they identified for other age intervals were not statistically significant. To evaluate the program, we averaged this effect out to a reduction of 0.075 hours per day for adults. Schultz (2000a) reports that the monthly wage for an average worker in urban areas is 1,300 pesos of 1996. We therefore priced the reduction of each leisure hour at $1,300/(8 \times 20) = 8.12$ pesos. Using demographic data from Behrman and Todd (1999) and Teruel and Davis (2000), we estimated that the total reduction in leisure time per month for our group of 100 households represented 5,457 pesos per month. Total monthly private costs were thus estimated to be 5,782 pesos.

Benefits of the project

Beneficiary households are found to have increased current consumption as a result of their participation in the program. Hoddinott, Skoufias, and Washburn (2000) estimated that, on average, a household increased its monthly consumption by 151 pesos at November 1998 prices. Deflated to 1996 pesos and multiplied by 100 households, this amounted to a level of monthly consumption equivalent to 10,203 pesos.

One of the major benefits of the program is an improvement in the educational outcomes of children. Behrman, Sengupta, and Todd (2001) analyzed the long-term effect of Progresa on education by simulating the outcome for a child belonging to a treated household and comparing it with the outcome for a child in an untreated household. To do so, they constructed transition matrices for each age for treated and non-treated children using data from baseline household surveys administered in October 1997 and March 1998 and from two follow-up surveys administered at approximately one-year intervals.

We assume that there are 22 states: "enrolled at grade j" for $j = 1 \dots 11$, and "dropped out at grade k" for $k = 0 \dots 10$. Let

$A^a_{T=0}$ $\left(A^a_{T=1}\right)$ be the 22 × 22 transition matrix of untreated (treated) individuals at age a, and let $f^i_{T=t}$ be the 22 × 1 vector indicating the distribution of educational status among individuals aged i after receiving treatment t. Finally, f^6 is the 22 × 1 vector of initial conditions (at age 6). Based on table A.4 in Behrman, Sengupta, and Todd (2001), we set initial conditions: 70% of individuals aged 6 attend first grade, 20% attend second grade, and 10% are not enrolled.

Note that the long-run outcome for a treated individual would be:

$$f^{15}_{T=1} = \left(\prod_{a=6}^{14} A^a_{T=1} \right) f^6$$

while the outcome for an untreated individual is:

$$f^{15}_{T=0} = \left(\prod_{a=6}^{14} A^a_{T=0} \right) f^6$$

Remember that we want to evaluate the effects of a two-year project. Therefore, our analysis is different from that of Behrman, Sengupta, and Todd (2001), since we are not interested in the effect of the program on one representative child who received treatment from age 6 to age 15; instead, we are interested in the project's effect on a population of 100 households that comprise several cohorts of students. The outcome of an individual aged s at the beginning of the program will therefore be computed as:

$$f^{15}_{T=1,s} = A^{14}_{T=0} \ldots A^{s+2}_{T=0} A^{s+1}_{T=1} A^s_{T=1} A^{s-1}_{T=0} \ldots A^6_{T=0} f^6 \text{ for } 5 \leq s \leq 14$$

In other words, we will apply a treatment transition matrix for two consecutive periods starting at period s. For untreated individuals, the outcome will always be $f^{15}_{T=0}$. To perform our calculation, we used the distribution of years of education at age 15 for each cohort.

We assume that wages are determined by the following Mincer equation:

$$\ln(w_i) = \alpha + \beta_1 exp_i + \beta^2 exp_i^2 + \gamma_1 pri + \gamma_2 sec$$

where *pri* is the number of primary years of education, *sec* is the number of secondary years of education, and *exp* stands for experience. Rewriting this expression we have:

$$w_i \cong e^\alpha [e(1 + \beta_1)]^{(exp)} [e(1 + \beta_2)]^{(exp^2)} [e(1 + \gamma_1)]^{pri} [e(1 + \gamma_2)]^{sec}$$

Let

$$S_i = [e(1 + \gamma_1)]^{pri_i}[e(1 + \gamma_2)]^{sec_i}$$

Legovini *et al.* (2001) estimate an earnings equation for Mexico and find that $\gamma_1 = 0.05$ and $\gamma_2 = 0.12$; therefore, we can construct the profile $S(e)$, where e is the number of years of education. For each cohort we can calculate the distribution of years of education, and thus, the expected S:

$$S^j = E(S(e)) = S(e)p^j(e)$$

where $p^j(e)$ is the distribution of e in cohort j. Then, S^j is the average income of cohort j in terms of the income of an uneducated worker with the same level of experience.

The following table shows the expected S for each cohort and the difference between it and the expected S without the program:

Average expected income for each cohort and difference attributable to the program

Age at program start	Normalized income	Difference attributable to the program
4	1.5833	0.0000
5	1.5838	0.0005
6	1.5863	0.0030
7	1.5888	0.0055
8	1.5923	0.0090
9	1.5914	0.0081
10	1.6159	0.0326
11	1.6329	0.0496
12	1.6374	0.0541
13	1.6167	0.0334
14	1.5862	0.0029
15	1.5833	0.0000

In Legovini *et al.* (2001), the coefficients of experience and squared experience are $\beta_1 = 0.064$ and $\beta_2 = -0.001$. Moreover, the constant term is $\alpha = 5.404$. Thus, we estimated the monthly wages of an uneducated worker at $exp(5.404) = 222$ pesos (1994 prices). In terms of 1996 pesos, this figure becomes 403 pesos. We built the flow of cohort income over time, assuming that individuals work from age 18 to 65.

The flow of benefits for each cohort is calculated as the difference between the flows of income in each counterfactual situation. The total benefits of the program are calculated as the weighted sum across cohorts of the present values of each cohort-specific flow of benefits. Weights are based on the expected number of individuals in that cohort in our 100 households.

In addition, several authors find that beneficiary households improved their health status. Needless is to say, assigning a price to outcomes such as reduced mortality rates is quite controversial. The only aim of our calculations is to provide some general idea of the order of magnitude of these health effects.

Beneficiaries of the program experienced improvements in their health status during their exposure to the program. Gertler (2000) shows that there is a reduction in the illness rate of about 11% (from 0.40 to 0.353 at ages 0–2 and from 0.28 to 0.248 at ages 3–5). For adults, the number of days of incapacity is also reduced. Finally, Barhman (2005) finds that the infant mortality rate is reduced from 0.018 to 0.016. We will quantify these effects using two different approaches: first, we will take advantage of information regarding the alternative cost of saving a life according to Summers (1992); secondly, we will quantify those effects in terms of DALYs. We will then show our results under two alternative DALY values: 1,000 and 5,000 dollars (average exchange rate in 1996: 7.61 pesos per dollar).

Summers (1992) suggests that World Bank estimates of the cost of saving a life through measles immunization were on the order of US$800 per life saved in the early 1990s. Behrman, Parker, and Todd (2004) state that, adjusting this cost for inflation in the next decade and for the distortion costs of raising these revenues, the alternative resource cost of saving an infant's life is estimated at about US$1,250.

Based on the demographic data, we estimate that there were 33.56 total live births in the 100 households during the two years of the program. In treated households, we would expect $0.016 \times 33.56 = 0.537$ infant deaths, while in untreated households deaths would total $0.018 \times 33.56 = 0.604$. The program effect is a reduction of 0.067 infant deaths, that is, a benefit of 638.52 1996 Mexican pesos, or a yearly benefit of 0.067 DALY for a lifetime (assumed to be 99 years).

Gertler (2000) shows that there is a reduction in the illness rate of about 11%. The illness rate is defined as the probability that a mother reports that her child experienced an illness in the four weeks prior to the survey. The reduction in the probability of illness is 0.047 in children aged 0–2 and 0.032 in children aged 3–5. Using our demographic data, we estimate the number of children aged 0–2 at 52 and the number of children aged 3–5 at 59 (in 100 households of 6 members). Therefore, the program results in a reduction of 4.33 monthly illness episodes. We assume that each illness episode lasts for a complete month (1/12 years) and that the disability weighting is 0.5. Thus, the effect of the program is a monthly benefit of 0.18 DALY for two years. Alternatively, we assume that each illness episode is valuated as a hundredth of the value of a life. In that case, the program's effect is estimated at 414 Mexican pesos per month for the two years that the program lasts.

As Gertler (2000) shows, there is no significant effect on the number of days of incapacity or of difficulty for people aged 6–17 years old. For people aged 18–50 and 51+ the results are in the following table.

Effect of the program in reducing the days of incapacity

Age	Days in bed	Days of incapacity	Days of difficulty
		Reductions in	
18–50	0.010	0.034	0.055
51 and older	0.243	0.330	0.360

One "day in bed" implies one "day of incapacity" and one "day of difficulty." Similarly, one "day of incapacity" implies one "day of difficulty," but the reverse is not true. We can alter this table so that the figure for "days of difficulty" will signify "days during which the individual had difficulty but was not incapacitated or in bed" and the figure for "days of incapacity" will mean "days that the individual was incapacitated but not in bed." Moreover, using our demographic data we calculate the effect on 100 households. We assume that a day in bed has a disability index of 1, a day of incapacity 0.8, and a day of difficulty 0.4. Finally, we calculate the benefits of the program as a flow of monthly DALY, for two years. If we want to avoid using DALYs in our estimation, we could valuate each incapacity day as a lost working day. If the average worker earns a monthly salary of 1,300 Mexican pesos, a day is worth a twentieth of that figure, or 65 Mexican pesos. In this case we did not place a price on days of difficulty (see table below).

Effect of the program in reducing the days of incapacity (valuing days)

	Reductions in		
	Days in bed	Days of incapacity	Days of difficulty
18–50	0.010	0.024	0.021
51 and older	0.243	0.087	0.030
In 100 households			
Days, 18–50	1.99	4.78	4.18
Days, 51+	24.18	8.66	2.98
Disability index (DI)	1	0.8	0.4
Monthly DALY			0.11

Improvements in health status also represent long-run investments. Behrman and Hoddinott (2000) and Gertler (2004) find that children aged 12–36 who receive treatment are, on average, 1 cm taller than those in the control group. We consider height as a proxy of health capital. The returns to this capital are hard to compute, however. Strauss and Thomas (1998) find that a 1% increase in height leads to 2.4% increase in lifetime earnings. Their estimation is based on survey data from men and women in Brazil. They state that "height is a cumulative measure reflecting both investments in nutrition during one's life (mostly as a child) and also, possibly, non-health human capital investments." We followed the approach taken by Behrman and Hoddinott (2000) to look at two scenarios: one under the assumption that the percentage change in adult height is equal to the change estimated for children; and the other under the assumption that the percentage change in adult height equals half of the estimated change for children (1 cm represents an increase of 1.2% – the mean height in the sample was about 84 cm for children aged 1–3 years old). Therefore, using the results of Strauss and Thomas (1998), we calculated the benefits of the program as a 2.86% increase in monthly wages in the first scenario and a 1.43% increase in the second. Using our estimation of a monthly income of 1,300 pesos (1996), the benefits of the program will be a monthly flow of 37.19 pesos per individual starting 17 years after the program began and lasting for 47 years (65–18). Using our demographic data, we estimated the monthly effect for our targeted population of 100 households at 1,222.60 pesos (611.29 pesos in the second scenario).

Table 8.9 *Program NPV*

Program NPV	Discount rate		
	3%	6%	8%
Not Using DALYs	$757,133.43	$250,878.41	$102,724.23
DALY Low (US$1,000)	$754,959.70	$241,602.41	$91,693.82
DALY High (US$5,000)	$1,026,998.64	$477,143.13	$315,044.02

Table 8.10 *Program B/C*

Program B/C	Discount rate		
	3%	6%	8%
Not Using DALYs	3.24	1.76	1.32
DALY Low (US$1,000)	3.23	1.74	1.28
DALY High (US$5,000)	4.03	2.45	1.98

Finally, comparing benefits and costs, we estimated the NPVs and BCRs in tables 8.9 and 8.10.

We conducted a series of robustness checks. Each robustness check departs from the estimates in table 8.10 using DALY Low estimates. First, we ignore all the health effects incorporated in the analysis in table 8.10. Second, we do not subtract the costs of the reduction in leisure costs incurred by beneficiary households. Third, we assume a homogenous 10% wage differential for each extra year of schooling. Finally, we assume a homogenous 5% wage differential for an additional year of schooling (table 8.11).

Early child development (ECD)

ECD projects are interventions that aim to improve the physical, intellectual, and social development of children early in their life, generally from ages 0 to 6. There is a wide range of interventions that belong to this category, some work directly with children – for instance, growth monitoring, daycare services, pre-school activities, or improved hygiene or health services; other work with parents to improve their parenting skills through home visits by trained professionals and parental training and education related to best childrearing

Table 8.11 *Program B/C robustness checks*

	Discount rate program's B/C	
Program B/C	3%	6%
No health effects (W)	3.09	1.74
No leisure costs	3.61	2.11
Average return to education 10%	2.46	1.36
Average return to education 5%	1.80	1.04

Note: W: We only consider as benefits the impact of Progresa on education and consumption and not on health as benefits. We reduce the costs by 20% since the government would not invest in health services and the households would not suffer costs in order to satisfy the health requirements of the program.

practices. Interventions may also include the provision of training services to teachers and caregivers, and the strengthening of institutional and community resources and capacities.

There are a great variety of program designs, divided primarily between formal vs. non-formal services. The former type corresponds to center-based programs, generally quite structured and controlled by professionals. Examples are daycare centers and pre-schools. The other kind of program is more flexible in format, is conducted primarily by paraprofessionals and mothers, is usually home-based, and significantly less expensive to administer. Some examples are home-based daycare programs, community kindergartens, or even lessons delivered over the radio.

It is well documented by medical and educational research that the brain is almost entirely developed by the time a child enters school, and it is estimated that half of all intellectual development potential is established by the age of 4. Poor nutrition at this age is related to delays in physical and motor development, impaired intellectual ability, concentration problems, and poor social skills (Martorell 1997). Probably most important is the fact that certain deficits can never be recovered later in life, so poorly developed children will never attain their full potential, helping to reproduce the well-known intergeneration cycle of poverty.

Engle *et al.* (2007) provide an extensive survey on the results of ECD interventions. They assess programs aiming at reducing iodine and iron deficiencies and child stimulation combined with nutrition and health program. They find positive effects on child development measures and that, in general, providing services directly to children is more effective than providing information only to parents; moreover, they note that: "The most effective child development... are targeted toward younger and disadvantaged children, are of longer duration, higher quality, higher intensity and are integrated with family support health, nutrition, or educational systems and services" (2007: 229).

ECD programs were found to have positive impacts on a great variety of outcomes, and some of the participants are old enough to offer the possibility of estimating long-term impacts, although most of them are conducted in the United States. Three well-known projects that use randomized evaluations are the Perry Preschool Project, the Carolina Abecedarian Project, and the Early Training Program. Participation in the first program mentioned increases the years of schooling: participants have 11.9 years of schooling as opposed to 11.0 years for the control group, and also increases high-school graduation rates from 45% to 66% (Schweinhart *et al.* 1993). There is also evidence of better performance on different tests at different ages. As regards to impacts on adult life, at the age of 40 it was found that program participants had median earnings more than one-third higher than non-participants, were more likely to be employed, and had better criminal performance (measured by fractions of lifetime arrests and months in prison sentenced) (Belfield *et al.* 2006). The Abecedarian Project also had a positive impact on achievement test scores and reduced the incidence of special education. An evaluation of another program, the Chicago Preschool Program, shows that the rates of school completion rose from 38.5 to 49.7%, drop-out rates dropped from 55% to 46.7%, grade retention dropped from 32.3% to 21.9%, and the need for special education decreased from 20.7% to 13.5% (Reynolds *et al.* 2002).

Impact estimates for the LAC region are scarcer, but there is evidence of some benefits of ECD projects. A review of nineteen evaluations of ECD programs in the region (Myers 1996) as well as a survey of thirteen programs in developing countries (Myers 1996) show that program participation is associated with improved school readiness, a higher probability of on-time primary school enrollment, lower rates of grade repetition and drop-out, and improved academic performance overall. Besides improving children's welfare, these programs have additional effects on other family members, especially on those previously in charge of childcare activities. Program participation frees women and older siblings to work outside the home, or to further their own education.

Hogares Comunitarios program in Colombia

Hogares Comunitarios (HC) is a large intervention based on a community nursery where poor children receive food (purchased by the government) and childcare from one of the mothers in the community. The program, which began in 1984, targeted poor neighborhoods and localities and encouraged eligible parents with children aged 0–6 to form 'parents' associations'. Each parents' association was registered with the program and elected a "madre comunitaria" (community mother). The madre comunitaria would receive in her house the children aged 0–6 of the parents belonging to the association. Each family would pay a tiny monthly fee (roughly equivalent to US$4), which would be used to pay a small salary to the madre comunitaria. The average number of children is around 12 (the maximum per madre comunitaria is 15 children). The parents' association would receive funds from the government to purchase food that would be delivered weekly at the house. The menu varied regionally and was established by a nutritionist. In addition, the children would also be given a nutritional beverage called bienestarina. Children were fed three times: lunch and two snacks. According to the office responsible for the program, the food received by the children (including the beverage) would provide them with 70% of the recommended daily amount of calories.

Attanasio and Vera-Hernández (2004) used Instrumental Variable (IV) estimation. They argue that given the evolution of the program and the high turnover of mothers in the last years, both the distance from the household to the nearest HC, and this distance averaged at the town level, will be good instruments. They present evidence showing the extent to which both the household distance to the nearest HC and its town average affects participation choices. Their identification assumption is that these two distances are unrelated to nutritional outcomes, conditional on the other control variables.

Attanasio and Vera-Hernández (2004) identify three key benefits from the program:

- **Better anthropometric measures**
  The authors estimate the effect of having attended an HC during the first six years of life as 3.78 cm for a boy (3.83 cm for a girl)

aged 72 months. At that age the median height of boys is 115.5 cm (114.5 cm for girls); therefore, the program effect is an increase over the median height of 3.3%.

- **Better school attainment and progress rates**
  The authors considered separately children aged 8–12 and those aged 13–17. While for the younger group they did not identify any significant effect, they found important effects for the older group. According to their tables the probability of progressing a grade among the younger group is 0.777, and 0.655 among the older group. The authors found that for each year a child attended an HC the probability of progressing increases by 0.07. Therefore, we simulated the education distribution for a child that attended one year at an HC and compared it with the distribution for a child that had not attended an HC at all. On average, a treated child accumulates 7.5 years of schooling against 7.15 for an untreated child.

- **Increased female labor supply**
  The program might have additional benefits caused by the child-care aspect that would allow mothers to work and earn additional resources. According to the authors, when they define as treatment a binary variable that is 1 if the mother has at least one child currently attending an HC, treated women increase their average number of hours in the labor market by 75 monthly hours.

Pre-primary education

Most OECD and many middle-income countries have turned to universal pre-primary education in order to give children a better start to their schooling life. Berlinski, Galiani, and Gertler (2009) examine the returns to pre-primary education by taking advantage of a large infrastructure program aimed at increasing school attendance for children between the ages of 3 and 5. Between 1993 and 1999, Argentina constructed enough classrooms for approximately 186,000 additional children to attend pre-school. By conditioning on region and cohort fixed effects, the construction program generated plausible exogenous variation in the supply of school facilities. Using an identification strategy similar to Rosenzweig and Wolpin (1988), Card and Krueger (1992), and Duflo (2001), among others, they exploit the variation in treatment intensity across regions and cohorts to estimate the effect of expanding pre-primary school facilities on subsequent achievement in primary school.

The results in Berlinski, Galiani, and Gertler (2009) show that attending pre-primary school had a positive effect on subsequent third-grade standardized Spanish and Mathematics test scores. They estimate that one year of pre-primary school increased average third-grade test scores by 8% of a mean or by 23% of the standard deviation of the distribution of test scores. They also find that pre-primary school attendance positively affected students' behavioral skills such as attention, effort, class participation, and discipline. This positive effect on behavioral skills provides evidence of possible pathways by which pre-primary might affect subsequent primary school test performance, as pre-school education facilitates the process of socialization and self-control necessary to make the most of classroom learning (Currie 2001). Moreover, behavioral skills are as important as cognitive skills to future success in life.

Berlinski, Galiani, and Manacorda (2008) (hereafter, BGM) estimate the effect of pre-primary education on school stay-on rates and levels of completed education among individuals aged 7–15. They exploit a rather unique feature of the Uruguayan Encuesta Continua de Hogares (ECH) for the years 2001–5 that collects retrospective information on the number of years of pre-school attended. In order to control for unobserved household characteristics that are common to all children in the household and that might simultaneously affect exposure to pre-primary education and school progression, they use a within-household estimator that only exploits variability in the outcome and treatment variables across siblings. A major expansion in the provision of public pre-primary education in Uruguay since the mid-1990s that led to an acceleration in pre-school attendance among subsequent birth cohorts and that mainly affected children from more disadvantaged backgrounds generates sufficient variation in exposure to pre-school attendance across siblings to warrant identification.

Nevertheless, parents may treat siblings differently, so that non-random selection within households is a potential threat to the consistency of the within-households estimates. Parental preferential treatment of some children, or changes in household resources along the family's life cycle, might imply that some siblings in the same households are both more likely to attend pre-school and to perform better in school or stay on longer. To address this potential threat to the identification, BGM rely on a variety of approaches. First, they control for some of the potentially spurious correlation between treatment and outcomes by conditioning on a number of children's characteristics, such as order of birth, gender, and mother's age at birth. Second, they present IV estimates that exploit average enrollment by cohort and locality as an instrument for treatment. Such source of variation is arguably uncorrelated with children's unobserved characteristics within each household, hence leading to consistent estimates of the treatment effects.

BGM find a significant positive effect of pre-school attendance on completed years of primary and secondary education. This works both through a fall in retention rates since the very early school years (from age 8 onwards) and a reduction in drop-out among teenagers (from age 13 onwards). The gains from having attended pre-school increase as children grow older, so that exposure to pre-primary education leads to gradually diverging paths in school performance between treated and untreated children. We speculate that early grade retention increases the incentives for early drop-out and raises the probability of grade failure later in the school life. Thus, pre-primary education appears as a successful policy to prevent early school failure and its long-lasting consequences.

In poor countries, a large share of the population is already excluded from the education system at an early age and well before completion of the compulsory schooling cycle. Exclusion from the school system encompasses in varying combinations failure to enroll, late entry, intermittent and irregular attendance, high retention rates, and eventually early drop-out.

In this context, early exposure to the school system appears as a possibly successful policy option. What makes pre-primary school different from primary school is that this is not generally conceived as an academic experience and children are not evaluated based on their performance. In Uruguay, as elsewhere, grade retention in pre-school is not an option (while it is in primary school), and children progress to the primary school cycle when they turn compulsory schooling age independently of their performance. This creates an environment for children to learn and socialize without some of the potentially distorted incentives linked to a formal evaluation system (such as competition among students or teachers) and guarantees a common starting ground for children from rather heterogenous backgrounds. If early success in school is a good predictor of later school performance, and if pre-school attendance strengthens early school outcomes particularly among children with worse school potential, then early interventions might yield high returns.

Comparing benefits and costs[11]

BGM estimated that, on average, the children who attended one year of pre-school at age 15 have accumulated around 0.79 more years of education than their non-treated siblings. They also found that untreated children are more likely to drop out from school than their treated siblings. By age 15 children who attended pre-school are 27 percentage points more likely to be in school. We can now use these estimates to compare the cost of offering 1 year of pre-primary education, say at kindergarten age, to the additional wealth generated by such intervention, under the assumptions that our estimates extend to all treated children and that the general equilibrium effects of it are not important. The better educational performance induced by attending 1 year of pre-primary education should translate into higher productivity and wages later in life. There is also evidence of other long-run benefits associated with education in general, and early interventions in education in particular, such as lower criminality, higher taxes revenue, and lower welfare payments (see Schweinhart *et al.* 1993 and Belfield *et al.* 2006). However, in our analysis we abstract from considering among the impacts of the intervention any possibly indirect effect for which we do not have direct evidence, in order to minimize the number of assumptions upon which the conclusion would rest.

One important issue related to pre-primary education is that of targeting it at the poor. Certainly, this can be done by means of geographically targeting supply of new rooms. This is regularly done in the LAC region. Still, someone might argue that it would be politically difficult to exclude the middle class from this intervention when they do not have access and target it at the poor. Still, since this intervention seems to be very cost-effective, extending the supply of pre-primary education beyond the poor seems a sensible policy.

We consider an intervention that consists of providing 1 year of public pre-primary education to one cohort of 50 students of 5 years of age. We estimate that in each new classroom can be fitted in 50 students per year in two shifts of 25 students each (see Berlinski, Galiani, and Gertler, 2009). In order to normalize the benefits and

[11] See also Damon and Glewwe's chapter 2 in this volume.

costs of the project in monetary terms, we transform all cash flows in terms of Uruguayan pesos of March 1997. We used the Uruguayan monthly Consumer Price Index published by the Instituto Nacional de Estadísticas (INE) and the monthly exchange rate published by the Banco Central del Uruguay. The exchange rate of March 1997 was UY$9.02 per US$.

The cost of this intervention is equal to the share of each cohort in the cost of constructing a new room, teacher wages, and other miscellaneous costs. There are also opportunity costs associated with acquiring higher education. For instance, students at school are consuming resources while individuals of the same cohort in the labor market might be contributing to the production of goods and services.

We fixed the cost of building a pre-primary classroom as US$35,000 according to Adminitracion Nacional de la Education Publica. A given cohort has to bear only a portion of this cost because the classroom will be utilizable by other cohorts of students in later years. Therefore, we assigned to the project the constant payment needed to cancel a loan of US$35,000 in 25 years using an annual interest rate of 10% per year. This assumption might be conservative since it implies that we fully depreciate the investment in 25 years. The spot price of the land over which the classroom is built is assumed to be US$5,000. We also assign to the cost of the project the interest over the value of the land also using an annual rate of 10%. Thus, taking into account both costs, we estimate the infrastructure cost of the intervention considered as UY$39,299.

We estimate the average monthly wage of schoolteachers using microdata from the ECH household survey for the period 1992–9. Wages were deflated into pesos of March 1997 and then averaged over the period. The monthly wage of a teacher that we assume attends both shifts is UY$4,460. Additionally, we estimate miscellaneous monthly costs as UY$2,230 (i.e. 0.5 of the monthly cost of a school teacher).

We estimated that the treated children would have higher enrollment rates during the subsequent school period considered. This also entails costs. First, there is the cost associated with the use of resources of the schooling system. In order to compute this cost, we multiply the estimated effect of attending 1 year of pre-primary education on enrollment by the estimated cost of supplying 1 year of education – which, for simplicity, we assume constant through the schooling system. We use the estimates in BGM's table 5 (column (4)) to calculate the effect of pre-school education on educational attainment. For instance, by age 15 treated children are 27 percentage points more likely to be in school. This means that 10 years after the intervention is executed, there is an additional cost that needs to be imputed to the project equal to 0.27 times the total cost of the first year of the program. We do this same computation for children aged 6–14; in each case, costs are properly discounted at the prevailing discount rate. Second, we also need to take into account the opportunity cost of attending school. We estimate that 27% of the children that are now in the school would have been in the labor market in the absence of the intervention. A portion of them would have been actually employed. The unemployment rate in Uruguay for the age group 15–24 years is 0.3. Therefore, we estimate the opportunity cost of the forgone labor income as the probability of being employed (0.7) times the proportion of children in school as a result of the intervention (e.g. 0.27 at age 15) times the mean income for children of each age (e.g. UY\$1,209 at age 15) times 50 children. We assume that only children older than 13 years of age participate in the labor market.

By age 15 treated children have accumulated 0.79 more years of education. We assume that this difference will be maintained beyond age 15. We adopt a rate of return to education of 10%. Therefore, a treated individual will earn 7.9% more per year than an untreated one. We estimated from the household survey age-specific average real wages over the period 1992–9, using the microdata gathered from the ECH.

We further assume that all individuals enter the labor market at age 16. Then, the benefits stemming from the intervention x years after it is carried out are calculated as: the age-conditional average yearly income of an individual $x + 5$ years old times 1 − the unemployment rate times 0.079. Benefits are computed this way for $x = 11 \ldots 60$. The net present benefit induced by the program is then calculated by adding the discounted benefits at each age $x + 5$ for $x = 11 \ldots 60$. The unemployment rate for individuals older than 24 years is 0.085.

Using alternative discount rates we find the NPVs and BCRs in table 8.12.

With these assumptions, the IRR of the intervention is 16%. These results are commensurate with those of other early child interventions. BCRs for the Perry Preschool Project range from 6.87 to 16.14 for annual discount rates of 7 and 3%, respectively (see Belfield

Table 8.12 *NPVs and BCRs*

Discount rate	NPV	BCR
0.03	UY$3,365,429	19.1
0.06	UY$1,220,804	8.2
0.08	UY$643,573	5.0

et al. 2006). The Chicago Child–Parent Center Program exhibited ratios ranging from 4.3 to 7.14 for discount rates of 7% and 3% (see Reynolds *et al.* 2002). Finally, the ratios for the Abecedarian project were 1.45–3.78, respectively (see Masse and Barnett 2003).

We have conducted some sensitivity analysis on these BCRs. Before, we assumed that one teacher works two shifts. However, it might be that even if they work for 8 hours per day, due to collective agreements or other rules, they in fact work only one shift. In this case, the IRR drops slightly to 14% and the BCR varies between 13.1 and 2.2, depending on the discount rate. Second, we assume that the return to 1 extra year of education is 8% instead of 10%. The IRR drops to 14.7% and the BCR varies between 15.2 and 2.5, again depending on the discount rate.

In sum, our data suggest that this policy intervention is highly cost-effective. Under the most conservative scenarios, we find an estimated rate of return to the expansion of pre-school education as high as 14% and BCRs greater than 2.2.

Taking stock

In the previous sections we have presented a set of interventions that, when properly targeted to the poor, appear to be, given our best estimates for their costs and benefits, decidedly cost-effective. These policies are being implemented in some countries of LAC, but surely there is scope for scaling them up to include other countries in the region.

We concluded that conditional cash transfers (CCTs) are cost-effective, and do not engender major disincentive effects. According to the experiences with CCTs described, there appear to be no reductions in employment among adults. In fact, there is some evidence that beneficiary households increased their participation in microenterprise activities and increased their agricultural production investments. In addition to these, the lack of evidence of changes in fertility rates implies that there has been no change in demographic incentives. CCT interventions also tend to reduce child labor, to promote the enhancement of the human capital of poor children, and to increase current consumption in poor households.

This last effect is of great importance, because even if other early childhood interventions were more cost-effective than CCT interventions, the corresponding analysis would not take into account intergenerational equity considerations. Furthermore, it is likely to be politically infeasible to conduct an anti-poverty program based solely on interventions that only affect the future income of the poor, even if these interventions were found to be more cost-effective than CCTs (an exception may be countries with low poverty rates).

There is another very relevant advantage of CCTs. As we mentioned, CCTs involve potentially high transfers to the poor, which in turn could have a substantial impact in reducing poverty and inequality. There may be other interventions that are highly cost-effective, but if the transfer is very small, their impact on poverty is limited. Thus, CCT programs should be at the core of the redistributive component of an integral strategy to reduce poverty in LAC.

In the previous sections we also emphasized the importance of education in avoiding the perpetuation of poverty and inequality in the region. We strongly consider that the region should invest heavily in education, attempting to achieve ten years of schooling for the poor (primary and basic secondary school plus at least one year of pre-primary education). A combination of CCTs and supply-side interventions to expand the supply of pre-primary education could be effective in achieving these goals.

Even though increasing the supply of education is key to overcoming poverty and inequality, the quality of education is also of great concern. Ferreira (2004) shows that, measured by international standards, the LAC region has, on average, middling levels of educational inequality but high levels of income inequality. This in part reflects the huge differences that exist in educational quality across income groups. Countries from LAC that participated in international tests have obtained substantially lower scores than the scores of countries from the OECD, East Asia and Eastern Europe countries. The result reflects not only a lower average but also a wide dispersion in LAC.

However, there is no consensus as to the best way to go about improving education quality.[12]

Finally, it is worth emphasizing that a progressive plan to reduce poverty in LAC should go beyond CCTs and early childhood interventions in nutrition and education. Therefore, in the next subsection, we briefly discuss other interventions which could potentially be effective in reducing poverty and inequality but for which we did not have enough information to assess their BCRs.

Other promising interventions

Education

Indigenous people as a group have been found to lag behind the general population in educational achievement. In recent years, there has been growing interest in bilingual education targeted at minority groups. This type of policy can improve the schooling achievements of the indigenous population (see Dutcher and Tucker 1994).

In order to promote social mobility and meritocracy, at least those countries with the lowest levels of poverty might consider adopting scholarship programs for tertiary education directed at the poor based on conditional merit (see Galiani 2007b). Such an intervention may well be cost-effective, since returns to education appear to be convex in the LAC region.

Property rights and land reform

Security of property rights is essential for investment and growth (see, among others, Acemoglu *et al.* 2001). In the LAC region, elites tend to have more secure property rights than the rest of society. This situation is especially troubling for the poor because they tend to own land for which titling is incomplete, which makes it harder to sell or mortgage. This, in turn, detracts from incentives for the poor to invest in productive activities and other assets.

Redistributive land reform has long been advocated as a source of both greater equity and greater efficiency. However, it is important to take into account the relationship between the size of landholdings and productivity. Small farms can be efficient units of production, but this depends on conditions specific to particular crops and associated

---

[12] See Damon and Glewwe's chapter 2 in this volume.

factors such as marketing and credit (see De Ferranti *et al.* 2004). In the case of Mexico, Finan *et al.* (2002) find that there is the potential for making large, poverty-reducing gains from landholdings as small as 1 or 2 ha.

Walton (2004) argues that it is important to distinguish between countries (and among areas within countries) with regard to where existing land rights are and are not contested. In the former case, there is greater scope for land reform to enhance both equity and efficiency. However, whether this type of intervention is cost-effective or not is something we cannot answer right now, although there are grounds for maintaining that such interventions may be useful in attaining large productivity gains. For example, Banerjee, Gertler, and Ghatak (2002) found that a reform of tenancy that forced landlords to raise the share of output going to the sharecroppers, and also gave them a secure right to the land, raised productivity by about 50%. Thus, in the LAC region, where land rights are contested, there appears to be scope for strengthening tenancy markets and for land titling programs. Indeed, the tenancy market in the region is severely under-developed. The primary reasons for this are weak property rights and a lack of conflict resolution mechanisms, sometimes combined with prohibitions on renting (Walton 2004).

However, the effectiveness of this policy should be weighed with caution, since there is a history of land reform failure in the region. De Janvry and Sadoulet (2002) argue that this is the result of incomplete reforms or poorly designed reforms which focused on ill-fated production cooperatives. Nevertheless, caution may still be called for in advocating land reform proposals as a means of reducing poverty, since there are large complementarities between the land market and the credit and commercialization markets. Also, access to infrastructure appears to be an important complement to land as a key input in income generation by small farmers. Land reform might easily fail in the absence of actions on other fronts.

The potential of urban land titling to serve as a powerful policy instrument to attack poverty has recently been brought to the fore in policy circles by the work of De Soto (2000). De Soto argues that titled property creates capital because formal landholders can use these assets as collateral for loans. In turn, this credit can be invested in capital goods to increase labor productivity and, hence, the income of the poor.

Galiani and Schargrodsky (2006) exploit a natural experiment to solve the problem of comparability between titled and untitled families. More than twenty years ago, a large number of comparable squatter families occupied a very small area of wasteland on the outskirts of Buenos Aires. The area was made up of different tracts of land, each with a different legal owner. An expropriation law was subsequently passed under which the land was to be transferred to the State in exchange for a monetary compensation. The purpose of the law was to allow the State to subsequently transfer legal titles to the squatters. However, only some of the original legal owners surrendered their land, which was then titled to the squatters. Other owners are still contesting the compensation payment in the slow-moving Argentine courts. As a result, a group of squatters obtained formal land rights, while others are still living on similar parcels without legal title.

Families that received formal title to their land between 7 and 14 years ago now own much better houses than the untitled families. Based on an analysis of a broad set of investment indicators, the study concludes that the titled houses are 40% better than the untitled ones. Do titled households have more access to credit? The evidence suggests that there is not much difference on this count: the effect is small. In addition, there are no differences at all between these two groups' actual earnings. This study also shows that the households that have titled parcels tend to be smaller in size and seem to invest more in the education and health of their children. This would seem to indicate that providing poor households with land titles prompts them to enhance their investments in both their houses and in the human capital of their children, which will reduce their poverty in the future.

Rural infrastructure

The expansion of infrastructure – rural roads, electrification, water and sanitation, and information and communication technologies – is considered to be an important component of poverty alleviation strategies (see, among others, Walton 2004). Increasing access to infrastructure reduces transaction costs and increases productivity by facilitating access to the markets for factors of production and final goods and by improving production technology. The expansion of infrastructure affects relative prices within the category of agricultural products and between agricultural and non-agricultural products, which in turn influences the allocation of time between different income-generating activities. Increasing access to infrastructure reduces the prices that poor households pay for services that they are currently purchasing: poor people often pay higher prices for services from informal infrastructure providers than they would be charged if the appropriate infrastructure were available.

Unfortunately, there are no credible experimental or quasi-experimental evaluations of the effects of rural infrastructure investments on earnings for the LAC region. Escobal and Torero (2005) present simple cross-sectional evidence on the effects of access to electricity, water, telephone lines, and roads on earnings in rural Peru. They also show evidence of complementarities between access to these different types of infrastructure, and their impact on income. Thus, we believe that this evidence points to an important opportunity for furthering the poverty-reduction agenda. Rigorous evaluation is urgently needed in this area.

The growth of agricultural activity in poor rural areas can drive poverty reduction through three broad mechanisms: the direct impacts of increased agricultural productivity and incomes on the rural poor who earn significant portions of their income as farmers or farm laborers; the benefits of cheaper food for both the urban and rural poor; and agriculture's contribution to growth and the generation of economic opportunity in the non-farm sector. Over time, this leads to structural economic change, as the non-farm economy grows in importance and the relative importance of the agricultural sector declines. The critical role of agriculture and agricultural markets in poverty reduction therefore applies only to poor economies that have not already achieved significant agricultural development.

Markets provide the most important mechanism for efficient, coordinated economic exchange. Promoting more efficient and extensive markets and providing more favorable market access to the poor are important elements in facilitating their access to exchange mechanisms. Development of agricultural markets could play such a role in extremely poor rural areas. Again, however, these types of interventions need to be rigorously evaluated before they can be scaled up throughout the poorest rural areas in the region.

Credit and insurance
The extensive cross-country literature on credit shows a strong correlation between "financial depth" and growth (see, for example, King and Levine 1993). However, the poor do not have access to banks

or other formal financial institutions (see, among others, Banerjee and Duflo, 2007). Credit from informal sources tends to be expensive. Rather than being attributable to high rates of default, this seems to be a result of the high costs of contract enforcement (Banerjee and Duflo, 2005). The poor also have little access to formal insurance.

One much-heralded innovation as regards the delivery of credit and insurance is that of microfinance institutions, which target the poor and rely on peer selection and peer monitoring to overcome the need for collateral. These schemes are typically operated by NGOs, but in some cases may need to be subsidized in order to operate properly. A policy of providing subsidies to microfinance institutions could be viewed as a type of intervention with the potential for reducing poverty by facilitating investment projects with very high rates of return (see Banerjee and Duflo 2005) and by smoothing the effects of severe shocks that seriously impact the poor (see, among others, Gertler and Gruber 2002).

However, it is worth noting that the success of microfinance initiatives may depend on the context, at least to a certain extent. The existence of opportunities to be capitalized upon by borrowers, the degree of stability of the economy, the level of development, and other such factors may directly affect the degree of success attained by the investment projects being financed by such institutions and, consequently, the degree of success of the microfinance projects as well. Thus, this idea requires further examination in terms of design and an extended period of evaluation before it can be scaled up to a region-wide level.

Parting thoughts

Stimulating economic growth should be at the core of any hope of substantially reducing poverty in the LAC region. However, in order to halve poverty in 10 years, *ceteris paribus, per capita* growth would need to accelerate to at least 3.5% per year, which even though it is not only well above the region's historical average for the last 40 years, but is also higher than the levels achieved during the 1990s, we believe is possible if the reform process initiated in the 1980s is invigorated and enhanced instead of depleted.

To accelerate economic growth, it is of key importance for the region to create an environment that reduces the distortions between the private and social returns to investments, thereby allowing entrepreneurs to appropriate a significant portion of the revenues generated by their investments and innovative projects.

Clearly, there are grounds for arguing that the high levels of inequality prevalent in the LAC region generate an excess burden of poverty over and above what would be expected given the region's level of development. Thus, reducing inequality is another powerful strategy for reducing poverty in the region. One striking feature is how little redistribution is carried out. Comparing income inequality between members of the OECD and the LAC countries, one sees that roughly half of all sharp income inequalities stem from differences in returns to factors of production, while the other half are the result of the more progressive taxation and transfer systems in existence in the OECD area.

Revenues from personal income taxes are low in the LAC region, even when compared with receipts in countries with similar income levels. This suggests that there is scope for increasing such revenues in order to improve the after-tax distribution of income. Property taxes are also currently under-utilized and could be used to increase redistribution. Nevertheless, the potential for achieving greater redistribution only via taxation is to some extent limited in developing countries by the fact that their tax systems rely heavily on indirect taxes.

Additionally, in most developing countries, and certainly in the LAC region, the poor operate primarily in the informal economy and are therefore beyond the reach of conventional tax and transfer mechanisms. Not only that, but a broad range of labor market policies dealing with such matters as minimum wages and wage subsidies for unskilled workers, although used in developed countries to affect the income levels of the working poor, are unlikely to be effective in most of the countries in the region. This fact represents a constraint for any strategy aimed at reducing poverty and inequality.

In this chapter, we have presented a set of interventions that, when properly targeted at the poor, are decidedly cost-effective. These policies are being implemented in some LAC countries, but surely there is scope now for scaling them up to include other countries in the region.

CCTs are not only cost-effective but, as we have seen, they also do not generate major disincentive effects. There is no evidence of reductions in employment among adults. To the contrary, there is some evidence that beneficiary households increased their participation in microenterprise activities and made larger investments in agricultural production activities. There is no evidence of significant changes in fertility rates, which in turn suggests that there has been no change in demographic incentives. CCT interventions also tend to reduce child labor. Finally, they not only promote the enhancement of the human capital of poor children, which may help them to escape poverty during adulthood, but they also increase current consumption in poor households. We want to emphasize this last effect here. Even if other early childhood interventions were more cost-effective than CCT interventions, the corresponding analysis would not take into account intergenerational equity considerations. Additionally, with the exception of countries where poverty is very low, it is likely to be politically unviable to conduct an anti-poverty program based solely on interventions that affect only the future income of the poor, even if these interventions were found to be more cost-effective than CCTs.

Another advantage of CCT interventions is that the transfers to the poor are potentially high and hence could have a substantial impact in reducing poverty and inequality. In other words, interventions that are highly cost-effective, but that transfer very small amounts of resources to the poor, are surely worth adopting, but are limited in their impact on poverty. Thus, we conclude that CCT programs should be at the core of the redistributive component of an integral strategy to reduce poverty in the LAC region.

Educational factors lie at the center of the perpetuation of poverty and inequality in the region. We believe that it should invest heavily in education, attempting to achieve 10 years of schooling for the poor (i.e. primary and basic secondary school) plus at least 1 year of pre-primary education (i.e. kindergarten). A combination of CCTs and supply-side interventions to expand the supply of pre-primary education could be effective in achieving these goals.

Certainly, a progressive plan to reduce poverty in LAC should go beyond CCTs and early childhood interventions in nutrition and education. We outlined a set of other promising interventions. For some of them there is credible evidence on its impact, while for others we still know less. We need more rigorous evaluations in these (and other) areas in order to assess the virtues of these potential interventions, but we also need better estimates of their cost functions in order to assess their cost-effectiveness.

Bibliography

Acemoglu, D., M.A. Bautista, P. Querubin, and J. Robinson, 2007. "Economic and Political Inequality in Development." NBER Working Paper **13208**

Acemoglu, D., S. Johnson, and J. Robinson, 2001. "The Colonial Origins of Comparative Development: An Empirical Investigation." *American Economic Review* **91**: 1369–1401

2005. "Institutions as a Fundamental Cause of Long-Run Growth." In P. Aghion and S. Durlauf, eds., *Handbook of Economic Growth*. Amsterdam: North-Holland

Adato, M., 2000. "Final Report: The Impact of Progresa on Community Social Relationships." Washington, DC: International Food Policy Research Institute

Aghion, P., M. Angeletos, A. Banerjee, and K. Manova, 2004a. "Volatility, R&D, and Growth." Harvard University, mimeo

Aghion, P., R. Blundell, R. Griffith, P. Howit, and S. Prantl, 2004b. "Entry, Innovation and Growth: Theory and Evidence." Harvard University, mimeo

Aghion, P. and P. Bolton, 1997. "A Theory of Trickle-Down Growth and Development." *Review of Economic Studies* **64**: 151–72

Alesina, A. and D. Rodrik, 1994. "Distributive Politics and Economic Growth." *Quarterly Journal of Economics* **109**(2): 465–90

Ashworth, A., 1998. "Effects of Intrauterine Growth Retardation on Mortality and Morbidity in Infants and Young Children." *European Journal of Clinical Nutrition* **52**, Supplement: S34–S42

Attanasio, O. and M. Vera-Hernández, 2004. "Medium and Long Run Effects of Nutrition and Child Care: Evaluation of a Community Nursery Program in Rural Colombia." University College London, unpublished manuscript

Banerjee, A. and E. Duflo, 2005. "Growth Theory through the Lens of Development Economics." In P. Aghion and S. Durlauf, eds., *Handbook of Economic Growth*. Amsterdam: North-Holland

2007. "The Economic Lives of the Poor." *Journal of Economic Perspectives*, **21**(1): 141–67

Banerjee, A., P. Gertler, and M. Ghatak, 2002. "Empowerment and Efficiency: Tenancy Reform in West Bengal." *Journal of Political Economy* **110**(2): 239–80

Banerjee, A. and A. Newman, 1993. "Occupational Choice and the Process of Development." *Journal of Political Economy* **101**(2): 274–98

Barhman, T., 2005. "Providing a Healthier Start to Life: The Impact of Conditional Cash Transfers on Infant Mortality." Department of Agriculture and Resource Economics, University of California at Berkeley, mimeo.

Beaton, G., R. Martorell, K. Aronson, B. Edmonston, G. McCake, A.C. Ross *et al.*, 1993. "Effectiveness of Vitamin A Supplementation in the Control of Young Child Morbidity and Mortality in Developing Countries."

Geneva: United Nations, Administrative Committee on Coordination and Subcommittee on Nutrition, mimeo

Belfield, C.R., M. Nores, S. Barnett, and L. Schweinhart, 2006. "The High/Scope Perry Preschool Program: Cost-Benefit Analysis Using Data from the Age-40 Follow-up." *Journal of Human Resources* **41**(1): 162–90

Benhabib, J. and M. Spiegel, 1994. "The Role of Human Capital in Economic Development: Evidence from Aggregate Cross-Country Data." *Journal of Monetary Economics* **34**: 143–73

Behrman, J., 1993. "The Economic Rationale for Investing in Nutrition in Developing Countries." *World Development* **21**(11): 1749–72

Behrman, J., H. Alderman, and J. Hoddinott, 2004. "Malnutrition and Hunger." Chapter 7 in Bjørn Lomborg, ed., *Global Crisis, Global Solutions*, 1st edn. Cambridge: Cambridge University Press

Behrman, J. and A. Deolalikar, 1988. "Wages and Labor Supply in Rural India: The Role of Health, Nutrition and Seasonality." In D. Sahn, ed., *Causes and Implications of Seasonal Variability in Household Food Security*. Baltimore, MD: Johns Hopkins University Press

Behrman, J. and J. Hoddinott, 2000. "An Evaluation of the Impact of PRO-GRESA on Pre-School Child Height." Washington, DC: International Food Policy Research Institute

Behrman, J.J. Hoddinott, J. Maluccio, A. Quisumbing, R. Martorell, and A. Stein, 2003. "The Impact of Experimental Nutritional Interventions on Education into Adulthood in Rural Guatemala: Preliminary Longitudinal Analysis." IFPRI, mimeo

Behrman, J., S.W. Parker, and P. Todd, 2004. "Medium-Term Effects of the Oportunidades Program Package, including Nutrition, on Education of Rural Children Age 0–8 in 1997." Technical Document **9** on the Evaluation of Oportunidades

2006. "Medium-Term Effects of the Oportunidades Program Package on Young Children." Revised version

2007. "Do School Subsidy Programs Generate Lasting Benefits? A Five-Follow-Up of *Oportunidades* Participants." Revised version

Behrman, J., P. Sengupta, and P. Todd, 2000. "Final Report: The Impact of PROGRESA on Achievement Test Scores in the First Year." Washington, DC: International Food Policy Research Institute

2001. "Progressing through PROGRESA: An Impact Assessment of a School Subsidy Experiment." University of Pennsylvania, mimeo

Behrman, J. and P. Todd, 1999. "Randomness in the Experimental Samples of PROGRESA (Education, Health, and Nutrition Program)." Washington, DC: International Food Policy Research Institute

Belfield C.R., M. Nores, S. Barnett, and L. Schweinhart, 2006. *The High/Scope Perry Preschool Program: Cost-Benefit Analysis Using Data from the Age-40 Follow-up. Journal of the Human Resources* **41**(1): 162–90

Berlinski, S. and S. Galiani, 2007. "The Effect of a Large Expansion of Pre-Primary School Facilities on Preschool Attendance and Maternal Employment." *Labour Economics* **14**: 665–80

Berlinski, S., S. Galiani, and P. Gertler, 2009. "The Effect of Pre-Primary Education on Primary School Performance." *Journal of Public Economics* **93**(2): 219–34

Berlinski, S., S. Galiani, and M. Manacorda, 2008. "Giving Children a Better Start: Preschool Attendance and School-Age Profiles." *Journal of Public Economics* **92**(5): 1416–40

Besley, T. and R. Burgess, 2003. "Halving Global Poverty." *Journal of Economic Perspective* **17**(3): 3–22

Bourguignon, F. and C. Morrison, 2002. "Inequality Among World Citizens: 1820–1992." *American Economic Review* **92**(4): 727–44

Brabin, B., M. Hakimi, and D. Pelletier, 2001. "An Analysis of Anemia and Pregnancy-Related Maternal Mortality." *Journal of Nutrition* **131**(2S-2): S604–S614

Burgess, S. and N. Stern, 1993. "Taxation and Development." *Journal of Economic Literature* **31**(2): 762–830

Busso, M., M. Cicowiez, and L. Gasparini, 2005. "Ethnicity and the Millennium Development Goals in Latin America and the Caribbean." Documento de Trabajo **27**, CEDLAS

Card, D. and A. Krueger,1992. "Does School Quality Matter? Returns to Education and the Characteristics of Public Schools in the United States." *Journal of Political Economy* **100**: 1–40

Carneiro, P. and J. Heckman, 2003. "Human Capital Policy." NBER Working Paper **9495**

Caulfield, L.E., S.A. Richard, J.A. Rivera, P. Musgrove, and R.E. Black, 2006. "Stunting, Wasting, and Micronutrient Deficiency Disorder." Chapter 28 in D.T. Jamison, J. Brenan, A. Measham, G. Alleyne, M. Claeson, D. Evans, P. Jha, A. Mills, and P. Musgrove, eds., *Disease Control Priorities in Developing Countries*, 2nd edn. New York and Oxford: Oxford University Press

Chen, S. and M. Ravallion, 2007. "Absolute Poverty Measures for the Developing World, 1981–2004." World Bank Policy Research Working Paper **4211**

Chu, K., H. Davoodi, and S. Gupta, 2000. "Income Distribution and Tax and Government Social Spending Policies in Developing Countries." United Nations University and World Institute for Development Economics Research Working Paper **214**

Coady, D., 2000. "Final Report: The Application of Social Cost-Benefit Analysis to the Evaluation of PROGRESA." Washington, DC: International Food Policy Research Institute

Coady, D., F. Ferreira, G. Perry, and Q. Woodon, 2004. "Taxation, Public Expenditure and Transfers." In D. De Ferranti, G. Perry, F. Ferreira, and M. Walton, eds., *Inequality in Latin America: Breaking with History?* Washington, DC: World Bank

Coady, D., M. Grosh, and J. Hoddinott, 2004. "Targeting Outcomes Redux." *The World Bank Research Observer* **19**(1): 61–85

Currie, J. 2001. "Early Childhood Education Programs." *Journal of Economic Perspectives* **15**(2): 213–38

Datt, G. and M. Ravallion, 1992. "Growth and Redistribution Components of Changes in Poverty Measures: A Decomposition with Applications to Brazil and India in the 1980s." *Journal of Development Economics* **38**(2): 275–95

Deaton, A., 1997. *The Analysis of Households Surveys: A Microeconometric Approach to Development Policy*, Baltimore, MD: Johns Hopkins University Press

  2006. "Measuring Poverty." In A. Banerjee, R. Benabou, and D. Mookherjee, eds., *Understanding Poverty*. Oxford: Oxford University Press

Deaton, A. and S. Zaidi, 2002. "Guidelines for Constructing Consumption Aggregates for Welfare Analysis." LSMS Working Paper **135**

De Ferranti, D., G. Perry, F. Ferreira, and M. Walton, 2004. *Inequality in Latin America: Breaking with History?* Washington, DC: World Bank.

De Janvry, A. and E. Sadoulet, 2002. "Land Reforms in Latin America: Ten Lessons toward a Contemporary Agenda." Paper prepared for the World Bank's Latin American Land Policy Workshop, Pachuca, Mexico, June 14

Deolalikar, A., 1988. "Nutritional and Labor Productivity in Agriculture: Estimates for Rural South India." *Review of Economics and Statistics* **70**(3): 406–13

De Soto, H., 2000. *The Mystery of Capital: Why Capitalism Triumphs in the West and Fails Everywhere Else*. New York: Basic Books

De Watcher, S. and S. Galiani, 2006. "Optimal Income Support Targeting." *International Tax and Public Finance* **13**(6): 661–84

Duflo, E., 2001. "Schooling and Labor Market Consequences of School Construction in Indonesia: Evidence from an Unusual Policy Experiment." *American Economic Review* **91**: 795–813

Duryea, S., S. Galiani, H. Ñopo, and C. Piras, 2007. "Educational Gender Gap in Latin America and the Caribbean." IADB, mimeo

Dutcher, N. and G. Tucker, 1994. "The Use of First and Second Languages in Education: A Review of Educational Experiences." World Bank, mimeo

ECLAC, 2005. *Objetivos de Desarrollo del Milenio: Una Mirada desde America Latiana y el Caribe.* Santiago: ECLAC

Engel, E., A. Galetovic, and C. Raddatz, 1998. "Taxes and Income Distribution in Chile: Some Unpleasant Redistributive Arithmetic." NBER Working Paper **6828**

Engle, P., M.M. Black, J.R. Behrman, M.C. de Mello, P.J. Gertler, L. Kapiriri, R. Martorell, M.E. Young, and the International Child Development Steering Committee, 2007. "Stategies to Avoid the Loss of Developmental Potential in More than 200 million Children in the Developing World." *Lancet* **369**: 229–42

Escobal, J. and M. Torero, 2005. "Measuring the Impact of Asset Complementarities: The Case of Rural Peru." *Cuadernos de Economia* **42**: 137–64

Ferreira, F., 2004. "Economic Mechanisms for the Persistence of High Inequality in Latin America." In D. De Ferranti, G. Perry, F. Ferreira, and M. Walton, eds., *Inequality in Latin America: Breaking with History?* Washington, DC: World Bank

Finan, F., E. Sadoulet, and A. de Janvry, 2002. "Measuring the Poverty Reduction Potential of Land in Latin America." Department of Agriculture & Resource Economics, UCB. CUDARE Working Paper **983**, October 1

Fishman, S., L. Caulfield, M. de Onis, M. Blossner, A. Hyder, L. Mullany, and R. Black, 2004. "Childhood and Maternal Underweight." In M. Ezzati, A. Lopez, A. Rodgers, and C. Murray, eds., *Comparative Quantification of Health Risks: Global and Regional Burden of Disease Attributable to Selected Major Risk Factors.* Geneva: World Health Organization

Foster, A. and M. Rosenzweig, 1993. "Information, Learning, and Wage Rates in Low-Income Rural Areas." *Journal of Human Resources* **28**(4): 759–79

Galiani, S., 2007a. "Mercado de Trahajo y Reforma Laboral en Latin America" Cepal, mimeo
    2007b. "Notes on Social Mobility." Document for the 7th Social Equity Forum. Inter-American Development Bank, Poverty Unit

Galiani, S. and E. Schargrodsky, 2006. "Effects of Land Titles." Universidad Torcuato Di Tella, mimeo

Galiani, S. and F. Weinschelbaum, 2007. "Modeling Informality Formality: Firms and Households." Universidad de San Andres, mimeo

Galor, O. and J. Zeira, 1993. "Income Distribution and Macroeconomics." *Review of Economic Studies* 60: 35–52

Gasparini, L., 2004. "Different Lives: Inequality in Latin America and the Caribbean." In D. De Ferranti, G. Perry, F. Ferreira, and M. Walton, eds., *Inequality in Latin America: Breaking with History?* Washington, DC: World Bank

2007. "A Guide to the SEDLAC: Socio-Economic Database for Latin America and the Caribbean." www.depeco.econo.unlp.edu.ar/cedlas/sedlac/guide.htm

Gasparini, L., F. Gutiérrez, and L. Tornarolli, 2006. "Growth and Income Poverty in Latin America and the Caribbean: Evidence from Household Surveys." *Review of Income and Wealth* 53(2): 209–45

Gertler, P., 2000. "Final Report: The Impact of PROGRESA on Health." Washington, DC: International Food Policy Research Institute

2004. "Do Conditional Cash Transfers Improve Child Health? Evidence from PROGRESA's Control Randomized Experiment." *American Economic Review* 94(2): 336–41

Gertler, P. and L.C. Fernald, 2004. "The Medium Term Impact of *Oportunidades* on Child Development in Rural Areas." unpublished manuscript

Gertler, P. and J. Gruber, 2002. "Insuring Consumption Againt Illness." *American Economic Review* 92(1): 51–70.

Gertler P.J., S. Martinez, and M. Rubio, 2006. "Investing Cash Transfers to Raise Long Term Living Standards." World Bank Policy Research Working Paper **3994**

Glewwe, P. and P. Olinto, 2004. "Evaluating the Impact of Conditional Cash Transfers on Schooling: An Experimental Analysis of Honduras's PRAF Program." Final Report for USAID. Washington, DC: International Food Policy Research Institute

Glewwe, P., P. Olinto, and P.Z. de Souza, 2003. "Evaluating the Impact of Conditional Cash Transfers on Schooling in Honduras: An Experimental Approach." University of Minnesota, Minneapolis mimeo

Grantham-McGregor, S., L. Fernald, and K. Sethuraman, 1999a. "Effects of Health and Nutrition on Cognitive and Behavioral Development in Children in the First Three Years of Life, Part 1. Low Birth Weight, Breastfeeding and Protein-Energy Malnutrition." *Food and Nutrition Bulletin* 20(1): 53–75

1999b. "Effects of Health and Nutrition on Cognitive and Behavioral Development in Children in the First Three Years of Life, Part 2. Infections and Micronutrients Deficiencies: Iodine, Iron and Zinc." *Food and Nutrition Bulletin* 20(1): 76–99

Hausmann, R., L. Pritchett, and D. Rodrik, 2004. "Growth Accelerations." NBER Working Paper **10566**

Heckman, J. and D. Masterov, 2007. "The Productivity Argument for Investing in Young Children." IZA Discussion Paper **2725**

Heymann, D., F. Navajas, and I. Warnes, 1991. "Conflicto Distributivo y Deficit Fiscal: Algunos Juegos Inflacionarios." *El Trimestre Economico* **58**: 101–37

Hoddinott, J. and E. Skoufias, 2004. "The Impact of PROGRESA on Food Consumption." *Economic Development and Cultural Change* **53**(1): 37–61

Hoddinott, J., E. Skoufias, and R. Washburn, 2000. "The Impact of PROGRESA on Consumption: A Final Report." Washington, DC: International Food Policy Research Institute

Horton, S., T. Sanghvi, M. Phillips, J. Fiedler, R. Perez-Escamilla, C. Lutter, A. Rivera, and A. Segall-Correa, 1996. "Breastfeeding Promotion and Priority Setting in Health." *Health Policy and Planning* **11**: 156–68

Huggett, M., G. Ventura, and A. Yaron, 2007. "Sources of Lifetime Inequality." NBER Working Papers **13224**, NBER

King, R.G. and R. Levine, 1993. "Finance and Growth: Schumpeter might be Right." *Quarterly Journal of Economics* **108**(3): 717–37

Kraay, A., 2006. "When is Growth Pro-Poor? Evidence from a Panel of Countries." *Journal of Development Economics* **80**: 198–227

Krueger, A. and M. Lindahl, 2001. "Education for Growth: Why and for Whom?" *Journal of Economic Literature* **34**: 1101–36

Legovini, A., C. Bouillon and N. Lustig, 2001. "Can Education Explain Income Inequality Changes in Mexico?" Washington, DC: IADB

Maluccio, J.A., 2004. "Education and Child Labor: Experimental Evidence from a Nicaraguan Conditional Cash Transfer Program." In P. Orazem, G. Sedlaceck, and Z. Tzannatos, eds., *Child Labor in Latin America.* Washington, DC: World Bank and Inter-American Development Bank

Maluccio, J.A., M. Adato, R. Flores, and T. Roopnaraine, 2005. "Red de Protección Social-Mi Familia. Rompiendo el ciclo de Pobreza." Washington, DC: International Food Policy Research Institute

Maluccio, J.A. and R. Flores, 2005. "Impact Evaluation of a Conditional Cash Transfer Program: The Nicaraguan Red de Protección Social." Reaserch Report 141. Washington, DC: International Food Policy Research Institute

Mariscal, E. and K. Sokoloff, 2000. "Schooling, Suffrage, and Inequality in the Americas, 1800–1945." In S. Habber, ed., *Political Institutions and Economic Growth in Latin America.* Stanford, CA: Hoover Institution Press

Martorell, R., 1997. "Undernutrition During Pregnancy and Early Childhood: Consequences for Cognitive and Behavioral Development." In M.E. Young, ed., *Early Childhood Development: Investing in Our Children's Future*, International Congress Series **1137**. Amsterdam: Elsevier Science

Martorell, R., K. Khan, and D. Schroeder, 1994. "Reversibility of Stunting: Epidemiological Findings in Children from Developing Countries." *European Journal of Clinical Nutrition* **48**, Supplement: S45–S57

Masse L.N. and W.S. Barnett, 2003. *A Benefit Cost Analysis of the Abecedarian Early Childhood Intervention*. D: National Institute for Early Education Research, New Brunswick, NJ: Rutgers University.

Mookherjee, D., 2006. "Poverty Persistence and the Design of Antipoverty Policies." In A. Banerjee, R. Benabou, and D. Mookherjee, eds., *Understanding Poverty* Oxford: Oxford University Press

Myers, R., 1996. *The Twelve Who Survive: Strengthening Programs of Early Child Development in the Third World*, 2nd edn. Ypsilanti, MI: High/Scope Press

North, D., 1990. *Institutions, Institutional Change and Economic Performance*. Cambridge: Cambridge University Press

Parker, S.W. and E. Skoufias, 2000. "The Impact of PROGRESA on Work, Leisure and Time Allocation." Washington, DC: International Food Policy Research Institute

Paxson, C. and N. Schady, 2007. "Does Money Matter? The Effects of Cash Transfers on Child Health and Development in Rural Ecuador." World Bank Policy Research Working Paper **4226**

Perry, G., O. Arias, J. Humberto Lopez, W. Malloney, and L. Serven, 2006. *Poverty Reduction and Growth: Virtuous and Vicious Circles*. Washington DC: World Bank

Pollit, E., 1990. *Malnutrition and Infection in the Classroom*. Paris: UNESCO

Ravallion, M., G. Datt, and D. van de Walle, 1991. "Quantifying Absolute Poverty in the Developing World." *Review of Income and Wealth* **37**: 345–61

Reynolds, A., Judy A. Temple Dylan L. Robertson, and Emily A. Mann, 2002. *Age 21 Cost-Benefit Analysis of the Title I Chicago Child–Parent Centers*. Educational Evaluation and Policy Analysis, **24**(4): 267–303

Rivera, J., D. Sotres-Alvarez, J.P. Habicht, T. Shamah, and S. Villalpando, 2004. "Impact of the Mexican Program for Education, Health, and Nutrition (Progresa) on Rates of Growth and Anemia in Infants and Young Children. A Randomized Effectiveness Study." *Journal of the American Medical Association* **291**(21): 2563–70

Rodrik, D., 2005. "Growth Strategies." In P. Aghion and S. Durlauf, eds., *Handbook of Economic Growth*. Amsterdam: North-Holland

Ross, J. and F. Thomas, 1996. "Iron Deficiency Anemia and Maternal Mortality." Academy for Education Development", Profiles, 3, Working Notes Series, 3. Washington, DC: Academy for Education Development: 185–213

Rozensweig, M.R. and K.I. Wolpin, 1988, "Evaluating the Effects of Optimally Distributed Programs: Child Health and Family Planning Interventions." *American Economic Review* 76: 470–82

Schady, N., 2006. "Early Childhood Development in Latin America and the Caribbean." *Economia* 6(2): 185–213

Schady, N. and M.C. Araujo, 2006. "Cash Transfers, Conditions, School Enrollment and Child Work: Evidence from a Randomized Experiment in Ecuador." World Bank Policy Research Working Paper 3930

Schultz, P., 2000a. "Final Report: The impact of PROGRESA on School Enrollments." Washington, DC: International Food Policy Research Institute

2000b. "School Subsidies for the Poor: Evaluating a Mexican Strategy for Reducing Poverty." Washington, DC: International Food Policy Research Institute

2000c. "Impact of PROGRESA on School Attendance Rates in the Sampled Population." Washington, DC: International Food Policy Research Institute

2001. "School Subsidies for the Poor: Evaluating a Mexican Strategy for Reducing Poverty." Center Discussion Paper 834. Economic Growth Center, Yale University

2004. "School Subsidies for the Poor: Evaluating the Mexican Progresa Poverty Program." *Journal of Development Economics* 74: 199–250

Schultz, T., 1997. "Assessing the Productive Benefits of Nutrition and Health: An Integrated Human Capital Approach." *Journal of Econometrics* 77(1): 141–57

Schweinhart, L.J., H.V. Barnes, and D.P. Weikart, with W.S. Barnett, and A.S. Epstein, 1993. *Significant Benefits: The High/Scope Perry Preschool Study Through Age 27*. Monographs of the High/Scope Educational Research Foundation, 10. Ypsilanti, MI: High/Scope Press

Skoufias, E., 2005. "PROGRESA and Its Impacts on the Welfare of Rural Households in Mexico." Research Report 139. Washington, DC: International Food Policy Research Institute

Strauss, J. and D. Thomas, 1998. "Health, Nutrition, and Economic Development." *Journal of Economic Literature* 36(2): 766–817

Summers, L.H., 1992. " Investing in All the People." *Pakistan Development Review* 31(4): 367–406.

Talvi, E., 2001. "Latin American Macrowatch." Presentation at the IDB Research Department, May

Teruel, G. and B. Davis, 2000. "Final Report: An Evaluation of the Impact of Progresa Cash Payments on Private Inter-household Transfers." Washington, DC: International Food Policy Research Institute

Thomas, D. and J. Strauss, 1997. "Health and Wages: Evidence on Men and Women in Urban Brazil." *Journal of Econometrics* 77(1): 159–87

Todd, P.E., J.R. Behrman, and S.W. Parker, 2007. "Medium-Term Effects of the Opportunidades Program Package on Young Children." *Economic Development and Cultural Change*

UN, 2005. *5th Report on the World Nutrition Situation.* New York: United Nations

Wodon, Q., 2000. "Poverty and Policy in Latin America and the Caribbean." World Bank Report **467**

World Bank, 1990. *World Development Report: Poverty.* Oxford: Oxford University Press

2001. "Poverty and Income Distribution in a High Growth Economy: The Case of Chile 1987–98." World Bank Report **22017**

8.1 Reducing poverty: an alternative view

STEPHEN D. YOUNGER*

1 Introduction

Sebastian Galiani's chapter 8 proposes three solutions to the challenge of poverty and inequality in Latin America: nutritional interventions, conditional cash transfers (CCTs), and early childhood development (ECD) programs. His coverage of these topics is careful and thorough, leaving me with only a few concrete objections to his benefit-cost (B/C) estimates that may be useful for the Expert panel. Most of these are questions about the external validity of benefits and costs estimated from studies conducted outside of the LAC region. I will present these fairly limited comments in the second part of this alternative view. But my main criticism is that the scope of the solutions that Galiani offers is too narrow, in two ways. First, his B/C calculations focus on average benefits, without distinguishing benefits conditional on one's position in the income distribution. While this may aid comparability with other chapters in the volume, it seems an important oversight for a chapter on poverty and inequality, where distributional considerations should be of prime importance. Second, the main focus of Galiani's solutions is investments in children's human capital which will reduce (income) poverty only in the future. This reflects a widespread but somewhat outdated perception that it is not realistic to reduce immediate income poverty in developing countries because tax and transfer

* Many people helped me to prepare this alternative view. I had several helpful conversations with Harold Alderman, who suggested that distributional concerns should be an important part of this challenge; with David Coady, who provided me with several helpful papers and data from the evaluation of Progesa/Oportunidades; and with Peter Glick and David Sahn, who commented on early drafts and ideas. I received advice on references and the state of knowledge in various fields from Chris Barrett, Steven Beckman, Flavio Cunha, Teresa Gonzalez, Sue Horton, Chessa Lutter, Becky Stoltzfus, and Edy van Doerslaer. Thomas Walker provided excellent research assistance. Of course, all remaining errors are my own.

498

systems are difficult to implement there. Yet the recent success of several transfer payment schemes in the LAC region should have changed this perception.

To underscore this criticism, I will dedicate a significant share of this alternative view to showing the importance of weighting solution benefits based on recipients' position in the income distribution. I will do this in B/C language to highlight for the Expert panel the importance of considering not just the average costs and benefits of the proposed solutions, but the distribution of those costs and benefits across the income distribution.[1] This is especially true of any solutions to the challenge of poverty and inequality. The one exception to this is benefits that are non-monetary and intrinsically important in the sense of Sen's capabilities: things like good health, cognitive ability, political voice, security, etc. I see no compelling reason to value these capabilities more for the rich or the poor, though others certainly disagree.[2] At first, this might seem to include many of the solutions that the Expert committee will see, including those in chapter 8. However, in that chapter, and in many of the other chapters in this volume, these intrinsic benefits do not factor into the B/C calculations explicitly.[3] Instead, health and education benefits are valued based on their ability to produce *monetary* benefits (future income or savings in healthcare costs) alone. Those monetary benefits should be weighted. Using simple quantitative examples, I will show that quite reasonable social welfare weights can produce BCRs for (some of) Galiani's solutions that are significantly or dramatically higher than his estimates.

2 Review of Galiani's solutions

Nutritional interventions

This solution draws directly on Behrman, Alderman, and Hoddinott (2004, hereafter BAH), the Malnutrition and hunger chapter in the 2004 Copenhagen Consensus process volume. This is a sensible choice, since that chapter's solutions were ranked highly in 2004. I will follow

---

[1] This is not my original observation. Simon Appleton (2004) suggested it in his Alternative Perspectives paper 7.2 in Lomborg (2004).

[2] For example, the literature on the gradient approach to health inequality (Wagstaff, Paci, and van Doorslaer 1991; van Doorslaer *et al.* 1997).

[3] This point is also made by Appleton (2004).

Galiani's lead and refer the Expert panel to Simon Appleton's (2004) alternative perspectives for that chapter, which makes several insightful comments which I include below.

Promotion of breastfeeding

The evaluation of breastfeeding promotion relies on the estimates of Horton *et al.* (1996) and, in particular, BAH (2004), who appear to use the lowest cost per infant death averted in their chapter, from \$100–\$200 (in 1993 dollars). However, those costs were estimated for breastfeeding programs that were established in hospitals that had previously promoted formula feeding. Hospitals in the LAC region no longer do this, so the more relevant costs per death averted are the higher ones in Horton *et al.* (1996) \$549–\$807 – which were estimated for cases in which the comparison hospital did not promote formula use, but also did not have focused promotion and support for breastfeeding. This is the relevant comparison group in the LAC region today, so the estimated BCR should be 2.75 (549/200) to 8 (807/100) times lower than those reported in BAH (2004), and also in Galiani. The adjustment makes this solution unattractive. I should add that I do not want to argue that breastfeeding is a bad idea; quite the contrary. It is just that we have already made good progress and captured much of the benefits in the LAC region. The remaining effort – to promote *exclusive* breastfeeding for longer periods (up to 6 months) – has a lower return.

On the other hand, Horton *et al.* (1996) consider only the benefits from reduced diarrheal and respiratory infections. The study also ignores any benefits from reduced morbidity and mortality that breastfeeding after 6 months of age might produce. Each of these would increase our estimate of the benefits, but I cannot quantify that adjustment.

Micronutrient supplementation and fortification

The micronutrient interventions have the really eye-popping BCRs reported in BAH's table 7.9 and summarized in Galiani's table 8.7 (p. 447). Two of Appleton's comments bear repeating here. First, it is difficult to understand how BAH get from their very comprehensive review of the literature's cost and benefit estimates in the text to the ranges of costs and benefits reported in table 7.9. I have every confidence in their work, but it is difficult to consider the external validity of their results if we cannot be sure of the circumstances surrounding the estimates that they use. Second, given the very low cost of these interventions, it may not be possible to spend $10 billion on them. For example, at $0.25 per person for iron fortification, the cost per year for all of the LAC region is about $150 million. Iodine supplementation may not cost much more, and vitamin A, which has to be targeted only at young children, would be $60–$600 million per year. One way to think about this is that the marginal benefit to these interventions declines quickly: once someone has adequate micronutrient intake, further consumption has limited value.

This last observation raises a concern about the external validity of the studies used for the B/C estimates. BAH draw from studies around the world to estimate both benefits and costs of micronutrient interventions. Whether these studies are applicable to the LAC region is an open question. Galiani's tables 8.5 and 8.6 show that protein-calorie deficiency is less pronounced in the region than most other developing areas. This matters because the standard approach to these micronutrient deficiencies is to treat everyone regardless of whether s/he is deficient because the cost of testing outweighs the benefits of savings from treating fewer people, and the treatment dosages are not harmful even to those who are not deficient. As BAH note, the benefits for such a protocol vary in inverse proportion to the share of the population that is deficient. Since the LAC region has generally lower deficiencies, BCRs are lower here than elsewhere.[4] Much like the breastfeeding solution, it may be that we have already picked the low-hanging fruit in the region.

On the other hand, an interesting editorial in the *American Journal of Clinical Nutrition* (Rasmussen and Stoltzfus, 2003) notes that the results for iron deficiency in pregnancy that BAH use (from Nepal) were quite similar to results for low-income women in Cleveland. These two populations probably bracket a large share of the LAC region, so for iron deficiency, at least, the external validity of the BAH results may be good.

---

[4] Ideally, I would compare deficiencies in the LAC region to the pre-treatment deficiencies at the study sites cited in BAH (2004) but, as Appleton (2004) has noted, it is not easy to understand which results they used, and from what sites, in their B/C calculations.

Conditional cash transfers (CCTs)

The calculations for this solution are quite clear and careful, so I have
only three comments, only one of which is likely to change its estimated
BCRs significantly. First, on the increase in household consumption,
it makes more sense to simply use the amount transferred to households (13,311 pesos) rather than the estimated change in consumption
(10,203 pesos). Even if households chose not to spend all of the transfer
immediately, they presumably benefit from the savings at some future
period, so that should be included in the benefits. That will raise the
overall benefits slightly. Second, the simulations seem to assume that
no one works before age 18, even if s/he drops out of school. But
most children who drop out do so in order to work. This income
would reduce the income differences attributable to the program
somewhat.

The one comment that will have a substantial effect on the estimates
is that the benefits should be weighted by the beneficiaries' place in
the income distribution. As I show below, this increases the social
BCR significantly because Progesa/Oportunidades is well targeted at
the poor.

Early childhood development (ECD)

The analysis of this solution is also quite detailed and careful, so my
comments again are few. The inclusion of new B/C analyses for pre-
primary schooling in Uruguay is especially helpful, because the other
cited studies from developing countries (Bolivia, Jordan, and Turkey)
have relatively low BCRs. The studies from the United States – the
Perry Preschool and Abecedarian projects – have much higher BCRs,
but I worry about their external validity for the LAC region. The children in those programs will have "graduated" to high-quality school
systems. If there is complementarity between education investments
across time, as suggested by Galiani (see also the influential paper by
Cunha and Heckman 2004), then the returns to ECD may be lower
for children who will eventually attend poor-quality schools. Cunha
(2007) estimates a CES production function for cognitive skill acquisition and finds that pre-school and later investments are more complementary than a Cobb–Douglas specification. In the extreme case of
Leontief production functions, the returns to pre-school could be zero

if the complementary investments in primary and higher education are not also made. It is reassuring, then, to see high B/C estimates for the Uruguayan case, though I still wonder about the comparability of school systems in Uruguay and other LAC countries.

For the Hogares Comunitarios case, I am concerned about the extremely high estimate for the impact on child heights and would be uncomfortable if this accounted for a large share of the estimated benefits. For comparison, the estimated impact of the protein-calorie supplementation in the INCAP trial, an intervention specifically designed to reduce stunting, was only 2.45cm (Habicht, Martorell, and Rivera 1995). It is also worth noting that at least some of the benefits of this program, and perhaps a large share, come from increased parents' labor supply. That is a benefit, to be sure, but not a benefit to the children's human capital from ECD, but rather a benefit from a more efficient organization of parents' time. There appear to be economies of scale to childcare, so pooling care with the madre comunitaria enables parents to free up time without (presumably) reducing the quality of their children's care. That may make this a good program, but it is not an ECD investment *per se*.

Finally, it is worth noting that program coverage for pre-primary education in the LAC region is far from universal, and the incidence of smaller public services is often not very good. The middle class often succeeds in capturing these programs, even if they are intended for the poor. Thus, Galiani's assertion that such services can be effectively targeted to the poor merits some skepticism.

3 The scope of Galiani's solutions

The survey results that led to the inclusion of poverty and inequality as a challenge for the San José Consultation show that inequality figures prominently in respondents' opinions (Berkman and Cavallo 2006). Of those responding that poverty and inequality are a main challenge, 88% cited "unequal distribution of income and wealth" as a reason for choosing this challenge, vs. 68% for "incidence of poverty." Most of the other reasons cited for choosing this challenge – concentration of political power; social, ethnic, and racial discrimination; and concentration of land property – also reflect concerns about inequality more than poverty. Indeed, the reasons for citing some of the *other* challenges also reflect concerns about inequality; 60% of those choosing education as a challenge cite "disparities in access to quality higher education" as a reason: 86% of those choosing health cite "disparities in access to quality healthcare" as a reason. It is hard to see how this meeting can ignore inequality in the face of these results.

It is true that Galiani's solutions, and any of the other solutions that the Expert panel considers, will reduce both poverty and inequality *if* they are targeted at the poor, but there is nothing in the quantitative part of his analysis that actually values such targeting. This is because Galiani implicitly uses a social welfare function that values each person's wellbeing equally.[5] That is inconsistent with a concern for poverty, and especially inequality. Below, I will show how changing this assumption can increase significantly the social benefits of policies that are well targeted at the poor.

A second limitation is the strong focus on solutions whose benefits will mostly not come to fruition until the beneficiaries, today's children, enter the labor market in 15 years or so. The same LAC public that expresses concern about poverty and inequality may not be so patient as to have a 6% discount rate, and thus may not be satisfied with solutions that take effect only in the future. Indeed, the political popularity of conditional cash transfers in the LAC region is due to their combination of investments in human capital *and* current transfers. While CCTs are one of Galiani's proposed solutions, the only way that we find benefits greater than costs for CCTs is through the returns to the human capital investments. The transfer itself has a ratio less than 1, with the benefits (current consumption) less than the cost (the value of the transfer plus administration costs).

To be fair, Galiani does briefly consider transfer payments, but rejects them as unworkable: "Given the high levels of inequality prevalent in the region and the deficient capacity that exists for redistribution through conventional tax and transfer mechanisms, a package of cost-effective policies targeting poor households is needed to build up the present and future income-generation capacity of the poor." Indeed, this was the dominant view among development economists until recently, as reflected in the Besley and Burgess (2003) survey that Galiani cites. But the economic and political success

---

[5] Galiani is not alone in this. With only minor exceptions, all of the Copenhagen Consensus process contributions in Lomborg (2004) made the same assumption.

of CCTs is changing opinions rapidly. These transfer schemes can be achieved with modest administrative costs (Caldés, Coady, and Maluccio 2006) and significant redistributive benefits (Coady, Grosh, and Hoddinott 2004; Coady 2006). Further, transfer payments are a cornerstone of developed countries' anti-poverty programs. Sooner or later, they will have to gain importance in the LAC region as well though, as Galiani's figure 8.2 makes clear, relatively little redistribution currently takes place here.

4 Why weight?

Let me now run through some calculations to illustrate the importance of weighting benefits across the income distribution. I do this by considering a pure transfer payment scheme, which cannot have a BCR greater than 1 if everyone's benefits are valued equally, because it is not an investment and it does not increase productivity by resolving any market failure.[6] Thus, the only way that such a scheme will be attractive is if we weight the benefits for poorer people more heavily than benefits to the rich.

The choice of a particular social welfare function is arbitrary, but applied policy analyses such as this one generally prefer simple ones such as Atkinson's (1970):

$$W = \int_0^{y_{\max}} U(y) f(y) dy, \quad U(y) = \frac{y^{1-\varepsilon}}{1 - \varepsilon} \text{ if } \varepsilon \neq 1,$$

$$U(y) = \ln(y) \text{ if } \varepsilon = 1 \tag{1}$$

Important limitations of this function are its additive separability and the constant relative inequality aversion of $U(y)$. Nevertheless, the parameter ε allows us to vary the degree of inequality aversion, and that is the key requirement for this example. The weight that this function gives someone with income y_i relative to a reference income y^* is

$$\beta_i = \left(\frac{y^*}{y_i} \right)^{\varepsilon} \tag{2}$$

---

[6] One possible exception to this is if there are poverty traps, in which case a transfer may generate positive returns if it helps people change from a low- to a high-level equilibrium. These are potentially quite important, but I know of no evidence for this in the LAC region. Note that Gertler, Martinez, and Rubio-Codina (2006) find that households did invest 12% of their cash benefits from Progresa/Oportunidades at an average rate of return of 18%.

benefits than s/he pays in taxes for the transfers. The numerator could be positive or negative, but will be positive if the program succeeds in making progressive transfers. Here, we have to think of spending the IDB's $10 billion not on transfers, but on the costs of running a transfer scheme.

Another important difference is that we cannot ignore the efficiency costs of raising the funds to transfer. The typical Copenhagen Consensus process assumes that the money to invest is "free" in that it ignores how it is raised (or assumes that it was raised with non-distortionary taxes). The previous simulation follows that precedent. Here, however, the money would actually be used to bring about a transfer scheme that itself involves deadweight losses, so we have to account for them. Unfortunately, I have not found an estimate of the deadweight loss associated with a VAT or taxes in general in the LAC region. Instead, I use 25%, which is about the mid-point of both Feldstein's and Ballard, Shoven, and Whalley's well-known estimates of the deadweight loss of taxes in the United States.[10] I add to that the 12% administrative and beneficiary costs from the last simulation to arrive at costs equal to 37% of total transfers.

Here, the social BCRs are considerably higher. For Progresa, they are comparable to many of Galiani's proposed investments, though much less so if the less-well-targeted Jamaican food stamp distribution of benefits is used. What is clear from both simulations is that if benefits are well targeted at the poor and if we use any value of ε that is not near 0, then the social benefits of pure transfer payments are larger than the costs of making those transfers, and perhaps considerably larger.

Adjusting Galiani's (and others') estimates

In addition to highlighting the social benefits of redistribution, the previous subsection also shows that if we modify Galiani's (and everyone

---

[10] It is difficult to know if this is a good assumption. VAT is usually less distortionary than other taxes, though my choice of VAT is perhaps unrealistic. (I use it because I can observe expenditures easily in household data.) Tax systems in developing countries are very different, and probably more distortionary, than that in the United States. On the other hand, Coady and Harris (2004) argue that a benefit of cash transfer programs is that they free the tax authorities to focus on minimizing distortions because they are no longer responsible for redistribution.

Table 8.1.2 *Social BCRs: income transfers – alternative calculation*

	ε				
	0.2	0.5	1.0	2.0	3.0
Progresa, net benefits	1.12	2.87	6.00	12.53	18.01
Jamaica distribution, net benefits	0.50	1.13	1.94	2.94	3.43

else's) B/C calculations to include their distributional consequences, we may get very different social B/C estimates. Unfortunately, very few impact evaluations study the distribution of impacts across income. The exception is for Progresa, to which I now turn.

Conditional cash transfers

Coady (2000) shows that the incidence of different aspects of Progresa – school attendance, health visits, and cash – is roughly comparable, so we can use the estimates in table 8.1.2 to adjust Galiani's estimates of the investment benefits of Progresa with welfare weights. Note that Galiani's estimated benefits are based on the average impact across the sample, so the best that we can do is multiply dy_i in (3) by his average B/C estimate.[11] So, for example, if we take the net benefit weights of the first row of table 8.1.2, the benefits to Progresa's CCTs are now much more attractive (table 8.1.3). Galiani's rather modest estimates start to look much better.[12]

---

[11] The fact that it is very difficult to find studies that examine the distribution of benefits across the income distribution – e.g. returns to schooling or iron supplementation by income deciles – is disconcerting. Galiani cites the survey Engle *et al.* (2007), but they do not give their distributional results in sufficient detail to make calculations with different values of dy_i across the income distribution. Such information is important if we want to take the distributional aspect of B/C analysis seriously. It may be, for example, that iron fortification benefits poorer households more, because their diets are less rich in iron. But the reverse may be true: richer households may be more likely to buy the fortified products. Weighting these results with β_is as in (3) will then give different values for the social benefits than a simple average.

[12] There is one difficult issue that this simple calculation does not address. Presumably, a currently poor person who attends more school because of Progresa will eventually move up in the income distribution, so we should lessen the distributional weight that we assign to her. But doing this would require long panel data that are simply not available in the LAC region.

Table 8.1.3 *Modification of Galiani's estimated BCRs: Progresa's CCTs*

ε:	0		0.5		1		2		3	
discount rate %:	3	6	3	6	3	6	3	6	3	6
Not using DALYs	3.50	2.01	10.05	5.77	21.01	12.07	43.87	25.19	63.03	36.20
Using DALY = $5,000	4.28	2.69	12.29	7.73	25.69	16.15	53.64	33.71	77.07	48.44

Table 8.1.4 *Headcount poverty indices: different populations*

Institution	Total population %	Urban population %	Microfinance clients %
BancoSol (Bolivia)	58	51	49
MiBanco (Peru)	52	22	27
SogeSol (Haiti)	48	34	37

Note: Headcounts are for national poverty lines in each country.
Source: Marulanda and Otero (2005).

A note on microcredit

While not one of his "solutions," Galiani does mention microcredit in his conclusions. However, table 8.1.4 shows that in the LAC region, microcredit is not particularly well targeted at the poor.

5 Conclusions

Such a brief alternative view requires little in the way of summary. Galiani's solutions are mostly good ones, likely to improve the well-being of poor people in the LAC region by amounts far greater than their costs. I have three general comments on these solutions, and for the others that the Expert panel will see as well. First, it is important to consider the external validity of studies used to make the B/C calculations. In the case of promotion of breastfeeding and perhaps some of the micronutrient interventions (though not iron supplementation), the benefits are likely to be less in the LAC region today than those reported in the underlying studies. Another way to state this is that the marginal benefits of a proposed solution may not equal the observed average benefits. Economists should know to make decisions on the margin, but much of our evidence is actually average treatment effects.

Second, it is important to consider the likely incidence of a solution's benefits and costs. Many programs in the LAC region that are justified politically as being "pro-poor" nevertheless get captured by the middle classes, though the recent (conditional) cash transfer programs are an important exception. Third and most importantly, we should weight a solution's benefits and costs based on its incidence across the income distribution. For programs that are well targeted at the poor, this can make a very large difference in our estimates of the social B/C ratios. In the only case for which I can do this quantitatively – Progresa's CCTs – the BCRs are much more attractive than Galiani suggests once we weight the outcomes, even for conservative values of welfare weights.

Bibliography

Amiel, Y., J. Creedy, and S. Hurn, 1999. "Measuring Attitudes Towards Inequality." *Scandinavian Journal of Economics* 101: 83–96

Appleton, Simon, 2004. "Malnutrition and Hunger." Alternative Perspectives Paper 7.2 in Bjørn Lomberg, *Global Crises, Global Solutions*, 1st edn. Cambridge: Cambridge University Press

Atkinson, Anthony, 1970. "On the Measurement of Inequality." *Journal of Economic Theory* 2: 244–63

Ballard, Charles, John B. Shoven, and John Whalley, 1985. "General Equilibrium Computations of the Marginal Welfare Costs for Taxes in the United States." *American Economic Review* 75(1): 128–38

Behrman, Jere, Harold Alderman, and John Hoddinott, 2004. "Malnutrition and Hunger." Chapter 7 in Bjørn Lomborg, ed., *Global Crises, Global Solutions*, 1st edn. Cambridge: Cambridge University Press

Berkman, Heather and Eduado Cavallo, 2006. "The Challenges in Latin America: Identifying What Latin Americans Believe to be the Main Problems Facing Their Countries." Inter-American Development Bank, mimeo

Besley, Timothy and Robin Burgess, 2003. "Halving Global Poverty." *Journal of Economic Perspectives* 17(3): 3–22

Caldés, Natalia, David Coady, and John A. Maluccio, 2006. "The Cost of Poverty Alleviation Transfer Programs: A Comparative Analysis of Three Programs in Latin America." *World Development* 34(5): 818–37

Caulfield, Laura E., Stephanie A. Richard, Juan A. Rivera, Philip Musgrove, and Robert E. Black, 2006. "Stunting, Wasting, and Micronutrient Deficiency Disorders." Chapter 28 in D.T. Lamison, J. Brenan, A. Meashan, E. Alleyne, M. Claeson, D. Evans, P. Jha, A. Mills, and

P. Musgrove, eds., *Disease Control Priorities in Developing Countries*, 2nd edn. New York and Oxford: Oxford University Press: 551–68

Coady, David P., 2000. "The Application of Social Cost-Benefit Analysis to the Evaluation of PROGRESA:" Washington, DC: International Food Policy Research Institute, December

2006. "The Welfare Returns to Finer Targeting: The Case of Progresa in Mexico." *International Tax and Public Finance* 13: 217–39

Coady, David, Margaret Grosh, and John Hoddinott, 2004. "Targeting Transfers in Developing Countries: Review of Lessons and Experiences." World Bank Regional and Sectoral Studies, Washington, DC: World Bank

Coady, David and Rebecca Harris, 2004. "Evaluating Transfer Payments within a General Equilibrium Framework." *The Economic Journal* 114: 778–99

Cunha, Flavio 2007. "A Time to Plant and a Time to Reap." University of Chicago, mimeo

Cunha, Flavio and James Heckman 2004. "The Technology of Skill Formation." University of Chicago, mimeo

Dasgupta, Partha 2006. "Accounting for Well-Being." Cambridge University, mimeo

de Benoist, B. *et al.*, eds., 2004. "Iodine Status Worldwide." WHO Global Database on Iodine Deficiency. Geneva: World Health Organization

Engle, P., M.M. Black, J.R. Behrman, M.C. de Mello, P.J. Gertler, L. Kapiriri, R. Martorell, M.E. Young and the International Child Development Steering Committee, 2007. "Strategies to Avoid the Loss of Development Potential in More than 200 Children in the Development World." *Lancet* 369: 229–42

Feldstein, Martin, 1978. "The Welfare Cost of Capital Income Taxation." *Journal of Political Economy* 86(2), S29–S51

Gertler, Paul J., Sebastian Martinez, and Marta Rubio-Codina, 2006. "Investing Cash Transfers to Raise Long Term Living Standards." World Bank Policy Research Working Paper **3994**

Habicht, Jean-Pierre, Reynaldo Martorell, and Juan A. Rivera, 1995. "Nutritional Impact of Supplementation in the INCAP Longitudinal Study: Analytic Strategies and Inferences." *Journal of Nutrition* 125(4), Supplement: 1042–50

Horton, S., T. Sanghvi, M. Phillips, J. Fiedler, R. Perez-Escamilla, C. Lutter, A. Rivera, and A. Segall-Correa, 1996. "Breastfeeding Promotion and Priority Setting in Health." *Health Policy and Planning* 11: 156–68

Lomborg, Bjørn, 2004. *Global Crises, Global Solutions*, 1st edn. Cambridge: Cambridge University Press

Marulanda, Beatriz and María Otero, 2005. "The Profile of Microfinance in Latin America in 10 Years: Vision and Characteristics." Boston: Acción International

Pirttila, J. and R. Uusitalo, 2007. "Leaky Bucket and the Real World: Estimating Inequality Aversion Using Survey Data." Helsinki School of Economics, Labour Institute for Economic Research Discussion Paper **231**

Rasmussen K.M. and Stoltzfus R.J., 2003. "New Evidence that Maternal Iron Supplementation Improves Birth Weight, which Raises New Scientific Questions." *American Journal of Clinical Nutrition* **78**: 673–4

Stern, Nicholas, 2007. *The Economics of Climate Change – The Stern Review*. Cambridge: Cambridge University Press

van Doorslaer, E. *et al.*, 1997. "Income-Related Inequalities in Health: Some International Comparisons." *Journal of Health Economics* **16**(1): 93–112

Wagstaff, A., P. Paci, and E. van Doorslaer, 1991. "On the Measurement of Inequalities in Health." *Social Science and Medicine* **33**: 545–57

9 | Public administration and institutions in the LAC region

SUSAN ROSE-ACKERMAN[*]

1 Introduction

Most LAC countries have democratic constitutions, functioning bureaucracies, and professional judiciaries. The institutions are in place, but their operation varies widely across the region. Some institutions function well in some countries, sometimes surpassing the performance of those in comparable, wealthier countries. Others, however, are plagued with waste and corruption, impose needless costs on the population, and do not accomplish their missions well. I highlight the most pressing problems in the LAC region and discuss potential solutions, drawing on existing experiments and reform initiatives. Reform priorities ought to differ across countries. Although most occupy the middle range on cross-country measures of corruption and government effectiveness and in terms of economic wellbeing and growth, the key pressure points vary. I highlight good and bad performers on a number of dimensions and argue that broad regional similarities imply that successes in one country can provide lessons for reformers elsewhere.

I concentrate on public administration and the judiciary, but improvements in these areas can complement other types of reform. For example, Latin American democracies have traditionally had weak legislatures.[1] If legislative capacity is strengthened, it can play a stronger oversight role with respect to the executive. Similarly, if violence and organized crime make ordinary state functioning

[*] Thanks to Paul Lagunes, a doctoral student in Political Science, Yale University, for his very helpful work in summarizing some of the sources and in reading Spanish language material and to the referees at the Copenhagen Consensus and the Inter-American Development Bank for their comments on an earlier draft.
[1] Mainwaring and Shugart (1997); Spink (1999); Moreno, Crisp, and Shugart (2003).

problematic, then improved law enforcement is a necessary condition for other types of reform to succeed.[2]

Political realities determine whether a country enacts reforms in the first place and affect the quality and sustainability of their implementation. Studies of state reform in the LAC region from the colonial period to the present highlight the way the loci of political power influence which reforms are feasible and which can survive over time.[3] I deal with this issue only indirectly in discussing the design of reforms and the value of improving routes for citizen access and monitoring. My primary focus is on isolating reforms that appear to have been successes, with the aim of providing guidance to those willing to push for change.

Reform of public administration can take three routes: (1) reform of the state in its interaction with private citizens and businesses, (2) internal reform of the civil service system to improve its professionalism and honesty, and (3) reforms that open up the operation of government to oversight by those both inside and outside the government. In discussing reform of the legal system, I concentrate on: (a) reform in the selection and performance of judges and their staff, and (b) reform of the legal system as a whole. If the judiciary can be reformed, then not only will it more effectively resolve private law disputes but will also play an oversight role *vis-à-vis* government – monitoring the performance of the public administration to be sure that public officials obey both substantive and procedural law (Rose-Ackerman 2004a).

Unfortunately, few reform options have been subjected to rigorous testing in the LAC region. I highlight the studies that exist but stress the importance of setting priorities on a country-by-country basis and of considering reforms that have not yet been tested in practice. As Dani Rodrik argues, the search for uniform "blueprints" or "best practices" is an elusive quest. Rather, in each country, reformers need to isolate its most serious problems and design policies that fit its situation (Rodrik 2006). There is much room for creative experimentation, but experiments should be carried out with an evaluation component that

---

[2] Chapters 1 and 10 in this volume deal with strengthening democracy and with combating crime and violence.

[3] See Spink (1999) for an overview and critique of past efforts. Geddes (1994) shows how reform occurred in LAC countries under grand coalitions of the major political parties. For the particular case of revenue authorities see Talierco (2001).

produces quantitative measures of success or failure. Successes cannot be automatically reproduced elsewhere, but they will, at least, suggest options for reformers to consider.

This chapter begins in section 2 by outlining the significant weaknesses of LAC states while highlighting cross-country differences. Obviously, many of the problems I isolate will sound familiar to readers from other regions, including wealthier societies, but I concentrate here on this one region in the hope that highlighting the variety of experience there can help our understanding. Section 3 proposes responses to these challenging problems. Section 4 collects existing information on the costs and benefits of alternative policies.

2 The challenge

Global cross-country research supports the claim that institutions matter for growth and demonstrates that poorly functioning government institutions are associated with harmful outcomes.[4] However, the consequences of weak institutions are difficult to distinguish from the causes. Take the controversy over corruption, for example. Corruption limits growth, but low growth encourages corruption and makes it difficult to improve government effectiveness.[5] There are feedback mechanisms from low growth to high corruption and, conversely, from high growth to low corruption; the growth process cannot begin unless reasonably well-functioning institutions are in place. Other empirical regularities raise similar problems of causation. High levels of corruption are associated with greater inequality and poverty, a larger shadow economy, a smaller and less productive capital stock, and distorted allocations of public and private resources.[6] These factors are consequences of corruption, but they could also be causes. In any case, corruption standing alone is not the essential problem. Rather, corruption symbolizes and highlights underlying weaknesses in the operation of the state and its interactions with citizens and businesses.

---

[4] Rivera-Batiz (2002); Feld and Voight (2003); Kaufmann, Kraay, and Mastruzzi (2006); Lambsdorff (2006)
[5] For a debate on the issue of causation and other questions raised by the cross-country research, see the interchange in the *Journal of Politics* in 2007: Kurtz and Schrank (2007a, 2007b), Kaufmann, Kraay, and Mastruzzi (2007a, 2007b).
[6] See Rose-Ackerman (2004b) for citations to the relevant literature.

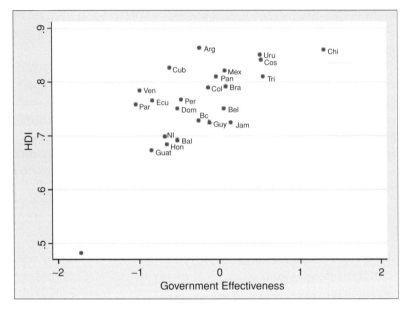

Figure 9.1 Government effectiveness
Sources: Government Effectiveness, see table 9.1, p. 522; HDI; UNDP

I concentrate here on an important class of government institutions
that can produce either a competent and fair state, if they function
well, or a corrupt, unfair, and ineffective state, if they operate poorly.
My focus is the operation of both the public administration and the
judiciary, leaving to chapter 1 a discussion of electoral politics and the
interactions between elected presidents and legislatures.

   The LAC countries are mostly in the broad middle range in both
per capita income and wellbeing and in measures of government effectiveness and institutional quality. Figure 9.1 shows a generally positive
relationship in the region between high government effectiveness, on
the one hand, and high levels of the UN Human Development Index
(HDI), on the other.[7] A similar pattern holds for corruption. However,
there are countries that do not fit the pattern. For example, measured

---

[7] Corruption is measured using Transparency International's Corruption
  Perceptions Index (TI–CPI) that ranges from 0 to 10 with high numbers
  representing lower levels of corruption. Government effectiveness is an index
  compiled by the World Bank Institute from various sources. The Human
  Development Index (HDI) is a weighted average of GDP *per capita* and
  measures of education and health.

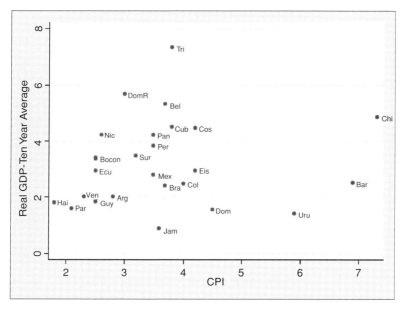

Figure 9.2 Corruption perceptions index (CPI): LAC countries
Sources: CPI: TI, see table 9.1, p. 522; HDI; UNDP

by the HDI, Chile is getting little marginal benefit from its low corruption and high government effectiveness compared to other relatively high-performing countries.[8] Conversely, Argentina reports high corruption and low confidence in the bureaucracy but is in relatively good shape economically. Figure 9.2 relates the Transparency International (TI) Corruption Perceptions Index to the ten-year growth rate of real GDP. Here the pattern is mixed. Those with the worst corruption are among those with the lowest growth rates, but some countries, such as Uruguay (a relatively wealthy country), have low growth and low corruption. Conversely, some high-growth counties are quite corrupt. For countries in the middle range, there is no clear pattern in the raw data. Thus, although bearing out the general claim that institutions matter for economic and social wellbeing, the figures suggest the need to disaggregate country-level summary indices to see what is happening in

---

[8] It is, however, important to recognize that that result is partly a function of the way the HDI is calculated. Income enters logarithmically so that its marginal impact on the index falls at higher incomes.

Figure 9.3 State corruption and organized crime
Source: Edgardo Buscaglia, "Análisis Económico de la Corrupción y de la delincuencia Organizada." Power Point presentation, 2004–5, Buscaglia and van Dijk (2003).

particular sectors and to analyze the underlying causes of economic growth.

Beyond simple measures of wellbeing such as the HDI, government competence and fairness affect people's daily lives in other ways. Of particular importance is the basic level of security and the effectiveness and fairness of law enforcement. The cross-country data, summarized by Buscaglia and van Dijk (2003), argue that countries with high levels of corruption, a signal of a weak and ineffective state, also have high levels of organized crime and of public insecurity, and this pattern applies to the LAC countries in their data (figure 9.3).[9] However, within the region there is considerable variation. Although organized

---

[9] The corruption levels are defined as follows and refer in particular to organized crime corruption of state institutions: Primer Nivel: Corrupcion aislada; Segundo Nivel: Frecuente corrupcion en la misma agencia; Tercer Nivel: Penetracion de la estructura a niveles operativos e intermdios; Cuarto Nivel; Infiltracion de la estructura a nivel de mandos; Quinto Nivel; Infiltration en el espacio politico. Detailed definitions are provided in Buscaglia and Gonzalez Ruiz (2006).

crime and corruption generally go together, Colombia's levels of organized crime is especially high relative to its level of corruption. In other work, Buscaglia and Gouzalez Ruiz (2006) show that public insecurity is generally related to extensive low-level corruption, but that some countries – Argentina, Bolivia, Brazil, Costa Rica, and Paraguay – report similar levels of public insecurity but widely different levels of low-level corruption.

Another negative effect of corrupt and ineffective governments is the lack of political legitimacy that they produce (Anderson and Tverdova 2003). High levels of administrative corruption are linked with negative perceptions of bureaucratic quality (Buscaglia and van Dijk 2003:18). This effect may be over and above the impact on economic wellbeing and personal security. Surveys carried out in four LAC countries (Bolivia, El Salvador, Nicaragua, and Paraguay) in 1998 and 1999 showed that those exposed to corruption had both lower levels of belief in the political system and lower interpersonal trust (Seligman 2002). In Nicaragua, respondents were asked if the payment of bribes "facilitates getting things done in the bureaucracy." Interestingly, those who agreed that corruption gets things done were *less* likely to believe in the legitimacy of the political system (Seligman 2002: 429).

To get a better sense of government functioning, we need to consider more focused measures that go beyond perceptions of "corruption" and government effectiveness. To begin, table 9.1 collects several indices of the quality of government, two of which are included in the figures 9.1 and 9.2 above. Chile, Costa Rica, and Uruguay top the governance rankings, and Paraguay and Venezuela are near the bottom.[10] Some countries' rankings, however, suggest the need for in-depth country-level analyses. For example, El Salvador is reputedly less corrupt than most others in the region, but it ranks low in government effectiveness and the rule of law. In contrast, Guatemala, one of the least-developed countries, is thought to be very corrupt and to have a poor property regime, but it ranks quite well in one measure of government effectiveness and in the rule of law.[11] Four major countries

---

[10] See also the regional and country reports at www.govindicators.org. That website contains the background material for World Bank (2007). For the LAC region, the same three countries are in the top rank. Countries that rank below the 50th percentile for the global survey on all six of their indices include Nicaragua, Honduras, Ecuador, and Bolivia, besides Paraguay and Venezuela.

[11] For a comparison of these countries, see Dodson and Jackson (2003), who highlight accountability problems in both countries.

Table 9.1 *Governance indicators*

	Corruption CPI rank 2005[a]	Corruption CPI score 2005[a]	Functioning of government (Freedom House)[b]	Gov. effectiveness percentile rank 2005[c]	Rule of law percentile rank 2005	Property rights 2007[d]
Chile	21	7.3	12	86.1	87.4	90
Uruguay	32	5.9	11	68.9	61.8	70
Costa Rica	51	4.2	11	64.1	65.7	50
El Salvador	51	4.2	7	13.9	22.7	50
Colombia	55	4.0	7	53.1	32.4	30
Brazil	62	3.7	7	55.9	43.0	50
Mexico	65	3.5	9	57.4	39.6	50
Panama	65	3.5	9	58.9	51.2	30
Peru	65	3.5	7	33.0	28.5	40
Argentina	97	2.8	8	47.8	36.2	30
Honduras	107	2.6	6	31.6	27.5	30
Nicaragua	107	2.6	5	24.9	32.9	30
Bolivia	117	2.5	5	23.9	27.1	30
Ecuador	117	2.5	4	41.1	33.3	30

Guatemala	117	2.5	5	45.9	44.0	30
Guyana	117	2.5	7	29.7	14.5	40
Venezuela	130	2.3	5	23.0	9.2	30
Paraguay	144	2.1	3	23.4	16.4	30

Notes:

[a] CPI rank and CPI score were obtained from Transparency International's 2005 report with data on 159 countries. The CPI score, in particular, measures perceptions of corruption as seen by business people and country analysts and ranges between 10 (highly clean) and 0 (highly corrupt).

[b] Functioning government data was obtained from Freedom House's 2005 comparative assessment of political rights and civil liberties, which covers more than 180 countries and some 14 related and disputed territories. Note: a higher number is associated with a better functioning government.

[c] The governance indicators presented here reflect the statistical aggregation of responses on the quality of governance given by a large number of enterprise, citizen, and expert survey respondents in industrial and developing countries, as reported by a number of survey institutes, think tanks, NGOs, and international organizations.

[d] Property rights is an assessment of the ability of individuals to accumulate private property, secured by clear laws that are fully enforced by the state. Property rights are graded using a scale from 0 to 100, where 100 represents the maximum freedom. A score of 100 signifies an economic environment or set of policies that is most conducive to economic freedom. The grading scale is continuous, meaning that scores with decimals are possible.

Sources: Transparency International www1.transparency.org/cpi/2005/cpi2005_infocus.html; Freedom House, www.freedomhouse.org/template.cfm?page=276; Kaufmann, Kraay, and Mastruzzi (2006); Governance Matters V: Governance Indicators for 1996–2005; The Heritage Foundation www.heritagefoundation.org.

Table 9.2 Doing Business in 2006

Country	Starting a business				Licenses			Property		Taxes		Export/Import		Contracts		GNI (per capita US$)
	Rank	Time (days)	Cost (% income per capita)	Cost (US$)	Time (days)	Cost (% income per capita)	Cost (US$)	Time (days)	Cost (% property value)	Time (hours per year)	Payable (as % of gross profit)	X: time (days)	M: time (days)	Days	Cost (% of debt)	
LAC																
Argentina	77	32	13.4	498	288	47.9	1,782	44	8.3	580	97.9	23	30	520	15.0	3,720
Bolivia	111	50	154.8	1,486	187	268.2	2,575	92	5.0	1,080	64.0	43	49	591	10.6	960
Brazil	119	152	10.1	312	460	184.4	5,698	47	4.0	2,600	147.9	39	43	546	15.5	3,090
Chile	25	27	10.3	506	191	125.2	6,147	31	1.3	432	46.7	23	24	305	10.4	4,910
Colombia	66	43	25.3	506	150	697.3	13,946	23	3.5	432	75.1	34	48	363	18.6	2,000
Costa Rica	89	77	23.8	1,111	120	150.3	7,019	21	3.6	402	54.3	36	42	550	41.2	4,670
Ecuador	107	69	38.1	831	149	100.0	2,180	21	6.7	600	33.9	20	42	388	15.3	2,180
El Salvador	76	40	118.0	2,773	144	204.2	4,799	52	3.6	224	32.7	43	54	275	12.5	2,350
Guatemala	109	39	58.4	1,244	294	667.8	14,224	69	4.7	260	53.4	20	36	1,459	14.5	2,130
Honduras	112	62	64.1	666	199	759.6	7,824	36	5.8	424	43.2	34	46	545	33.1	1,030
Mexico	73	58	15.6	1,056	222	159.0	10,764	74	5.3	536	31.3	18	26	421	20.0	6,770
Panama	57	19	24.8	1,104	128	114.3	5,086	44	2.4	424	32.9	30	32	355	37.0	4,450
Paraguay	88	74	147.8	1,729	273	544.5	6,371	48	2.0	328	37.9	34	31	285	30.4	1,170
Peru	71	102	38.0	897	201	366.3	8,645	33	3.2	424	50.7	24	31	381	34.7	2,360
Uruguay	85	45	43.9	1,734	146	95.0	3,752	66	7.1	300	80.2	22	25	620	25.8	3,950
Venezuela	120	116	15.7	631	276	547.2	21,977	33	2.1	864	48.9	34	42	445	28.7	4,020
Europe/United States																
France	44	8	1.2	361	185	78.0	23,470	183	6.5	72	42.8	22	23	75	11.7	30,090
Portugal	42	54	13.4	1,789	327	57.7	7,703	83	7.4	328	45.4	18	18	320	17.5	13,350
Spain	30	47	16.5	350	277	77.1	16,353	25	7.2	56	48.4	9	10	169	14.1	21,210
Unites States	3	5	0.5	207	70	16.9	6,997	12	0.5	325	21.5	9	9	250	7.5	41,400

Source: World Bank and International Finance Corporation (2006).

Note:

in the region – Argentina, Brazil, Columbia, and Mexico – are at or above the regional median on all measures. Peru, although comparable to Mexico on the corruption index, appears to have an especially ineffective government.

A second way to compare countries is through the *Doing Business* measures compiled by the World Bank and the International Finance Corporation (2006). These concentrate on the legal costs imposed on business, not the entire operation of the state. Thus, they provide no direct evidence on, for example, the quality of education, welfare, or healthcare. Furthermore, some measures that are costly for business may be beneficial for other actors, such as workers or ordinary citizens. Nevertheless, these data highlight areas of concern in individual countries. If a country is an outlier, then its government has the burden of proof to demonstrate that the high costs provide corresponding benefits. Overall, the LAC countries are not at the top or the bottom of the 155 countries in the basic study but, as table 9.2 illustrates, some countries do stand out as especially strong or weak along some dimensions.[12] The measures only reflect the views of a small number of country experts on the formal law. They do not take account of the ways in which businesses cope, and they ignore other aspects of the business environment such as threats of crime and violence, the level of domestic demand, the costs of inputs, and transportation costs of exports or imports.

Table 9.2 compares the continental LAC countries that have a French legal heritage with each other and with France, Portugal, Spain, and the United States. Overall, the lowest-ranked countries, beginning with the worst first, are: Venezuela, Brazil, Honduras, Bolivia, Guatemala, and Ecuador. There is a large gap between those countries and the next group. Only Chile is superior to the European benchmarks overall. Table 9.2 includes those components of the index most closely linked to the operation of the public administration or the courts. In each column, the three worst LAC countries are highlighted. If any of

[12] Table 9.2 includes each country's overall rank and the details for most of the components that are related to the operation of the state. It omits information on minimum capital requirements for formally registering a business, labor and credit regulations, investors' protections, and the costs of closing a business. The data on all the sections listed in table 9.2 also include information on the number of transactions. I omit these because they are closely associated with the time and money costs of compliance. For the complete data set, see World Bank and International Finance Corporation (2006).

the benchmark countries is in the range of the three bottom LAC countries, they are also highlighted. Table 9.2 can be used as a diagnostic tool at the country level. Presumably, if a country ranks poorly on these measures, one should expect both that economic activity is hampered and that businesses try to get around the formal rules through bribes, family or political connections, or avoidance – using such techniques as operating off the books, under-paying taxes, smuggling across borders, or enlisting organized crime as contract enforcers.

Legal processes that are costly in terms of *either* time *or* money are pressure points. If both are high, as with taxation in Brazil or licensing in Guatemala, the problem is especially serious. Some sectors in some countries seem to be in crisis. Thus the courts in Guatemala appear to be very dysfunctional for contract disputes, and starting a formal business in Bolivia, El Salvador, and Paraguay looks very expensive relative to each country's wealth. A similar result obtains for licensing, and the large time cost, at least relative to the United States, suggests that many LAC counties have excessive requirements.

The *Doing Business* project calculates set-up and licensing costs as a fraction of each country's GDP *per capita*, but businesses with international options might also be interested in the absolute costs, not normalized by *per capita* income. Thus, table 9.2 also reports the absolute costs in US dollars. On that measure, Brazil is the cheapest place to establish a business in monetary terms although it imposes large time costs. Colombia and Chile are close behind, and out-of-pocket costs (OOP) are lower in most of the LAC region than in Spain and Portugal. El Salvador and Paraguay, however, continue to stand out as especially costly along with Uruguay, a relatively prosperous country. Licensing costs remain highest in Colombia and Guatemala but they are now joined by relatively prosperous Venezuela. Notice, however, that France and Portugal impose licensing costs that exceed all but those in Venezuela.

Tables 9.1 and 9.2 do not always paint a consistent picture. For example, in table 9.2 Guatemala appears to have a dysfunctional business licensing system and a judiciary with long delays, but it ranks quite well on some measures in table 9.1 (for example, rule of law). Nevertheless, its high level of corruption may be related to efforts to circumvent the difficulties highlighted in table 9.2.

Tables 9.1 and 9.2 indicate that policy responses need to be tied to the details of each country's situation. At the extremes, the situation is clear. In very weak polities, state failure is so pronounced that the government cannot carry out pro-growth policies. When the state is competent, macroeconomic policies can be effective, and citizens support high taxes because their funds are used effectively to provide public services. But most LAC countries fall in the middle range, and here the connection is complex. Countries with similar rankings on the most widely used governance and corruption indices may have quite different business climates because costly legal requirements and corruption are concentrated in different sectors. In addition, indices based on the perceptions of business investors and legal professionals may miss the problems experienced by ordinary people. Furthermore, if growth rates vary widely across a country's subregions or across sectors, some may benefit from reform while others lose – or, at least, receive a smaller share of the gains. Given the already high levels of inequality in most countries in the region, this is a particularly important consideration.[13]

Within individual countries, some institutions function well while others are deeply dysfunctional. Table 9.2 provides some evidence on this for government actions that affect business, but the point is more general. Within an individual country, healthcare may be effectively provided to the poor, but primary education may be of low quality. Judicial processes may be speedy and effective, but the police may be corrupt. Even for countries in the bottom half in terms of overall government functioning, there are pockets of high performance (Kaufmann, Mastruzzi, and Zaveleta 2003), and it is important for reformers to identify and strengthen the good performers, as well as to use these examples to provide models for other less-well-functioning institutions.

The remainder of this section distinguishes between problems that arise in administering public programs in the executive branch and problems in the operation of the judiciary and law enforcement. These two aspects of government complement each other. Although some court disputes involve purely private controversies under contract and tort law, many arise from governments' efforts to hold the private

---

[13] De Ferranti *et al.* (2004) document the high levels of inequality in the LAC region and discuss its historical roots and political consequences. You and Khagram (2005) show how inequality and corruption can reinforce each other, as wealthy elites use corrupt inducements to hold back redistributive pressures in unequal societies.

sector to account or from efforts by private individuals and organizations to hold government to account. If the public administration functions poorly, especially in areas of law enforcement or inspections, the public can break the law in ways that never reach court. If both program administration and the courts are ineffective or corrupt, those who complain about maladministration will have no recourse.

Public administration

A strong and competent public sector is the backbone of programmatic reform. Cross-country research supports the view that a well-functioning bureaucracy contributes to economic growth (Evans and Rauch 1999: 750–3). Furthermore, few of the proposed solutions to the other Copenhagen Consensus process challenges will be possible unless the state is capable of administering complex public programs. Figure 9.4 is a measure of the quality of the public administration compiled by researchers at the IDB (Lora 2007a, based on Echabarría and Cortázar 2007). The figure reflects recent reform efforts in Brazil and Chile, as well as Costa Rica's tradition of competent public administration.[14] It also indicates that several countries, particularly in Central America, have very poorly operating public sectors, at least as measured by the IDB.

In discussing the public administration, I take as given a political process that generates a set of policy goals and translates them into laws. Although many statutes and rules can be criticized on substantive grounds, I leave such critiques to other chapters and, instead, concentrate on government failures that can undermine even the most socially beneficial programs. A scholar seeking to explain why certain programs exist and why they operate poorly would need to analyze the underlying political coalitions and their ways of wielding power. I assume this political context as background and assess the way ineffective institutions impose costs. This means, of course, that some of the reforms I will later propose will not be politically feasible in some countries. My goal is not to suggest ways to reform politics but, instead, to illustrate that failure to reform the state is costly for ordinary people

---

[14] Earlier work by Evans and Rauch (1999), based on data from 1970–90 and using a different methodology, showed that Brazil and Chile were in the middle of the countries they studied in terms of merit-based recruitment and the quality of public sector careers.

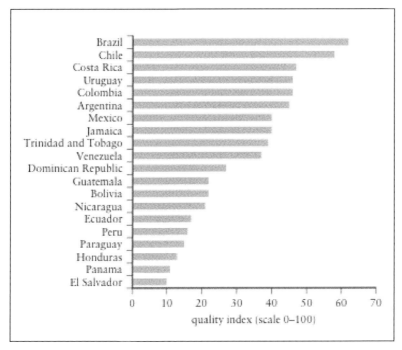

Figure 9.4 Quality of public administration
Source: Lora (2007a), figure 1.2, p. 17, calculated from data compiled by IDB staff; see Echebarría and Cortázar (2007)

and for economic progress.[15] Recognizing that states must impose costs on citizens and businesses in order to provide valuable goods and services, the problem for reformers it not to dismantle government but to locate waste and inefficiency and to limit their impact without undermining state functioning.

There are several interlocking ways in which the public administration can perform poorly. The sources of failure are: the lack of professionalism in the civil service; vague, complex, and confusing legal rules; poor management of government finances; poor distribution of tasks across levels of government; a lack of transparency in government processes; and the difficulty of holding officials to account for their actions. Weaknesses in any or all of these dimensions create

---

[15] On the connection between democracy, governance, and economic growth, see Rivera-Batiz (2002).

incentives for corruption and other forms of self-dealing and capture and for simple laziness and incompetence.[16]

One key to the functioning of the modern bureaucratic state is the separation of roles. Government officials do not own their offices and must distinguish between actions appropriate to their roles as public agents and their roles as family members and friends. One way to facilitate such role division is specialized training that separates decisionmaking procedures inside government from one's day-to-day life outside it. Thus, officials may use CBA to make choices or refer to an agency manual for guidance, but use quite other criteria in their free time. Internal bureaucratic rules forbid favoring friends and family or taking gifts in return for favors, but such practices are common outside government. The indoctrination of professional norms and technical expertise are not sufficient.

Separation of roles will be impossible if official salaries are below their private sector equivalents. Low pay is an inducement to moonlighting and corruption. Adequate pay is a necessary condition for competent bureaucratic performance, and rules must constrain conflicts of interest with other sources of wealth in the official's family. However, adequate pay is clearly not sufficient, as documented by evidence of corrupt and self-serving officials at the highest government levels.

Second, even if the civil service is exemplary, the underlying legal structure may be either vaguely defined or overly complex. Resources of money, time, or expertise may be scarce relative to the tasks assigned to officials. Then temptations to corruption, capture, and shirking will be high. Bribes are a short-cut around such laws; capture favors those with political influence, and shirking reflects officials' hopelessness in the face of a chaotic legal reality. Accepting bribes or favoring the powerful may even be seen as a reasonable way to carry out an otherwise impossible set of tasks. If a weak civil service combines with a poor legal framework, officials face the temptation to create additional arbitrary rules and regulations and use them to extort payoffs or justify inaction.

Third, if the government has no unified budget and does not audit and track spending either inside the bureaucracy or through an independent controller, room is opened up for inefficiency caused by

---

[16] On corruption, see Rose-Ackerman (1999, 2004b).

self-dealing or laziness. If officials need not account well for their spending, some will be tempted to keep a portion of their budgets for themselves, or to spend it on useless official perks. Of course, a professional civil service can help ameliorate this problem, but when the temptation is high a government should not rely on prior training and moral norms as the only defense. A self-selection mechanism may filter those likely to succumb to temptation into the civil service. Further, key positions in the bureaucracy may be filled mostly by those with close links to powerful private interests – be they legitimate economic interests or, in truly pathological cases, organized crime groups.

Fourth, tasks need to be allocated to levels of government or to levels of the hierarchy within a unified government. Too much decentralization risks capture by local elites who benefit themselves and impose costs both on neighboring governments and on those higher up. Too much centralization can lead to a frozen, rigid hierarchy that poorly reflects diverse local conditions. Cross-country work is inconclusive on the issue of decentralization, although several studies conclude that federalism is associated with corruption. I do not take on the complexities of this issue here, but instead, concentrate on one aspect: grassroots, directly democratic participation in policymaking.

Fifth and sixth, government operation needs to facilitate monitoring by citizens, watchdog groups, the media, and opposition political parties. If government does not inform the public about what it is doing and does not provide a way for people to lodge complaints, officials can operate with impunity subject only to oversight by their superiors who may collude in their malfeasance, shirking, or capture by narrow groups. People need to be able to find out what government is doing through both published documents and freedom-of-information requests for unpublished material. However, information is of no value if it cannot be used to hold governments to account. This implies both that private groups such as NGOs or independent media can organize and that the state has a means for taking and responding to complaints. An active political opposition with real electoral prospects is valuable, but is not sufficient. In addition, other routes for intervention are needed, such as an Ombudsman, public hearings for the making of rules, and so forth. These provisions for public input and oversight can constrain even a weak civil service charged with enforcing vague and complex laws, but they will have only a limited impact in such cases. Oversight can be most effective when the other elements of a well-working administrative system are in place. They cannot be expected to cure systemic problems but can help prevent an adequate system from collapsing into corruption, capture, and sleeping on the job.

Finally, one needs to acknowledge the particularly serious problems that arise when corruption or capture reaches the top of the bureaucratic hierarchy to include senior civil servants or political appointees – bringing the state to the edge of outright failure and undermining the economy. In some cases, a branch of the public sector may be organized as a bribe-generating machine. For example, top police officials may organize large-scale corrupt systems in collaboration with organized crime groups, who are given a *de facto* monopoly on illicit activities. Policing is probably the most dramatic example, but tax collection agencies and regulatory inspectorates can also degenerate into corrupt systems where high-level officials manage and share in the gains of their inferiors. In other situations, governments engage in projects that have a significant effect on the wealth of domestic and foreign businesses. High-level politicians can then use their influence to collect kickbacks from private firms. The relative power of government officials and private interests may, in practice, be difficult to sort out. The extremes are kleptocracy, on the one hand, and state capture by powerful private interests, on the other (Johnston 2005).

Public administration reform needs to link the corruption, waste, and inefficiency observed in practice with the underlying economic and political incentives that make them possible. Criminal prosecutions and exhortations to observe high moral standards in both the public and private sector are all very well, but they cannot be the only responses to problems that are fundamentally structural.

The judiciary and law enforcement

If a state operates under "the rule of law," statutory and constitutional provisions constrain both private actors and public officials. There are two linked issues here. First, given any set of legal rules, how do they affect the behavior of public and private actors? No one expects 100% compliance with any legal rule, but in well-functioning systems laws have marginal effects on behavior. Second, are the substantive laws themselves appropriate to further reform goals? Here, of course, there will be debate about what the laws ought to require. A system with honest and competent courts and police forces that enforce repressive laws is operating under "the rule of law" as defined by that country's rules but may be deeply dysfunctional with respect to goals such as the promotion of individual freedom, the encouragement of economic growth, or the alleviation of poverty.[17] Recognizing the importance of this second issue, this section, nevertheless, concentrates on the first question.

A necessary condition for the establishment of the "rule of law" is an independent and competent judicial system. In cross-country statistical work the independence of the judiciary is associated with higher levels of political and economic freedom, stronger economic growth, and more developed credit markets.[18] Other work shows that organized crime levels are lower in countries with independent judiciaries, holding other factors constant.[19] Some complementary evidence comes from country-level studies. Thus, in Ecuador a survey found that judicial uncertainty and delays in contract enforcement deterred investment (Messick 1999: 121). Another study based on in-depth interviews of Brazilian entrepreneurs suggested that investment would go up 10% if the judiciary were on a par with those in advanced economies (Messick 1999: 121, citing Castelar Pinheiro 1998). The judiciary can both constrain the state and structure private interactions; hence, corrupt and incompetent courts may be especially damaging to both the consolidation of democratic regimes and to the promotion of the free market economy.

Unfortunately, in most of the LAC region between 20% and 40% of those surveyed by Latinobarometer expressed "no confidence" in the judiciary (figure 9.5). These responses are suspect, however, because they include many people with no experience with the courts. To deal with this problem, a household survey in Peru distinguished between those who had and who had not interacted with particular types of officials. It revealed that the judiciary was the most corrupt institution. The incidence of bribery was high, and 42% of reported bribe revenues were paid to the judiciary, even though it represented only 2% of citizen interactions (Hunt 2006).

---

[17] On Chile under Pinochet, see Barros (2002). Venezuela's low rank on the "rule of law" column in table 9.1 is determined by Freedom House and presumably represents that group's view of the substantive law. It seems unlikely that the score represents especially severe problems with street crime.

[18] La Porta *et al.* (2004); Dam (2006): 93–4 and sources cited therein.

[19] Buscaglia and van Dijk (2003): 13

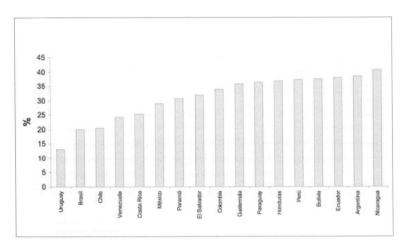

Figure 9.5 Public confidence in the judiciary: percentage of survey respondents expressing "no confidence"
Source: Latinobarómetro

Another subjective measure of judicial independence from the World Economic Forum (WEF), shown in figure 9.6, provides a different ranking (Sousa 2007). The judiciaries of Chile, Costa Rica, and Uruguay, which rank highly according to the WEF, are low on public confidence in the Latinobarometer. The disjunction may represent higher expectations in those countries, indicate that independence is not all that matters, or represent attitudes not informed by experience with the system. In any case, outside of those ranked at the top by the IDB, most of the region appears to need judicial reform of some sort.

Even if the judiciary functions well, corrupt police forces and prosecutors can cement patterns of illegality. The police can impose costs and coerce payoffs more effectively than other public officials, so it is not surprising that payoffs are frequent. In Peru, it was the second most corrupt institution. Although the individual payoffs were not large, 37% of those who had an interaction reported paying a bribe, compared with 17% for the judiciary and under 5% for most other agencies (Hunt 2006). Public sector reform should not ignore the police, prosecutors, and other aspects of law enforcement, but I leave those issues to chapter 10 on the control of crime and violence – recognizing, of course, that the police play multiple roles.

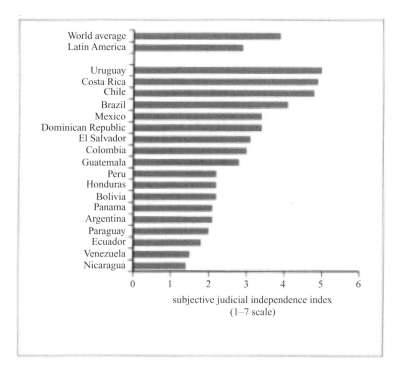

Figure 9.6 Subjective indicators of judicial independence: selected LAC countries
Source: Sousa (2007), figure 3.2, p. 106

Overall, the judicial system includes not just the trial but also preliminary stages of both the civil and the criminal process, and the enforcement of judgments. In the private law, the service of process starts a legal challenge, and if one wins at trial, the judgment must be enforced. In cases brought by the state against private parties or by private individuals against the state, there are investigations *ex ante* and enforcement *ex post*.

To help one understand the operation of the private litigation process, the Lex Mundi project, supported by the World Bank, chose two routine legal problems facing business: evicting a tenant for non-payment of rent and collecting on a bounced check (Djankov *et al.* 2003). Unfortunately, the project did not deal with judicial processes where a state agency was a party. Law firms in each country provided data on the exact procedures used by litigants and courts.

The researchers then constructed an index of legal formalism and showed that it was associated with higher expectations of judicial delay, less consistency, honesty, and fairness in the courts; and more corruption. Because higher levels of formalism are correlated with legal systems based on European civil law models, the authors conclude that the transplanted system is partly to blame. One need not accept that controversial conclusion,[20] however, to extract some valuable lessons from this research.

All of the countries in the continental LAC region, with the exception of Belize and Guyana, have private law systems derived from French models, and neither of these former British colonies stands out as a model of the rule of law. Furthermore, legal origin is not a policy variable in the LAC region in the twenty-first century. Thus, it seems more fruitful to concentrate on cross-country variations in the operation of the legal system.

One symptom of problems in the litigation system is delay. For example, the household survey in Peru revealed extensive delays in the court system due, in part, to the poor training of judges.[21] Other research shows that the percentage of filed cases adjudicated in one year was 58% in Brazil and 42% in Bolivia in the mid-1990s. Some countries had hundreds of thousands of pending cases (Dakolias 1996: xi–xiii). The Lex Mundi project provides data on the expected duration of legal processes derived from surveys of lawyers. There are estimates of time for service of process, duration of trials, and the time it takes to enforce a judgment. One should expect that in the countries with long delays in the formal processes businesses will find other ways to solve problems. These might be modifications in business practices, such as requiring payment before delivery of goods and doing business only with friends and family; corruption of the judicial system; or resort to informal methods of dispute resolution, perhaps in the extreme calling on organized crime as an enforcer.

---

[20] Thus, with respect to the bounced check hypothetical, paper checks are much less common in civil law countries than in the United States. Rather, bank drafts are the most familiar ways of paying bills including automatic debiting of accounts. As the internet spreads into more households and postage rates increase, such methods of payment are becoming more common in the United States. For a critique of work comparing civil and common law systems in the aggregate, see Dam (2006) and Rose-Ackerman (2007).

[21] See Hunt (2006).

Table 9.3 *Days elapsed for completion of each stage in the process*

	Eviction of tenant				Check collection			
	Service of process	Trial	Enfor-cement	Total	Service of process	Trial	Enfor-cement	Total
LAC								
Argentina	60	300	80	440	20	200	80	300
Bolivia	14	60	20	94	14	360	90	464
Brazil	30	60	30	120	30	90	60	180
Chile	15	200	25	240	15	140	45	200
Colombia	139	279	82	500	165	216	146	527
Costa Rica	20	90	30	140	10	180	180	370
Ecuador	38	40	30	108	38	235	60	333
El Salvador	45	60	45	150	25	15	20	60
Guatemala	10	180	90	280	10	120	90	220
Honduras	15	30	30	75	30	90	105	225
Mexico	20	60	100	180	33	99	151	283
Panama	36	50	48	134	76	86	35	197
Paraguay	12	50	140	202	25	32	165	222
Peru	41	135	70	246	81	135	165	441
Uruguay	120	120	90	330	150	120	90	360
Venezuela	30	300	30	360	30	300	30	360
Europe								
France	16	75	135	226	16	75	90	181
Portugal	20	280	30	330	20	280	120	420
Spain	60	55	68	183	49	69	29	147

Source: Derived from table V in Djankov *et al.* (2003).
Shading: Dark: Best in European group plus LAC countries that meet or exceed that level. Light: 3 worst LAC performers in each column plus any of the European countries in the range of the these 3 worst.

Table 9.3 shows the wide variation in expected delays across the region, using the Lex Mundi data, and compares the delays to the estimates for France, Portugal, and Spain because those represent the European countries that are the source of most private law. Cells marked in light gray are the three worst cases for the LAC region in each category plus any of the European countries comparable to these worst cases. Cells marked in dark gray are those that perform at least as well as the best of the European countries. We can see that a number of countries reach that level, at least along some dimensions. Of course, describing speedy processes as better than slow processes implies a value judgment. Clearly, procedures, especially trials, can be too fast. However, the model cases were constructed to leave little room for judgment. The courts are simply enforcement mechanisms. Hence, one should be careful about generalizing to more complex legal disputes. To see this, compare the columns on contract enforcement in table 9.2 with the data on the judicial process in table 9.3. For example, Guatemala where contract disputes take over three years to resolve seems to rank less poorly for the routine legal problems in table 9.3. Obviously, businesses are finding ways to get around the delays of the formal system.

Those interested in the reform of legal processes in a particular country might consult table 9.3 as a starting point. Columbia and Uruguay appear to need to improve the service of process. Delays in scheduling and completing trials seem a problem in Argentina, Bolivia, Colombia, Ecuador, and Venezuela. The enforcement of judgments is much delayed in Argentina, Colombia, Costa Rica, Paraguay, Peru, and Venezuela. Table 9.3 also contains some regional role models that do well, at least for one of the hypothetical disputes included in the study. Overall, El Salvador seems a model of speed, especially for the check collection case; it ranks better than the United States on speed. However, a case study in the early 2000s highlights problems with the courts in El Salvador, in spite of an influx of resources and international technical assistance (Dodson and Jackson 2003). The difficulties concern the persistence of political influence, an issue that is unlikely to affect the routine use of the courts to resolve private disputes.[22]

The limits of the Lex Mundi data suggest the value of gathering more direct experience on the operation of courts. A World Bank project headed by Linn Hammergren attempted to do just that in Argentina and Mexico. The group studied a random sample of cases in first-instance courts, obtaining a detailed view of the operation of this part of the legal system. Consistent with table 9.3, they confirmed that enforcement of judgments needs attention. Judges appeared unbiased

---

[22] Figure 9.5 indicates that over 25% had "no confidence" in the judiciary, and Dodson and Jackson's (2003) own survey found that 47.1% described the judiciary as "corrupt." Most survey respondents, however, had no direct experience with the judicial system.

and delays were not as long as reported in the *Doing Business* data for contracts cases, but were comparable to those in table 9.3 (223 days for debt collection in Mexico and 300 for a broader mixture of cases in Argentina). Many cases were never resolved in court, however, so it is unclear if they were settled informally or whether they should be counted into time-to-resolution data. In Mexico, 81% were abandoned (World Bank 2002). This figure suggests that going to court can be a thankless exercise, and that many disputes probably never reach court at all.

Problems with the judiciary mean that people and businesses in the LAC region try to avoid using the courts to resolve disputes.[23] Non-judicial alternative dispute resolution (ADR) processes, such as arbitration and mediation, will in some cases be a viable or even superior alternative, but they cannot entirely substitute for weak or venal courts.[24] Even the best of such systems, however, needs the courts as a backstop in case they misfire. Thus, judicial reform ought to have priority in most countries in the region. At the very least, there is a crisis of confidence, and, at worst, that lack of confidence is well deserved.

3 Solutions

This section outlines possible solutions. It begins with reform of the public administration to increase its competence and efficiency. However, structural reforms of the bureaucracy are unlikely to be sufficient. Without oversight, the bureaucracy may simply act to enrich itself at the expense of the state.[25] Thus, the next subsection discusses oversight and accountability inside and outside the government. The next subsection separately considers reform of the justice system, with its dual roles as an institution to resolve private disputes and as a check on the rest of the state. Based on the material in this section, section 4, which concludes the chapter, isolates some specific reforms from the broad menu outlined here and sketches their costs and benefits.

---

[23] Buscaglia (1995): 8–13; Dakolias (1996).

[24] Buscaglia and Stephen (2005) demonstrate the value of alternative dispute resolution mechanisms, especially for the resolution of land disputes involving low-income people.

[25] Tommasi and Spiller (2007) claim that this is the case in Argentina, which has experienced high presidential turnover. Nane (2007) has made a similar argument with respect to Nigeria.

Public administration

Cross-country research suggests the value of reforms that streamline and simplify regulations and that encourage competition.[26] Unfortunately, however, such reforms may be difficult to implement if a country is caught in a vicious cycle. Thus, Tommasi and Spiller (2007, chapter 6) worry that in Argentina the country's "poor bureaucracy worsens the policymaking environment, and [its] poor policymaking environment is unlikely to create a quality bureaucracy." Increases in civil service salaries are not a sufficient policy response; structural reforms are also needed. Countries with more independent and professional civil servants tend to have higher-quality bureaucracies and less corruption. High-level corruption is worse if the civil service is not insulated from political pressure and interference.[27]

One way to improve the administration of public programs is to go to the root and change the way goods and services are provided and programs managed. This is a large topic, but I discuss five important options for the LAC region: the reform of customs and tax collection, procurement reform, reform of the interface between business and government, privatization, and contracting out. This subsection concludes with a more generic issue: reform of the civil service.

Revenue collection

LAC governments vary in the level of taxes they collect from their citizens. For some, this reflects the importance of natural resource rents in revenues, but in most cases it also signals the importance of tax evasion. The countries fall into three groups according to data collected by Gómez Sabaini (2006). At the top are those that collected over 20% of GDP in taxes during the period 1995–2004 – Argentina, Brazil, and Uruguay. At the bottom, collecting under 13% are, in ascending order, Haiti, Guatemala, Venezuela, Ecuador, Mexico, and Paraguay – a mixture of resource-rich and resource-weak states. Furthermore, even when governments do collect taxes, they may be imposed in ways that

[26] For example, one study of the business environment in Asia estimated that if Calcutta had the investment climate of Shanghai, the share of firms exporting would nearly double from 24% to 47% and the share of foreign-invested firms would increase from 2.5% to 3.9% (Dollar, Hallward-Driemeier, and Mengistae 2006).
[27] Buscaglia and van Dijk (2003): 18.

are either highly distortionary or so full of exemptions that most tax-payers can avoid high tax bills.[28] A government that has difficulty collecting taxes will be severely crippled. If tax evasion, achieved through under-reporting or payoffs, is high, other proposals to reform the public administration are likely to founder.

Since 1990, every country in the LAC region has implemented reforms in the area of taxation (Stein *et al.* 2005: 186). Most of these reforms consist of a mixture of simplified tax schedules that are affordable to taxpayers and importers, automation of operations, better auditing, and improvements in the training, oversight, and incentives of officials. These reforms can have a real impact, but are not always easy to implement successfully.

In Bolivia, where these reforms were combined with overall civil service reforms, corruption and smuggling declined in the customs service, and the proportion of the VAT lost went from 42% in 2001 to 29% in 2004 after reforms. Unfortunately, however, smuggling appears to be on the rise (Escobar 2004; Zuleta, Leyton, and Ivanovic 2007). Gómez Sabaini (2006) reports that tax collections as a share of GDP in Bolivia rose from 8.2% in 1990 to 20.5% in 2000 and to 23.0% in 2004.[29]

When Peru reformed customs collection, tariff revenues went from 23% of revenues in 1990 to 35% in 1996 and increased four-fold in dollar terms despite reductions in duties (OECD 2003: 9). Peru also reduced total staff from 4,700 in 1990 to 2,540 in 2002 and increased the share of professionals from 2.5% to 60% (Goorman 2004). An additional benefit from streamlined customs procedures is the time saved by importers and exporters. The average clearance times fell from 2 days to 2 hours and, in Costa Rica, under a similar reform, times fell from 6 days to 12 minutes (OECD 2003: 22). Overall tax collections as a share of GDP in Peru were 11.6% in 1990, rising to 15.4% in 1995, before falling back to 14.9% in 2004 (Gómez Sabaini 2006).

A comparison of reforms in Chile and Argentina designed to increase compliance with VAT shows how similar policies can have different results (Bergman 2003). The average VAT compliance coefficient is

---

[28] Stein *et al.* (2005): 186 single out Colombia as a case of highly inefficient and distortionary taxes, and Costa Rica and Paraguay as examples of tax systems that are full of exemptions.
[29] See also Lora (2007b).

Table 9.4 *Revenue authorities: LAC region*

	Input indicators			Output and outcome indicators			
	Personnel management	Collection costs	Collections	Registration	Compliance	Taxpayer services
MEXICO **SAT**	No retrenchment No pay increase policy	Low collection costs	No major change	No major progress	No major change	Some improvement
VENEZUELA **SENIAT**	Voluntary retrenchment Initial reduction in staff complement Salary increases	Low collection costs	Moderate increase in tax/GDP ratio	Focus on large taxpayers with mixed results	Low audit coverage of large taxpayers	Some improvement
PERU **SUNAT**	Quasi-voluntary radical retrenchment Sub-stantial salary increase Overall staff reduction In-house training program	Low collection costs	Substantial increase in tax/GDP ratio (trend)	Focus on large taxpayers very successful Ex-pansion of tax base	Improve-ment in audit coverage since reform Improved audit procedures Moderate rate of audit coverage of large taxpayers	Some improvement, especially for large taxpayers

Source: Derived from table 4 in Taliercio (2004). © World Bank.

77.6% in Chile and 54.3% in Argentina. After examining and rejecting other explanations, the author concludes that the difference can be explained by the greater credibility of Chile's reform because the tax agency was stable and had broad autonomy. Hence it was better able to induce voluntary compliance because of its more credible deterrence capacity. However, Chile, with considerable revenue from the copper industry, may simply find tax administration easier because it does not have to tax its citizens as highly. Taxes as a share of GDP were 26.3% in 2004 in Argentina and only 17.3% in Chile (Gómez Sabaini 2006).

These results are consistent with one specific reform that has received detailed study: the creation of a semi-autonomous revenue authority. Although these come in several variants, Taliercio's (2004) study of such authorities in three African and three LAC countries is broadly favorable. He studied Mexico, Peru, and Venezuela (although Mexico's revenue authority was too new at the time of his study in 1998–9 to permit much evaluation).[30] Table 9.4 summarizes the main features of each country's authority. The reforms appear to be very cost-effective. Though some countries had better experiences than others, revenue collection improved. In Peru, total tax revenues increased from 8.4% of GDP in 1991 to 12.3% in 1998 at the same time as many tax rates were reduced.[31] The number of registered taxpayers increased from 895,000 in 1993 to 1,766,000 in 1999. Revenue also increased in Venezuela, although this was partly due to new taxes.[32] Mexico had little increase between 1996 and 1997, but its reform was the least far-reaching. Another measure of the effectiveness of revenue authorities is the ratio between GDP generated by VAT to the VAT rate. Here, Peru is the most productive at 0.32, followed by Mexico 0.26, but the accuracy of this data for cross-country comparisons depends on the nature of the tax base which is much narrower in Mexico than in Peru.

Peru's reform was the most far-reaching and involved an up-front cost of retrenchment in the form of severance payments and the cost of

---

[30] For a complementary study of the politics of fiscal reform in Ecuador, see Mejía Acosta *et al.* (2006).

[31] Including social security contributions, the tax share increased from 11.6% in 1990 to 14.0% in 2000. However, the share fell between 1995 and 2000 from a high of 15.4% (Gómez Sabaini 2006).

[32] In Venezuela, taxes as a share of GDP went from 4.4% in 1990 to 8.9% in 1995, and 11.0% in 2004. The low shares obviously reflect the importance of oil revenues to the state.

hiring new employees on the basis of merit. Mexico, as noted above, did not have a civil service when the reforms were introduced and did not create a special career track for the revenue authority. The same was true for Venezuela. Survey evidence confirmed that the public in Peru found tax officials better qualified, relative to other officials, compared to Venezuela or Mexico (85% vs. 75% and 52%, respectively). In Peru, 81% said that agency employees were substantially or much more qualified than before the reform compared with 61% in Venezuela, and 16% in Mexico. They were also perceived as less corrupt than before the reform by 85% of Peruvians and only 26% and 21% of those in Venezuela and Mexico, respectively. Talierco (2004) points to a range of factors that contributed to increased revenue collection for a modest administrative cost. It is not possible to measure the marginal costs of the reform, but they appear low or even negative. Overall, the cost of revenue collection as a share of revenues collected ranges from 1.7% to 2% for the LAC cases. Talierco concludes that the best performer was Peru, whose agency was the most independent from the executive and whose leaders were most able to motivate employees by creating a professional organizational culture. Talierco does, however, recognize the need for accountability and recommends the Mexican model under which the authority reports to the legislature.

Unfortunately, when Talierco checked to see if the reforms had been sustained over time, he found a disappointing pattern of backsliding in all the cases he studied (Talierco 2001, see also Geddes 1994).[33] He argues that the political coalition in favor of independent revenue authorities is likely to be fragile, and demonstrates that this is so. Officials in the Ministry of Finance oppose the revenue authorities, especially if they seem competent and professional and, as a consequence, seek to be involved in tax policy, not just tax collection. Furthermore, taxpayers may also object. However, at the time of Talierco's study, the one bright spot was Peru, where the organized business community supported the independent revenue authority because it was able to collect taxes more evenhandedly from all business and because it promised certainty and limited official extortion.

---

[33] Stein *et al.* (2005): 186, 192 also found that countries, such as Colombia, are forced to pass reform after reform because each gets watered down in the approval process.

Procurement and business regulation

Outside of the revenue authorities, private businesses interact with the government in two main ways: by selling it goods and services and by complying with or evading its regulations. Each can be a source of waste and corruption or reflect the simple incompetence of public officials and the lack of public concern in the business world.

Table 9.2 (p. 524) summarizes cross-country differences in the costs of government regulations and practices for business, but it ignores the possible social benefits of the rules and regulations. If one supposes that those benefits are fairly constant across the hemisphere, there appears to be room for improvement in most of the region. Jansson and Chalmers (2001) argue the case for reform. They claim that costly regulations drive firms off the books into the informal sector, thus losing the benefits of formal legal status. These benefits include better access to financing, access to government support programs, ability to sign legally enforceable contracts, and lack of fear of being caught and punished for one's informal status. Reducing the costs of operating on the books will, they argue, stimulate economic growth. Their goal is not to eliminate informality but to shift the trade-off so that more firms choose to register.

Even if sufficient funds are collected, government will be ineffective if procurement expenses are padded with corruption and waste. In that regard, internet procurement systems that limit corrupt opportunities appear promising. This is being tried in LAC countries such as Colombia and Mexico. In Mexico, the government estimated that every dollar invested in an internet procurement system earned a social return of \$4.[34] Of course, not all government purchases are so standardized that they can be reduced to an impersonal form, but the benefits of such systems suggest that governments should also re-examine what they purchase to see if off-the-shelf products used in the private sector can substitute for some specially made goods and services. The government would go "shopping" rather than have to use specially designed procurement systems (Rose-Ackerman 1999: 59–68).

[34] Robert Kossick, "Best Practice Profile: CompraNet," May 10, 2004, www.undp.org/surf-panama/egov/docs/programme_activities/bpractices/e-procurement_in_mexico-compranet.pdf, accessed September 13, 2006.

Privatization and contracting out

Difficulties with tax collection and procurement can be limited if the state simply reduces its reach. Although the government obviously cannot stop collecting taxes,[35] other problems with public administration can be resolved by ending state involvement in the provision of one or another service. In particular, LAC countries were active in the 1990s in privatizing public utilities such as water, electricity, and telecoms, with some going further to contract for private toll roads and other services (Chong and Benavides 2007).

An IDB study documents the overall favorable impact of privatization in economic terms (Chong and López-de-Silanes 2003), but the LAC experience with the privatization of public utilities has been mixed. For example, in telecomms privatization has eliminated unmet demand by raising prices so that many households still lack service.[36] Barrera-Osorio and Olivera (2007) find that privatization of water supply in Colombia was beneficial overall, especially for town and city dwellers; however, the price rises that accompanied higher quality had a strongly negative effect on poor rural households' access to water. Some transfers to private ownership were marred by corruption and patronage and imposed costs on ordinary citizens. The familiar trade-off between maximizing the revenue earned by the government from the sale vs. creating a competitive market without monopoly profits was evident in many programs, and was often resolved in favor of giving private firms monopoly power (Manzetti 1999; Hoffmann 2007). The privatization of electric power in Brazil was designed to clean up the central government's core budget in a way that ultimately transferred liabilities to an off-budget state development bank (Prado 2007). The most successful cases involved transparent and homogenous procedures, speed, and limited restructuring prior to privatization (Chong and Lopez-de-Silanes 2003).

---

[35] Some have recommended the revival of "tax farming" systems such as those practised by European monarchs in the past. Under such systems, the state sells the right to collect revenues to private individuals. The state receives a guaranteed payment and the "tax farmer" has an incentive to collect as much a possible from the taxpayers. The system creates obvious opportunities for abuse but has occasionally worked well when effective complaint and monitoring systems are in place and tax liabilities are relatively clear. See Rose-Ackerman (1999): 86 and sources cited therein.

[36] Hoffmann (2007): 10, quoting a study by the International Telecommunications Union (2000, 3).

At present, the LAC region is experiencing something of a backlash against privatization of for-profit firms (Bonnet *et al.* 2006; Chong and Benavides 2007: 265–7), a trend that highlights the importance of public sector reform. Privatization efforts are often highly politically salient and unpopular. For example, in Costa Rica efforts to privatize telecomms and electricity beginning in the late 1980s generated widespread opposition, and were never carried out.[37] Furthermore, once privatized as monopoly providers, the industry needs to be regulated, and the LAC experience there has also been mixed (see, e.g. Levy and Spiller 1996 on telecommunications, and Chong and López-de Silanes 2003). This mixed experience with privatization suggests that it should not be priority going forward. Rather, efforts should be made to consolidate the benefits of past efforts by improving regulatory quality and increasing the benefits flowing to the poor.

Privatization is also having an impact on public service delivery, as LAC governments sign contracts with private firms. Here the government still funds the program and sets eligibility criteria, but does not provide the service itself. A promising option is to use NGOs as service providers. Loevinsohn and Harding (2005) review ten evaluations of contracting out in the delivery of primary health and nutrition services in developing countries. Two cases were from the LAC region – Bolivia and Guatemala. Compared with government provision, both showed positive results from management contracts, as measured by coverage of the program, and in rural Guatemala benefits flowed from service delivery contracts as well. Even in Guatemala, where the researchers faulted the government's management of the contract, implementation still succeeded and over time the program expanded to cover more than one-quarter of the country. No cost data were available for Bolivia, but in Guatemala the cost averaged $6.25 per head with 3.4 million covered. The authors do point to factors that limit the generality of the results. Of particular importance is the nature of the services provided – primary care and nutrition services. These are services where outputs are quite easy to monitor so that the contractors can be held to account not only by public officials but by the beneficiaries themselves. The authors conclude that contracting out should be considered, but that

---

[37] Hoffmann (2007). Actually, a law did pass in 2000, but was withdrawn a few months later in the face of massive popular opposition and intervention by the courts. Ratification of DR-CAFTA, however, will put the issue back on the political agenda.

rigorous evaluation should go along with experiments. The results also suggest the value of combining contracting out with some type of bottom-up public accountability, as discussed below.

If privatization is not a quick fix and leads to organized political opposition, state ownership is likely to continue.[38] This political reality gives even more urgency to programs of internal state reform. Although the public corporations that operate state enterprises are frequently not formally part of the civil service system, the issues of personal training, motivation, and pay arise there as well. Vested interests will seek to block internal reform, but it may be more feasible than additional large-scale privatizations in the current political environment in much of the LAC region. Perhaps a combination of contracting out some activities to non-profit organizations/NGOs, civil service reforms, and improved external monitoring can work to produce favorable results.

Civil service reform

Most LAC democracies need to strengthen the overall capacities of the civil service. According to Stein *et al.* (2005: 67), the region has traditionally had large but weak institutions, with little capacity to respond to the needs of citizens. Thus, it is crucial that these countries train the new generation in tools of policy analysis and program design and set favorable civil service employment conditions so as to attract high-quality applicants. Figure 9.4 (p. 529), based on IDB research carried out between 2002 and 2005, indicates the extent of the problems in the region in general terms. It combines three subindices that measure: (1) the strategic consistency of public administration with government priorities, (2) the extent to which merit is a criterion for selection promotion and discharge, and (3) the functional capacity of the bureaucracy with respect to management systems.[39] The IDB data-gathering exercise was influenced by the NPM literature, with its emphasis on managing for results, but the subindices do not provide much additional nuance compared to the averages in figure 9.4 and have not been reproduced here (Echabarría and Cortázar 2007:

---

[38] For a general discussion of corrupt opportunities in privatization processes, and some suggestions for limiting them, see Rose-Ackerman (1999): 35–8, 42–4.

[39] In addition, Stein *et al.* (2005): 67 stress the value of a stable professional bureaucracy. However, stability is not itself desirable if the existing system performs poorly.

138–41). The top six performers are identical, with some variation in order. These top performers (Brazil, Chile, Costa Rica, Uruguay, Argentina, and Colombia) are followed by Mexico, Jamaica, Trinidad and Tobago, and Venezuela, with the rest clustered at low scores. A comparison with the earlier work by Evans and Rauch (1999; see Rauch and Evans 2000) suggests that some countries, such as Brazil and Chile, have made important gains, but clearly there is much room for improvement in the region, with some countries in a particularly weak condition on all three measures.

Rauch and Evans (2000) found that recruitment and promotion on merit was the key to good performance.[40] In the thirty-five countries they studied, salary levels played little role in performance, but presumably that was partly because recruitment on merit can hardly succeed unless salaries are adequate. In a study using data from the 1990s, Panizza (2000) concluded that pay levels were not the primary weakness of the public administration in the LAC region.[41] Table 9.5 shows that most countries pay public sector workers more than private sector workers – in part, because of strong unions and the difficulty of firing officials. Women especially benefited from government jobs because their options in the formal private sector were poor. This suggests that women face more discrimination in the private than in the public sectors and also reflects the large number of public sector jobs in teaching and healthcare. Both Uruguay and Mexico have promulgated civil service reform laws that seek to professionalize the civil service through more promotion and recruitment on merit and a reduction in purely political appointments. The Mexican law was passed in 2003 and so in not reflected in table 9.5. Uruguay's law dates from 1996, and the survey data are from 1981 to 1997 so its reforms are also not included (Panizza and Philip 2005). If the data in table 9.5 reflect current realities in other LAC countries, they suggest that most countries provide employment opportunities for women that dominate those available in the private sector, and that men also do well. Panizza's data for formal sector workers confirm this pattern; although the differences are smaller, they remain significant in many of the countries surveyed. For men, the only countries where low pay seems to be a problem

---

[40] See also Stein *et al.* (2005): 68 who express a similar view.
[41] Echebarría and Cortázar (2007): 134, citing Panizza (2000). Panizza's data are from the 1980s and 1990s.

Table 9.5 *Public sector wages relative to
private sector wages, 1990s*

	Men	Women
Bolivia	−0.17*	0.01*
Brazil	0.02	−0.08*
Chile	−0.025	0.17*
Colombia	0.16*	0.27*
Costa Rica	0.17*	0.47*
Ecuador	0.30*	0.26*
El Salvador	0.27*	0.67*
Guatemala	−0.045	0.40*
Honduras	0.01	0.60*
Mexico	0.11*	0.23*
Nicaragua	−0.02	0.02
Panama	0.11*	0.49*
Paraguay	0.11	0.28
Peru	0.05	0.11*
Dom. Rep.	−0.37*	0.23
Uruguay	−0.015	−0.04
Venezuela	−0.001*	0.27

Note: * = Significant at 1%.
Source: Panizza (2000), table A2; surveys from
various dates in the 1990s.

are Bolivia and the Dominican Republic. For women, low pay is a
significant problem only in Brazil, and that finding reverses when the
sample is restricted to formal sector only – there, the pay premium in
the public sector was 0.24 (Panizza 2000, table A2).

Thus, it seems that except for a few pockets of low pay, reform
should concentrate on motivating and reorganizing the public administration, not providing across-the-board pay raises. Brazil has been the
most active reformer in the region. Although the data in figures 9.1,
9.2, and 9.3 and in tables 9.1 and 9.2 suggest continuing problems,
studies of the reform suggest that they have had real benefits, some
of which have been sustained to the present. Although some public
sector employees were recruited on an on-merit basis as early as 1937,
it took the 1988 constitution to mandate a comprehensive federal civil
service system and the Cardoso administration to obtain a further

amendment and to implement the new program (Gaetani and Heredia 2002; Echebarría and Cortázar 2007: 127–8). The reform "tried to avoid the pitfalls of the Weberian civil service model and promoted greater flexibility, greater managerial autonomy, decentralization and results-based forms of administration and control" (Gaetani and Heredia 2002: 2). It also promoted: "(1) an alignment between public and private sector wages; (2) bonuses based on performance; (3) more flexible allocation of public personnel; and (4) the National School of Public Administration for training all types of public employees in all areas" (Gaetani and Heredia: 15). Beginning in 1996, the share of new civil servants with a university degree jumped dramatically from 39.2% in 1995 to 63.6% in 1996, rising again to 94.1% in 2001 (Gaetani and Heredia 2002: 6, table 5). However, there were few short-term benefits from the reform during Cardoso's first term. Rather the gains were in an improved system of human resource management (HRM) and the strengthening of career paths that helped pave the way for more effective reforms during Cardoso's second term.

Chile has also implemented reforms based on management agreements and evaluation by results plus a system, established only in 2003, that created a merit-based system of selection for senior civil servants and a professional career path. The gradual introduction of reforms gave them staying power (Echebarría and Cortázar 2007: 128, 131–2).[42] There is an ongoing debate about the appropriate model that should guide civil service reform – a Weberian model or the NPM. I do not attempt to adjudicate this debate here, partly because many of the mostly urgently needed reforms do not turn on this difference.[43] A more professional, merit-based civil service that is paid and trained well and rewarded for competence is the bedrock on which other reforms must be built and needs to be introduced more broadly in many LAC countries.

Even before one considers which reforms are best, however, one must ask how such reforms can obtain political support, given the

---

[42] Peru also attempted reform of a somewhat different sort in 1995–7, but it was not implemented (Echebarría and Cortázar 2007: 128, 131–2).

[43] Compare Evans and Rauch (1999), who follow a Weberian model and study merit recruitment and professional career paths, with Echebarría and Cortázar (2007), who stress these factors but also include a broader range of measures. Evans and Rauch (1999), however, mention other factors related to NPM, but they have not developed ways to measure them in their expert surveys (1999: 752, n. 9).

vested interests that benefit from the status quo. A study of successful legal change in other countries can help one identify when a window of opportunity exists (Rose-Ackerman 1999: 198–224). Echebarría and Cortázar (2007: 132) outline the conditions that made reform possible in Chile and to some extent in Brazil, while it failed in Peru. They stress the value of gradual reform as a way to avoid politicizing the process and to permit lessons to be learned from any initial missteps. Linking public administration reform to other issues such as economic policy can increase support. Panizza and Philip's (2005) study of Uruguay and Mexico, in contrast, stresses the importance of seizing, the perhaps fleeting, moment when conditions are favorable and of recognizing political constraints that will limit the range of reform. On the one hand, they point to the key role of ideas and of people willing to advocate for reform policies. For example, in Mexico a coalition of public policy intellectuals pushed for reform with support from international agencies and outside experts (Panizza and Philip 2005: 684–5). On the other hand, the authors emphasize the need for an alliance between policy entrepreneurs and economic interests that limits or obscures the costs imposed on potential losers (2005: 671). In Mexico, an opportunity was presented by the election of the first president from outside the traditional ruling party. Even though he himself was not a strong advocate for reform, reformers formed a broad coalition that included legislators from the old ruling party who had lost their base of patronage in the bureaucracy. In a bow to political realities, the reform was limited to the top of the federal bureaucracy and did not challenge either the powerful public sector unions or the newly important state and local governments (2005: 685). Similarly in Uruguay, many of the most important patronage jobs, such as appointments to the boards of public utilities, were not covered by the reform (2005: 678–83).

These compromises with political reality, however, should not obscure the impact of the reforms. In Uruguay, the number of public employees fell, as did the number of operational units in the central government. The state established an evaluation system although its implementation may have lacked consistency (2005: 676–7). Reform in Mexico is too new for evaluation, but it has sharply reduced the number of patronage positions in the central government from tens of thousands to a few hundred. The aim is to develop a career civil service, although incumbents are given some priority if they receive training and favorable job evaluations (2005: 677).

One way to convince doubters is to provide data on the value of reform. Unfortunately, the success of the NPM in improving service delivery and citizen satisfaction relative to more conventional bureaucratic models has not been rigorously tested in the LAC region. The theory behind the NPM model is plausible, and it has apparently been successful in New Zealand, where it has been most intensively implemented, but there is a need for research to study its benefits and costs as actually applied in middle-income countries. In Brazil, hints that all is not well in practice come from the data in table 9.2 that suggest, at least for the business community, that the state continues to impose costly obstacles relative to its neighbors. Nevertheless, a few studies point the way in showing positive relations between the pay and the presumed status of government jobs and between measures of state performance and favorable economic outcomes.

Oversight and public accountability

Internal reforms are not sufficient; oversight is also necessary. Accountable executive branch policymaking requires participation and oversight by a range of interested actors, but it also requires that the resulting policy be effective, transparent, and capable of assessment by the voters. The establishment of an accountable government, then, is a tricky balancing act. Public bodies must be responsive to the concerns of citizens and yet remain insulated from improper influence. They must be both competent experts and democratically responsible policymakers. There are two broad responses – government institutions charged with oversight, and empowerment of citizens. Sometimes the two go together, as when an Ombudsman attempts to resolve citizen complaints and uses them as a guide to more wide-ranging inquires.

Many LAC governments have state-financed institutions of accountability that operate with various degrees of independence of the rest of government. Some report to the legislature; others can bring court cases. Appointments are more or less independent of the government in power. These are what O'Donnell (1999) calls institutions of "horizontal accountability." They perform important checking roles although as Moreno, Crisp, and Shugart (2003) point out, their impact varies, depending not only on their independence from those they monitor but also on whether or not they can impose sanctions.[44] The authors' useful compilation categorizes each country's high courts, attorneys general and prosecutors, human rights Ombudsmen, and controllers general in terms of their methods of appointment and the ratio of their terms to the terms of the body that appoints them (figure 9.7). Although they are unable to measure how effectiveness varies with independence, they argue, quite plausibly, that monitoring agencies cannot do their jobs well if they are dependent on the body that they must oversee. Independence is a necessary but not sufficient condition.

As Moreno, Crisp, and Shugart (2003) point out, these ostensibly independent institutions are often dependent on other parts of the government, and have a mixed record. This suggests the importance of providing more direct routes for citizens to act as a check on government. However, they can do this only if the government provides information on its actions and gives citizens a convenient means of lodging complaints that protects them against possible reprisals. Collective action problems limit the impact of aggrieved citizens, but if the costs are low enough they may nevertheless band together to protest government action. The state should facilitate such organization, but in a way that avoids creating groups that are merely captives or puppets of powerful political forces. Furthermore, government officials must find it in their interest to respond to complaints from both individuals and groups. To assure accountable policymaking, the executive must make its policy processes open to outside scrutiny, and officials must be required to listen to the opinions and expert views of those outside the government.

The World Bank's surveys of public officials in Bolivia provide some statistical backing for the view that low corruption and high levels of transparency and "voice" are beneficial to the actual performance of government and help the poor (Kaufmann, Mastruzzi, and Zaveleta 2003). A study based on 1,200 interviews with public officials in many different national agencies and local governments demonstrated wide inter-agency and inter-government variation. The study found that the quality of public service delivery is negatively

---

[44] In fact, Moreno, Crisp, and Shugart (2003) argue that the term "horizontal accountability" is an oxymoron. To them, accountability implies a degree of vertical authority to impose sanctions.

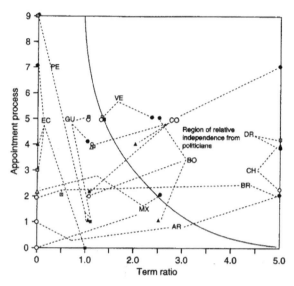

FIG. 4.3. *Independence of high courts and superintendence agencies in Latin America*

(*Source*: Appendix Tables.)

Key to scale on appointment process:

Legislative-dominant: appointment by:

0. Legislative majority only
1. Legislators, with opposition participation

Mixed: appointment by:

2. Legislators and elected president
3. State entity other than legislature or elected president (e.g. weak upper house or head of state)
4. Judges and politicians
5. Civic groups and politicians

Judicial-dominant: appointment by:

6. Supreme court or council of judges with participation by state entity other than legislature or elected president
7. Supreme court or council of judges

Civil-society-dominant: appointment by:

8. Commission of lawyers, academics, etc., with participation by state entity other than legislature or elected president
9. Commission of lawyers, academics, etc.

Key to country abbreviations

AR   Argentina
BO   Bolivia
BR   Brazil
CH   Chile
CO   Colombia
CR   Costa Rica
DR   Dominican Republic
EC   Ecuador
GU   Guatemala
MX   Mexico
PE   Peru
VE   Venezuela

Key to symbols

● Supreme Court
▲ Constitutional Tribunal
△ Attorney General
⊟ Prosecutor General
∎ Ombudsman or Defender of human rights
○ Controller General or audit court

Figure 9.7 Accountability deficit: LAC countries
Source: Figure 4.3 in Moreno, Crisp, and Shugart (2003).

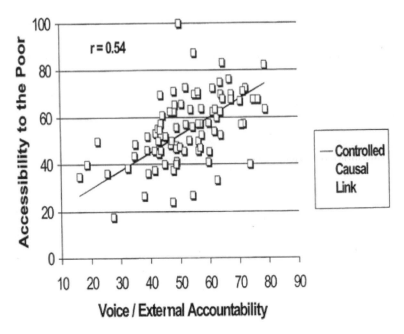

Figure 9.8 External accountability/feedback improve access of the poor to public services (Bolivia GAC diagnostic)
Source: Based on Kaufmann, Mehrez, and Gurgur (2002)
Note: The sample of institutions includes 44 national, departmental, and municipal agencies that provide services to the poor. Each point depicts an institution

associated with corruption and positively with the external voice of users and with transparency. Bribery and corruption are higher in more politicized units of government and in those with lower transparency and less meritocracy. Transparency is affected positively by voice and negatively by corruption and politicization. Municipal governments perform worse than central government agencies on average, but do sometimes provide better access for the poor. Measures of civil service management and individual ethical commitments have no independent impact although they may obviously be associated with some of the other data (Kaufmann, Mastruzzi, and Zavaleta 2003: 383). Figure 9.8 illustrates one result. Higher levels of voice and accountability are associated with greater accessibility of the poor to public services (Kaufmann 2003: 24).

The judiciary and its relationship to prosecutors are, of course, one source of oversight. I defer discussion of those institutions to p. 568. Here, I discuss public information and auditing, the media and public opinion, grassroots participation, and administrative law.

Public information and auditing

A precondition for citizen influence is information. Open government includes telling citizens what their government is doing by publishing consolidated budgets, data on tax collections, statutes and rules, and the proceedings of legislative bodies (Premchand 1993). Financial data should be audited and published by independent authorities such as the Government Accountability Office (GAO) in the United States or the Supreme Audit Offices in many LAC countries.[45] These institutions are independent of the government agencies that they audit – a necessary condition for credibility. LAC audit agencies vary in professionalism and independence. Carlos Santiso (2007) has evaluated the audit agencies in ten LAC countries (table 9.6). He finds that all have weaknesses but that overall Brazil, Chile, and Colombia are best and Argentina and Ecuador are worst.[46] Santiso ranks them in terms of independence, credibility, timeliness, and enforcement. Although most agencies rank fairly well in terms of formal independence and enforcement powers, they do less well in measures related to actual performance – credibility and timeliness. Although the number of data points is too small to draw firm conclusions, there is a positive relationship between the effectiveness of external audit agencies in the LAC region and the quality of fiscal governance defined by the efficiency of the bureaucracy, the control of corruption, and the strength of public institutions. They are less important as checks on the executive. Of course, these results may just show that some good things go together.

---

[45] The GAO has changed its name from the General Accounting Office, to the General Accountability Office, to signal its broader mission. It monitors the federal executive branch and reports directly to Congress. It resolves contracting disputes, settles the accounts of the US government, resolves claims of or against the United States, gathers information for Congress, and makes recommendations to it (Abikoff 1987: 1539–62).

[46] Notice the divergence between Santiso's (2007) ranking of audit agencies and their position in figure 9.7. This appears to result from the fact that most are appointed by the legislature, a fact that seems less problematic for audit agencies than for the other institutions included in the table that they categorize.

Table 9.6 *Index of effectiveness of AAAs: LAC region*

Country	Index of institutional effectiveness	Independence	Credibility	Timeliness	Enforcement
ARG	0.28	0.46	0.22	0.13	0.33
BRA	0.63	0.88	0.42	0.24	1.00
CHI	0.60	0.81	0.40	0.18	1.00
COL	0.61	0.78	0.46	0.21	1.00
CRI	0.50	0.69	0.48	0.16	0.67
ECU	0.28	0.67	0.14	0.00	0.33
SLV	0.41	0.58	0.08	0.00	1.00
MEX	0.36	0.61	0.38	0.12	0.33
NIC	0.43	0.82	0.20	0.03	0.67
PER	0.33	0.82	0.12	0.04	0.33
LAC10	0.44	0.71	0.29	0.11	0.67

Note: Indicators are on a scale from 0 to 1, with lower scores representing lower performance.

Sub-index of independence of audit agencies: Based on the constitutions, organic budget laws, financial administration laws, and organic laws of fiscal control and government auditing based on twelve key variables.

Sub-index of credibility of audit findings: Based on the IBP indicator of the credibility of external auditing.

Sub-index of timeliness of audit reports: Based on the IBP indicator of the quality and timeliness of information.

Sub-index of enforcement powers of audit agencies: Derived from a proxy indicator measuring the enforcement powers of AAAs, provided by the UNDP. It reflects the binding nature of audit decisions and AAAs' capacity to enforce sanctions. According to Santiso, the construction of this dummy is not very robust.

Source: Santiso (2007), which includes information on the calculations and the under-lying sources.

One would have to do more detailed case study research to make any causal inferences. This has been done for Argentina, Brazil, Chile, and Mexico in a way that provides much more nuance (Santiso 2007 for the first three, and Ackerman 2007 for Mexico). Even for audit institutions that rank relatively well in the LAC region, the authors locate serious problems. Perhaps most interesting is Santiso's conclusion that Chile's Contraloría General de la Republica is *too* independent so that it is insulated from political accountability. Santiso claims that its over-sight is excessively legalistic and procedural.

Ferraz and Finan (2007) have made an interesting effort to measure the impact of audits on political success in Brazil. They benefited from a natural experiment under which the federal government randomly audited the accounts of municipal governments and revealed the results to citizens before elections. In an encouraging result for democrats, voters withdrew their electoral support for mayors of municipalities with problematic accounts, especially if local radio stations existed to publicize the results. The study shows how the state can use technical expertise in auditing to enhance democratic accountability. Information that no citizen could uncover alone was, with the help of an independent audit and media exposure, decisive in determining electoral outcomes.

In general, however, audit agencies are not so independent of the governments they audit, and they report to the legislature. Although they may help citizens evaluate state functioning, they are part of the government structure. Thus, in addition, many countries facilitate direct citizen oversight through FOIAs that permit citizens and organizations to access government information without having to give a reason for their interest in the material (Ackerman and Sandoval-Ballesteros 2006; Neuman and Calland 2007). This is the essence of FOIAs insofar as they are a tool for government accountability. The United States FOIA (5 U.S.C. §§552) sets out the basic principles, including a range of exceptions, time limits on bureaucrats, and provisions to help agencies manage the process, including guidelines on fees and recordkeeping requirements. However, the US law has one weakness. There is no government agency charged with overseeing its administration and resolving disputes. Instead, those with complaints must go to court – a costly and time-consuming process. In contrast, some countries have independent agencies that monitor and manage the implementation of the law. Examples are Canada, Hungary, Jamaica, and Mexico (Rose-Ackerman 2005: 149–53; Neuman and Calland 2007: 204–5).

FOIAs are effective only if the government actually collects data that citizens find useful. Some FOIAs mandate the collection and dissemination of particular types of information, including requirements for open web access to certain materials.[47] Furthermore, the cost of complying with information requests encourages agencies to take steps

---

[47] See the amendment to the US FOIA, calling for improved e-government.

ex ante to organize their files and to make more of them available on line. As of 2005, only six LAC countries had enacted FOIAs (Ackerman and Sandoval-Ballesteros 2006), but in countries with strong laws (such as Mexico) it will be important to study their impact on the overall management of information throughout the government, not just on formal compliance with requests. Neuman and Calland (2007) outline the implementation challenges. A strong civil society can help keep pressure on the state to perform, and such groups should concentrate on the procedures for information management and disclosure. Successful implementation is quite expensive both in start-up costs and in the ongoing response to requests. Poorer countries will need to find ways to keep costs down without undermining the law's purposes. To get a sense of the costs, the authors take the example of Mexico, one of the few countries where budgetary figures are available. In its first year, the Mexican Federal Institute for Access to Information (IFAI) had a budget of US$25 million, a new building, a staff of over 150, and an advanced Internet-based system "that would make major corporations jealous" (Neuman and Calland 2007: 193). The budget of the IFAI was 0.033% of GDP compared to 0.0007% in the United States and 0.004 in Canada (Neuman and Calland 2007). The benefits of a FOIA have never been systematically examined, although a few studies do show how the provision of information can be a cost-effective way to limit corruption (Di Tella and Schargrodsky 2003; Reinikka and Svensson 2005).

The media and public opinion

Even a government that keeps good records and makes them available to the public may operate with impunity if no one bothers to analyze the available information – or if analysts are afraid to raise their voices. If the aim is to pressure government to act in the public interest, both the media and organized groups are important.

The media can facilitate public discussion if it is privately owned and free to criticize the government without fear of reprisal. Nominal press freedom will be insufficient if most of the media is associated with political parties. Governments can also keep the press in line through advertising, printing contracts, and payments to journalists. Another subtle form of control is to overlook under-payment of taxes by editors and media companies, retaining the possibility of prosecution as a threat.[48] The LAC media is mostly ranked as free or partly free by Freedom House (table 9.2). Some of the poorest countries with the weakest institutional quality are also those where the press is only partly free.

The forms of political control are usually more subtle than outright censorship. But, in the extreme, a sitting government may simply buy off the media with regular payments conditional on their subservient behavior. A study of the Fujimori/Montesinos regime in Peru demonstrates the importance of a free media in maintaining democracy. McMillan and Zoido (2004) studied the tapes made by Vladimer Montesinos, President Fujimori's top advisor. The videos recorded his payoffs to legislators, judges, and the media, the relatively large size of the payoffs to television stations suggests their importance. McMillan and Zoido show how a state with exemplary formal constitutional rules, providing for elections and checks and balances, can be undermined by corrupt high-level officials. However, it was not sufficient to pay off public officials; Montesinos recognized that the information available to the public had to be manipulated at well. In fact, the one independent cable station, which was not corrupted, ultimately brought the system to light and led to the downfall of the government. This paper gives one a rough measure of the value of press freedom in maintaining democratic accountability. Another data point is the Ferraz and Finan (2007) study mentioned above, where radio broadcasts were a critical part of a strategy that helped punish corrupt incumbents at the polls.

Private associations and non-profit organizations

Laws that make it easy to establish private associations and non-profit corporations can help improve accountability. Political economic analysis stresses the free-rider problems that plague the organization of advocacy organizations. In reality, however, in all societies

---

[48] "It Happened in Monterrey," *New York Times*, November 29, 1991, discusses the resignation of a newspaper editor after pressure was put on his paper through the cancellation of government advertising and printing contracts. When a leading editor was arrested in Mexico City in 1996 for tax evasion, the editor claimed that the arrest occurred in response to the paper's newly asserted independence. The tax authorities claimed that the editor adopted a more outspoken line only after the investigation had begun (*Mexico Business Monthly*, October 1, 1996).

some altruistic individuals bear the costs, although economic interests are generally better organized and financed. This fact suggests that more groups will organize if the costs are low. Yet, some governments, worried that NGOs will be used by political opponents, limit such groups, or make it very costly for them to organize. Formal legal constraints may be high, and members may be subject to surveillance and harassment. Once registered, non-profits may face onerous formal reporting requirements and require state approval before undertaking new projects.

Another problem is cooptation. Some non-profits organize and administer development programs for the poor. Their financing may be provided by the state or by aid funds administered by the state: their very existence thus depends upon cooperation with public authorities. As a consequence, they may be reluctant to criticize officials openly. To avoid such tensions, an NGO that takes on a mandate to work for law reform should avoid participation in service delivery. LAC non-profits sometimes have an adversarial relationship with their governments (Bratton 1989: 567–87). Thus, these existing groups may be able to perform a monitoring role.

However, in emerging democracies with moderate income levels it is difficult to create a group of strong NGOs capable of participating in national policymaking. In the LAC region, the role of civil society is limited partly by the low incomes of citizens and partly by the structures of political power that limit their role. A key issue is to find ways to strengthen such groups without turning them into mere extensions of the state. A first step is to remove obstacles to the formation of groups while improving checks on the use of the NGO form as a fraudulent effort to avoid taxes or otherwise disguise profitmaking activities. Secondly, positive incentives can be created actively to encourage the formation of groups.

Grassroots participation in government decisionmaking

A framework with good access to information, a free media, and a collection of organized groups and concerned citizens constitutes one side of the efforts to make government more accountable. On the other side is the government itself. The state needs to design structures that permit people and organizations to participate in a meaningful way. Otherwise participation will be limited to organized elites with inside connections who can shape the law in their interest. The goal is not to have the state abdicate its responsibilities but instead to find ways to use bureaucratic and executive expertise to complement political empowerment (Ackerman 2004). Government ought to open up its processes at all levels. To take the extremes, this subsection discusses grassroots participation; the next concerns participation in national policymaking.

Sometimes the problem of public participation is deep-seated and is limited by fear of intimidation. This needs to be a high priority although it is, of course, more difficult to remedy than a policy of more open public records.[49] If the problem is acute at the local level, higher levels of government need to prevent local officials from operating with impunity so that local people are intimidated and afraid. The LAC democracies need to be sure that the routes for public participation are open to those at the bottom of the income ladder, and that fears of intimidation are addressed in an open and straightforward fashion. Long-standing patron–client relationships between politicians and local elites, on the one hand, and ordinary citizens, on the other, operate in some areas to make independent participation difficult.

Much of the research on the role of grassroots participation draws on cases in South Asia and Africa but the general findings are relevant for the LAC region as well (Rose-Ackerman 2004b: 316–22). As Deininger and Mpuga (2005: 172) conclude, "both governments and donors might be well advised to focus on ways by which ordinary citizens can hold (elected and appointed) bureaucrats to account as a means to improve outcomes in the public sector."

In the LAC region, numerous attempts have been made both to involve rural people in the design and monitoring of agricultural development programs and to increase the participation of city dwellers in government decisionmaking. The rural development programs were designed to improve the targeting of programs to the needs of the farmers and to increase accountability to beneficiaries (Parker 1995; Das Gupta, Grandvoinnet, and Romani 2000). The urban cases, of

---

[49] For example, in Mexico in 2000 farmers in Guerrero complained about illegal logging that they claimed involved corrupt deals involving local political bosses and the army. The ensuing dispute, which led to the arrests of some farmers, raised claims that the army and local politicians were acting outside the law. Unfortunately, many of these allegations could not be proven. "A Farmer Learns about Mexico's Lack of the Rule of Law," *New York Times,* October 27, 2000.

which the most famous is Participatory Budgeting (PB) in Porto Alegre, Brazil, had the explicitly political goal of increasing democratic participation in opposition to existing clientelistic structures (Abers 1998; Sousa Santos 1998; Torres Ribeiro and de Grazia 2003; Ackerman 2004: 451–2). Of course, an implication is that the process affected the relative strength of various political parties and groups, and that fact will determine which politicians will support or oppose PB (Goldfrank and Schneider 2006). The successful cases in both settings gave citizens better information about what to expect from government and developed their capacity to hold public officials to account. Evaluations of the Porto Alegre case found that it reduced clientelism and reduced corruption (Gret and Sintomer 2005). A World Bank study of Porto Alegre (Shah and Wagle 2003) showed that services improved and tax collections increased although, of course, one cannot attribute those benefits entirely to public participation. PB was expanded to over 300 Brazilian municipalities between 1998 and 2004, so there will be an opportunity to evaluate its impact in a more diverse set of environments (Avritzer and Wampler 2005). As Goldfrank and Schneider (2006) show in their study of PB at the state level in Brazil, one can expect mixed results that do not support either the extremely positive or the sharply negative position.

The World Bank is studying the links between empowerment, participation, and development worldwide (Empowerment Project and Participation and Civic Engagement Project, www.worldbank.org). In addition, the World Bank Group's International Finance Corporation (IFC) is beginning to incorporate local participation and assistance to local governments into the mining investment projects in which they participate. A report to the World Bank Board provides some background in connection with the Yanacocha gold mine in Peru and the Marlin gold mining project in Guatemala. The project in Peru is designed to increase the capacity of local governments near the mine so that they can make effective use of the funds they are receiving from the project. In Guatemala, unrest and protests in some surrounding communities spurred efforts to improve dialogue with neighboring communities and to create a community environmental monitoring committee.[50] Although the process cannot always be

---

[50] *Implementation of the Management Response to the Extractive Industries Review*, Report to the World Bank board, December 9, 2005, boxes 1, 3.

applied successfully (Wampler 2007), it seems a promising innovation worth further study. At present, however, outside of individual case reports, only two studies have considered a wide range of cases, and they lack any consideration of the economic and social effects.[51]

The case studies of the performance of participatory programs suggest that they require a long-term commitment from established governments, along with technical and organizational help. They also work better if governments are not too sharply resource-constrained so that many participants can see an upside to the process (Goldfrank and Schneider 2006). Furthermore, people who are not used to political power need time to learn how to exercise it responsibly. The variety of experience at both the rural and urban level suggests the factors that need to be considered, but can hardly produce the "blueprints" or "best practices" preferred by the international lending organizations. These examples suggest that a number of factors must come together before productive partnerships between government reformers and low-income people can succeed. The successes have proved difficult to replicate elsewhere, but this experience teaches us something about how to facilitate grassroots participation. Increases in local control do not necessarily increase transparency and accountability (Das Gupta, Grandvoinnet, and Romani 2000). In a worst-case scenario, such policies enhance the power of local patrons and entrenched interests. The interest of the cases outlined above is that they were designed explicitly to deal with this problem, and have sometimes had quite marked success.

National policymaking

Grassroots participation concerns only local problems, but many government policies are national in scope. Central government policymaking needs to be managed through a transparent and accountable system of administrative law. This involves not just the application of the law in individual cases but also rulemaking in the executive branch, where broadly drafted statutes are implemented through the promulgation of general rules. Rulemaking should be structured to assure adequate participation and transparency. The public also needs

---

[51] In connection with his research on participatory democracy, Paolo Spada, a doctoral student in Political Science at Yale provided many of the sources cited here. Torres Ribeiro and de-Grazia (2003) is a descriptive comparative report; Wampler (2007) studies the diffusion process only in Brazil.

avenues for appeal to the judiciary if the government has not followed its own procedures, or has acted lawlessly. One goal is to make corruption and self-dealing harder to hide by forcing review of both the process and the substantive outcome. Furthermore, administrative law should help in the creation of good substantive policies that are both competent and reflect democratic values.

One model is the US administrative process as reflected in the Administrative Procedure Act (APA).[52] Although these procedures were developed in light of the US constitutional and government structures, they nevertheless respond to general problems related to the accountable operation of the public sector. I focus on the "notice and comment rulemaking," provisions of the APA, where an agency makes policy free of the strictures of a judicialized process. The APA requires that draft rules be publicly announced, and the agency must have a hearing open to anyone with an interest in the subject at hand. Final rules must be accompanied by a statement that explains the statutory basis of the rule and justifies the outcome. Rules can be reviewed in court for conformity with the underlying statute and with the Constitution, and for conformity with APA procedures. Frequently, rules are found wanting, but the courts seldom correct the problems themselves; rather, the agency is required to reconsider its decision or follow improved procedures. There are many practical problems in the American rulemaking process, but in principle it tries to cope with the challenge of balancing expertise and bureaucratic rationality against popular concerns for openness and accountability.

Of course, a major caveat may be the limited transferability of the US model. In using US practice as a guide to reform in LAC countries, one must recognize the differences in political structure and in the organization of society. Furthermore, partial reforms may not have the expected consequences. For example, the introduction of greater participation rights without effective judicial review can lead to policy distortions. Adding notice and an ability to comment may have little effect if agencies are not required to give reasons and are not subject to judicial oversight.[53]

---

[52] The APA passed in 1946 is at 5 U.S.C. §§551–559, 701–706.

[53] The Taiwanese APA has notice and comment rulemaking with no requirement for reason giving and limited judicial review. The Act provides only limited public accountability (Cheng 2005).

The introduction of notice and comment rulemaking may be politically difficult to achieve. Both career bureaucrats and political officials may resist increased participation and transparency on the grounds that they threaten to delay action and to distort choices. Critics argue that the problems with participation are delay, bias, irrelevance, displacement to other methods such as adjudication and curbs on agency implementation. However, most appear to be the result of poorly designed and biased procedures, not participation *per se*.

Of course, some delay is an inevitable counterpart of expanded participation. Agencies must take the time and trouble to consult. However, the extremely long time between proposed and final rules in the US experience seems to be driven more by strategic considerations than by cost of the process *per se*.[54] Some rulemakings attract the interest of only a few groups that submit comments. Examination of a random sample of forty-two rulemakings found that the median number of comments was about thirty (West 2004). Furthermore, advances in communication and information technology can speed up the comment process. Most US agencies have developed comprehensive and user-friendly web sites, and many permit comments on draft rules to be submitted via email. Of course, the agencies still need to be able to process comments in an effective manner, but information technology can make the processing of comments more cost-effective.

Displacement of agency activity to non-binding guidelines and to implementation through the adjudication of individual cases occurs. However, neither seems to be a general problem given the large number of rules that US agencies continue to issue.[55] In any case, the problem of displacement can be overcome if the legislature includes rulemaking requirements in statutes and if the courts resist adding incremental procedural requirements. The proponents of participatory

---

[54] Kerwin and Furlong (1992). A major rulemaking at the Environmental Protection Agency (EPA) averages almost three years and requires many hours of input from both bureaucrats and outside interests from industry and the environmental community. Many rules are challenged in court before they go into effect, introducing further delay (Coglianese 1997).

[55] Between 1992 and 2001, the number of final rules issued each year ranged from 4,132 in 2001 to a high of 4,937 in 1996. Of the 4,509 rules in the pipeline in October 2001, 149 were major rules, defined as those with at least a $100 million economic cost. Clyde Wayne Crews, Jr., *Ten Thousand Commandments: An Annual Snapshot of the Federal Regulatory State* (Washington, DC: Cato Institute, 2002: 11–16).

processes need to consider the actual workings of procedural innovations. Rigid, cumbersome, and biased processes are obviously not an improvement.

The costs of the rulemaking process ought to be balanced against the benefits. In the well-functioning cases the benefits were of several kinds. The most important benefit is that officials draft proposed rules in the light of the forthcoming public participation processes. Even if they consult with a biased selection of interest groups before the public hearing process, officials must consider how their proposals will be greeted by the public and the media when they are publicly posted, and later, when they are subject to judicial review.[56]

Public hearing processes can raise the salience of an issue with the public and increase public knowledge about a regulatory issue. Furthermore, studies of the hearing process suggest that US bureaucrats are not the captives of well-funded groups.[57] Successful efforts at public involvement can lead to choices that better reflect public values and are substantively strong – although, of course, fair and open procedures can not entirely overcome partisan biases.

Open procedures cost time and money; LAC democracies will need to make some compromises to avoid gridlock and to assure that processes are not just for show. Practical implementation requires a realistic understanding of the tradeoffs involved.

The judicial system

An effective system of law enforcement and dispute resolution provides a crucial background condition for state reform and for the operation of the market economy. The professionalism and honesty of the judiciary is a central concern, but other aspects of the system matter as well. Judges depend on litigants and prosecutors to bring cases before them and do not enforce their judgments on their own. Furthermore, many legal disputes are resolved outside of the formal adjudicatory system. The quality of ADR institutions for both ordinary people and

---

[56] West (2004) found that a common reason for delay was agency lawyers' efforts to withstand court challenges. In one rule that was substantially changed after notice and comment he quotes an official who claimed that the agency staff had "failed to do their homework on this one" by neglecting to consider the interests of some of the producers affected by the rule.

[57] See, for example, Magat, Krupnick, and Harrington (1986); Mendelson (2003).

businesses, and their relationship to the courts, are important aspects of private dispute settlement under law. If it works well, ADR provides speedy and well-accepted services; if it does not, informal dispute resolution may be captured by local elites or dominated by organized criminals who "enforce' judgments.

Judicial independence is commonly believed to be a necessary hallmark of a modern legal system. Widner provides a serviceable definition – independence is "the insulation of judges and the judicial process from partisan pressure to influence the outcomes of individual cases" (Widner 1999: 177–8). However, independence is not inherently valuable. Taken alone, it carries the risk of impunity. Because judicial decisions help to determine the distribution of wealth and power, independent judges can exploit their positions for private gain. An honest government administration will be difficult to establish if the judiciary is venal. A corrupt judiciary can undermine reforms and over-ride legal norms. When dealing with such courts, the wealthy and the corrupt operate with the confidence that a well-placed pay-off will resolve any legal challenges they face. However, even honest judges can cause concern if they overturn or fail to enforce legislative and executive branch decisions. Because of these worries, no country has an entirely independent judiciary. Some form of broad-based accountability to the government and the citizens is consistent with a well-functioning judiciary, and it is needed as a check on corruption and other forms of self-dealing.

Given the importance of a fair judiciary, judicial reform is a crucial part of the state-building process in emerging democracies. States need to create a judicial system that is convenient and fair and that gives judges and litigants incentives to behave responsibly and not to exploit the system for private gain. Unfortunately, assessments of past judicial reform efforts in the LAC region suggest that success is difficult to achieve. Stein *et al.* (2005: 81) claim that: "Historically, in much of the region the judicial branch has been characterized by dependence on the executive and a lack of activism in interpreting the law, in challenging the legality of executive actions, or in reviewing the constitutionality of laws." Hammergren (2002) claims that, in the LAC region: "Judiciaries are never the leaders in adopting modern management techniques or new technologies, and it is not uncommon for them to be decades behind the rest of the public sector in this regard. Arcane personnel practices, procedural requirements, and even equipment are the norm not the exception."

Table 9.7 *Judicial quality indicators*

Indicators	Costa Rica	Chile	Argentina	Panama	Paraguay	Bolivia	Dominican Republic	El Salvador	Guatemala	Honduras
Total	18	15	8	3	-1	-2	-3	-3	-10	-16
Judicial powers	5	5	4	5	3	3	2	3	1	1
Operating guarantees	4	3	5	2	2	0	0	-1	-3	-4
Financing resources	2	1	1	-1	-2	-1	0	2	2	-1
Judges' rating and selection	1	3	-1	-3	-1	0	0	-2	-2	-3
Transparency and responsibility	5	2	-1	1	1	-3	-2	-3	-3	-4
Efficiency	1	1	0	-1	-4	-1	-3	-2	-5	-5

Note: Larger numbers indicate better-quality reforms.
Source: Sousa (2007), chapter 3.

The IDB has attempted to rank countries on the basis of the quality of their judicial systems, using criteria that stress independence and the professionalism and resource base of the courts. Table 9.7 presents their finding using a scale of −5 to +5 for each component and adding up the scores. Obviously, one can quarrel with the particular scores and with the decision to give each factor the same weight, but the table is a helpful way of locating pressure points, especially when combined with table 9.3, which measures delays in routine cases including judicial involvement in trials. Thus, Argentina, ranked quite well by the IDB, has long court delays, much longer than in Honduras which is at the bottom, both overall and in terms of "efficiency." Viewing these tables together suggests the need to study the way nominal measures of institutional quality play out in practice when citizens or business contemplate bringing a dispute to court or are forced into court by private plaintiffs or public agencies.

In addition to adequate budget and salaries, a fundamental issue is the method of selection of judges and prosecutors. For ordinary courts, judicial careers in most civil law countries, such as those in Latin America, are influenced by bureaucratic review processes and affected by budgetary appropriations. In the best cases, they are independent professionals; in the worst, they are captured by powerful private interests and may be organized into a corrupt hierarchy.

As table 9.7 (p. 570) shows, constitutional and supreme courts are nominally among the most independent institutions of accountability in the LAC region. However, in practice, the selection of judges in most countries is not independent of the other branches of government, and political considerations are generally relevant in the selection of justices of constitutional courts and other high courts with a role in the oversight of the government. The selection of high court judges has been politicized at the same time, as lower-court judges mostly operate like civil servants with lifetime career paths as judges. Even with nominal independence and terms that overlap presidential terms, chief executives have frequently determined supreme court composition upon taking office and also may be able to appoint prosecutors. This has led to fairly short average tenure for supreme court justices, as table 9.8 shows. Even so, justices are not simply rubber stamps, at least in Argentina (Tommasi and Spiller 2007), although they do tend to defer on sensitive political issues (Dix 2004).

One response is the creation of judicial councils (consejos de la magistratura) charged with the task of selecting judges on the basis of merit.

Table 9.8 *Supreme court justices' average tenure in selected countries, 1960–90 (number of years)*

Country	Judicial term
Brazil	7.2
Nicaragua	7.1
Chile	5.7
Argentina	4.4
Peru	4.0
Dominican Republic	3.6
Mexico	3.3
Honduras	2.8
Colombia	1.9
Ecuador	1.9
Guatemala	1.8
Paraguay	1.1

Source: Computed by Witold Henisz, sent to the author in a personal communication, and used in Henisz (2000).

However, LAC experience with this institution has been largely negative (Popkin 2005: 25). One study pointed to El Salvador as the only positive case, in part, because the Council is broadly representative (Dakolias 1996: 12). However, another case study casts some doubt on this positive view (Dodson and Jackson 2003: 236–7). The authors show that the Council was quite dependent on the supreme court until the 1999 reforms that excluded the judiciary from membership, and that it did not actively police judicial corruption. Nevertheless, its experience since 1999 ought to be worth studying. One commentator suggests that such councils might work better if required to operate more transparently and to develop participatory processes that consult with concerned citizens (Popkin 2005).

The organization and independence of prosecutors is another dimension for reform. Some, as in the United States, are part of the executive branch. In other countries, they are part of the judiciary. Either option can create problems with independence and professionalism. One interesting experiment is the Brazilian public prosecutor (Ministerio Público) system that is largely independent of the rest of government and has been able to achieve a level of prestige and professionalism unknown under the previous system (Sadek and Batista Cavalcanti 2003). In addition to its criminal law responsibilities it is also charged with defending minority rights and with providing oversight of the state. Nevertheless, it needs resources to function well and cannot achieve reform on its own. According to Sadek and Batista Cavalcanti, the offices lack staff and technical support (2003: 210). Some prosecutors express frustration with the police, on the one hand, and with the judiciary, on the other – either or both of which may be under-resourced, corrupt or incompetent.[58] Hence the prosecutors' performance varies from state to state (2003: 211–13). Furthermore, its very independence risks the sort of impunity that can also be a problem with an overly insulated judiciary (2003: 217–22). In spite of the difficulties outlined in this study, the Brazilian case seems worth careful scrutiny to see if its positive traits might be copied elsewhere.

Considerable research has been done on the LAC judiciary, mostly by Edgardo Buscaglia and his associates. Their focus is on the use of the courts to resolve private disputes similar to the focus of the Lex Mundi project summarized in table 9.3 (p. 537) and the *Doing Business* finding on contract enforcement in table 9.2 (p. 524).

As table 9.3 indicates, delay seems to be a problem in the operation of the legal system throughout the LAC region. Within the courts, one explanation is the amount of time judges must spend on non-adjudicative tasks. One study found that Argentine judges spent 70% of their time on such tasks (Buscaglia and Ulen 1997). No wonder it takes an estimated 520 days to resolve a contract dispute and 200–300 to get a trial verdict on a routine business matter (tables 9.2 and 9.3). Buscaglia and Ulen's (1997) study of Argentina and Venezuela shows how improving judicial efficiency stimulates demand for judicial resolution so that delays reappear. They conclude that, in addition to relieving judges of many non-adjudicative tasks, reforms should focus on streamlining procedures, improving the professionalism of court personnel, and introducing computer technology to speed up case processing and limit the discretion of clerks.[59]

---

[58] "In order to conduct an investigation Brazilian prosecutors not only need support from the police, but also authorization from a judge to obtain access to classified information" (Sadek and Batista Cavalcanti 2003): 220.

[59] Dakolias (1996) comes to similar conclusions. She also emphasizes the importance of strengthening bar associations, and argues that they should play a more active role in monitoring the legal profession.

With a focus on corruption, Buscaglia (2001) studied a sample of 450 commercial cases in the Argentina, Ecuador, and Venezuela courts and conducted an annual survey between 1991 and 1999 of judges, lawyers, and business people. None of these countries is among the worst three in table 9.2, but all have substantial trial delays for at least one of the items in table 9.3. Buscaglia distinguished between administrative corruption that violated formal procedures (for example, to speed up processing) and operational corruption where the judge benefited personally from making a ruling. The former was apparently more common. Similar reforms in the mid-1990s in all three countries appear to have had beneficial results. The reforms simplified processes and made them more transparent and eliminated some of the clerks' discretion. The reforms that seemed most effective were: (1) use of computer systems for information provision and the reporting of corruption, (2) reducing the time to disposition and the number of administrative or procedural steps, and (3) increasing options for alternative public and private methods of dispute resolution. Unfortunately, however, the results are dependent upon the trustworthiness of those surveyed and do not include any quantitative measures of either costs or benefits.

Hammergren (2002, 2003; World Bank 2002) has a somewhat different take on the best way to reform the courts. Delay is a problem in the first instance courts in Ecuador and Peru, but some courts operate quite well, such as justice of the peace courts in Peru and Mexico's civil and justice of the peace courts (Hammergren 2003). However, Hammergren is less concerned about overall delay and more concerned about the large number of abandoned cases. For example, in Mexico 80% of cases did not reach final disposition and in Ecuador only 39% of controversies had been closed in a three–four year period. This suggests that the best dilatory tactic may be simply not to show up in court (Hammergren 2003). Thus, Hammergren would focus on creating institutions to facilitate out-of-court settlements and on improving the execution of court judgments. Table 9.3 suggests that service of process is a key bottleneck in some countries. Hammergren argues that the judiciary does a poor job of setting priorities, so that backlogs develop and cases are considered with little attention to the relative importance of a speedy resolution.

Consistent with Hammergren's critique, some look to ADR as a way around these problems with courts. However, because such systems

Table 9.9 *Comparative analysis of total costs of access to dispute resolution mechanisms for resolving land disputes (as % of money at stake)*

(%)	Civil courts	Complaint Board	Socha[a] (courts only)
Lowest 1–5	27.6	9.0	30.4
Lowest 5–10	25.7	7.0	26.2
Lowest 10–15	16.1	9.1	18.1
Lowest 15–20	11.9	10.7	13.7

Note: [a] Socha is a jurisdiction with no Complaint Board and dysfunctional courts.
Source: Colombia Survey (2000) cited in Buscaglia and Stephen (2005), chart 5.

are generally less transparent than courts and harder for the state to control, they carry their own risks. One study, based on survey work in Colombia, shows the promise of ADR for poor rural households facing land title disputes (Buscaglia and Stephen 2005). In the survey areas, few households used the courts, and few obtained a final resolution to the cases they brought.[60] The obstacles most mentioned were lack of information, costs in money and time, and corruption (2005: 98). A system of Complaint Boards or Panels, composed of respected local volunteers, was introduced into parts of rural Colombia around 2000. The study shows that they operated much more effectively to resolve land disputes. Even though their decisions are only advisory, the local governments accepted Board rulings in recording ownership. As a result, land values rose for those using that system compared to those using the courts, with the relative gains for the poorest being especially high. These gains went along with much lower costs as a percentage of the money at stake (table 9.9). However, comparing the results in table 9.9 with the *Doing Business* data in table 9.2, one sees that urban businesses fare even better, with costs estimated at only 3.5% of the money at stake, a number that may reflect economies of scale in dispute resolution. Nevertheless, so long as the litigants

---

[60] Of those interviewed, 3.75% had attempted to use the courts and only 0.2% (9 of 4,500) households had resolved a land dispute through the courts. Thus only 5% of cases filed had been resolved at the time of the interview. In the district with no ADR system, the average case took 3.5 years, and the courts were reputedly corrupt and dysfunctional. In addition, the formal court system seemed particularly to disadvantage women (Buscaglia and Stephen 2005): 97, 99, 101.

accept the outcome, the Complaint Boards seem a clearly beneficial innovation. They apparently raise property values and cost less. One assumes that there must be some losers, but the costs of uncertain land titling are sharply reduced and the system itself is cheaper. Nevertheless, as Buscaglia and Stephen (2005) point out, these results should not lead one to abandon court reform in favor of a wholesale shift to ADR. Such processes cannot be used for cases where "the public interest is at stake and where, consequently *ex ante guidance* is required (i.e. civil and political liberties cases)" (2005: 103). The problem of court reform cannot be abandoned but can perhaps be integrated with the creation of bottom-up informal institutions of the kind studied here.

4 Costs and benefits of alternative policies

The challenge faced by the weakness of LAC public institutions is not one that has a "solution" in any simple and straightforward way. There are three fundamental reasons for this.

First, the problem itself is multi-faceted and can hardly be reduced to a single quantifiable metric expressed in monetary terms. Part of the problem is the inefficient provision of public services and the wasteful administration of regulatory, law enforcement, and revenue-generating activities. This waste can, in principle, be measured. However, the consequences of institutional weakness go beyond inefficiency and include challenges to the legitimacy of the democratic state in its dealing with the public. These costs may create risks to the survival of democracy in some countries, but even if they do not, they can lead to a lack of engagement with the democratic project and open the way for both the dominance of narrow economic interests and a growth in the influence of organized crime.

Second, as with any policy reforms that affect the organization of the state, the main problems of implementation may not be the economic costs but rather the strength of political interests that benefit from the status quo. Everyone may agree that the judiciary is ineffective or that the customs service is corrupt, and no one may justify that state of affairs, but reform may, nevertheless, be difficult.

Finally, although most countries in the region are in the middle range in terms of income and of state functioning, there is a wide variety once one focuses on particular pressure points. Tables 9.1–9.3 highlight the differences, and this divergence must be part of any regional reform strategy. Not all countries need the same degree of customs or tax reform. Not all need the same reforms in the civil service or the judiciary. Nevertheless, from the broad agenda laid out above, I have selected five promising areas for reform.

Although hard data are difficult to come by, some public sector reforms are free in B/C terms. They involve cost savings for the government in reduced personnel and limits on paperwork that can provide benefits to both the government and to the bulk of the private sector. True, some officials lose because they are not receiving transfer payments in the form of bribes, but these are just funds that go from one pocket to another and in the process distort public priorities. Such officials will oppose reform, but under B/C criteria, the reform is justified.

The five options that I have isolated from the range of possibilities are: (1) reform of revenue collection, procurement systems, and business regulation; (2) civil service reform and selective contracting out with NGOs; (3) improving oversight of the public sector by independent public organizations; (4) improving grassroots participation in government decisionmaking, and (5) improvements in judicial professionalism and enhanced ADR possibilities. Box 9.1 summarizes the options, drawing on the detail in the rest of the chapter.

An alternative way to think about policy reform is to examine information, such as that in tables 9.2 and 9.3, that provides measures of weak government performance on a country-by-country basis. One would then work back from these pressure points to predict where reforms could make a difference. For example, tables 9.2 and 9.3 suggest that Brazil has a problem with bureaucratic delays and time-consuming tax and regulatory laws, but that its court system works rather well, at least for routine matters. Colombia seems to have a particularly dysfunctional court system. Mexico has trouble enforcing court judgments and is a relatively costly place to do business honestly. However, it is not at the crisis level and compares quite well on some dimensions with legally similar European countries. One needs to interpret the data in these tables with caution, but they do suggest a place to start as officials in individual countries set reform priorities. Benchmarking, however, should go beyond state actions that affect the business climate to include the effectiveness of spending on social

---

Box 9.1. Options to improve the operation of government: each option should include funds for impact evaluation to develop benchmarks

Option 1

- *Improve performance and limit corruption in regulation and in revenue raising and in procurement*
- *Special emphasis on automated, computer-based systems for procurement and revenue collection*
- *Examination of regulatory climate for business to eliminate or streamline the rules.*

Benefits
Encourages formation of new businesses and increases economic value of existing businesses. Improves the operation of government and provision of services. End result is more robust and productive economic growth. For government, better service delivery to those at all income levels.

Costs
OOP costs for technical consultancies and program evaluation. Other costs are close to zero for pure "red tape", but one needs to include benefits forgone from ending programs with social value. Costs of monitoring and reforming bureaucracies may include improvements in salaries and working conditions for oversight officials. Concern for political sustainability if independent revenue authorities are used.

BCRs
Of course, not all programs are successful, but existing cases of procurement and revenue reform have B/C ratios as high as 100:1, with others in the 3:1 or 10:1 range.

Positive cases of tax and customs reform
In Bolivia, the proportion of VAT lost went from 42% in 2001 to 29% in 2004 after reforms. In Peru, total tax revenues increased from 8.4% of GDP in 1991 to 12.3% in 1998, at the same time as many tax rates were reduced. Taxpayers increased from 895,000

---

in 1993 to 1,766,000 in 1999. Tariff revenues went from 23% of revenues in 1990 to 35% in 1996 and increased four-fold in dollar terms despite reductions in duties. Peru reduced total staff from 4,700 in 1990 to 2,540 in 2002 and increased the share of professionals from 2.5% to 60%. The average clearance times fell from 2 days to 2 hours. In Costa Rica, times fell from 6 days to 12 minutes. It is not possible to measure the marginal costs of reforms, but they appear low or even negative. Overall, the cost of revenue collection as a share of revenues collected ranges from 1.7% to 2% for the LAC cases.

Option 2

- *Merit recruitment and promotion in the civil service and increased contracting out to NGOs for service delivery.*

Costs
Costs of testing for recruitment and better monitoring of performance of civil servants. Costs of organizing the contracting process with NGOs and monitoring *ex post*. Modification of program design to make it feasible for contracting out. Program evaluation costs.

Benefits
Higher efficiency and better service delivery from civil service. Performance incentives for contractors who desire repeat business.

Positive cases
Civil service: Costa Rica, Brazil, Chile with, at least, marginal improvement. *NGO provision*: Bolivia and Guatemala – primary care and nutrition services. Cost in Guatemala $6.25 per head with 3.4 million people covered. Studies showed net benefits.

Option 3

- *Government monitoring: audit agencies, Ombudsmen, etc.*

Costs
Costs of setting up and staffing new organizations and on-going budgetary support for new and reformed agencies.

Benefits
More transparency with respect to government activities leading to cost saving, less corruption, better priority setting.

Positive cases
Audit agencies in Brazil, Chile, Colombia (although all are weak on timeliness). Brazilian audits of municipalities. Costs are probably similar across all LAC cases so these may have lessons for the others.

Option 4

- *Grassroots monitoring with technical assistance and information provision provided centrally by government or NGOs.*

Costs
Opportunity cost of people's time; costs of consultants and central government officials to help design programs and provide information. Demoralization costs if government does not respond to citizen complaints.

Benefits
Cost savings on existing programs that have ranged as high as 400% in pilot projects outside the LAC region. Better overall economic performance and access of the poor to public services.

Positive cases
Brazilian urban participatory democracy. Community monitoring in goldmining areas of Peru and Guatemala.

Option 5

- *Improvements in judicial and prosecutorial independence and performance; enhanced ADR possibilities.*

Costs
Judiciary: higher salaries for judges and clerks, better computer systems and other equipment, automation of some functions may reduce numbers of personnel. Eliminating pure red tape is costless.

Prosecutors: Costs of setting up and staffing a new, independent system. *ADR*: May be staffed with volunteers in rural areas. One cost is lack of transparency and variation in decisions in similar cases.

Benefits
Judiciary: Less wasted time and more clarity for litigants. More widely accepted outcomes and less corruption. Better judicial oversight of rest of government. *Independent prosecutors*: better oversight of rest of government if complemented by police and court reform. *ADR*: quicker and more acceptable resolution of routine local disputes in areas such as land titling.

Positive cases
Judiciary: Chile and El Salvador stand out as having court systems that function with low levels of delay, although others are superior on some dimensions. El Salvador's relative poverty and high donor involvement make it an especially interesting case. *ADR*: Land title disputes resolved with Community Boards in rural Colombia.

benefits and infrastructure; the regulation of everyday life through the police and health, safety, and environmental inspectors; and the regulation of the labor market. How is education quality related to spending levels? How far does regulatory performance depart from statutory mandates? How easy is it for employers to ignore labor and environmental standards? In many of these areas reasonable cross-country estimates could be developed that would help governments see where they were falling short in regional terms and where they were approaching the levels achieved by wealthier countries with similar political and legal systems.

Bibliography

Abers, Rebecca, 1998. "From Clientalism to Cooperation: Local Government, Participatory Policy, and Civic Organizing in Port Alegre, Brazil." *Politics and Society* **26**: 511–37

Abikoff, Kevin T., 1987. "The Role of the Comptroller General in Light of Bowsher *v*. Synar." *Columbia Law Review* **87**: 1539–62

Ackerman, John M., 2004. "Co-Governance for Accountability: Beyond 'Exit' and 'Voice'." *World Development* 32: 447–63

2007. *Organismos Autónomos y Democracia: El Caso de México*, Mexico City MX: Siglio Vientiumo Editores

Ackerman, John M. and Irma E. Sandoval-Ballesteros, 2006. "The Global Explosion of Freedom of Information Laws." *Administrative Law Review* 58: 85–130

Anderson, Christopher J. and Yuliya V. Tverdova, 2003. "Corruption, Political Allegiances, and Attitudes Toward Government in Contemporary Democracies." *American Journal of Political Science* 47: 91–109

Avritzer, L. and Brian Wampler, 2005. "The Spread of Participatory Democracy in Brazil: From Radical Democracy to Good Government." *Journal of Latin American Urban Studies* 7: 37–52

Barrera-Osorio, Felipe and Mauricio Olivera, 2007. "Does Society Win or Lose as a Result of Privatization? Provision of Public Services and Welfare of the Poor: The Case of Water Sector Privatization in Colombia." Research Network Working Paper R-525, www.iadb.org/topics/Home. cfm?topicID=RM&parid=2&language=English

Barros, Robert, 2002. *Constitutionalism and Dictatorship: Pinochet, the Junta, and the 1980 Constitution.* Cambridge: Cambridge University Press

Bergman, Marcelo S., 2003. "Tax Reforms and Tax Compliance: The Divergent Paths of Chile and Argentina." *Journal of Latin American Studies* 35: 3–28

Bonnet, Céline, Pierre Dubois, David Martimort, and Stéphane Straub, 2006. "Empirical Evidence on Satisfaction with Privatization in Latin America: Welfare Effects and Beliefs." University of Toulouse, draft paper for IDB\World Bank project on the Political Economy of Private Participation, Social Discontent, and Regulatory Governance

Bratton, Michael, 1989. "The Politics of Government–NGO Relations in Africa." *World Development* 17: 567–87

Buscaglia, Jr., Edgardo, 1995. "Judicial Reform in Latin America: The Obstacles Ahead." *Journal of Latin American Affairs* 3: 8–13

2001. "An Analysis of Judicial Corruption and Its Causes: An Objective Governance-Based Approach." *International Review of Law and Economics* 21(2): 233–49

Buscaglia, Jr., Edgardo and Samuel Gonzalez Ruiz, 2006. "The Factor of Trust and the Importance of Inter-Agency Cooperation in the Fight against Transnational Organised Crime: The US–Mexican Example." In Marina Caparini and Otwin Marenin, eds., *Borders and Security Governance: Managing Borders in a Globalised World.* Geneva: LIT Verlag: 269–80, www.dcaf.ch/publications/kms/details. cfm?lng=en&id=22189&nav1=4

Buscaglia, Jr., Edgardo and Paul B. Stephen, 2005. "An Empirical Assessment of the Impact of Formal Versus Informal Dispute Resolution on Poverty: A Governance-based Approach." *International Review of Law and Economics* **25**: 89–106

Buscaglia, Jr., Edgardo and Jan van Dijk, 2003. "Controlling Organized Crime and Corruption in the Public Sector." *Forum on Crime and Society* **3**(1 and 2): 3–34

Buscaglia, Jr., Edgardo and Thomas Ulen, 1997. "A Quantitative Assessment of the Efficiency of the Judicial Sector in Latin America." *International Review of Law and Economics* **17**: 275–91

Castelar Pinheiro, D., 1998

Cheng, Wen-Chen, 2005. "Alternative Agenda(s) in Constitutional Reengineering: Ensuring the Rule of Law and Political Trust in Taiwan." In the *Proceedings of the International Conference on Constitutional Reengineering in New Democracies: Taiwan and the World*, October 28–29, Taipei: 397–400

Chong, Alberto and Juan Benavides, 2007. "Privatization and Regulation in Latin America." In Eduardo Lora, ed., *The State of State Reforms in Latin America*. Washington, DC: Inter-American Development Bank

Chong, Alberto and Florencio López-de-Silanes, 2003. "The Truth about Privatization in Latin America." IDB Research Network Working Paper

Coglianese, Cary, 1997. "Assessing Consensus: The Promise and Performance of Negotiated Rulemaking." *Duke Law Journal* **46**: 1255–1349

Dakolias, Maria, 1996. "The Judicial Sector in Latin America and the Caribbean: Elements of Reform." World Bank Technical Paper **319**

Dam, Kenneth, 2006. *The Law–Growth Nexus: The Rule of Law and Economic Development*. Washington, DC: Brookings Institution

Das Gupta, Monica, Helene Grandvoinnet, and Mattia Romani, 2000. State-Community Synergies in Development: Laying the Basis for Collective Action." World Bank Policy Research Working Paper **2439**

Deininger, Klaus and Paul Mpuga, 2005. "Does Greater Accountability Improve the Quality of Public Service Delivery? Evidence from Uganda." *World Development* **33**(1): 171–91

De Ferranti, David *et al.*, 2004. *Inequality in Latin America: Breaking with History?* Washington, DC: World Bank

Di Tella, Rafael and Ernesto Schargrodsky, 2003. "The Role of Wages and Auditing During a Crackdown on Corruption in the City of Buenos Aires." *Journal of Law and Economics* **46**: 269–92

De Wulf, Luc and José B. Sokol, 2004. *Customs Modernization Initiatives: Case Studies*, Washington DC: World Bank

Dix, Sarah, 2004. *Judicial Politics in Argentina*. PhD dissertation, Department of Political Science, Yale University

Djankov, Simon, Rafael La Porta, Florencio Lopez-de-Silanes, and Andrei Shleifer, 2003. "Courts." *Quarterly Journal of Economics* **118**: 453–517

Dodson, Michael and Donald W. Jackson, 2003. "Horizontal Accountability and the Rule of Law in Central America." In Scott Mainwaring and Christopher Welna, eds., *Democratic Accountability in Latin America.* Oxford: Oxford University Press: 228–65

Dollar, David, Mary Hallward-Driemeier, and Taye Mengistae, 2006. "Investment Climate and International Integration." *World Development* **34**: 1498–1516

Echabarría, Koldo and Juan Carlos Cortázar, 2007. "Public Administration and Public Employment Reform in Latin America." In Eduardo Lora, ed., *The State of State Reforms in Latin America.* Washington, DC: Inter-American Development Bank: 123–55

Escobar, Flavio, 2004. "Bolivia." In Luc De Wulf and José B. Sokol, *Customs Modernization Initiatives: Case Studies.* Washington, DC: World Bank: 7–18

Evans, Peter and James E. Rauch, 1999. "Bureaucracy and Growth: A Cross-National Analysis of the Effects of 'Weberian' State Structures on Economic Growth." *American Sociological Review* **64**: 748–65

Feld, Lars P. and Stefan Voight, 2003. "Economic Growth and Judicial Independence: Cross-Country Evidence Using a New Set of Indicators." *European Journal of Political Economy* **19**(3): 497–527

Ferraz, Claudio and Frederico Finan, 2007. "Exposing Corrupt Politicians: The Effects of Brazil's Publicly Released Audits on Electoral Outcomes." Institute for the Study of Labor (IZA) Discussion Paper **2836**, www.iza.org/publications/dps/

Gaetani, Francisco and Blanca Heredia, 2002. "The Political Economy of Civil Service Reform in Brazil: The Cardoso Years." *Red de Gestión y Transparencia del Diálogo Regional de Politica del Banco Interamericano de Desarrollo.* Washington, DC: Inter-American Development Bank

Geddes, Barbara, 1994. *Politicians' Dilemma: Building State Capacity in Latin America.* Berkeley, CA: University of California Press

Goldfrank, Benjamin and Aaron Schneider, 2006. "Competitive Institution Building: The PT and Participatory Budgeting in Rio Grande do Sul." *Latin American Politics & Society* **48**(3): 1–31

Gómez Sabaini, Juan, 2006. "Evolución y Situación Tributaria Actual en América Latina: Una Serie de Temas para la Discusión." In Comisión Económica para América Latina y el Caribe, ed., *Tributación en América Latina: En Busca de Una Nueva Agenda de Reformas.* Santiago: Santiago de Chile Naciones Unidas: Comisión Económica para América Latina y el Caribe

Goorman, Adrien, 2004. "Peru." In Luc De Wulf and José B. Sokol, *Customs Modernization Initiatives: Case Studies*. Washington, DC: World Bank: 65–84

Gret, Marion and Yves Sintomer, 2005. *The Porto Alegre Experiment: Learning Lessons for Better Democracy*, trans. Stephen Wright. London and New York: Zed; New York: Palgrave Macmillan

Hammergren, Linn, 2002. *Fifteen Years of Judicial Reform in Latin America: Where We Are and Why We Haven't Made Much Progress*. New York: United Nations Development Program

2003. *Uses of Empirical Research in Refocusing Judicial Reforms: Lessons from Five Countries*. Washington, DC: World Bank, www1.worldbank.org/publicsector/legal/UsesOfER.pdf

Henisz, Witold, 2000. "The Institutional Environment for Economic Growth." **12**(1): 1–31

Hoffmann, Bert, 2007. "Why Reform Fails: The 'Politics of Policies' in Costa Rican Telecommunications Liberalization." GIGA Research Unit, Institute of Latin American Studies, Working Paper **47**

Hunt, Jennifer, 2006. "Why Are Some Public Officials More Corrupt Than Others?" In Susan Rose-Ackerman, ed., *International Handbook on the Economics of Corruption*. Cheltenham: Edward Elgar: 323–51

Jansson, Tor and Geoffrey Chalmers, 2001. "The Case for Business Registration Reform in Latin America." *Sustainable Development Department Best Practice Series* **25**. Washington, DC: Inter-American Development Bank

Johnston, Michael, 2005. *Syndromes of Corruption: Wealth, Power, and Democracy*. Cambridge: Cambridge University Press

Kaufmann, Daniel, 2003. "Rethinking Governance: Empirical Lessons Challenge Orthodoxy." World Bank Discussion Draft, http://ssrn.com/abstract-386904

Kaufmann, Daniel, Aart Kraay, and Massimo Mastruzzi, 2006. "Measuring Governance Using Cross-Country Perceptions Data." In Susan Rose-Ackerman, ed., *International Handbook on the Economics of Corruption*. Cheltenham: Edward Elgar: 52–104

2007a. "Growth and Governance: A Reply." *Journal of Politics* **69**(2): 555–62

2007b. "Growth and Governance: A Rejoinder." *Journal of Politics* **69**(2): 570–2

Kaufmann, Daniel, Massimo Mastruzzi, and Diego Zaveleta, 2003. "Sustained Macroeconomic Reforms, Tepid Growth: A Governance Puzzle in Bolivia." In Dani Rodrik, ed., *In Search of Prosperity: Analytic Narratives on Economic Growth*. Princeton, NJ: Princeton University Press

Kaufmann, Daniel, Gil Mehrez, and Tugrul Gurgur, 2002. "Voice or Public Sector Management? An Empirical Investigation of Determinants of

Public Sector Performance Based on Survey of Public officials." World Bank Research Paper, http://ssrn.com/abstract=31686

Kerwin, Cornelius M. and Scott R. Furlong, 1992. "Time and Rulemaking: An Empirical Test of Theory." *Journal of Public Administration Research and Theory* 2: 125–31

Kurtz, Marcus and Andrew Schrank, 2007a. "Growth and Governance: Models, Measures, and Mechanisms." *Journal of Politics* 69(2): 538–54

2007b. "Growth and Governance: A Defense." *Journal of Politics* 69(2): 563–9

Lambsdorff, Johann Graf, 2006. "Causes and Consequences of Corruption: What Do We Know from a Cross-Section of Countries?" In Susan Rose-Ackerman, ed., *International Handbook on the Economics of Corruption.* Cheltenham: Edward Elgar: 3–51

La Porta, Rafael, Florencio Lopez-de-Silanes, Christian Pop-Eleches, and Andrei Shleifer, 2004. "Judicial Checks and Balances." *Journal of Political Economy* 112(2): 445–70

Levy, Brian and Pablo Spiller, eds., 1996. *Regulations, Institutions and Commitment.* Cambridge: Cambridge University Press

Loevinsohn, Benjamin and April Harding, 2005. "Buying Results? Contracting for Health Service Delivery in Developing Countries." *Lancet* 366: 676–81

Lora, Eduardo, 2007a. "State Reform in Latin America: A Silent Revolution." In Eduardo Lora, ed., *State of State Reform in Latin America.* Washington, DC: Inter-American Development Bank: 1–56

2007b. "Trends and Outcomes of Tax Reform." In Eduardo Lora, ed., *The State of State Reform in Latin America.* Washington, DC: Inter-American Development Bank: 185–212

Magat, Wesley A., Alan, J. Krupnick, and Winston Harrington, 1986. *Rules in the Making: A Statistical Analysis of Regulatory Agency Behavior.* Washington, DC: RFF Press

Mainwaring, Scott and Matthew S. Shugart, eds., 1997. *Presidentialism and Democracy in Latin America.* Cambridge: Cambridge University Press

Manzetti, Luigi, 1999. *Privatization South American Style.* Oxford: Oxford University Press

McMillan, John and Pablo Zoido, 2004. "How to Subvert Democracy: Montesinos in Peru." *Journal of Economic Perspectives* 18: 69–92

Mejía Acosta, Andrés, María Caridad Araujo, Aníbal Pérez-Liñán, and Sebastián Saiegh, 2006. *Veto Players, Fickle Institutions and Low-Quality Policies: The Policymaking Process in Ecuador (1979–2005).* Research Department, Inter-American Development Bank

Mendelson, Nina A., 2003. "Agency Burrowing: Entrenching Policies and Personnel Before a New President Arrives." *New York University Law Review* **78**: 557–666

Messick, Richard E., 1999. "Judicial Reform and Economic Development: A Survey of the Issues." *World Bank Research Observer* **14**(1): 117–36

Moreno, Erika, Brian F. Crisp, and Matthew Soberg Shugart, 2003. "The Accountability Deficit in Latin America." in Scott Mainwaring and Christopher Welna, eds., *Democratic Accountability in Latin America*, Oxford: Oxford University Press: 79–131

Nane, Grimot, 2007. "New Rules of the Game for Rent Seeking: The Civil Service in Nigeria." Paper presented at the World Meeting of the Public Choice Society, Amsterdam, March 29–April 1

Neuman, Laura and Richard Calland, 2007. "Making the Law Work: The Challenges of Implementation." In Ann Florini, ed., *The Right to Know: Transparency for an Open World*. New York: Columbia University Press: 179–213

O'Donnell, Guillermo, 1999. "Horizontal Accountability in New Democracies." in Andreas Schedler, Larry Diamond, and Marc R. **Plattner**, eds., *The Self-Restraining State: Power and Accountability in New Democracies*. Boulder, CO: Lynner Rienner: 29–51

Organization for Economic Cooperation and Development (OECD), 2003. "Trade Facilitation Reforms in the Service of Development." Trade Committee Working Paper **TD/TC/WP(2003)11/FINAL**

Panizza, Francisco, 2000. "The Public Sector Premium and the Gender Gap in Latin America: Evidence for the 1980s and 1990s." IDB Research Department Working Paper **431**

Panizza, Francisco and George Philip, 2005. "Second Generation Reform in Latin America: Reforming the Public Sector in Uruguay and Mexico." *Journal of Latin American Studies* **37**: 667–91

Parker, Andrew N., 1995. "Decentralization: The Way Forward for Rural Development?" World Bank Agriculture and Natural Resources Department Policy Research Paper **1475**

Popkin, Margaret, 2005. "Participación Ciudadana en la Reforma de la Justicia." In Centro Nacional para Tribunales Estatales: Fundación para el Debido Proceso Legal, ed., *Sociedad Civil y Reforma Judicial en América Latina*. Washington, DC: Due Process of Law Foundation: 23–32

Prado, Mariana Mota, 2007. "The Challenges and Risks of Creating Independent Regulatory Agencies: A Cautionary Tale from Brazil." University of Toronto, Legal Studies Research Paper **983907**

Premchand, A., 1993. *Public Expenditure Management*, Washington, DC: International Monetary Fund

Rauch, James and Peter Evans, 2000. "Bureaucratic Structure and Bureaucratic Performance in Less Developed Countries." *Journal of Public Economics* 75: 49–71

Reinikka, Ritva and Jakob Svensson, 2005. "Fighting Corruption to Improve Schooling: Evidence from a Newspaper Campaign in Uganda." *Journal of the European Economic Association* 2(2–3): 259–67

Rivera-Batiz, Francisco L., 2002. "Democracy, Governance, and Economic Growth: Theory and Evidence." *Review of Development Economics* 6: 225–47

Rodrik, Dani, 2006. "Goodbye Washington Consensus, Hello Washington Confusion? A Review of the World Bank's Economic Growth in the 1990s: Learning from a Decade of Reform." *Journal of Economic Literature* 45(4): 973–87

Rose-Ackerman, Susan, 1999. *Corruption and Government: Causes, Consequences, and Reform.* Cambridge: Cambridge University Press

2004a. "Establishing the Rule of Law." In Robert I. Rotberg, ed., *When States Fail: Causes and Consequences.* Princeton, NJ: Princeton University Press: 182–222

2004b. "Governance and Corruption." Chapter 6 in Bjørn Lomborg, ed., *Global Crises, Global Solutions*, 1st edn. Cambridge: Cambridge University Press: 301–62

2005. *From Elections to Democracy: Building Accountable Government in Hungary and Poland.* Cambridge: Cambridge University Press

ed., 2006. *International Handbook on the Economics of Corruption.* Cheltenham: Edward Elgar

2007. "Judicial Independence and Corruption." In Transparency International, *Global Corruption Report 2007.* Cambridge: Cambridge University Press: 15–24

Sadek, Maria Theresa and Rosângela Batista Cavalcanti, 2003. "The New Brazilian Public Prosecution: An Agent of Accountability." In Scott Mainwaring and Christopher Welna, eds., *Democratic Accountability in Latin America.* Oxford: Oxford University Press: 201–27

Santiso, Carlos, 2007. "Eyes Wide Shut? The Politics of Autonomous Audit Agencies in Emerging Economies." Working Paper based on PhD, Johns Hopkins, Baltimore, MD: University, http://ssrn.com/abstract=982663

Seligman, Mitchell, 2002. "The Impact of Corruption on Regime Legitimacy: A Comparative Study of Four Latin American Countries." *Journal of Politics* 64: 408–33

Shah, P. and S. Wagle, 2003. "Case Study 2 – Porto Alegre, Brazil: Participatory Approaches in Budgeting and Public Expenditure Management." World Bank Social Development Notes 71: 1–5

Sousa, Mariana, 2007. "A Brief Overview of Judicial Reform in Latin America: Objectives, Challenges, and Accomplishments." In Eduardo Lora, ed., *The State of State Reform in Latin America*. Washington, DC: Inter-American Development Bank: 87–121

Sousa Santos, Boaventura de, 1998. "Participatory Budgeting in Porto Alegre: Toward a Redistributive Democracy." *Politics & Society* 26: 461–510

Spink, Peter, 1999. "Possibilities and Political Imperatives: Seventy Years of Administrative Reform in Latin America." In Luiz Carlos Bresser Pereira and Peter Spink, eds., *Reforming the State: Managerial Public Administration in Latin America*. Boulder, CO: Lynne Rienner

Stein, Ernesto, Mariano Tommasi, Koldo Echebarría, Eduardo Lora, and Mark Payne, 2005. *The Politics of Policies: Economic and Social Progress in Latin America*. Washington, DC: Inter-American Development Bank and The David Rockefeller Center for Latin American Studies at Harvard University

Taliercio, Jr., Robert, 2001. "Unsustainably Autonomous?: Challenges to the Revenue Authority Model in Latin America Tax Agencies in Developing Countries." Washington, DC: World Bank, mimeo

2004. "Designing Performance: The Semi-Autonomous Revenue Authority Model in Africa and Latin America." World Bank Policy Research Working Paper 3423

Tommasi, Mariano and Pablo T. Spiller, 2007. *The Institutional Foundations of Public Policy in Argentina: A Transactions Cost Approach*. Cambridge: Cambridge University Press

Torres Ribeiro, Ana Clara, and Grazia deGrazia, 2003. *Experiências de orçamento participativo no Brasil: período de 1997 a 2000*. Petrópolis: Fórum Nacional de Participação Popular and Vozes

You, Jong-Sung and Sanjeev Khagram, 2005. "A Comparative Study of Inequality and Corruption." *American Sociological Review* 70: 136–57

Wampler, Brian, 2007. *Participatory Budgeting in Brazil: Contestation, Cooperation, and Accountability*. State College PA: Penn State University Press

West, William F., 2004. "Formal Procedures, Informal Processes, Accountability, and Responsiveness in Bureaucratic Policy Making: An Institutional Analysis." *Public Administration Review* 64: 66–80

Widner, Jennifer, 1999. "Building Judicial Independence in Common Law Africa." In Andreas Schedler, Larry Diamond, and Marc F. Plattner, eds., *The Self-Restraining State: Power and Accountability in New Democracies*. Boulder, CO: Lynne Rienner

World Bank, 2002. "Reforming Courts: The Role of Empirical Research." PREM Notes 65

2007. *A Decade of Measuring the Quality of Governance: Governance Matters 2007, Worldwide Governance Indicator 1996–2006.* Washington, DC: World Bank

World Bank and International Finance Corporation, 2006. *Doing Business in 2006.* Washington, DC: World Bank

Zuleta, J.C., A. Leyton, and E.F. Ivanovic, 2007. "Combating Corruption in Revenue Administration: The Case of VAT Refunds in Bolivia." In J.E. Campos and S. Pradhan, eds., 2006. *The Many Faces of Corruption: Tracking Vulnerabilities at the Sector Level.* Washington, DC: World Bank: 339–66

9.1 Public administration: an alternative view

UGO PANIZZA[*]

1 Introduction

Chapter 9 by Susan Rose-Ackerman is a *tour de force*. It contains a comprehensive survey of the literature and a careful description of the main challenges for institutional reform in Latin America. Since the chapter is so comprehensive, it is almost impossible to focus on something that was not already mentioned in it and to prepare an alternative view highlighting the chapter's weaknesses.

An easy but, in my view, unfair way to criticize the chapter would be to say that the discussion of solutions to the challenge is short and lacks a detailed CBA. This would be unfair because the challenge that Rose-Ackerman was faced with was almost mission impossible. In fact, I can think of five types of challenges for a project like that of the Copenhagen Consensus. (1) There are challenges for which we know the solution and for which we also know how to estimate their costs and benefits (think about preventing the spread of a disease for which there is a known vaccine). (2) There are also challenges for which we do not know the exact solution but for which we have an idea of what may work well and, if we knew the solution, it would be easy to estimate its costs and the benefits (think about preventing the spread of a disease for which we still do not have a vaccine). (3) There are also challenges for which we know the solution but for which we do not have a clear idea of the costs and benefits (for instance, reducing inflation). (4) Next, there are challenges for which we do not know the solution and have no idea about the costs and benefits of such a solution (for instance, preventing earthquakes). (5) Finally, there are

[*] All the opinions expressed in this alternative view are my own, and should not be attributed to any organization I am or have been affiliated with. I would like to thank Mandana Hajj, Monica Yañez, Francesca Recanatini, Ernesto Stein, and the Expert panel of the San José Consulta for helpful suggestions and discussion. The usual caveats apply.

challenges for which we do not know the solution, we have no ideas about the costs and benefits, and we even have problems in defining and measuring the challenge (how do we measure institutions?). This is the type of challenge Rose-Ackerman had to deal with. Criticizing her chapter for not providing a detailed set of solutions with a CBA would be utterly unfair.

Moreover, Rose-Ackerman correctly makes the point that the quest for blueprints is not likely to bear any fruits, for at least two reasons. First, LAC countries are facing different constraints. For some, the most pressing need may be a tax reform; for others, the most pressing need may be a judicial reform or a custom reform. Second, blueprints may not work even for countries that have problems in the same area. A given solution may work well in one country, but may not be appropriate in another.

There are three plus two fundamental areas of intervention for improving the quality of a country's public sector. The first consists of keeping the rules as simple as possible and eliminating unnecessary red tape. The second has to do with providing civil servants with the incentives to be efficient, honest, and hard-working. The third has to do with providing civil servants with the tools, organizational set-up, and continuous training necessary to perform their job.

Of course, there are close interactions among these three areas of intervention. On the one hand, lack of a proper work environment and the presence of Byzantine rules are likely to have a negative effect on the incentives of civil servants. On the other hand, providing dishonest civil servants who lack motivations and initiative with lots of resources might be a waste of money, at best, and counterproductive, at worst.

Even assuming that we know how to deal with the three issues outlined above, nothing will happen if politicians do not have the incentives to improve public administration. Hence, the fourth area of intervention has to do with politics.

Finally, reformers need to recognize that improving institutional quality is a dynamic process. As there are no blueprints, each country needs to find its own way to implement institutional reforms, and these reforms need to be subject to constant evaluation. Constant evaluation and monitoring is the fifth necessary element of any policy aimed at improving institutional quality.

As it is almost impossible to find a crucial point that was not mentioned in the chapter, I shall use my alternative view to highlight a few points that were mentioned in the chapter but, in my opinion, not emphasized enough. The main point that I want to make is that incentive problems dominate everything else, and that providing the right incentives is not necessarily costly.[1] This point is illustrated by the fact that when we look across countries we find almost no correlation between the amount spent in maintaining the public administration and its efficiency. This suggests that most countries are far from the efficiency frontier and that things can be improved at no cost.

This alternative view is organized as follows. In section 2, I provide evidence of the lack of correlation between public expenditure and quality of government, and conduct back-of-the-envelope estimates of possible benefits of improving public administration. In this section, I also make the point that low public sector wages are not the problem (again, this is discussed in the chapter but, in my view, not emphasized enough) and that high public sector wages may even be a symptom of the problem. In section 3, I briefly discuss reforms aimed at providing politicians with the incentives to improve the public sector. This is probably the only important topic not covered in the chapter. In section 4, I highlight the role of transparency and a free press and discuss a "crazy" proposal for increasing the monitoring role of the press. Section 5 drews some brief conclusions.

2 Money can't buy you a good public administration

This section discusses the relationship between institutional quality and public expenditure. The main point of the section is that increasing public expenditure is not an efficient way to improve government quality.

I focus on three measures of institutional quality: government effectiveness, control of corruption, and the rule of law. All measures are from Kaufman, Kraay, and Mastruzzi (2006), and are expressed as averages for the 1996–2005 period (table 9.1.1 reports these indicators rescaled to take values between 0 and 100).

I also use three measures of public expenditure all expressed in USD *per capita* and averaged for the 1995–2004 period. The first (GEGS)

---

[1] This perception might be wrong and due to the fact that my formal training was in economics and "Most of economics can be summarized in four words: 'People respond to incentives.' The rest is commentary" (Landsburg 1995).

Table 9.1.1 *Governance indicators*

	Levels			Residuals		
	(1) Government effectiveness	(2) Control of corruption	(3) Rule of law	(4) Government effectiveness	(5) Control of corruption	(6) Rule of law
ARG	53	41	49	37	30	31
BHS	85	90	91	80	76	76
BOL	44	30	42	60	46	56
BRA	55	53	50	56	65	56
CHL	92	100	94	100	100	100
COL	51	40	38	56	54	41
CRI	70	79	78	71	79	78
DOM	43	39	46	38	43	41
ECU	31	26	39	38	46	53
GTM	39	28	33	39	39	33
GUY	49	41	48	63	52	52
HND	40	29	35	56	45	44
HTI	14	11	15	20	29	17
JAM	52	41	47	55	46	41
MEX	60	44	48	57	45	41
NIC	37	37	37	46	52	44
PAN	55	45	57	64	54	63
PER	46	46	42	53	61	49
PRY	26	19	31	21	22	24
SLV	49	41	46	56	52	48
TTO	70	58	64	69	58	54
URY	71	76	72	70	71	66
VEN	30	25	30	25	36	29
LAC						
Mean	51	46	50	53	52	49
St. dev.	18	22	19	19	18	17

Note: The level data were computed as averages of the 1996, 1998, 2000, 2002, 2003, 2004, and 2005 data on Government effectiveness, Control of corruption and Rule of law indicators compiled by Kaufman, Kraay, and Mastruzzi (2006). The averages were then rescaled to range between 0 and 100 (the higher the value, the better the governance indicator). The Residuals data were computed as the residuals of an OLS regression of the level data over the log of GDP *per capita* (measured in PPP), latitude, legal origin, ethno-linguistic fractionalization, log country area, log population, and a LAC dummy.

is central government expenditure in public services minus public debt transactions (mostly interest payments) and transfers between levels of government.[2] In theory, GEGS should capture the cost of running the government. However, countries might not be consistent in classifying public expenditure. Therefore, I also use primary expenditure (PRIEXP), which is a more comprehensive measure of public expenditure. The third measure of public expenditure is expenditure for public order and safety (L&O EXP). This should be a good proxy of the cost of maintaining the rule of law. For all three variables, I use data both in current dollars and in purchasing power parity (PPP) adjusted dollars (table 9.1.2).

As a first way of looking at the relationship between expenditure and institutional quality, I regress institutional quality over public expenditure controlling for GDP *per capita* measured in PPP.[3] I focus on a sample that includes all developing countries for which I have data and on a subsample of LAC countries.

When the dependent variable is Government effectiveness or Control of corruption (Panels A and B of table 9.1.3), I measure expenditure using both GEGS and primary expenditure. When I focus on the Rule of law (Panel C in table 9.1.3), I use expenditure for public order and safety. The regressions indicate that GEGS has no significant effect on institutional quality, while primary expenditure has a statistically significant effect on government effectiveness and control of corruption. This is surprising, because GEGS should be a better measure of the cost of running the government. The results might be driven by the fact that countries do not classify public expenditure in a homogenous way. I also find that expenditure for public order and safety has a statistically significant effect on Rule of law. These results hold for both the sample that includes all developing countries and for the LAC subsample.

Although the coefficients are statistically significant, the economic impact is small. For instance, Panel A shows that a 10-point increase in government effectiveness would require an increase in PPP-adjusted

---

[2] All data are from the IMF Government Finance Statistics. I use data from the central government because data for other levels of government are often not available.

[3] I control for GDP *per capita* because richer countries are likely to spend more for running the government (because real wages tend to be higher) and are also likely to have better working governments. Of course, GDP *per capita* is endogenous with respect to institutional quality, but I have no way to deal with this issue.

Table 9.1.2 *Public expenditure* per capita

	Current dollars			PPP dollars		
	GEGS	PRIEXP	L&O EXP	GEGS	PRIEXP	L&O EXP
ARG	96.29	891.50	36.45	157.49	1568.88	68.60
BOL	21.50	214.69	17.04	52.02	530.45	42.00
BRA	148.73	846.97	28.11	219.39	1257.90	41.57
CHL	41.06	983.57	58.50	77.92	1868.45	111.71
COL		476.46			1518.70	
CRI	43.98	722.26	54.34	89.88	1492.94	111.82
DOM	29.13	303.01	13.04	84.09	895.10	38.70
JAM	239.45	667.21	62.13	306.94	851.57	78.67
MEX	122.97	532.11	11.81	215.97	945.79	20.39
NIC	15.70	148.78	10.34	64.79	620.66	42.68
PAN	72.08	748.35	67.96	109.51	1138.51	103.39
PER		344.48			742.34	
SLV	11.52	156.99	25.05	25.52	347.72	55.54
TTO	262.59	1283.68	97.56	365.54	1827.76	134.56
URY	134.63	1581.82	58.84	179.83	2233.77	79.59
VEN	276.17	679.30	35.00	374.93	981.56	47.51
LAC						
Mean	108.27	661.32	41.16	165.99	1176.38	69.77
St. dev.	93.47	402.80	26.02	116.14	534.02	34.46
Min.	11.52	148.78	10.34	25.52	347.72	20.39
Max	276.17	1581.82	97.56	374.93	2233.77	134.56
All developing countries						
Mean	83.22	561.25	38.83	181.93	1297.56	87.37
St. dev.	71.44	498.09	32.96	123.76	1079.90	70.30
Min.	1.52	28.60	1.35	12.57	122.59	5.22
Max	276.17	1788.89	137.40	513.55	4488.82	293.53

Notes: All data are from the IMF Government Finance Statistics and are computed as averages for the 1995–2004 period. GEGS is computed by subtracting lines 7017 and 7018 from line 701. Primary expenditure is line 2 minus line 24, Law and order is line 703. The PPP adjustment is from the World Bank's World Development Indicators.

per capita primary expenditure ranging between $700 and $2,500.[4] Panel B suggests that a 10-point increase in control of corruption would

[4] For instance, column (7) of Panel A estimates that 1 extra dollar in PPP-adjusted primary expenditure yields a 0.004 point increase in government

require an increase in PPP-adjusted *per capita* primary expenditure ranging between $400 and $1200. The Rule of law seems to be cheaper. Column (4) of Panel C suggests that a 10-point increase in the Rule of law would require an increase in PPP-adjusted *per capita* expenditure in public order and safety ranging between $33 and $120.

One problem with the estimates of table 9.1.3 is that they do not recognize that historical and geographical factors are key determinants of institutional quality, and that excluding these factors might distort the relationship between institutional quality and public expenditure. In table 9.1.4, I address this issue by re-estimating the equations of table 9.1.3, controlling for geography and history. The results are similar.[5]

It is possible to use the estimates of table 9.1.4 to do a back-of-the-envelope CBA of a policy aimed at improving institutional quality through an increase in public expenditure. Kaufman, Kraay, and Zoido-Lobatón (1999) estimate that a 1 standard deviation increase in governance can lead to an increase in GDP *per capita* that ranges between 150% and 300%. I take the upper bound of this range and assume that the transition to the new steady state takes about 30 years. These assumptions imply that a 1 standard deviation increase in governance leads to an increase in the growth rate of GDP *per capita* of approximately 3.7%. The present value (PV) of this increase will depend on the initial GDP. If we are in a country with an income *per capita* of $1,000, the *per capita* benefit in the first year will be $37. Assuming a discount rate of 3%, the PV of the second-year benefit will be $0.037*1037/1.03 = $37.3. The PV of third-year benefit will be $0.037(1.037)*1037/(1.03*1.03)$, and so on. If we focus on a 30-year horizon, the *per capita* PV of the increase in growth will be $1226.[6]

---

effectiveness. Hence, a 10-point increase requires $10/0.004 = 2,500$ PPP-adjusted dollars. Note that I am interpreting the relationship as causal (i.e. I assume that an increase in primary expenditure has an effect on government effectiveness). While reverse causality is likely to be a serious issue, it is worth noting that addressing causality would probably make the coefficient even smaller and hence strengthen my argument.

[5] The estimations of table 9.1.4 do not control for settler mortality (Acemoglu, Johnson, and Robinson 2001). I exclude this variable to maximize sample size. Including the variable would not alter my basic results.

[6] A 100-year horizon would increase the benefits by approximately $500. This small increase is due to the fact that (by assumption) the growth effect ends after 30 years.

Table 9.1.3 Institutional quality and public expenditure

	(1)	(2)	(3)	(4)	(5)	(6)	(7)	(8)
				A: Government effectiveness				
GEGS	0.003	−0.032						
	(0.07)	(0.64)						
GEGS_PPP			0.006	−0.031				
			(0.27)	(0.77)				
PRIM_EXP					0.012	0.013		
					(3.04)***	(2.26)**		
PRIM_EXP_PPP							0.004	0.014
							(2.08)**	(1.98)*
GDP_PC	15.799	22.052	15.362	22.622	9.450	9.853	11.054	3.870
	(5.79)***	(2.51)**	(5.16)***	(2.52)**	(3.31)***	(1.49)	(3.68)***	(0.56)
Constant	−79.16	−132.26	−76.39	−135.48	−34.33	−39.791	−46.36	3.38
	(3.91)***	(1.83)*	(3.53)***	(1.85)*	(1.60)	(0.73)	(2.07)**	(0.06)
Observations	52	14	52	14	59	17	59	17
R²	0.57	0.39	0.58	0.40	0.61	0.40	0.60	0.45
				B: Control of corruption				
GEGS	0.007	−0.060						
	(0.17)	(1.17)						
GEGS_PPP			0.005	−0.056				
			(0.17)	(1.36)				
PRIM_EXP					0.021	0.020		
					(3.92)***	(2.73)**		

PRIM_EXP_PPP						0.007	0.024
						(2.90)***	(2.90)**
GDP_PC	14.094	27.729	13.963	28.660	4.339	10.755	7.668	-0.065
	(3.94)***	(2.26)**	(3.24)***	(2.30)**	(1.25)	(1.00)	(2.13)**	(0.01)
Constant	-72.08	-183.74	-71.31	-188.96	-3.14	-57.10	-27.80	21.40
	(2.69)***	(1.85)*	(2.30)**	(1.88)*	(0.12)	(0.65)	(1.03)	(0.30)
Observations	52	14	52	14	59	17	59	17
R²	0.41	0.37	0.41	0.39	0.54	0.41	0.49	0.50

C: Rule of law

LO_EXP	0.219	0.295		
	(2.38)**	(2.68)**		
LO_EXP_PPP			0.096	0.309
			(2.87)***	(2.99)**
GDP_PC	8.088	14.809	8.677	12.422
	(2.47)**	(2.07)*	(2.94)***	(2.10)*
Constant	-23.809	-86.409	-28.623	-75.057
	(0.98)	(1.43)	(1.29)	(1.50)
Observations	49	14	49	14
R²	0.51	0.47	0.51	0.63
Sample	All	LAC	All	LAC

Notes: Robust *t*-statistics in parentheses.

* Significant at 10%; ** significant at 5%; *** significant at 1%.

Table 9.1.4 Regressions with controls

	(1)	(2)	(3)	(4)	(5)	(6)	(7)	(8)	(9)	(10)
	Government effectiveness				Control of corruption				Rule of law	
GEGS	0.003 (0.08)				0.015 (0.35)					
GEGS.PPP		0.012 (0.52)				0.022 (0.77)				
PRIM.EXP			0.015 (3.18)***				0.021 (3.87)***			
PR.EX.PPP				0.009 (3.83)***				0.013 (5.03)***		
LO.EXP									0.184 (1.58)	
LO.EXP.PPP										0.116 (2.16)**
GDP.PC	15.250 (5.16)***	14.285 (4.67)***	8.671 (3.04)***	7.385 (2.76)***	12.041 (3.08)***	10.837 (2.59)**	3.333 (1.03)	1.488 (0.53)	8.581 (2.17)**	7.646 (2.33)**
Latitude	31.275 (1.73)*	33.513 (1.83)*	27.219 (1.50)	27.364 (1.64)	48.803 (2.20)**	50.901 (2.36)**	39.960 (1.89)*	40.178 (2.08)**	38.948 (1.95)*	33.851 (1.72)*
French code	-3.470 (0.73)	-2.662 (0.58)	-4.208 (1.04)	-4.411 (1.12)	0.768 (0.13)	1.805 (0.32)	-0.327 (0.07)	-0.619 (0.14)	-3.325 (0.65)	-3.328 (0.70)
Soc. Code	-14.440 (2.48)**	-15.043 (2.69)**	-14.801 (2.75)***	-19.200 (3.51)***	-19.898 (2.49)**	-20.900 (2.74)***	-20.462 (2.93)***	-26.824 (4.16)***	-20.841 (3.33)***	-22.650 (3.61)***

ELF	7.050	7.444	3.862	5.367	2.554	3.235	−0.133	2.048	−2.787	−0.498
	(0.96)	(1.04)	(0.61)	(0.88)	(0.29)	(0.38)	(0.02)	(0.31)	(0.31)	(0.06)
Log(Area)	−1.064	−1.131	−0.727	−0.408	−0.491	−0.565	0.179	0.641	0.467	0.588
	(0.68)	(0.71)	(0.49)	(0.28)	(0.25)	(0.29)	(0.10)	(0.37)	(0.22)	(0.28)
Log(Pop)	−0.102	−0.037	0.319	−0.265	−2.079	−2.075	−1.667	−2.513	−2.356	−2.401
	(0.06)	(0.02)	(0.20)	(0.15)	(0.92)	(0.94)	(0.87)	(1.25)	(1.08)	(1.00)
Constant	−66.838	−62.010	−28.033	−14.084	−26.542	−19.478	24.996	45.085	3.023	8.597
	(2.64)**	(2.25)**	(1.10)	(0.52)	(0.84)	(0.55)	(0.89)	(1.55)	(0.09)	(0.27)
Observations	51	51	55	55	51	51	55	55	48	48
R^2	0.62	0.62	0.68	0.70	0.51	0.52	0.62	0.66	0.59	0.61

Notes: Robust t-statistics in parentheses.

* Significant at 10%; ** significant at 5%; *** significant at 1%.

Table 9.1.5 CBA

Initial income *per capita*	1,000	2,500	5,000	10,000
A. PV of 1 standard deviation increase in institutional quality	1,226	3,066	6,133	12,226
B. PV of the cost of a 1 standard deviation increase in control of corruption achieved by increasing primary expenditure		28,140		
C. PV of the cost of a 1 standard deviation increase in the Rule of Law achieved by increasing expenditure in public order and safety		2,886		
NPV A–B	−26,914	−25,074	−22,007	−15,874
NPV A–C	−1,660	180	3,247	9,380

Notes: Assumptions: a 1 standard deviation increase in institutional quality increases long-run growth by 3.7% per year for 30 years. The discount rate is 3% and the cost of increasing institutional quality is based on the estimates of table 9.1.4.

Of course, the higher the initial income *per capita*, the higher the PV. Thus, in a country with an initial GDP *per capita* of $10,000, the *per capita* PV of the increase in growth will be $12,226 (table 9.1.5).

But what would the cost of this policy be? Let us start with a policy aimed at increasing the control of corruption. The standard deviation of the index measuring control of corruption is approximately 18. The point estimates of table 9.1.4 suggest that with an additional PPP dollar we can increase control of corruption by 0.013 (column (8)). Hence, increasing control of corruption by 1 standard deviation will cost $1,394 per year. The PV over 30 years is $28,142. As the benefits range between $1,226 and $12,226, table 9.1.5 shows that trying to increase the control of corruption by increasing primary expenditure is a very bad deal. Even in the best-case scenario, the NPV of such a policy is negative and large (–$15,874, table 9.1.5).[7]

---

[7] I obtain similar results if, rather than focusing on control of corruption, I focus on government effectiveness.

Trying to increase the Rule of law by spending more on public order seems to be a better strategy. The standard deviation of the Rule of law index is 17 and the point estimates of table 9.1.4 suggest that an additional PPP dollar in expenditure in public order and safety can increase the Rule of law by 0.12 points. Therefore, increasing the Rule of law by 1 standard deviation would cost $143 per year. The PV of this increase in expenditure is $2,886. In this case, the net NPV will be positive for countries with an initial income *per capita* of at least $2,500.

While the above example suggests that targeting public expenditure towards promoting the Rule of law might be a good strategy for middle-income countries, it is not clear whether a country can double its expenditure on public order and safety (in the LAC region, average expenditure on public order and safety is about $70 PPP) without increasing other types of public expenditure. Moreover, the estimates of Kaufman, Kraay, and Zoido-Lobatón (1999) do not consider interactions among various measures of institutional quality and assume a linear (or log linear) relationship between the Rule of law and GDP *per capita*. Hence, it is not clear whether increasing the quality of the Rule of law (assuming that this is possible) while leaving the other measures of institutional quality unchanged will have a large impact on GDP growth. Moreover, too much Rule of law (keeping the other institutional characteristics constant) may have a negative effect on growth, as nobody will dare do anything which may lead to some probability of violating the law.

As an alternative experiment, I regress institutional quality over the same set of variables included in table 9.1.4, but without controlling for public expenditure. The residual of this regression can be interpreted as a measure of institutional quality that nets out the role of history and geography.[8] I report the values of this "residual" institutional quality in columns (4)–(6) of table 9.1.1 (again, the values are rescaled to range between 0 and 100).[9] As these residuals should not depend on the level of development and on geographical and historical factors,

---

[8] Although the regressions use all countries for which I have data, from now on I will limit my analysis to Latin America.

[9] Appendix figures 9A.1.1, 9A.1.2 and 9A.1.3 plot the actual and residual values of institutional quality. Countries above the 45° line have levels of institutional quality which are higher than those predicted by the regression (i.e. given their history and geography, they are doing relatively well) and countries that are below the 45° line have levels of institutional quality which are lower than those predicted by the regression.

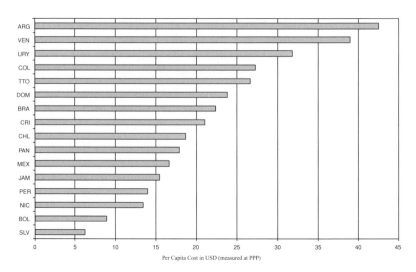

Figure 9.1.1 Primary expenditure cost: residual unit of government effectiveness

I can divide them by PPP-adjusted *per capita* public expenditure and obtain a measure of the "unit cost" of government quality under the assumption that all countries have the same history, geography, and level of development.[10] Figures 9.1.1 and 9.1.2 plot the unit cost of government effectiveness and the Rule of law and show that there are enormous differences in the *per capita* unit cost of institutional quality. A unit of government effectiveness costs more than 30 PPP-adjusted dollars in Argentina, Venezuela, and Uruguay and less than 20 PPP-adjusted dollars in Chile, Panama, Mexico, Jamaica, Peru, Nicaragua, Bolivia, and El Salvador. The same is true for the unit cost of the Rule of law which ranges from more than 2 PPP-adjusted dollars in Trinidad and Tobago and Argentina to less than 1 PPP-adjusted dollar in Nicaragua, Dominican Republic, Bolivia, Brazil, and Mexico.

Of course, these differences might be due to the fact that in richer countries everything is more expensive. Hence, it is not surprising that running the government is more expensive in Argentina than in

---

[10] In the case of government effectiveness, I focus on primary expenditure because I found no statistically significant relationship between GEGS and government effectiveness. In the case of the Rule of law, I use expenditure in public order and safety.

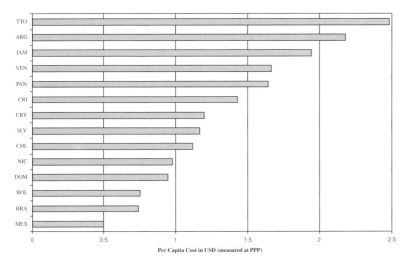

Figure 9.1.2 Cost of a residual unit of law

El Salvador. However, I am partly controlling for this by using PPP-adjusted figures. Moreover, figure 9.1.3 shows that the correlation between GDP *per capita* and the unit cost of the Rule of law is far from being tight.[11]

In order to evaluate the benefits of increasing the efficiency of the public sector, I can focus on the countries with the highest unit cost and evaluate how much institutional quality could improve if their unit costs were equal to the LAC median. Figure 9.1.4 focuses on government effectiveness and shows the level of residual government effectiveness (the light bars are from column (4) of table 9.1.1), and the additional level of government effectiveness (the dark bars) that these countries could obtain by maintaining their expenditure constant but becoming as efficient as the median LAC country. Figure 9.1.5 repeats the experiment, focusing on the Rule of law.

It is possible to use the increase in efficiency plotted in figures 9.1.4 and 9.1.5 and the estimates of Kaufman, Kraay, and Zoido-Lobatón

---

[11] Appendix figures 9A.1.4 and 9A.1.6 measure the unit cost as a share of GDP *per capita*. This affects the position of some countries (Argentina being the most notable example) but does not alter the basic message of figures 9.1.1 and 9.1.2 (see also figures 9A.1.5 and 9A.1.7, which plot the relationship between the cost measured in PPP dollars and the cost measured as a share of GDP *per capita*).

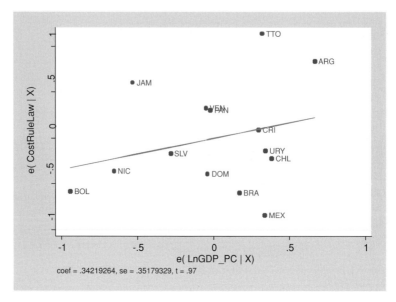

Figure 9.1.3 Correlation between the cost of Rule of law and GDP *per capita*

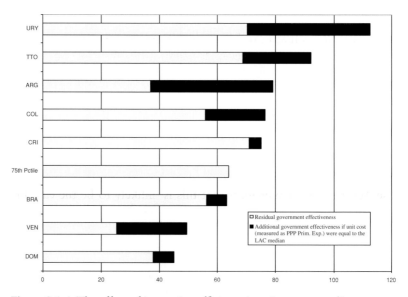

Figure 9.1.4 The effect of increasing efficiency in primary expenditure

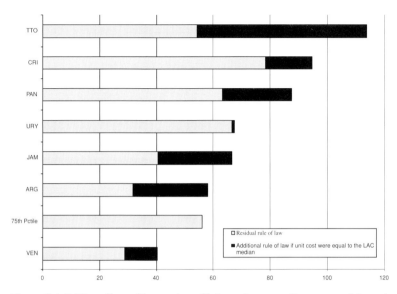

Figure 9.1.5 The effect of increasing efficiency in expenditure on public order and safety

(1999) to calculate the PV of increasing efficiency (note that there is no cost because, by assumption, I am keeping total expenditure constant). Table 9.1.6 shows that in some countries these benefits are extremely large; in some cases, several times the country's GDP *per capita*.

The above analysis suggests that improving institutional quality can lead to very large benefits at basically no cost. Of course, these are back-of-the-envelope calculations based on a series of unrealistic assumptions.[12] However, they illustrate my main point: money is not the issue.

It is often claimed that public sector workers lack incentives because they are under-paid. If this were the case, money would be an issue. Rose-Ackerman's chapter hints that this is unlikely to be the case in the LAC region. My views on this topic are even more extreme than hers. She points out that "Increases in civil service salaries are not a sufficient policy response" (p. 540). I think that in most cases such

---

[12] First, they assume that the estimates by Kaufman, Kraay, and Zoido-Lobatón (1999) are correct and apply to all countries. However, several authors have emphasized that poor governance is not the binding constraint in each country (Hausmann, Rodrik, and Velasco 2005, UNCTAD 2006). Second, they assume a causal and linear relationship between expenditure and government quality.

Table 9.1.6 Per capita *benefit (PPP USD) of having the same average cost of the median LAC country*

	GE PEXP	RL
ARGENTINA	93,816	32,493
BRAZIL	3,188	
COLOMBIA	12,119	
COSTA RICA	2,052	10,980
DOMINICAN REPUBLIC	2,968	
JAMAICA		9,734
PANAMA		16,052
TRINIDAD AND TOBAGO	25,015	227,859
URUGUAY	70,257	352
VENEZUELA	13,394	4,173

Notes: The benefits are computed as the PV (using a discount rate of 3%) of the additional growth in GDP *per capita* brought about by an increase in the efficiency of government expenditure.

increases are not even necessary. There are two problems with the "poorly paid" civil servants argument.

First, it is not true that, on average, LAC civil servants are underpaid (for evidence, see Panizza 2000, 2001a; Panizza and Qiang 2005). What is true is that public sector wages are more compressed than private sector wages. Hence, there is often a premium for low-skilled public sector workers and a penalty for high-skilled public sector workers (Panizza 2001a). This suggests that incentives could be corrected at basically no cost by increasing the steepness of the public sector pay scale. Of course, this may have no financial costs but serious political and social costs. I will say something about this in the concluding section 5.

Second, the evidence that higher public sector wages lead to lower corruption or better bureaucratic quality is, at best, mixed. Rauch and Evans (2000) find that there is no relationship between average public sector pay and bureaucratic quality. What matters is meritocracy. In my own work on Latin America (Panizza 2001a), I find the same result. Moreover, it is possible to use an efficiency-wage model to show that countries characterized by poor institutions pay higher (rather than lower) public sector wages (Panizza, 2002). If this is the case, high public sector wages are a symptom of the problem rather than a solution.

Di Tella and Schargrodsky (2003) find that higher public sector wages can reduce corruption, but only with high levels of auditing. Van Rijckeghem and Weder (2001) find a negative relationship between public sector wages and corruption, but also find that reducing corruption through higher public sector wages is an incredibly expensive strategy. In particular, they find that if the average developing country wants to reduce corruption to the level of the average OECD country, it should push public sector wages to anything between 2 and 8 times average private sector wages. Thus, the findings of Van Rijckeghem and Weder (2001) are consistent with my back-of-the-envelope calculations. In this sense, the title of this section is wrong. Money *can* buy you a good public administration, but you really need a lot of money, and this seems to be an inefficient way to proceed.[13]

3 Reforming the reformers

One thing missing from Rose-Ackerman's chapter is an analysis of the relationship between institutional quality and the political process. This is a conscious choice. On p. 516 of the chapter, the author explicitly states that her "primary focus is on isolating reforms that appear to be successes, with the aim of providing guidance to those willing to push for change." On p. 528, the author states that she takes "as given a political process that generates a set of policy goals and translates them into laws" and that her goal is "not to suggest ways to reform politics but, instead, to illustrate that failure to reform the state is costly for ordinary people and for economic progress." It is understandable why Rose-Ackerman decided to stay out of the large literature that studies the links between politics and institutional quality. A complete survey of this literature would have added at least twenty pages to an already long chapter.

However, it is important to note that politics does play an important role in institutional quality, not only because politicians write the law

---

[13] A friend who teaches at Harvard University once told me the following: "You know that old saying that you cannot throw money at a problem. At Harvard I realized that this saying is wrong. If you throw enough money at it, the problem will go away." In 2006, Harvard had an income of $150,000 for each enrolled student.

but also because they decide how to implement it and enforce it. In fact, any reform of the public administration needs to start in the political arena. If politicians do not have the incentives to improve institutional quality, nothing will ever happen. Hence, it is necessary to go beyond a purely technocratic approach to policymaking. As pointed out by Inter-American Development Bank (2005) in its report, the *Politics of Policies*, the political process and the policymaking process are inseparable and failing to understand the former one risks failure with the latter.

One important link between politics and institutional quality goes through the electoral system. Research has found that electoral rules affect institutional quality because they play a key role in shaping politicians' incentives. In particular, Persson, Tabellini, and Trebbi (2003) find that corruption tends to be higher in countries with proportional electoral systems and lower in countries with majority-based electoral systems. Focusing on the degree of "Political Particularism" (Seddon-Wallack *et al.* 2003), I find that electoral systems characterized by intermediate levels of political particularism are associated with better institutional quality (Panizza 2001b).

Another important mechanism is decentralization.[14] Through yardstick competition, decentralization can give politicians (especially at the local level) the right set of incentives for an efficient provision of public goods, and thus reduce corruption and increase the efficiency of the public sector. Moreover, decentralization can increase the variety of local public goods and tailor the supply of these goods to the preferences of the local population (Tiebout 1956).[15] However, decentralization can also lead to "commons" problem and fiscal profligacy. Moreover, local governments might be inefficient because of their small scale (Panizza 1999) and local bureaucrats may be poorly trained and thus inefficient in delivering public goods and services. Tanzi (1996) suggests that these imperfections may prevent the realization of benefits from decentralization.

These considerations suggest that the relationship between decentralization and institutional quality can go either way. Fisman and Gatti (2002) were among the first to study the cross-country relationship between decentralization and corruption and found a negative

---

[14] Decentralization is briefly discussed on p. 551 of the chapter.
[15] For an empirical analysis of the links between heterogeneity of preferences and decentralization, see Panizza (1999).

relationship between these two variables, suggesting that decentralization reduces corruption. However, Nupia (2005) shows that this result does not hold within developing countries. In assessing the possible effect of decentralization it is thus necessary to go beyond cross-country analyses and look at case studies. A study of the experiences of Uganda and the Philippines shows that decentralization has the potential for improving the delivery of public services, but that this potential is often not realized (Azfar, Kahkonen, and Meagher 2001). This is clearly an area that requires more research.[16]

4 Subsidizing transparency

Rose-Ackerman correctly points out that auditing and transparency can play an important role in increasing institutional quality. I agree with her that setting up auditing agencies and improving existing ones is likely to be a cost-effective way to improve public service delivery and reduce corruption (Recanatini, Prati, and Tabellini 2005, provide evidence of the importance of internal and external auditing).[17] I also agree with her analysis suggesting that effective auditing agencies may require independent media, and that in several countries the government has subtle ways to influence the media and limit their monitoring role. Moreover, in several countries newspapers and TV channels are often perceived to be partisan. Reporting of government corruption by an opposition newspaper can often be dismissed as being motivated by a political agenda. On the other hand, reporting by prestigious international newspapers is often perceived to be more balanced and impartial and hence more effective in exposing corruption and misgovernment.[18] The news produced by the international newspaper can then be disseminated within the country by local newspapers and bloggers.[19]

---

[16] Tulchin and Selee (2004) discuss the experience with decentralization of six LAC countries.

[17] The chapter and Recanatini, Prati, and Tabellini (2005) also point to the importance of increasing the available flow of information. In particular, Recanatini, Prati, and Tabellini (2005) show that agencies that make their budget, procurement, and staffing decisions publicly available have lower levels of corruption.

[18] There are, of course, some exceptions. Reporting by a US newspaper on a country with explicit anti-US policies is unlikely to be perceived as impartial.

[19] The importance of the blogsphere should not be under-estimated. See, for instance, the *Financial Times* article (July 28, 2007, "Quick off the Blog") that

One problem is that the market does not supply enough of such reporting. The *New York Times* is more likely to publish a story about Paris Hilton than a story about corruption in some unknown LAC country which does not even have a Hilton Hotel. As a consequence, able freelance investigative journalists will have more incentives to write stories about Paris Hilton than about corruption in Latin America.

How can this situation be changed? Here is a "crazy" proposal. The IDB could establish a list of ten or so prestigious international newspapers and magazines (of the caliber of the *New York Times* and *The Financial Times*, for instance) and pay a $20,000 premium to each journalist who manages to publish a major story (where "major" is defined as being above some minimum number of words) about either bad or good government in the LAC region in one of these journals. An important feature of this proposal is that the premium should be automatic. After the author publishes the article she can directly collect the money from the IDB, no questions asked. Otherwise, member countries that are offended by a given article could prevent the IDB from awarding the prize, or accuse the IDB of being biased against a given country and/or government. Given that the decision of whether to publish the article or not is in the hands of the editorial board of the newspaper and the prize is automatic, nobody can accuse the IDB of being biased against a given country.[20]

Of course, this premium will provide incentives to write articles but not to publish them. However, if the prize increases the supply of good articles, it is likely that the newspapers will publish some of them. Moreover, even if an article does not get published in a major journal, it is still likely to be published elsewhere and have some effect on reporting on corruption and bad/good government. The impact may be smaller, but the marginal cost of this article will be zero.

What would the costs and benefits of such policy be? As the conditions for paying the prize are easily verifiable, managing such an

shows how a single blogger fuelled the scandals which led to the dismissal of Senate Majority Leader Trent Lott and the incarceration of US vice-president top aide, I. Lewis "Scooter" Libby. However, while bloggers can play a key role in disseminating information, they do not have the resources to conduct the investigative journalism which is necessary to uncover a scandal.

[20] Member countries that think that they would not be treated fairly by the international press could opt out (either totally or partially) in advance (i.e. at the beginning of each year), but not after the article was published.

award will have very low administrative costs – and, for the sake of simplicity, I will assume no administrative costs. Hence, the only cost would be the prize itself. Assume that the prize generates 50 articles per year (clearly an upper bound) and that each article reduces average corruption in the region by 0.017 points in our 0–100 scale (this is one-hundredth of 1 standard deviation).[21] Then, the cost would be $1,000,000 per year and the benefit would be an increase in yearly *per capita* GDP growth of 1.85% (half of 3.7%, see the calculations in section 2). If I assume an average GDP *per capita* of 7500 PPP-adjusted dollars (this is close to the current LAC PPP-adjusted GDP *per capita*) and use all the assumptions of section 2, I find that a 1.85% increase in GDP *per capita* has a PV of 3,500 *per capita* PPP-adjusted dollars. Since this is a *per capita* value, we need to multiply it by the LAC population, which is about 500 million, yielding a total of 1.7 trillion PPP-adjusted dollars.

These are back-of-the-envelope calculations, and I am sure that the 1.7 trillion figure is a gross over-estimation of the potential effect of my proposal. My assumptions on the effect of the program on corruption are probably too generous and so are my assumptions on the effect of corruption on growth. Moreover, I am comparing actual dollars with PPP-adjusted dollars.[22]

However, the costs are so low (0.2% of IDB's administrative expenses) and the potential benefits so large that it may be worth trying.[23] In fact, the program would still yield a net benefit even if the benefits were one thousand times smaller than I estimated.[24]

---

[21] This reduction of corruption will be driven by both the direct and indirect effects of greater transparency. Brunetti and Weder (2003) find that freedom of the press has a large effect on corruption. Besley and Burgess (2002) find that local governments are more responsive in Indian states with higher newspaper circulation.

[22] Another criticism of my proposal is that it may not generate the desired number of publications. However, this would have no effect on the cost-benefit ratio (unless there are important non-linearities), because if there are no publications there is no cost.

[23] Paraphrasing Nils Bohr, the experiment might be crazy enough to yield some positive result.

[24] Here I am cheating because I am considering the $1,000,000 as a once-for-all expenditure. If the program is maintained every year, the PV of the cost would be $20,000,000 and the program would break even only if the actual benefits of the program are about 180 hundred times smaller than my estimates.

5 Conclusions

If the organizers of the San José Consulta had asked a public administration scholar to write this chapter, they would have probably received a text with a series of detailed proposals on how to organize a public sector office. Given my training, I could only focus on much broader proposals aimed at improving incentives.[25] Moreover, since I fundamentally agree with most of Rose-Ackerman's conclusions, rather than presenting an fully alternative view, I used my space to reinforce some of the points made in the chapter.

My main point is that money is not the problem. Most countries are far from the efficiency frontier and hence they should be able to increase the quality of their institutions without increasing public expenditure. So, in theory, the costs are minimal and the benefits enormous. This is true in theory. In practice, things are more complicated.

First, we still know little about how to improve public institutions and more research in this field could have high returns (the chapter points to the need of more research on p. 558). Interestingly, the World Bank has spent a large amount of resources on collecting micro-level data that could be of great help in understanding how to improve institutional quality, but these lie largely unused or under-used.[26] One exception is Recanatini, Prati, and Tabellini (2005). This paper uses data on corruption at the public agency level in six LAC and African countries, and derives a rich set of anti-corruption policy prescriptions. More papers along these lines could be of great help in devising anti-corruption policies. Rather than hiding its data, the World Bank should advertise them and create incentives for using them (maybe establishing an award for the best paper written using them).

Second, reforms of public administration need political support and gathering such support may be difficult. Rose-Ackerman correctly points out that policy reforms may have no economic cost but a

---

[25] I have not discussed reforms aimed at improving any specific branch of the public administration. However, since the chapter explicitly discusses the case of tax evasion, it should probably discuss Ordoñez's (2001) clever incentive scheme for tax evasion reporting.

[26] See Panizza (2007) for a discussion on possible uses of the World Bank's BEEPS data. Some of these data are available to the research community but not well advertised, and some are available only to World Bank staff.

large political cost. In several countries, public sector workers' unions have been very active in protecting the status quo and blocking reforms. The chapter points out that implementing reforms is easier during certain historical periods, but that in most cases reforms need to proceed very cautiously. An alternative approach would be to follow the suggestion of Delpla and Wyplosz (2007) and compensate the losers.[27] In particular, reformers could evaluate whether it is worth buying back the privileges acquired by the group that will be damaged by the reform process and, if the reform is worth the price, buy back those privileges (assuming that the seller can commit to not asking for the privileges back). This would be a cool experiment in CBA.

Appendix

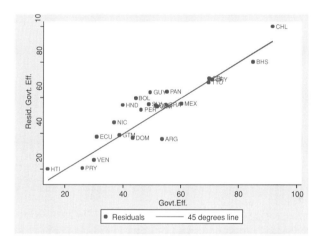

Figure 9A.1.1 Regression residuals and actual governance effectiveness

---

[27] Sometimes compensating the losers will be the morally correct thing to do and sometimes it won't (Alex Tabarrok at www.marginalrevolution.com reports a probably apocryphal story which says that while the British Parliament was debating how much slave owners should be compensated for their losses a furious John Stuart Mill rose to his feet thundering, "I should have thought it was the slaves who should be compensated."). The point is that some reforms will not be feasible without compensating the losers. Hence, we may go ahead with compensation even when it is not morally justified.

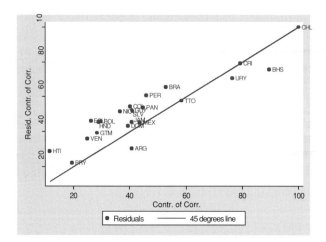

Figure 9A.1.2 Regression residuals and actual control of corruption

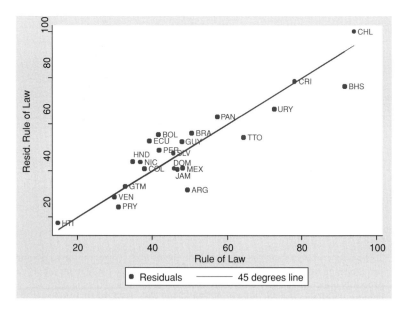

Figure 9A.1.3 Regression residuals and actual Rule of law

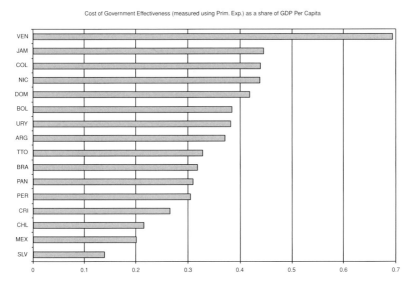

Figure 9A.1.4 Cost of government effectiveness (measured using primary expenditure) as share of GDP

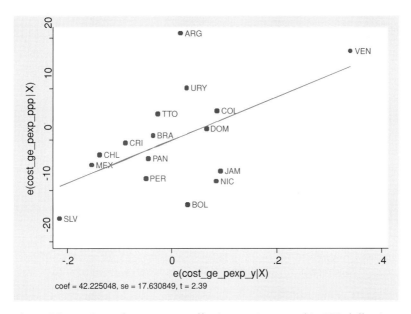

Figure 9A.1.5 Cost of government effectiveness (measured in PPP dollars) vs. cost of government effectiveness (measured as share of GDP)

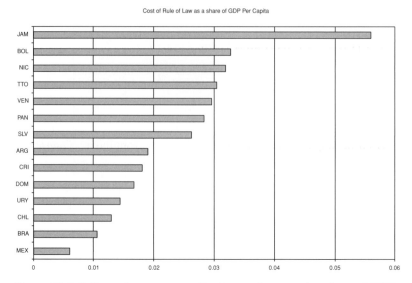

Figure 9A.1.6 Cost of government effectiveness (measured as share of GDP)

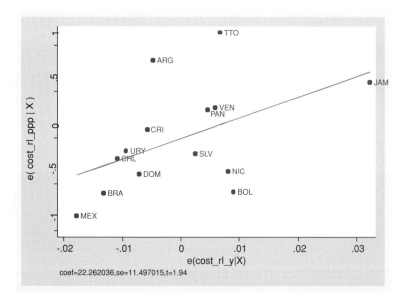

Figure 9A.1.7 Cost of Rule of law (measured in PPP dollars) vs. cost of Rule of law (measured as share of GDP *per capita*)

Bibliography

Acemoglu, Daron, Simon Johnson, and James Robinson, 2001. "The Colonial Origins of Comparative Development: Empirical Investigation." *American Economic Review* **91**: 1369–1401

Azfar, Omar, Satu Kahkonen, and Patrick Meagher, 2001. "Conditions for Effective Decentralized Governance: A Synthesis of Research Findings." University of Maryland, mimeo

Besley, Timothy and Robin Burgess, 2002. "The Political Economy of Government Responsiveness: Theory and Evidence from India." *Quarterly Journal of Economics* **117**: 1415–51

Brunetti, Aymo and Beatrice Weder, 2003. "A Free Press is Bad News for Corruption." *Journal of Public Economics* **87**: 1801–24

Delpla, Jacques and Charles Wyplosz, 2007. *La fin des privilèges*. Paris: Hachette

Di Tella, Rafael and Ernesto Schargrodsky, 2003. "The Role of Wages and Auditing During a Crackdown on Corruption in the City of Buenos Aires." *Journal of Law and Economics* **46**: 269–92

Fisman, Raymond and Roberta Gatti, 2002. "Decentralization and Corruption: Evidence across Countries." *Journal of Public Economics* **83**: 325–45

Hausmann, Ricardo, Dani Rodrik, and Andres Velasco, 2005. "Growth Diagnostics." Harvard University, mimeo

Inter-American Development Bank, 2005. *The Politics of Policies*. Cambridge, MA: Harvard University Press

Kaufman, Daniel, Aart Kraay, and Massimo Mastruzzi, 2006. "Governance Matters V: Governance Indicators for 1996–2005." World Bank, mimeo

Kaufman, Daniel, Aart Kraay, and Pablo Zoido-Lobatón, 1999. "Governance Matters." World Bank Policy Research Working Paper **2196**

Landsburg, Steven, 1995. *The Armchair Economist*. New York: Free Press

Nupia, Oskar, 2005. "Decentralization, Corruption, and Political Accountability in Developing Countries." Universitiat Pompeu Fabra, mimeo

Ordoñez, Guillermo, 2001. "Let the Mouse Hunt the Cat: A Way to Evade Evasion Corrupting Corruption." UCLA, mimeo

Panizza, Ugo, 1999. "On the Determinants of Fiscal Centralization: Theory and Evidence." *Journal of Public Economics* **74**: 97–139

2000. "The Public Sector Premium and the Gender Gap in Latin America: Evidence from the 1980s and 1990s." IDB Research Department, Working Paper **431**

2001a. "Public Sector Wages and Bureaucratic Quality: Evidence from Latin America." *Economia* **2**: 97–151

2001b. "Electoral Rules, Political Systems and Institutional Quality." *Economics and Politics* 13: 311–42

2002. "The Strange Case of the Public Sector Premium." *Public Finance and Management* 2: 334–5

2007. "Comment on 'Judicial Reform in Developing Economies: Opportunities and Constraints,' by M. Stephenson, and 'Transforming Judicial Systems in Europe and Central Asia,' by J. Andersen and C. Gray." *Annual Bank Conference on Development Economics, Europe*. Washington, DC: World Bank

Panizza, Ugo and Christine Zhen-Wei Qiang, 2005. "Public–Private Wage Differential and Gender Gap in Latin America: Spoiled Bureaucrat and Exploited Women?" *Journal of Socio-Economics* 34: 810–33

Persson, Torsten, Guido Tabellini, and Francesco Trebbi, 2003. "Electoral Rules and Corruption." *Journal of the European Economic Association* 1: 958–89

Rauch, James and Peter Evans, 2000. "Bureaucratic Structure and Bureaucratic Performance in Less Developed Countries." *Journal of Public Economics* 75: 49–71

Recanatini, Francesca, Alessandro Prati, and Guido Tabellini, 2005. "Why are some Public Agencies Less Corrupt than Others? Lessons for Institutional Reform from Survey Data." International Monetary Fund, mimeo

Seddon-Wallack, Jessica, Alejandro Gaviria, Ugo Panizza, and Ernesto Stein, 2003. "Political Particularism Around the World." *World Bank Economic Review* 17: 133–43

Tanzi, Vito, 1996. "Fiscal Federalism and Efficiency: A Review of Some Efficiency and Macroeconomic Aspects." In M. Bruno and B. Pleskovic, eds., *Annual World Bank Conference on Development Economics*. Washington, DC: World Bank

Tiebout, Charles, 1956. "A Pure Theory of Local Expenditures." *Journal of Political Economy* 64: 416–24

Tulchin, Joseph and Andrew Selee, 2004. *Decentralization and Democratic Governance in Latin America*. Washington, DC: Woodrow Wilson Center

UNCTAD, 2006. *Trade and Development Report*. Geneva: UNCTAD

Van Rijckeghem, Caroline and Beatrice Weder, 2001. "Bureaucratic Corruption and the Rate of Temptation: Do Wages in the Civil Service Affect Corruption and By How Much?" *Journal of Development Economics* 65: 307–31

10 Violence and crime in the LAC region

MARK A. COHEN AND MAURICIO RUBIO*

1 Challenges

Background

The public survey that was conducted by the IDB for the Copenhagen Challenge process identified the problem of "crime and violence" as one of the areas of major concern in the LAC region. In particular, the following items were identified (in descending or perceived priority): (a) high incidence of crime, (b) drug trafficking, (c) proliferation of violent youth gangs, (d) pervasiveness of money laundering, and (e) frequency of domestic violence. In conducting the research for this chapter, we evaluated the nature of the evidence on the extent to which these perceived issues would rise to the level of being "significant," as well as the evidence on "what works" and what the benefits and costs are from programs that have been shown to be effective.

Setting the boundaries of our analysis was a difficult task, but one that we needed to do in order to arrive at a document that would be of value to policymakers. For example, while most incidents of crime and violence are essentially "local," the causes and potential solutions to crime may lie well outside the local or even national jurisdiction. This is true globally – where many types of crimes are clearly of a global character and require more than local solutions.

There are several very stark examples of this problem in the case of crime and violence in the LAC region. For example, the demand for drugs in the United States and Europe will have an impact on the

---

* The views expressed are those of the authors and not necessarily any of the sponsoring organizations or our home institutions.

supply of drugs in various LAC countries – and hence will impact organized crime and gang-related violence. Because these markets operate outside of traditional legal institutions, enforcement of property rights disputes, for example, also takes place outside normal legal channels – hence contributing to the demand for violence itself. Moreover, because the demand for drugs is coming from outside of the LAC region and suppliers are large and sophisticated, any attempt to reduce the supply of drugs in one "hot spot" country in the region will ultimately backfire as drug production is shifted to another country to keep up with the demand. There is good evidence that this has happened repeatedly in the region. Thus, without global solutions, a LAC solution to this problem is unlikely to succeed.

Drug and terrorism policy in the United States and Europe can also affect crime and violence in the LAC region. For example, the US war on drugs has led to the extradition of drug lords – something that has destabilized the Colombian drug market, for example, with the ultimate effect of more violence between organized drug cartels to gain control over local areas. This contrasts with the approach taken in Europe which is largely to treat drugs as a "consumption" problem at home.

Similarly, some researchers have suggested that US immigration and prison policies affect crime and gang-related violence in the LAC region. For example, illegal immigrants who have committed crimes while in the United States will serve time in prison and then be deported to their home country. To the extent that returning prisoners have joined gangs in US prisons and transfer knowledge and experience back to their home countries, this exacerbates the gang violence problem in the home country.

In this chapter, we take these factors as exogenous and beyond the scope of our immediate concern – which is to identify the most cost-beneficial programs that can be implemented in the region to reduce crime and violence, given the current situation and institutions within which we have to work.

Policy discussions over crime and violence have oftentimes been framed using political and ideological themes. Thus, for example, calls for more police and tougher prison sentences are often seen as attempts by the "right" to control the underclass. Similarly, calls for prevention programs through better education, jobs, and an enhanced standard of living to reduce the desirability of illegal occupations are often seen as "socialist" solutions by the right. Given this political backdrop, as well as the fact that the field of criminology itself has historical roots in sociology, there is scant empirical evidence on either the extent of criminal behavior or the effectiveness of prevention or control strategies in the LAC region. Police records are notoriously poor, due to poor training, lack of resources, and few incentives for good reporting. Moreover, they are often generated by corrupt politicians or police administrations to support their own point of view. There have only been a few comprehensive victimization surveys in some countries, and any significant cross-country comparisons that can be made are of only limited value, unlike the more detailed surveys in the United States and Europe. There are also no reliable indicators of drugs or arms trafficking or the influence of organized crime. Measures of these problems are largely indirect and subject to considerable uncertainty. Thus, in the following discussion of the extent of crime and violence in the region, the uninitiated reader might be struck by the lack of solid data – but this is a persistent problem in measuring crime and violence.

Basic facts on crime and violence

Incidence of crime and violence

Although a recent rise in crime and violence in the LAC region is almost taken for granted,[1] the available evidence is not conclusive. Moreover, existing sources of reported crime and violence data are often contradictory – oftentimes with no apparent method of reconciliation. Instead, if any pattern is clear, it is that crime and violence are highly variable across countries and even across localities within countries. Nevertheless, the evidence is clear that crime and violence is a serious problem, that has a significant impact on the health, wellbeing, and economic development of the region. In this section, we review the empirical evidence on crime and violence, to provide a context in which our solutions are proposed.

For the period 1995–2002, the annual increase in homicides (2.1%) was slightly higher than the rise in population (1.6%) for the LAC region as a whole.[2] However, this rise in homicides was concentrated

[1] WOLA (2006). [2] OPS (2005).

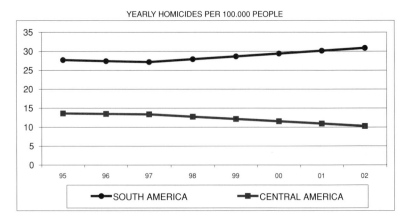

Figure 10.1 Homicide rate, 1995–2002
Sources: Calculations based on CELADE (2003); OPS (2005)

	1995	1996	1997	1998	1999	2000	2001	2002
Argentina	5,0	4,9	4,9	5,3	5,8	6,2	6,6	7,0
Brasil	26,6	27,3	28,1	28,7	29,2	29,8	30,4	31,0
Chile	2,9	2,9	2,9	3,4	3,9	4,3	4,8	5,3
Colombia	91,6	86,0	80,4	81,2	82,1	82,9	83,8	84,6
Costa Rica	5,4	5,5	5,6	5,7	5,9	6,0	6,1	6,2
Cuba	6,1	6,6	7,1	7,1	7,1	7,1	7,1	7,0
Ecuador	14,0	14,1	14,1	14,4	14,7	15,1	15,4	15,7
El Salvador	35,7	43,0	50,4	49,0	47,6	46,2	44,8	43,4
Guatemala	21,6	22,3	23,1	...	...	...	...	...
Honduras	0,0	...	...	...	...	...	...	...
México	17,1	16,4	15,7	14,8	13,9	13,0	12,1	11,1
Nicaragua	11,3	11,1	11,0	11,3	11,5	11,8	12,0	12,3
Panamá	11,1	11,1	11,1	11,6	12,1	12,6	13,2	13,7
Paraguay	15,6	16,4	17,3	17,5	17,7	17,9	18,1	18,4
Perú	6,2	5,3	4,5	...	...	...	...	...
Puerto Rico	22,8	22,6	22,4	21,7	20,9	20,2	19,4	18,7
R Dominicana	11,2	11,1	11,1	...	...	...	...	...
Uruguay	4,8	4,9	5,0	5,1	5,1	5,1	5,2	5,2
Venezuela	15,6	16,0	16,3	19,6	22,8	26,0	29,2	32,0

Figure 10.2 Homicide rate, 1995–2002
Source: OPS (2005)

in South America. In Central America, there was a continuous drop in homicide rates, as shown in figure 10.1.

According to the Pan American Health Organization (PAHO-OPS) figures, the evolution of homicides varies among countries, as shown in figure 10.2.

Yet, in Nicaragua, where PAHO-OPS figures show a small rise in homicide rates, official Policía Nacional figures show a decline from 1992 to 2000, as shown in figure 10.3.

In some high-violence countries, the rise in homicide rates is far from clear. For example, according to Policía Nacional data in Colombia,

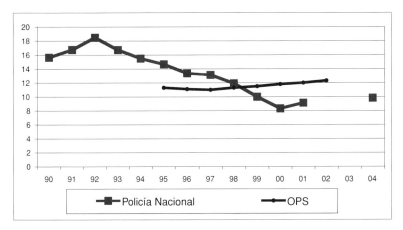

Figure 10.3 Homicide rate: Nicaragua, 1990–2004
Sources: 1990–6, Cuadra (2000); 1997–2001, Valle and Argüello (2002)

there has been a sharp and continuous drop since the 1990s, as shown in figure 10.4.[3]

In Honduras, estimates of homicide rates differ but it is not easy to say that violence is on the rise, as shown in figure 10.5.

In El Salvador, another high-violence country, victimization rates show a continuous drop, as shown in figure 10.6.

Despite this mixed picture, it is important to put the problem of violence into perspective relative to other countries. For example, the WHO estimates that the number of homicides committed with firearms in the region – between 73,000 and 90,000 a year – has reached three times the world average. Further, violence is the leading cause of death among Latin Americans between the ages of 15 and 44. The homicide rates reported above for the countries of Colombia,

---

[3] We are aware that there is a discrepancy between the reported drop in homicides in Colombia in this table and the PAHO-OPS data shown on p. 624 that suggests there has been no such drop. While we believe the Policía Nacional data tend to be reasonably reliable, we have not been able to reconcile these figures with the PAHO-OPS data where we are uncertain about methodology or reliability. Nonetheless, this illustrates our points that (a) there is a lack of good data on crime and violence in the LAC region, and (b) it is difficult to make reliable comparisons across countries or between Latin America and crime rates in other parts of the world.

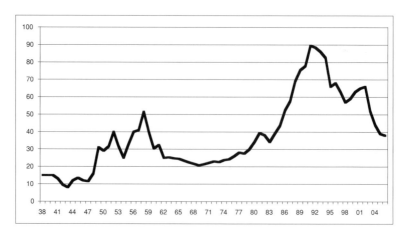

Figure 10.4 Homicide rate: Colombia, 1938–2005
Sources: Rubio (1999); Policía Nacional – DANE

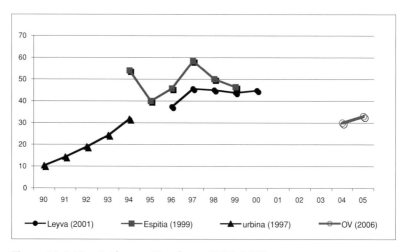

Figure 10.5 Homicide rate: Honduras, 1990–2005

El Salvador, Venezuela, and Brazil are among the highest in the world.

While it is difficult to make world-wide comparisons of homicide rates, it is even more difficult to do so with non-fatal crimes and violence due to differences in definitions, reporting rates, and survey methodologies. Partly for that reason alone, homicide is often used

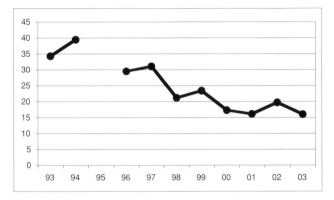

Figure 10.6 Victimization rate: El Salvador, 1993–2003
Source: IUDOP–FESPAD (2004)

as a barometer of overall crime, and hence the best crime for such international comparisons.

High variance of homicide and violence rates

More consistent with available information is the statement that crime and violence rates have a large variance in both time and space. For example, PAHO-OPS figures on homicide rates show ratios of almost 1:30, as shown in figure 10.7. It is not easy to find such large differences across countries in any other social/economic indicator in the region. In Venezuela, homicide rates were up almost 50% in less than one decade.

In urban areas, differences are just as big, as shown in figure 10.8. For example, homicide rates in Recife, or Medellín are 10 or 20 times as high as those observed in Ciudad de Panamá, Santiago, or Buenos Aires.

Even within a country, homicide rates depend greatly on local factors. As shown in figure 10.9, in Honduras, for example, the homicide rate by departamento varies from 107 in Cortés to 8 per 100,000 in Colón.

Similar differences are found in Guatemala, as shown in figure 10.10, where homicide rates range from less than 5 in Huehuetenango to more than 90 per 100,000 in Izabal.

Even in a small geographical area, or within a municipality, differences in the level of violence can be staggering. This is illustrated

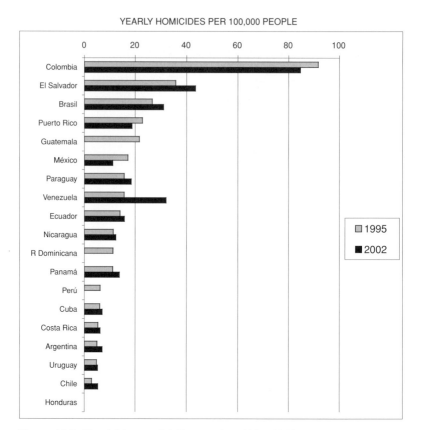

YEARLY HOMICIDES PER 100,000 PEOPLE

Figure 10.7 Homicide rate: LAC countries, 1995–2002
Source: OPS (2005)

in figure 10.11. For example, in San Pedro Sula, Honduras, homicide rates reach almost civil war levels. Yet, neighboring villages like Omoa or Santa Rita show a very small incidence of murder. Some barrios in San Pedro Sula show rates that are 4 or 8 times the city average.

Victimization rates also show some differences that do not always correspond to differences in homicide rates. Colombia, for example, has been the indisputable leader in homicides and kidnapping. However, as shown in figure 10.12, Colombia is behind Venezuela, Mexico, Ecuador, Argentina, Peru, and Brazil in terms of non-fatal victimization.

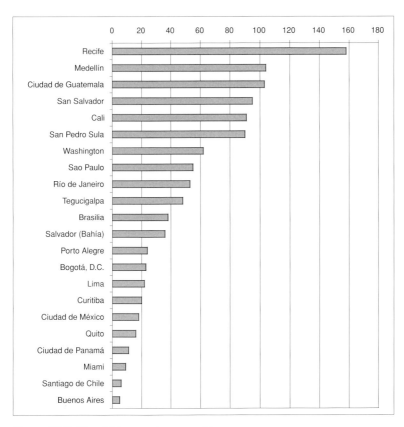

Figure 10.8 Homicide rates in some cities
Source: Mockus and Acero (2005)

Similarly, as shown in figure 10.13, victimization rates in Panama are about 25% lower than in peaceful Costa Rica, and less than half the rate of Guatemala. Yet, in figure 10.7, it shows that Panama's homicide rate is significantly higher than that of Costa Rica.

Gang membership

Gang membership in Central America shows the same pattern of high variance. As shown in figure 10.14, according to estimates reported by USAID (2006) there are 500 gang members per 100,000 people in Honduras. In El Salvador the figure is 153, in Guatemala 111, and in Nicaragua 40.

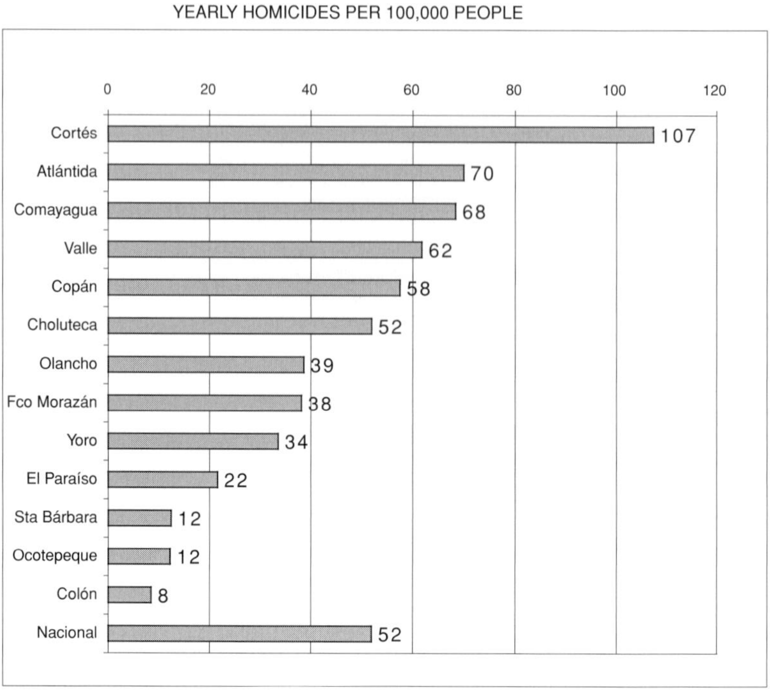

YEARLY HOMICIDES PER 100,000 PEOPLE

Figure 10.9 Homicide rates, by departamento: Honduras, 2000
Source: Leyva (2001)

According to random, representative self-report surveys, gang membership among students varies from 5.5% in Panama to less than 1% in San Pedro Sula (Rubio 2007), as shown in figure 10.15.

Estimates of gang incidence from self-report surveys are quite different from those calculated from police records. According to the former, gang membership in Nicaragua is higher than in Honduras (Tegucigalpa and San Pedro Sula). However, according to police records, gang membership in Honduras is 10 times higher than in Nicaragua. Due to the difference in data collection methodologies, it is impossible to reconcile these discrepancies.

The problem of gang violence is further complicated by the possibility that some gangs in the region might be controlled by members in the United States – often in prison themselves. Moreover, it has often been stated that deportation of gang members and other violent

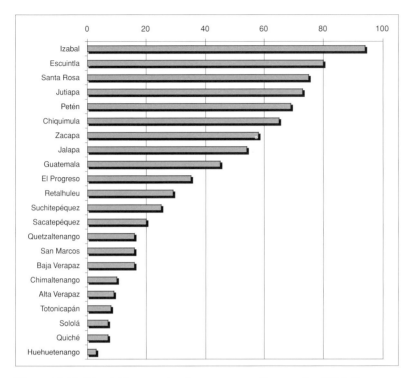

Figure 10.10 Homicide rates, by departamento: Guatemala, 1996–8
Source: BID–CIEN (2000)

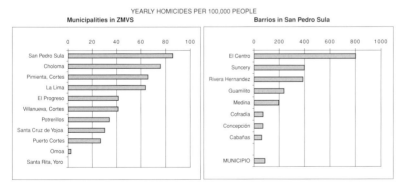

Figure 10.11 Homicide rates, Zona Metropolitana del Valle del Sulla (ZMVS): Honduras, 2000
Source: Rubio and DIEM (2003)

PROPORTION (%) OF HOUSEHOLDS VICTIMS OF CRIME

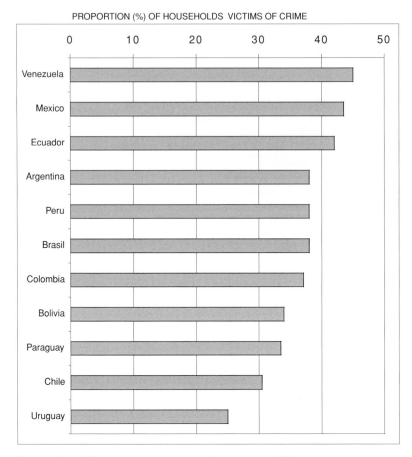

Figure 10.12 Victimization rates: South America, 1999
Source: Latinobarómetro, from Gavira and Pages (1999)

offenders from US prisons exacerbates the gang problem, as those who
return to their home countries are more likely to become active and
dangerous gang members.[4] This view has, however, been contradicted

---

[4] See for example, "Somos la mano de obra del crimen organizado: las pandillas
Centroamericanas," *El País* (Spain), 10 May, 2005; *Economist* "After the
Massacre," January 15, 2005; "Combating El Salvador's Gangs," BBC News,
March 20, 2004; "Derrière la violence des gangs du Salvador," *Le Monde
Diplomatique*, March 2004; "La lutte contre les gangs," *Le Monde*, November
26, 2005; *Boston Herald*, January 2005; *Washington Post*, July 2005.

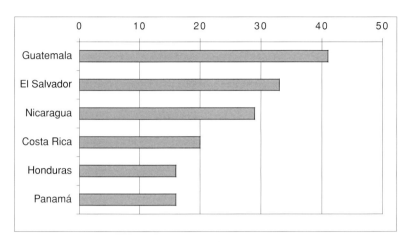

Figure 10.13 Victimization rates: Central America, 1999
Source: Barómetro Centroamericano, from BID-CIEN (2001)

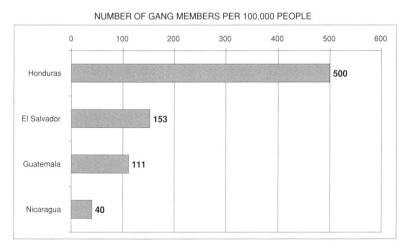

Figure 10.14 Gang membership: Central America
Sources: Gang membership, USAID (2006); Population 2005, United Nations

by several researchers (see e.g. WOLA 2006). The problem of gang violence is multi-faceted – and even if part of any ultimate solution involved dealing with these external political forces (e.g. immigration/ deportation issues), the problem of youth gangs and violence will still

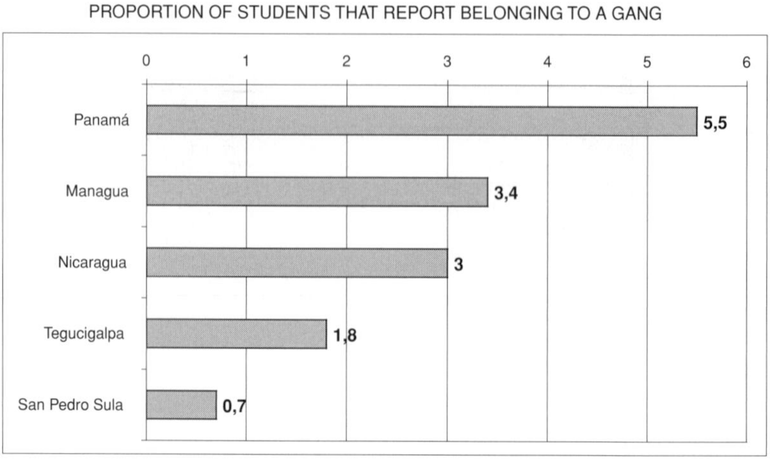

PROPORTION OF STUDENTS THAT REPORT BELONGING TO A GANG

Figure 10.15 Gang membership among students
Source: Self-report surveys, Rubio (2007)

persist. Ultimately, we focus on these internal problems of preventing youth violence in the community – as well as rehabilitation and re-entry of youth into a community once they have started down a path of crime. While international and/or other country policies might have an impact on LAC gang activity, we believe these programs, if implemented, will have a positive effect irrespective of these external factors.

Offenders mostly young men

Most LAC crime and violence seems to be committed by young men. However, it is difficult with available information to estimate the exact contribution of young men to violence, for many reasons. Since clearance rates are very low (i.e. number of arrests per committed offense), the profile of perpetrators is mostly unknown. Moreover, reporting rates are low relative to other parts of the world (Levitt and Rubio 2000).

To make matters even more difficult, clearance and reporting rates are negatively associated with the levels of violence. If crime is very high, the criminal justice system, from prosecutors to judges to prisons, simply cannot keep up. Also, as criminals get more power, victims

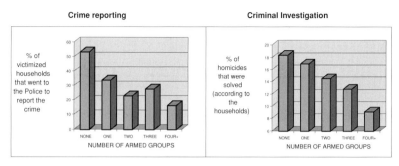

Figure 10.16 Colombia: armed groups' influence and criminal justice
Source: Cuéllar de Martínez (1997)

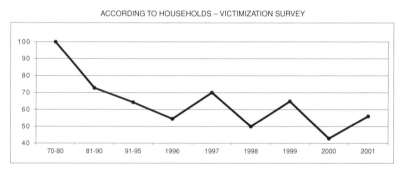

Figure 10.17 Honduras: proportion of homicides reported to the police
Source: Rubio (2002)

report less to official authorities. In Colombia, for example, a victimization survey made in regions under the influence of different illegal armed groups (e.g. guerrillas, paramilitary, narcos), showed that as violence gets worse, in terms of stronger influence of mafias, victims rely less on the official criminal justice system – which, in turn, is less able to perform (see figure 10.16).

A similar pattern over time can be deduced from data on reporting of murders to the police in Honduras. As shown in figure 10.17, as homicide rates went up during the 1980s–1990s, the proportion of cases reported to the police decreased.

This scenario of "no justice" or "private justice," instead of dealing with crime through the official criminal justice system, can be relevant

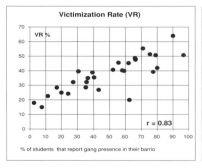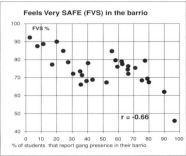

Figure 10.18 Gang incidence and security in the Barrio
Source: IADB Self-report surveys; Data by municipalities; Rubio (2007)

both in neighborhoods where organized crime and/or gangs have political control or where paramilitaries regain it.

Some indirect evidence of the role that young people play in crime
and violence is the strong relationship between gang presence in the
barrios and insecurity – both victimization rates and feelings of safety
among students, as shown in figure 10.18.

In spite of the difficulty of assessing the share of young people in
crime and violence, two facts seem corroborated by different kinds
of evidence – testimonial, police records, victimization and self-report
surveys: (i) youth gangs work closely with organized crime and (ii)
among young people, the most serious violence is committed by gang
members.

A random household victimization survey done in Honduras asked
respondents to rate the influence of both maras (gangs in Central
America) and organized crime. Respondents were asked to rate maras
and organized crime on a seven-point scale from "irrelevant" to "very
highly relevant." As shown in figure 10.19, both of these phenomena
are closely related.

The same type of scenario has been found in Cali and Medellín in
Colombia.

The IADB self-report surveys done in Central America show that
gang membership significantly increases the probability of a young
person committing an offense (Rubio 2007). The difference between
the frequency of offending among gang members and students varies
across the sample, but is always higher than 50%, as shown in

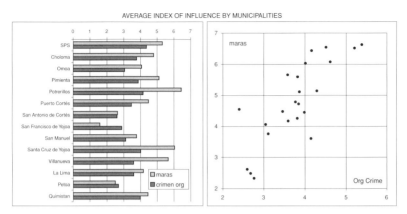

Figure 10.19 Maras (gangs) and organized crime: Honduras
Source: Rubio (2002)

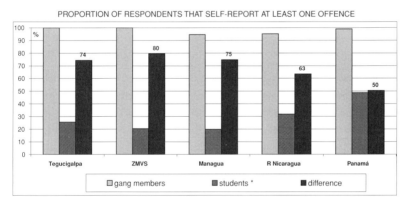

Figure 10.20 Frequency of offending: gang members and students
Note: *Students that do not belong to a gang
Source: IADB Self-report surveys; Rubio (2007)

figure 10.20. It seems to be higher where gangs are highly organized. Such is the case of the maras in Honduras (Tegucigalpa and
ZMVS).

For serious offenses, such as homicides, the difference between gang
members and students is larger. Gangs almost monopolize extreme violence among young people. As shown in figure 10.21, the incidence of

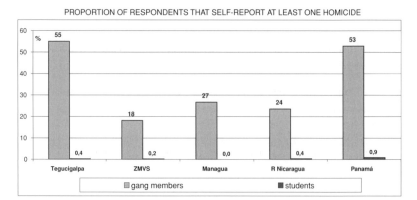

Figure 10.21 Self-reporting of homicide: gang members and students
Notes: Includes serious injuries.
Source: IADB Self-report surveys; Rubio (2007)

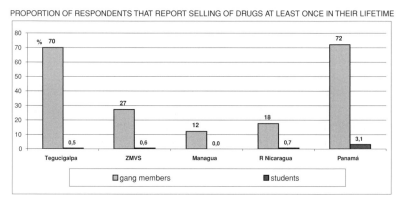

Figure 10.22 Self-reporting of selling of drugs: gang members and students
Source: IADB Self-report surveys; Rubio (2007)

homicide among gang members can be quite high: 55% in Tegucigalpa and 53% in Panama.

There is a lot of evidence that relates high homicide rates with illegal markets, especially with drugs (see Levitt and Rubio 2000), so it does not come as a surprise that high self-report of homicides is closely associated with drug-selling among young people. This kind of offense is also concentrated in gang members, as shown in figure 10.22.

Risk factors for juvenile delinquency and gang membership

According to a USAID report on gang violence in five countries studied in Latin America (El Salvador, Guatemala, Honduras, Mexico, and Nicaragua):

The root causes of gang activity in the five countries are similar – marginalized urban areas with minimal access to basic services, high levels of youth unemployment compounded by insufficient access to educational opportunities, overwhelmed and ineffective justice systems, easy access to arms and an illicit economy, dysfunctional families, and high levels of intra-familial violence. A demographic youth bulge has created a cohort of youth without jobs, decent education, or realistic expectations of employment. The four Central American countries have a combined total population of nearly 30 million people and approximately 60% are under 25 years old. The Mexican states assessed (Chiapas, Baja California, Chihuahua, and Tamulipas) have an estimated population of 9.6 million people and nearly 50% are under 25 years old. Underemployment and unemployment ranges from less than 20% in Guatemala, to about 25% in Mexico, to over 50% in the remaining three countries. Although many of these youth represent untapped economic potential for their countries, they face a much bleaker future than their parents did at the same age. (USAID 2006: 17)

The above study correctly paints LAC violence and gang member-ship as a complex social issue. While it might be "common knowledge" to many that poverty itself is a strong risk factor for gang membership and juvenile delinquency, the facts suggest that this finding may be partially a consequence of sampling bias error. Normally, gang stud-ies have limited their field work to low-income barrios. In the IADB self-report surveys (Rubio 2007), a random sample of students, repre-sentative of all income strata, was taken. Also, a non-random sample of school drop-outs was taken, looking for gang members to answer the same questionnaire that was applied to the control group of students.

As shown in figure 10.23, the distribution of the perceived social class among students was, as expected, a normal distribution. Among school drop-outs, a higher percentage of respondents perceived them-selves as belonging to the lower strata.

These distributions are very similar among gang members, as shown in figure 10.24. For those that are still in school, the social class dis-tribution is almost an inverted U-shaped normal distribution. Only among gang members that dropped out of school is there a higher participation of lower strata.

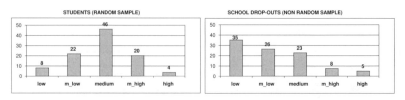

Figure 10.23 Distribution of perceived social class: students and school drop-outs
Source: IADB Self-report surveys

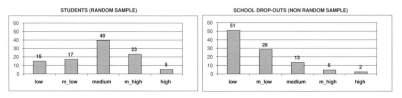

Figure 10.24 Distribution of perceived social class among gang members
Source: IADB Self-report surveys

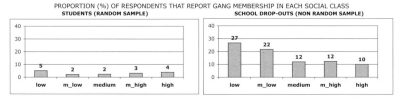

Figure 10.25 Gang membership and social class: students and school drop-outs
Source: IADB Self-report surveys

So it is not surprising to find that, among students, gang membership is almost independent of social class. Only in the non-random sample of school drop-outs can one find a negative relationship between social class and gang membership. Similar results are found using other variables of economic background (see figure 10.25).

So poverty does not look like a necessary condition for gang membership. Lower-income gangs have gotten more attention, probably because they are more visible in the streets. Dropping-out of school, which is likely related to poverty, looks like a stronger risk factor than poverty by itself. However, it is not possible to quantify the impact

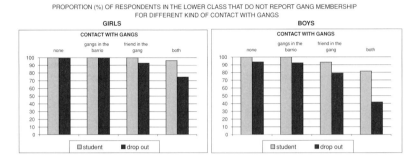

Figure 10.26 Poor young people out of gangs
Source: IADB self-report surveys

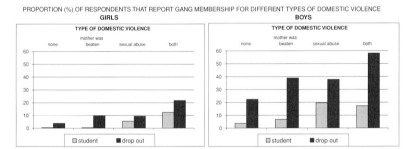

Figure 10.27 Gang membership and domestic violence
Source: IADB Self-report surveys

of dropping-out on gang membership. The sampling method used for these surveys surely over-emphasizes its effect.

On the other hand, poverty is far from being a sufficient condition for gang membership. The vast majority of the poorest students in the sample do not belong to a gang even if there is one in the barrio. As shown in figure 10.26, even when poor young boys live in a barrio with gangs and report having friends in a gang, a high proportion of them (80%) are not gang members. However, a combination of poverty and dropping-out of school does appear to be a high risk factor for gang membership.

Finally, domestic violence has been repeatedly identified as a risk factor of juvenile violence. Self-report surveys also corroborate this claim, as shown in figure 10.27.

Domestic violence rates are high

While the data are based on a few surveys in selected locations, there appears to be ample evidence that domestic violence rates are high in the LAC region. As reported in UNICEF (2000), for example, 11% of women surveyed in a representative sample in Santiago reported at least one episode of "severe violence" by a partner, while an additional 15% reported at least one episode of less severe violence. In a Colombian survey of over 6,000 women, 19% reported being physically assaulted by their partner at some point in their lifetime. In a 1997 survey of 650 women in Guadalajara 30% reported at least one episode of physical violence by a partner, with 13% reporting physical violence during the past year. Finally, in a 1996 representative sample of women in León 52% reported being physically abused by a partner at least once, with 27% reporting being abused within the past year.

While these rates are high, there are no systematic data available by which we could judge the relative severity of the LAC domestic violence problem compared to elsewhere.[5] In fact, even when there is evidence of an increase in domestic violence, it is oftentimes unclear whether that represents more domestic violence or more reporting. Nevertheless, there is evidence that the costs of domestic violence are high. Domestic violence not only takes the form of physical or sexual abuse against a partner, but also commonly against children. Even when children are not direct victims, they oftentimes become indirect victims upon witnessing their parent's abuse.

The consequences of domestic violence are varied, and can be extremely harmful and costly to society. In addition to physical harm, medical costs, and lost wages, victims often suffer severe psychological harm. However, there is little documentation of the social costs of domestic violence in the region. Further, the only evidence to date is correlational – not causal. One study of more than 300 women each in Santiago and Managua found strong evidence that victims of domestic violence had significantly lower earnings than women who were not victimized – with potential losses in productivity being as high as 2% of GDP (Morrison and Orlando 1999: 66). However, findings were mixed with respect to the impact on employment and healthcare utilization. A study by Ascencio (1999) in Mexico City included data from vital statistics from 1990–5, along with death certificates on cause of

---

[5] Morrison's alternative view provides some more recent evidence on the extent of the problem in Brazil and Peru.

death, files on autopsies, and surveys with victims of non-fatal domestic violence. Ascencio estimated the total (DALYs) lost from domestic violence including number of days of life lost, plus non-fatal losses of reproductive health, sexually transmitted diseases, and psychological health.[6] He estimated that DALYs lost in Mexico City in 1995 totaled 27,200 – 53% from physical injury and 47% from non-physical injury. In fact, this totaled 8.1% of total DALY losses for women in Mexico City – the third leading cause of lost DALYs behind diabetes and birth-related disorders. Particularly hard hit were young girls under the age of 5 and women of childbearing years.

Domestic violence – especially sexual abuse of children – has been found to be a significant risk factor for gang membership, youth crime, and prostitution in Central America (Rubio 2007). Thus, the value of preventing child abuse has important positive spillovers beyond the benefits to the child's immediate welfare.

Studies outside the region also find domestic violence to be a huge share of the problem of overall violence. For example, a US study concluded that the cost of child abuse and domestic violence accounted for nearly 30% of the cost of crime (Miller, Cohen, and Wiersema 1996). Given the fact that domestic violence rates appear to be as high if not higher in the LAC region, we would not be surprised to find similar results.

2 Proposed solutions

The most comprehensive review of the evidence on "what works" in criminal justice and prevention programs was published in 1997 by Sherman *et al.*, following the commission of a comprehensive study by the US Congress. While the literature has progressed beyond this seminal work, the basic findings are largely intact, and both our assessment of proposed solutions and subsequent OBA are based on the most current data available at the time we conducted our study in early 2007.[7]

---

[6] The DALY is a measure of the health gap that includes both the number of life years lost due to premature death as well as the number of years in which an individual is in a poor health state. For a complete definition, see WHO, www.who.int/healthinfo/boddaly/en/index.html.

[7] Morrison's alternative view mentions several more recent studies, some of which we had considered but others that were not even available at the time that we were working on this chapter. For example, he cites systematic reviews

Sherman *et al*. (1997, 1998) undertook a very comprehensive review of the existing literature on US crime prevention program effectiveness. They examined hundreds of studies to determine the strength of scientific evidence and whether or not one could draw conclusions about the effectiveness of individual programs. The study included:

- **Community-based crime prevention** – such as community organizing and mobilization against crime, gang violence prevention, community-based mentoring, and after-school recreation programs.
- **Family-based crime prevention** – such as home visitation of families with infants, pre-school education programs involving parents, parent training for managing troublesome children, and programs for preventing family violence, including battered women's shelters and criminal justice programs.
- **School-based prevention** – such as Drug Abuse Resistance Education (DARE, a series of classroom lessons taught by police), peer-group counseling, gang resistance education, anti-bullying campaigns, law-related education, and programs to improve school discipline and social problem-solving skills.
- **Labor markets and crime risk factors** – such as training and placement programs for unemployed people, including Job Corps, vocational training for prison inmates, diversion from court to employment placements, and transportation of inner-city residents to suburban jobs.
- **Preventing crime at specific locations** – the effectiveness of practices to block opportunities for crime at specific locations such as stores, apartment buildings, and parking lots, including such measures as cameras, lighting, guards, and alarms.
- **Policing for crime prevention** – such police practices as directed patrols in crime "hot spots," rapid response time, foot patrols, neighborhood watch, drug raids, and domestic violence crackdowns.
- **Criminal justice and crime prevention** – such as prisoner rehabilitation, mandatory drug treatment for convicts, boot camps, shock incarceration, intensively supervised parole and probation, home confinement and electronic monitoring.

and meta-analyses – one on "hot spots" and one on "cognitive behavioral therapy," both of which were published by the Campbell Collaboration later in 2007. This illustrates the fact that the state-of-the-art in "what works" and "what pays" for criminal justice programs is still in its infancy.

Sherman *et al.* (1997) reviewed each study and classified the strength of the evidence based on the scientific rigor in conducting the study. Unfortunately, they concluded that:

Very few operational crime prevention programs have been evaluated using scientifically recognized standards and methodologies, including repeated tests under similar and different social settings. Based on a review of more than 500 prevention program evaluations meeting minimum scientific standards, the report concludes that there is minimally adequate evidence to establish a provisional list of what works, what doesn't, and what's promising. (Sherman *et al.* 1998)

Unfortunately, most of the evidence that Sherman *et al.* found was in the United States and to a lesser extent in the United Kingdom or Europe. There is even less systematic information available in the LAC region, as programs are often carried out by different agencies and NGOs, with no coordination at all. The few programs that have been evaluated or reported on as being promising have not had the benefit of independent reviews and thus should not be considered as reliable evidence. Indeed, it is not easy to find even a rough inventory of what is being done.

From their extensive analysis, Sherman and his colleagues drew numerous conclusions about what program works, what doesn't and what's promising. They developed a consistent set of criteria to evaluate the scientific rigor of each study. Studies were rated based primarily on three factors:

- Control of other variables in the analysis that might have been the true causes of any observed connection between a program and crime.
- Measurement error from such things as subjects lost over time or low interview-response rates.
- Statistical power to detect program effects (including sample size, base rate of crime, and other factors affecting the likelihood of the study detecting a true difference not due to chance).

Before declaring that a program "works" or "doesn't work," they required two or more evaluations of a reasonably high quality, along with the preponderance of other evidence. In some cases, where they had only one such study but significant other evidence pointing in that direction, they determined that a program "looks promising."

Sherman *et al.* (1997) did not attempt to quantify cost-benefit ratios, however, and instead focused on which programs had adequate scientific evidence to determine that they "worked." More recently, Steve Aos and his colleagues at the Washington State Institute for Public Policy (WSIPP) have systematically reviewed the literature and conducted a meta-analysis of program effectiveness studies (see e.g. Aos *et al.* 2004, 2005; Aos, Millar, and Drake 2006). They have largely followed and updated the work of Sherman *et al.* (1997, 1998) as well as augmenting this information with additional data. Not only have they updated Sherman's inventory of effectiveness studies, they have gone beyond it by modeling the costs and benefits of each program. While one might disagree with certain assumptions that had to be made throughout the process, it is a very transparent approach and researchers can both replicate and conduct sensitivity analyses with their model. More importantly, it provides a consistent framework from which policymakers can compare programs that all have the same basic goal of reducing crime. For purposes of this chapter, the Aos methodology is especially useful since we have been able to directly compare the costs and benefits of a myriad of programs designed to reduce crime and violence.

Based on the analysis conducted by Aos and our review of the literature, the following four programs are considered to have the highest BCR and to be most appropriate to the identified problems and potential solutions for the Latin American context.

Solution 1: comprehensive programs targeting at-risk mothers and young children under age 5

There is growing evidence that behaviors learned and reinforced in early childhood can have significant consequences throughout an individual's lifetime. Accordingly, certain programs targeting the youngest children who are at risk of child abuse, neglect, and lack of proper social skills reinforcement have been shown to reduce subsequent juvenile and adult offending behavior. These programs often have additional benefits such as improved high-school graduation rates, reduced substance abuse, and other positive social outcomes. Two programs appear to be particularly beneficial and cost-effective. The first targets low-income, pregnant women and very young children from birth to age 2, while the second program targets very young children age 3 and 4.

The program targeting young mothers was developed in Colorado and tested through a randomized control study involving 735 pregnant women (Olds *et al.* 2002). The program involves approximately 27 home visits by trained nurses (in the trial, there were an average of 6.5 visits during pregnancy and 21 visits from birth through age 2). In addition to a control group, one-third of participants received visits by paraprofessionals. Only those who received visits by nurses, however, showed any significant effects. Among the benefits noted were better pre-natal care (e.g. reduced smoking or other risky behavior, more use of healthcare services, etc.), fewer subsequent pregnancies, improved educational achievement and workforce participation by the mothers, better mother–infant interactions, improved family home environment, as well as improvements in the child's emotional and developmental wellbeing (e.g. language and mental development, temperament, behavioral problems). This program is particularly well suited to the LAC region, given the very high rate of low-income single-mother households – the group targeted by the program.

The second program picks up where the first one ends, by focusing on very early childhood education for children in low-income families. Well-known examples of such US programs include pilot/demonstration programs such as the Perry Preschool Project (see Barnett 1993) and large-scale programs such as Project Head Start. Aos *et al.* (2004) conduct a meta-analysis of over 50 studies of these programs. Although their features vary, and this is not the venue to analyze them in detail, all of them target low-income 3- and 4-year-old children and bring them into a classroom setting. The benefits of these programs include lower incidence of child abuse and neglect, higher graduation rates from high school, and lower delinquency and long-term adult offending behavior.

Solution 2: comprehensive program to deal with youth and gang violence

While not all gangs are the same in terms of their root causes, extent of violence, age ranges, etc., all gangs recruit from the pool of available youth in a community. This is particularly true in the LAC region, since the high-school drop-out rate is so high and there is a large pool of youth from which gangs can recruit. One obvious solution beyond the scope of this chapter is to increase the high-school graduation rate – something that will have numerous benefits including lowered crime rates. However, since crime reduction is a secondary byproduct of such a program, and education is the subject of chapter 2, we do not focus on that solution. Clearly, however, any successful program that increases graduation rates will have some crime-reduction benefits.

Aside from educational programs, several US model programs have been found to significantly reduce gang violence and membership. These programs are coordinated inter-agency efforts that involve considerable integration of activities across police, courts, schools, social service agencies, and community groups. Perhaps the most well-known and successful model was instituted in Boston (see Piehl, Kennedy, and Braga 2000). The scope of the Boston youth gang project was all-encompassing, with participation by the local police, state juvenile justice correction facilities, probation and parole agencies, the district attorney, the US Bureau of Alcohol, Tobacco, and Firearms, as well as numerous community and clergy groups.

As described in Piehl, Kennedy, and Braga (2001), Boston used a two-pronged approach – starting with a crackdown on trafficking of illegal handguns to youth. The second prong was to communicate and confront gang members directly. Formal meetings were held in community centers, juvenile detention centers for those under supervision, and elsewhere between police, community leaders, and gang members. The message was clearly communicated that gang violence would not be tolerated and that there would be a severe crackdown. This crackdown would focus on the worst offenders, gang leaders, etc. At the same time, there would be a positive offer of assistance to others who were not the most violent offenders – job training assistance and other social services. A group of clergy and other community workers made themselves available to work with these youth. This approach appears to have provided an 'out' for many youth who were on the verge of becoming more severe offenders.

While the details of each program vary, and Boston's approach might not be applicable to all cities (e.g. the focus on the availability of illegal handguns to youth would not be appropriate if guns were not widely available in one jurisdiction), there are several important lessons to be learned from the Boston experience. First, there is value in implementing a community-based problem-solving approach. In Boston, a working group was established consisting of members of all agencies interested in youth violence. This working group met regularly to assess the nature of the youth gang problem in their community as well as to coordinate a response that was tailored to their city's needs. Second, it is clear that the multi-pronged approach, whereby there is both a carrot and stick, works best. Cracking down on gang violence will not solve the underlying problems of troubled youth looking for an outlet. Thus, a successful program must "get tough" on the worst offenders in conjunction with a program designed to rehabilitate and encourage youth to go down a better path. The comprehensive approach we recommend has also been reviewed and advocated in a USAID report on gangs in Central America and Mexico (USAID 2006).

While we believe a comprehensive, community-based, gang violence program might be appropriate in some communities, it will not work everywhere – and could in some cases be counterproductive. Any program needs to be tailored to local needs – taking into account the relationship between schools, community leaders, and governmental institutions. In fact, this point is consistent with the Boston approach, whereby there was ongoing dialogue among community members about the source of problems and the best possible solutions. Moreover, as researchers on gang violence have cautioned, sometimes drawing attention to gangs only reinforces their existence and legitimacy in the minds of local community youth – in other words, it can make matters worse. This might be a particular problem in some communities where gangs serve as protection for many community members.

Beyond the comprehensive gang-control model described above, according to Sherman *et al.* (1997), the following specific treatment programs have been shown to "work":

- Various comprehensive, school-based programs have been shown to reduce delinquency and crime, such as: building capacity to initiate and sustain innovation; and communicating norms about behavior through rules, reinforcement of positive behavior, and school-wide initiatives (such as antibullying campaign). (We note that in the LAC context, even more basic needs to maintain school building infrastructure could be of value in providing a safe, secure, school environment.)

- Social competency skills curriculums, such as Life Skills Training – which teach over a long period of time such skills as stress management, problem-solving, self-control, and emotional intelligence – reduce delinquency and substance abuse.
- Training or coaching in thinking skills for high-risk youth – using behavior modification techniques or rewards and punishments – reduces substance abuse.
- "Schools within schools" programs such as Student Training Through Urban Strategies (STATUS) – that group students into smaller units for more supportive interaction or flexibility in instruction – have reduced drug abuse and delinquency.
- Job Corps, an intensive residential training program for at-risk youth, in one study reduced felony arrests for four years after participants left the program and increased earnings and educational attainment, although it also produced higher rates of misdemeanor and traffic arrests.
- Family therapy and parent training about delinquent and at-risk pre-adolescents reduce risk factors for delinquency.
- Rehabilitation programs for juvenile offenders using treatments appropriate to their risk factors reduce their repeat offending rates.

In addition, however, there were other programs shown to be "promising" based on preliminary evidence and theory, but that did not pass the strict tests of Sherman *et al.* In many cases, that meant there was only one study of sufficient quality as well as additional collaborative evidence, but not enough to pass their test of "what works." Some of the programs appear to have a positive BCR based on the further (and more updated) analysis by Aos *et al.* (2004) and Aos, Millar, and Drake (2006). In particular, Sherman *et al.* (1997) found the following programs to be "promising":

- Community-based mentoring by Big Brothers/Big Sisters of America substantially reduced drug abuse in one experiment, although evaluations of other programs with mentoring as a major component did not.
- Community-based after-school recreation programs may reduce juvenile crime in the areas immediately around the recreation center. Similar programs based in schools, however, have failed to prevent crime.

- Intensive supervision and aftercare of minor juvenile offenders, primarily status offenders like runaways or truants, reduced future offending. The finding held true for first offenders but not for those with prior delinquency in one experiment.
- Intensive supervision and aftercare of serious juvenile offenders in a Pennsylvania program reduced rearrests compared to putting offenders on probation.
- Gang offender monitoring by community workers and probation and police officers can reduce gang violence, although similar programs can increase gang crime if they increase gang cohesion.

In analyzing the various programs that have been proposed and evaluated, we took into account the best available research on costs and benefits, as well as how the existing programs might be adapted to the LAC situation. For example, certain school-based programs might be particularly difficult to implement in a decentralized manner due to lack of adequate teaching staff. Pilot programs, centralized training and staff, and other such modifications would likely be needed to successfully implement many of these programs in the LAC context.

We focus on several programs that target juvenile offenders that have been found to significantly reduce recidivism and other socially costly outcomes such as high-school drop-out and drug abuse. These programs all involve some form of intensive monitoring/supervision of the offender and include involvement by the family and/or community in a meaningful way. Based on our review of the literature, we have chosen three such programs as models by which a comprehensive program could be developed and adopted in conjunction with the crackdown on gang violence mentioned above. These programs have been validated in numerous studies and have also been analyzed in the meta-analysis conducted by Aos *et al.* (2004). Of course, implementing these programs in the LAC region would likely require some amount of tailoring and modifications – and would best be approached slowly through pilot testing.

One program, called "Functional Family Therapy," involves a systematic family intervention with regular visits by a trained counselor (see www.fftinc.com). This program has been used successfully with at-risk youth ages 10–18 with alcohol, drug abuse, and/or delinquency issues. In some cases, the program is administered through a juvenile court, but that is not a necessary component. The second program,

"Adolescent Diversion Project," involves a diversion from juvenile court (usually for first-time offenders) whereby a youth is prevented from being labeled a delinquent (see Smith *et al.* 2004). Youth are matched up with trained mentors who work with them on behavioral changes. While most LAC criminal justice systems already have something like this in place, where first-time offenders are diverted from the courts, the program we advocate requires strong involvement by trained mentors and adequate monitoring. The risk of not doing this well – i.e. simply diverting first-time offenders into an alternative with some form of minimal supervision – is that this could make matters worse by "identifying" good prospects for gang recruitment.

The third program, called "Aggression Replacement Training," targets aggressive adolescents and children, and teaches them pro-social behaviors, anger control, and moral reasoning (see www.uscart.org/new.htm). In both this case and the functional family therapy program, there will be a need to build the infrastructure for identifying participants in addition to the actual program itself. In other words, there needs to be adequate training and awareness by school officials, for example, to identify at-risk children who could benefit from these programs. Then, the students can be treated by trained professionals – whether based in the schools or elsewhere in the community.

While other programs have been found promising, we have chosen those with the highest BCR and that are most likely to fit in to the needs and abilities of the LAC context. The only program Aos *et al.* (2004) identified targeting youth violence with a higher BCR is a set of programs they call "interagency coordination programs." These programs are "wrap-around" efforts to coordinate existing community services on an individualized basis for juvenile offenders. Given the dearth of existing social service programs in most LAC communities, we do not believe this program is widely applicable in our context. Thus, we have not included it in our list of recommended solutions.

An important issue we believe worth mentioning in the context of youth violence is that "where" attention and resources are placed might be as important as "what" programs are instituted. We note that in most cases resources have flowed to the worst areas and the highest-risk youth – with virtually no chance of success. This is problematic, for two reasons. First, in some areas, gang control and violence is so pervasive that nothing short of military-type action will likely have an effect. Tackling individual youth issues one-on-one might not only be "too little too late" for these areas, it is much less likely to be effective even on an individual basis in such a "war zone." Second, we note that targeting resources to the very worst areas while ignoring those where there are strong community ties and the rule of law exists, sends the wrong signals about the availability of government assistance. We believe that a higher success rate and higher BCR could be obtained by better targeting resources into *communities where the likelihood of success is highest* – which, unfortunately, might not always be those communities with the most "need."

Solution 3: comprehensive prison treatment and reintegration program

Offenders who are released from prison have extremely high recidivism rates. Thus, programs that target these offenders while in prison can have a high payoff if they are successful in reducing recidivism. Three such programs – if implemented correctly – have been shown to reduce recidivism: (a) drug treatment, (b) educational and vocational programs, and (c) cognitive behavioral therapy. While these programs have been found to be effective, additional benefits may accrue when similar (and additional) programs extend to offenders upon their release from prison – to assist in their reintegration into society.

While reintegration programs are relatively new, a comprehensive study (including a CBA) was conducted of a successful program in Baltimore, Maryland. According to Roman *et al.* (2007: 1–2), the Reentry Partnership Initiative (REP):

was designed as a community–justice partnership in which public agencies and community based organizations work together to provide continuous case management as prisoners transition into the community. The REP model addresses prisoner reentry needs at three levels: *individual, community,* and *systems.* At the individual level, returning prisoners are matched to social and medical services tailored to their needs and designed to help them successfully reintegrate into the community. Services are delivered by community-based organizations, which also seek to strengthen returning prisoners' support networks, enhance informal social controls within the target neighborhoods, improve community service availability and accessibility, and increase offender accountability. At the systems level, REP brings together corrections agencies and community service providers to coordinate services, share information, and ensure continuous case management during the transition to the community.

In the Baltimore case, the REP program was managed by an independent non-profit agency – first The Enterprise Foundation, and later Catholic Charities. Thus, the program was a coordinated, community-wide partnership. In a quasi-random experimental design where program participants were matched with non-participants, Roman *et al.* (2007) found a small reduction in the number of rearrests – although the estimated crime reduction from program participation also tended to be for the most severe crimes. It is particularly difficult to evaluate these programs because oftentimes the services that are provided to offenders out of prison are also available in the community. Hence, the added value is in the improved coordination of services and presumably increased offender participation rates in the right programs targeted to their needs. While the evidence is not overwhelming, these programs are not very expensive, and the evidence to date suggests they are well worth the cost. Of course, they must be coupled with the actual services.

Thus, our proposed solution involves both well-designed treatment programs in prison and out of prison, as well as a coordinated approach to identify appropriate service needs and to offer a supportive re-entry program once the offender is released. While we do not suggest that these ideas are necessarily "new" in the LAC region – and, indeed, there are many reintegration programs, we are unaware of any systematic review of the effectiveness of these programs and are certain that much can be learned from the best practices we have identified in this chapter. Thus, we suggest as a starting point such a review of existing programs with an eye towards adding to – or replacing them – with the solutions identified here.

Solution 4: domestic violence prevention and control

While it is one thing to identify domestic violence as an important problem, finding solutions is another matter. Among the factors most closely linked (through correlations – not necessarily a causal connection) to domestic violence are poverty, unemployment, and the lack of a social support network (Gonzales de Olart and Llosa 1999: 45).

Cultural factors are also key. As a study by UNICEF (2000: 13–14) noted:

Domestic violence is a complex problem and there is no one strategy that will work in all situations. To begin with, violence may take place within very different social contexts, and the degree to which it is sanctioned by a community will naturally influence the kind of strategy needed.

Considering the interconnections between the factors responsible for domestic violence – gender dynamics of power, culture and economics – strategies and interventions should be designed within a comprehensive and integrated approach. A multi-layered strategy that address[es] the structural causes of violence against women while providing immediate services to victim-survivors ensures sustainability and is the only strategy that has the potential to eliminate this scourge.

Key areas for intervention include:

- advocacy and awareness-raising
- education for building a culture of non-violence
- training
- resource development
- direct service provision to victim survivors and perpetrators
- networking and community mobilization
- direct intervention to help victim survivors rebuild their lives
- legal reform
- data collection and analysis
- early identification of 'at-risk' families, communities, groups, and individuals.

According to Sherman *et al.* (1997), two programs have been shown to "work" in reducing domestic violence. First, they found that the same programs we identified in Solution 1 – programs targeting at-risk mothers beginning with pre-natal through age 2 – were beneficial in reducing child abuse and neglect. Second, they note that a program to train police officers to arrest domestic violence offenders has been shown to be effective in reducing both domestic violence incidents by the perpetrator in the future, and also in the neighborhood where the offender lived. However, the evidence on this second program is of some concern, as it was found to be effective only with perpetrators who were employed and in neighborhoods where most households had an employed adult. The reasons why these findings hold – and whether they would hold in another culture outside the United States – are not known. In addition, Sherman *et al.* noted that one "promising" program was a battered women's shelter, which had been found to reduce repeat victimization – at least in the short term (six weeks).

While the 2000 UNICEF report calls for many other pieces of the puzzle – including programs to raise awareness, education and training, and legal reforms, we are unaware of any systematic studies of the effectiveness of such programs. Larraín (1999) reviews existing programs across the LAC region – including victim hot lines, battered shelters, special police units, and education programs. While many of these programs seemed to have been beneficial, we are unaware of any attempts to systematically document their effectiveness, or to assess costs and benefits. Nonetheless, it does make sense to work on these issues as part of a comprehensive solution that will have a long-term impact. While we have proposed some solutions, these might be duplicative of efforts already underway in some areas. Thus, it would be useful to conduct a more systematic review of existing programs in the region and to focus attention where effective programs are not yet in place. It would also seem worthwhile to study the effect of domestic violence and child abuse programs on youth crime and gang membership.

3 CBA

Valuing benefits of crime-reduction programs

Programs that are designed to reduce crime may do so in two basic ways: (1) by changing the situational conditions under which crime occurs – such as increased lighting in a parking lot, installing security fences, or removing a child from a home where they have been abused, or (2) by affecting the behavior of potential offenders – such as drug treatment programs designed to rehabilitate juvenile offenders, or increasing penalties in order to deter potential offenders from committing crimes. Similarly, we can measure the benefits of these programs either based on the reduced number of incidents occurring in these specific situations, or on the number of offenses that have been deterred. In the first case, we are not targeting individual offenders and we might instead measure the number of generic crimes that have been averted. In the second case, however, we are directly affecting individuals, and instead of counting generic crimes we are interested in crimes that those particular individuals would have otherwise committed. This suggests that there are two approaches that one could use to measure the benefits of crime control policies. In the first approach, we measure crimes. In the second approach, we measure criminal careers.

We now briefly review the literature on the "cost of crime" to illustrate the magnitude of the problem. We turn first to the measurement of the cost of individual crimes.

The costs of crime/benefits of crime reduction

The benefits of crime reduction are difficult to quantify – and even the most inclusive estimates inevitably leave out significant cost components. The most comprehensive estimates of the cost of crime (and hence benefits of crime reduction) have been made in the United States (Miller, Cohen, and Wiersema 1996; Cohen *et al.* 2004) and the United Kingdom (Dubourg, Hamed, and Thorns 2005). Briefly, the costs of crime (see Cohen 2005) include:

(1) Victimization costs (including OOP losses, pain, suffering, and lost quality of life from victimization). This could be direct costs to victims but also to their families who might suffer both economically and psychologically.
(2) Precautionary expenditures by individuals and businesses.
(3) Avoidance behaviors by individuals.
(4) Criminal justice system.
(5) Government prevention and rehabilitation programs.
(6) Residual effects on individuals (e.g. fear).
(7) Residual effects on community (e.g. loss of tax base).
(8) Over-deterrence (e.g. activities not undertaken by innocent people for fear of being accused of criminal activity).[8]
(9) "Justice" costs (e.g. costs incurred solely to ensure that "justice" is done).
(10) Burden imposed on incarcerated offenders and their families.

Building up these cost estimates requires a tremendous amount of data, assumptions, and varied methodologies. At best, the various estimates are "ballpark" and under-estimate the true social costs of crime,

---

[8] We note that policies of one country – such as tough immigration policies for fear of bringing in foreign criminals – might be an example of how over-deterrence in one country can affect the population (and crime) in another.

as various components are inevitably left out due to lack of data or appropriate methodologies. However, the "state-of-the-art" in estimating the costs of crime has developed to the point where it is being used by policymakers. For example, the US National Institute of Justice requires virtually all program evaluations to include a CBA in their final report. The legislature in the State of Washington has required a systematic review of all existing government programs designed to prevent or control crime – with the understanding that programs not found to be cost-beneficial will be replaced by those where benefits are estimated to exceed costs. The UK Home Office engages in an ongoing research program to estimate the costs of crime. In fact, there is beginning to be some consistency across estimates, and this growing body of literature has developed to the point where the European Commission has funded a two-year study to identify best practices and promote a common methodology for estimating the cost of crime.[9] Thus, "cost of crime" estimates have developed to the point where policy analysts are beginning to feel comfortable using them to compare the effectiveness of programs and to conduct CBAs.

One of the more difficult costs of crime to estimate is the loss to communities when there is a significant crime problem. Most of the effort to date has gone into estimating the cost of victimization, the criminal justice system, and to some extent precautionary expenditures (e.g. burglar alarms). More difficult, and thus often overlooked, are costs to the public at large – such as fear of crime and losses to the community. However, some methodologies have taken a 'top-down' approach that in theory encompasses all costs by using surveys of the public's WTP to reduce crime (Cohen *et al.* 2004; Cohen 2008). Many of these non-victim costs are likely to be non-linear – and in fact, they are expected to increase at the margin (not decrease, as many other 'costs' are assumed to in economics). For example, if crime is very low and people are unafraid to walk in the park at night, there are likely to be many people in the park and the risk of crime may even be tempered by the fact that many people are walking around and thus deter criminals at very little cost. Yet, if crime is very high, few people will venture out at night and the risk of walking alone in a park

[9] The program, entitled, "Mainstreaming Methodology for the Estimation of the Costs of Crime," is being managed by the Centre for Criminal Justice Economics and Policy, University of York. Professor Cohen is a member of the research team on that project. See www.york.ac.uk/criminaljustice/MMECC.

is very high. In such a high-crime situation, local residents might take very expensive precautionary measures like purchasing burglar alarms, taking taxis at night, and also suffer from residual fear when simply waiting outdoors for a taxi or getting from their car to their home. Thus, the marginal cost of crime might be much higher in high-crime areas than in low-crime areas. In the LAC context, there is evidence that an additional cost of crime (falling into the "community cost" category, perhaps) is the fact that victims of crime have little confidence in governmental institutions. Residents in high-crime areas are often likely to set up or hire a "justiciero" gang or a paramilitary group – or, in extreme cases, even favor a military coup.[10] While it might be difficult to place a dollar value on the loss in confidence in democratic institutions, this is a real burden of a high crime rate in the region. Similarly, since high crime rates can be a significant deterrent to new businesses and economic activity, unless a policy has a large enough impact on crime to change perceptions about a city's or country's crime rate, it is unlikely to bring about economic development benefits.

What this discussion suggests is that in thinking about BCRs and policy options, a program that has a very significant impact on crime might have a much higher BCR than one that has a relatively modest impact on crime – even if costs are linear. In addition, it is quite possible that in order to have a significant impact on crime, there will need to be multiple and perhaps integrative programs. For example, a program targeting at-risk youth to prevent them from joining a gang might have a small impact. Similarly, a police crackdown on gang violence might reduce incidents somewhat. However, a coordinated attack on both the kids who are likely to join a gang as well as a crackdown on gang violence will likely result in better results than the sum of the two programs. This has been shown (as discussed above) in gang violence. However, there are other examples where this might be true. Returning to the earlier example of the impact of violence on the confidence in democratic institutions, programs that have small effects are unlikely to have an impact on the level of confidence even though they have an impact on the cost to individual victims. Only when there

---

[10] See USAID (2006: 9). The victim survey results are from LAPOP (various years). The findings about public attitude towards military coups are contained in UNDP (2004).

are multiple and large-scale programs might the additional benefit of public confidence begin to kick in.

The costs of a criminal career

If an individual embarks on a criminal career, he is likely to engage in a variety of crimes over a period of years and also runs the risk of being arrested, convicted, and incarcerated. Based on the model described in Cohen (1998), the external costs imposed by a typical criminal career are:

$$\text{Lifetime cost} = \sum_{ij} (1 - \beta)^{j-1} \lambda_{ij} [(VC_i + CJ_i + CI^*T_i + W^*T_i]$$

(1)

where λ = mean number of offenses
VC = victim cost of crime
CJ = cost of criminal justice investigation, arrest, adjudication
CI = cost of incarceration (in days)
T = average time served (in days)
β = discount rate
W = opportunity cost of offender's time
i = crime 1 through crime I
j = year 1 through year J of crime career

Inside the square brackets are four terms: VC_i (average cost to victims for each type of crime); CJ_i (average criminal justice cost per crime); CI^*T_i (average cost of incarceration per crime); and W^*T_i (opportunity cost of incarceration, as measured by a convicted offender's legitimate wages). Each of these terms is multiplied by λ_{ij}, the number of offenses committed by a career criminal each year. The resulting annual cost can be converted into a lifetime cost by adding average annual costs, discounted to PV by the social discount rate β.

Cohen (1998) estimated the PV of external costs imposed by a typical career criminal to be $1.3 million–$1.5 million in 1997 dollars. However, the worst offenders impose costs as high as $36 million. This excludes any cost associated with drug abuse (which could amount to an additional $150,000–$364,000 if the career criminal is also a heavy drug user). Cohen and Piquero (2009) have updated these estimates and provide further details by type of offender.

To date, there have only been a few attempts to estimate the costs of crime in the LAC region. A series of studies funded by the IADB in 1999 estimated the cost of violence in Brazil, Colombia, El Salvador, Mexico, Peru, and Venezuela, to range between 0.3% and 5.0% of GDP. These papers used similar methodologies to that used in the United States and United Kingdom. While a first step in the process, those earlier papers had many shortcomings. More recently, the UNDP financed a study "Cuanto Cuesta la Violencia a El Salvador?" ("How Much Does Violence Cost El Salvador?") (PNUD 2007), in which the costs of violence were estimated to be approximately 11.5% of GDP.

While direct comparisons are difficult, it is interesting to compare the LAC estimates to those in the United States and United Kingdom. Adding the costs of criminal victimization in Miller, Cohen, and Wiersema (1996) to the costs of the US criminal justice system, yields an estimate of over $600 billion – about 5% of GDP. Similarly, the Home Office estimates place the cost of UK crime at about $60 billion – about 2.6% of GDP.

CBA of proposed solutions

To date, there have only been a handful of cost-benefit studies in the criminal justice arena. For example, McDougall *et al.* (2003) conducted a systematic review of cost-benefit studies in the area of sentencing – including both custodial and non-custodial sentencing options such as incarceration, intensive supervision, day reporting centers, home confinement, shock incarceration programs, electronic monitoring, community service, fines, and treatment programs – or other interventions that were part of a sentencing option. Yet, only six studies where a valid cost-benefit conclusion could be drawn were identified. These six studies involved (a) pre-trial diversion into a drug treatment program for drug offenders, (b) in-prison treatment for sex offenders (two studies), (c) intensive supervision as an alternative to incarceration, (d) longer prison sentences for adults convicted of felonies, and (e) family and juvenile offender treatment programs. Only two of these studies included the intangible costs of crime.

The most common US approach to valuing the non-monetary cost of victimization has been to rely upon the estimates in a National Institute of Justice Report by Miller, Cohen, and Wiersema (1996). These estimates are based on US jury awards for pain and suffering.

However, a study by Cohen and Miller (2003) reviewed these and other jury awards and compared them to estimates of the statistical value of a life. They found that the implied value of a statistical life using the jury award methodology to value crime victimization was approximately $3.8 million in 1995 – very close to the estimated value of a statistical life in the United States that economists have derived from numerous market-based studies. In the appendix, we convert this figure into an estimate of the value of a life year, and a DALY, and also provide a methodology for converting US costs into the LAC context for purposes of this study.

The remainder of this section considers the costs and benefits of each of our four solutions in turn.

Solution 1: comprehensive programs targeting at-risk mothers and young children under age 5

Aos *et al.* (2004) estimate the cost of a home visitation program where nurses work directly with pregnant women and young children to be $9,188 in 2003 dollars. They estimate benefits to be $26,298, or 2.88 times the costs. Benefits included in this analysis are reduced child abuse and neglect of the children, as well as reduced juvenile and criminal offending behavior of these children, and increased high-school graduation rates. Note that the educational benefits account for about 12.6% of this total ($3,325 out of $26,298), with the remaining value being reductions in child abuse and neglect ($5,686, or 21.6%), drug or alcohol abuse ($850 or 3.2%), and criminal offending behavior ($16,437, or 62.5%).

In addition, we propose a comprehensive pre-kindergarten program for low income 3- and 4-year-old children. Aos, Millar, and Drake (2006) estimate the cost of this program to be $7,301 per child in 2003 dollars, with benefits being $17,202, for a BCR of 2.36:1. Benefits include reduced child abuse and neglect, improved educational outcomes, and reduced crime later in life.

Combining these programs would cost a total of $16,419 per child (over a four-year period), with benefits of $43,500 – for a BCR of 2.65:1. This BCR is a based on a 3% discount rate. However, because the benefits of these programs accrue many years beyond the treatment (Aos, Millar, and Drake carry benefits out through age 33), using a 6% discount rate would lower the benefits of the early childhood education programs approximately 50%.[11] Similar reductions would need to be made for the home visitation program by nurses. Thus, using a 6% discount rate, in the table below we estimate total benefits of approximately \$21,750 compared to costs of \$16,419 – for a BCR of 1.32 : 1.

Solution 1 – *Early childhood programs benefits and costs (based on US dollars)*

	Benefits ($)	Costs ($)	BCR (3%)	BCR (6%)
Nurse family partnership	26,298	9,188	2.86	1.43
Early childhood	17,202	7,301	2.36	1.18
Combined	43,500	16,489	2.64	1.32

While it is not easy to translate these cost-benefit ratios to the LAC context, a few adjustments can be made to account for differences in the valuations used in the Aos, Millar, and Drake studies and the "standardized" DALY value that is used in this alternative view. The methodology used to do this is explained in the appendix. Note that reduced DALYs account for only about 30% of the cost of criminal victimization, with the remaining 70% being the cost

Solution 1 – *Early childhood programs benefits and costs (based on adjustments for this chapter)*

DALY ($)	Discount rate = 3%			Discount rate = 6%
	Benefits ($)	Costs ($)	BCR	BCR
Low (1,000)	5,700	2,650	2.2	1.1
High (5,000)	6,100	2,650	2.3	1.1

---

[11] Personal communication with S. Aos, March 31, 2007. Note that throughout this chapter we have reduced the BCR by 50% in the case of early childhood programs and 25% in the case of programs targeting youth and adult offenders. While Aos and his colleagues have appropriately discounted both costs and benefits, we do not have the year-by-year costs or benefits from which we could report the revised dollar figures using a 6% discount rate. Thus, we report only on the revised BCRs when using a 6% discount rate.

of lost wages, medical costs, criminal justice costs, etc. The result is the following table that lists the benefits and costs under varying assumptions about discount rates and DALYs.

Solution 2: comprehensive program to deal with youth and gang violence

As discussed, our proposed solution is a two-pronged approach including a comprehensive program cracking down on gang violence, coupled with a rehabilitative program for juvenile offenders. While we have identified several cost-benefit studies for the juvenile offender programs, we are unaware of any cost-benefit studies of the gang violence aspects of our proposed solution. For example, the authors of the most comprehensive study of the successful program in Boston claim that "Operation Ceasefire did not impose additional costs on the participating organizations, but was implemented by using existing resources more strategically." In Boston, state, local, and federal enforcement officials coordinated and focused their attention on gang violence, guns, etc. However, in addition to cracking down on gangs, they also coordinated with local juvenile justice and service agencies, as well as local clergy and community groups. Unfortunately, most LAC cities are unlikely to have the same level of existing police and community resources in place. Thus, additional resources might be required. Depending upon existing capacity in a city, this might be a relatively small investment – perhaps one or two dedicated police officers and case managers. Less certain, however, is the existence of community-level organizations such as clergy or community volunteers who are willing and able to devote their energy to such a project. While we have not included the cost of these additional resources, as discussed below, the BCR of the juvenile offender rehabilitation program is so high that we are confident of a significant positive BCR on balance.

For the juvenile rehabilitation programs, we assume that each of the three programs will be needed in equal amounts. This is an arbitrary assumption, but each city will require different combinations of these programs, depending upon the mix of juvenile offenders. Moreover, as shown, all three have relatively high BCRs and, regardless of the weights, they will more than pay for themselves. Aos *et al.* (2004) estimate the cost of a "functional family therapy" program for juvenile offenders to be $2,140. They estimate benefits to be $28,356, or

13.25 times the costs. The adolescent diversion project is estimated to cost $1,777 per participant, and result in benefits of $24,067, or 13.54 times the costs. The aggression replacement training program is estimated to cost $758 per participant, with benefits of $15,606 – 20.59 times the costs. In all three cases, the only benefits included in the analysis are reduced juvenile delinquency. Not included, but also potential benefits, are reduced substance abuse and the value of increased long-term wage productivity to the extent that these juvenile offenders stay in school and ultimately have more successful working lives than they would without treatment. Assuming an equal percentage of each program, the average cost per participant is estimated to be $1,559, with average benefits being $22,676 – for a BCR of 14.54.

Once again, the Aos, Millar, and Drake (2006) estimates are based on a 3% discount rate. Unlike early child education programs, the benefits of these programs begin to accrue immediately. However, discounting is also a factor, as Aos, Millar, and Drake estimate criminal activities through age 33. Thus, using a 6% discount rate, we have estimated a reduction of 25% from the benefits that accrue using a 3% discount rate. Thus, benefits are estimated to be $17,007 compared to costs of $1,559, a BCR of 10.91:1.

Solution 2 – *Youth violence benefits and costs (based on US dollars)*

	Benefits ($)	Costs ($)	BCR (3%)	BCR (6%)
Functional family therapy	28,356	2,140	13.25	9.94
Adolescent diversion	24,067	1,777	13.54	10.16
Aggression replacement training	15,606	758	20.59	15.44
Average	22,676	1,559	14.54	10.91

To translate these figures into the LAC context and to be consistent with the other chapters in this volume, we use the same methodology as used in solution 1 to transform intangible crime control benefits into DALYs and convert wage rates from the US to LAC levels. In this case, all the benefits that have been estimated are crime reductions, hence the DALY adjustment is made to 30% of benefits, with the wage adjustment being made to the remaining 70%. Doing this provides the benefit and cost figures in the table below.

Solution 2 – Youth violence benefits and costs (based on adjustments for this chapter)

DALY	Discount rate = 3%			Discount rate = 6%
($)	Benefits ($)	Costs ($)	BCR	BCR
Low (1,000)	2,600	250	10.4	7.8
High (5,000)	2,900	250	11.5	8.7

We also note that we have not included programs specifically targeting education – such as "stay in school" education programs and incentives to graduate high school. While many of these programs appear to have significant crime-related benefits – often high enough to justify the programs solely on the basis of crime reductions – these are programs that are more appropriately reviewed in a paper on education because that is where their primary benefit accrues. However, it would be important that the authors of that paper take into account the likely crime-reduction benefits as well.

Solution 3: comprehensive prison treatment and reintegration program

Offenders who are released from prison have extremely high recidivism rates. Thus, if a program targets these offenders while in prison, it might have a high payoff if successful in reducing recidivism. Three such programs – if implemented correctly – have been shown to reduce recidivism: (a) drug treatment, (b) educational and vocational programs, and (c) cognitive behavioral therapy. While these programs have been found to be effective, additional benefits may accrue when similar (and additional) programs extend to offenders upon their release from prison – to assist in their reintegration into society.

Drug treatment programs have been found to be cost-beneficial both in prison and in the community. Community drug treatment is often an alternative to prison, so that it is much less expensive, but has generally been found to be cost-effective only for drug offenders – not those who are also property crime offenders (see Aos 2005).[12]

---

[12] Morrison's alternative view mentions a study by Miller and Levy (2000) as finding lower B/C numbers. However, Miller and Levy (2000) actually uses the

Aos, Millar, and Drake (2006) estimated the cost of drug treatment in prison to be $1,604, compared to drug treatment in the community of $574. Benefits were similar, totaling $10,628 in the community (BCR = 18.5) and $9,439 in prison (BCR = 5.88). Cognitive behavioral therapy – either in prison or in the community – has been estimated to cost $105 per offender, with a benefit of $10,404 – nearly 100 times the cost. In all cases, these benefits only include the value to taxpayers through lower criminal justice costs as well as savings to crime victims – they do not include any benefits to the offender or society through increased labor productivity or reduced drug use itself.

Aos, Millar, and Drake (2006) also estimate that educational programs in prison cost $962 per offender on average, compared to benefits of $11,631 – for a BCR of 12.09. Vocational education programs in prison are estimated to cost $1,182 per participant, with benefits of $14,920 – for a BCR of 12.62. Similarly, employment and job training programs for recently released offenders have been estimated to cost $400 per offender, with total benefits of $4,759 – a BCR of 11.89. In all cases, these benefits are restricted to criminal justice and criminal victimization outcomes – not the increased labor productivity associated with improved employment outcomes. Thus, benefits are expected to be considerably higher.

Roman *et al.* (2007) estimate the cost of the Maryland re-entry program to be $1.2 million annually, with 176 offenders being treated. This cost of $6,900 per offender includes the cost of the treatment programs themselves – including transitional housing – but we do not have information on the details of the programs received. Benefits were estimated to be $31,824, although these findings were not statistically significant by standard measures ($p < 0.15$). The BCR for this program is thus 4.6:1. Note that this finding is based on a five-year follow-up to post-release. Presumably, benefits stretch beyond that point. The measured benefits include reduced cost to the criminal justice system and to victims. They do not include any potential benefit to the offender and society through improved labor outcomes or reduced drug abuse.

Roman *et al.* (2007) also conduct a hypothetical benefit-cost study of re-entry programs for jailed inmates – often used as a pre-trial diversion. Comparing actual costs of two programs to potential benefits,

Aos (1999) figures which do not include many of the non-criminal justice benefits of early childhood programs.

they find that the "break-even" effectiveness rate is approximately 5% reduced recidivism or less. In other words, to pay for themselves, these programs would need to reduce recidivism by 5% more than the rate non-treated offenders would be expected to recidivate. Roman *et al.* (2007) also provide detailed cost estimates for two programs – ranging from $489 to $672 per offender, with a "high-end" program costing $3,000. These programs provide differing services, ranging from education and employment assistance, healthcare, transportation assistance, and case managers that help coordinate and find local community services for released offenders.

In assessing the benefits and costs of our comprehensive program for treatment and reintegration of offenders, we have used the lower-cost estimate of the jail re-entry program (as opposed to the prison re-entry program, since that includes many services that would likely be double-counted with our treatment programs). Thus, we estimate costs of $672 per offender. We do not include any benefits for this portion of our program – since the benefits of the actual treatments are high enough, and the benefits of the actual reentry services are not fully documented. In other words, we have been careful to be conservative in estimating benefits – they are clearly higher than estimated here. Moreover, to achieve the most benefit from these treatment programs, we believe it is important to employ some form of coordinated reentry program.

Combining these programs, we assume that educational programs, employment programs, and cognitive behavioral treatment programs are needed for all offenders, while drug treatment is required for 50% of offenders. Assuming that an equal portion of drug treatment will be done in prison and in the community, the total costs per adult offender are thus estimated to be $2,794 ($105 for cognitive behavioral therapy, $1,072 average for educational programs, $400 for employment programs, and $672 for reentry assistance; plus 50% × $1,089 average for drug treatment).

While we have provided benefits estimates for each program, it is not necessarily true that we can simply add them all up. While we are certain that providing both drug treatment and educational programs to offenders will offer higher benefits than simply providing one or the other, we do not know if the combined benefits will be less than or more than the sum of the two. It is quite possible that there are synergistic effects, and that the combined effect will be more than the sum of the parts. However, to be conservative, we assume a diminishing marginal benefit from adding each program. At one extreme, we could assume the highest level of benefits for one program and no benefits for each additional program. If we took this approach, benefits would be $13,275 based on the average benefit for educational and vocational programs in prison. With total costs of $2,794 per offender, the BCR would be 4.75. Alternatively, if we adopted the assumption used in Aos, Millar, and Drake (2006), and reduced each additional program by 25%, benefits would be $28,603 [($13,275 + 75% × 10,404 + 75% × ($10,628 + $9,439)/2)]. This would yield a BCR of 10.2.

Once again, the above figures are based on a 3% discount rate. If we assume a 6% discount rate, benefits would be reduced by approximately 25%, so that the BCR would range between 3.6 and 7.7.

Solution 3 – *Prison treatment and reintegration program*

Program	Benefits ($)	Costs ($)	BCR (3% discount)	BCR (6% discount)
Drug treatment in prison	9,439	1,604	5.9	4.4
Drug treatment in community	10,628	574	18.5	13.9
Cognitive behavioral therapy	10,404	105	99.1	74.3
Educational programs in prison	11,631	962	12.1	9.1
Vocational programs in prison	14,920	1,182	12.6	9.5
Job training programs upon release	4,759	400	11.9	8.9
Reentry coordination program	0	672		
Average[a]	13,275–28,603[b]	2,794	4.8–10.3	3.6–7.7

Notes:
[a] See text: assumes 50% drug treatment (equal shares in and out of prison); 100% educational or vocational programs in prison; 100% job training upon release.
[b] Lower figure based only on average benefits from educational/vocational programs. Higher figure adds to this 75% of additional program benefits.

To convert these estimates into the appropriate figures for this project, we once again convert 30% of crime benefits into DALY estimates and the remaining costs and benefits using the differential in US vs. LAC wage rates. It is important to keep in mind that all of these estimates are conservative, as they exclude the benefits from improved labor productivity that are likely to accrue from these programs and instead focus only on crime control benefits.

Solution 3 – *Prison treatment and reintegration benefits and costs (based on adjustments for this chapter)*

| DALY ($) | Discount rate = 3% | | | Discount rate = 6% |
	Benefits ($)	Costs ($)	BCR	BCR
Low (1,000)	1,545–3,329	450	3.4–3.8	2.6–2.8
High (5,000)	1,705–3,673	450	7.4–8.1	5.5–6.1

Solution 4: domestic violence prevention and control

The evidence on the benefits and costs of domestic violence programs is sparse. Unfortunately, we were unable to find studies that examine the comprehensive approach recommended by UNICEF. We were also unable to find studies that estimate the costs and benefits of domestic violence interventions by police or battered women's shelters.[13]

The only CBA we are aware of involving domestic violence programs is the new mother/early-childhood program targeting at-risk families for children under age 2, which was discussed in detail under solution 1 (p. 662). Aos *et al.* (2004) estimate that about 21.6% ($5,686 out of $26,298) of the benefits of that program are due to reduced child abuse and neglect – with the remaining benefits being apportioned to improved educational outcomes (12.6% – $3,325/$26,298), reduced crime by the children once they become older (62.5% – $16,437/26,298), and alcohol and drug abuse (3.2% – $850/26,298).

---

[13] Morrison's alternative view paper, 10.1, cites a US study that conducted a B/C analysis of the Violence Against Women's Act. However, that study did not focus solely on domestic violence – it included all violence against women. More importantly, it did not look at specific programs. Instead, it compared all violence against women before and after implementation of a federal law that was designed to reduce violence against women – hence, it assumed that all benefits were due to the law and did not control for other intervening factors. Thus, the study did not use a valid methodology to sort out the impact of domestic violence policies.

Summary tables of costs and benefits and concluding remarks

Before presenting our summary tables on the costs and benefits of our proposed solutions, we want to emphasize another recommendation arising from our review of the evidence. Before recommending "changes" and "new programs," it is important to inventory and assess existing LAC programs. There is a glaring need to obtain better information on what existing programs are being used – and which have promise based on external studies (such as those we identified in this chapter) or through localized studies.

We proposed four solutions based on our considered judgment about the severity of the problem, the availability of effective policy options, and the benefits and costs of implementation. In all cases, we propose "comprehensive" programs that focus on different aspects of the problem we believe need to be implemented in tandem for maximum benefits: (1) programs targeting at-risk mothers and young children under age 5, (2) programs to deal with youth and gang violence, (3) prison treatment and reintegration programs, and (4) domestic violence prevention and control programs.

Morrison (in the alternative view paper) proposes three additional solutions: (1) programs designed to keep youth in high school, (2) "hot spot" and community policing, and (3) crime prevention through environmental design ("situational crime prevention") – the last of which he identifies as the priority item. Morrison's recommendations are largely sound and we encourage the reader to study his alternative view. We agree on the importance of the "stay in school" programs, and he is quite correct that we could have included that as a priority item ourselves – although we made the decision to leave that proposal to the researchers studying educational programs. As both we and Morrison note, programs designed to improve educational outcomes oftentimes have tremendous crime-reduction benefits as well. We also agree with Morrison's conclusion that situational crime prevention programs have been found to be cost-beneficial. We left them out, primarily because their main demonstrated benefit to date has been in the area of property crime – something that is not within the purview of this chapter. However, to the extent that these programs can be shown to reduce the risk of violence in addition to property crimes, they are worthy of consideration. Finally, while we also agree that there is evidence of cost-beneficial policing programs in both the United States and the United Kingdom, we deliberately left these out of our proposed solutions due to our concern about the extent to which they can be "imported" to the LAC context. Corruption is a major concern (and is the subject of chapter 9 in this volume), and public distrust for police might reduce the benefits of "hot spot" and "community" policing, or even make matters worse. We do believe, however, that this is an area for promising future research.

The table below contains a summary of the estimated benefits and costs of the four solutions proposed in this chapter. We note that these estimates are meant more to be "illustrative" than definitive, as they are largely based on extrapolations from the US experience. While there is evidence that the proposed programs can work and provide benefits that far exceed costs, translating them from the US to the LAC experience would require pilot testing, tailoring of programs to suit local needs, etc. As noted above, there might be existing programs in some locations that are similar to those that are known to work from the US experience. These should be followed closely to determine if they are appropriately designed or could benefit from minor modifications. They are likely to have already been adapted to local circumstances, and much can be learned from their experiences. In addition, the cost and benefit estimates themselves are largely based on US wage rates, the value of intangible harms from crime, etc. These have been conservatively converted into LAC values, but once again they are meant to be more illustrative of the type of benefits that one can achieve with these programs.

It is also important to note that the BCRs shown here are based on very conservative assumptions as indicated in the "Notes" section of the table. In some cases, even though improved educational outcomes, and hence long-term productivity gains, are to be expected, they were not included in our estimates due to data limitations. Moreover, benefits are generally extended out no more than 33 years (and 15 years for adult offenders). Especially for early childhood education and domestic violence programs, the benefits might continue beyond that timeframe.

Finally, we understand that the most controversial aspect of placing monetary values on crime is the valuation of the intangible losses to crime victims and to communities. While these have been included through the monetization of DALYs as called for in the Copehagen Consensus process, it is important to emphasize that most of the benefits that have been valued are savings from reduced criminal justice and court costs, and the reduced OOP losses to victims – such as property losses, wages, and medical costs. Intangible costs in our estimates generally represent only about 5% of benefits or less. Thus, even ignoring these benefits would not change our basic recommendations.

Summary of BCRs for crime and violence solutions

Solution	Discount rate 3%		Discount rate 6%		Notes
	DALY $1,000	DALY $5,000	DALY $1,000	DALY $5,000	
1. Early childhood	2.2	2.3	1.1	1.1	
2. Youth violence	10.4	11.5	7.8	8.7	Excludes benefits of drug abuse and education; excludes cost of gang violence coordinator
3. Prison treatment and Re-integration	3.4– 3.8	7.4– 8.1	2.6– 2.8	5.5– 6.1	Excludes benefits of drug abuse and education
4. Domestic violence	?	?	?	?	Solution 1 includes benefits from child abuse reduction.

Appendix Conversion of US wage rates and value of statistical life estimates

In this appendix, we provide details on the assumptions used to convert the costs and benefits from the various US studies by Aos and his colleagues to the LAC context. This requires both converting dollars of tangible losses into an equivalent value in the LAC region, as well as converting the intangible losses into a DALY equivalent.

The largest cost component of criminal justice, crime prevention, and treatment programs is labor. According to the 2006 World Bank Development Indicators (World Bank 2006, table 2.6), the average cost of a US manufacturing worker was $28,907 during the 1995–9 time period, the last reported data available. LAC data during the same time period ranged from a low of $1,806 in the Dominican Republic to a high of $14,134 in Brazil. The average for the fifteen LAC countries included in the survey was $4,705.[14] This is 16.2% of the cost of labor

---

[14] Countries included were: Argentina, Bolivia, Brazil, Chile, Colombia, Costa Rica, Dominican Republic, Ecuador, Guatemala, Honduras, Mexico, Panama, Paraguay, Uruguay, and Venezuela.

in the United States. Thus, in our final B/C estimates, we multiply all costs and all tangible benefits by 16.2%.

The guidelines for the Copenhagen Consensus solution papers recommend that authors standardize the valuation of DALYs at a range of $1,000–$5,000. However, the intangible crime benefits valued by Aos and his colleagues are based on the intangible costs of crime estimated by Miller, Cohen, and Wiersema (1996). While the latter are oftentimes used in B/C analyses and by policy analysts, we do not need to adopt those figures here. Instead, we have used the information from Miller, Cohen, and Wiersema (1996) and related studies to infer a DALY loss from crime that can then be valued based on the standard $1,000–$5,000 range.

Miller, Cohen, and Wiersema (1996) used the same source of data on jury awards to crime victims that was used by Miller, Cohen, and Wiersema (1996), to estimate the implied statistical value of a life from jury awards. They found that jury awards, on average, valued a statistical life in $3.8 million 1995 dollars. Reducing this to account for tangible wage losses, this implies a value of intangible losses to be $2.8 million. Based on an approximate 50-year remaining life-span for the typical crime victim, this implies a value of the intangible portion of a statistical life year of approximately $100,000.[15] This is between 20 and 100 times larger than the DALY estimate recommended here. Thus, we have adjusted the intangible benefit downwards to account for this difference. To do this, we multiply intangible crime victim benefits by either 0.05 or 0.01.

To illustrate how we have adjusted the estimates, consider the home visitation program recommended as part of solution 1. According to Miller, Cohen, and Wiersema (1996), approximately 30% of the costs of crime (including criminal justice and crime victim costs) are due to intangible effects on the quality of life to crime victims. Moreover, of the $43,500 estimated benefits from solution 1, $28,935 are due to

---

[15] We note that this $100,000 figure is considerably less than the current estimate of the statistical value of a life year of $300,000, as suggested by Viscusi (see, e.g. Aldy and Viscusi 2007). However, we use the $100,000 figure because that was derived directly from the source of the data that was used to value crime victimization. We also note that the "value of a statistical life year" is not the same as the value of a DALY. However, these figures should generally be close, and there is no other way to estimate a comparable figure based on the guidelines for the Copenhagen Consensus process. Ultimately, the DALY calculations account for a very small portion of benefits.

reduced crime with the remaining $14,565 being improved productivity through reductions in drug abuse, alcohol abuse, and increased educational attainment. Thus, about 30% of the $28,935 benefit – or $8,680 – is estimated to be the value of improved quality of life to victims. This would translate into approximately 0.087 of a DALY in the United States (based on the valuation of $100,000 per DALY). Using the range of $1,000–$5,000 per DALY required in the Copenhagen Consensus project, this translates into a range of $87–$435. Of course, the remaining 70% of benefits also needs to be valued. Using the 16.2% estimate discussed above, this portion of benefits totals $5,641 ($34,820 × 0.162). Added to the DALY values, benefits range between $5,723 and $6,076.

Of course, costs also need to be adjusted. Thus, the estimated per-participant cost in the United States of this program has also been multiplied by 16.2% – resulting in a cost estimate of approx. $2,650 ($16,419 × 0.162). Ultimately, this leaves a BCR ranging from 2.2–2.3. This same procedure is used throughout the chapter to convert US dollars into LAC-based equivalents.

Bibliography

Aldy, J. and W.K. Viscusi, 2007. "Age Differences in the Value of Statistical Life: Revealed Preference Evidence." *Review of Environmental Economics and Policy* 1: 241–60

Aos, S., 2005. "Washington's Drug Offender Sentencing Alternative: An Evaluation of Benefits And Costs." Olympia, WA: Washington State Institute for Public Policy, www.wsipp.wa.gov/rptfiles/06-10-1201.pdf

Aos, S., R. Lieb, J. Mayfield, M. Millar, and A. Pennucci, 2004. "Benefits and Costs of Prevention and Early Intervention Programs for Youth." Olympia, WA: Washington State Institute for Public Policy, www.wsipp.wa.gov/pub.asp?docid=04-07-3901

Aos, S., M. Millar, and E. Drake, 2006. "Evidence-Based Public Policy Options to Reduce Future Prison Construction, Criminal Justice Costs, and Crime Rates." Olympia, WA: Washington State Institute for Public Policy

Ascencio, R.L., 1999. "The Health Impact of Domestic Violence: Mexico City." In A.R. Morrison and M.L. Biehl, eds., *Too Close to Home: Domestic Violence in the Americas*. New York: Inter-American Development Bank: 81–97

Barnett, W.S., 1993. "Benefit-Cost Analysis of Preschool Education: Findings from a 25-Year Follow-Up." *American Journal of Orthopsychiatry* 63: 500–8

BID, 1999. *Notas técnicas prevención de la violencia.* Washington, DC: Banco Interamericano de Desarrollo

BID-CIEN, 2001. Encuesta para el proyecto "Magnitud y Costos de la Violencia en Guatemala" realizada por Borge y Asociados, http://centroamericajoven.org/fileadmin/contenido/Documentos/Publicacoines/85-23.pdf

Botello, S. and Á. Moya, 2005. *Reyes Latinos. Los códigos secretos de los Latin King en España.* Madrid: Temas de Hoy

Braga, A.A. and D.M. Kennedy, 2003. "Reducing Gang Violence in Boston." In *Responding to Gangs: Evaluation and Research* 266–288. Washington, DC: National Institute of Justice, www.ncjrs.gov/pdffiles1/nij/190351.pdf

Carranza, E., 1997. *Delito y Seguridad de los Habitantes.* Mexico: Siglo XXI Editores

CELADE, 2003. "América Latina: Población por años calendario y edades simples, 1995–2005." *Boletín Demográfico* 71, Enero, www.eclac.cl/celade/default.asp

Cohen, M.A., 1998. "The Monetary Value of Saving a High Risk Youth." *Journal of Quantitative Criminology* 14: 5–33

2005. *The Costs of Crime and Justice.* New York: Routledge

2008. "Valuing Crime Control Benefits Using Stated Preference Approaches." In Terence Dunworth, ed., *Cost and Benefits of Crime.* Washington, DC: Urban Institute Press, ssrn.com/abstract=1091456

Cohen, Mark A. and Ted R. Miller, 2003. "Willingness to Award Non-monetary Damages and the Implied Value of Life from Jury Awards." *International Review of Law and Economics* 23: 165–81

Cohen, M.A. and A. Piquero, 2009. "New Evidence on the Monetary Value of Saving a High Risk Youth." *Journal of Quantitative Criminology* 25(1): 25–49

Cohen, M.A., R. Rust, S. Steen, and S. Tidd, 2004. "WTP for Crime Control Programs." *Criminology* 42: 86–106

Cuadra, E., 2000. "Proliferación y control de armas en Nicaragua." Fundación Arias par ala Paz y el Progreso Humano, www.arias.or.cr/documentos/armasliv/niarmasdiag.pdf

Cuéllar de Martínez, M.M., 1997. *Valores y capital social en Colombia.* Bogotá: Corporación Porvenir y Universidad Externado de Colombia

Delisi, M. and J.M. Gatling, 2003. "Who Pays for a Life of Crime? An Empirical Assessment of the Assorted Victimization Costs Posed by Career

Criminals." *Criminal Justice Studies: A Critical Journal of Crime, Law and Society* **16**: 283–93

Dubourg, R., J. Hamed, and J. Thorns, 2005. *The Economic and Social Costs of Crime Against Individuals and Households, 2003–4*. Home Office Online Report **30–05**

Espitia, V. E., 1999. *Consultora, Asesoría en sistemas de Vigilancia de Violencia en Tegucigalpa (Honduras)*. Tegucigalpa: OPS

Fajnzylber, P., D. Lederman, and N. Loayza, 2001. *Crimen y violencia en América Latina*. Washington, DC: Banco Mundial y Alfaomega

FESPAD, 2004. *Propuesta de política criminal y seguridad ciudadana para El Salvador*. San Salvador: Fundación de Estudios para la Aplicación del Derecho, www.fespad.org.sv/portal/html/Archivos/Descargas/PPCPES2005.pdf

Gavira, A. and D. Pages, 1999. "Patterns of Crime Victimization in Latin America." Washington, DC: IABO, mimeo

Gonzales de Olarte, E. and P.G. Llosa, 1999. "Social and Economic Costs of Domestic Violence: Chile and Nicaragua." In A.R. Morrison and M.L. Biehl, eds., *Too Close to Home: Domestic Violence in the Americas*. New York: Inter-American Development Bank: 35–49

Guerrero, R., A. Gaviria, and J.L. Londoño, 2001. "Asalto al desarrollo: Violencia en América Latina." New York: Inter-American Development Bank

Ibanez, A.M. and C.E. Velez, 2005. "Civil Conflict and Forced Migration: The Micro Determinants and the Welfare Losses of Displacement in Colombia." http://economia.uniandes.edu.co/var/rw/archivos/cede/documentos/d2005–35.pdf

INCEP, 2004. *Centroamérica: Balance de escenarios econoómicos, sociales y políticos, asií como las perspectivas 2005–2006*. Guatemala: Instituto Centroameriicano de Estudios Políticos, www.incep.org/images/content/Balance.pdf

Larraín, S., 1999. "Curbing Domestic Violence: Two Decades of Action." In A.R. Morrison and M.L. Biehl, eds., *Too Close to Home: Domestic Violence in the Americas*. New York: Inter-American Development Bank: 106–29

Latin American Public Opinion Project (LAPOP), various years. *Americas-Barometer*. Vanderbilt University, www.lapopsurveys.org

Levitt, S. and M. Rubio, 2000. "Understanding Colombia's Crime Situation and the Institutional Reforms Required to Alleviate the Problem." In A. Alesina, ed., *Institutional Reforms: The Case of Colombia*. Cambridge, MA: MIT Press

Leyva, H., 2001. *Delincuencia y criminalidad en las estadísticas de Honduras, 1996–2000*. Serie Sociedad y Cultura, Documento de Trabajo **3**. Tegucigalpa: FIDE–PNUD

McDougall, C., M.A. Cohen, A. Perry, and R. Swaray, 2003. "The Costs and Benefits of Sentencing – A Systematic Review." *Annals of the American Academy of Political and Social Science* **587**: 160–77

Miller, T.R., M.A. Cohen, and B. Wiersema, 1996. *Victim Costs and Consequences: A New Look*. National Institute of Justice Research Report, NCJ-155282, www.ncjrs.org/pdffiles/victcost.pdf

Miller, T.R. and D. Lexy, 2000. "Cost–Outcome Analysis in Injury Prevention and Control." *Medical Care* **386**: 562–82

Mockus, A. and H. Acero, 2005. *Criminalidad y violencia en América Latina: la experiencia exitosa de Bogotá*, www.iigov.org

Morrison, A.R. and M.B. Orlando, 1999. "Social and Economic Costs of Domestic Violence: Chile and Nicaragua." In A.R. Morrison and M.L. Biehl, eds., *Too Close to Home: Domestic Violence in the Americas*. New York: Inter-American Development Bank: 51–80

Olds, D.L., J. Robinson, R. O'Brien, D.W. Luckey, L.M. Pettitt, C.R. Henderson, Jr., R.K. Ng, K.L. Sheff, J. Korfmacher, S. Hiatt, and A. Talmi, 2002. "Home Visiting by Paraprofessionals and by Nurses: A Randomized, Controlled Trial." *Pediatrics* **110**: 486–96

OPS, 2005. *Iniciativa regional de datos básicos en Salud; Sistema de información técnica en Salud*. Washington, DC: Organización Panamericana de la Salud, Área de Análisis de Salud y Sistemas de Información Sanitaria, Washington, www.paho.org/Spanish/SHA/coredata/tabulator/newTabulator.htm

Piehl, A.M., D.M. Kennedy, and A.A. Braga, 2000. "Problem Solving and Youth Violence: An Evaluation of the Boston Gun Project." *American Law and Economics Review* **2**: 58–106

PNUD, 2007. "Cuanto Cuesta la Violencía a El Salvador?" Programa de las Nauones Unidas para el Desarrollo. San Salvador: PNUD, www.pnud.org.sv/2007/content/view/27/83?idpubl.=64

Rocha, José Luis, 2006. "Why no Maras in Nicaragua?" *Revista Envío* **301**, www.envio.org.ni/articulo/3351

Roman, J., L. Brooks, E. Lagerson, A. Chalfin, and B. Tereshchenko, 2007. *Impact and Cost-Benefit Analysis of the Maryland Reentry Partnership Initiative*. Washington, DC: Urban Institute www.urban.org/UploadedPDF/311421_Maryland_Reentry.pdf

Rubio, M., 1999. *Crimen e Impunidad: Precisiones sobra la Violencia*. Bogotá: CEDE-Tercer Mundo

    2002. *La violencia en Honduras y la Región del Valle del Sula*. Serie de Estudios Económicos y Sectoriales. Washington, DC: Banco Interamericano de Desarrollo

    2007. *De la pandilla del barrio, a la Mara Salvatrucha. Migración, pobreza, mujeres y violencia juvenil*. Bogotá: Univerdidad Externado de Colombia–Banco Interamericano de Desarrollo

Rubio, M. and DIEM, 2003. *Resultados de la "Encuesta de Auto Reporte de Conductas entre Jóvenes,"* en la Zona Metropolitana del Valle del Sula. Banco Interamericano de Desarrollo, Informe Final de Consultoría

Sherman, L.W., D. Gottfredson, D. Mackenzie, J. Eck, P. Reuter, and S. Bushway, 1997. *Preventing Crime: What Works, What Doesn't, What's Promising: A Report to the United States Congress.* Washington, DC: National Institute of Justice, www.ncjrs.gov/works/

1998. *Preventing Crime: What Works, What Doesn't, What's Promising?* National Institute of Justice Research in Brief, NCJ **171676**, www.ncjrs.gov/pdffiles/171676.pdf

Smith, E.P., A.M. Wolf, D.M. Cantillon, O. Thomas, and W.S. Davidson, 2004. "The Adolescent Diversion Project: 25 years of Research on an Ecological Model of Intervention." *Journal of Prevention & Intervention in the Community* **27**: 29–47

UNICEF, 2000. *Domestic Violence against Women and Girls.* Innocenti Digest **6**, Florence

United Nations, 2006. *Observatorio de la violencia*, **1**, Honduras, www.un.hn/PNUD_Observatorio_Violencia.htm

United Nations Development Programme (UNDP), 2004. *Democracy in Latin America: Towards a Citizens' Democracy.* New York: UNDP

United States Agency for International Development (USAID), 2006. *Central America and Mexico Gang Assessment*, April. New York: USAID

Urbina, M.A., 1997. *La situación en Honduras – La perspectiva Policial.* en Carranza

Valle, M. and A. Argüello, 2002. *Diagnostico de seguridad ciudadana en Nicaragua.* Proyecto: Apoyo a la implementación de una estrategia de seguridad ciudadana en Nicaragua. Managua: PNUD

Washington Office on Latin America (WOLA), 2006. *Youth Gangs in Central America. Issues in Human Rights, Effective Policing, and Prevention.* Washington, DC: Washington Office on Latin America Special Report

World Bank, 2006. *World Development Indicators.* Washington, DC: World Bank

10.1 | *Violence and crime: an alternative view*

ANDREW MORRISON*

1 Overview of chapter 10

Chapter 10 (i) reviews the evidence on levels and trends in crime and violence in the LAC region; (ii) discusses, in summary fashion, the evidence on good practices in crime and violence reduction; and (iii) presents four proposed solutions for LAC countries, with BCRs provided for three of the four proposed solutions.

Cohen and Rubio recognize the heroic nature of the quest to provide a CBA of crime and violence prevention initiatives for Latin America:

Unfortunately, most of the evidence [on what works is]... in the United States and to a lesser extent in the United Kingdom or Europe... The few programs [in the LAC region] that have been evaluated or reported on as being promising have not had the benefit of independent reviews and thus should not be considered as reliable evidence. Indeed, it is not easy to find even a rough inventory of what is being done.

Faced with such a weak knowledge base from which to formulate public policy recommendations, Cohen and Rubio have few options. They adopt an eminently sensible strategy: survey the developed-country literature on what works and what doesn't; locate B/C estimates for those interventions which have been identified as having been successful in reducing crime; and propose as solutions for the region some of the interventions with attractive BCRs.

While an eminently reasonable strategy, there are some problems in execution, and these limitations will be discussed in more detail below. It is important to emphasize at the outset, however, that Cohen and Rubio have produced a solid attempt. They have been creative in

---

* The views expressed in this chapter are those of the author and not of the World Bank.

identifying promising approaches to crime and violence reduction for the region, despite quite serious limitations of available information.

2 Strengths of chapter 10

There is much to be praised in the chapter. As noted in section 1, the overall strategy adopted is sensible given the data constraints faced by the authors – principally, the lack of program evaluations for interventions that might reduce crime and violence.

The authors are also correct in debunking the notion that crime and violence are spiraling out of control in the region, correctly noting that the evidence on *trends* "is not conclusive." At the same time, they also accurately note that the *levels* of violence in the region – at least as measured by the homicide rate – make the region one of the world's most violent.

The four solutions to reduce crime and violence proposed by Cohen and Rubio are:

- Comprehensive programs targeting at-risk mothers and young children under age 5
- Comprehensive program to deal with youth and gang violence
- Comprehensive prison treatment [*sic*] and reintegration program
- Domestic violence prevention and control.

These solutions fall within mainstream approaches to crime and violence prevention. UNODC and World Bank (2007) identified three sector-specific approaches to violence prevention (criminal justice, public health, and conflict transformation and human rights) and three cross-sectoral approaches (crime prevention through environmental design, citizen security/public safety, and community-driven development/social capital). Three of the solutions proposed by Cohen and Rubio can be categorized primarily as public health approaches (although domestic violence and youth/gang violence prevention, depending upon the approach used, may also be labeled as criminal justice or human rights interventions.) Only one of the proposed solutions – comprehensive rehabilitation of inmates and reintegration of ex-offenders – falls unambiguously under the category of criminal justice. No cross-sectional approaches are recommended, presumably because of lack of B/C estimates.

3 Different views on the problem and its solutions

While the chapter offers reasonable proposed solutions, it also has a few serious shortcomings which should be addressed, which I shall consider in turn:

- an incomplete discussion of domestic violence
- an over-reliance on one landmark paper on the cost-benefit ratios of crime prevention measures
- use of a somewhat outdated paper on what works in violence and crime prevention, instead of more recent meta-analyses that could provide information on the relative effectiveness of specific approaches to crime reduction
- lack of attention to several promising (and potentially cost-effective) approaches to crime reduction.

Incomplete discussion of domestic violence

Cohen and Rubio claim that "there is no systematic data available by which we could judge the severity of the domestic violence problem in the LAC region compared to elsewhere." While this was the case several years ago, it no longer is: the WHO has undertaken a multi-country study in which it administered a comparable survey on intimate partner violence (see n. 3) in fifteen locations across ten countries (WHO 2005).[1] Two of the fifteen countries – Brazil and Peru – are in the LAC region. The results distinguish between lifetime and current physical and sexual violence committed by intimate partners, and between rates in rural and urban areas. The prevalence rate of physical violence in rural Peru was higher than in any other country or area in the sample, and the rate of physical violence in urban Peru was the third-highest rate among any country or area.[2] Prevalence rates

---

[1] The term "domestic violence" is currently very infrequently used. Domestic violence implies that the violence takes place in the home, when in fact it can take place in public spaces or in the workplace. It also fails to distinguish between violence against women, child abuse, and elder abuse. Thus, I use the term "violence against women," which includes both intimate partner violence (IPV) and sexual coercion by non-family members. For a fuller discussion, see Morrison, Ellsberg, and Bott (2004).

[2] Demographic and Health Surveys also frequently contain questions about women's experience with violence. Although there are problems about

of physical violence in Brazil, on the other hand, were at the lower end of the spectrum.[3] In terms of rates of sexual violence by intimate partners, neither country ranked particularly high. The bottom line is that there is evidence that the prevalence rate of physical violence is unusually high in Peru; of course, whether this is the case in other LAC countries must await expansion of the WHO survey.

There are also problems with the discussion of the risk factors for intimate partner violence (IPV). Cohen and Rubio identify the close correlates of IPV as poverty, unemployment, and the lack of a social support network. These conclusions are based on a single – albeit inter-esting – study from Peru. More serious work on the risk factors for IPV identifies many more factors operating at the individual, relationship, community, and societal levels, including witnessing IPV as a child, suffering abuse as a child, differences in age between male and female partners, neighborhood rates of crime, cultural norms that support violence, and norms that support male dominance over women (Heise 1998; Morrison, Ellsberg, and Bott 2007).

Over-reliance on one landmark paper on the cost-benefit ratios of crime prevention measures

Cohen and Rubio base their four proposed solutions with high BCRs "on the analysis conducted by Aos and our review of the litera-ture." There is no doubt that Aos' (2005) work and that of Aos *et al.* (2004) and Aos, Millar, and Drake (2006) on estimating BCRs is of seminal importance.

But there are several other studies that should have been consulted and which might have modified the list of proposed solutions. One key source is the series of B/C studies for the United States summarized by Miller and Levy (2000). In particular, Miller and Levy are significantly

comparability of surveys and questions across different DHS surveys Kishor and Johnson (2004) corroborates that Peru may have unusually high rates of physical violence: Peru had the second-highest rate of lifetime physical violence of the nine countries included in Kishor and Johnson's analysis (second only to Zambia).

[3] By way of illustration, 27.2% and 48.6% of women in urban Brazil and urban Peru, respectively, had suffered physical violence at some time in their lifetime. This compares with rates of lifetime physical violence in urban areas of 12.9% in Japan, 22.8% in Serbia and Montenegro, 22.9% in Thailand, 30.6% in Namibia, 32.9% in Tanzania and 39.7% in Bangladesh. See WHO (2005) for details.

less optimistic about BCRs of prisoner rehabilitation than are Aos *et al.* (2006).[4] This finding is of particular relevance for the LAC region, since prisons and social service agencies are far less prepared to offer rehabilitation services than their counterparts in developed countries. In particular, the infrastructure of prisons in LAC countries is so precarious that significant investments in improving the physical environments would be needed before investments in rehabilitative services for inmates would have any possibility of being successful. This raises the cost of the total intervention package, and – given the significantly lower B/C ratios for prisoner rehabilitation programs provided by Miller and Levy for the United States – calls into question whether such programs are an attractive investment for crime prevention in the LAC region.

Cohen and Rubio report that they are unable to find BCRs for programs designed to reduce IPV, and it is true that the standard sources (Miller, Cohen, and Wiersema 1996; Aos *et al.* 2006) do not report BCRs on programs to reduce IPV. Indeed, the only B/C analysis available in this area examines the cost-effectiveness of the US 1994 Violence against Women Act, which provided US$1.6 billion over five years to "increase penalties for perpetrators and improve resources for police, prosecutors, and victim service providers" (Clark, Biddle, and Martin 2002). Clark, Biddle, and Martin, using cost components of crime developed by Miller, Cohen and Wiersema (1996), find a BCR of

---

[4] While Aos *et al.* cite BCRs of drug treatment inside and outside of prison as a crime prevention strategy at 5.9 and 18.5, respectively, Miller and Levy's (2000) estimates for these programs are 0 and 2.9, respectively. Similarly, in-prison vocational education and basic education have much higher BCRs in Aos than in Miller and Levy. On one key point the two authors are in full agreement: cognitive-behavioral therapy for inmates or ex-offenders is extremely cost-effective. Even here, however, the precise BCRs diverge significantly. While Aos *et al.* report a BCR of almost 100 for cognitive-behavioral therapy in prison or the community, Miller and Levy report a much lower (but still impressive) ratio of 33 for moral reconation therapy, one of the leading forms of cognitive-behavioral therapy. These significant differences in BCRs between Aos and Miller and Levy buttress the need to broaden the scope of the BCRs used to inform policy selection in chapter 10.

Even within the stream of research by Steve Aos and his co-authors, it seems that Cohen and Rubio are using a less-than-up-to-date version of this work. Citing Aos *et al.* (2004), Cohen and Rubio provide a BCR of 2.88 for a home visitation program by nurses. More recent research by Aos, Millar, and Drake (2006), however, provides a BCR of 18.5 and 21.6, depending on whether the visiting nurse works with the mother or children, respectively.

9.25. While there are no BCRs available for developing-country initiatives to prevent violence against women generally, or IPV specifically, the C/B estimates for the Violence against Women Act are particularly relevant for large number of LAC countries which have adopted national plans to address violence against women.[5]

Finally, there is one "pseudo" cost-effectiveness study that provides important information on the potential cost-effectiveness of nine important crime and violence prevention initiatives in Brazil (World Bank 2006).[6] The terms "pseudo" and "potential" are used because – in the absence of studies on the effectiveness of the specific interventions in Brazil – effectiveness data were imported from meta-evaluations of substantially similar interventions in developed countries and compared to data on the cost of these interventions in Brazil. While this procedure is subject to a host of criticisms (most importantly, that individual initiatives in Brazil will not have the mean effectiveness of similar initiatives conducted in other countries), it does provide the first-ever estimates of cost-effectiveness for violence and crime prevention initiatives in a LAC country; as such, these estimates are highly relevant for chapter 10. This study finds that the secondary prevention interventions Fica Vivo and Paz nas Escolas are the two most cost-effective of the nine prevention and control initiatives examined.[7]

---

[5] Even more basic studies on the effectiveness of programs to address violence against women are rare for developing countries. For a study which summarizes the small amount of evidence about what works in developing countries, see Morrison, Ellsberg, and Bott 2007.

[6] It is important to distinguish between cost-effectiveness and CBA. Cohen (2000) provides a useful definition: "Unlike benefit-cost analysis, which requires all benefits and costs to be expressed in monetary terms, cost-effectiveness only requires that costs be monetized. Benefits still need to be expressed in some common denominator – such as comparable crimes, comparable injuries, lost years of life, and so forth."

[7] Fica Vivo (Stay Alive) is a homicide prevention program that originally targeted a poor neighborhood (Morro das Pedras) in Belo Horizonte characterized by very high homicide rates. It has since been expanded to all of Belo Horizonte and to the state of Minas Gerais. The program is classified as "secondary prevention" because of extensive activities targeting at-risk youth, but also has important elements of problem-oriented and "hot-spot" policing. It also attempts to improve coordination between law enforcement and social service providers. For more details on the program, as well as a serious evaluation of its impacts, see Almeida de Matta and Viegas Andrade n.d. The program Paz nas Escolas (Peace in Schools) works with teachers, student organizations and

Use of out-dated information on what works in violence and crime prevention

The authors rely on the seminal paper by Sherman *et al.* (1997) to identify what works and what doesn't in crime and violence prevention. In large part due to the short time available to complete their study, Sherman *et al.* simply classify "what works" as all programs that have at least two reasonably rigorous studies supporting effectiveness and an effect size (if reported) of at least one-tenth of a standard deviation.

To put it quite bluntly, the literature has advanced significantly since the Sherman paper, and more sophisticated analyses of what works in crime and violence prevention are now available. In particular, the meta-evaluations produced by the Campbell Collaboration and by Mark Lipsey and his (cf. Lipsey 1992; Lipsey and Wilson 1998; Lipsey, Wilson, and Cothern 2000) co-authors are particularly valuable.[8] By surveying a critical mass of impact evaluations and presenting their results with a common yardstick, meta-analyses provide a very careful measure of the impact of specific approaches to crime and violence prevention. To the extent that the outcome measures used are consistent across meta-evaluations, they can also provide information on the relative effectiveness of specific approaches to crime reduction.[9] In contrast, Sherman's study classified interventions into three very broad categories (works, doesn't work, promising), frequently based on a very small number of impact evaluations.

---

police to promote non-violence in schools. For more information on the program, see www.mj.gov.br/sedh/paznasescolas.

[8] The Campbell Collaboration has conducted meta-analyses in many areas; some of those most relevant to chapter 10 are incarceration-based drug treatment, correctional boot camps, custodial vs. non-custodial sentences, non-custodial employment programs, "hot-spots" policing, Scared Straight and other juvenile awareness programs, and police-led drug enforcement strategies. Many more meta-analyses are under way within the Campbell Collaboration, including cognitive-behavioral programs, CBA and cost-effectiveness of sentencing, school bullying prevention programs, closed circuit television surveillance, face-to-face restorative justice, street lighting, school-based cognitive–behavioral anger interventions, electronic monitoring, mentoring programs, police strategies for reducing illegal possession and carrying of firearms, programs for violent and chronic juvenile offenders in secure correction facilities, and neighborhood watch. See www.campbellcollaboration.org for details.

[9] Meta-evaluations, of course, do not address either cost-effectiveness or cost-benefit, but simply effectiveness.

Lack of attention to several promising approaches to crime reduction

As Cohen himself notes (Cohen 2000), one of the major shortcomings of the Aos *et al.* B/C analyses is that they do not include policing and sentencing policies. Nor do they include the cross-sectoral approaches outlined above: crime prevention through environmental design, citizen security/public safety, and community-driven development/social capital.[10] Thus, it is not surprising that chapter 10 does not propose actions in these areas, since it bases its recommendations almost exclusively on the B/C estimates of Aos *et al.*, supplemented by Sherman's analysis.

Policing policy has undergone a veritable revolution in recent years. "Hot-spot" policing, community policing, and problem-oriented policing – to name just three of the most commonly used and analyzed approaches – have been used both in OECD countries and in the LAC region.

Randomized experiments have shown the utility of "hot-spot" policing in the United States as a crime control strategy (Braga 2001). One might suspect that "hot-spot" policing might be an even more important and effective strategy in the LAC region, given the very low clearance rates for many crimes. The only evidence on that score comes from the study by Almeida da Matta and Viegas Andrade (n.d.), which shows that the Fica Vivo program in a low-income neighborhood of Belo Horizonte (which involved both prevention initiatives oriented towards youth and "hot-spot" policing) led to a reduction in crime that was 2.7% larger than that obtained in the city as whole.

There are very few studies examining the impact of community policing on crime in the LAC region; tentative evidence from Guatemala and Costa Rica seems to suggest that these programs are much more effective at improving police–civil society relations than they are at reducing crime victimization (Chinchilla 1998, 2004). Unfortunately, B/C estimates are not currently available for these various approaches to policing.

The lack of attention to crime prevention through environmental design (CPTED) is a serious omission, since this has been shown

---

[10] Admittedly, the latter two approaches are more common in developing than in developed countries – so it is not surprising that they were omitted from a US B/C study.

to generate significant reductions in crime in quite short time horizons; a meta-analysis of multiple-component CPTED initiatives in the United States finds that they decrease robberies between 30% and 84% (Casteel and Peek-Asa 2000).[11] A careful impact evaluation of the Transmilenio public transit program in Bogota, which has important CPTED elements, found that it decreased commercial robberies by 78%, robberies of individuals by 90%, and homicides by 95% along one corridor where Transmilenio was built (Moreno Garcia 2005). Unfortunately, B/C or cost-effectiveness estimates for CPTED do not seem to be available.

The Cohen and Rubio's decision to exclude from consideration programs designed to keep youth in school is perplexing, especially given their recognition that "many of these programs appear to have significant crime-related benefits – often high enough to justify the program solely on the basis of crime reductions."[12] Conditional cash transfer (CCT) programs are a common feature of the LAC landscape and perhaps the most common approach to maintaining at-risk youth in school. Not only are they one of the easiest crime prevention initiatives to bring to scale (of course, they have multiple benefits beyond crime reduction), but they have been the subject of several high-quality impact evaluations that demonstrate their effectiveness (at least in the cases of Bolsa Escola in Brazil and Oportunidades in Mexico).[13]

---

[11] CPTED relies on physical modification of the built environment to reduce criminality. It usually involves improving natural surveillance, access control, territorial reinforcement (to promote ownership of space), and maintenance. Recently, the concept of "place-specific crime prevention" has begun to supplant CPTED. Place-specific crime prevention goes beyond environmental design to include considerations of *management* of physical space (Feins, Epstein, and Widom 1997). It should be noted that some authors (see Roman and Farrell 2002) are skeptical of the ability of existing B/C methodologies to capture all the relevant benefits of situational crime prevention.

[12] Cohen and Rubio justify this exclusion only by noting that "these are programs that are more appropriately reviewed in a paper on education." This is peculiar logic, since the same argument could be used to relegate comprehensive programs targeting at-risk mothers and young children – one of the proposed solutions – to a paper on early childhood development. The basic point is that programs which have multiple benefits beyond crime reduction should be included in the analysis.

[13] In the cost-effectiveness study in Brazil cited above (World Bank 2006), Bolsa Escola was found to be the fifth most cost-effective crime prevention program out of nine studied in Brazil.

Finally, citizen security approaches – incorporating interventions across sectors to address multiple risk factors and multiple forms of crime and violence – have been employed with notable success in several LAC cities (Lamas, Alda, and Buvinic 2005).

In sum, Cohen and Rubio face a serious dilemma: there are several extremely promising approaches to crime and violence reduction for which B/C estimates are not available, but for which evidence of effectiveness is available from OECD countries and, in some cases, from the LAC region itself. The authors have established the precedent for including as a proposed solution an intervention (domestic violence prevention) for which they claim no B/C estimates are available.[14] Why, then, should policing reform, CPTED, and the integrated-citizen security approach be excluded?

4 An additional solution

The rules of the game of the Copenhagen Consensus and the Consulta de San José 2007 limit authors of alternative views to proposing *one* additional solution. CBA, the metric of the Copenhagen Consensus, cannot be used to rank the relative attractiveness of the promising approaches (policing reform, CPTED, and the integrated-citizen security approach) that were omitted from the chapter; C/B estimates are simply not currently available for these approaches. Nor is it appropriate to exclude these approaches from consideration, since reasonably persuasive evidence for their effectiveness is available.

Given this situation, what type of logic can guide the choice of solution? Any additional solution should:

(i) have a *preponderance of evidence* showing its effectiveness
(ii) produce impacts in a *relatively short time horizon*, given the important role that discount rates play in determining BCRs[15]
(iii) be relatively *simple to implement*.

---

[14] Though, as was documented above, there is at least one study which does provide a B/C estimate of a national program to address violence against women. It is worth emphasizing once again that this alternative view strongly supports the inclusion of the prevention of violence against women as one of the proposed solutions. The relatively high BCR found for the US Violence against Women Act simply buttresses Cohen and Rubio's intuition that this is an attractive policy option.

[15] Obviously, the size of costs and benefits (and their distribution over time) also matters, but at this time there is no information on these costs and benefits for these interventions.

One the basis of criterion (i), integrated-citizen security approaches cannot be strongly recommended. They are indeed promising, but the impact evaluation evidence is not yet strong enough. As noted above, there is scientific evidence of the effectiveness of both CPTED and "hot-spot" policing in terms of reducing criminality – and, in both cases, there is at least one impact evaluation study documenting that the approach has worked in the LAC region.

Both CPTED and "hot-spot" policing are capable of producing results in a very short time frame. CPTED, however, has the advantage in terms of simplicity of implementation. "Hot-spot" policing requires significant institutional change in the police. Data from geographic information systems (GIS) must be made available to police in real time in order to both allocate resources and to evaluate results. Police decisionmaking must be decentralized, and decentralized commanders must be held accountable for their performance. This shift toward information-based and decentralized decisionmaking is nothing less than a seismic shift in police culture and organization – and consequently is far from simple to implement.[16] CPTED, on the other hand, requires modification only in the built environment. Even the more sophisticated place-specific crime prevention, which adds the management of the physical environment (see n. 11), is well within the capabilities of most municipal governments in Latin America. Thus, while "hot-spot" policing will pay high dividends if successfully implemented, **CPTED must be recommended as the additional solution because it has more realistic probabilities of success.**

Bibliography

Almeida da Matta, Rafael and Monica Viegas Andrade, n.d. "Avaliação economica do impacto do programa de controle de homicídios Fica Vivo." www.anpec.org.br/encontro2005/artigos/A05A153.pdf

Aos, Steve, 2005. "Washington's Drug Offender Sentencing Alternative: An Evaluation of Benefits and Costs." Olympia, WA: Washington State Institute for Public Policy

Aos, Steve, R. Lieb, J. Mayfreld, M. Millar, and A. Pennucci, 2004. "Benefits and Costs of Prevention and Early Intervention Programs for

---

[16] Despite these challenges, success in implementing "hot-spot" policing has been achieved in Belo Horizonte (see the discussion of the Fica Vivo program in n. 7) and – although the evidence is still tentative – in the Barrios Seguros program in the Dominican Republic (see World Bank 2007).

Youth." Olympia, WA: Washington State Institute for Republic Policy, www.ws.pp.wa.gov/pub.asp?/docid=04-07-3901

Aos, Steve, M. Millar, and E. Drake, 2006. *Evidence-Based Public Policy Options to Reduce Future Prison Construction, Criminal Justice Costs and Crime Rates*. Olympia, WA: Washington State Institute for Public Policy

Braga, Anthony, 2001. "The Effects of Hot Spots Policing on Crime." *Annals of the American Academy of Political Science* 578: 104–25

Casteel, Carri and Corinne Peek-Asa, 2000. "Effectiveness of Crime Prevention through Environmental Design (CPTED) in Reducing Robberies." *American Journal of Preventive Medicine* 18(4S): 99–115

2004. "El caso de Villa Nueva, Guatemala." in H. Fruhling, ed., *Calles más seguras: Estudios de policía comunitaria en América Latina*. Washington, DC: Inter-American Development Bank

Chinchilla, Laura, 1998. "Experiencias locales de prevención del delito en América Central." Paper presented at the forum "Seguridad Ciudadana y Consolidación Democrática en América Latina." Santiago: Woodrow Wilson Center and the Instituto de Ciencias Políticas de la Universidad de Chile

Clark, Kathryn Andersen, Andrea Biddle, and Sandra Martin, 2002. "A Cost-Benefit Analysis of the Violence Against Women Act of 1994." *Violence against Women* 8(4): 417–28

Cohen, Mark, 2000. "Measuring the Costs and Benefits of Crime and Justice." *Measurement and Analysis of Crime and Justice* 4. Washington, DC: United States Department of Justice, Office of Justice Programs, National Institute of Justice

Feins, Judith, Joel Epstein, and Rebecca Widom, 1997. *Solving Crime Problems in Residential Neighborhoods: Comprehensive Changes in Design, Management and Use*. Washington, DC: US Department of Justice, Office of Justice Programs, National Institute of Justice

Heise, Lori, 1998. "Violence against Women: An Integrated, Ecological Framework." *Violence against Women* 4(3): 262–90

Kishor, Sunita and Kiersten Johnson, 2004. *Profiling Domestic Violence: A Multi-Country Study*. Calverton, MD: ORC Macro

Lamas, Jorge, Erik Alda, and Mayra Buvinic, 2005. *Emphasizing Prevention in Citizen Security*. Washington, DC: Inter-American Development Bank

Lipsey, Mark, 1992. "Juvenile Delinquency Treatment: A Meta-Analytic Inquiry into the Variability of Effects." in T.D. Cook *et al.*, eds., *Meta-analysis for Explanation: A Casebook*. New York: Russell Sage

Lipsey, Mark and David Wilson, 1998. "Effective Interventions for Serious Juvenile Offenders: A Synthesis of Research." in R.L. Loeber and D.P.

Farrington, eds., *Serious and Violent Juvenile Offenders: Risk Factors and Successful Interventions*. Thousand Oaks, CA: Sage

Lipsey, Mark, David Wilson, and Lynn Cothern, 2000. *Effective Intervention for Serious Juvenile Offenders*. OJJDP Bulletin **181201**. US Department of Justice, Office of Justice Programs, Office of Juvenile Justice and Delinquency Prevention

Miller, Ted, Mark Cohen, and B. Wiersema, 1996. *Victim Costs and Consequences: A New Look*. Washington, DC: US Department of Justice, Office of Justice Programs, National Institute of Justice

Miller, Ted and David Levy, 2000. "Cost-Outcome Analysis in Injury Prevention and Control." *Medical Care* 38(6): 562–82

Moreno Garcia, Alvaro José, 2005. "Impacto del transmilenio en el crimen de la Avenida Caracas y sus vecindades." CEDE Working Paper **2005–55**. Bogotá: Universidad de los Andes

Morrison, Andrew, Mary Ellsberg, and Sarah Bott, 2004. "Addressing Gender-Based Violence in the Latin American and Caribbean Region: A Critical Review of Interventions." World Bank Policy Research Working Paper **3438**

2007. "Addressing Gender-Based Violence: A Critical Review of Interventions." World Bank Research Observer 22(1): 25–51

Roman, John and Graham Farrell, 2002. "Cost-Benefit Analysis for Crime Prevention: Opportunity Costs, Routine Savings and Crime Externalities." in N. Tilly, ed., *Evaluation for Crime Prevention. Crime Prevention Studies* **14**. Monsey, NY: Criminal Justice Press

Sherman, L., D. Gottfredson, D. Mackenzie, J. Ecoc, P. Reuter, and S. Bushway, 1997. *Preventing Crime: What Works, What Doesn't, What's Promising. A Report to the United States Congress*. Washington, DC: National Institute of Justice, www.ncjrs.gov/works/

United Nations Office on Drugs and Crime (UNODC) and World Bank, 2007. *Crime Violence and Development: Trends, Costs and Policy Options in the Caribbean*. Washington, DC: World Bank

World Bank, 2006. "Crime, Violence and Economic Development in Brazil: Elements for Effective Public Policy." Report **36525-BR**. Washington, DC: World Bank

2007. "Crime, Violence, and Development: Trends, Costs, and Policy Options on the Caribbean." World Bank Report **37820**

World Health Organization, 2005. *WHO Multi-Country Study on Women's Health and Domestic Violence against Women*. Geneva: WHO

Conclusion

BJØRN LOMBORG

Since the first global event held in 2004, the Copenhagen Consensus process has been used successfully as a means of reviewing challenges for the United Nations and UNICEF, but this is the first time it has been applied to look at the problems of a single region. Inevitably, when global problems are covered, the focus of attention is on the world's poorest people, and particularly on the overwhelming challenges facing Africa and parts of southern Asia. In comparison, LAC countries are quite prosperous, with problems which by most measures do not compare with the miseries of Africa. Nevertheless, problems there are, and this volume represents a clear-headed and well-argued attempt to address these on a regional basis.

Although the performance of most countries in the region is around the global average when assessed by common economic indicators, they have a long way to go to fulfill their potential and catch up with the world's richest countries. At the same time, their performance is in danger of being overshadowed by the rise of China and other dynamic Asian economies. As readers will have learned for themselves, many countries in the LAC region still have structural problems in the economic and political system, holding back development to the disadvantage of entire populations.

Perhaps more worrying is the seemingly ingrained level of inequality in the region. Despite rising middle-class living standards and a small number of the very wealthy, there remains a stubborn problem of poverty for large swathes of the population. Disproportionately, this means those who live in rural areas, particularly indigenous populations. The poor bear the brunt of problems such as malnutrition, disease, and low standards of education. In urban areas, they are also the victims of the frighteningly high level of violence found in many LAC cities and towns.

The ten challenges which form the heart of this book cry out for our attention. The authors make convincing cases for cost-effective interventions in each case. But, in the real world, there are simply not enough resources to do justice to all these in parallel. Indeed, trying to tackle too many issues at once is likely to dilute the effectiveness of each and divert resources from where they can do most good. Prioritization is essential, hard as that may be to say out loud. Economic CBA is, we believe, the best tool available for this prioritization. It is by no means perfect, but if we are aware of its limitations then at least it provides a rational basis for decisionmaking.

There are two key problems. First, valuation of benefits can be difficult. What is the real value of biodiversity? How can we, in all conscience, place a value on human life? These are indeed thorny problems, both practically and ethically, but refraining from answering them will not make them go away. Whatever our views on these issues, we still make policy choices that implicitly rank both biodiversity and human life; rejecting an objective economic framework for this simply makes them less clear, less well argued and most likely less effective. Second, we need data from real-life case studies to be able to project costs and benefits for the particular solutions proposed, and sometimes hard evidence can be very elusive.

Despite this, the experts did a great job in looking at the available evidence for the LAC region and giving us the first, regional, economically based priority list. The Consulta de San José Expert panel has assessed the evidence and come up with their own prioritization, ranking solutions to problems of poverty/inequality, fiscal policy, infrastructure, and education as their top five of 29 listed. Were they right? The Youth Forum priorities seem to confirm many of the hard choices made. Nevertheless, you may think differently. It is up to all of us to look as objectively as possible at what has been put forward by the authors of the individual chapters and come to our own views. Do you think that the figures put forward are realistic? Are authors being too optimistic about their favored projects? Are there other, and perhaps more radical, solutions which should be adopted?

You can make your own choice. The important thing is that you use some rational, logical framework to make that choice. Heart-rending as many of the problems are, we cannot simply let our emotions lead us into knee-jerk reactions. Using BCA gives us the best chance of really doing something to make life much better for the poor and disadvantaged.

Not only that, but it is the means for us to monitor progress on policy initiatives. It is no good investing scarce resources in a promising intervention, only to find ten years later that it hasn't worked. Outcomes need to be reviewed and hard choices made in the light of reality. Successful projects can be continued or even expanded, problematic ones can be revamped, and failing ones replaced by other projects next in line. This, of course, is also an excellent reason for revisiting the LAC priority list in 2011, both to see what we have learned and where we should go next.

But for now, this volume shows us that, although the LAC region does have its own problems, it also has a large number of great and promising solutions to draw on, and shows some of the best ways in which the problems can be tackled cost-effectively. We hope that this will catalyze a debate which will use our approach to decide on policies which address the pressing needs of each country as efficiently as possible. This is a first step. Words alone are not the answer; action is now needed from those with the resources.